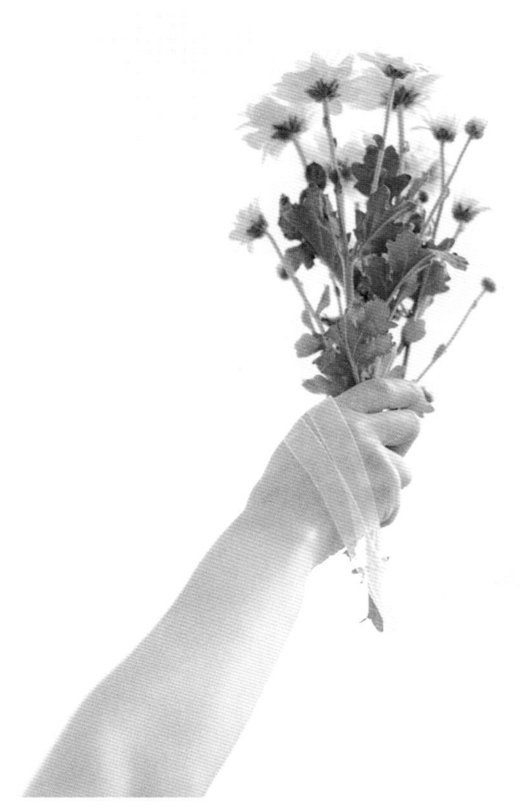

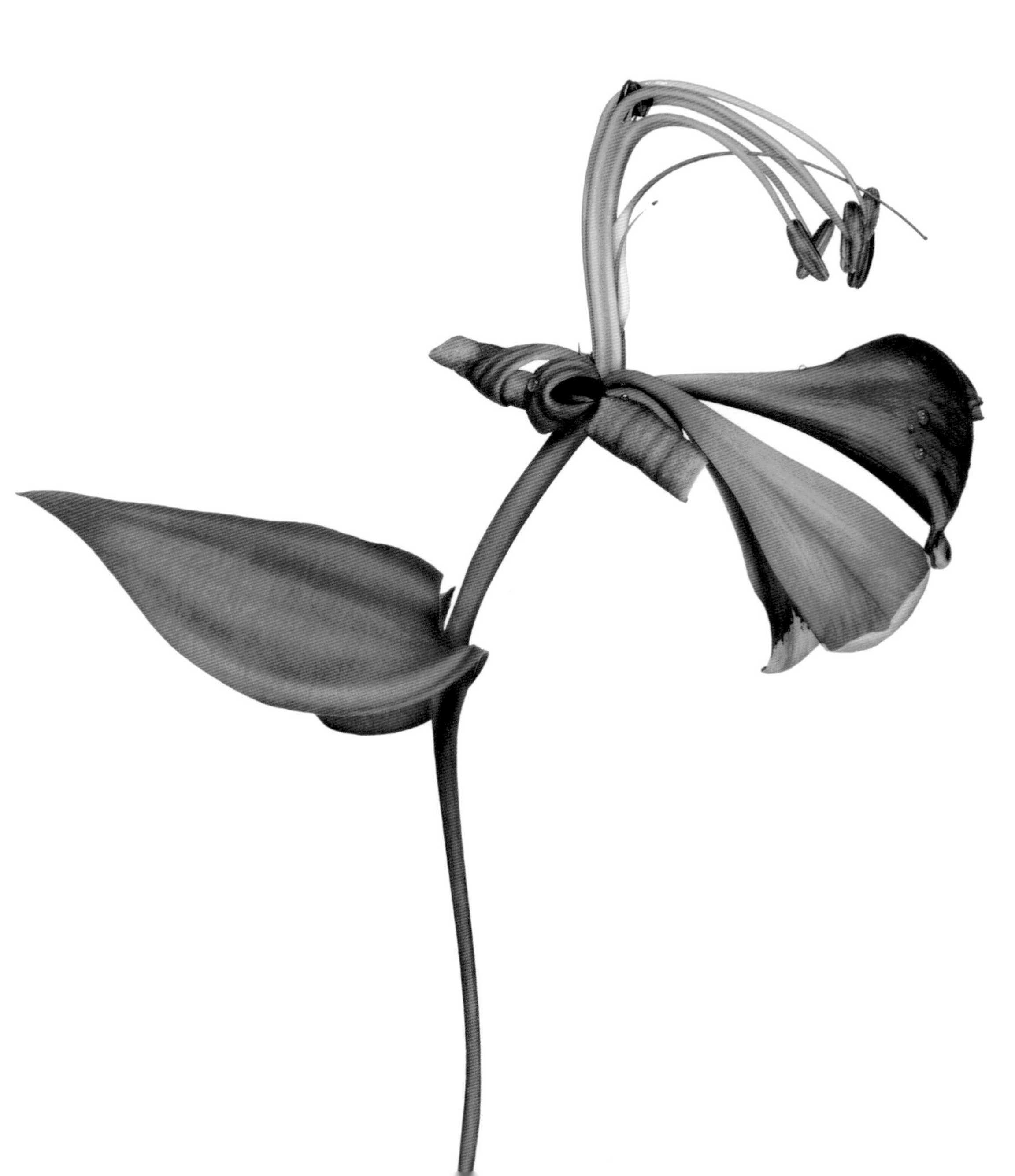

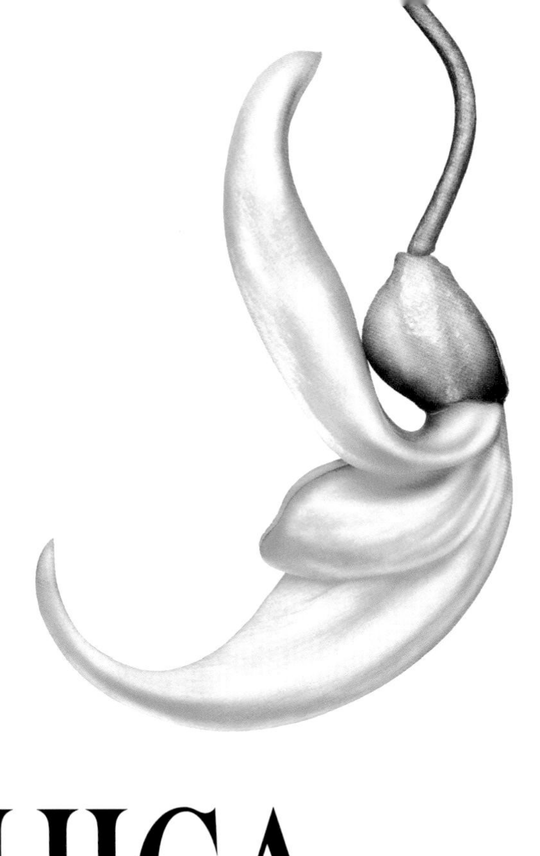

FLORA PHOTOGRAPHICA

THE FLOWER IN CONTEMPORARY PHOTOGRAPHY

WILLIAM A. EWING AND DANAÉ PANCHAUD

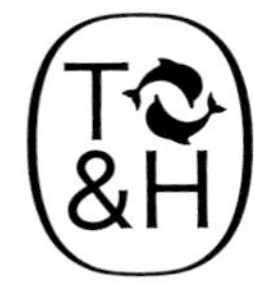

First published in the United Kingdom in 2022 by Thames & Hudson Ltd, 181A High Holborn, London WC1V 7QX

First published in the United States of America in 2022 by Thames & Hudson Inc., 500 Fifth Avenue, New York, New York 10110

This paperback edition published in 2024

Cover designed by Sarah Boris

British Library Cataloguing-in-Publication Data
A catalogue record for this book is available from the British Library

Library of Congress Control Number 2021943304

ISBN 978-0-500-29755-1

Printed and bound in China by RR Donnelley

FSC www.fsc.org MIX Paper | Supporting responsible forestry FSC® C144853

On the cover
front: Erwan Frotin, *Freesia sp.*, from the series *Flora olbiensis*, 2007, Courtesy the artist
back: Leonce Raphel Agbodjelou, *Untitled (Musclemen series)*, 2012, Courtesy Jack Bell Gallery, London

Page 1
Jędrzej Nowicki
14.08.2020 Minsk, Belarus, 2020
A woman stands near the detention centre on Okrestina Street in Minsk, Belarus. She is holding a bouquet of white flowers tied with a white ribbon. The remand prison became a symbol of the oppression of the Alexander Lukashenko regime. Here, protesters detained by the security services were beaten and tortured. Red and white flowers and ribbons became a symbol of the Belarusian protests.

Page 2
Andrew Zuckerman
Amherstia nobilis 295, 2012

Page 3
Andrew Zuckerman
Strongylodon macrobotrys 41, 2012

Page 4
Andrew Zuckerman
Euphorbia punicea 100, 2012

WILLIAM A. EWING is a curator of photography whose exhibitions have been seen at hundreds of museums worldwide over the past fifty years. His many publications on photography include *Flora Photographica: Masterpieces of Flower Photography* (1991), *The Body, Landmark: The Fields of Landscape Photography, Edward Burtynsky: Essential Elements, William Wegman: Being Human* and *Civilization: The Way We Live Now*. He is an Officer in the French Republic's Ordre des Arts et des Lettres, and a winner of the Royal Photographic Society's Award for Outstanding Service to Photography.

DANAÉ PANCHAUD is a curator and lecturer specializing in photography. She has held positions at several Swiss institutions in the fields of photography, contemporary art, design and science. She was the director of the Photoforum Pasquart in Biel, 2018–21, and currently serves as director of the Centre de la photographie Genève, one of the leading Swiss institutions for contemporary photography.

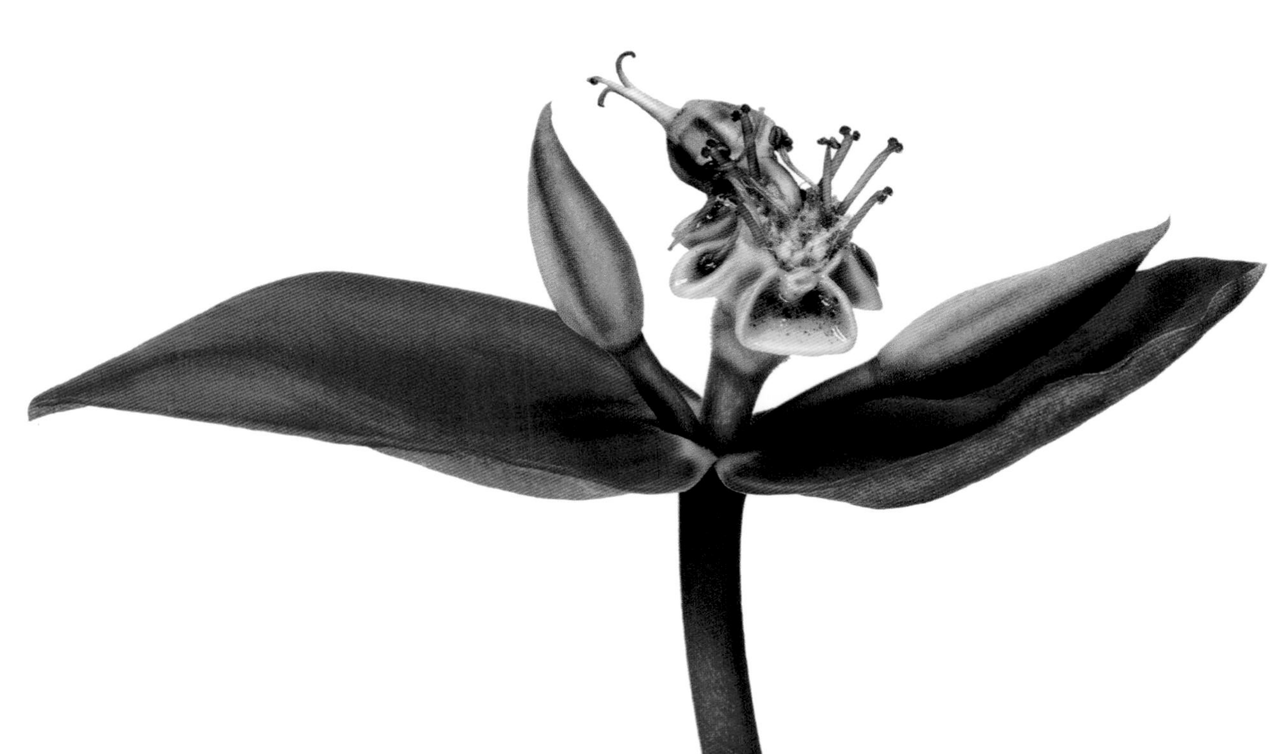

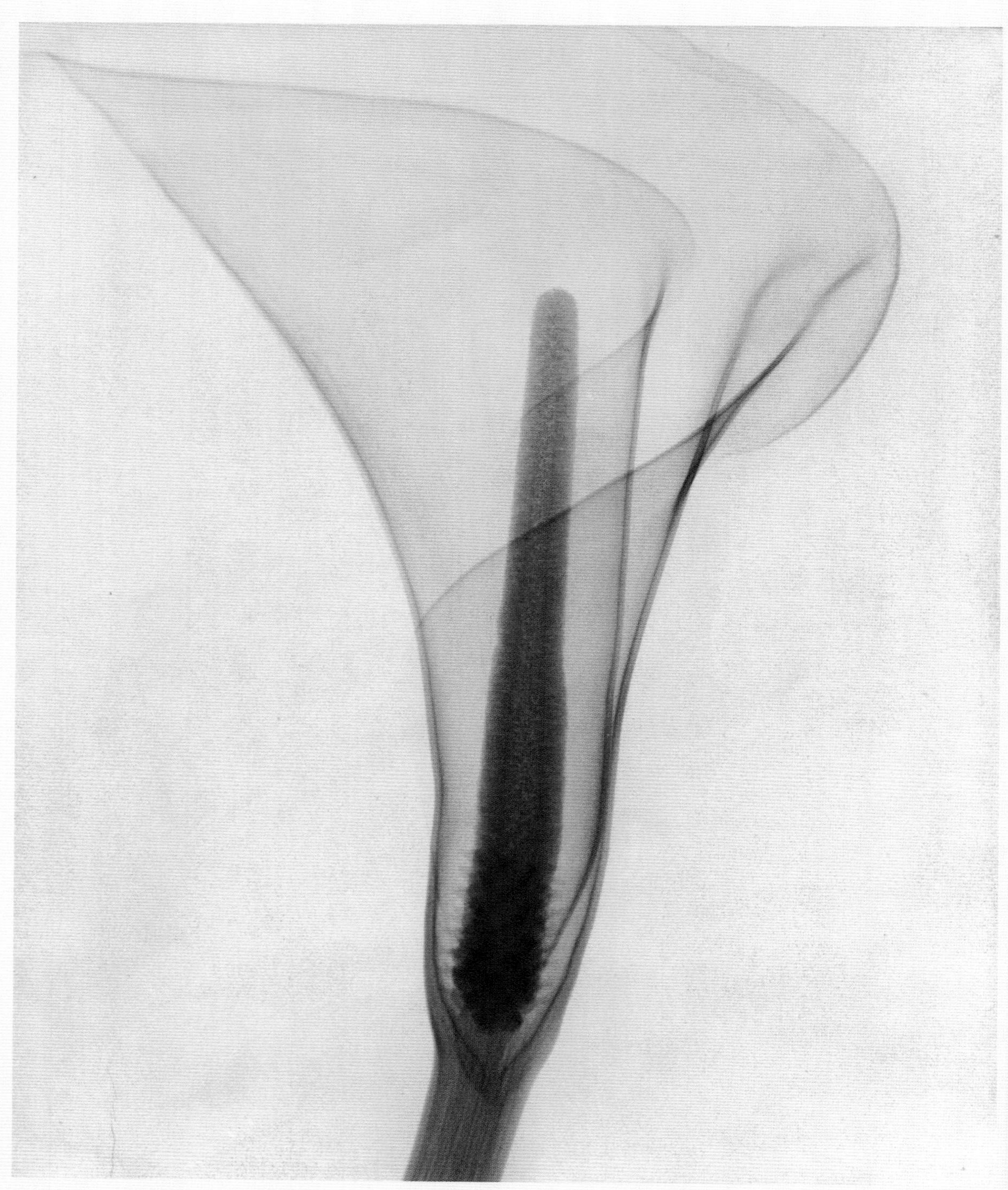

DR DAIN TASKER
Lily – An X-ray, toned gelatin silver print, 1930

By 1930 floral radiography was not new, having been published as early as 1913. Dr Tasker's eloquent imagery, however, imbued with a sense of fluid motion, did much to popularize it.

INTRODUCTION

Beneath the lenticular eye,
the secrets of the flower fall one by one.

Colette, 1932[1]

Colette was mostly thinking about the role of the microscope when she wrote these words almost a full century ago, but being an ardent lover of both flowers and contemporary art, she might well have been aware of the superb floral photographic studies being produced during her time. The much-admired Karl Blossfeldt, for example, argued persuasively that art forms grew out of forms found in nature.[2] The equally prolific Edwin Hale Lincoln, earlier in the century – and way ahead of his time, ecologically speaking – took hundreds of plants from their New England habitats to photograph meticulously in his studio, then returned them to their homes, never disclosing their whereabouts for fear of plant hunters who might 'tear my friends up by the roots', while leaving to posterity an editioned portfolio of 400 magnificent platinum prints.[3]

It is quite likely that Colette was familiar with the work of Blossfeldt. To say the same of Lincoln is perhaps a stretch, given the state of transatlantic communications at the time and his lower profile, being a self-publisher whose sights were set more locally. But Colette might well have been thinking of such bold American modernists as Charles Sheeler, Alma Lavenson, Edward Weston and Imogen Cunningham, who did have an international profile at the time, and perhaps of the great Japanese photographer, printer and publisher Kazumasa Ogawa, whose seminal book *Some Japanese Flowers* (1896) had found a following in Europe and America. All these photographers zeroed in on flowers and showed their parts in such exquisite detail as to evoke miraculous miniature worlds, not to mention demonstrating a surprising kinship of flowers with machine-made objects. And, since she mentioned the microscope, Colette might also have had in mind the sensuous X-ray studies by Dr Dain Tasker, the more scientifically focused 'floral radiographs' of Hazel Engelbrecht and even, in light of increasingly powerful imaging systems, electron microscopy, which had been publicized only the year before she penned her observation.[4]

Now it's another era, and another sensibility – concerning flowers, concerning nature and concerning ourselves. This is the era baptized Anthropocene, with its heightened awareness of the profound impact human presence has on our planet, including, of course, on its plant forms, which, botanists tell us, were successfully rooted more than one hundred million years before our earliest human ancestors came along. If anything, today we find *more* floral photography than ever. It seems those lenticular eyes have not yet penetrated all the recesses of Colette's secret garden.

Flower photographs are to be found in every period of photographic history, in every movement and in every genre. Obviously we expect to find them in landscape practice – and we often do, particularly where the focus is on parks and gardens – but surprisingly, they appear with regularity in a wide range of documentary work. Street photographers note flowers in the most unlikely urban environments, presenting them as symbols of tenacity in the inhospitable terrain of glass, steel and concrete. And, as we shall see, even the unlikely fields of industrial photography and war photography occasionally offer up notable floral images.

But mostly we look to the studio tradition for the mainstay of floral imagery. Here, in controlled environments, with cut flowers (real or artificial), photographers strive to do something pictorially and/or conceptually that no other photographer has done before, or never done *quite like this*. It is a tall order, but then no one else has had these particular specimens, in this particular combination, with this particular light.

Flowers have also abounded in the genres of the portrait and the nude (following cultural conventions, until very recently almost exclusively associated with women), and have long been staples in diverse domains of commercial photography. Where would fashion photography be, for instance, without its flower-bedecked models? How would advertising for beauty products be possible without

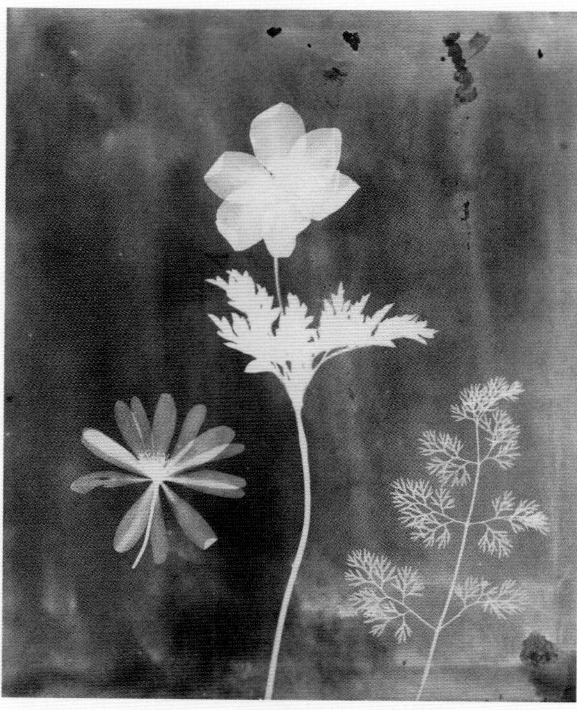

WILLIAM HENRY FOX TALBOT
Untitled, photogenic drawing, *c.* 1838
This photogenic drawing, or contact negative, is attributed to William Henry Fox Talbot. Botanical specimens were the ideal experimental material for this pioneering scientist and inventor: easily laid flat; of variable size, shape and density; readily accessible in Talbot's garden; and, of course, expendable.

images of floral perfection adorning boxes and bottles of perfumes, lotions and drugs?

Amateur photography has also provided a profusion of floral imagery, and today the fields of social media are brimming with blossoms, mostly following time-worn conventions – something that is ironic, given the widespread belief that innovation and disruption are assets of the new visual platforms. And, last but far from least, we have the field of professional botanical illustration, which, having slowly and grudgingly taken to photography after keeping it at arm's length for the better part of a century, eventually produced its own superb imagery.

As the reader of this book will soon see, this sketch is very much a simplification. (We might even add to our list the genre of pornography, given that prim flower arrangements are sometimes employed as counterpoints to vigorous human couplings; see page 11.) The point we wish to underline is this: flowers are indeed to be found everywhere in photography.

Cutting across all these diverse genres are the principal inclinations of the photographer: a scientific versus artistic intent; a sharp-focus realism versus an atmospheric 'Pictorialism' (we see echoes of this influential late nineteenth-century movement in current practice); a modernist minimalism versus a baroque profusion; a colour palette ranging from muted to bold, or even reverting to the rich language of black and white; the living flower in nature versus the cut flower in the studio; analogue versus digital (or some combination thereof); the straight photograph versus the manipulated image – collaged, montaged, painted over, enhanced using graphics software, or otherwise computer-manipulated. Realism, surrealism, abstraction, symbolism: we find examples of all these and more in photography's flower garden. Perhaps this explains the ubiquity of flowers in photography: they simply cater to every aesthetic taste, while providing a fertile ground for myriad symbolic and metaphorical interpretations. It should therefore not come as a surprise to read the words 'poet' and 'visual poet' in the Artists' Statements found later in this book. We might remind ourselves that among the symbolic attributes of flowers are love (from platonic to erotic), exoticism, youth, beauty, purity, rarity, fragility, strength, ephemerality, transience, complexity, simplicity, extravagance, spirituality, even life and death. Small wonder, then, flowers' perennial attraction.

Photographers tend to be deeply appreciative of earlier art forms. Many are those who use the seventeenth-century Dutch still life – often referred to as a 'flower piece' – as a point of departure, or at least a reference. Others have been inspired by engravings, etchings and lithographs of the past few centuries. Moreover, it would be a mistake to assume that photography stepped into the field in the 1840s and shoved entrenched floral painting aside. In fact, over time, photography *did* force painters to change direction and find fresh terrain where the new medium could not follow, but at the beginning of photography, it wasn't much welcomed by artists. Who wanted a tiny black-and-white picture of flowers on a metal plate at which one had to squint in order to read it satisfactorily, when one could have a beautifully drawn and vibrantly coloured Redouté ('the Raphael of Flowers') engraving a hundred times larger? Or, if one had seen

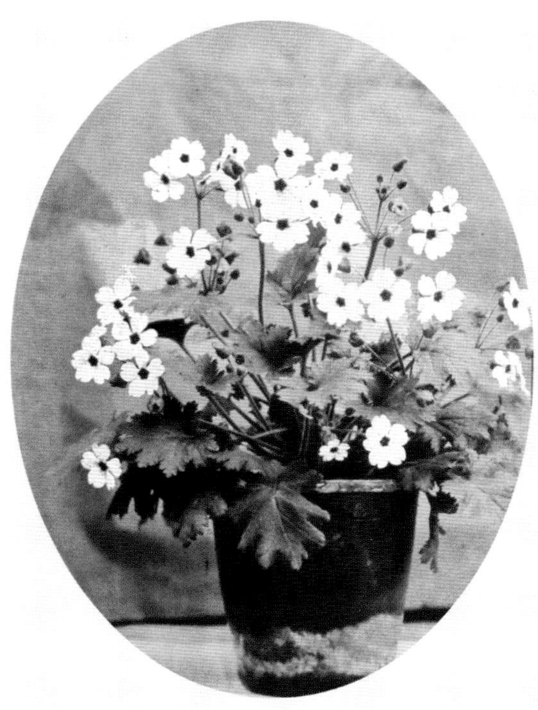

JOHN DILLWYN LLEWELYN
Chinese Primrose (Primula chioantha), salted paper print, *c.* 1854
Llewelyn's prolific photography earned him the respect of William Henry Fox Talbot, who considered him the first serious botanical photographer.

Robert John Thornton's sumptuous *Temple of Flora* (1799–1807), with its richly decorative engravings from the exquisite paintings of Philip Reinagle, who would settle for a positive print from a fuzzy paper negative, in a pale brownish tint, such as those William Henry Fox Talbot was producing? Given the option, it was far more likely that they would choose to gaze upon the splendour of a Dutch still life by Rachel Ruysch or Jan van Huysum, pictures so realistic that the viewer might be tempted to brush a fly off a petal.

In 1842 John Dillwyn Llewelyn, a keen horticulturalist and one of the earliest botanical photographers, wrote to the director of Kew Gardens in London of his experiments with the new medium: 'I have amused myself with making Daguerreotype portraits [of several flowers], and from their exact accuracy they are interesting, though the want of colour prevents them being beautiful as pictures.'[5] 'Prevents them being beautiful'! And this admission not from a casual amateur, who might have dabbled with 'sun pictures', or a disgruntled painter whose livelihood was being threatened, but from a champion of floral photography, who also successfully produced albumen and salted paper prints from paper negatives and, later, from wet collodion glass plates. Llewelyn knew that while he and a few pioneering photographers were working on their relatively tiny, monochrome, often splotchy and fast-fading prints, a flower-besotted public could turn their gaze to paintings that were always much larger, more vibrant and more imposing than any existing photograph, and which could take any bright light shone on them without 'wilting' as the flimsy paper images were wont to do. Together, drawings, watercolours, paintings and prints had achieved such high standards of expression, exactitude and permanence that *any* new medium would find matching them an almost insurmountable challenge. Photographers would have to struggle even to find a foothold.

Botanists were among the sceptics. A trained illustrator's own hand-drawn depiction of a flower would be in the form of a synthetic composite of several different specimens, in order to get a trustworthy rendering of a 'typical' plant (the best illustrators were trained to generalize or synthesize thus). A botanically minded photographer, on the other hand, was stuck with a single specimen, as always in monochrome (although perhaps afterwards hand-coloured, usually unconvincingly), which might not serve at all well as a single exemplar of the species, being abnormally small, spindly, sickly, etc. Moreover, true colour was not seen to be anywhere on the horizon. As late as 1887 the *Photographic News*, a highly influential journal published in London from 1858 to 1908, could write scathingly:

> It is needless in these days, when a scientific primer can be bought for one shilling, to point out the boastful absurdity and inherent nonsense of any pretentions to photograph colours directly. To do so would be to attempt to rival the exploits of those wise old gentlemen of Laputa whom Lemuel Gulliver discovered engaged in the process of extracting sunbeams from cucumbers.[6]

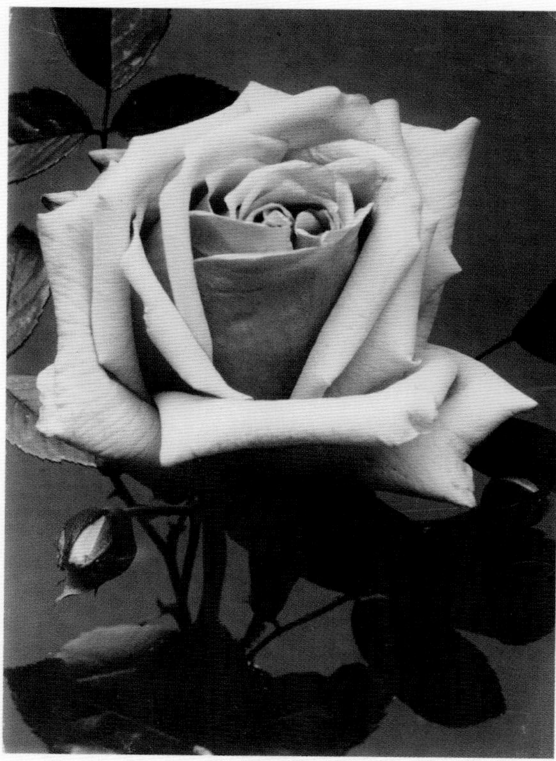

CHARLES JONES
Rose, gold-toned gelatin silver print, *c.* 1900.
As the curator Robert Flynn Johnson has rightly observed of Jones, 'the close-up view, the long exposure (necessary to achieve depth of field and a full range of values in his subjects and their shadows) and spare arrangements anticipate later modernist photography.'[9]

Small wonder, then, that the botanists preferred the proven illustrative arts. The nail in the botanical photography coffin, moreover, was the simple fact that for many decades after their medium's invention, photographers could not reproduce their work in books and journals: woodcut engravings from photographs were the best they could do. Is it any surprise, then, that many botanically minded photographers thought: Why bother?

Yet despite all these obstacles, a small number of photographers persisted. The very first issue of *Photographic News* heralded a new kind of artist, the photographer, who 'scientifically utilized the object of pagan worship [i.e. the sun], and made his golden rays subservient to the purposes of an artificial life...It paints for them pictures instinct with life and beauty, and with a fidelity so true that art cannot imitate it.'[7]

So it is not surprising that some early nineteenth-century photographers took up the challenge of flowers, with varying degrees of success, and for a variety of reasons. While the horticulturalist/gardener/photographer Charles Jones wanted to record prize specimens for his own wants (record-keeping? Aesthetic pleasure? We know only that he never felt the desire to exhibit his photographs publicly), enterprising professionals such as Adolphe Braun and Charles Aubry took a 'the more the merrier' position with regards to getting their work seen by the public, not as artworks in their own right, but as source material for wallpaper designers and textile firms. In the botanical arena, a handful of determined photographers such as Pietro Guidi saw a means to get around the synthetic composite conundrum by simply including different specimens of the same plant side by side in the frame.

If connections can be drawn with earlier art forms, there is another sense in which photography has much deeper roots, roots going off in all directions. Photographers working today might well be drawing on their historical understanding, personal concepts, ideologies and sensory impressions, and not really thinking much about history, if at all. But also, even unconsciously, they are counting on a latent storehouse of cultural antecedents – the history of botanical investigation, horticultural advances going back to the first agrarian revolution, the great importations during the age of exploration, the proliferation of botanic gardens (which continually traded new plants with one another), the breeding and commercialization of flowers, and, more generally, concepts of leisure, pleasure and refinement.

For hundreds of years flowers have also been 'invented' to meet consumer demand, and today geneticists are designing flowers for industrial-scale production. Any photographer who claims to be 'only interested in nature' is ignorant of the fact that the blossoms in his or her still life are largely *cultural* fabrications. The famous rose known as 'Black Velvet' was just such a creation in 2006, costing investors more than $4 million. And such invention, and investment, is nothing new. As the anthropologist Jack Goody reminds us, 'the culture of flowers took off in the Hellenistic period

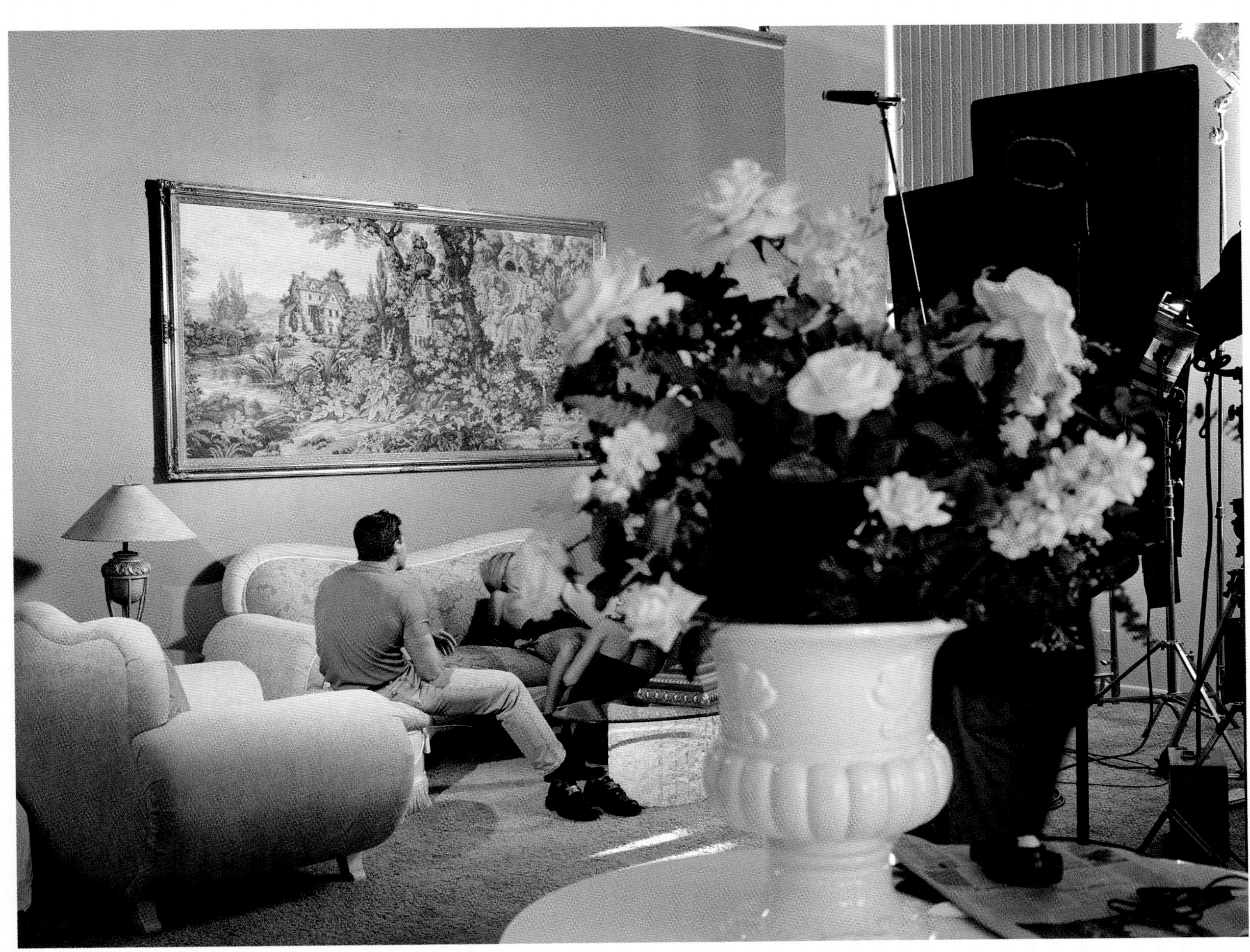

LARRY SULTAN
Mulholland Drive #2, from the series *The Valley*, 2000 © Estate of Larry Sultan

The photographer's partial masking, with a lush floral arrangement, of the sexual couplings going on during the shooting of a pornographic film acts as a tongue-in-cheek tease – just as the 'adult' film itself was intended to do.

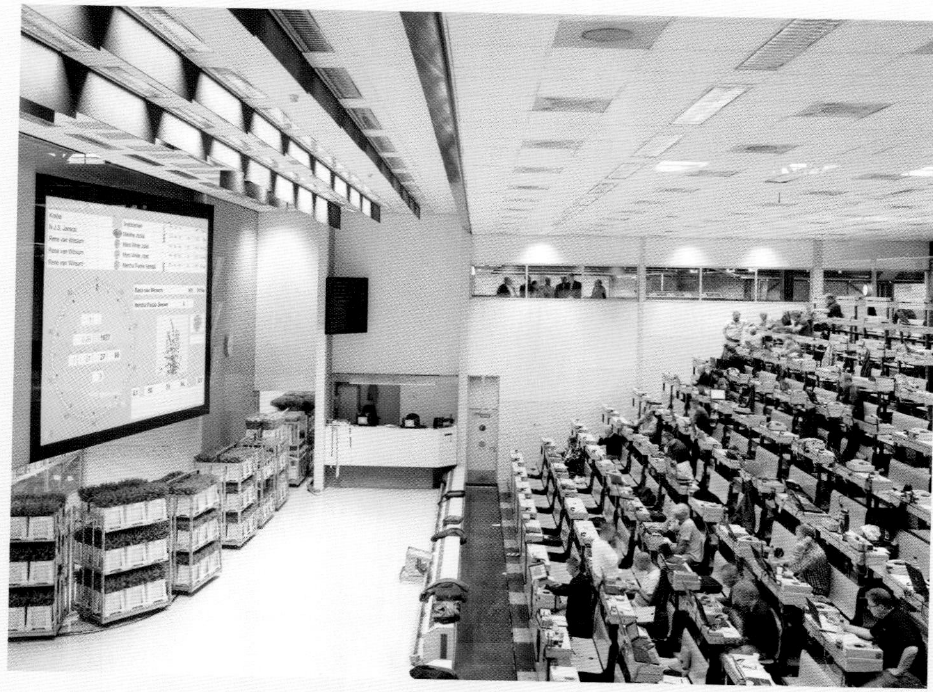

HENRIK SPOHLER
One of the World's Largest Flower Auctions in Aalsmeer, The Netherlands, 2010
The *Global Cut Flowers Market Report 2021* projected that global sales will reach a value of approximately $50 billion by 2028, a figure that underlines the centrality of flowers in human affairs.

[323–30 BC], both in actuality and in representation.'[8] While it is true that many photographers are not particularly interested in these cultural roots, or perhaps are simply not aware of them, nonetheless they benefit from all that has gone before. After all, roots usually are out of sight.

For those with a historical curiosity, which is to say an interest in the photography of flowers before the period covered by this book (1990–2020), we suggest a look at *Flora Photographica: Masterpieces of Flower Photography from 1835 to the Present* (1991), which opens with Fox Talbot's simple photograms of the 1830s; Anna Atkins's iconic cyanotypes of British and other flowering plants of 1854; and an extremely rare floral daguerreotype (c. 1845); and then moves through all manner of nineteenth-century experimentation to austere modernist masterpieces by Blossfeldt, Edward Steichen (a great gardener and plant breeder as well as photographer), Cunningham and many others. The anthology ends with the melancholy studies of dying plants by Chris Enos, the hilariously artificial hybrids of Joan Fontcuberta and the stylish, almost aggressively erotic forms of Robert Mapplethorpe. Readers of the present book will find much continuity with the first volume, but will undoubtedly be struck by a major difference, a logical consequence of time's passage: the first book was 90 per cent black and white; the present volume is 90 per cent colour. As for the digital 'revolution', the reader will most likely conclude that although much has shifted in that direction, analogue has more than held its own. The *Flora Photographica* of 1991 was also more Eurocentric, with the majority of contributors coming from France, Britain, Germany and the United States, and only a few from further afield. The internet has given us curators much greater reach, and the present study represents photographers from around thirty countries.

The photographers in this volume, which might be viewed as a sequel to the first, range from those who have specialized in the subject, sometimes for many years, to the exclusion of anything but flowers or plants, through those who have focused on flowers in depth but for only a short time – even, say, for a single project – to those who in the course of their work have from time to time found themselves with a promising flower subject, and pursued it briefly. Lastly, a few photographers are represented here who have simply occasionally found themselves making a picture with a flower in it – even admitting afterwards that they hadn't really *seen* the flower when taking the picture, only later realizing it was a key component.

Some specialists are more interested in the botany, aesthetics being secondary; others privilege the aesthetics, and the botanical element is secondary, or even dismissed (one or two even admit to having no interest in flowers as such, only finding them useful objects for the study of colour and form). Some photograph real flowers; others delight in the artificial variety, on occasion even fabricating the blooms themselves. Some delight in the centuries-old trope of the floral arrangement in a vase; others take a more freewheeling approach, dispensing with traditional containers. Some stand back, taking in a lavish display; others delve into a petal or a stem – often to the point of pure abstraction.

What *Flora Photographica* does not claim to do is gather all the fine flower photographers worldwide in one book; there are

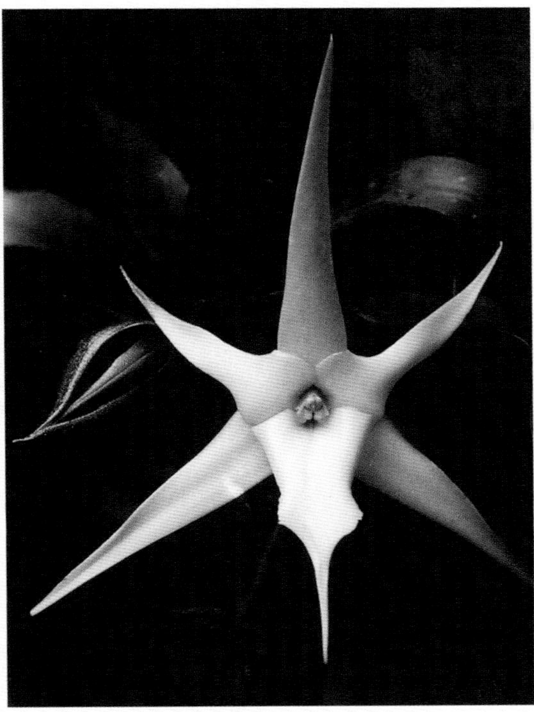

SCOWEN & COMPANY
Angraecum sesquipedale, Ceylon, c. 1870
The work of this early photographer might easily be confused with that of a modernist photographer fifty years later. The quality of the work by the firm's founder, Charles T. Scowen, 'demonstrates considerable skill', notes the historian John Falconer: 'The brilliantly lit and simply composed studies...argue a long familiarity with the medium.'

far too many – enough for an entire series of *Florae Photographicae*! But we do claim to cover the main approaches, with fine examples of each. As we have seen, the flower can be seen as a symbol. It can also be an emblem (standing for a person, a group, a corporation, etc.). It can be studied as an object of curiosity or admiration. It can be employed as a decorative motif, stripped of all but the most general symbolic associations (would one ever ask a woman wearing a floral dress what the individual flowers stood for?). And it can be seen as a token in social exchange, or considered as a product or commodity.

A few of the specialist flower photographers, here represented by one or two images, have books of their own where the fullness of their work can be appreciated. And a number of those who have made flowers a specific project (among others) have produced monographic publications. It's a big field, and *Flora Photographica* is best thought of as a guide.

The book is structured in thematic chapters, nine in all. Each in turn will be briefly introduced, but the reader is first owed an explanation of our curatorial methodology. The choice of works for *Flora Photographica* was made from many tens of thousands of individual pictures, via a slow process of careful pruning. The final selection was then laid out at playing-card size, to allow the hundreds of photographs to be seen all together – a curatorial aerial view, so to speak. The pictures then began to coalesce naturally: here were images clearly referencing previous art forms (*Roots*); there, variations on the still life (*Arrangements*); in some we noted a minimalist approach (*Essence*); in others a botanical interest (*Enquiries*). Some photographs exhibited a concern with symbolic attributes, or employed mixed media (*Hybrids*). If for some practitioners the intent was a classic still life, or a botanical enquiry, for others it was an opportunity for a mischievous or subversive theme (*Imposters*). Whereas some photographers placed their emphasis on the 'still' in still life, others toyed with movement and rhythm (*Fugue*). Many were pictures of cut flowers arranged in vases (again, *Arrangements*); others were of flowers found in nature or depicted in cultural contexts (*In Situ*). And while some approaches were carefully observant and sober, others preferred flights of fancy (*Reverie*).

Initially some twenty such thematic chapters suggested themselves. Some were then seen to be unsustainable, and were abandoned, while others proved their staying power, resulting in the final nine. While we admit to subjective categorization (readers are free to imagine reassigning pictures on their own, or even to invent alternative chapters), the process was considered, not arbitrary. And by juxtaposing pictures that share similarities of some kind, we hope to trigger further associations, even suggest alternative interpretations – and maybe even prod aspiring photographers to take up the challenge of flowers.

Composing this book has felt a little like composing a sumptuous bouquet. It is our hope that this modern-day florilegium will give pleasure on the one hand to those who care deeply about flowers, but for whom photography is merely a convenient window through which to gaze admiringly on their charms; and on the other, to those who feel deeply about photography and perhaps less about flowers, and marvel at the creativity of 'lens-based' artists who seem to find endless new ways to probe the secrets of Colette's garden.

ROOTS

Photographers of our time who decide to accept the challenge of depicting flowers have at their fingertips a wealth of historical precedent, garnered not only from Odilon Redon's 'good ground of reality' (see page 110) but also from that vast new, largely uncharted terrain of the virtual. A few clicks, and up on the screen pop a Roman floral mosaic, an early still life by the pioneer Ambrosius Bosschaert, a sinuous, opulent still life by Rachel Ruysch, or any one of a host of Impressionist and Modernist masterpieces, let's say by Pierre-Auguste Renoir, Henri Matisse or Vincent van Gogh. Or a botanically minded photographer looking for inspiration from the past might call up a Pierre-Joseph Redouté watercolour of such realism that it might easily be confounded with a photograph. We might also look to the rich traditions of the East and Near East, at exquisite Persian decorative motifs, or Utagawa Hiroshige's irises and cherry blossoms, or the bird and flower painting of China, already superbly fluent a thousand years ago.

Closer to our time, from the past century, we find Pop Art, Abstract Expressionism and Conceptual Art influences, while Surrealism has proved a particularly attractive ground for inspiration. And for flowers purely derived from the imagination we can look back to Jean-Baptiste Pillement, Giuseppe Arcimboldo and Redon. None of this is fanciful on an observer's part: the photographers credit their sources freely, and often with reverence.

Then, if we turn to shallower roots, photography itself offers up its icons: an extremely rare daguerreotype or two, cyanotypes by Anna Atkins, photograms by William Henry Fox Talbot, early still lifes by Adolphe Braun and Charles Aubry, the 'Art Deco' of Karl Blossfeldt, Edward Steichen's delphiniums and sunflowers, Man Ray's solarizations, Imogen Cunningham's magnolias, and later fine studies by Lee Friedlander, Chris Enos, Jan Groover and Robert Mapplethorpe. Portraits, nudes and street photography of the twentieth century: each genre proposes brilliant examples and challenges the contemporary photographer to match the accomplishment – or do one better.

All these precedents were of course analogue; we are now in the digital realm, with new sources to work from. But this changes nothing where inspiration is concerned. Photographers of both eras know that what is ultimately important is the result, not the road taken. The photographers in the following pages may well have the advantage of having this vast historical storehouse to draw from, but it also means the bar has been set high. How will they fare?

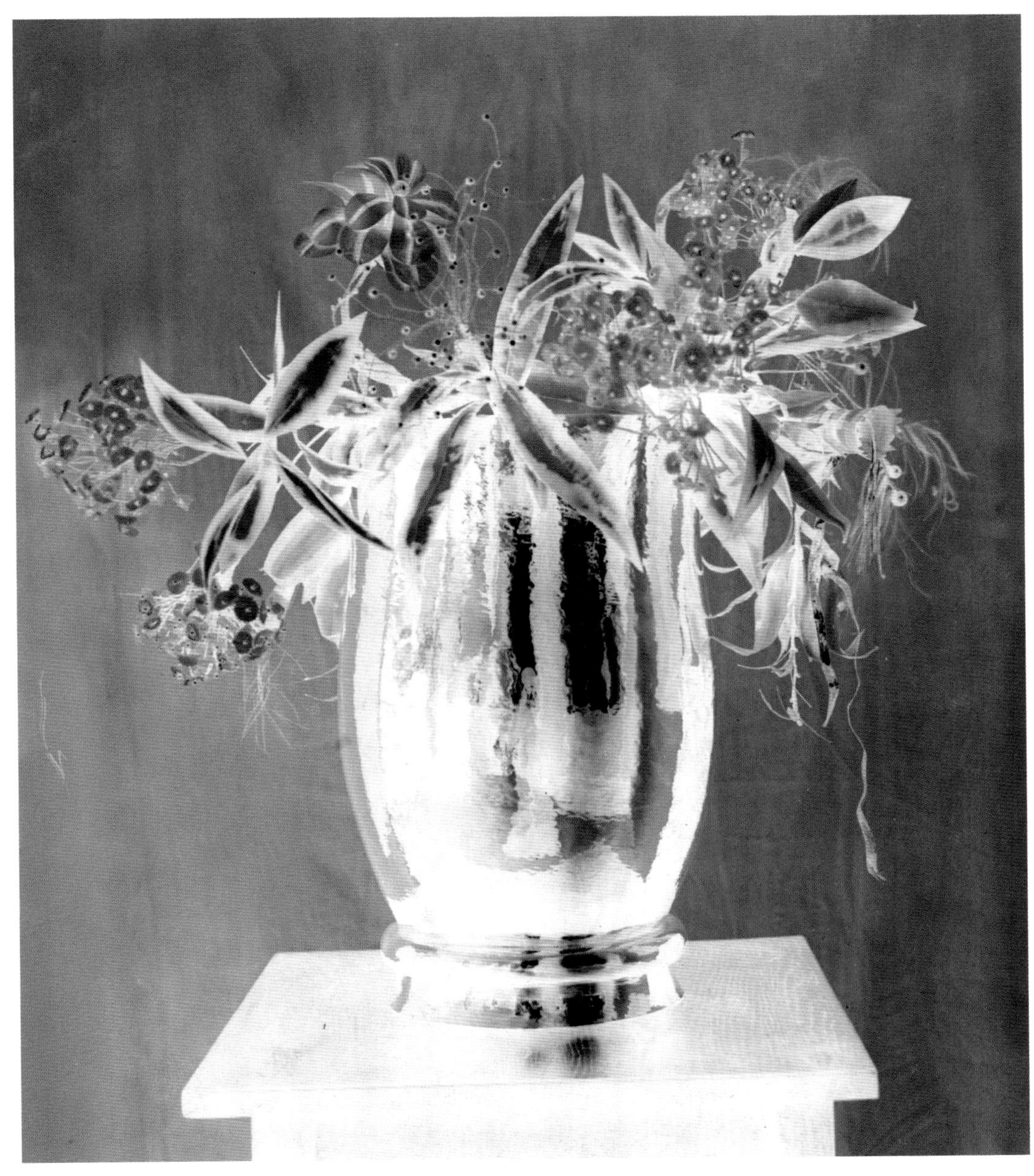

THOMAS RUFF
neg◊stil_02, 2015

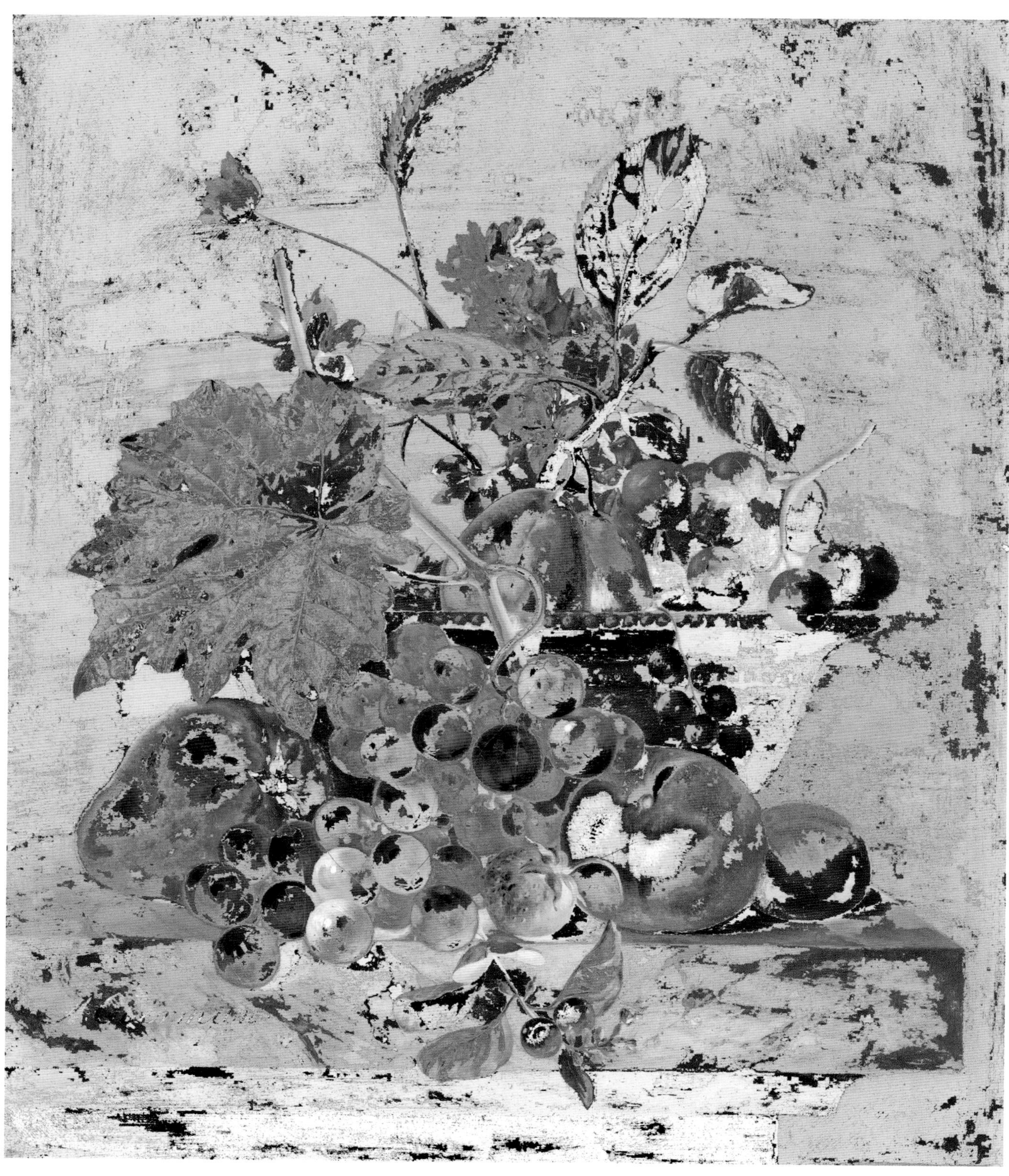

PAMELA ELLIS HAWKES
After Oberman, 2019

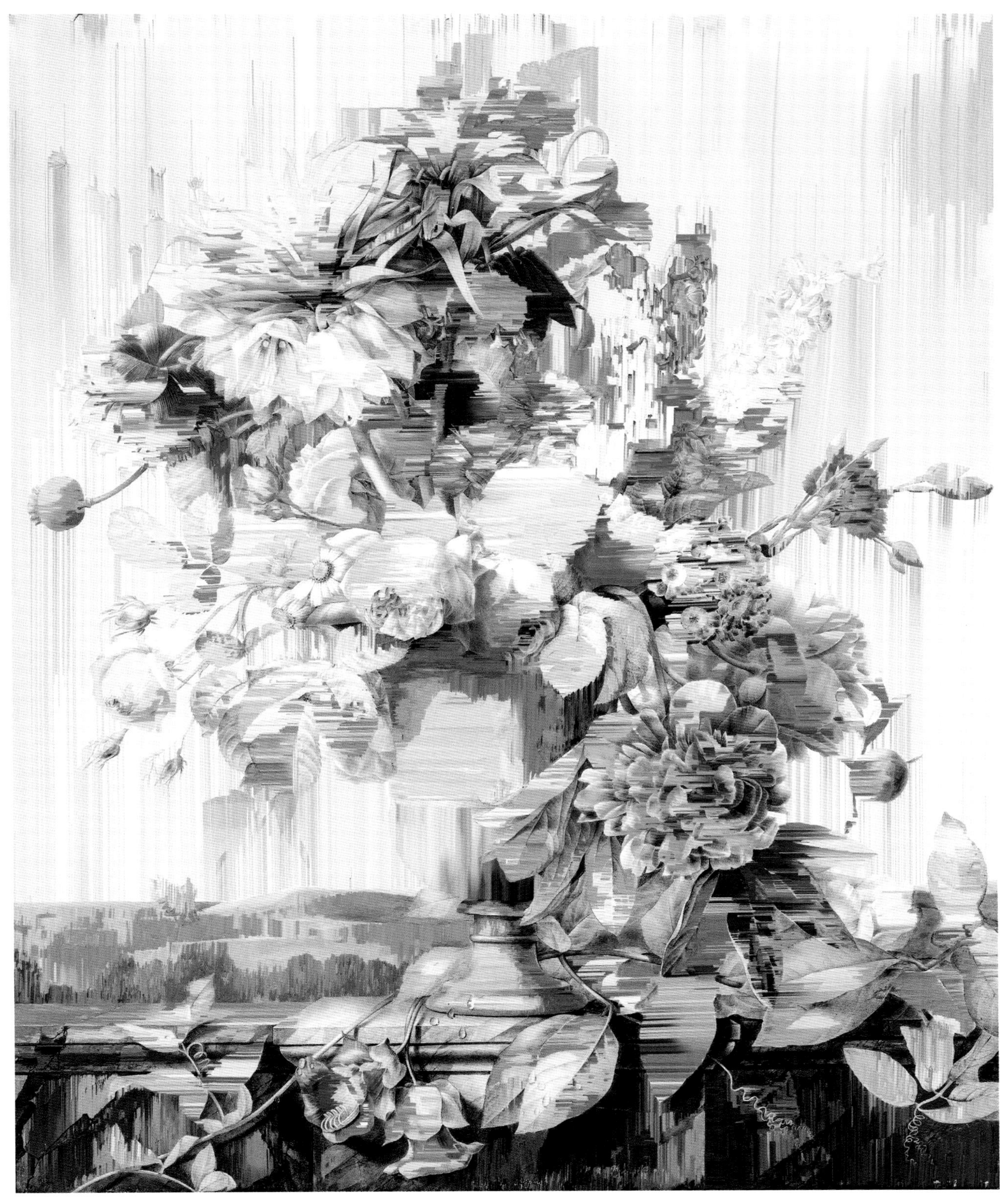

PAMELA ELLIS HAWKES
After Redoute, 2019

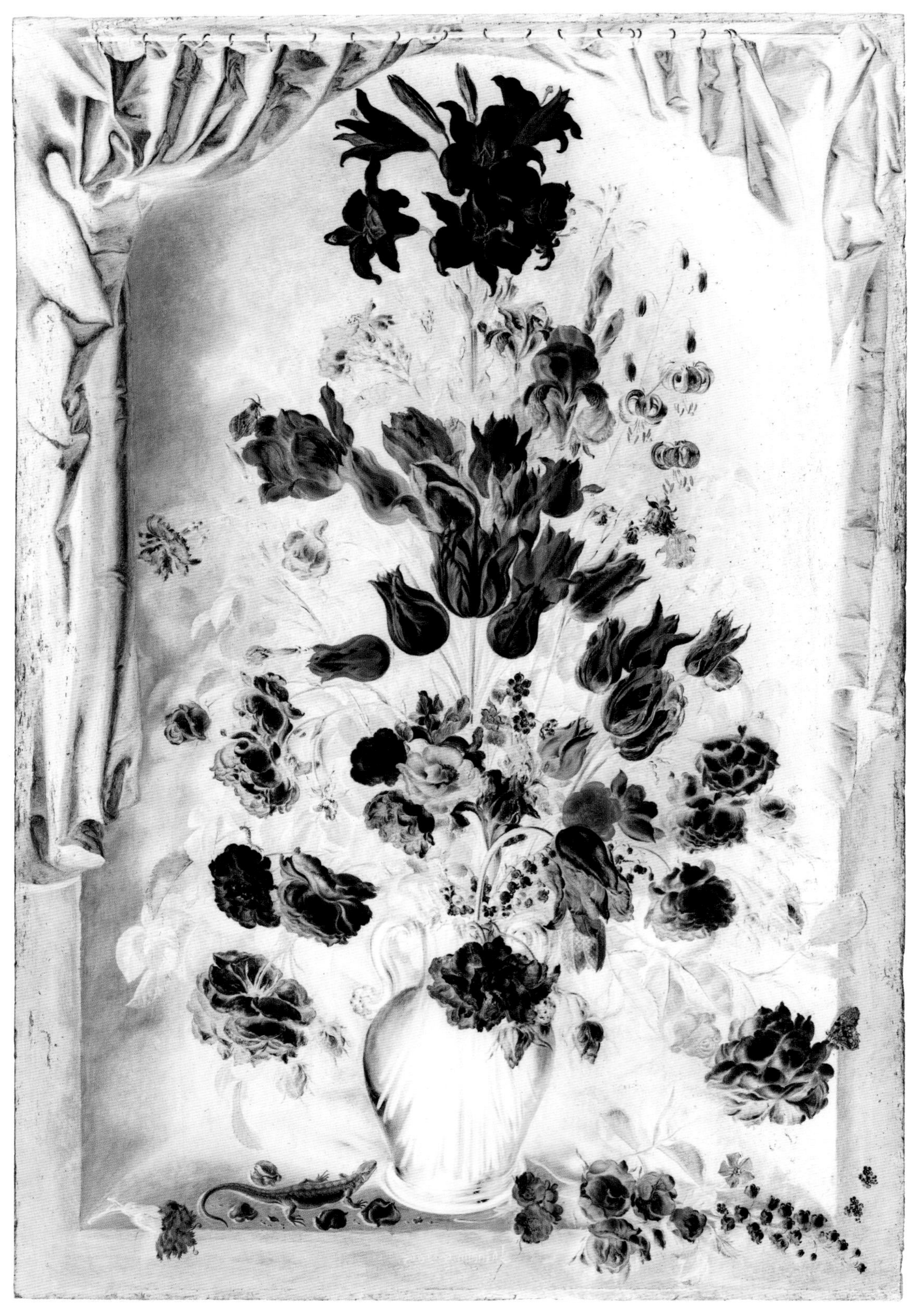

ROB AND NICK CARTER
Positive, Negative, Painting Photograph, 2016
After Jacob de Gheyn II (1565–1629), Vase of Flowers with a Curtain, 1615

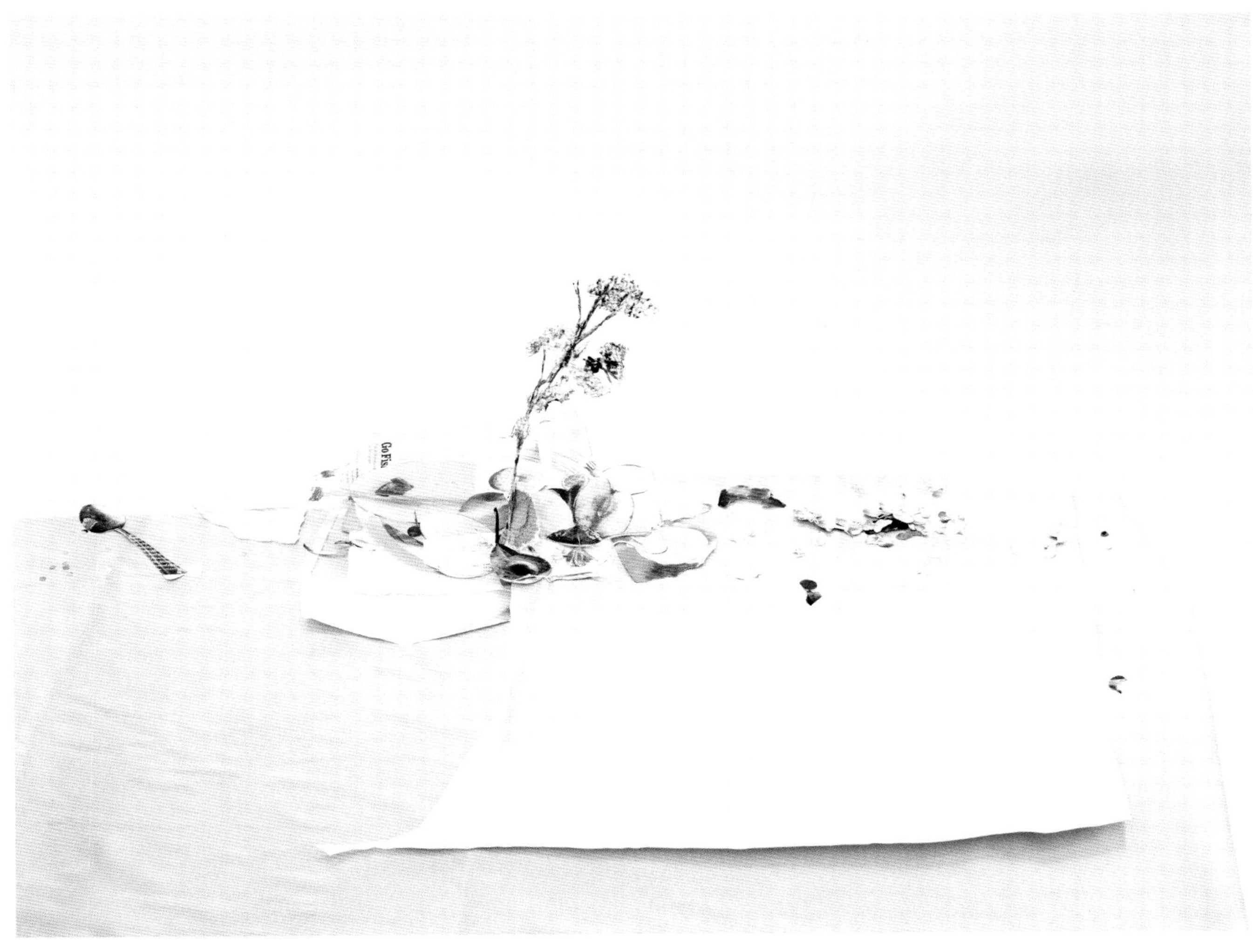

LAURA LETINSKY
Untitled 49, from the series *III Form and Void Full*, 2013

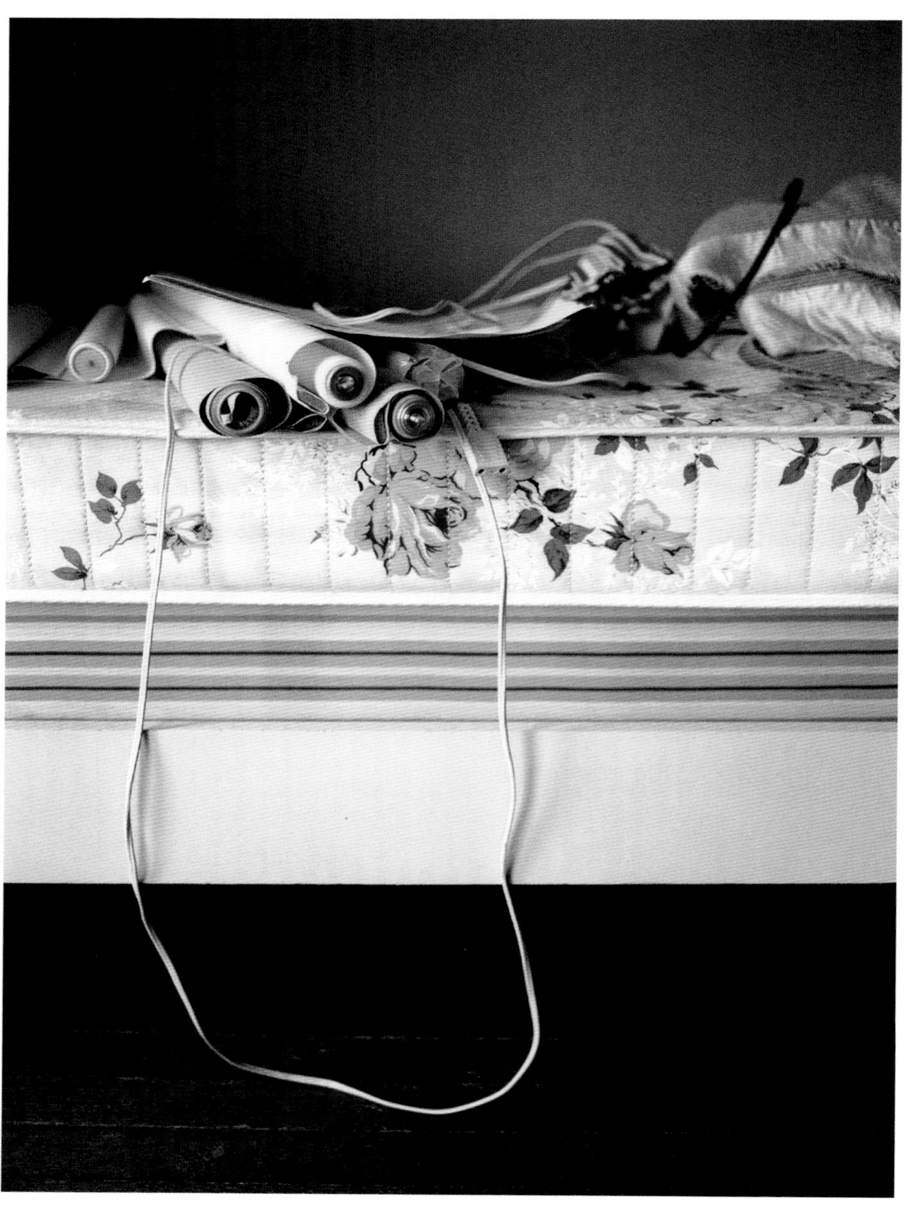

JESSICA BACKHAUS
Roses and Cables, 2007

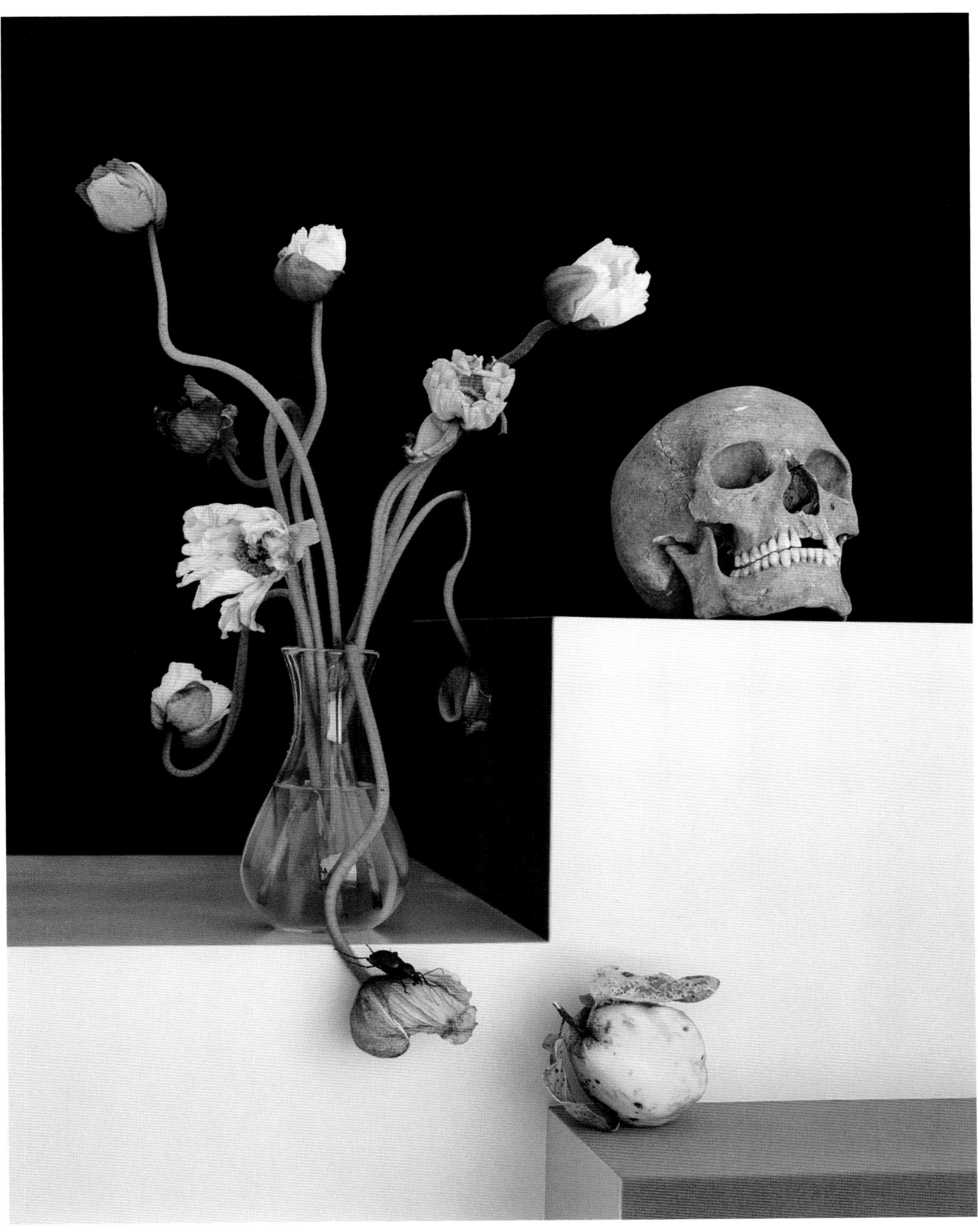

SHIRANA SHAHBAZI
[Stilleben-33-2009], 2009

THE THREAD OF A GREAT TRADITION

'Good art has got to be in the thread of the great tradition,' wrote the modernist photographer Charles Sheeler, whose own photographs of flowers were inspired by the Dutch still life. 'An underlying current goes through all the way to Renaissance, Egyptian, Chinese, back to cave painting.'[1] *Sheeler was correct, even with cave painting, although depictions of flowers are extremely rare in Stone Age art, the emphasis and pressing preoccupation being with animal life. Contemporary photographers, thanks to the unparalleled access to earlier floral forms via the internet, can not only find inspiration, but also myriad concrete examples of floral art from previous centuries – fine, decorative and applied – to play off against, extend in some clever fashion, or even subvert. Perhaps Sheeler's observation should be amended to read* threads *of the great* traditions.

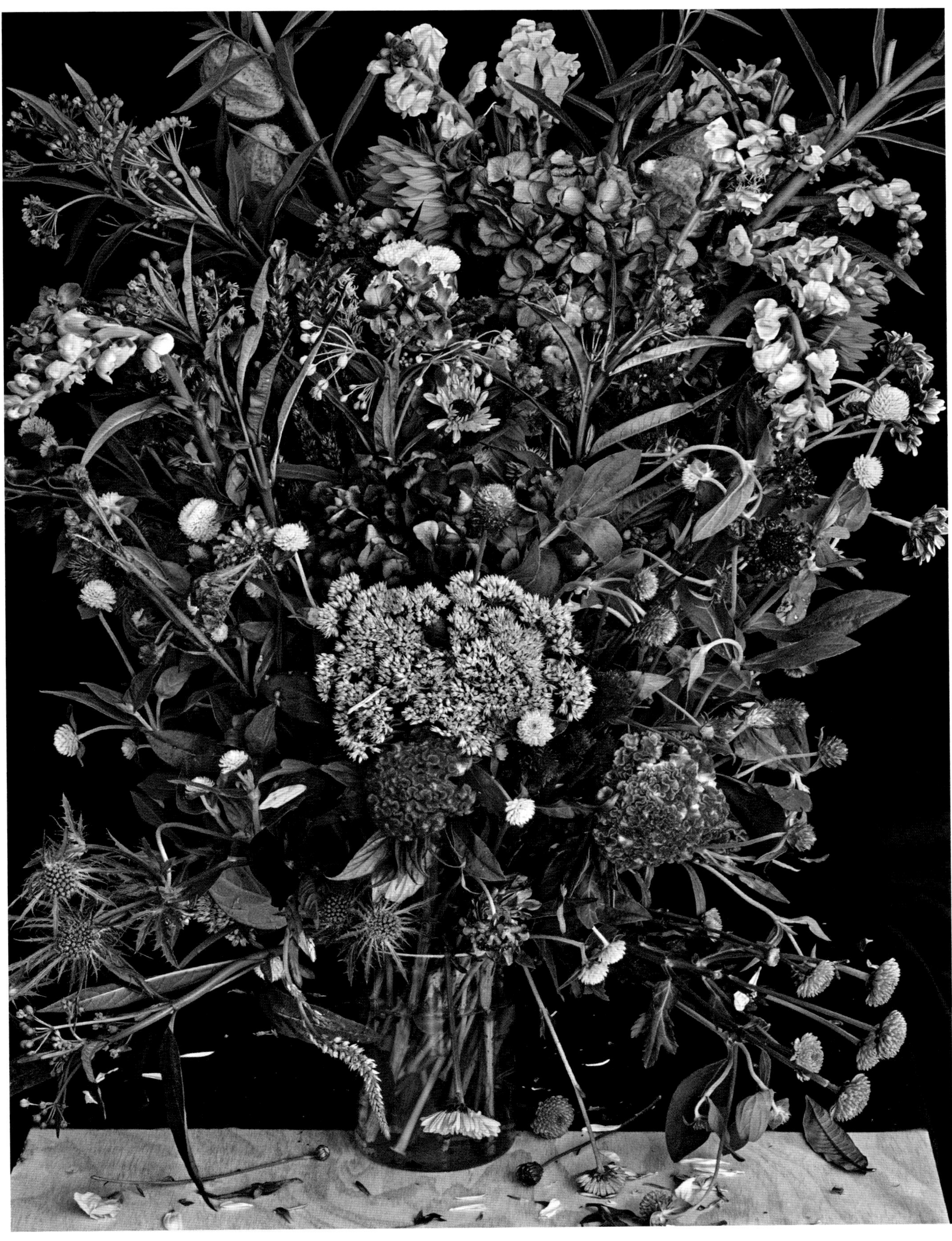

ABELARDO MORELL
2016 – Flowers for Lisa #26, 2016

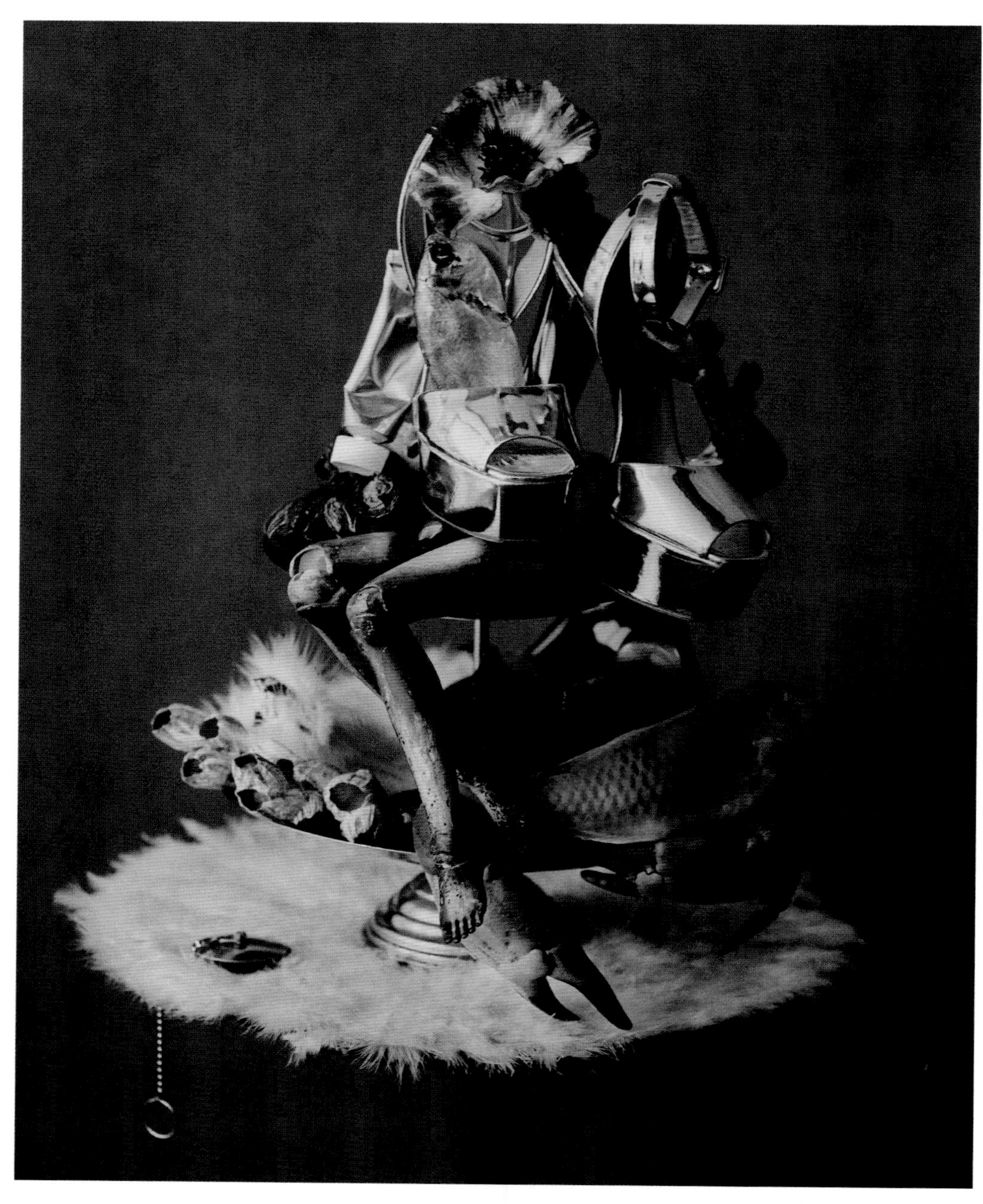

JULIA HETTA
Of Fish and Flowers, for *AnOther Magazine*, 2016

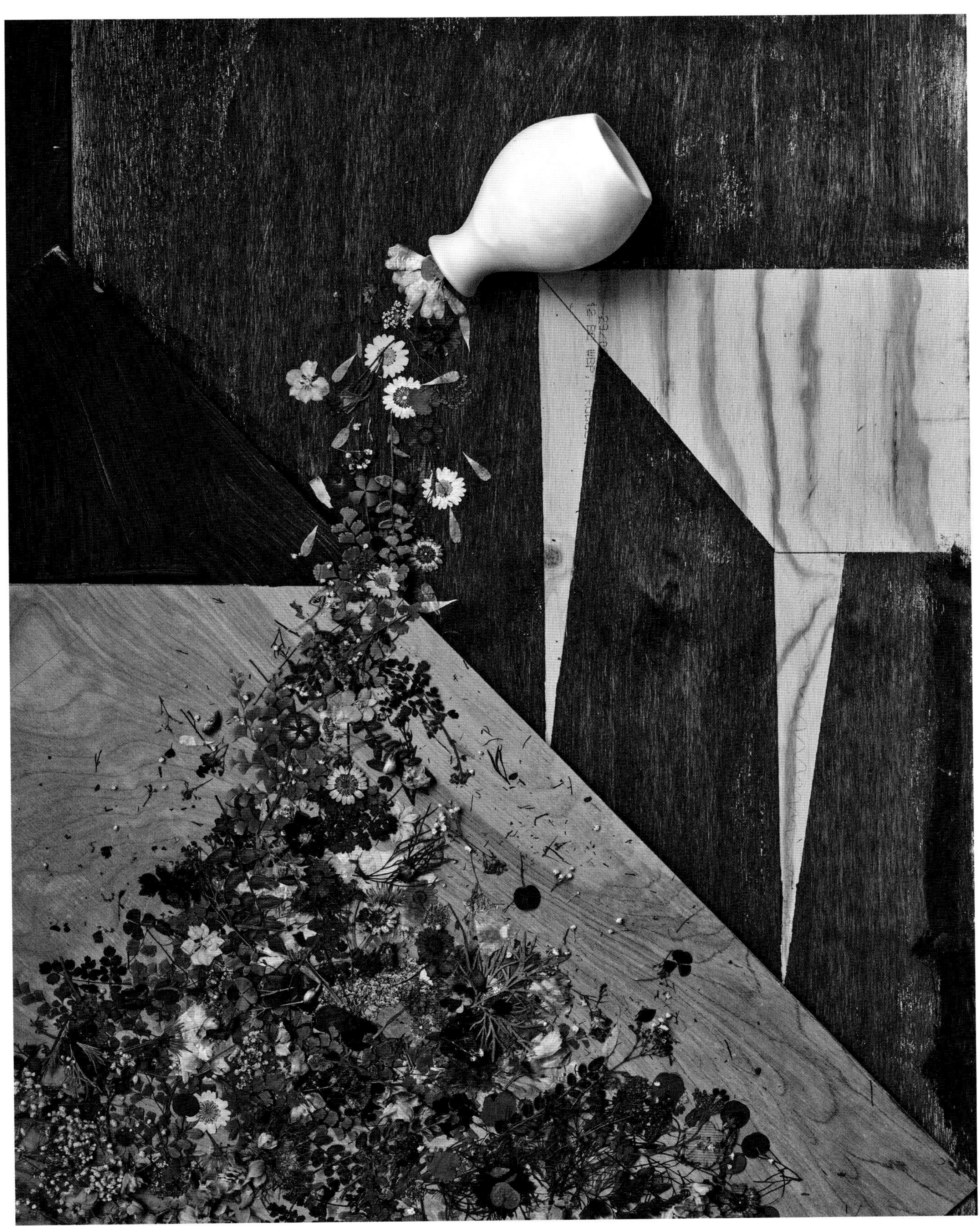

ABELARDO MORELL
2016 – Flowers for Lisa #30, 2016

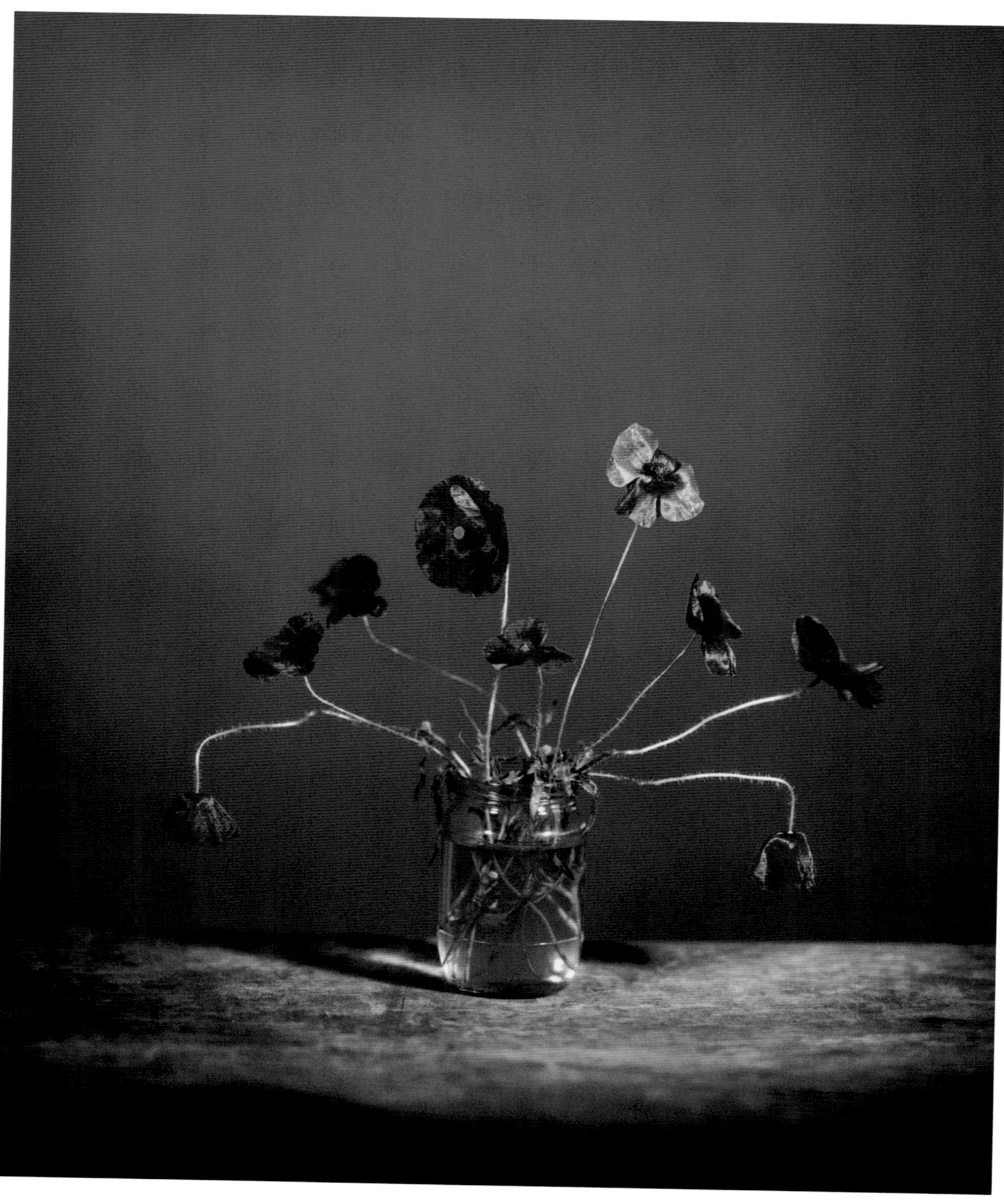

BRENDAN BARRY
Common Poppy, 2020

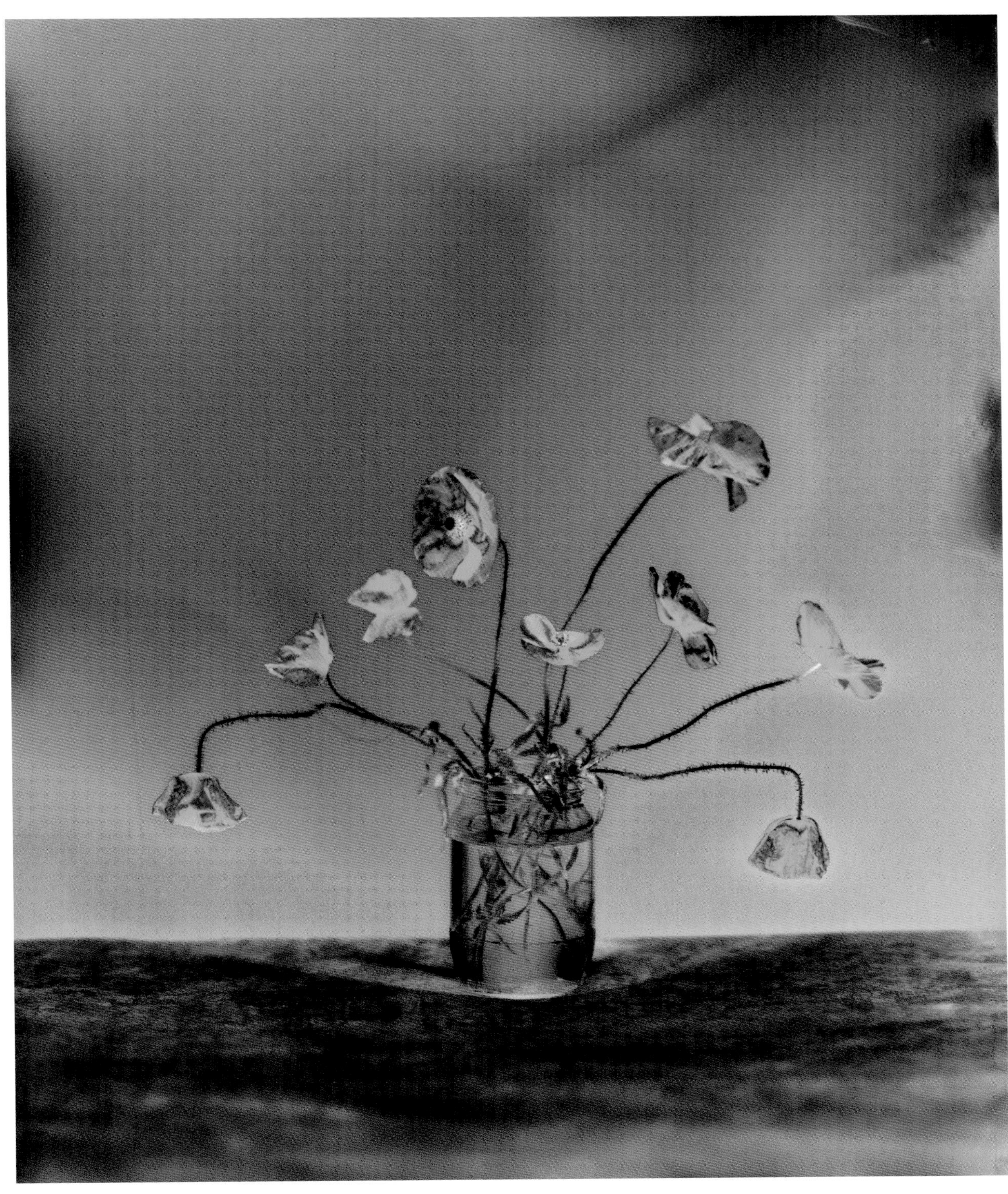

BRENDAN BARRY
Common Poppy, 2020

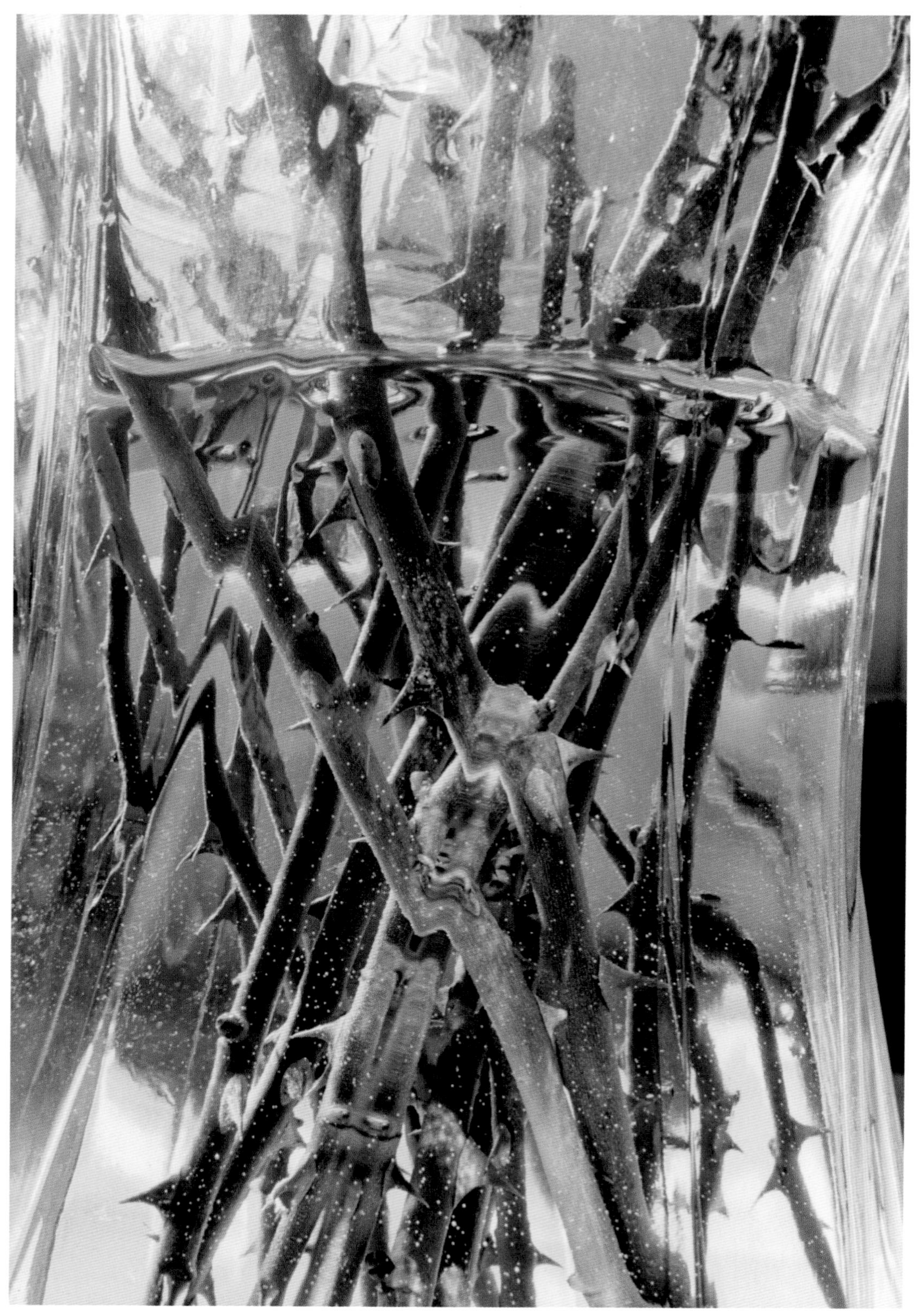

LEE FRIEDLANDER
Stem, 1999

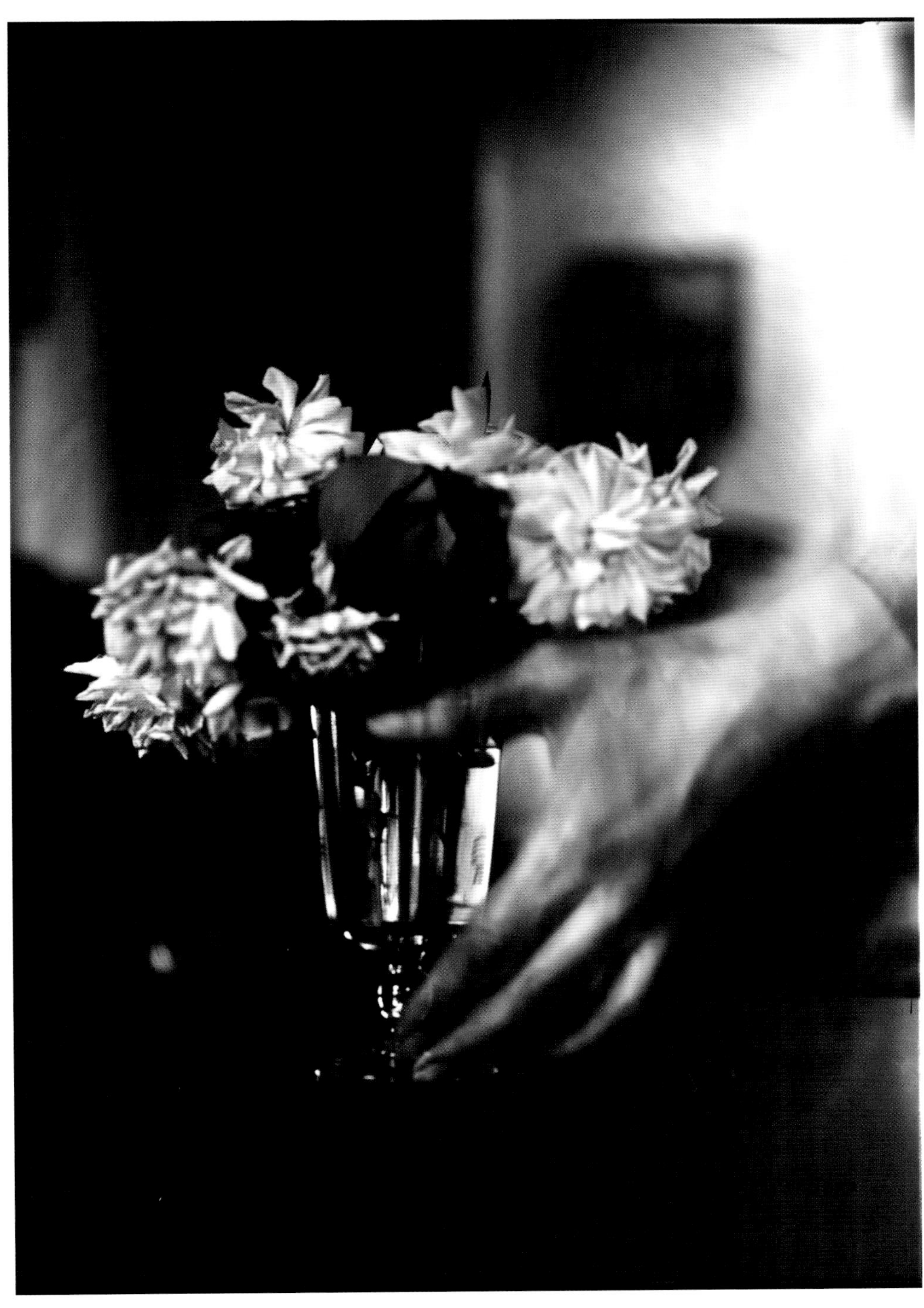

JOANNA EPSTEIN
Untitled, from the series *Isolation (Self)*, 2020

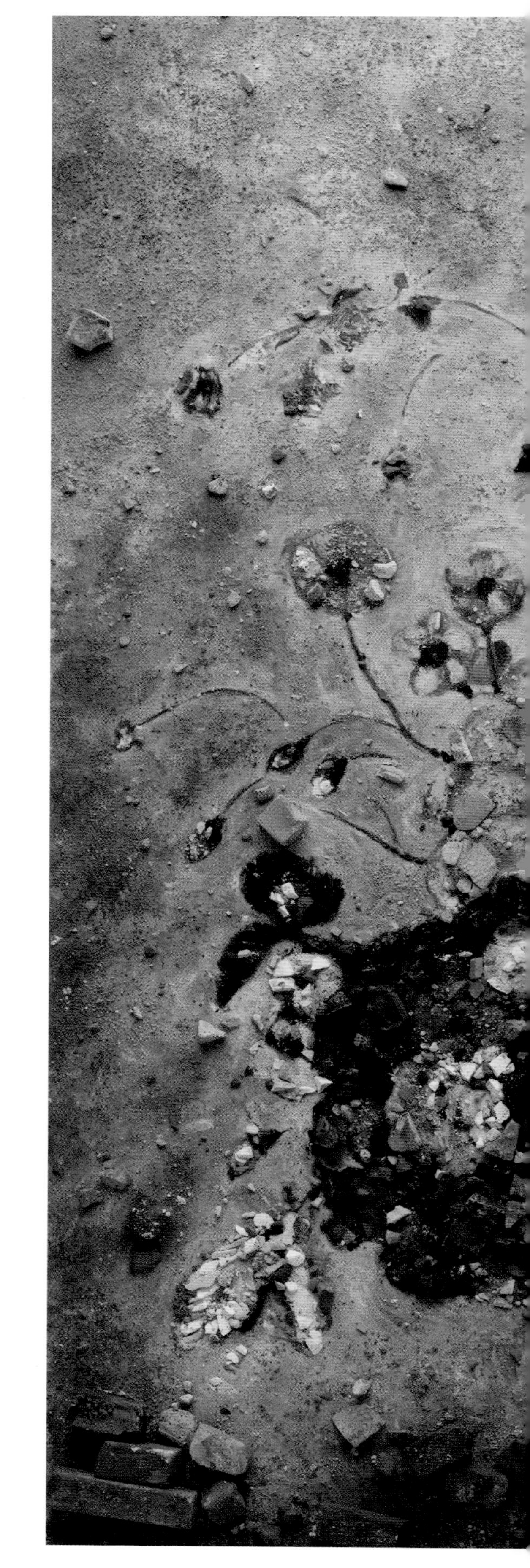

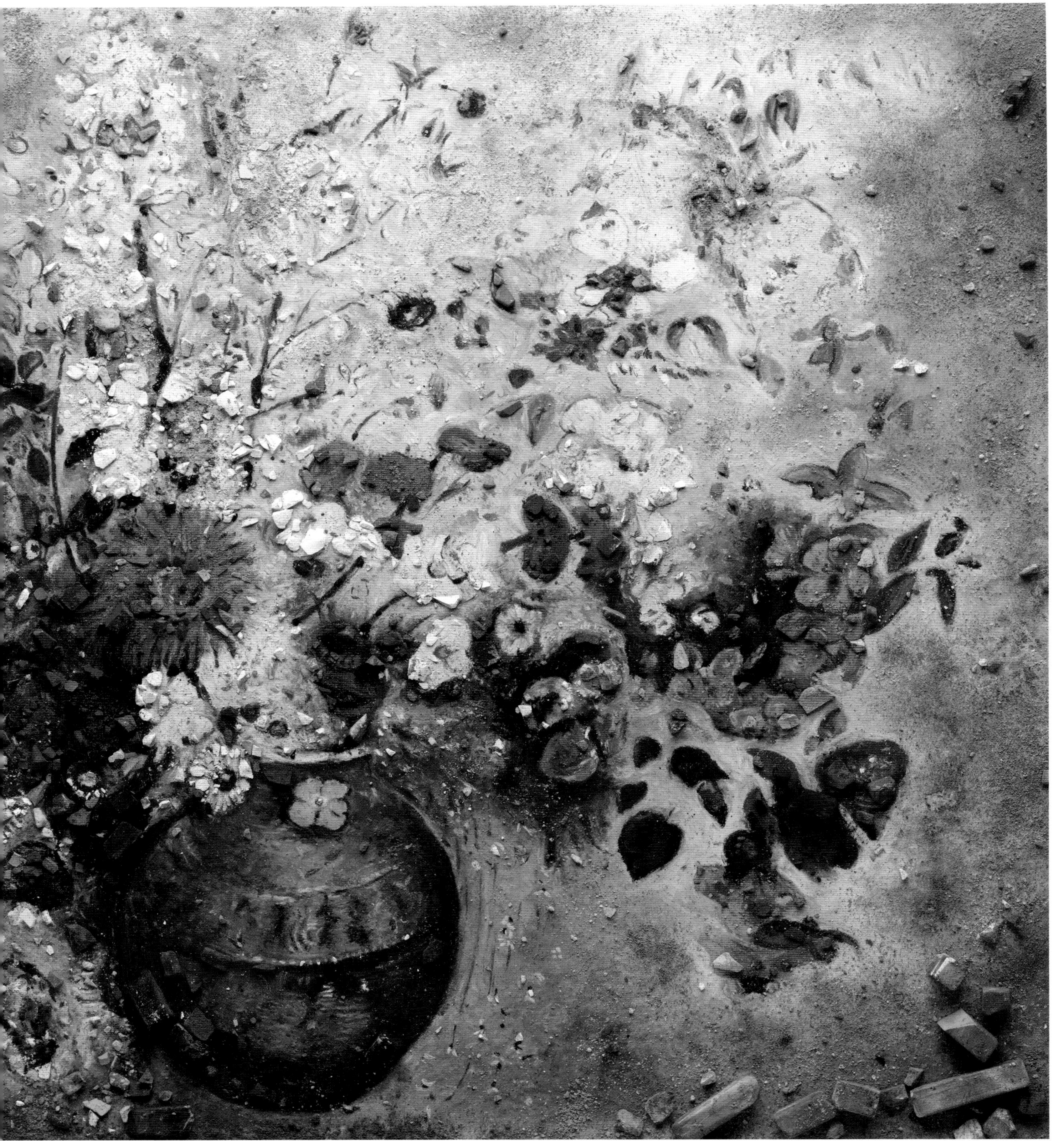

VIK MUNIZ
Metachrome (Flowers, after Redon II), 2016

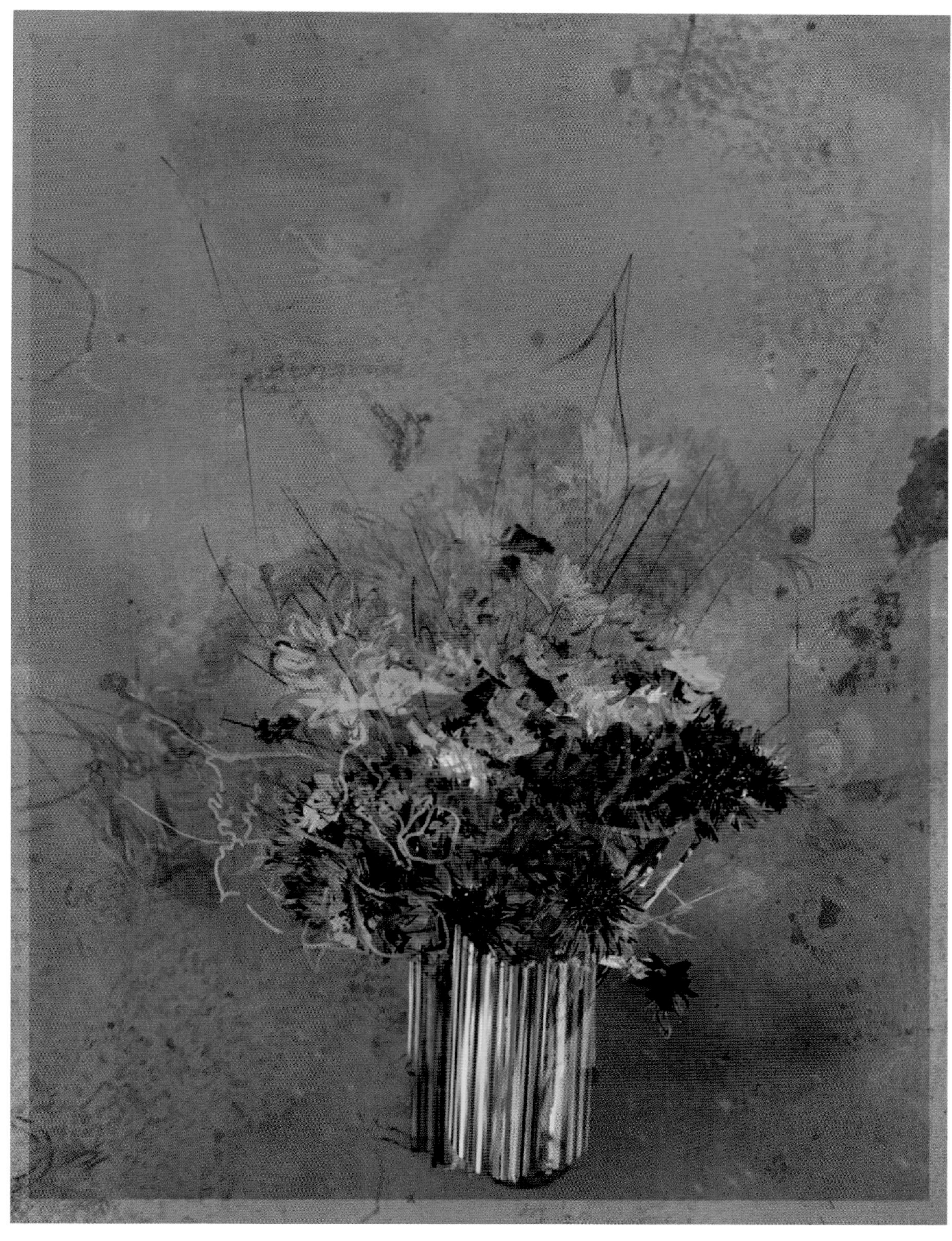

PETRA CORTRIGHT
PC_Flower_Vase 001, 2021

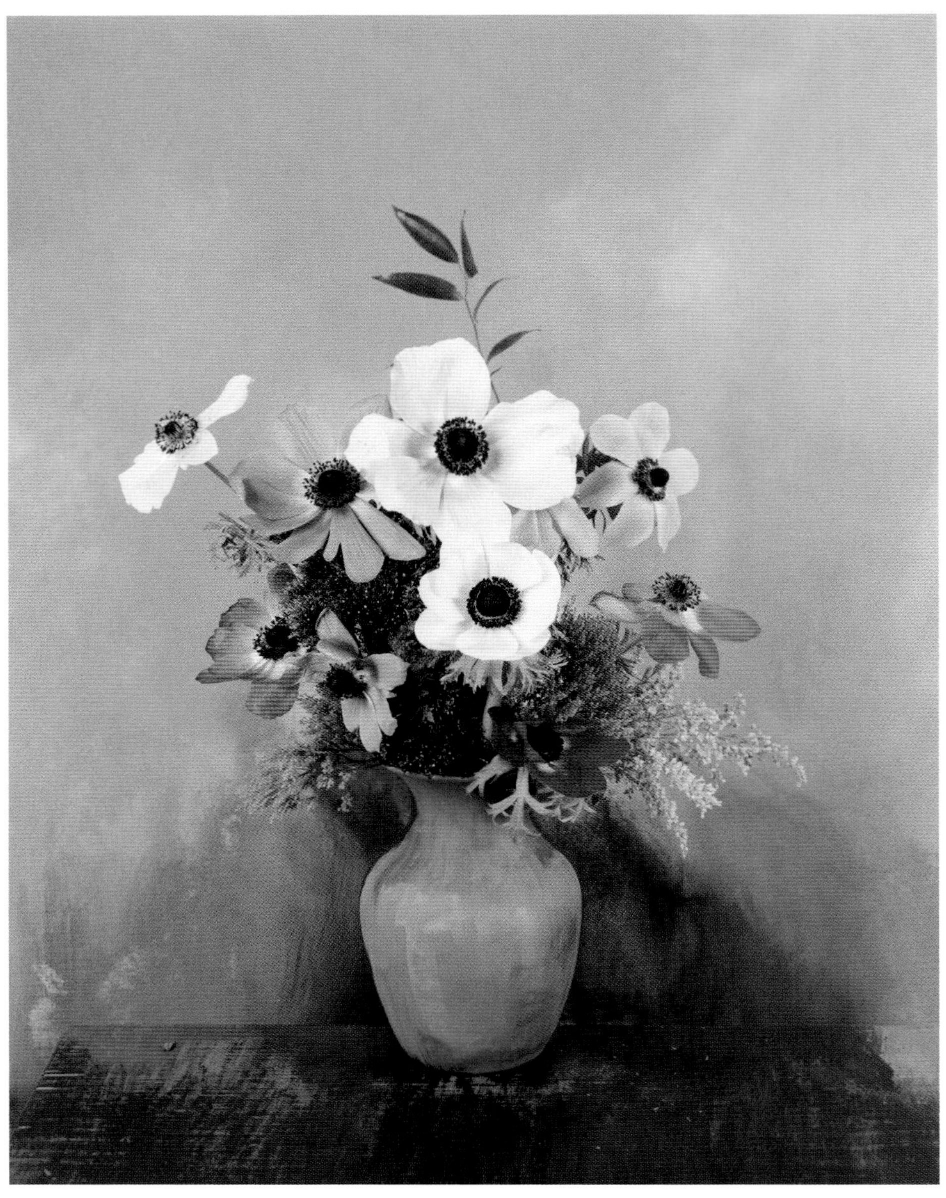

SHARON CORE
1905, 2011

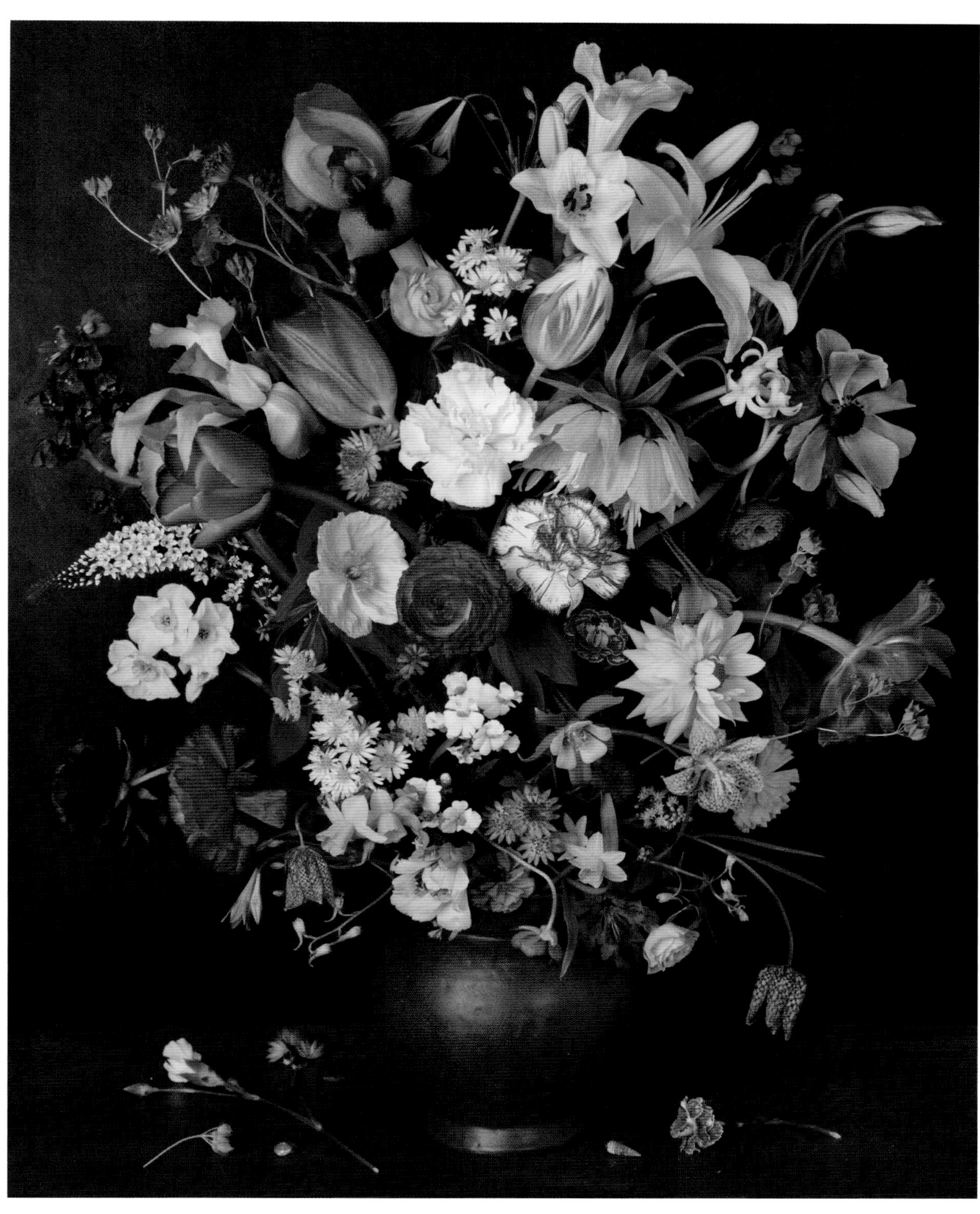

SHARON CORE
1634, 2011

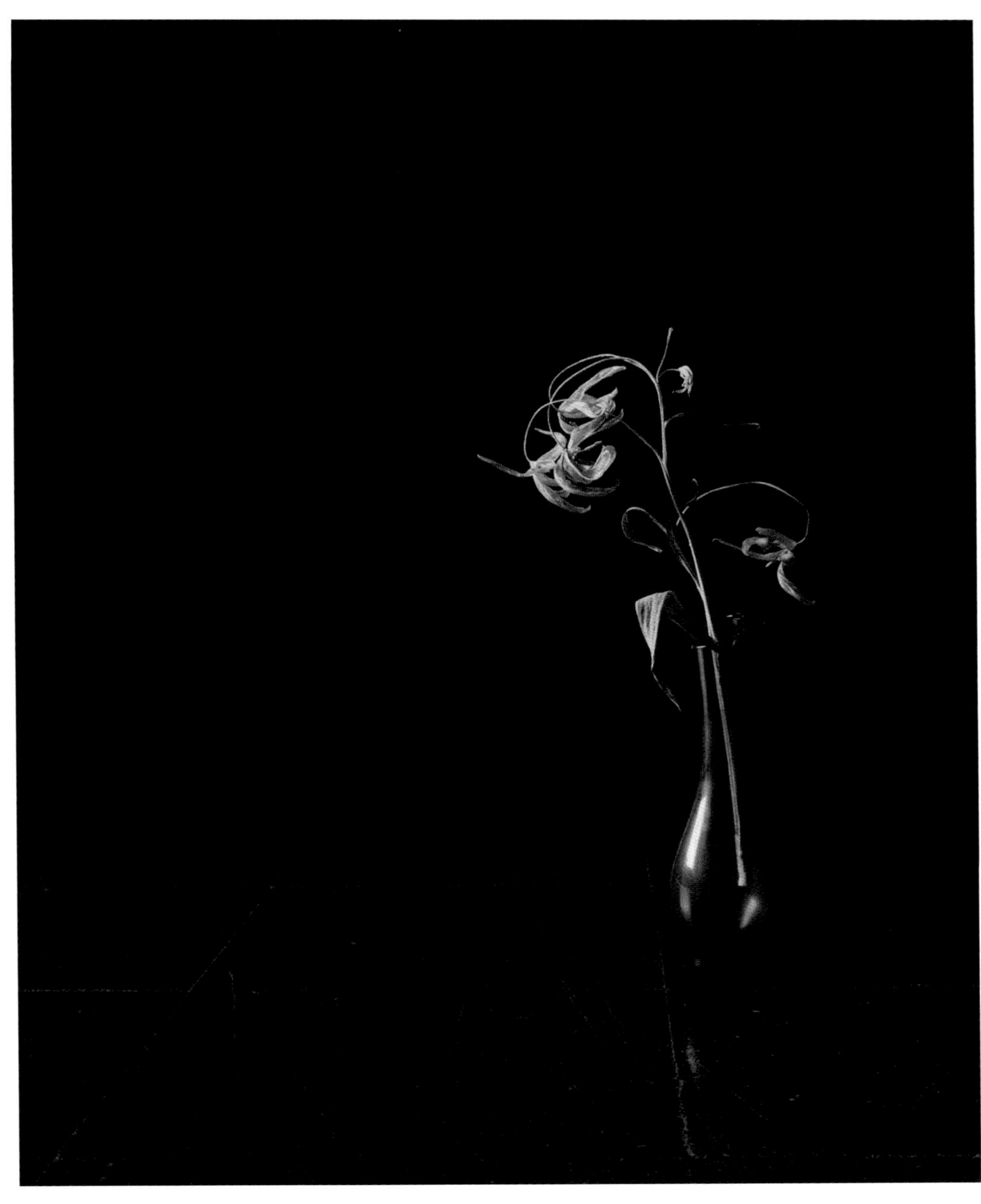

BRIGITTE LUSTENBERGER
Flowers XXI, from the series *Still Untitled*, 2014

IN SITU

For many of us, the photography of flowers carries an assumption that we're referring to *cut* flowers, artfully arranged in a vase by the photographer, most likely in a studio, a setting that allows the use of a background of choice, often (but not necessarily) neutral, and carefully controlled effects of light and shadow. But some photographers aren't interested in selecting and positioning the flowers themselves; they prefer to record the compositional efforts of others, finding colourful arrangements in a market stall, in a friend's house or even spied through an apartment window. For still others, the impulse to photograph flowers is best satisfied outdoors – in parks and gardens, tamed or wild, or on the vast tracts of commercial growers. For the urban photographer, the botanic garden is particularly fertile terrain, with its 'exotics' from the world over. Sometimes, though, it's the photographer's own cultivated patch of paradise that satisfies the desire.

Edwin Smith, the great twentieth-century British photographer of flowers and trees, argued that the photographer 'who lives in his eyes is continually confronted with scenes and spectacles that compel his attention, or admiration...Photography, to many of its addicts, is a convenient and simple means of discharging this ever-recurring debt to the visual world.'[1] For other visual addicts, the *un*natural world is the desirable realm: the streets of the city, so rich in spectacle, where a solitary flower might hold its own against acres of glass, steel and concrete. For some, the flower is merely an accessory to an intriguing scene, a supporting actor, so to speak, in an urban drama. Paradoxically, even situations of warfare offer up intriguing juxtapositions. Or, a flower may simply be chanced upon, and a fleeting moment seized. Such photographers often say that the world is interesting enough as it is, without the need to manipulate or rearrange anything. Others beg to disagree; the world of contemporary photography is all the richer for encompassing the two approaches.

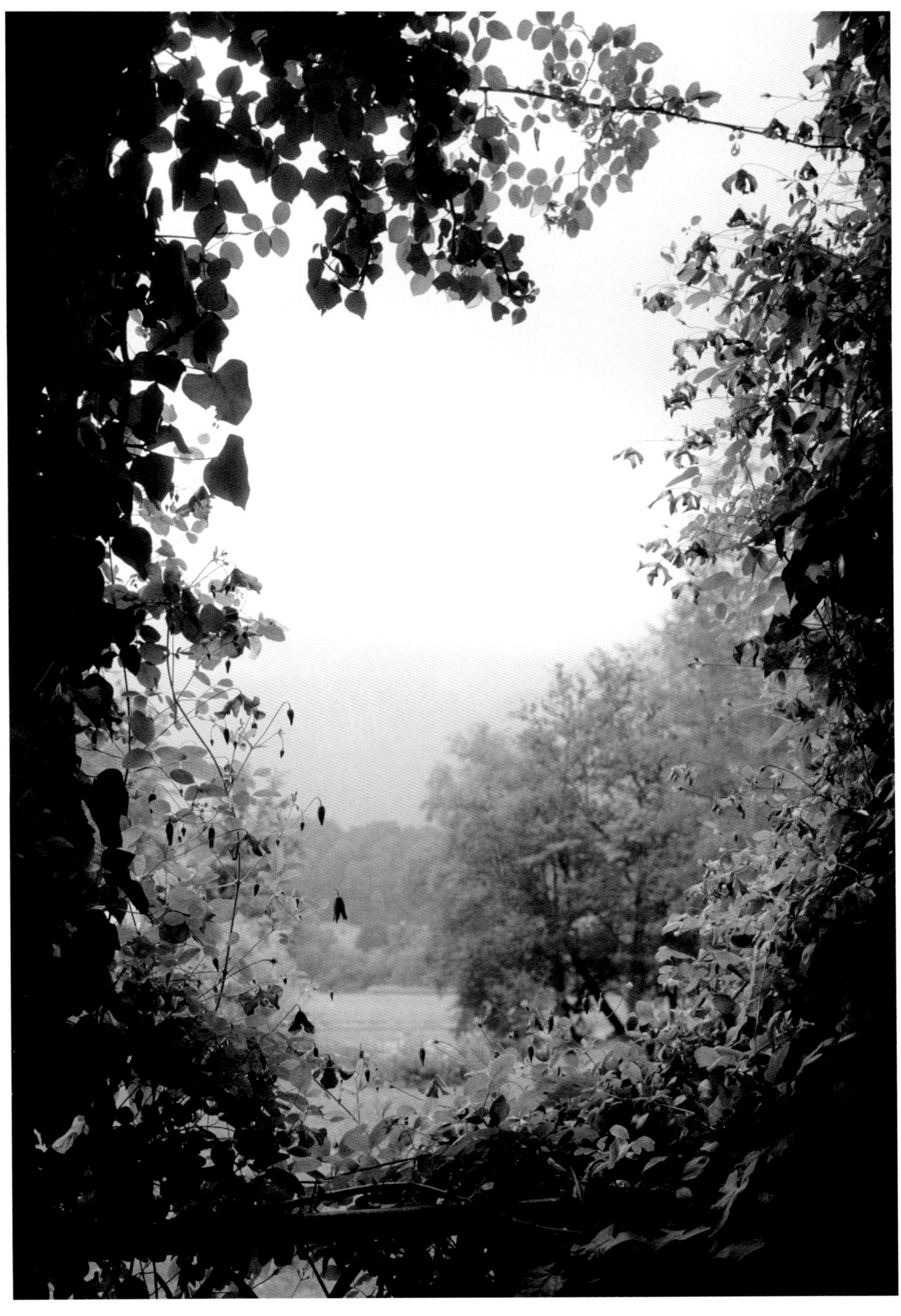

RICHARD DE TSCHARNER
Transparence, Switzerland, 2003

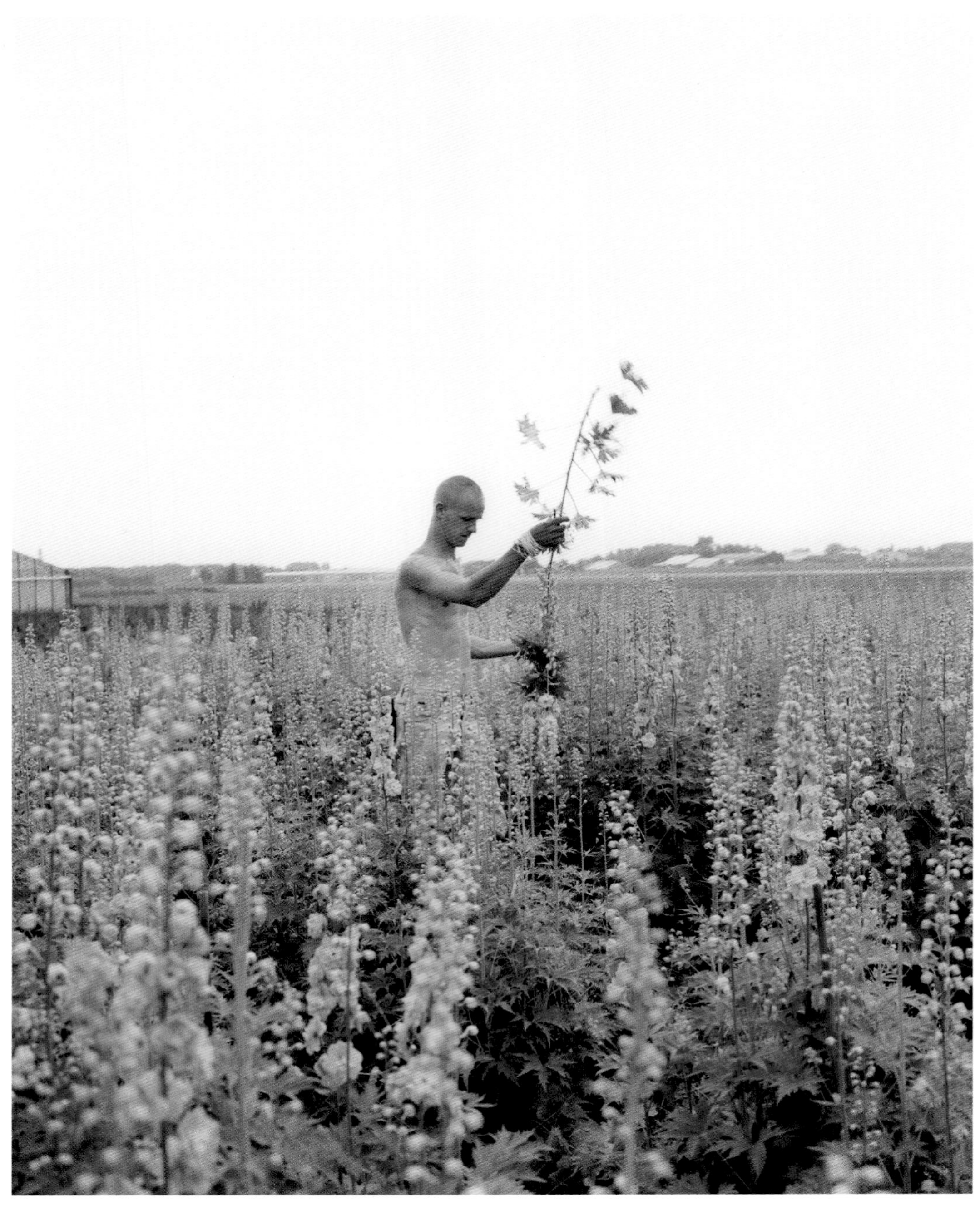

NOOR DAMEN
Delphinium Rose, from the series *Flower-picking Men*, 2000

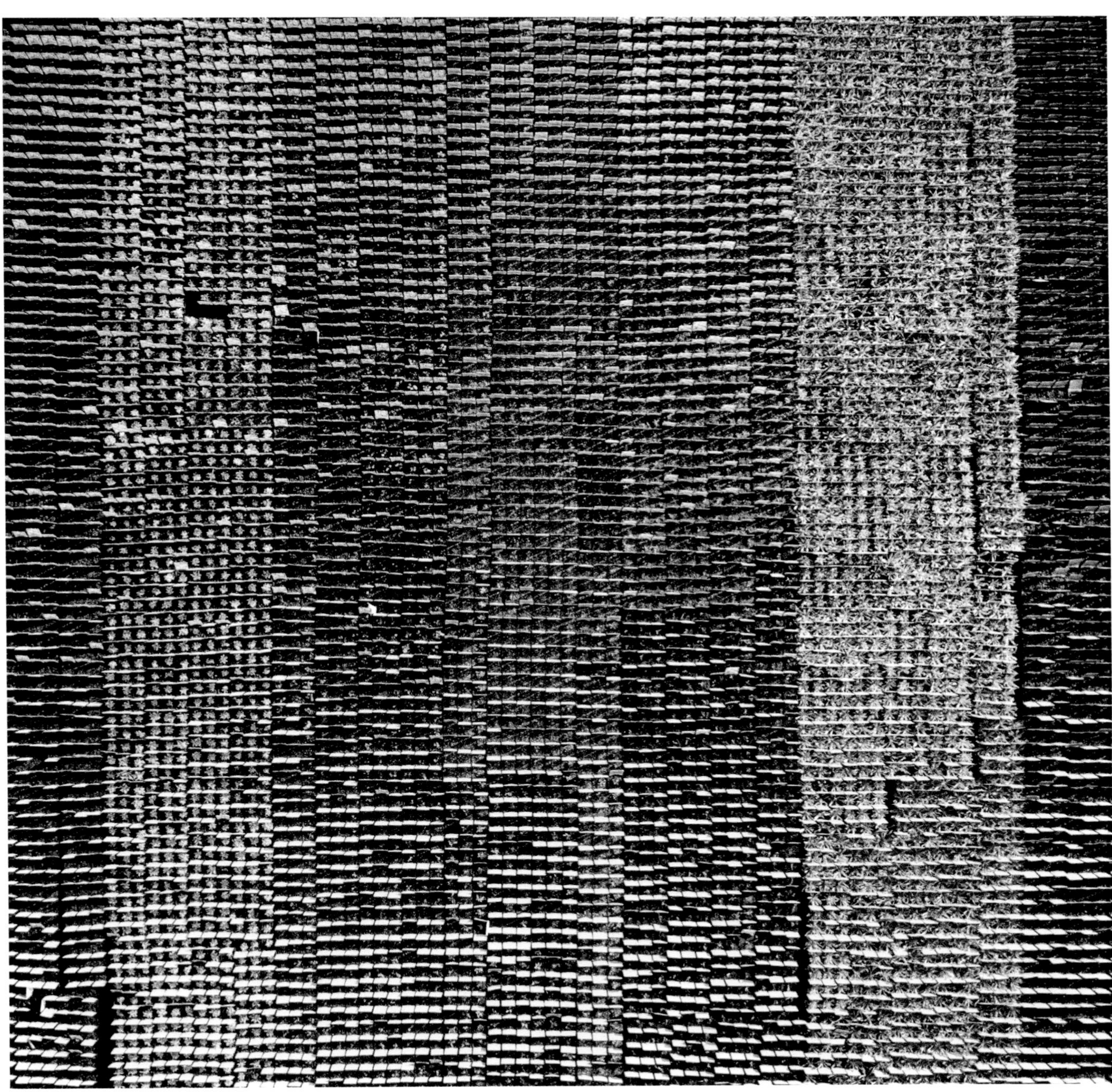

GERCO DE RUIJTER
Untitled (Perennials Etten-Leur), 2014

TO SHATTER THE NARROW SPHERE

A little more than 100 years ago, the Belgian writer Maurice Maeterlinck wrote a celebrated text, The Intelligence of Flowers (1907). *In soaring prose he described how the flower has one object: 'to escape above from the fatality below, to evade, to transgress the heavy and sombre law, to set itself free, to shatter the narrow sphere, to invent or invoke wings, to escape as far as it can, to conquer the space in which destiny encloses it, to approach another kingdom, to penetrate into an active and moving world'.*[2] *Although these sentiments do not appear radical today, it does not mean that they weren't perceived as such a century ago, when there was much talk of 'man's conquest' of nature, as if it were an adversary or, at the very least an unruly force that needed to be kept in its place. Human beings have indeed come a long way in understanding the non-human* intelligence *possessed by plants. Flower photographers (to use an admittedly awkward shorthand) do not restrict themselves to parks, gardens and household vases – the domesticated sphere. They describe flowers everywhere.*

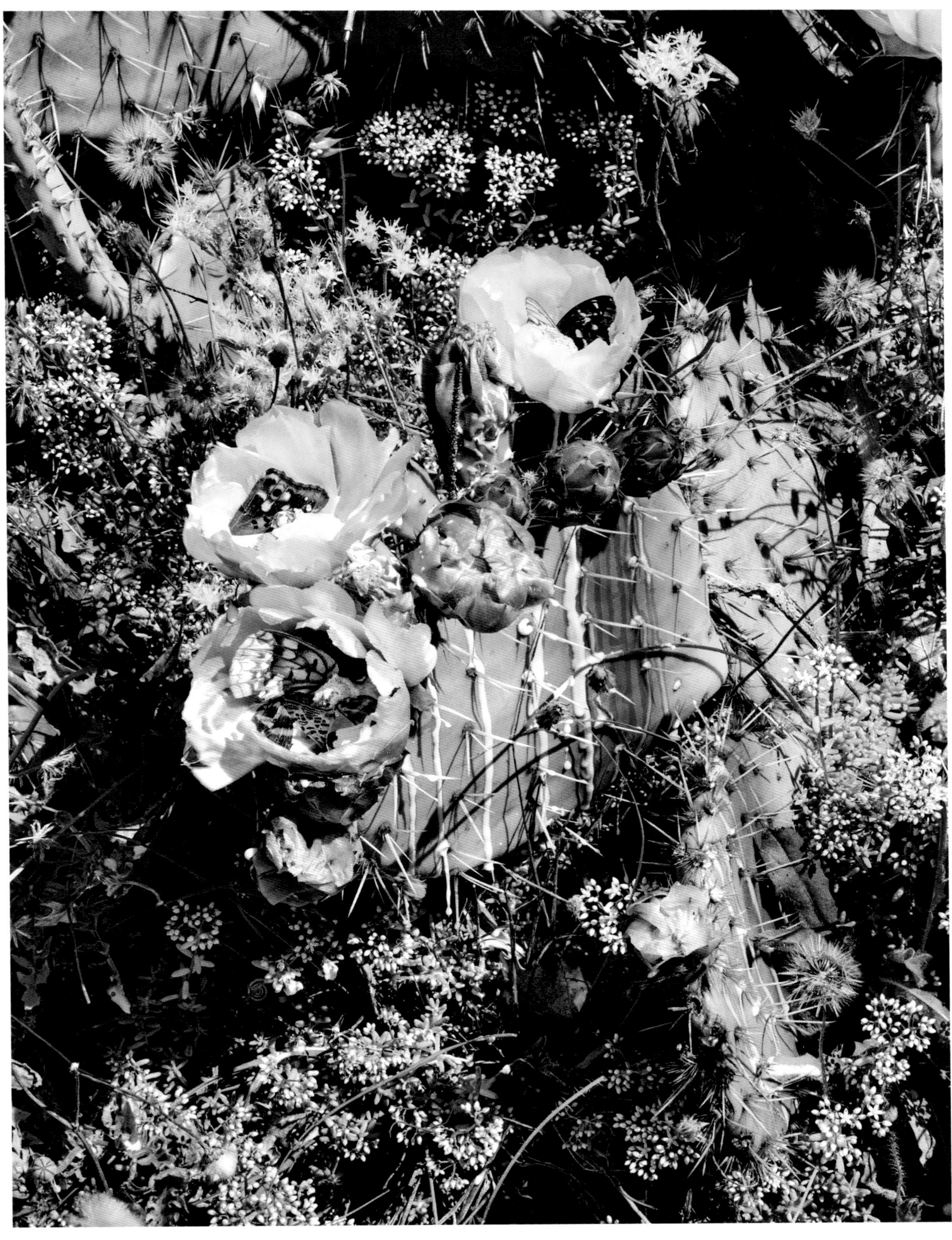

JOHN MACLEAN
Cactus, 2018

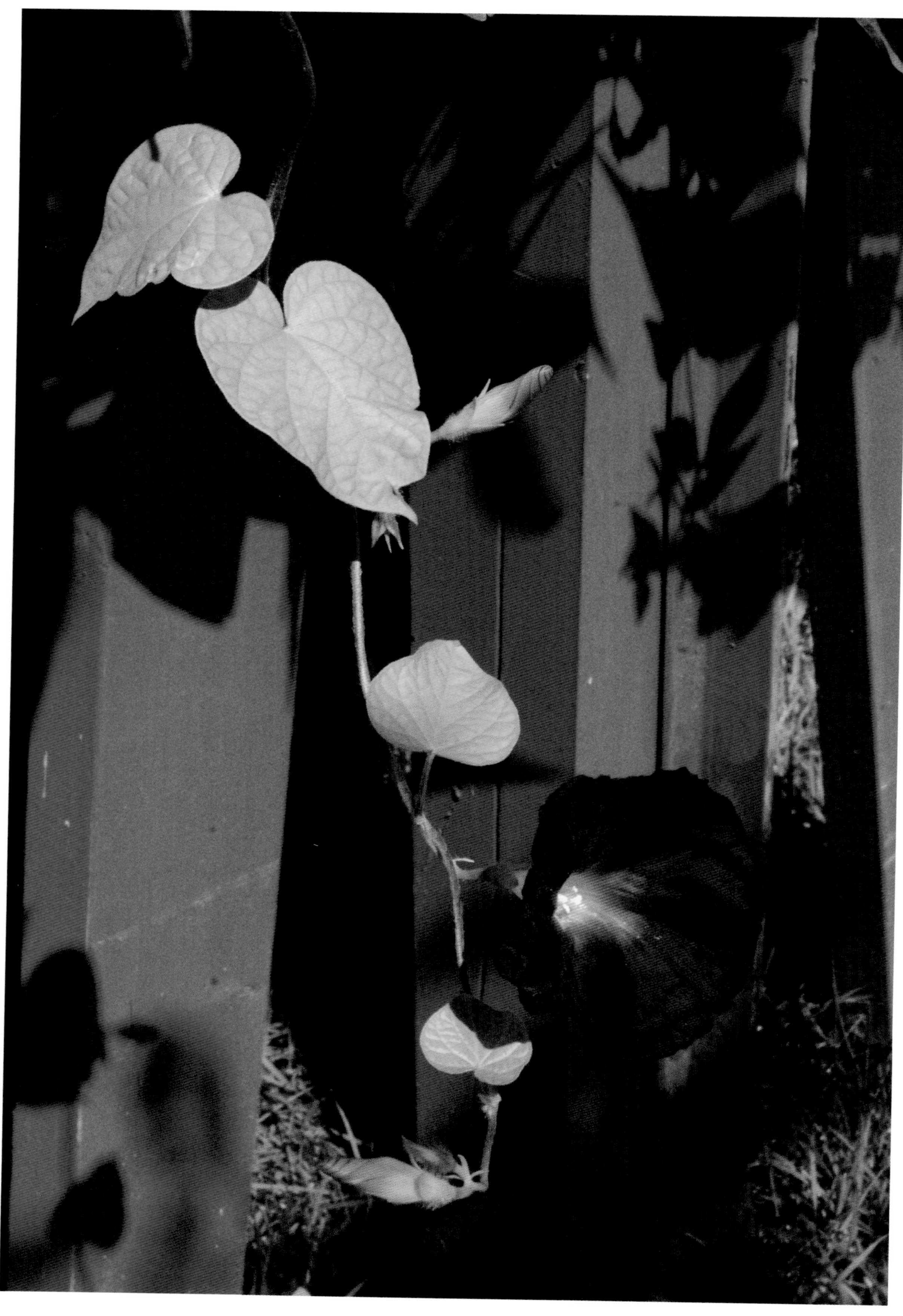

ROBERT WALKER
Montréal botanique #43, 2009

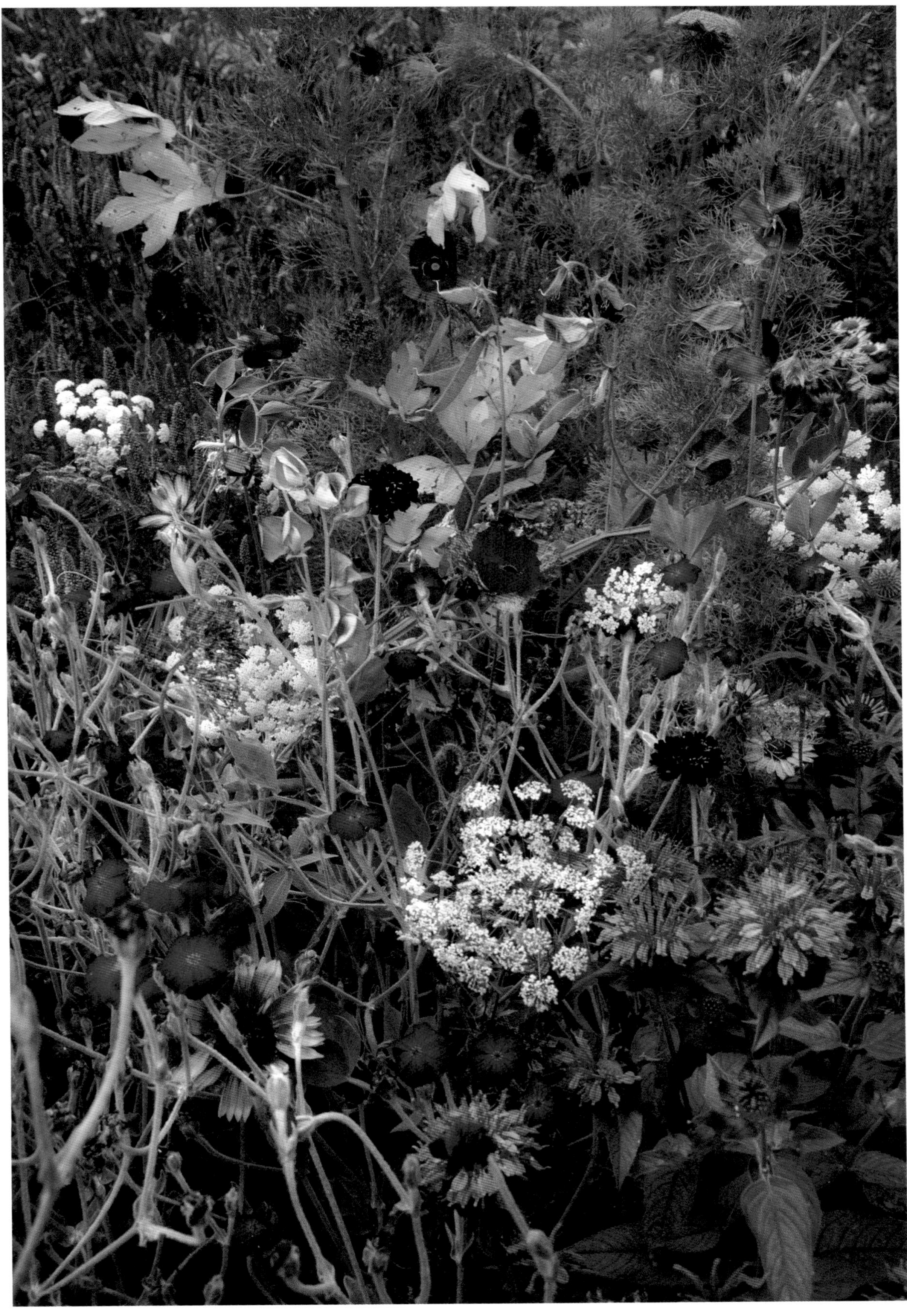

ELSPETH DIEDERIX
Mix, 2019

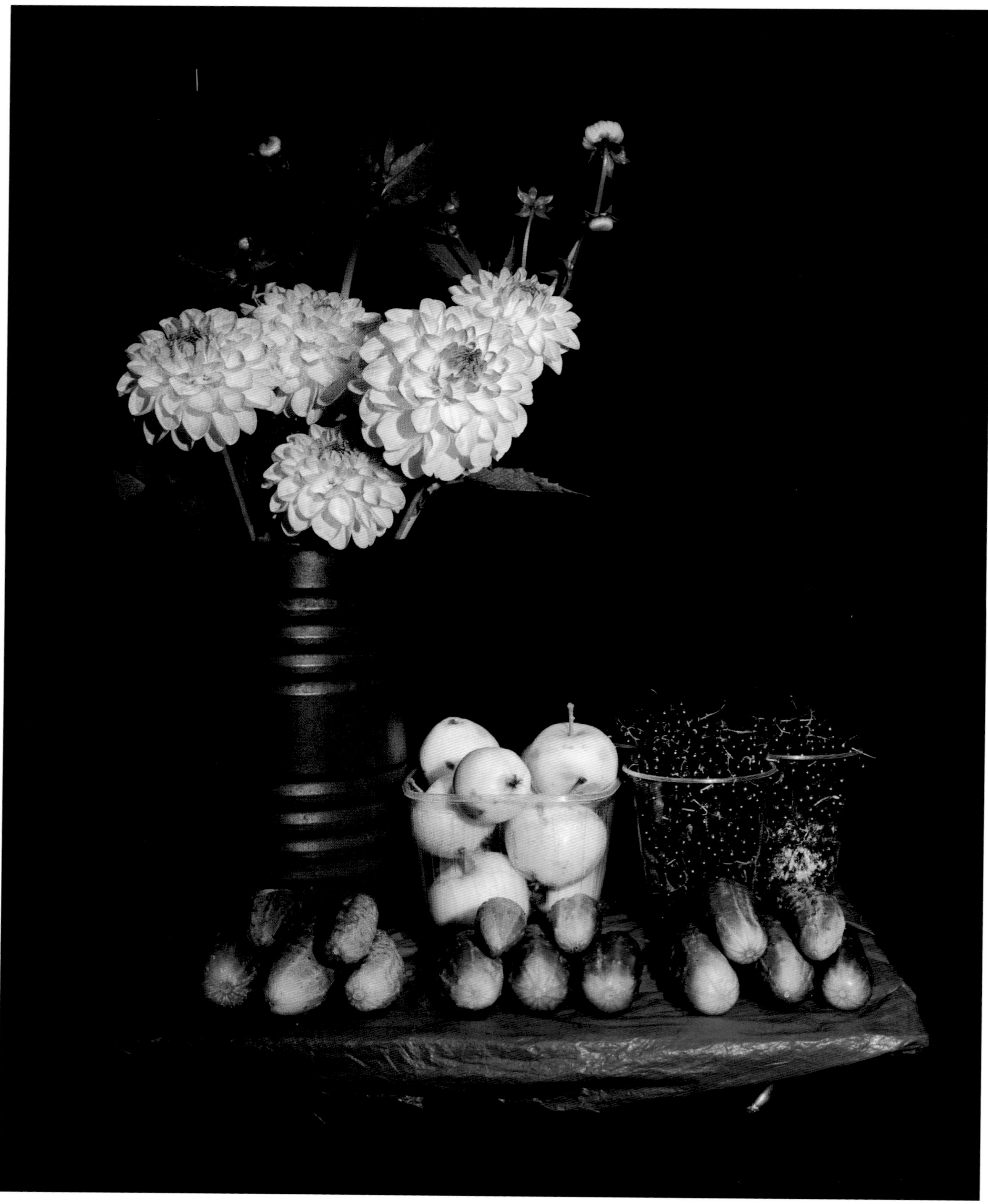

LIA DARJES
Stillleben mit Dahlien und Johannisbeeren, from the series *Tempora Morte*, 2016
Every day, in the Russian exclave of Kaliningrad, small, unofficial roadside markets pop up, where old women offer the modest harvest from their gardens or the nearby forest for sale to supplement their pensions.

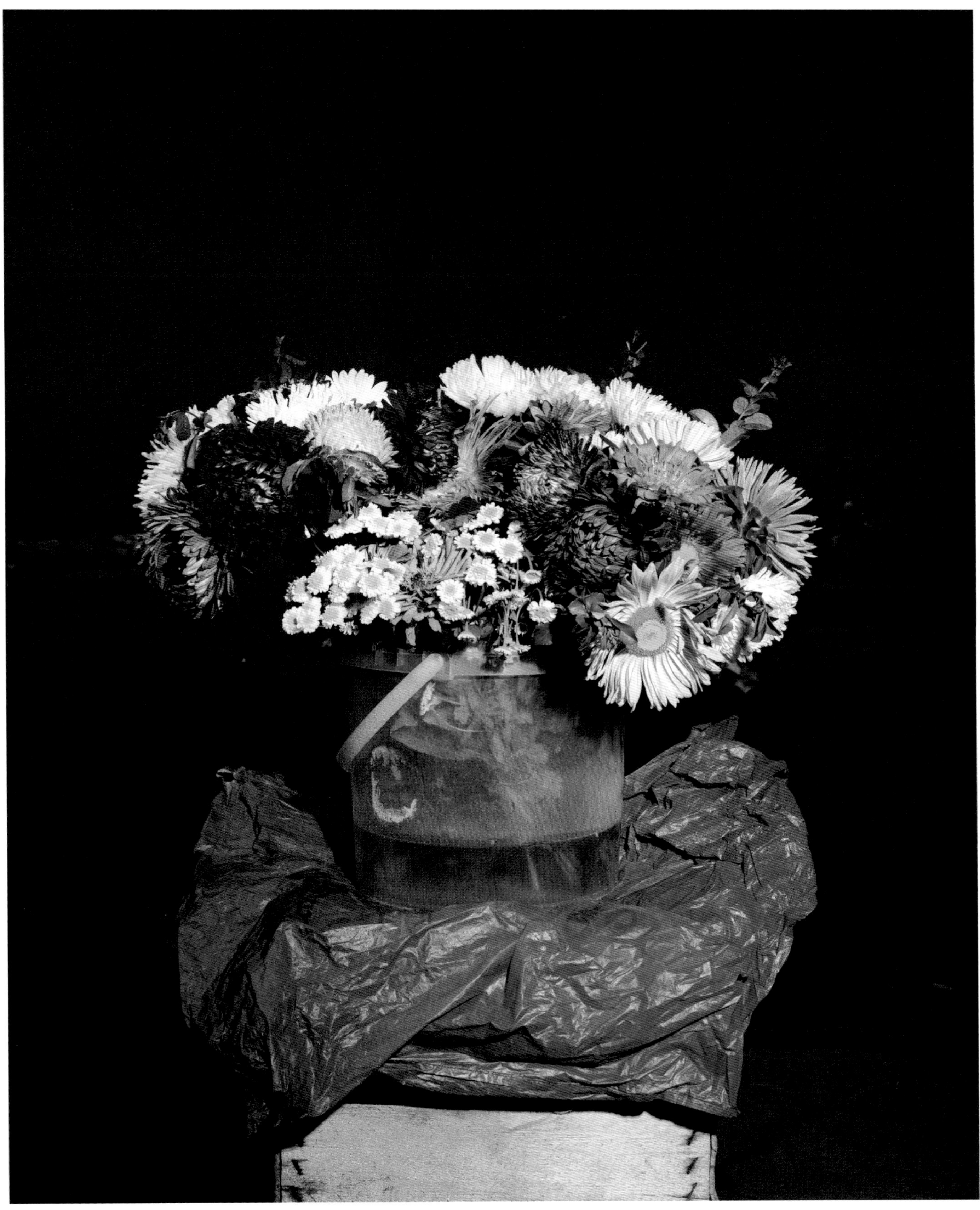

LIA DARJES
Stillleben mit Sommerblumen, from the series *Tempora Morte*, 2016

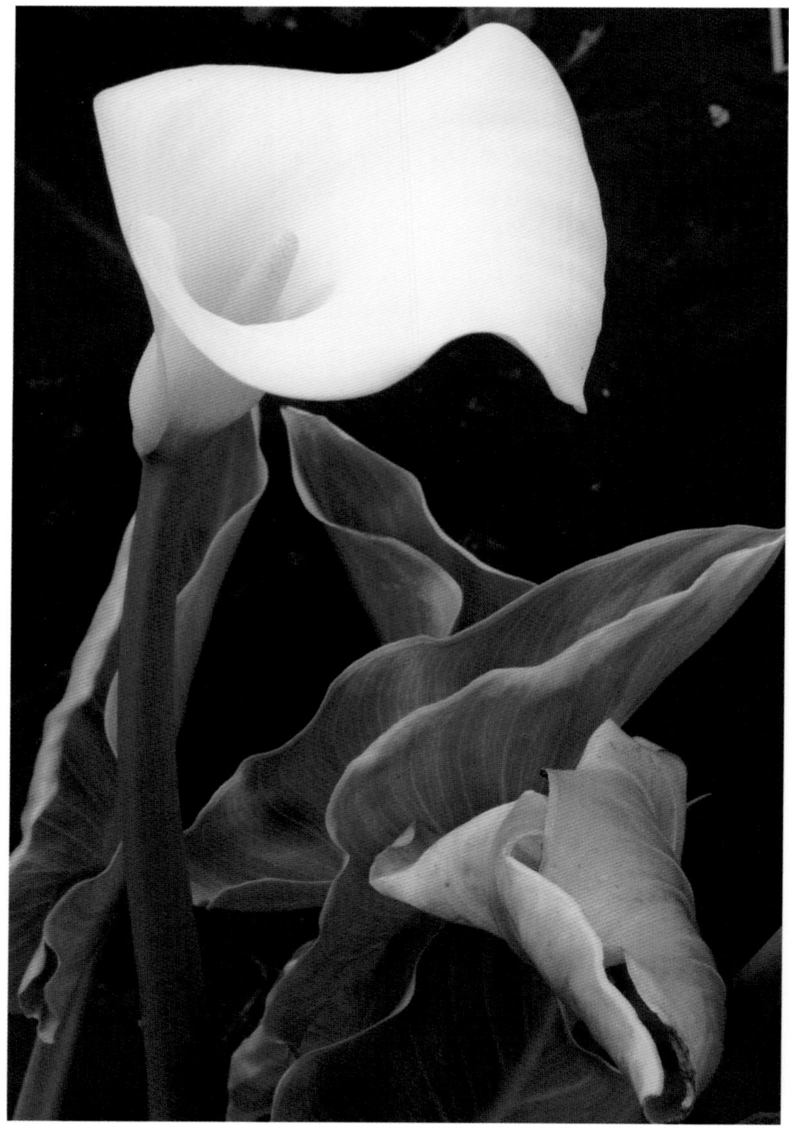

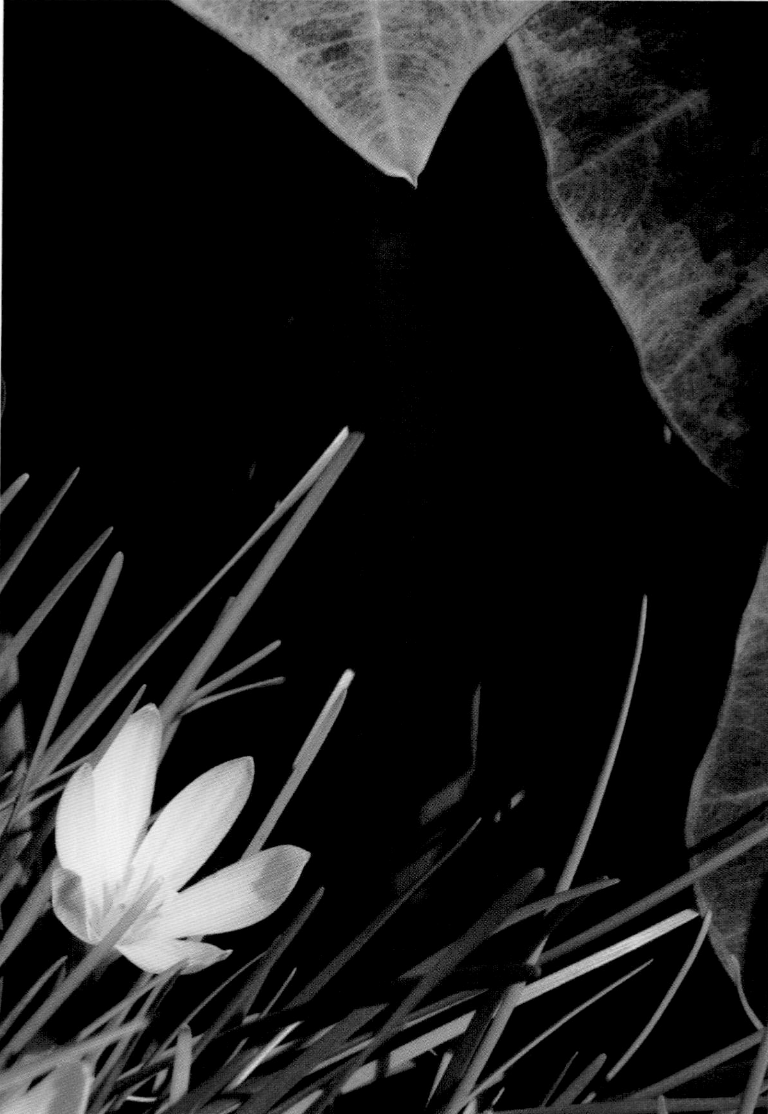

ROBERT WALKER
Montréal botanique #46, 2009 (left), and *Montréal botanique #38*, 2006

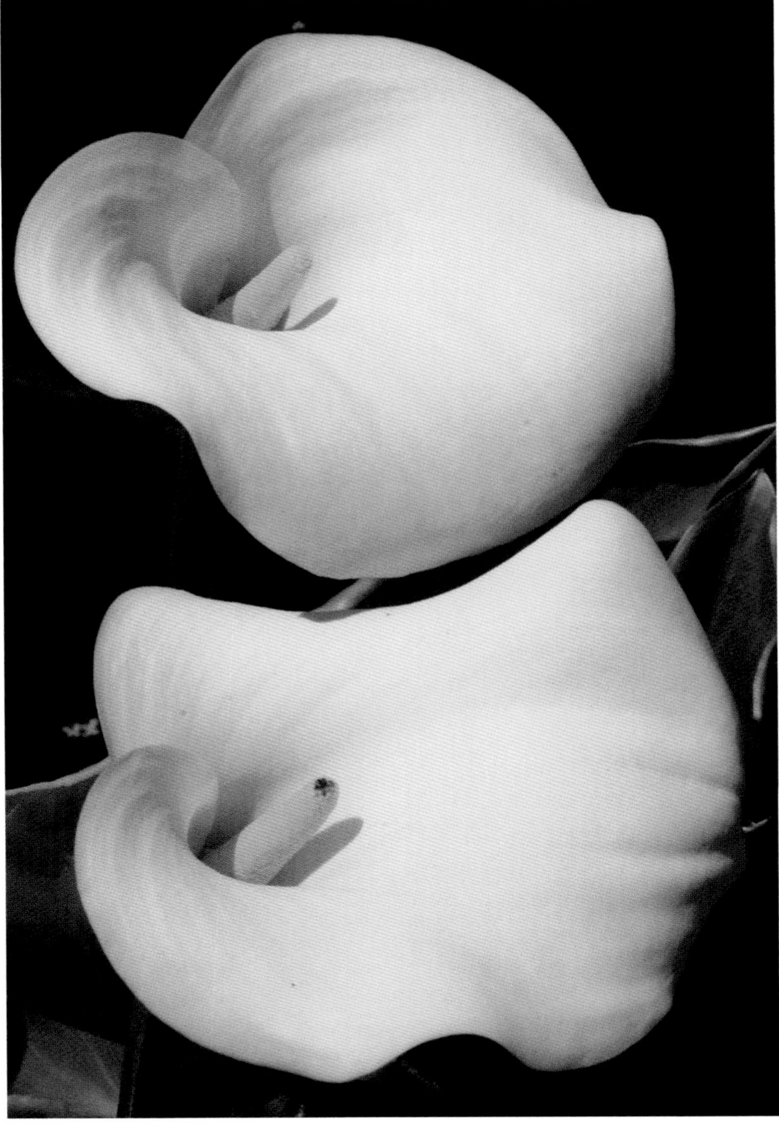

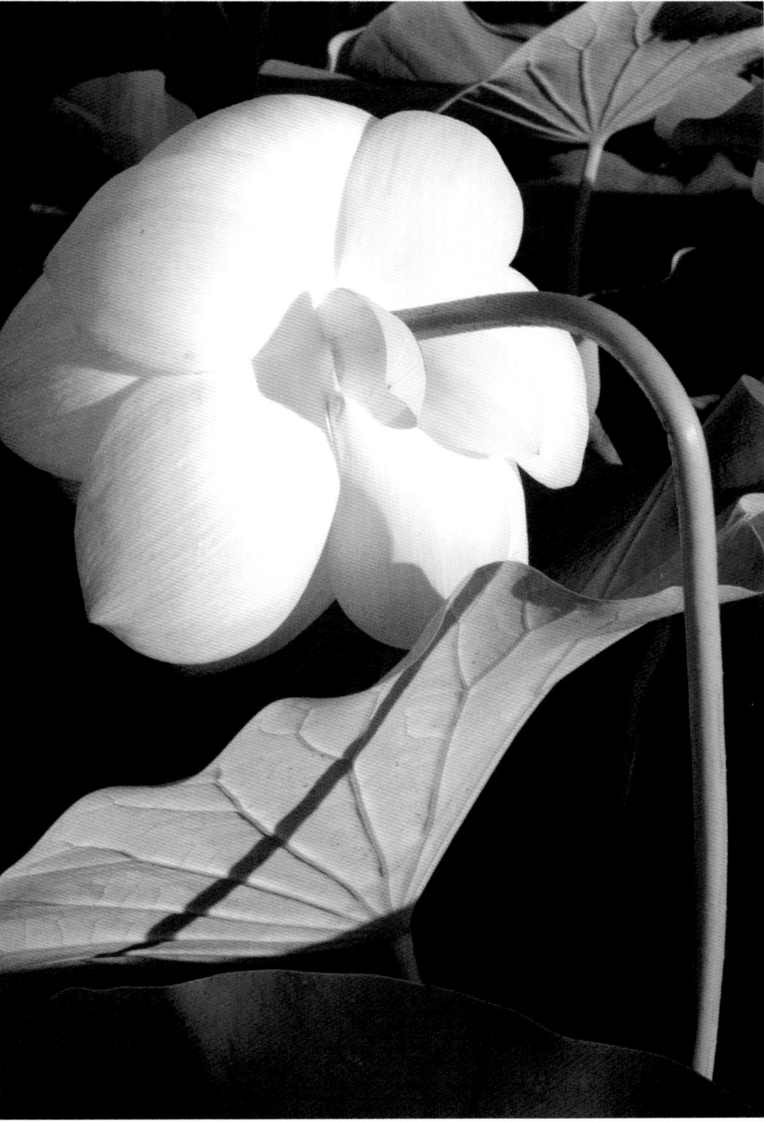

ROBERT WALKER
Montréal botanique #45, 2008 (left), and *Montréal botanique #44*, 2009

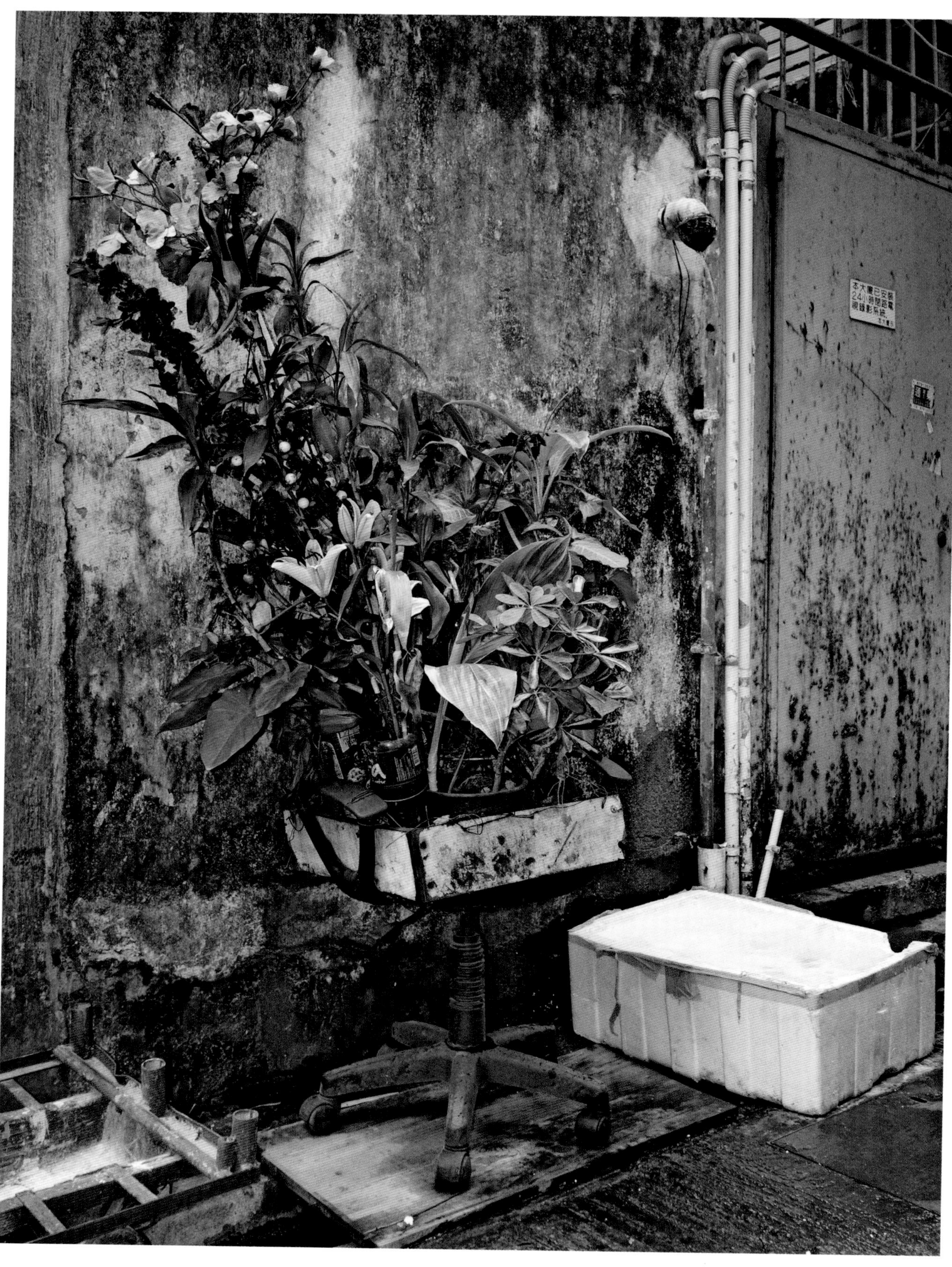

MICHAEL WOLF
Hong Kong Flora 8, 2015

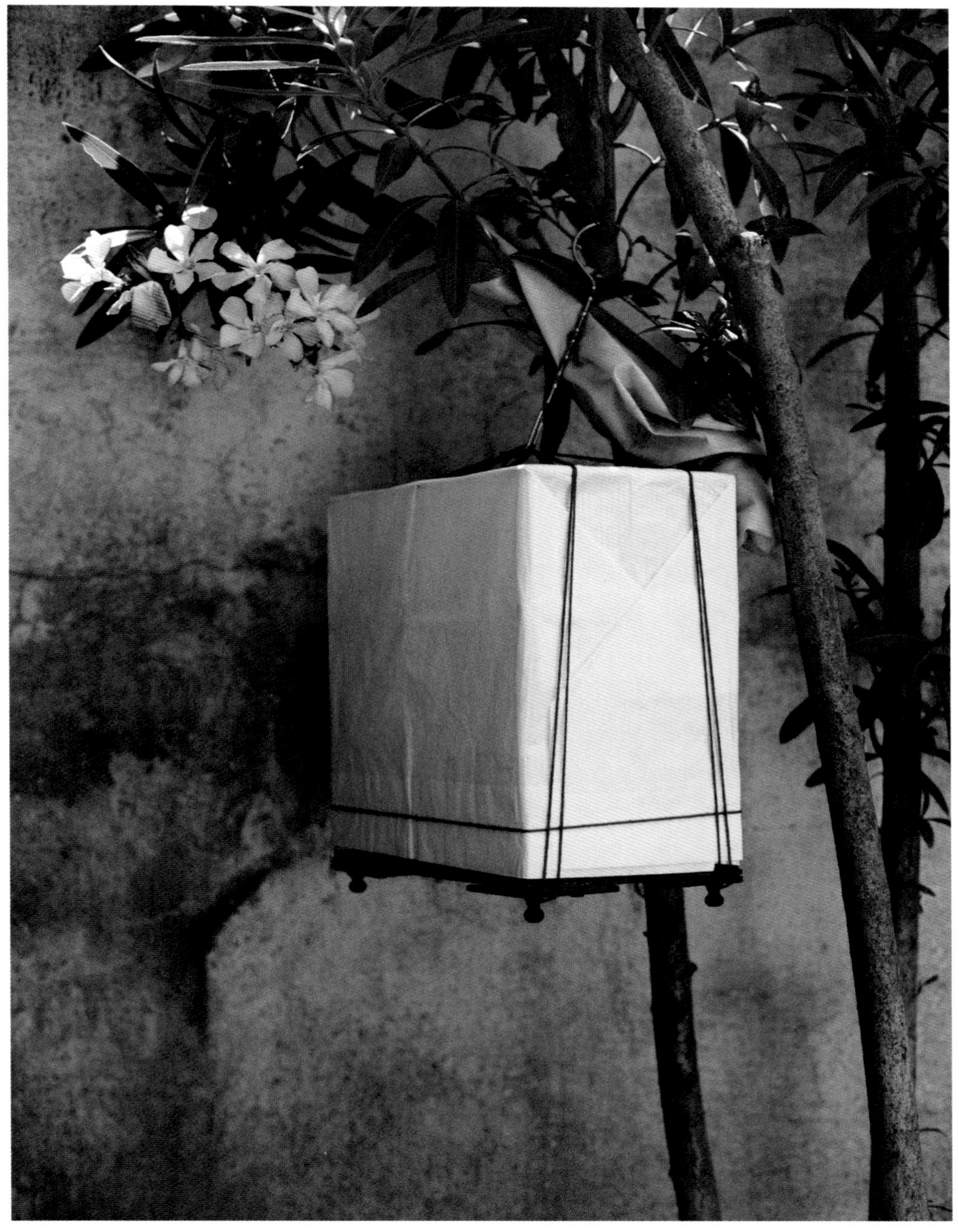

MARIA STURM AND CEMRE YEŞIL GÖNENLI
Cage #3, from the series *For Birds' Sake*, 2014

'We call this picture "the Japanese cage". It is just a regular cage inside the garden of a Birdman café, in Istanbul. Different Birdmen have different styles of wrapping the cage with paper, cloth or the way the strings are placed around the cage. Sometimes a cage will be wrapped in multiple layers of cloth or paper. The bird sings best in darkness, the Birdmen say.'

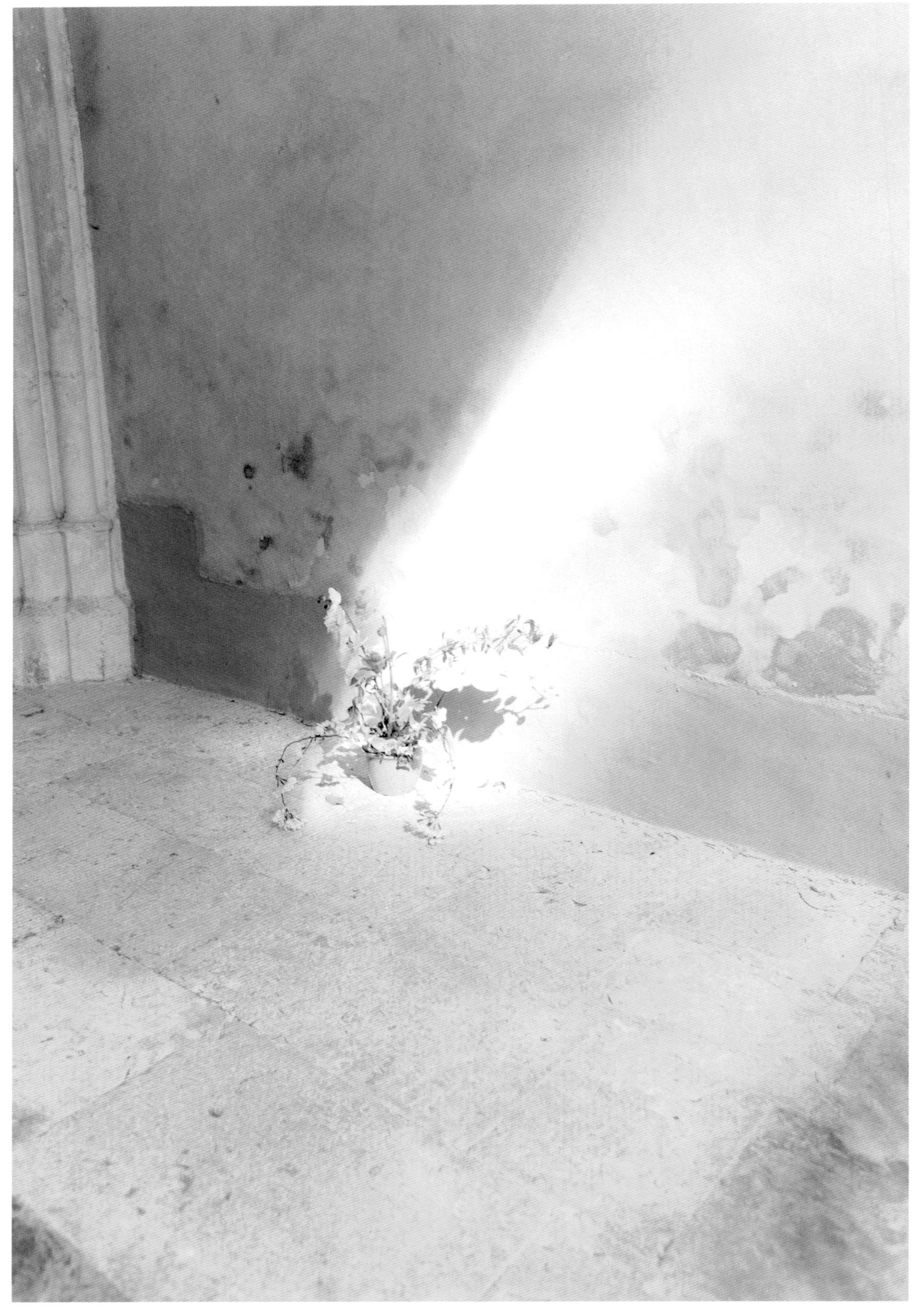

SARKER PROTICK
Flowerpot in chapel, Vendome, 2012

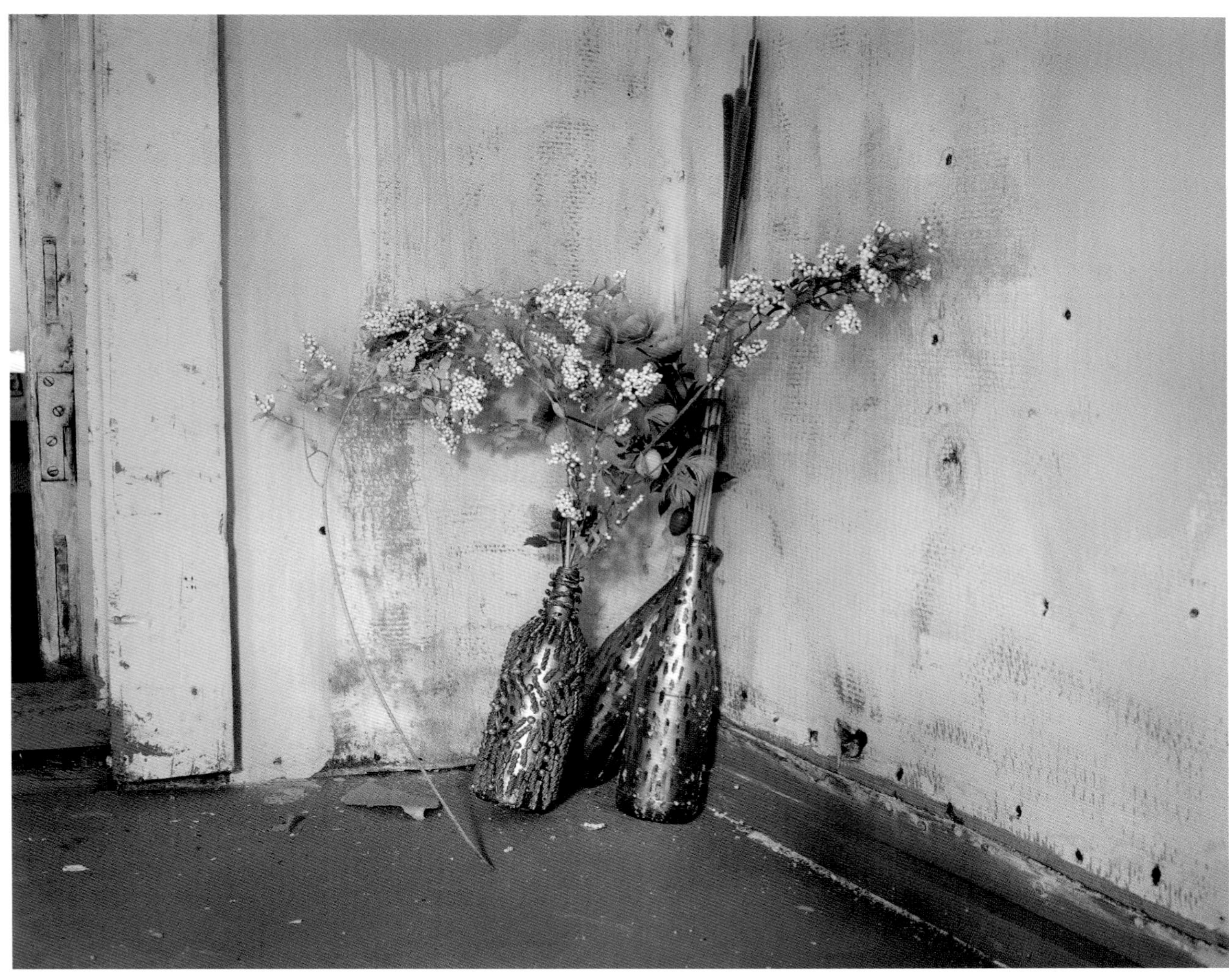

ESKO MÄNNIKKÖ
Rauha?, 2001

THE RAIN OF FLOWERS

War, it would seem, is an unlikely theatre for any kind of floral imagery, but nonetheless flowers are to be found here too, and for good reason: what other symbol can so eloquently speak of the fragility of life, and warn us of irretrievable loss? The historian Margaret Ann Donnell noted something similar in the domain of another art, that of poetry: 'A great number of wartime poetry incorporated a common, and perhaps unconventional, imagery: flowers.'[3] Aside from that obvious connotation of fragility, flowers in a war setting can also remind us of tenacity and rebirth. The one-time soldier and eminent German writer Ernst Jünger captured that ambiguity eloquently; speaking of his own experience as a young man, he wrote: 'We had set out in a rain of flowers to seek the death of heroes. The war was our dream of greatness, power and glory. It was a man's work, a duel on the fields whose flowers would be stained with blood. There is no lovelier death in the world.'[4]

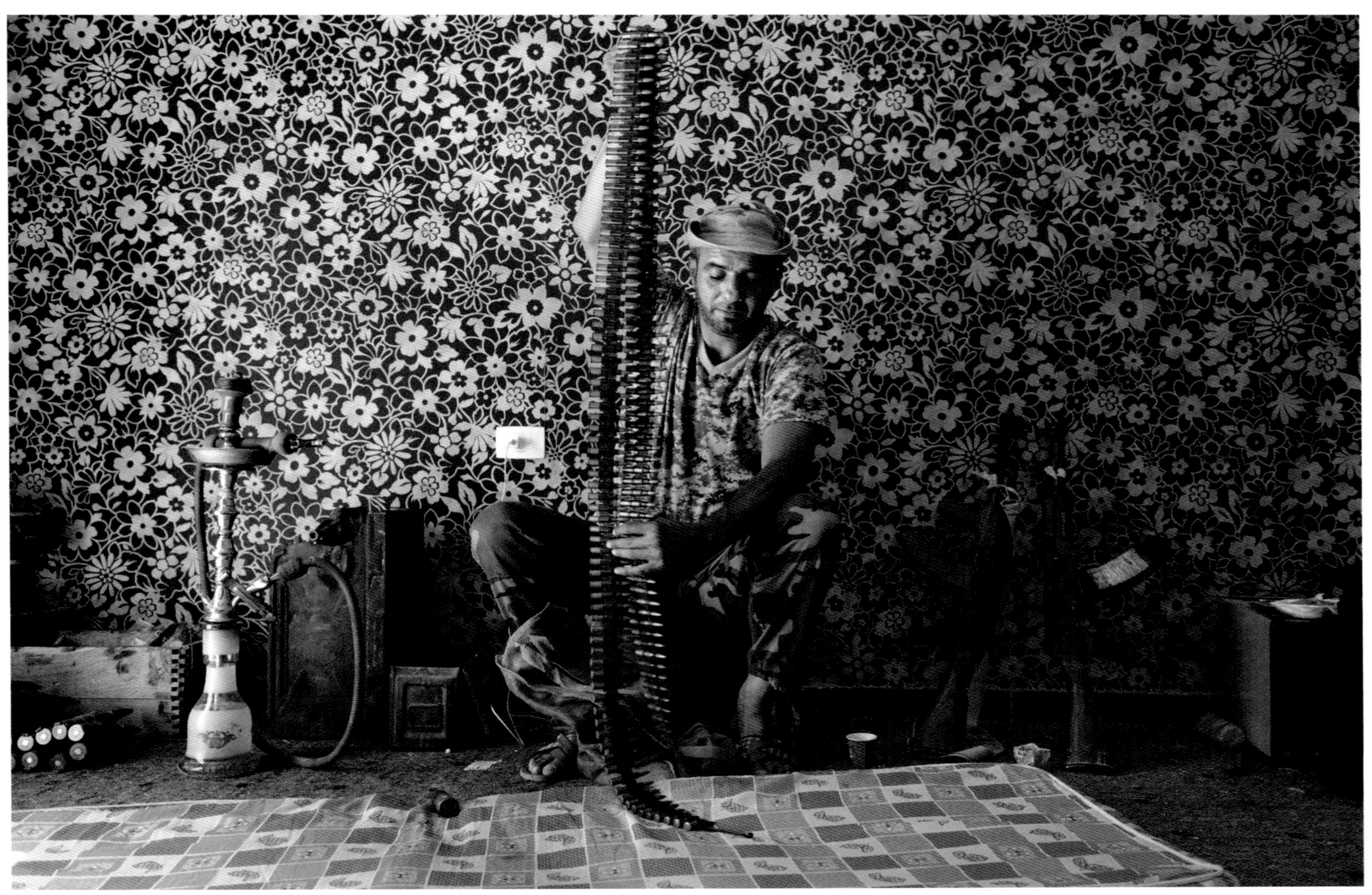

ALESSIO ROMENZI
Libya, Sirte: Captain Grandi, affiliated with Libya's Government of National Accord (GNA), prepares ammunition for machine guns before the battle for the 700 neighbourhood in Sirte, 30 June 2016

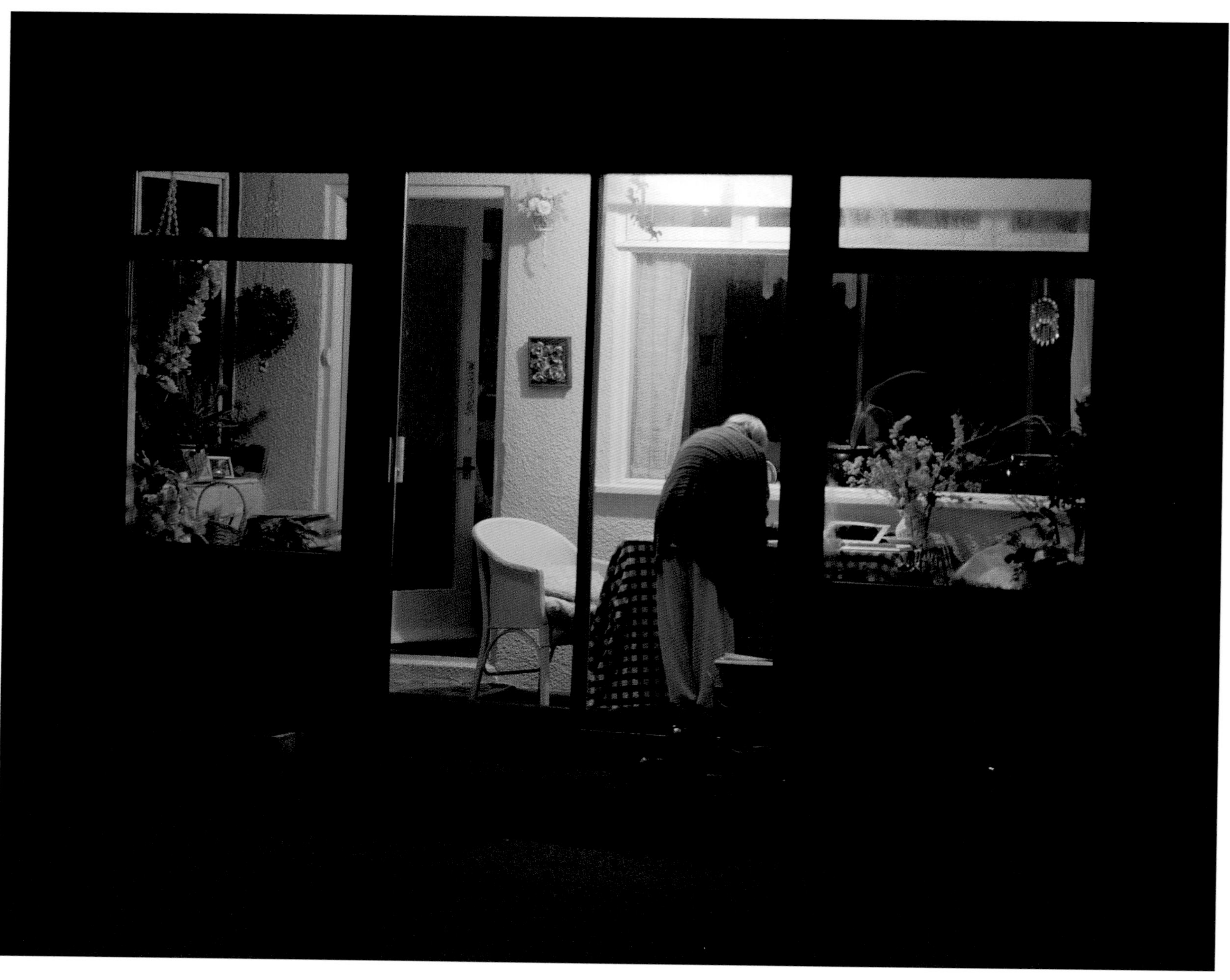

NADAV KANDER
Woman and Dried Flowers, from the series *The Parade*, 2002–4

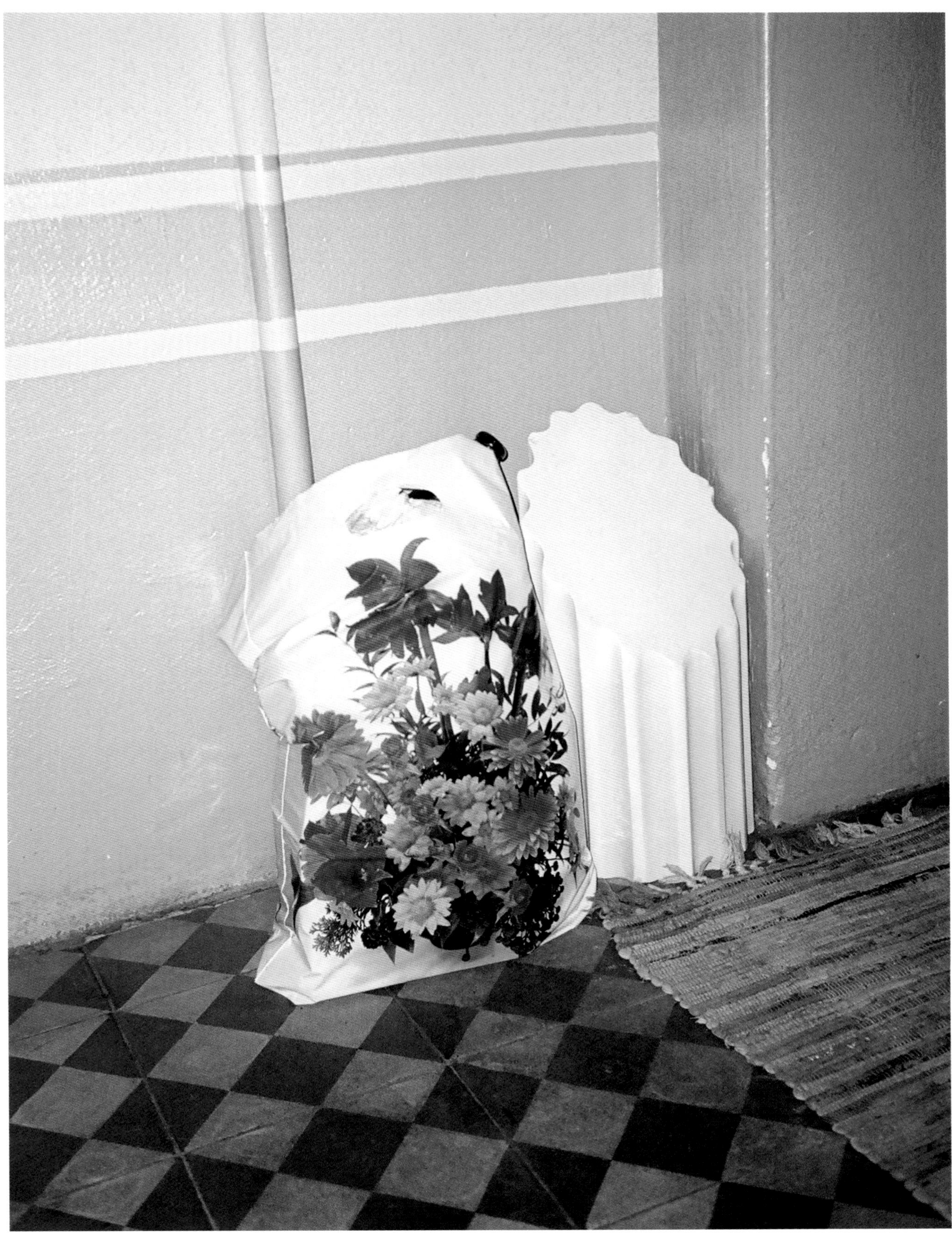

VICTOR DE CASTRO
Things are...Whatever things happen to be #7, 2008

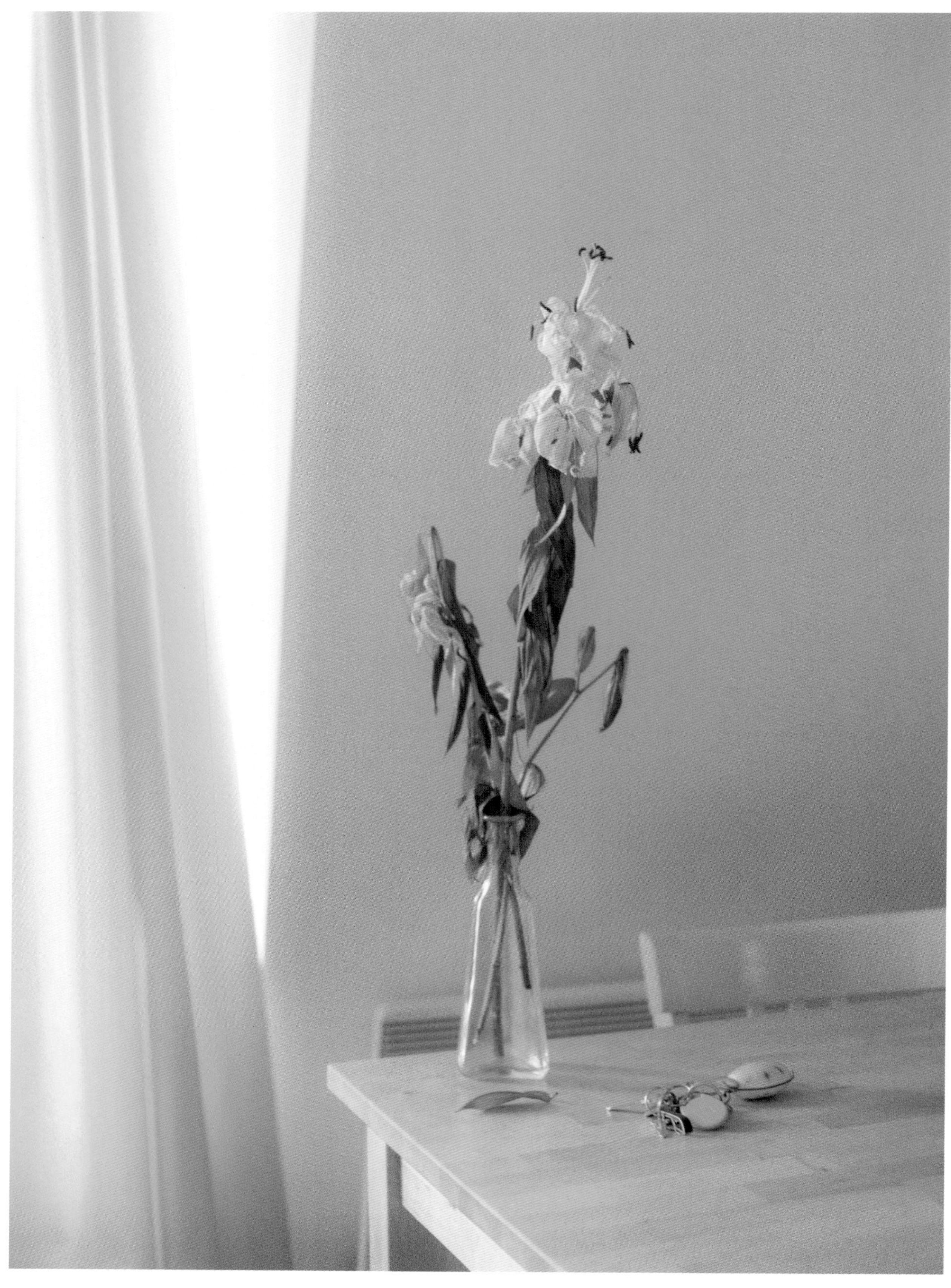

PAUL ROUSTEAU
Nature-Morte aux Clés, 2016

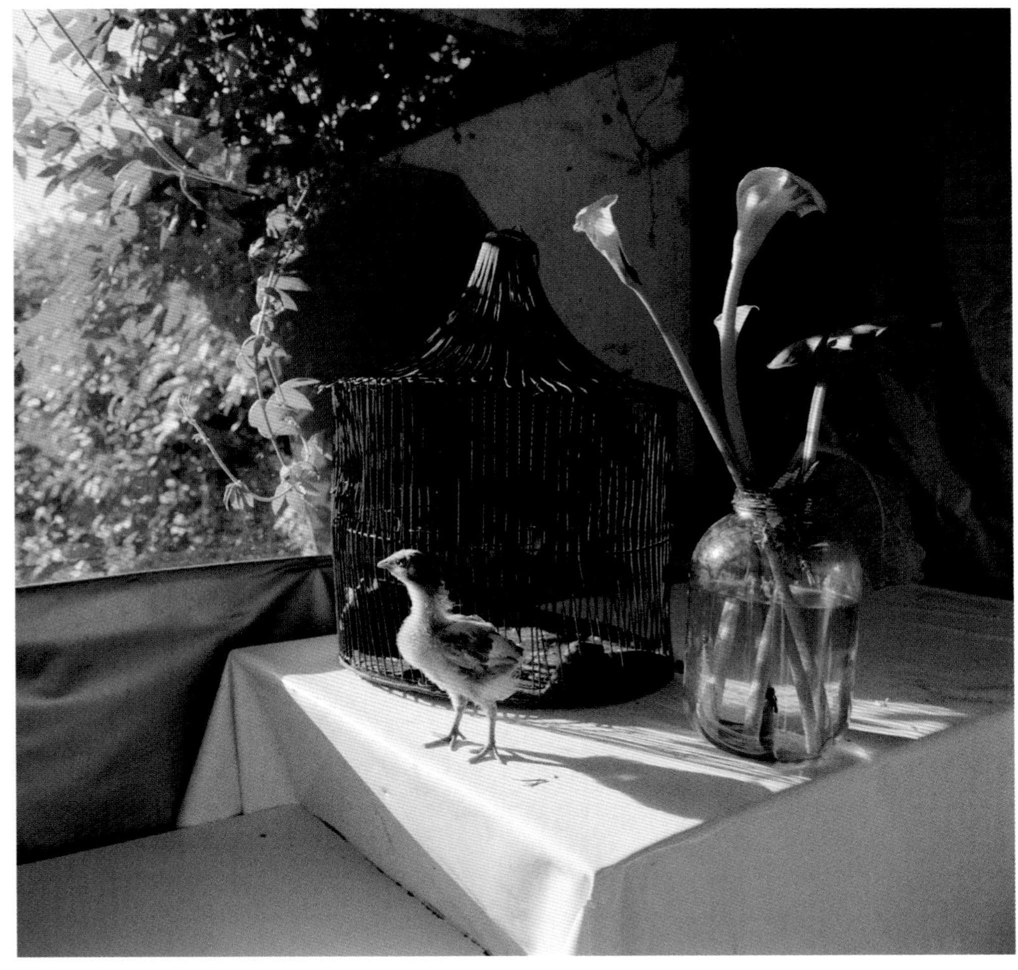

ALEC SOTH
Untitled 51, from the series *Dog Days, Bogotá*, 2003

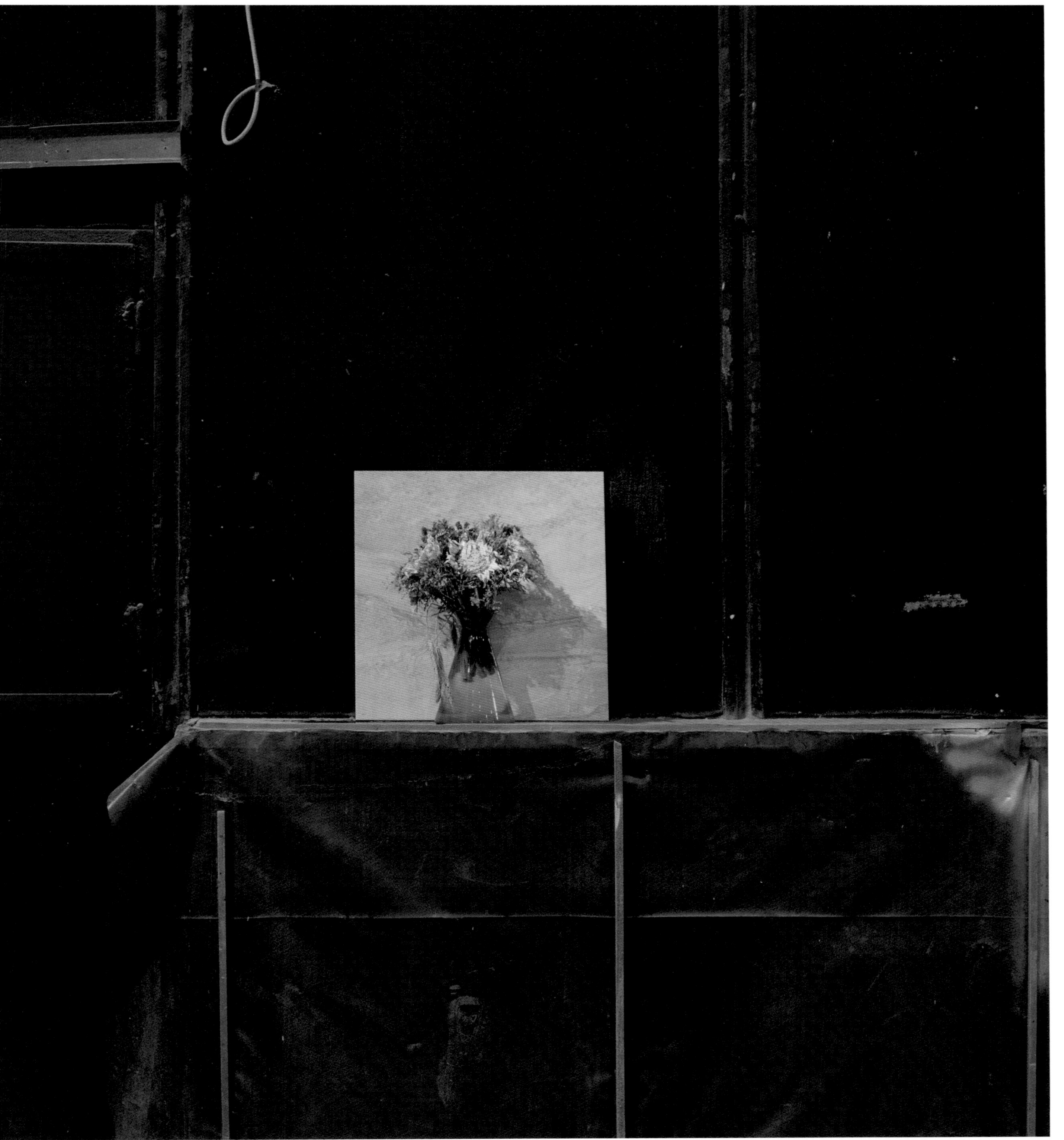

NADAV KANDER
Untitled VI, from the series *Isolation*, 2015

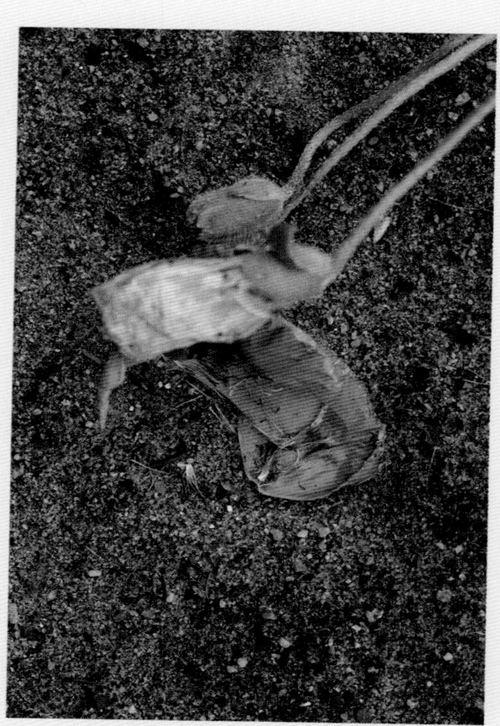

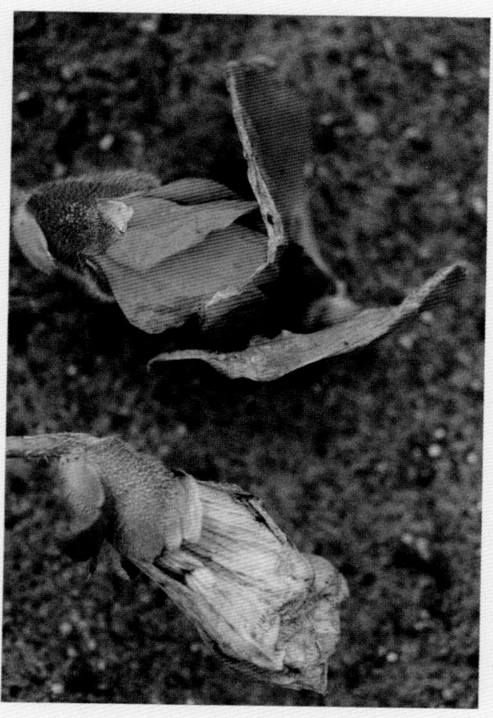

THOMAS STRUTH
Orientalischer Mohn (Papaver orientale) 1, Feldberger Seenlandschaft 2020

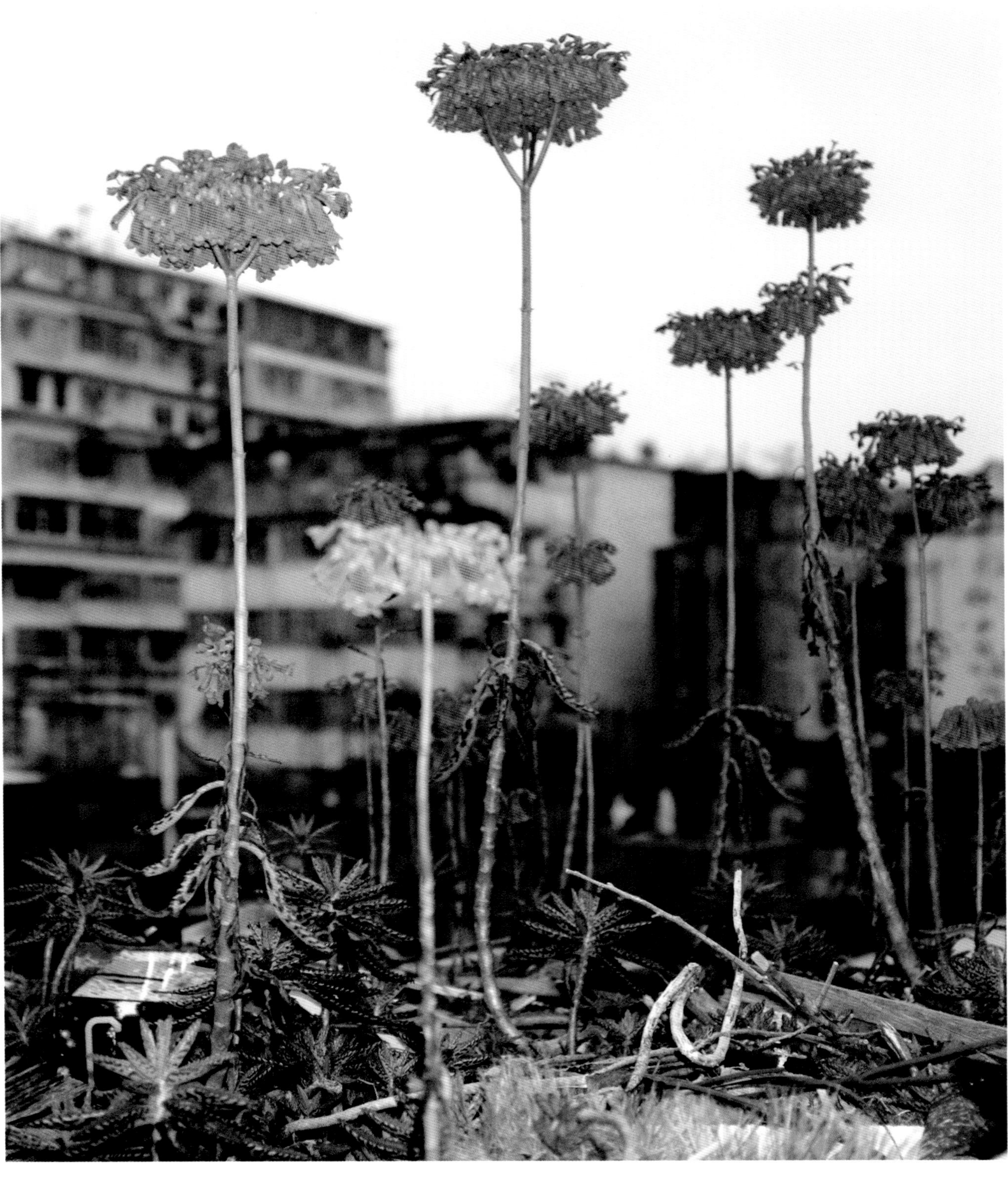

MICHAEL WOLF
Hong Kong Flora 53, 2014

PROUD ASSERTIONS

Flowers and fruits are always fit presents; flowers because they are a proud assertion that a ray of beauty outvalues all the utilities of the world. These gay natures contrast with the somewhat stern countenance of ordinary nature: they are like music heard out of a workhouse.

Ralph Waldo Emerson[5]

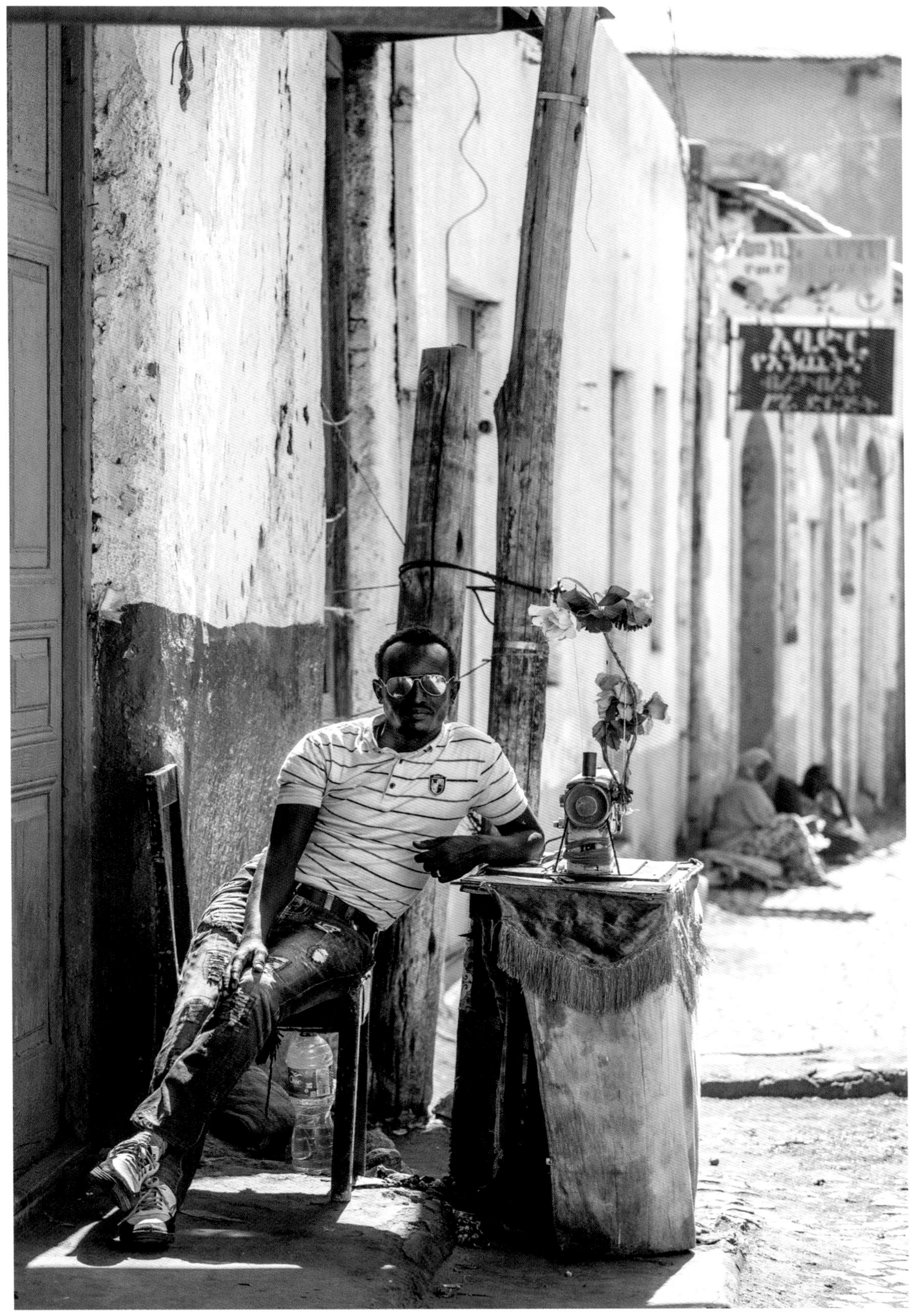

MARCUS WESTBERG
A tailor sits with his Singer sewing machine inside the old city quarter of Harar, Ethiopia, 2019

ENQUIRY

In his intriguing lecture 'Why Are Flowers Beautiful? (2007)', the quantum physicist David Deutsch makes the point that scientific enquiry and artistic enquiry are not poles apart, as we often assume. Both are trying to get at a truth they intuit is there to be grasped with sustained effort, provided certain steps are taken in a logical sequence.[1] Photographers of a scientific bent have worked in the service of botanical study for many years, although not as long as one might imagine; more than fifty years after Louis Daguerre had announced his invention, London's widely read *Photographic News* could state flatly, 'A photograph of a plant in the text books is as rare as that of a human face is common.'[2] It was not until the 1920s that textbooks began to accept photography, and they did so grudgingly.

Still today we find this persistent bias: botanists simply favour drawing. Some of the best botanical photographers in the world find themselves struggling against the entrenched enmity of the scientific discipline, despite superb pictorial achievements that indeed sometimes surpass the capacities of drawing. Botanical focus of course includes microscopic study, or studies in media of altered light, such as infrared and ultraviolet-induced visible fluorescence (UVIVF). Photographers do not have to be trained botanists, however, although openness to the field is a prerequisite. 'Botany, scientific imagery and history have informed my approach and nourished my explorations as much as the prospecting of my own walks,' explains one photographer, while another was so inspired by his altered-light experiences that he became an avid horticulturalist.[3]

Botanically-minded photographers of the twenty-first century have embraced digital technology while not abandoning analogue techniques. One of the field's pre-eminent practitioners tells us that 'a digitally created composite illustration is much the same as a traditional one, in being a scientific plant portrait clearly illustrating the diagnostic and characteristic features of the taxon,' but composed in an aesthetically pleasing manner.[4]

The enquiring artist knows that scientific procedures and methods may also be applied to his or her investigations, sometimes with tongue in cheek. So, for example, if plastic flowers have become a very real component of our civilization – culturally naturalized, so to speak – then they too deserve the scientific treatment. And exercises of taxonomy (naming, describing and classifying) may equally be applied to deep critiques of society and culture.

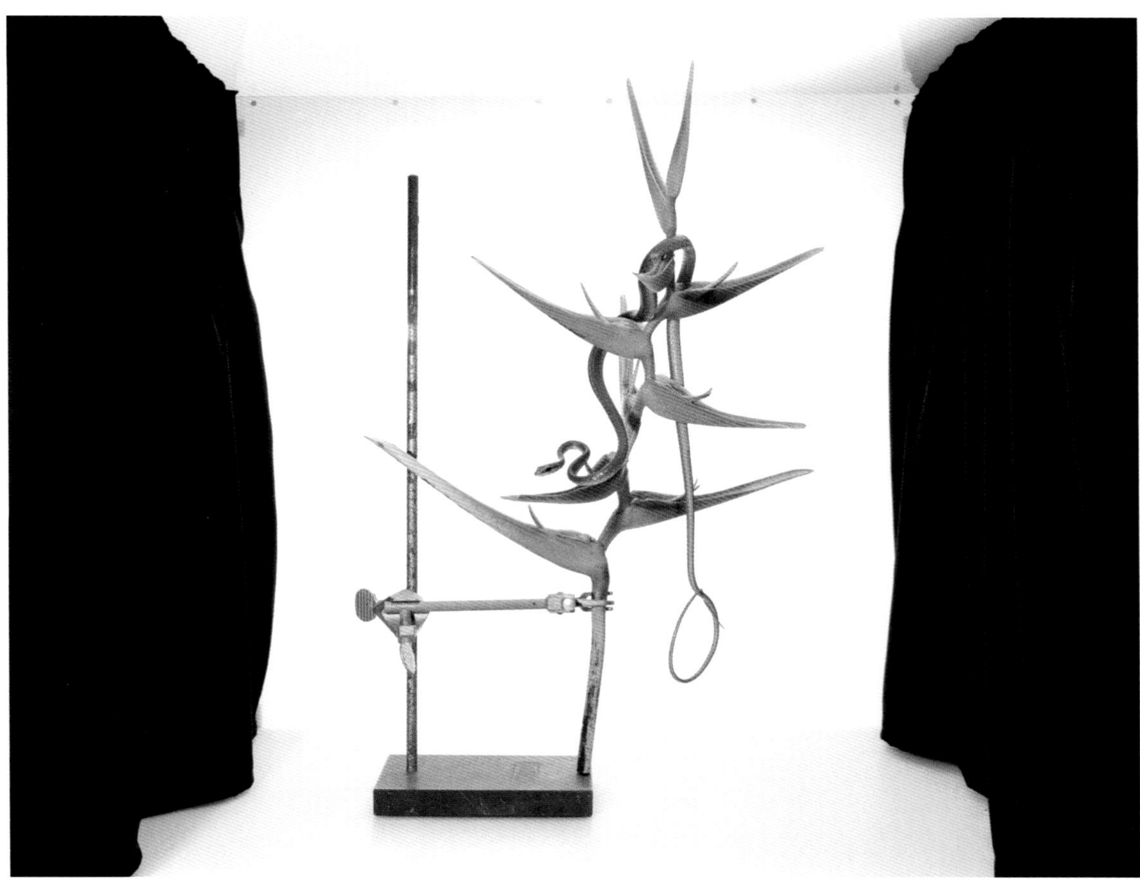

SANNA KANNISTO
Leptophis ahaetulla, 2016

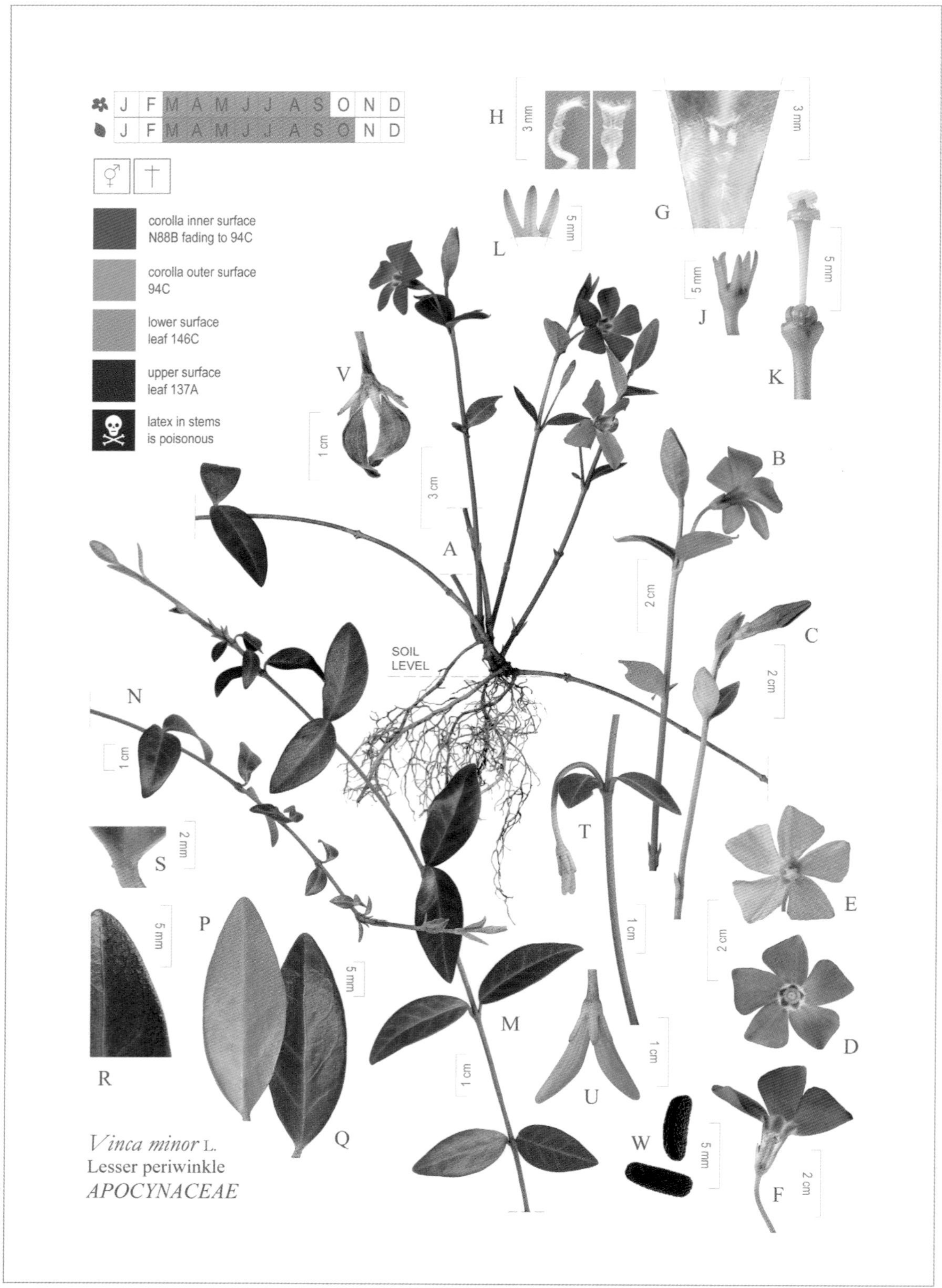

NIKI SIMPSON
Lesser periwinkle (Vinca minor), 2009
Family: APOCYNACEAE

A: flowering plant; B: erect flowering stem; C: flowering stem with bud; D: flower from above; E: flower from below; F: flower, vertical section; G: portion of corolla tube, showing stamen; H: stamen, side and adaxial views; J: calyx; K: gynoecium; L: portion of calyx opened out; M: arching vegetative shoot; N: vegetative shoot showing point of rooting; P: leaf, lower surface; Q: leaf, upper surface; R: leaf, apex and margin; S: leaf base showing petiolar glands; T: portion of stem with developing fruit; U: immature fruit of paired follicles; V: dehisced fruit; W: seeds.

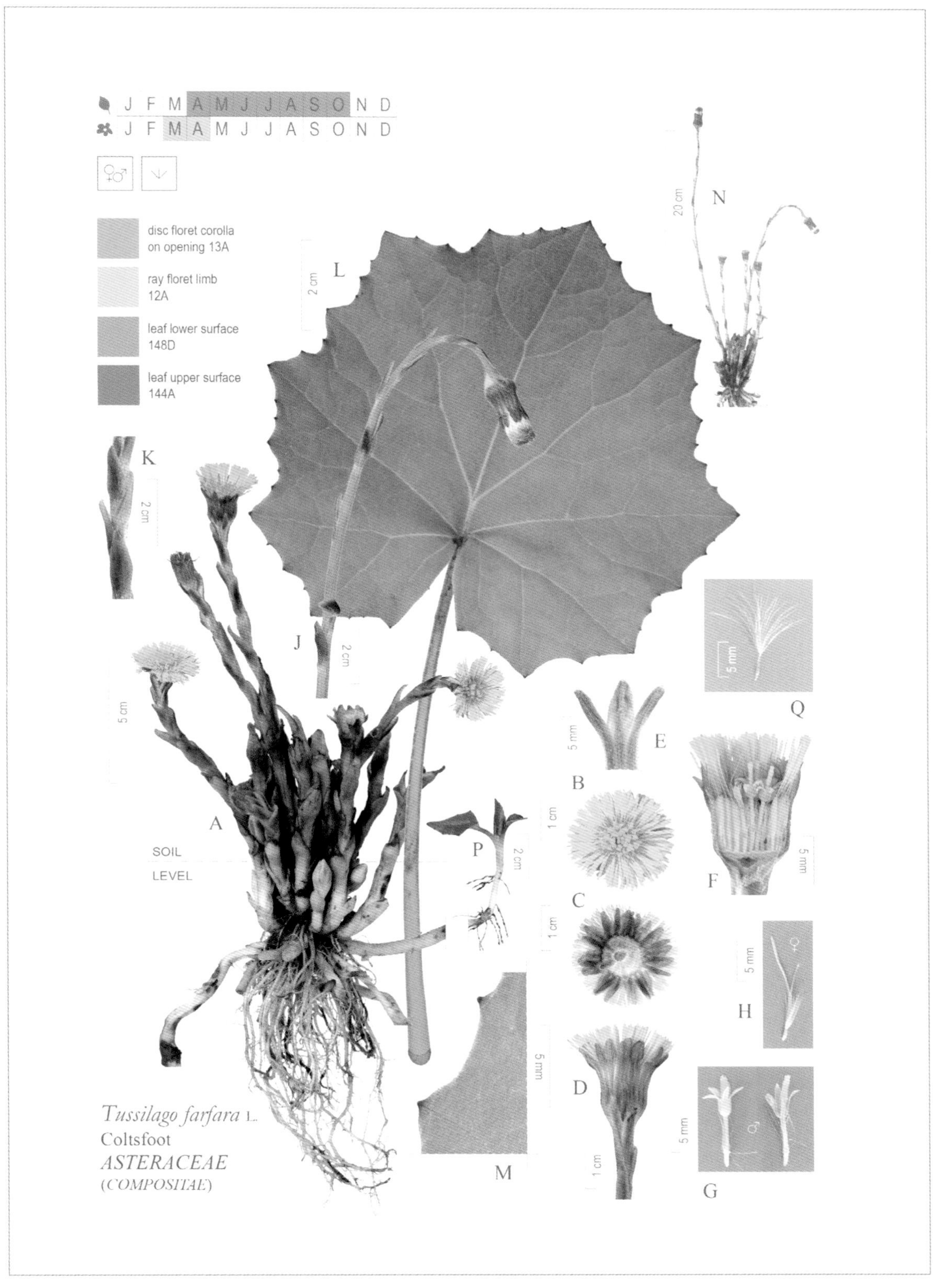

NIKI SIMPSON
Coltsfoot (Tussilago farfara), 2009
Family: ASTERACEAE
A: flowering plant (some flowering stems removed); B: flower head (capitulum) from above; C: flower head from below (some outer involucral bracts removed); D: flower head, side view; E: three involucral bracts; F: flower head, vertical section; G: disc floret and vertical section through disc floret (male); H: ray floret (female); J: developing fruiting head on elongating stem; K: bracts on flowering stem (scape); L: leaf, upper surface; M: leaf margin, lower surface, with hydathodes and arachnoid hairs; N: whole plant, showing flowering and fruiting habit; P: plantlet arising from stolon; Q: achene with pappus, developed from ray floret.

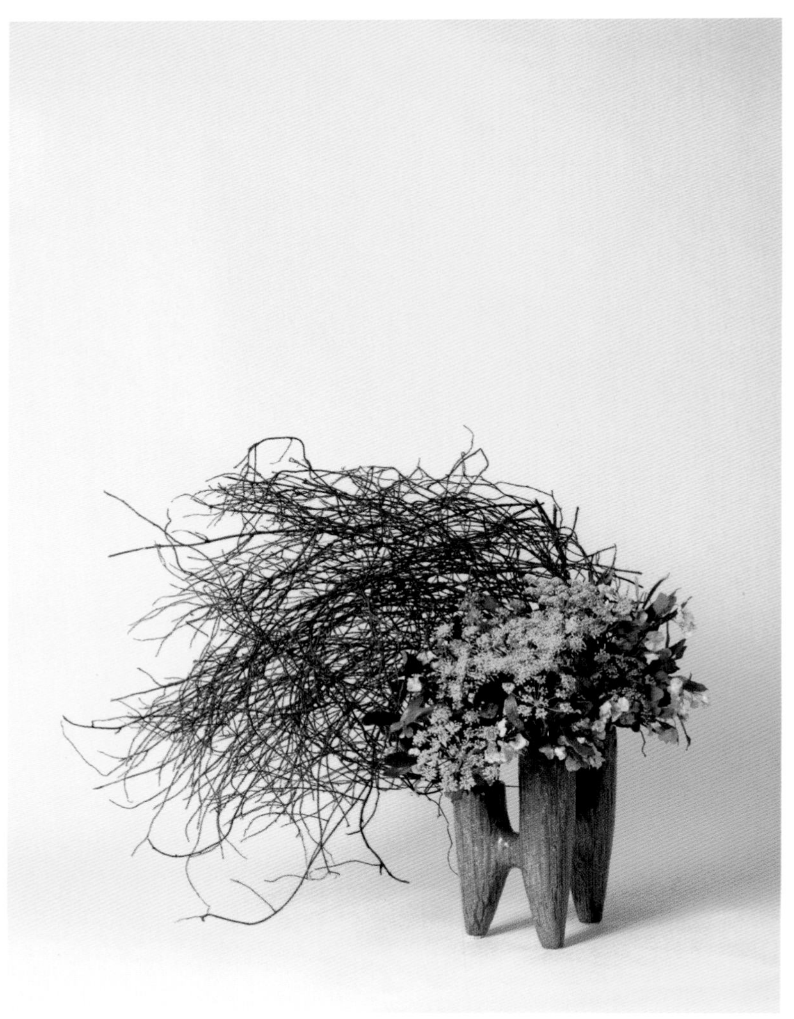

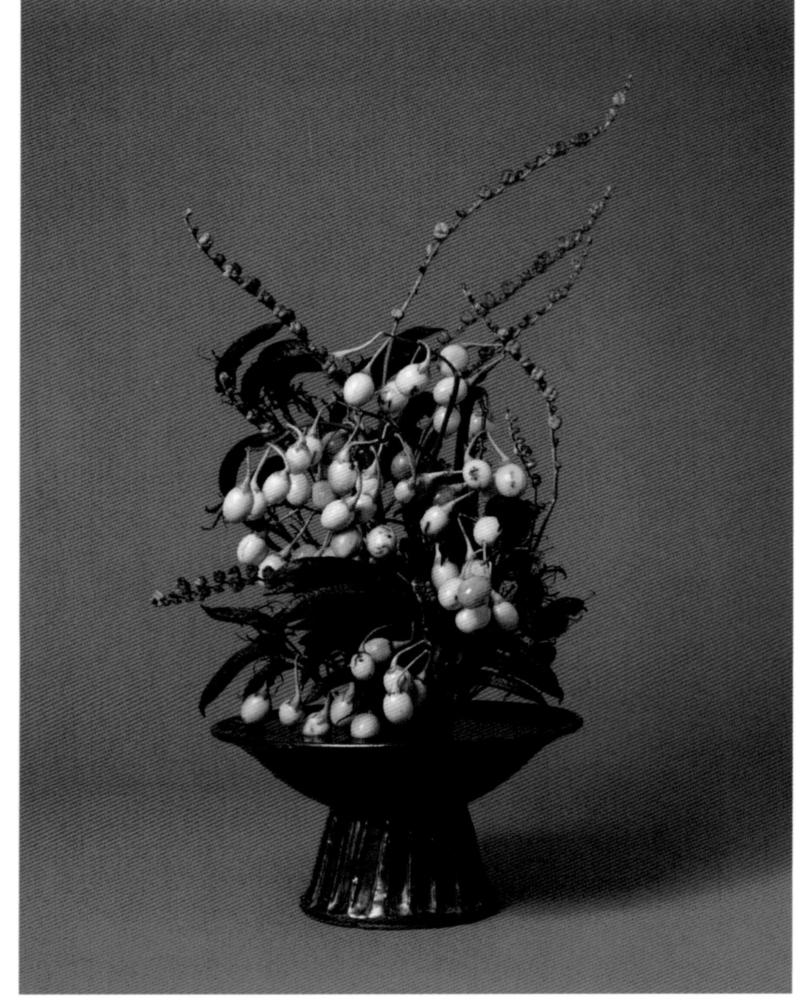

ANN SHELTON
*The Hysteric, Fennel (*Foeniculum *sp.)*, from the series *jane says*, 2015–ongoing

jane says allows us to examine of the loss of plant knowledge inside the secrecy of personal trauma. Two publications on the history of abortion in Aotearoa New Zealand by trail blazing feminist Margaret Sparrow are important touchstones for this body of work. They discuss the many women who died in the process of trying to find an effective means of control over their own bodies during the colonial period. The Hysteric, Fennel (Foeniculum *sp.*) reminds us of the incarcerating and 'so called' medical controls placed on women who transgressed the strict gender codes designated them by patriarchal Victorian and Colonial traditions. Fennel has reportedly been used historically to bring on Menstruation.

ANN SHELTON
*The Courtesan, Poroporo (*Solanum *sp.)*, from the series *jane says*, 2015–ongoing

Many Ancient medical practices incorporated herbal traditions into their healthcare regimes, allowing women to control their own reproductive health. The Courtesan, Poroporo (Solanum *sp.*), depicts poroporo which was used in Aotearoa by Māori people as a contraceptive. The Encyclopaedia of New Zealand Te Ara states that poroporo's efficacy is unknown, but that it was farmed commercially in Aotearoa in the 1970's for use in contraceptive pills.

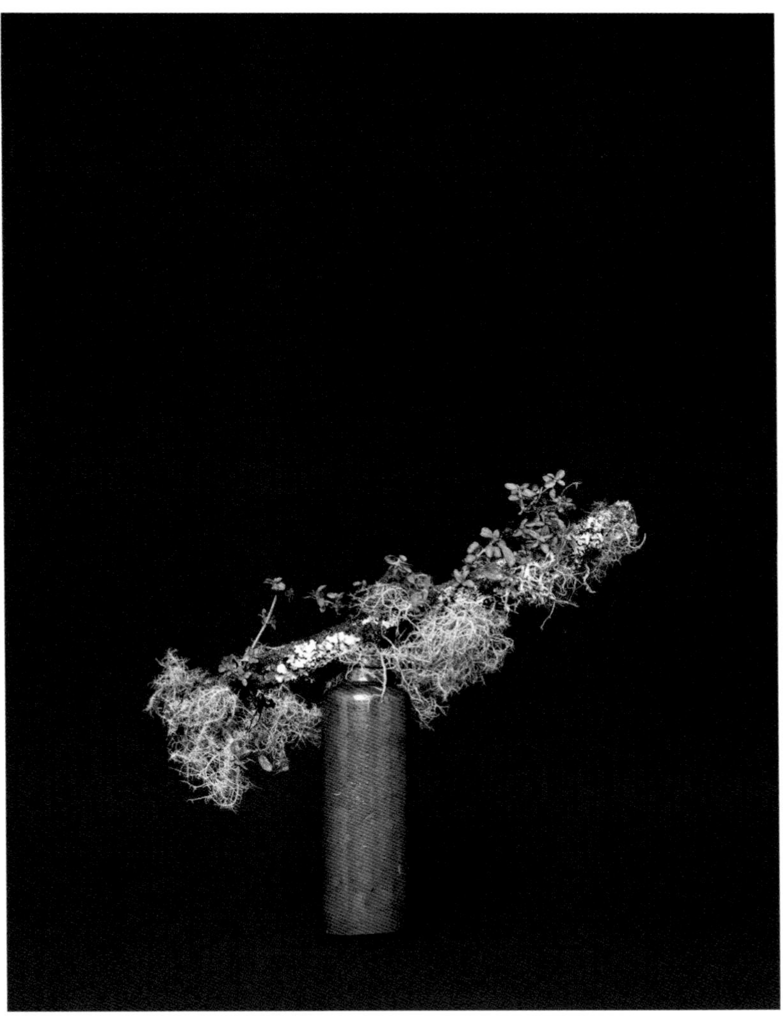

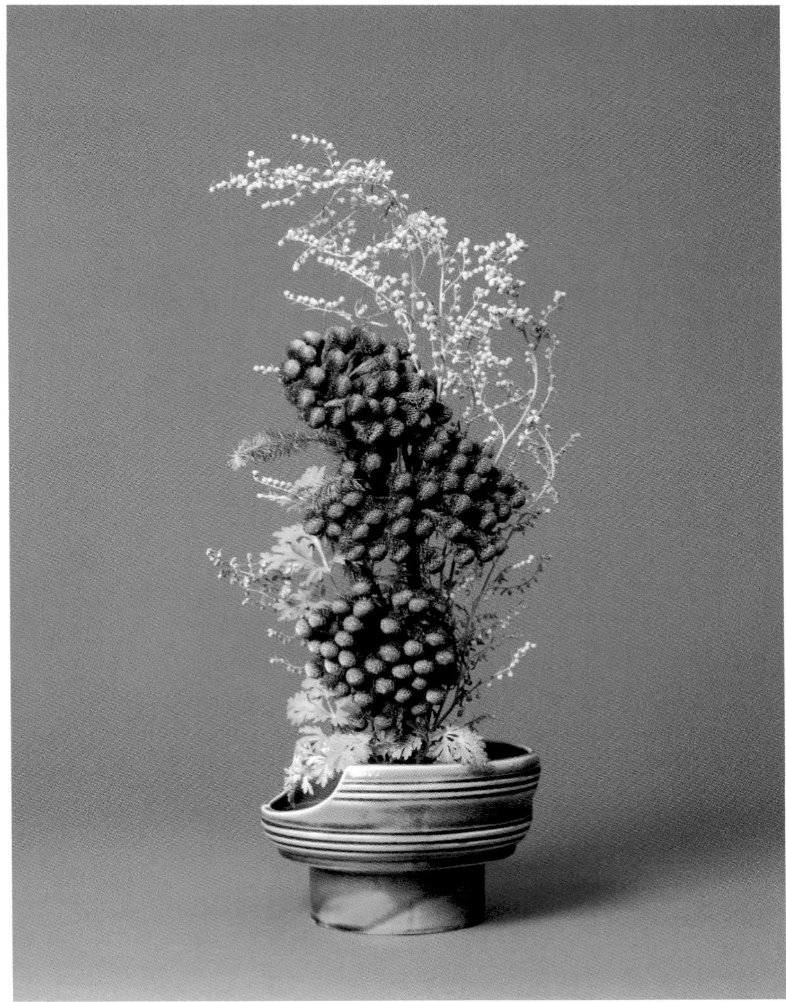

ANN SHELTON
*The Witch, Pennyroyal (*Mentha *sp.)*, from the series *jane says*, 2015–ongoing

The witch continues to be a maligned and misunderstood figure who has been, literally, persecuted to death. The holder of ancient wisdom and of old herbal knowledge she is also known as the wise woman or the wort cunner from a time when the function and aesthetics of plants were not yet separated. This work depicts penny royal, a highly toxic and dangerous plant from the mint family (do not mess with this plant), that is a known abortifacient with a history dating back to Roman times. The Witch, Pennyroyal (Mentha *sp.*), an arrangement I attempted to make unsuccessfully several times (because of the tiny scale of the plant), invokes the relationship between women's health and witchcraft and highlights the process whereby this knowledge was forcefully removed from women.

ANN SHELTON
*The Mermaid, Wormwood (*Artemisia *sp.)*, from the series *jane says*, 2015–ongoing

The Mermaid, Wormwood (Artemisia sp.) curves and towers over a sea of green reflecting on the shadowy and ancient archetype of the female sea dwelling creature. John Riddle remarks in Eve's Herbs (1997), "To the ancients this plant was of more noble standing, because it was the plant of Artemis, the goddess of woodland, forest, childbirth and fertility to man and beasts. Artemis looked after women in childbirth and, like birthwort, her plant was sometimes used to hasten or to assist delivery. Some herbs that were believed to stimulate menstruation were also thought to help in childbirth and, as the ancients expressed it, to remove the afterbirth. The plant artemisia was associated with the goddess for good reason. Artemisia had been found to be an effective antifertility agent."[5]

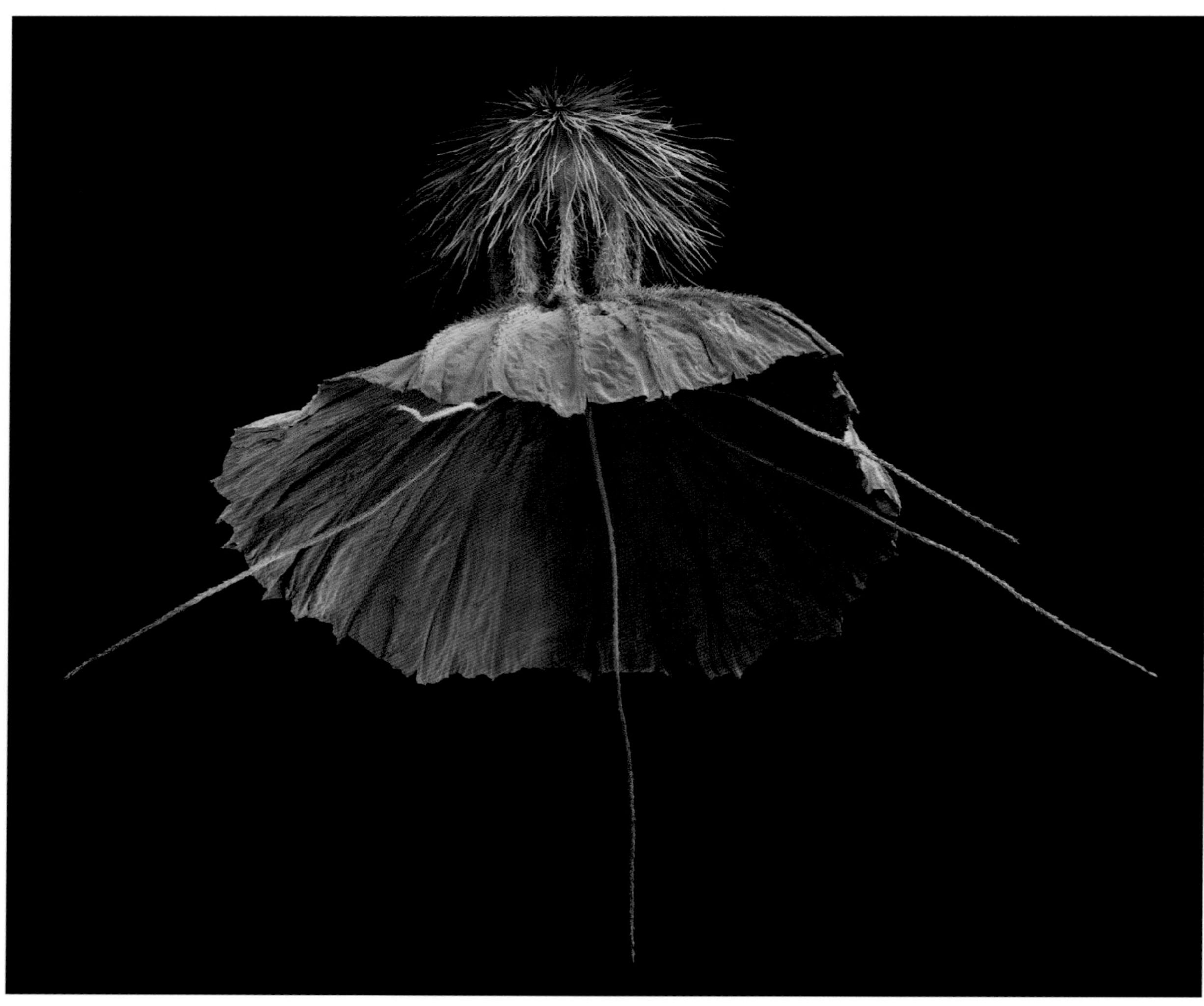

ROB KESSELER
Scabiosa crenata, hand-coloured electron micrograph, 2013

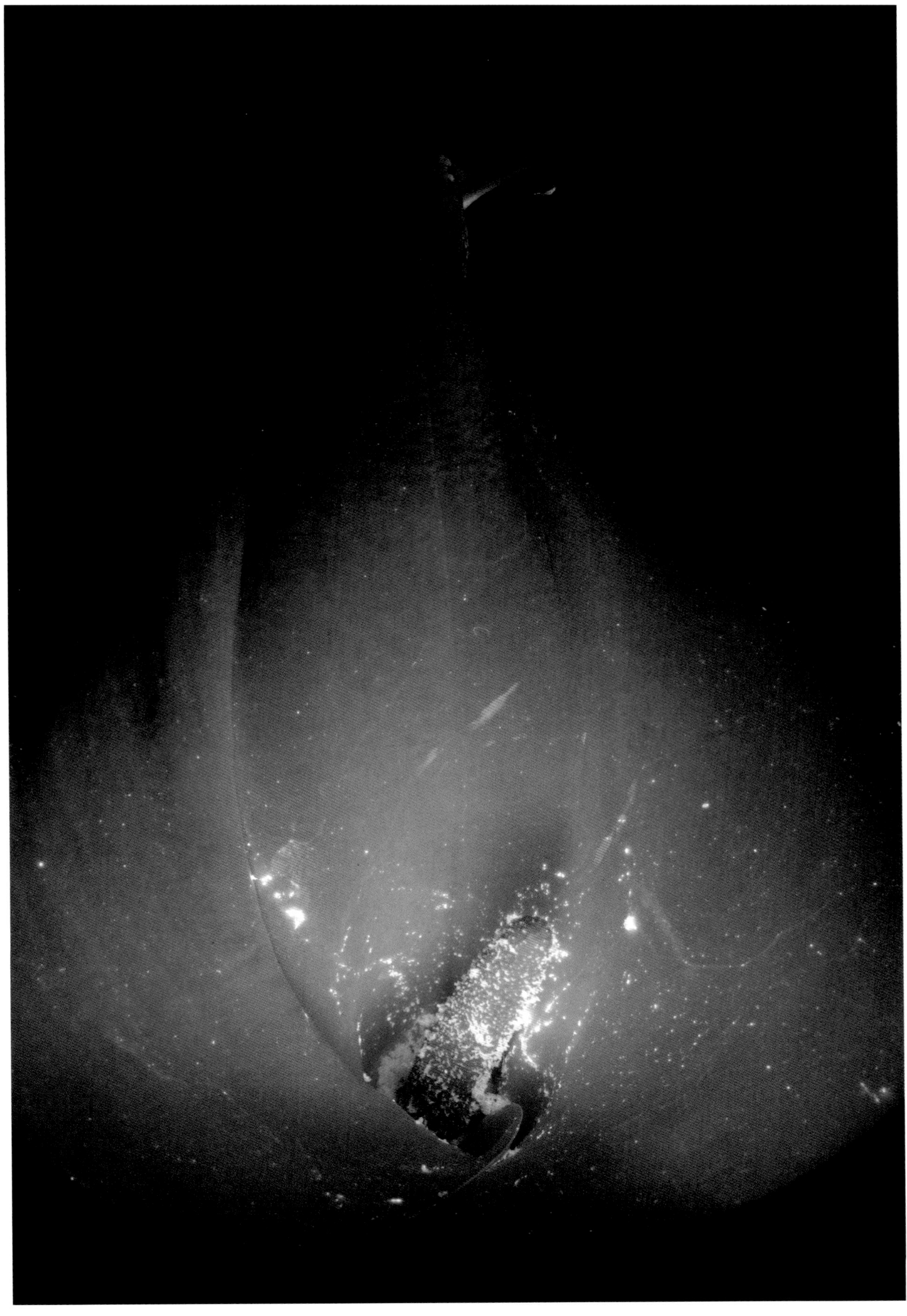

CRAIG P. BURROWS
Calla Lily, digital ultraviolet-induced visible fluorescence (UVIVF) photograph, 2016

THE SOUL OF THE FLOWER

The scientific urge and the aesthetic urge are hard to separate where the photography of flowers is concerned. One early voice arguing for high-quality photographs in the service of botany, R. H. Noailles, claimed in his The Hidden Life of Flowers *(1954) that 'the very soul of the flower' could be caught on the negative, and 'with the help of photography, these processes are brought right before the reader's eyes.'*[6] *Today contemporary photographers charged with botanical illustration – unlike the 'artist photographers', who of course have a free hand to do what they like – must put scientific accuracy before aesthetic considerations. Nevertheless, the botanical image-makers argue on the one hand that aesthetics are a necessary concomitant to their work, making their imagery attractive to the viewer, and on the other that scientifically accurate imagery is in itself, objectively, beautiful.*

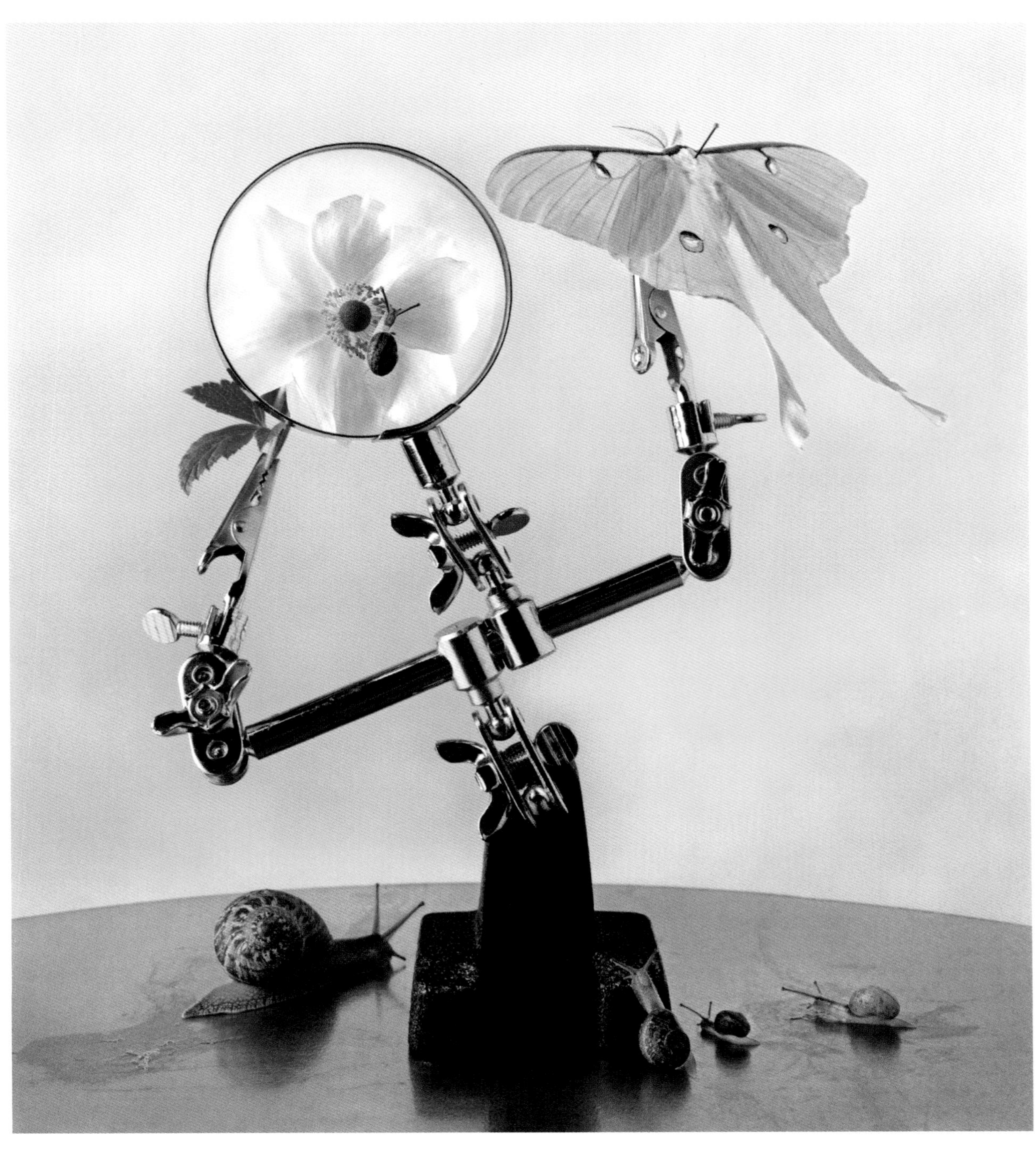

JO WHALEY
Analytical Behavior, 1994

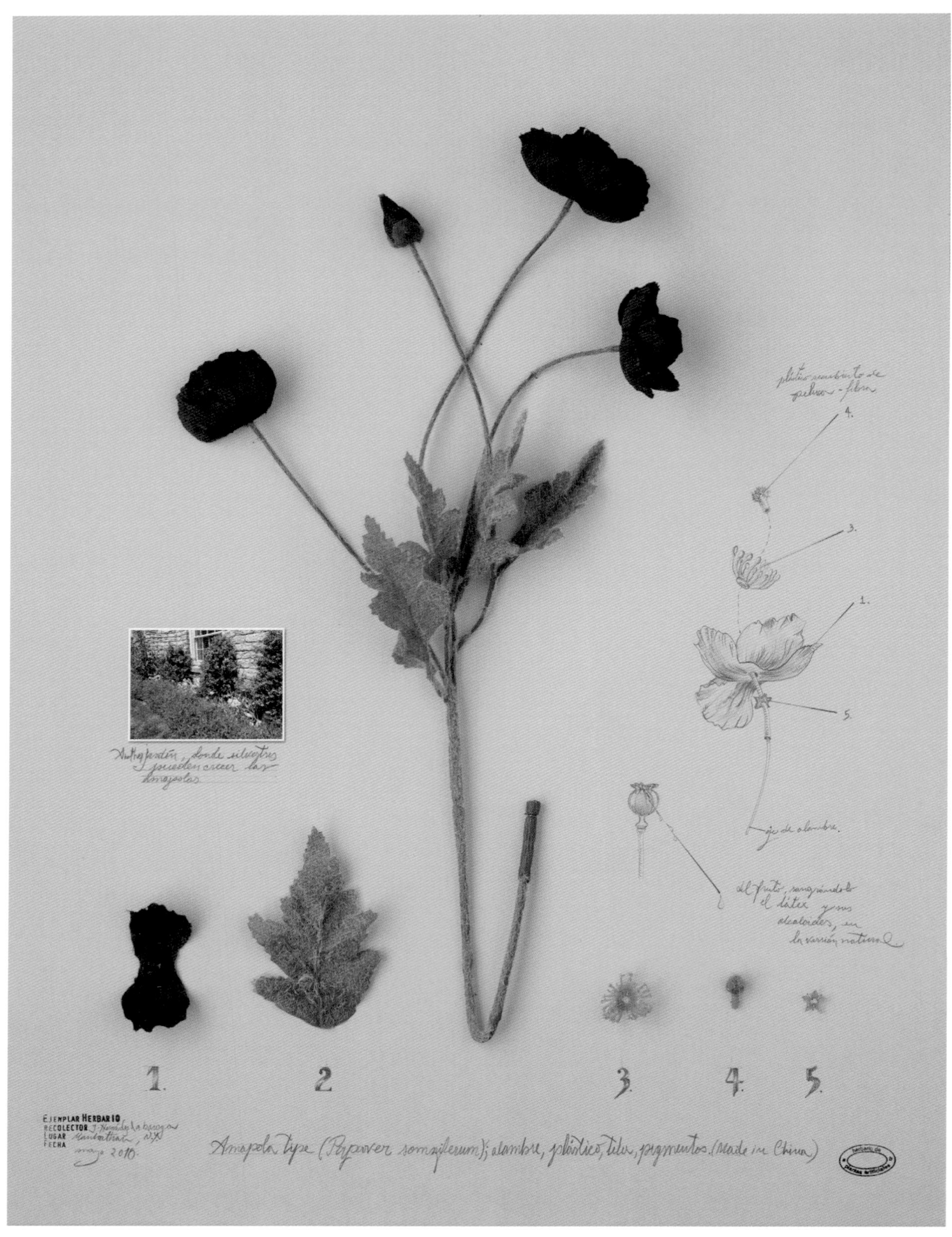

ALBERTO BARAYA
Another Amapola, from the series *Herbario de plantas artificiales*, 2018

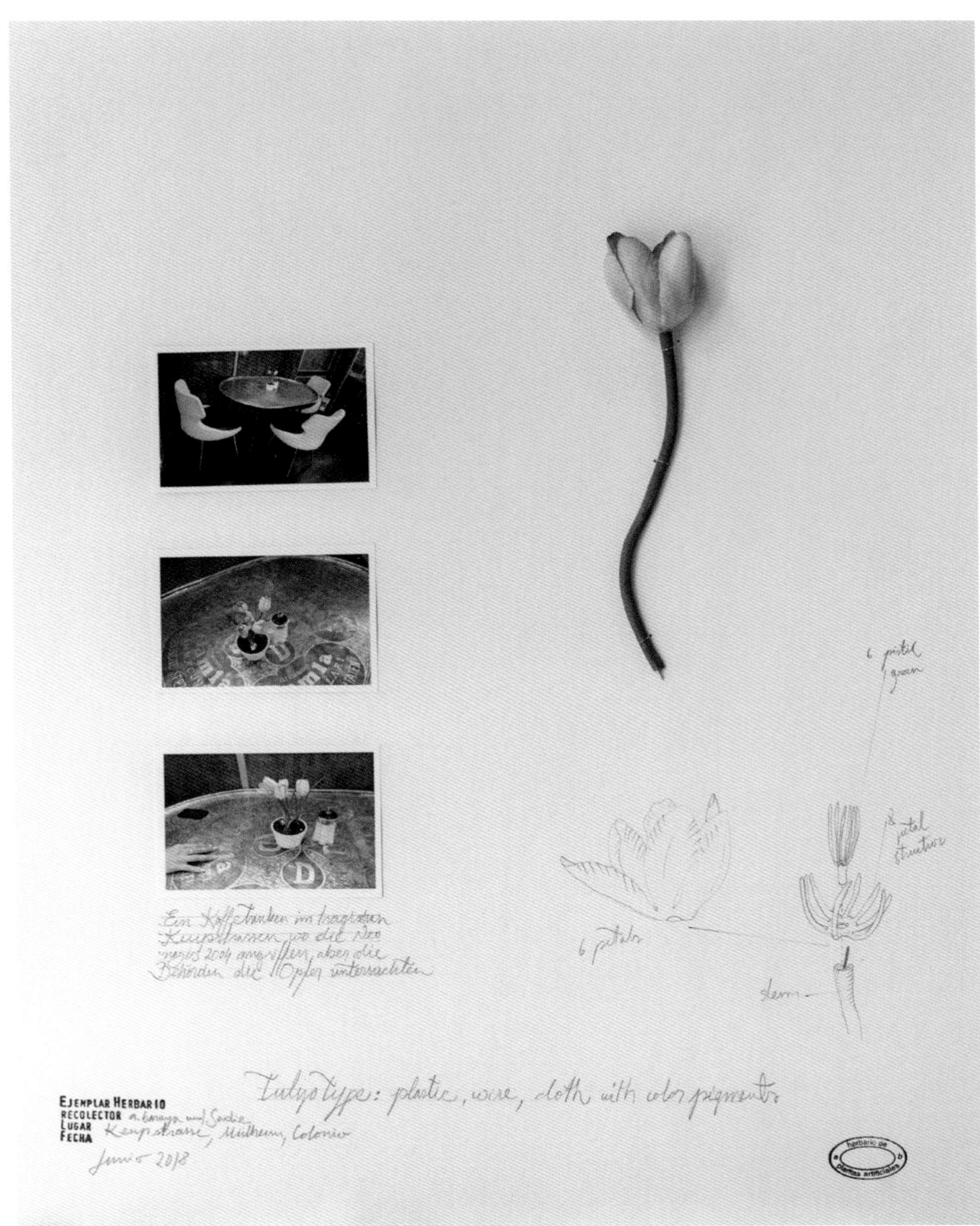

ALBERTO BARAYA
Tulip from Turkish Cafe, plate 3 from the series
Expedition Colonia, Herbario de plantas artificiales, 2018

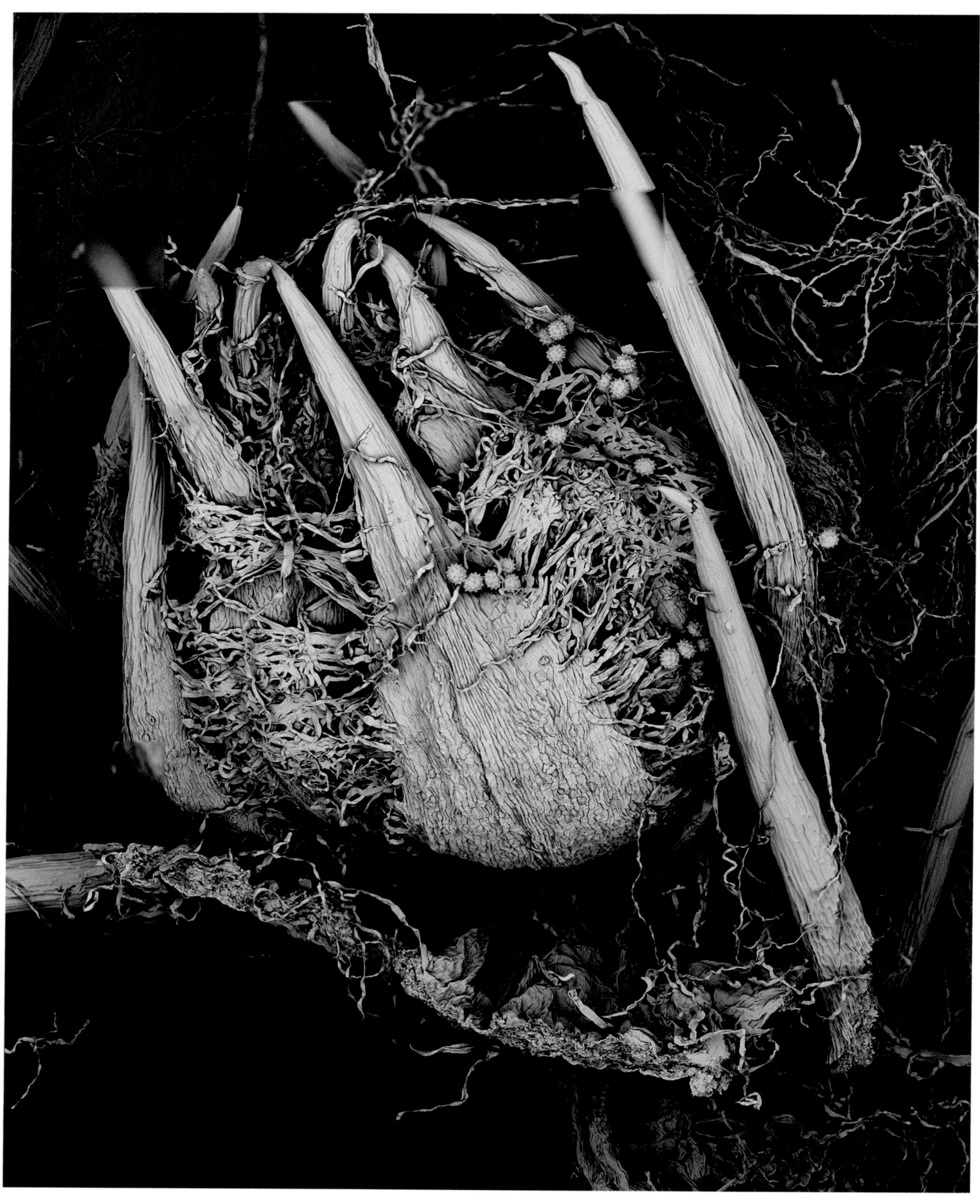

OLGA CAFIERO
Erigeron annuus (L.) Desf. 2, from the series *Flora Neocomensis*, scanning electron microscopy image, 2019

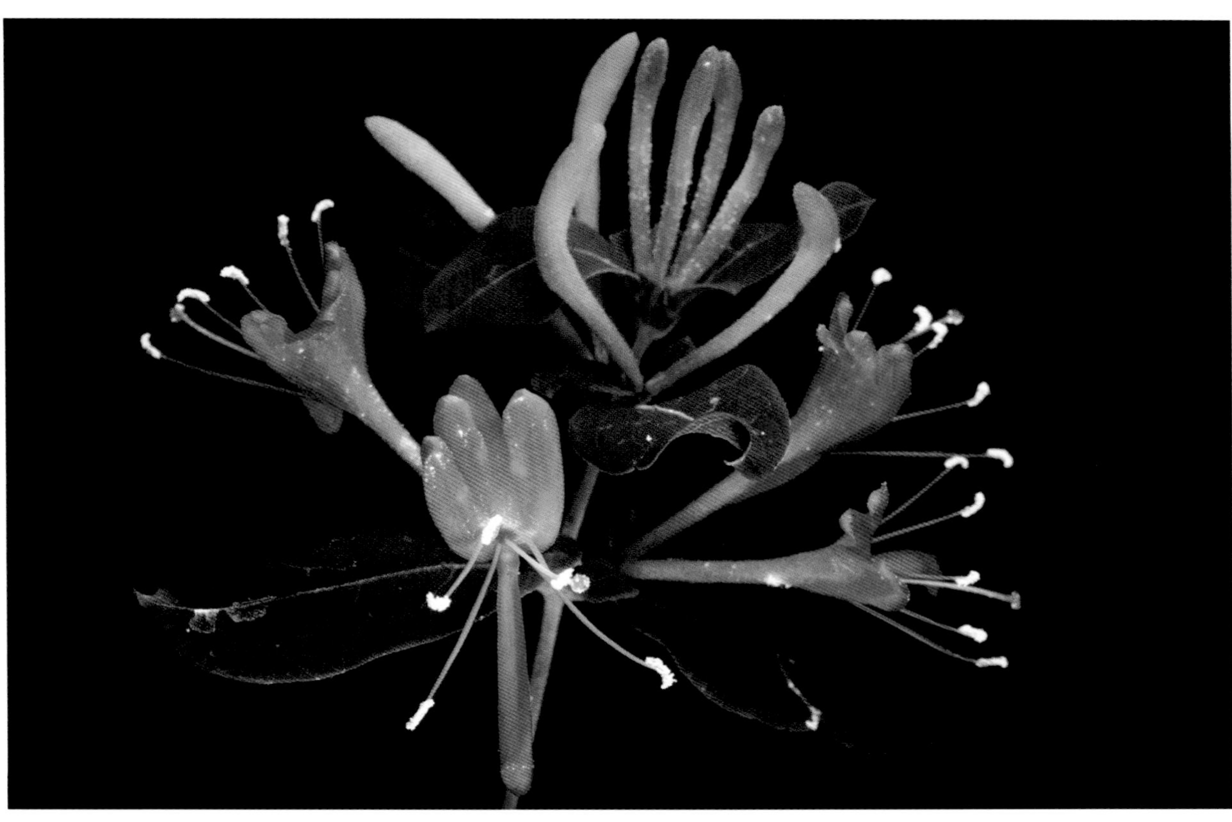

CRAIG P. BURROWS
Honeysuckle, digital ultraviolet-induced visible fluorescence (UVIVF) photograph, 2015

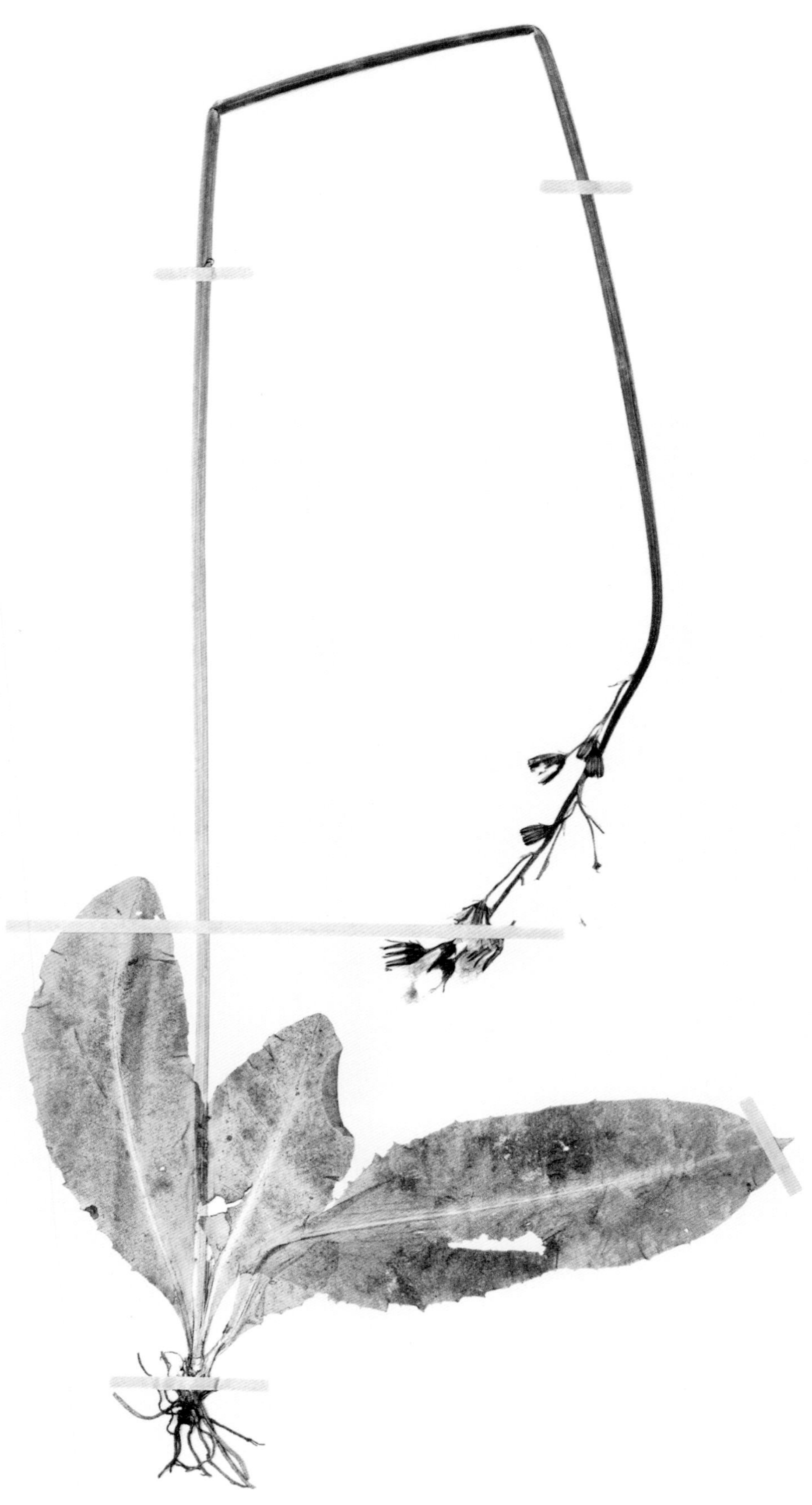

OLGA CAFIERO
Crepis praemorsa (L.) Walther, from the series *Flora Neocomensis*, 2019

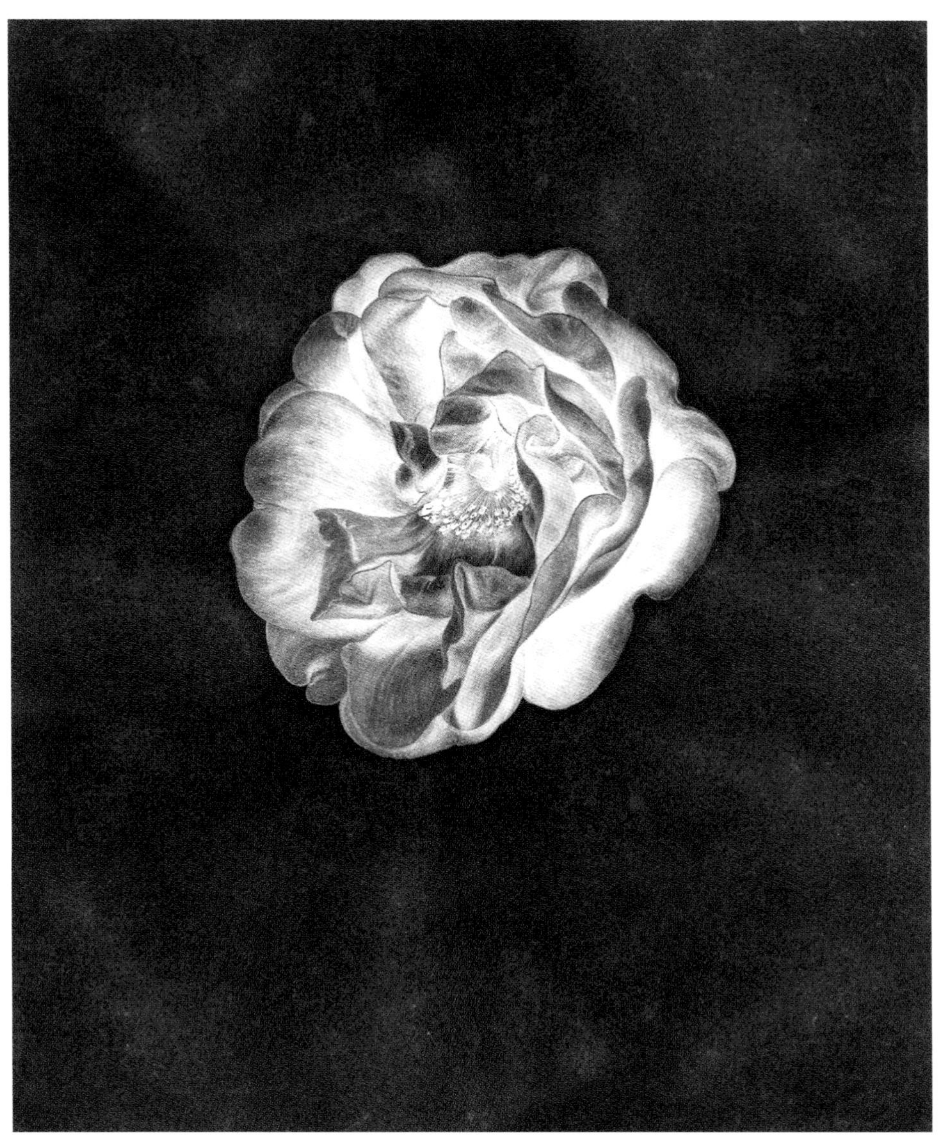

ROB AND NICK CARTER
Positive, Negative, Painting Photograph, 2016
After Jacob de Gheyn II (1565–1629), Three Roses, 1603

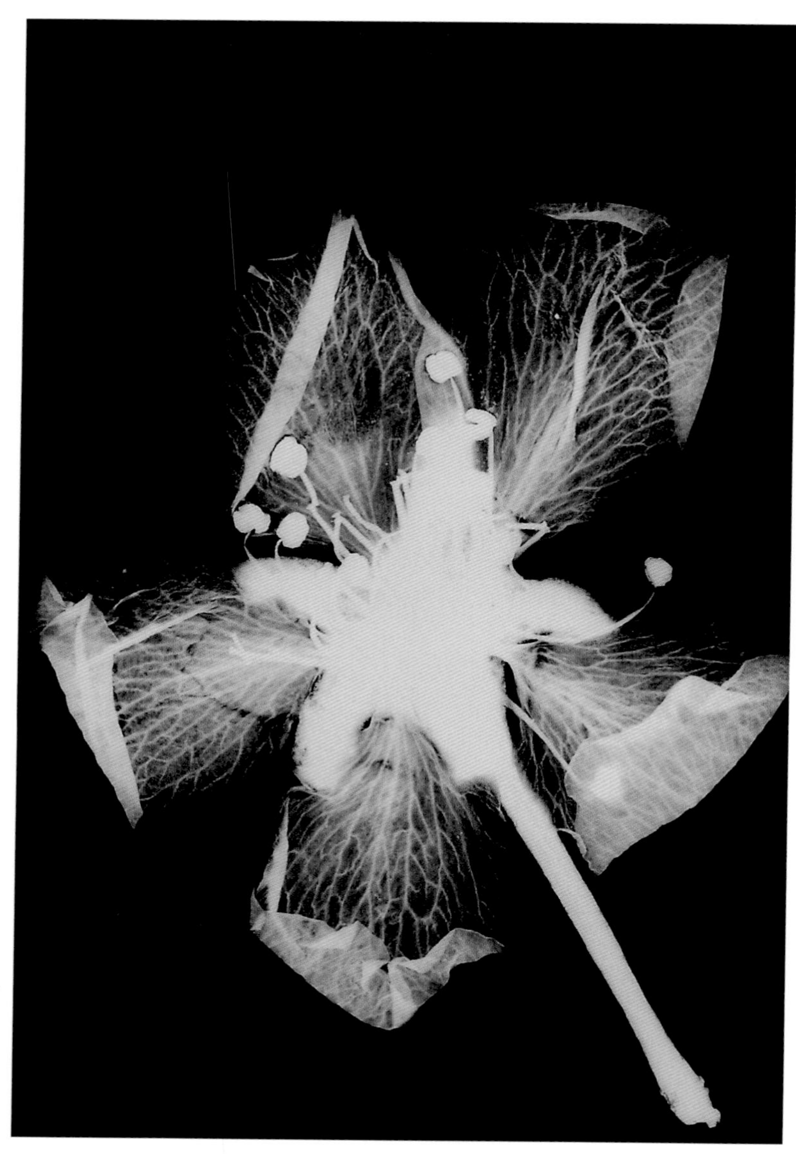

ZOÉ MENTHONNEX
Zombie, 2018

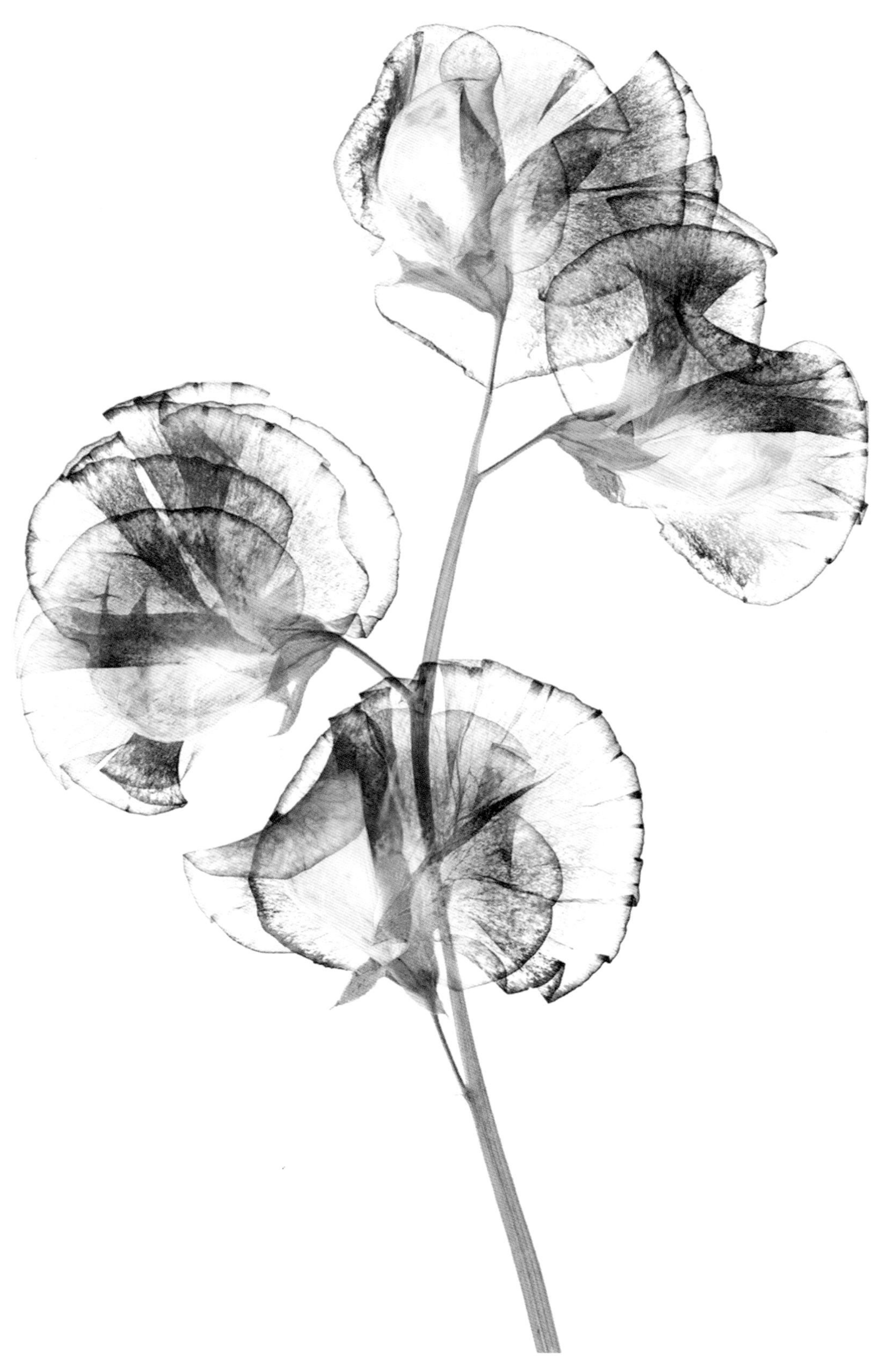

RON VAN DONGEN
Lathyrus odoratus 'Unwin's Butterfly Striped' study #2, 2013

The Ukrainian president Leonid Kuchma, Russian president Boris Yeltsin, United Kingdom prime minister John Major and United States president Bill Clinton signed a memorandum on security assurances that completed Ukraine's accession to the Treaty on the Non-Proliferation of Nuclear Weapons.

Ukraine voluntarily transferred the entirety of its nuclear stockpile to Russia in exchange for security assurances from the United States, the United Kingdom and Russia. Following the collapse of the Soviet Union, Ukraine reportedly inherited 15 per cent of Soviet nuclear inventory, including 460 warheads, each of which was 22 times more powerful than the bombs dropped at Hiroshima and Nagasaki. Technical control over the weapons remained with Russia, theoretically enabling the launch of 'Ukrainian' missiles by Moscow. Ukraine saw this inheritance as a geopolitical liability. Ukrainian government officials were also concerned about Russia's view of Ukraine as a 'seasonal state', and about Russia's continued attempts to undermine Ukraine's independence. In response to this perceived threat, the United Kingdom, the United States and Russia affirmed 'their obligation to refrain from the threat or use of force against the territorial integrity or political independence of Ukraine'. But the security assurances provided to Ukraine in the memorandum lacked clear enforcement provisions. In 2014 Russia invaded Ukraine's Crimean peninsula; the conflict remains unresolved.

Lilium 'Stargazer', Stargazer Lily, Netherlands

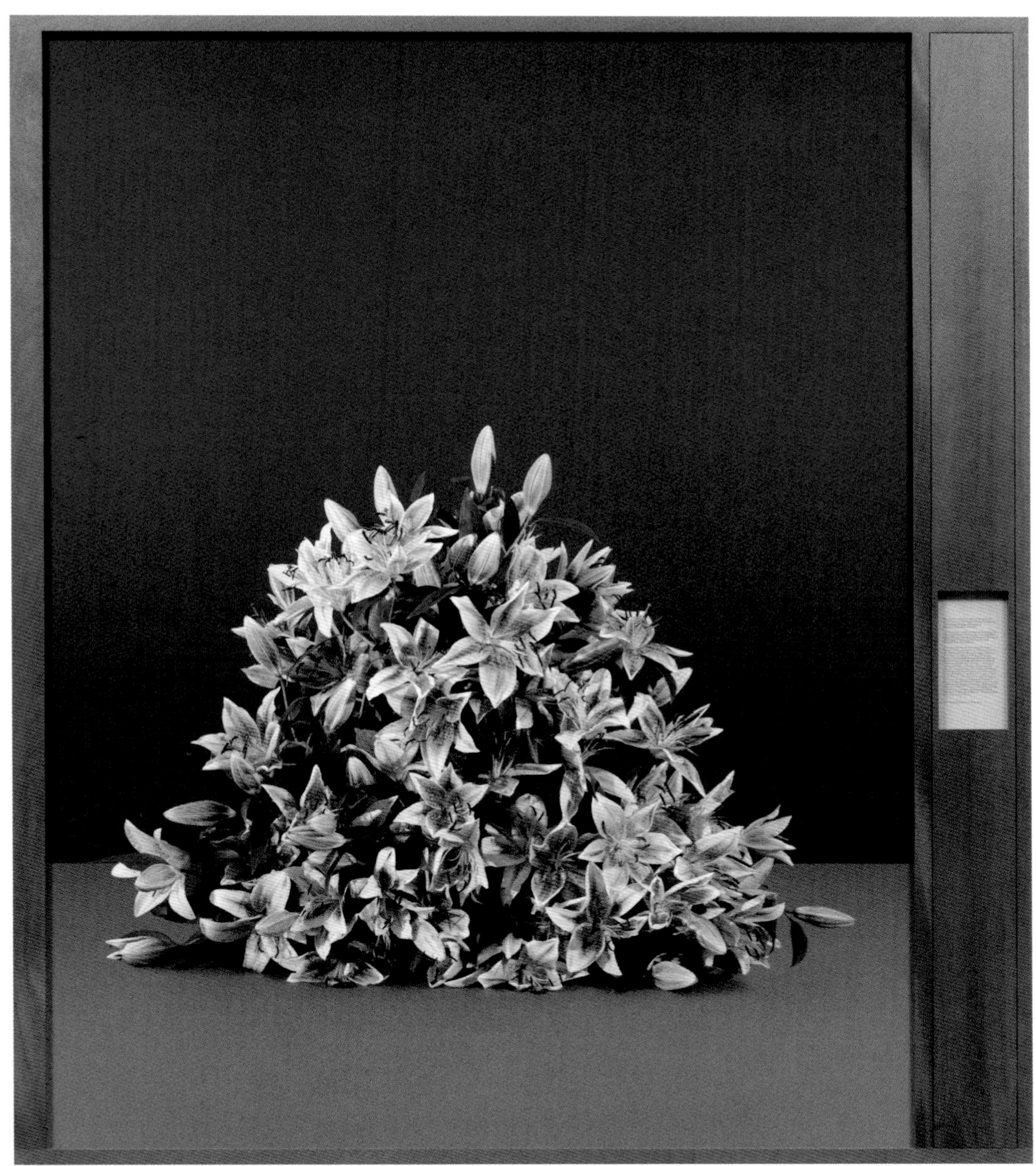

TARYN SIMON
Memorandum on Security Assurances in Connection with Ukraine's Accession to the Treaty on the Non-Proliferation of Nuclear Weapons (Budapest Memorandum), Budapest, Hungary, December 5, 1994.

Paperwork and the Will of Capital, 2015
Archival inkjet print and text on archival herbarium paper in mahogany frame
215.9 × 186.1 × 7 cm (85 × 73¼ × 2¾ in.). © Taryn Simon. Courtesy Gagosian

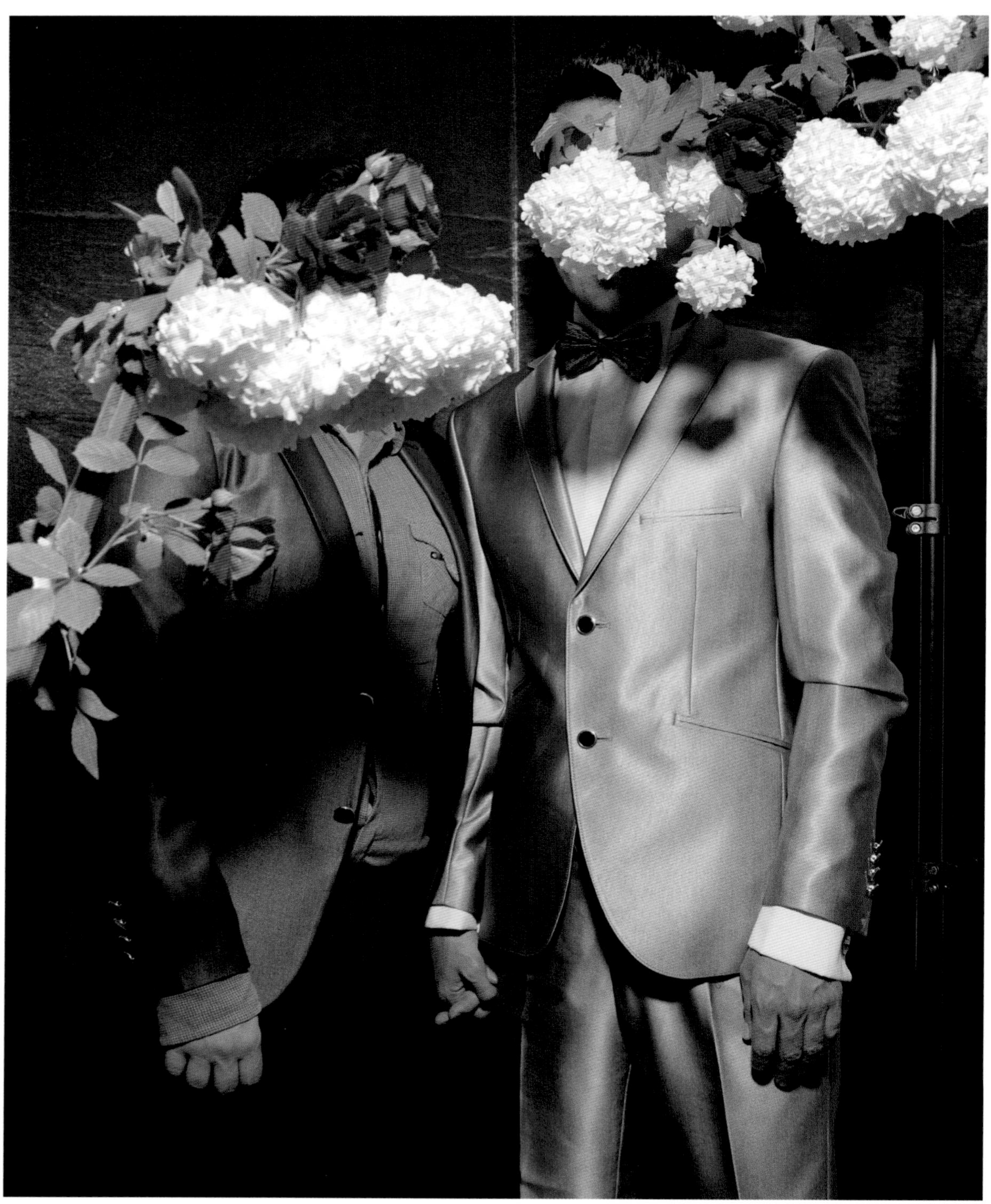

LAURENCE RASTI
Untitled, from the series *There Are No Homosexuals in Iran*, 2014–16

Laurence Rasti photographed Iranian gay refugees in transit in Denizli, Turkey. They flee their country, where their sexual identity is punishable by death. In this context of uncertainty, where anonymity is the best protection, this work questions the fragility of identity and gender concepts.

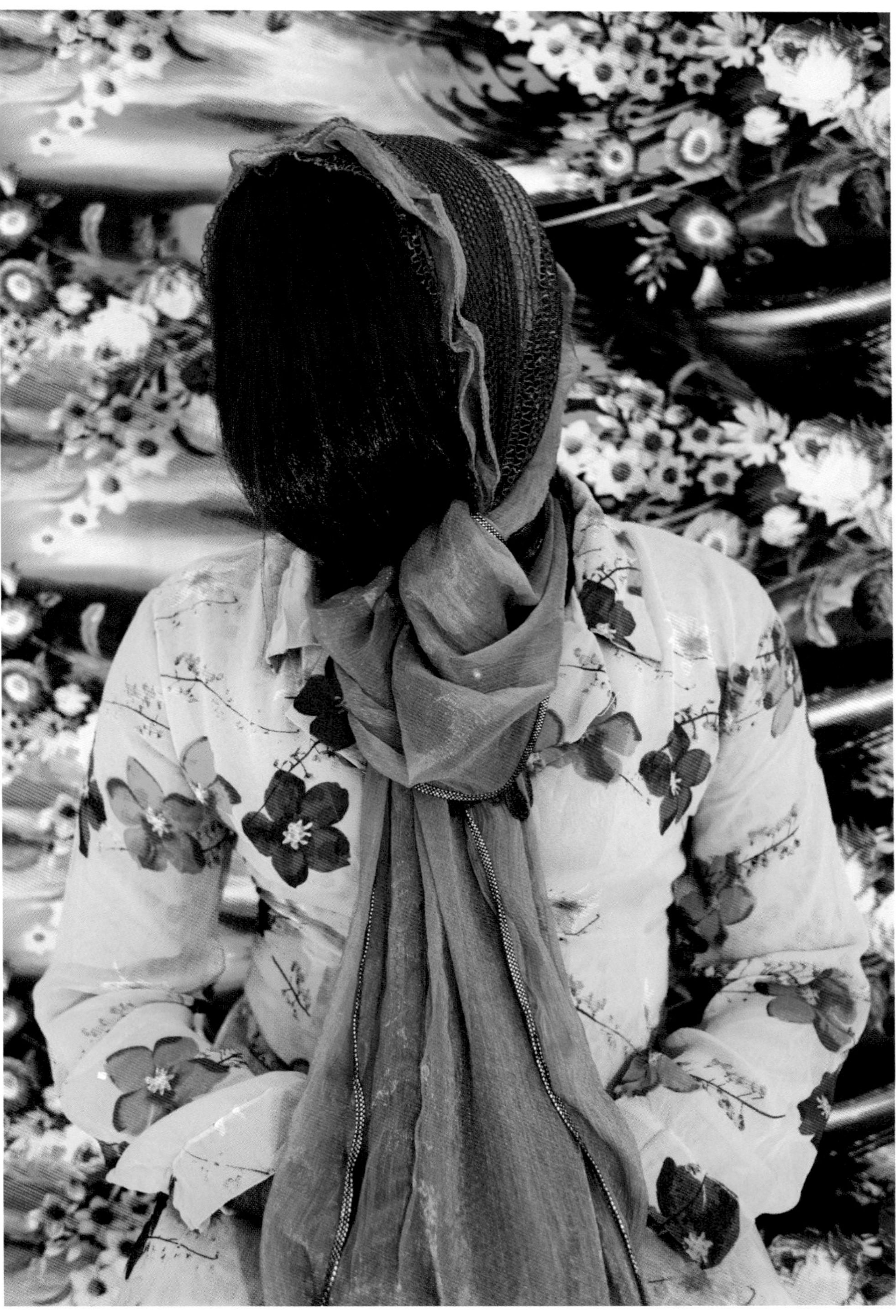

HABIBA NOWROSE
Concealed, 2014–18

'As women we are often compelled to portray our beautiful selves. In that path to avail beauty we are made to strip off our individuality, stories and traumas. Eventually we lose ourselves and become one with that fabricated image. We become anonymous even to ourselves and our identities remain concealed.'

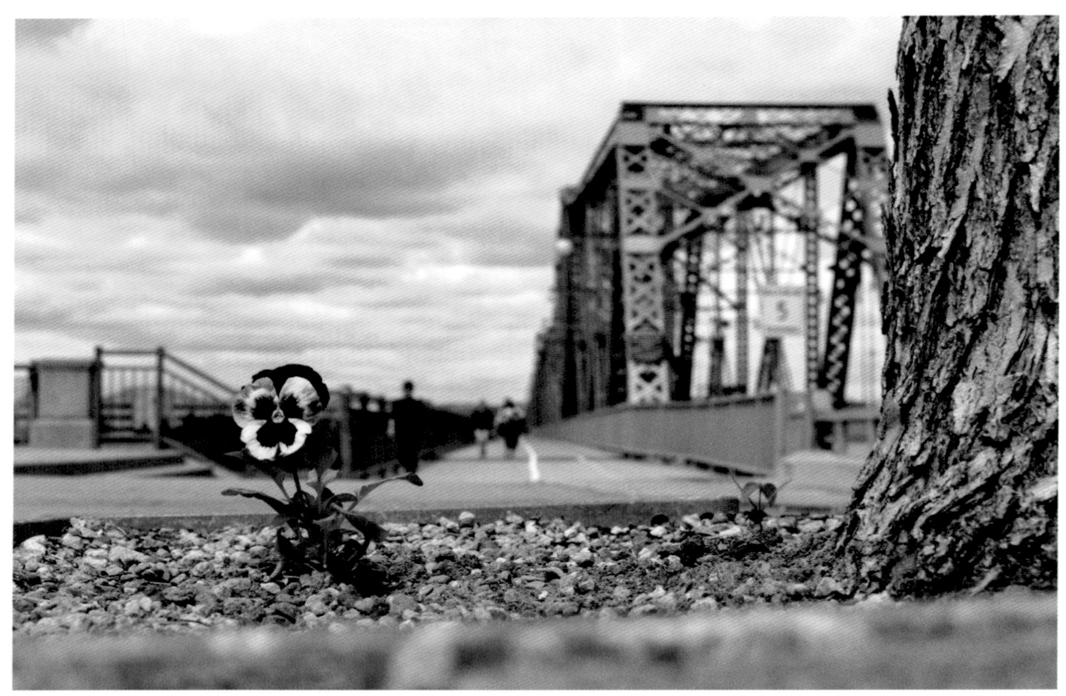

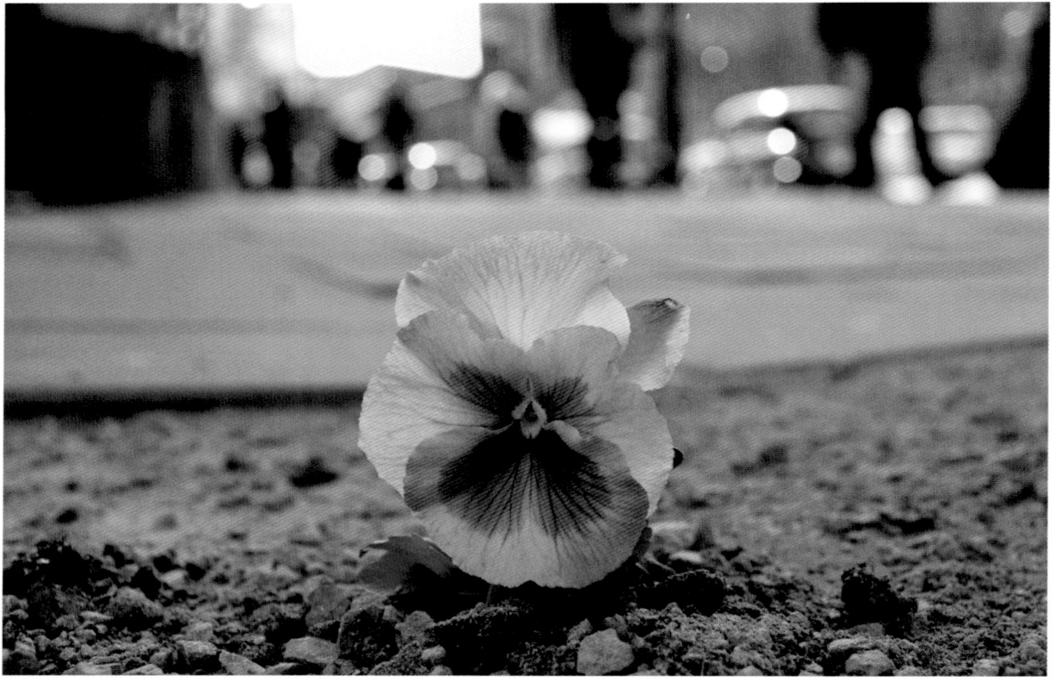

PAUL HARFLEET of The Pansy Project
'Nice Shoes, Faggot!' For Alain Brosseau. Alexandra Bridge, Ottawa, 2019 (top)
'Batty!' King's Cross, London, 2013

The artist Paul Harfleet plants pansies at the sites of homophobic abuse. The flower is then documented in its location, the image entitled after the abuse. These images reveal a frequent reality of LGBTQ+ experience, which often goes unreported to the authorities.

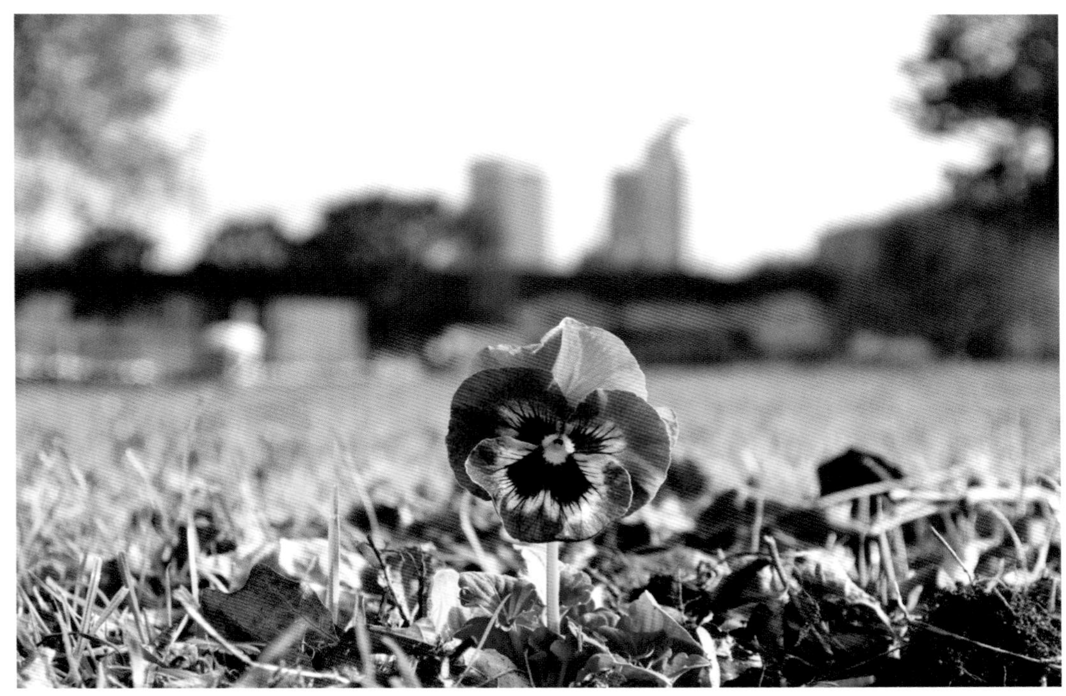

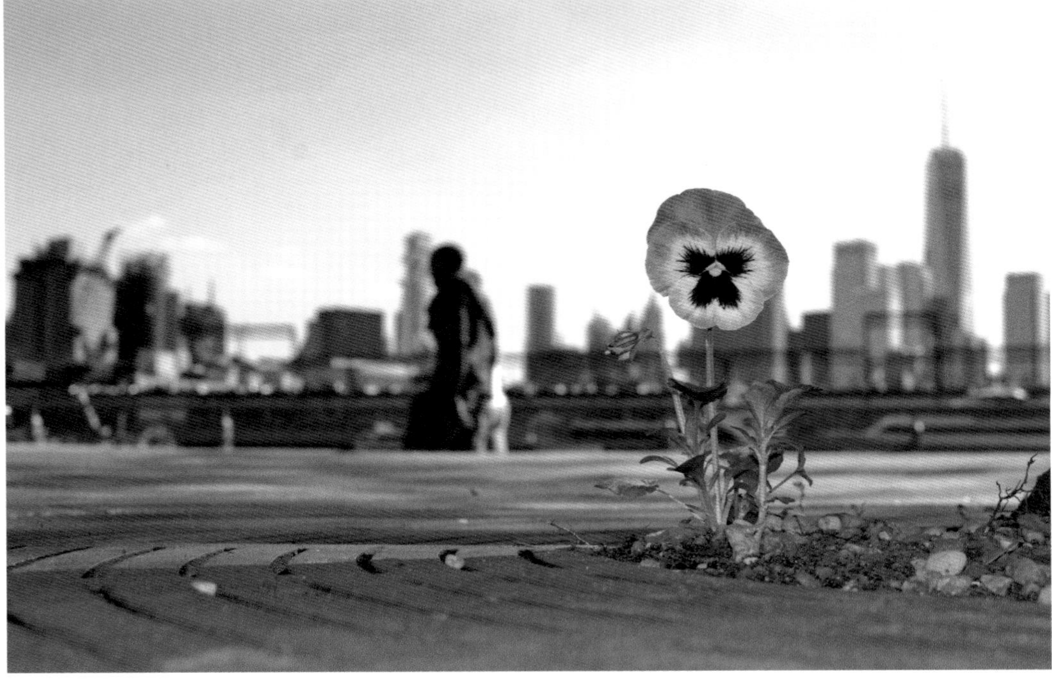

PAUL HARFLEET of The Pansy Project
'Batty Boy! – Tranny!' Regent's Canal, London, 2013 (top)
For Marsha P. Johnson. Christopher Street Pier, New York, 2019

L'Angoisse

Il y a un mal contre lequel l'opium est souverain
et ce mal s'appelle l'Angoisse.

(There is an evil against which opium is sovereign,
and this evil we call anguish.)

Antonin Artaud[7]

For the contemporary photographer seeking some insight into or elucidation of the mysteries of life, including its darker corners, the flower isn't to be admired – at least, not primarily – for its beauty, but for its capacity to stir deep in the soul a sense of foreboding, unease or longing. The seminal poetic work of the modern era, Baudelaire's Les Fleurs du Mal (1857)*, did just that, with the result that he was initially castigated by a bourgeois society that wished flowers to be merely pretty. Almost alone in his praise, Victor Hugo wrote to the poet:*
'Vos Fleurs du mal *rayonnent et éblouissent comme des étoiles. Continuez. Je crie bravo de toutes mes forces à votre vigoureux esprit' (Your* Flowers of Evil *shine and dazzle like the stars. Continue. I cry 'bravo' with all my soul to your vigorous spirit).*[8] *Photographers, too, can set aside the comfortable traditional associations of the flower, and inscribe on their petals and leaves their own anxieties, acknowledging the artist and educator Sister Corita Kent's wise, oft-quoted observation, 'Flowers grow out of dark moments.'*

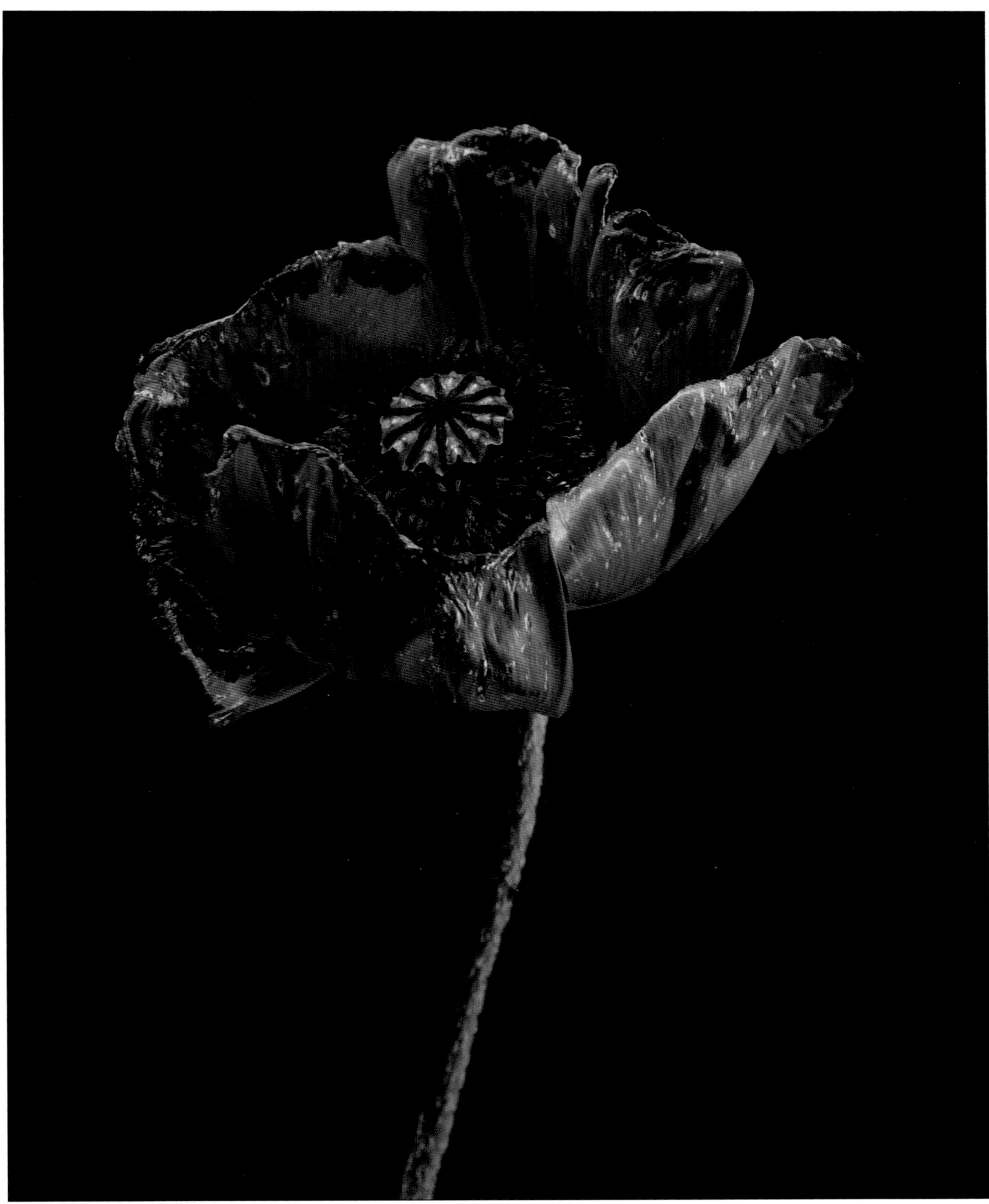

MATTHIEU GAFSOU
Papaver somniferum, from the series *Only God Can Judge Me*, 2012–14
Matthieu Gafsou explored the drug scene of the Swiss city of Lausanne for more than a year, creating a body of work documenting the harshness of the lives of drug addicts, alongside more poetic takes on their experience.

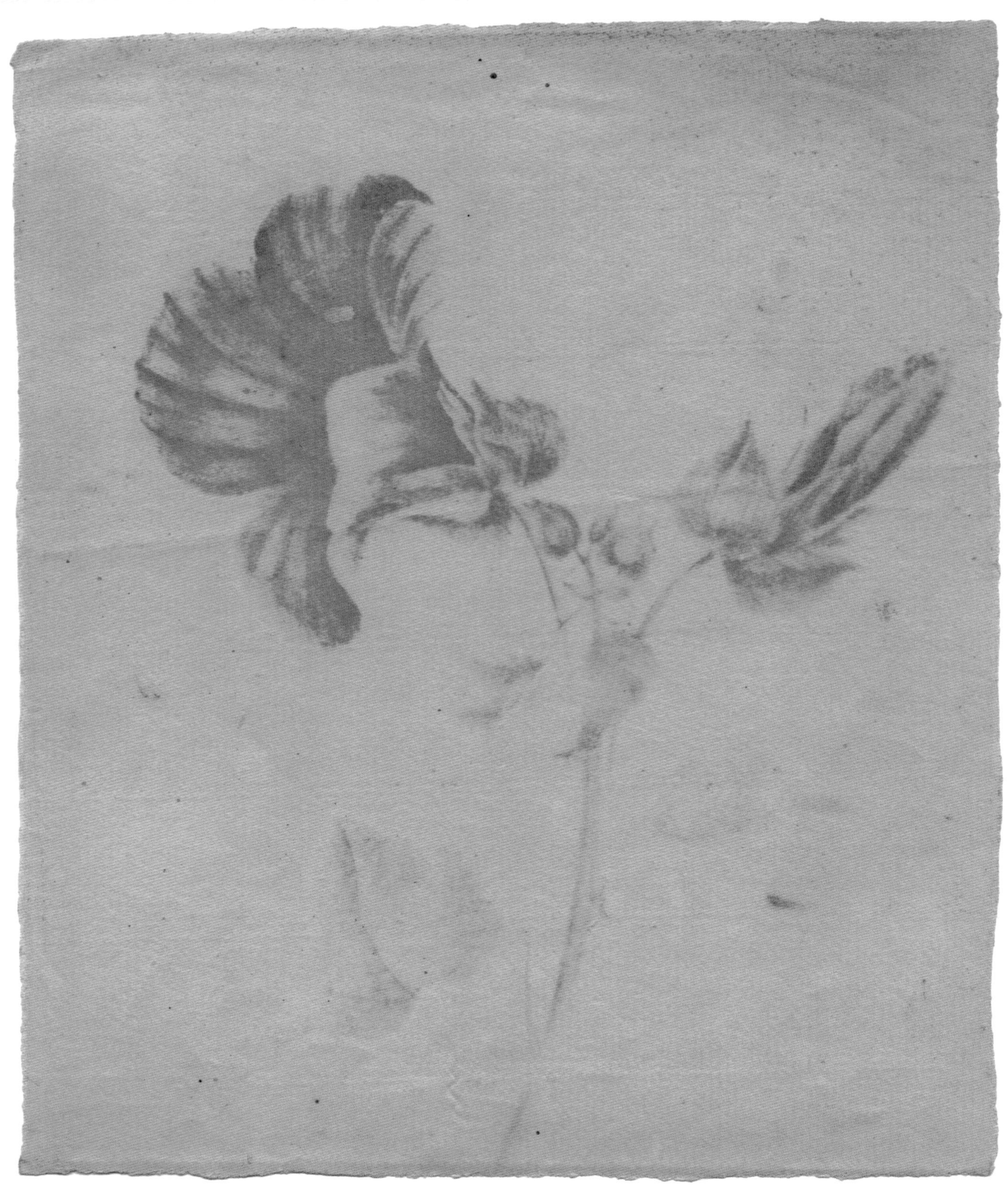

NEVIL STORY-MASKELYNE
Untitled, photogenic drawing?, *c.* 1844

A certain mystery surrounds this eloquent flower study by Nevil Story-Maskelyne, a geologist, mineralogist and enthusiastic disciple of William Henry Fox Talbot. At first glance it might appear to be a photogenic drawing, but its three-dimensionality suggests that either it was made with a camera, or it was a photogenic drawing contact negative from an engraving by a botanical artist.

A PHOTO-SYNTHESIS

We know that photographs (or, to be true to the historical moment, camera-less photograms, or 'photogenic drawings') of flowers began very early. Indeed, it was in 1834, five years before the official date of photography's 'invention', that William Henry Fox Talbot found their varied forms ideal for his experiments, along with leaves, lace and other materials easily laid flat. But while flowers have the honour of being the first objects ever photographed, as we have seen, it took many decades for them to find a secure place in the fields of photography. Today, as this book makes abundantly clear, floral imagery is ubiquitous. Once photographic technology developed sufficiently to rival other media – and, one might even argue, surpass them – the practice exploded, although it may only have been with the coming of reliable colour technology in the second half of the twentieth century that photography could do justice to that ever-so-vital floral characteristic. The hundreds of pictures selected for this book, by more than 120 photographers, necessarily represent only a tiny fraction of the excellent and varied studies produced over the past thirty years, although I'd like to think we've covered most of the main approaches. Clearly, flowers are a highly attractive subject, and for many, even a passion. Is this passion simply to be explained by colourful, shapely subject matter? Or is it something more deeply rooted?

BEFORE PHOTOGRAPHY

For the answer to such questions, we must look back thousands of years. The cliché 'since the dawn of humankind' is actually appropriate, and highly so, where flowers and humans are concerned. And we know now that this relationship is not restricted to *Homo sapiens*; for instance, certain Neanderthal burial sites show high concentrations of pollen, suggesting that ritual demanded some form of floral offering. Flowers have long been appreciated for their myriad forms and colours, their seductive fragrance, their utility in food, cosmetics and medicine, and their symbolic and emblematic power. 'Many kinds of meaning, philosophical and practical, have been derived from these long generations of observing,' notes the critic and novelist Raymond Williams.[1]

Worldwide plant transfers have an extremely long history, and where they were intentional (many were not) they required deep knowledge to succeed, much of it acquired well before written records began. Some scholars go so far as to argue that the ability to move species from one place to another is a defining element of human culture and consciousness, while the ecologist Matthew Chew has stated flatly that the 're-dispersal of biota by humans is a hallmark of civilization'.[2]

The key word here is 'civilization'. If an appreciation of flowers goes back thousands of years, the *culture* of flowers really begins with the Neolithic agricultural revolution around 12,000 years ago, which in turn laid the foundations for individual human civilizations everywhere. 'While flowers initially evolved to attract pollinating insects, they also proved pleasurable to much of agricultural mankind,' notes the anthropologist Jack Goody, who goes on to explain just how enriching plant knowledge became to human beings.[3] The Symbolist writer Maurice Maeterlinck, whose essay 'The Intelligence of Flowers' (1907) had a profound influence on the young photographer-cum-plant breeder Edward Steichen (who at one point came close to abandoning photography for horticulture), hints that we respond intelligently, *rationally,* to flowers, and not – as conventional wisdom would assert – emotionally, because we are in a symbiotic relationship with them. The need is mutual and profound:

> We could truly say that ideas come to flowers in the same way they come to us. Flowers grope in the same darkness, encounter the same obstacles and the same ill will, in the same unknown. They know the same laws, same disappointments, same slow and difficult triumphs. It seems they have our patience, our perseverance, our self-love; the same finely tuned and diversified intelligence, almost the same hopes and the same ideals. Like ourselves, they struggle against a vast indifferent force that ends by helping them.[4]

The photographer-philosopher Ernst Fuhrmann, whose macro-photographs of plants were widely published in his book *The Plant as Living Being* (1930), even proposed an organic-ecological way of thinking, or 'biosophy' as he termed it, and came up with a vivid image to convey the deeply rooted connection between plant and animal: the animal was simply a plant that had learned to pick up its roots and move around.

In 'Why Are Flowers Beautiful?', David Deutsch extends this thinking about symbiosis, arguing – quixotically, some might argue – that flowers have an *objective* beauty. This is not to say that we cannot have subjective reactions and read into flowers meanings that are well established by culture, 'but that there is such a thing as aesthetic value and that it is objective, independent of culture, independent of our personal preferences and tastes, and independent of our biological makeup'.[5] Flowers do indeed need us and we them (it would be wise to remember that they are one of the most successful life forms on Earth), and objective standards of beauty enable us to 'signal across the species divide'. The psychologist Jeannette Haviland-Jones and her colleagues cite several studies that seem to support this conclusion, namely, 'that cultivated flowers are rewarding because they have evolved [in order] to rapidly induce positive emotion in humans, just as other plants have evolved to induce varying behavioural responses in a wide variety of species leading to the dispersal or propagation of the plants'.[6]

With human civilization came record keeping, and where flowers are concerned, what a lengthy record it has been. New Kingdom Egyptian medicine, to take one particularly sophisticated example, incorporated knowledge of useful plants as far away as Persia and India, offering its doctors a pharmacopoeia of 700 plant-based ingredients. And if foods, medicines, dyes, insecticides and cosmetics might top the historical list, they hardly account for the rich culture of flowers that evolved in so many places, although the elaboration was sometimes disrupted by puritanical critics who condemned the worship of false idols, simply deplored the extravagance or, perhaps more persuasively, protested that the cultivation of flowers was encroaching on land that should have been consecrated to the growing of food.

Attitudes could always shift within a culture or over time, with flowers falling into or out of favour. During the European colonial era, for example, settlers often despised the local flora, considering it mere weed, preferring imports from the mother country – only to find that visitors from abroad were delighted with, and exported back home, the despised 'exotics'. (Ironically, once independence sentiments stirred, suddenly those 'weeds' were rehabilitated to serve proudly as nation symbols.) Flowers were also unwelcome in Europe for almost 600 years after the fall of Rome, while Goody noticed their absence from much of African culture, where animals predominated in art forms.[7] So although claims of a universal and unequivocal love of flowers should be qualified, the overall world picture is generally one of fascination, adoption and cultivation – both literally and figuratively. Flowers have been used in bodily decoration, as garlands worn on the head, and in and on clothing or on the skin (literally, or painted, printed or tattooed). Flowers are printed or embroidered on our dresses, jackets, shorts, shawls, ties and scarves, on our bed sheets and towels, on upholstery, wallpaper and curtains. They're woven into our carpets, fabricated in jewelry, carved into furniture, cast in glass or ceramic, printed on coins, flags, banknotes and product packaging of all kinds, and feature in myriad advertisements. They have inspired poets and writers of songs, ballets, operas, short stories and novels. After his visit to Colette, when he was given an exquisite 'millefiori' paperweight, the writer Truman Capote wrote a hymn of praise to it, and to the celebrated author, calling it 'The White Rose (1970)'.[8]

We can't seem to exist without floral ornament, and nor could our gardens, whether private or public – and often highly competitive (one of the most talked-about events of the British social calendar is the Chelsea Flower Show, held since 1888 in springtime London and costing untold millions, itself a proof of primary cultural significance). Even contemporary architecture may be flora-inspired: the lotus gave its form to the ArtScience Museum in Singapore; Shanghai's Qizhong Stadium was based on the petals of the magnolia; and the Burj Khalifa in Dubai took its cue from the spider lily.

Flowers mark important rituals and ceremonies, public and private. It is impossible to imagine a wedding or funeral without bouquets of flowers, and birthdays, anniversaries, Valentine's Day, all require floral offerings. In short, as Goody reminds us, flowers have been used quasi-universally, and 'above all in establishing, maintaining and even ending relationships, with the dead as with the living, with divinities as well as humans'.[9]

Yet how ironic it is that most of this 'flower power' remains, if not invisible, at least so taken for granted as to be virtually so. Indeed, how ironic: flowers or floral motifs are everywhere in our lives, from birth to death, but we hardly ever acknowledge this ubiquity, nor give much thought to its significance. One part of the explanation is obvious. Flowers are so intricately woven into our social lives that we don't have to think much about them. On the other hand, might this not be partially explained as an example of chauvinistic disdain? Flowers have almost everywhere been gendered feminine; men give, women receive, and women wear. Flowers have blossomed in the domestic sphere, while being decidedly excluded from the industrial domain. Any doubts about this feminine gendering are easily dispelled by a consideration of babies' names: is there a boy out there called Rose, Violet, Iris, Marguerite, Alyssia or Lily? While a portrait of an actress or singer with a flower in her hair is mundane, do we ever see a businessman or politician sporting one? A woman can wear a flower-patterned dress without eliciting any comment, but a man in a floral suit is still more likely to be seen on the catwalk or the stage than on the street. Still, in a world (or parts of it) where gender-fluidity is gaining ground, we can expect to see more men wearing flowers without causing comment.

Another partial explanation has to do with the association between flowers and innocence. Babies and small children can be given flowers or dressed in floral-patterned clothing, but associations with innocence seem to make adult men leery. Cultural prejudice is deep-rooted. The history of photography does show us that exceptions are made for gay men and male artists, both popularly considered 'to be in touch with their feminine side', but the exceptions prove the rule: Flora was, and remains, a goddess, not a god. The implication in all this historical baggage? That flowers are perfectly fine as decoration and enhancements to beauty – but ultimately frivolous.

That general sense that flowers are not 'serious', in the context of this book, was echoed in an email exchange with the British photographer Nadav Kander, who figured among the photographers who had never thought of themselves as flower enthusiasts and were therefore rather surprised to be invited to contribute. After thinking about it a bit, he fired off this response: 'And by the way, I love this

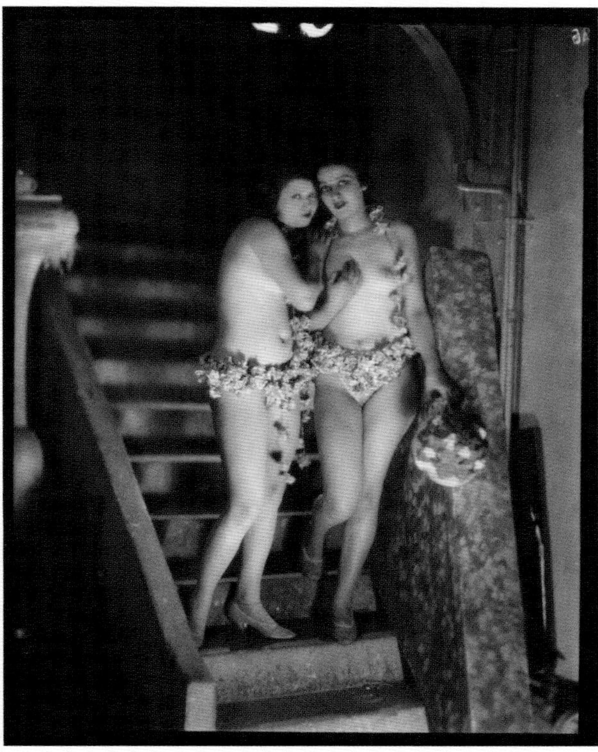

JAMES ABBE
The Dolly Sisters at the Folies Bergère, gelatin silver print, 1924
The flower as a symbol of youthful vitality, and of course sexual availability, has long been deeply embedded in Western culture. It is only in recent years that the idea has been vigorously contested.

idea of yours. For years I have disregarded any photograph of flowers as cheesy and simply *not* allowed.'

Nothing could be further from the frivolity charge, as Kander now admits. I might add to my list above the use of flowers as indicators of status or respect (both for the giver and for the recipient), or to convey subtle messages of love (or rejection), a language that became so evolved in Europe and America that by the nineteenth century there were extremely detailed manuals and etiquette books instructing (mostly) well-brought-up young ladies on the correct grammar and syntax. For instance, handing over a bouquet upside down meant the opposite of handing it over right side up; handing it tilted to the left meant 'me', to the right, 'you', etc., etc. In fact, few took the very bourgeois 'language of flowers' terribly seriously, and many of the 'meanings' of flowers were different from book to book; for example, acacia in one was 'bitterness', in another 'anxiety'. But even sceptics could agree that a rose meant love and a lily purity, associations that are deeply rooted in the past. The rose was long a symbol of sensual love, and the early Christian Church initially tried to suppress it, but eventually gave up and took the wiser course of bending it to its will, proclaiming it as a symbol of the Virgin Mary. Meanwhile, the chrysanthemum went from symbol of fertility and longevity in China to one of death, as it took the long road to Christian Europe; as Goody notes sardonically, 'neither party was interested in the symbolic meanings given to them abroad.'[10] And there are still modern Italians, French or Brazilians who won't have a white carnation in the house, with its associations of death. As for modern versions of 'the language', this sales pitch from a website shows that its appeal remains strong:

> Flower enthusiasts may have heard this term being thrown around every now and then, but what exactly is floriography you ask? Floriography is the language of flowers. All flowers hold different meanings, often based on the type of flower, the colour of the flower, or both. And floriography is the art of communicating through different flower types. Once you learn and understand the meaning of flowers, giving flowers as gifts becomes so much more thoughtful as you can convey just how you feel with a bouquet![11]

As for flowers being used to impress others, hierarchy and class have long played a role. Whereas wealthy folk of earlier centuries would seek to impress through masses of blooms, displays in today's chic house and garden magazines will privilege one or two exotic stems drooping over the lip of an austere vase – sending a subtle 'less is more' message. There is still something to this language of flowers, then. But the grammar isn't fixed, nor will it ever be. If flowers are living beings, so is their language; beyond being *things* they are also tokens, emblems and symbols. Potent ones, at that: it's a fact that at least one war has been waged in the name of a flower, and heated diplomatic spats have caused international incidents.[12] In 1911, the

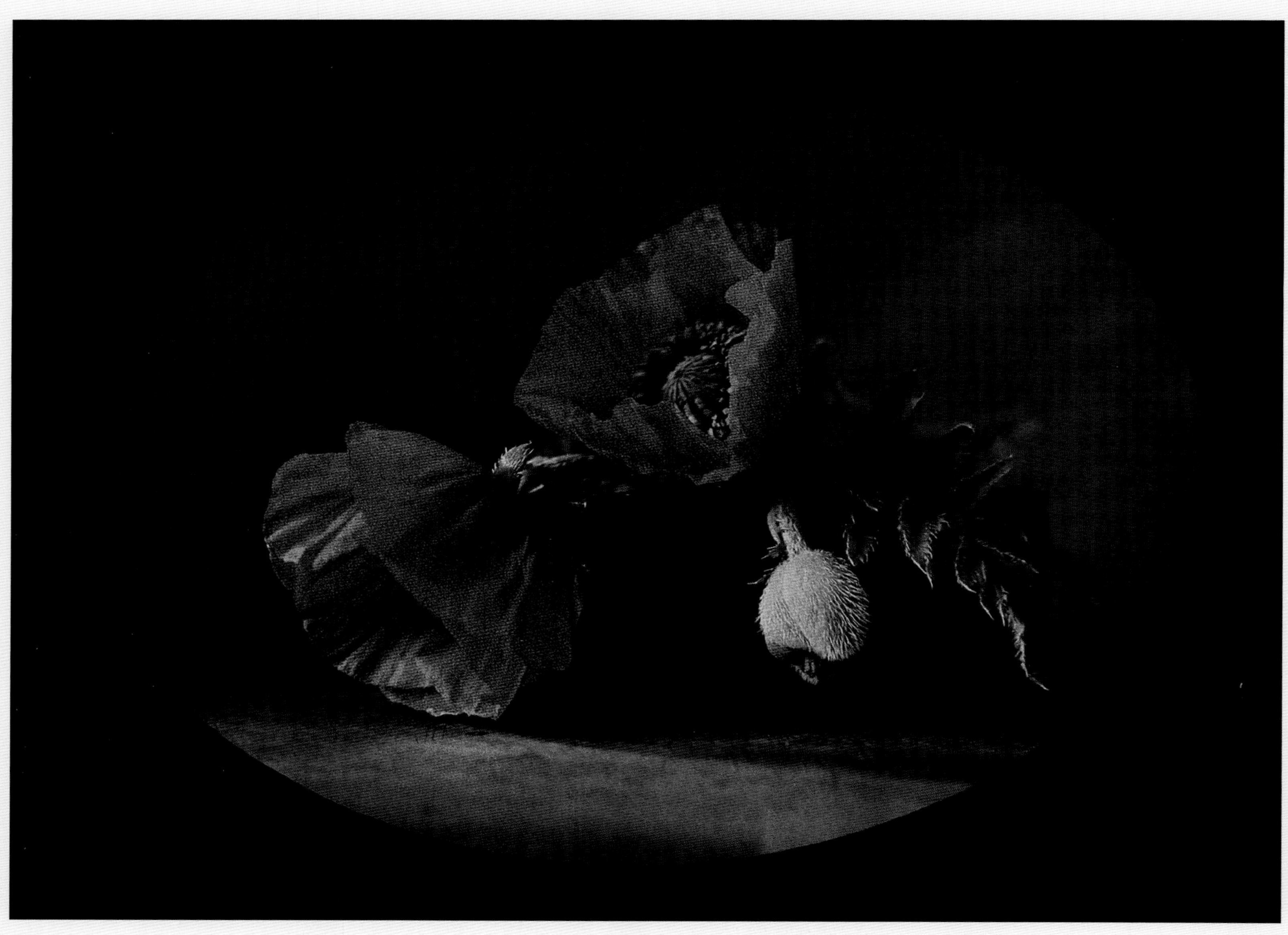

ANDRÉ CHAPON
Pavots, autochome, *c.* 1930

The autochrome, invented by the Lumière brothers and commercially available from 1907, finally allowed flower photography to rival painting, although this relatively cumbersome and expensive method was destined to fall out of favour during the modernist period.

recently established Union of South Africa chose a thornless acacia-like flower to represent it at King George V's coronation. When it was realized that the lack of thorns meant it was an Australian import, and not a native plant, thorns had to be hastily added. Flowers have even contributed to aspects of social order. The Romans would hang a rose as a token of secrecy over the council table where sensitive information would be discussed, hence the legal term *sub rosa*, meaning in secret.

Obviously, the quasi-universal appreciation of flowers, along with a passion for the exotic forms, meant the production (and cultivation) of flowers on increasingly vast scales, along with the development of correspondingly vast and quick-moving trading networks, a process that evolved over millennia. Two thousand years ago there was already a vigorous and reliable trade between Egypt and Rome, and thousands of roses and narcissi could arrive from the former in a single consignment. Centuries later, the heyday of the clipper ships, and later steamships, sped up the importation of exotics. Cut flowers were a top-down phenomenon; by the nineteenth century they were within the reach, at least for special occasions, of all but the poorest members of European society. The Industrial Revolution brought another practice into common use: those vases we take for granted were once the privilege of the wealthy, but mass production and much-lowered prices brought them into the homes of ordinary folk. Today, cargo jets filled exclusively with flowers ply the globe, with annual trade estimated at roughly $30 billion. For some human beings, flowers are evidently less carriers of symbolic meaning than luxury products to be bought and sold, although not quite like any other; their fragility and short lives see to that.

A full assessment of the role of the flower in human culture would involve every scholarly discipline imaginable, and we should not be surprised one day to discover a graduate school of floral studies at some progressive university. So profoundly rooted is our subject that we use the terms 'the flower of' or 'the flower*ing* of' to mean 'the best' state or stage of just about anything: 'the flower of youth'; 'the flowering of human consciousness'; 'the flower of democracy'; or the (aptly titled, given our book's subject) exhibition catalogue *The Flowering of Florence* (2002).[14]

It is not surprising, then, to find the fine arts to be a rich terrain of floral imagery. Aside from the highly developed arts of flower arranging and garden design, the two-dimensional representation of flowers has on the whole reached spectacular heights, achieving magnificence at various times in Asia, the Middle East and Europe. Our focus is on the art of photography, and this is not the place to delve into this rich history of painting, but it might be helpful to anchor our thoughts about photography with a succinct word from Peter Mitchell, author of *European Flower Painters* (1973): 'Painters...have never doubted the value of the flowerpiece as a challenge, as a means of instruction, and above all, as a subject the equal of any other.'[15]

The stage was set for photography long ago. The photographers in this book have taken to it with gusto.

A BIRD'S-EYE VIEW

How, and why, do contemporary photographers engage with flowers? Our book makes it clear that that they do so in infinite ways, sometimes following a particular tradition, sometimes going down a path of their own making. (The Artists' Statements at the back of this book help to contextualize each photographer's work, although some practitioners have declined to provide such a statement, preferring that the work 'speak for itself'.)

'Infinite' might suggest that the universe of floral imagery is without limit or structure. But pulling back and taking a bird's-eye view of the genre reveals interesting commonalities, or, we might say, constellations of images, even if those remain amorphous. The following synopsis might therefore serve the reader as a useful guide to these constellations, both major and minor. It is meant to complement the themes elaborated in the Introduction.

The act of photographing flowers may be *intended* as introspection or self-reflection – or may *result* in it – perhaps mirroring an emotion felt by the photographer. Or the photographic gesture may be intended as a contemplation of nature, an admiration of its myriad forms or a rumination on life and death. Some photographers question perception itself, or even human consciousness, exploring the fine line between reality and illusion. These contemplative or philosophical threads run through much contemporary work – not surprisingly, given the widespread anxiety about all things environmental. Moreover, given growing awareness of the many deleterious forms of human impact on the natural world, a number of photographers directly confront subjects such as pollution, radiation and genetic manipulation, feeling the need to issue a clear warning: *we can't go on like this*.

Other photographers follow a less political, more mystical path, expressing joy and wonderment at what in a previous and more innocent time would have been termed 'nature's bounty'. Often they cite poetry (or 'visual poetry') as their preferred approach. A number of these photographers also happen to be devout gardeners, finding both solace and renewal surrounded by the plants they grow, carefully nurture and finally preserve in imagery. Unlike commercial photographers, who are obliged to show flowers at the peak of perfection (with a lot of help from digital manipulation), art photographers tend to be at ease with wilting and even dead specimens, finding in them more pathos and tenderness than in their youthful and more perfect counterparts.

While ecology is a major concern for many photographers, others cite cultural or political issues as driving forces, seeing flowers as vivid metaphors for a host of social ills or their remedies, including struggles of gender identity, sexuality, ethnicity and the like. Given that flowers are quasi-universally gendered feminine, it makes them ideal targets of subversion – speaking symbolically – in the service of a reimagining of sexual politics. Meanwhile, commerce, industry and even capitalism come in for their share of subtle critique. On the other hand, countering this critical slant, some photographers celebrate the enduring nature of social rites in which flowers are essential components.

Interestingly, a number of practitioners cite chance, or accident, as factors in their floral imagery, simply having found themselves in particular places or situations where flowers (or a floral element) happened to be located, and slipped quite naturally into the picture. Indeed, sometimes photographers will admit to having realized the pictorial importance of that floral element only *after* they made the picture.

Another central constellation groups works concerning ideas about the depiction of flowers in art, whereby the photographer is inspired by, pays homage to, borrows from, develops, modifies, transforms or parodies artwork of the past or present, namely painting, drawing, watercolour, sculpture, botanical illustration and even imagery found on the internet. Collage, montage, mixed media...

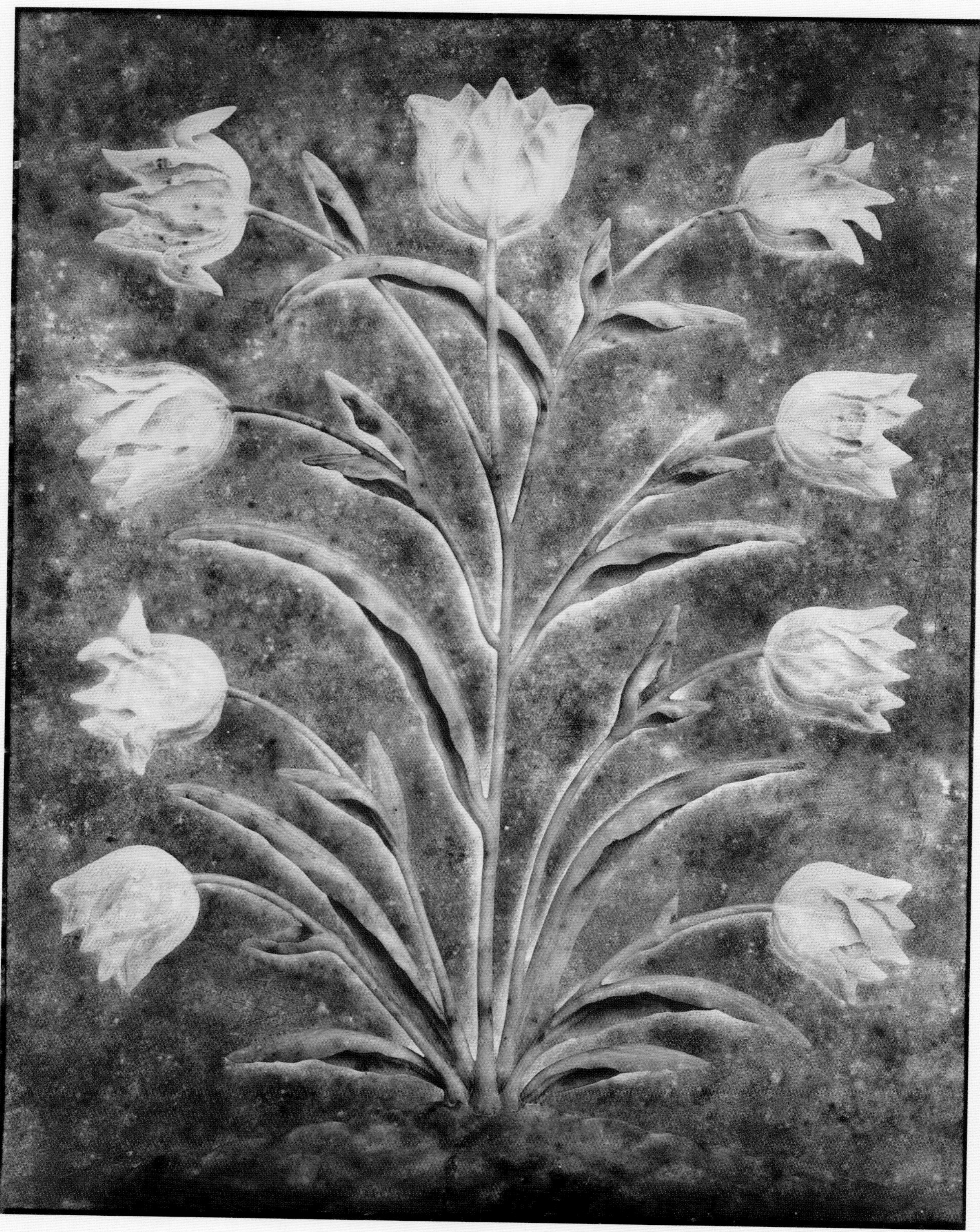

ADAM FUSS
Untitled, from the series *My Ghost*, 2014
A number of contemporary photographers have shown an interest in antique processes. Fuss's daguerreotype serves as a reminder of both the limitations and the promise of this mid-nineteenth-century medium.

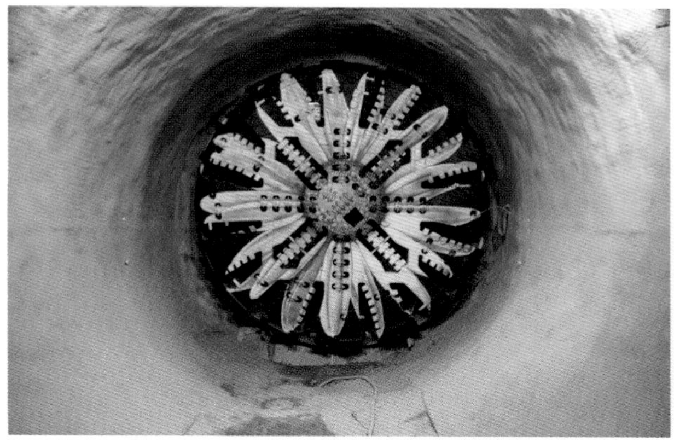

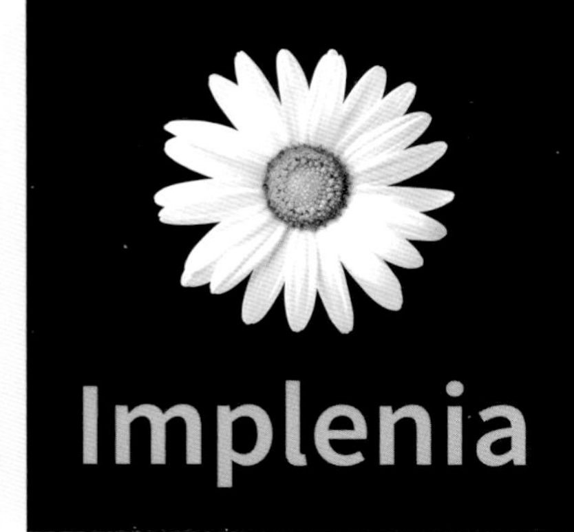

JÜRGEN STRESIUS
Implenia Tunnel-boring Machine in Operation on a Deutsche Bahn Construction Project (left), 2019

This Swiss construction company chose a flower as its emblem (right), a surprising choice that met initially with resistance from staff, given that construction was seen as a tough, 'manly' enterprise. Eventually, however, the choice was seen to have been a wise one. Clearly, it was the tunnel-boring machine that inspired the logo.

the principle here is that anything goes. I hasten to add that this category includes references to historical photographs themselves. Although not the only genre so referenced, the still life is the most important, a staple in art that has never lost its appeal.

A further constellation includes work with scientific intent, namely studies of flora, sometimes microscopic, clearly revealing structure, form and function. Many such studies involve isolated single specimens seen against neutral backgrounds, most often white, less often black, and occasionally coloured for contrast. This group includes plant studies modelled on traditional forms of botanical illustration. And yet, if scientific rigour is foremost in these photographers' minds, none of them discounts the importance of the aesthetic aspect, and all strive for an appropriate balance. At the other end of the botanical-interest spectrum, however, some photographers profess absolutely no interest in the flower per se, but instead see in texture, pattern, form, colour and so on a fabulous field for artistic license.

A fourth grouping coalesces around the found flower, as opposed to the cut or arranged variety, whether discovered in town or country, the wild, parks or gardens. Photographers may work outdoors, without interfering in what they find, or take flowers back to the studio, where they can do what they like with them. This might mean a variation on the classic still life of flowers in a vase, or something more inventive, even theatrical. Photographers sometimes even talk about their flowers as 'performers'. On occasion these flowers aren't flowers at all, or rather, not real flowers: those made in various kinds of plastic hold a particular fascination for photographers, especially since with clever lighting one can't always tell the difference; and, they ask, does it really matter? There are even mock 'botanical illustrations' of the *flora artificialia* genus.

A fifth category of images coalesces around explorations of photography's inherent character: its limitations, contradictions and particular strengths vis-à-vis other media, along with experimentation with the methods by which imagery can be reproduced. Negative and positive prints, montage, collage, multiple exposure, chemical manipulation, daguerreotypes, camera-obscura imagery, photograms, cyanotypes and new possibilities opened up by easy access to printers and scanners are among the techniques employed.

Cutting across all these tendencies is the powerful pull of symbolism, although usually not the conventional ones dimly associated with the Victorian 'language of flowers', tenacious though that idea is. The symbolism of the contemporary photographer is essentially personal, although the presentation of the work normally requires an explanation of, or at least a subtle reference to, the desired meaning. Political, social and cultural critique via floral imagery is a vital strand of contemporary practice. But the flower may also be symbol-free, or rather *specific symbol*-free, instead alluding to a mood, or beauty or harmony. Clearly, photographs encourage many readings, once the viewer gives them the attention they deserve. My co-curator Danaé Panchaud does just this with a number of them in her essay (pp. 176–183).

In my book *Flora Photographica* of 1991, I ended the introduction wondering if 'the flower' would remain of perennial interest to photographers. Would the twentieth century be seen in the future as *the* era of photography in floral art, or would some other medium have come along to displace it? Or would the flower simply lose its appeal for photographers in the twenty-first century? 'Most likely the flower *will* preserve its tenacious hold on our imagination.... The flower will appear in guises wholly new yet somehow familiar.'[16] Now, well into the new century and thirty years on from that first survey, it seems photography is as vibrant and floraphiliac as ever.

ARRANGEMENT

'The flower piece', as it was known – cut flowers in a vase – the most venerable of Western art forms, has never lost its attraction for artists working in a wide variety of disciplines. 'The old masters', wrote the great colourist Odilon Redon in 1868, 'have proved that the artist, once he has established his own idiom, once he has taken from nature the necessary means of expression, is free, legitimately free, to borrow his subjects from history, from the poets, from his own imagination.'[1]

No photographer would question this list. For a long time black-and-white or at least monochrome imagery was the default mode of photography, a limitation the finest photographers were able to exploit to the full or turn into a strength. 'I think it best', advised the great Japanese photographer Yasuhiro Ishimoto, 'if people who see the photos tint the flowers with whatever colours come to their minds.'[2]

Today the era of black and white is largely behind us, its application now a choice rather than a necessity. The contemporary photographer delights in the possibilities that rich colour media can offer. But the flower piece has shaken off its restricted abode and its traditional associations. Signs of the times have crept in. Today the container might be a plastic detergent bottle or a polythene bag, while a face mask or a hairdryer may creep into the composition. And while mostly we think of the word 'arrangement' in terms of flowers in a container, photographers like to think outside the vase: an arrangement of a body or bodies in space, or flowers worn as a crown. The old associations of the language have long faded, as have those of the venerable *vanitas*, the brevity of life, and so on. Yet something remains of that fascination with the metaphoric; life *is* short, beauty *is* ephemeral, and plants often *do* remind us of people we know.

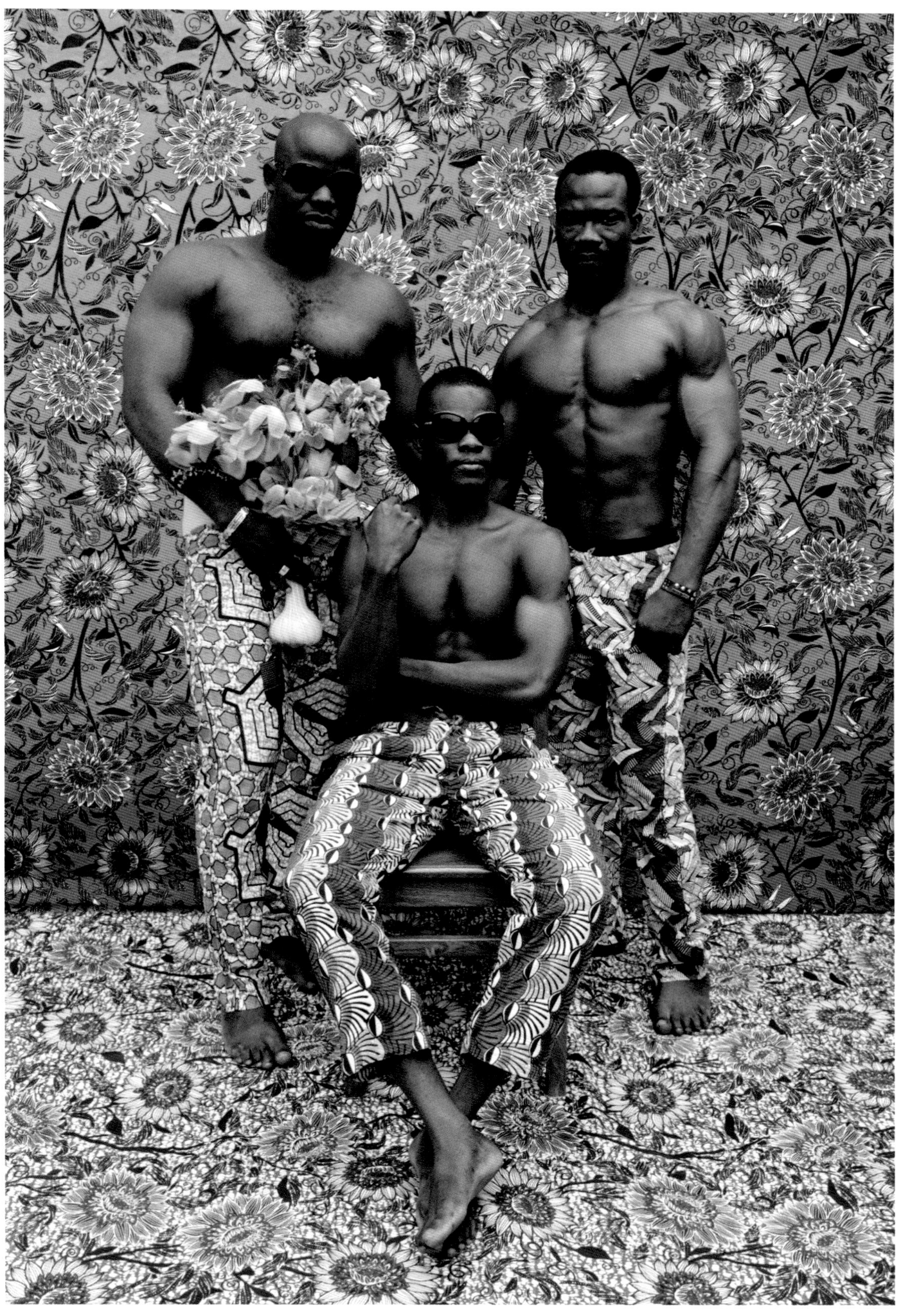

LEONCE RAPHAEL AGBODJELOU
Untitled (Musclemen series), 2012

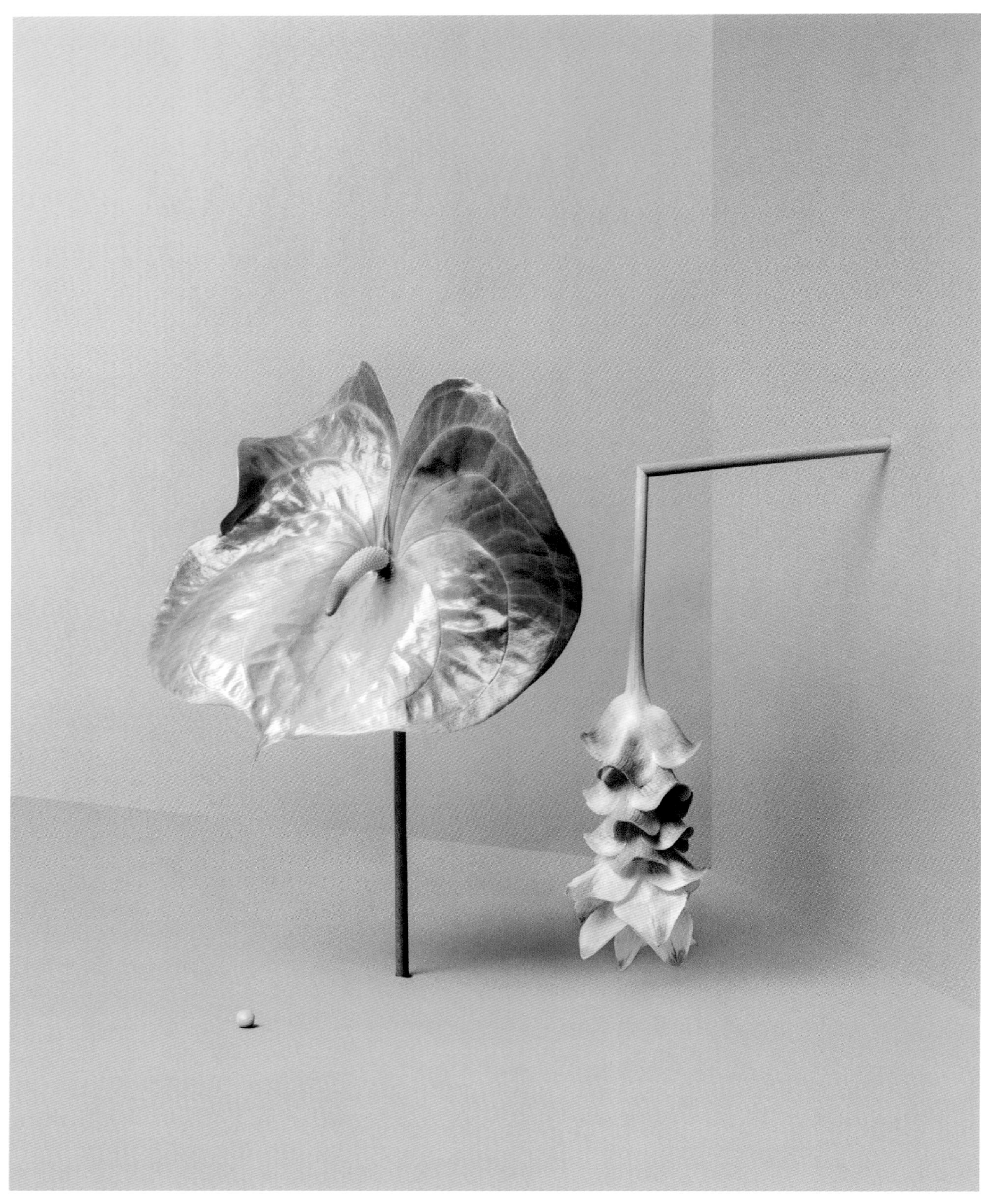

CARMEN MITROTTA
Geometric Leaves, 2016

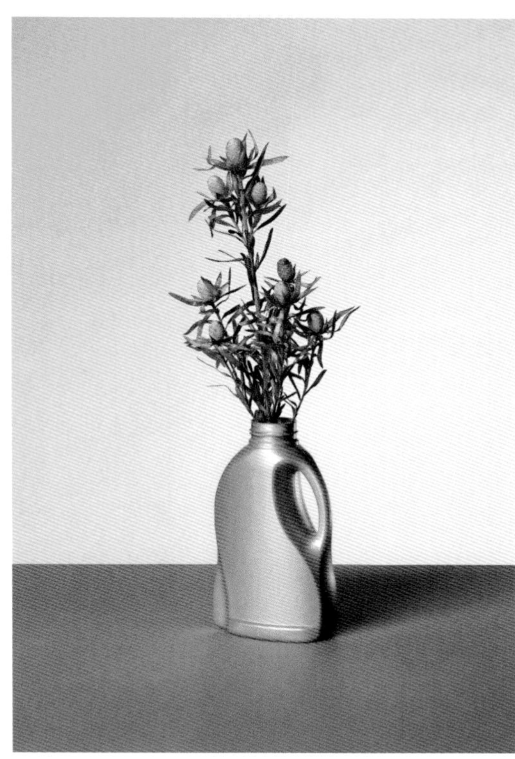

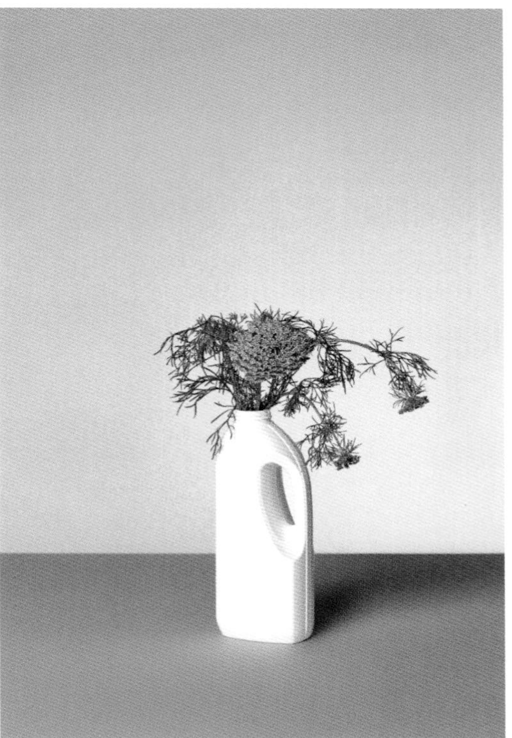

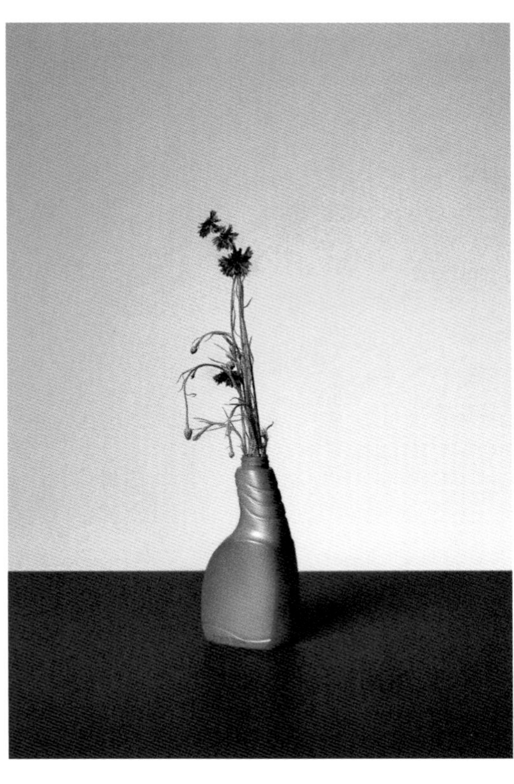

VANESSA LEISSRING
(from top) *Perwoll, Henkel, 2273*; *Denk Mit, Unknown, 2397*; *Febreze, Procter & Gamble, 2475*, from the series *Polyflowers*, 2020

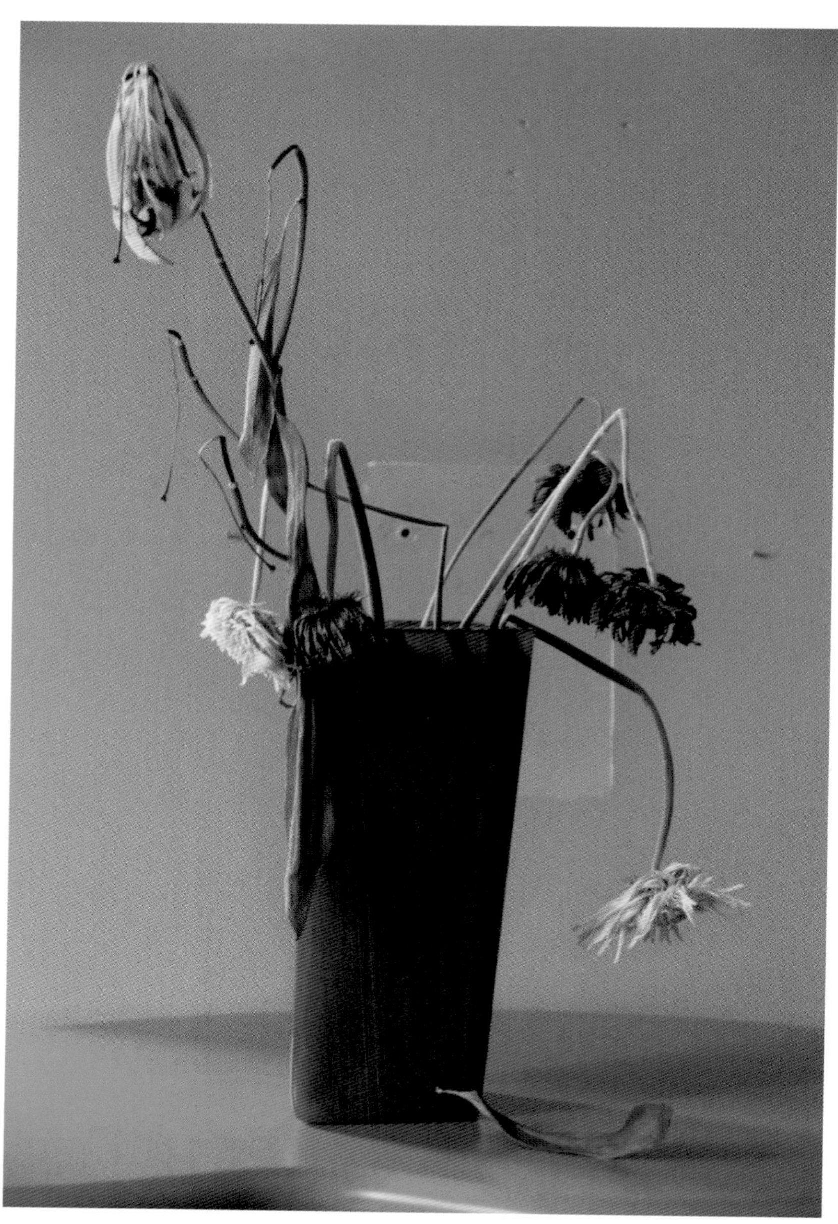

PEDRO ALMODÓVAR
Untitled 1, 2018

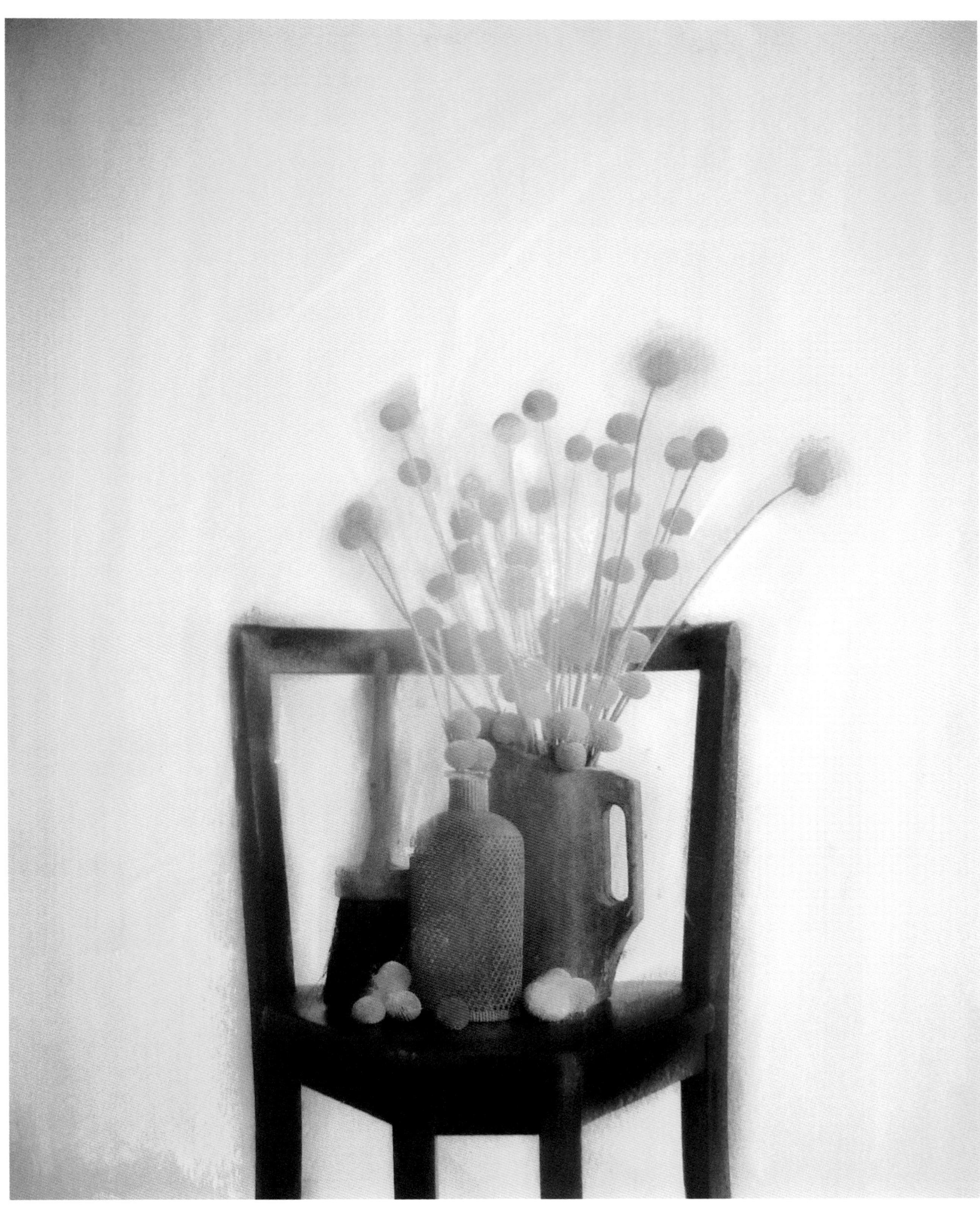

MARIE TAILLEFER
Bloom, Matte Flowers, New York, 2015

A FLORILEGIUM

Edward Steichen, a pioneering plant breeder and photographer, once said of his famed hybrids that flowers were the most emotional of the arts.[3] What other kind of object, thing, material or living being can trigger such a wide range of human feelings? Photographers have always found the subject irresistible, and, generation after generation, one of the games they love to play is that of the still life, not to mention its challenging sub-theme: the container. With this practice, they contribute to a collective florilegium. Historically, a florilegium was a book of flower imagery designed to show the decorative possibilities of flowers when arranged in vases and vessels. Simplicity vs complexity, symmetry vs asymmetry, flatness vs depth, the living vs the dead (or a state in between), polychrome vs monochrome – these and more offer variables that create infinite conceptual and aesthetic possibilities.

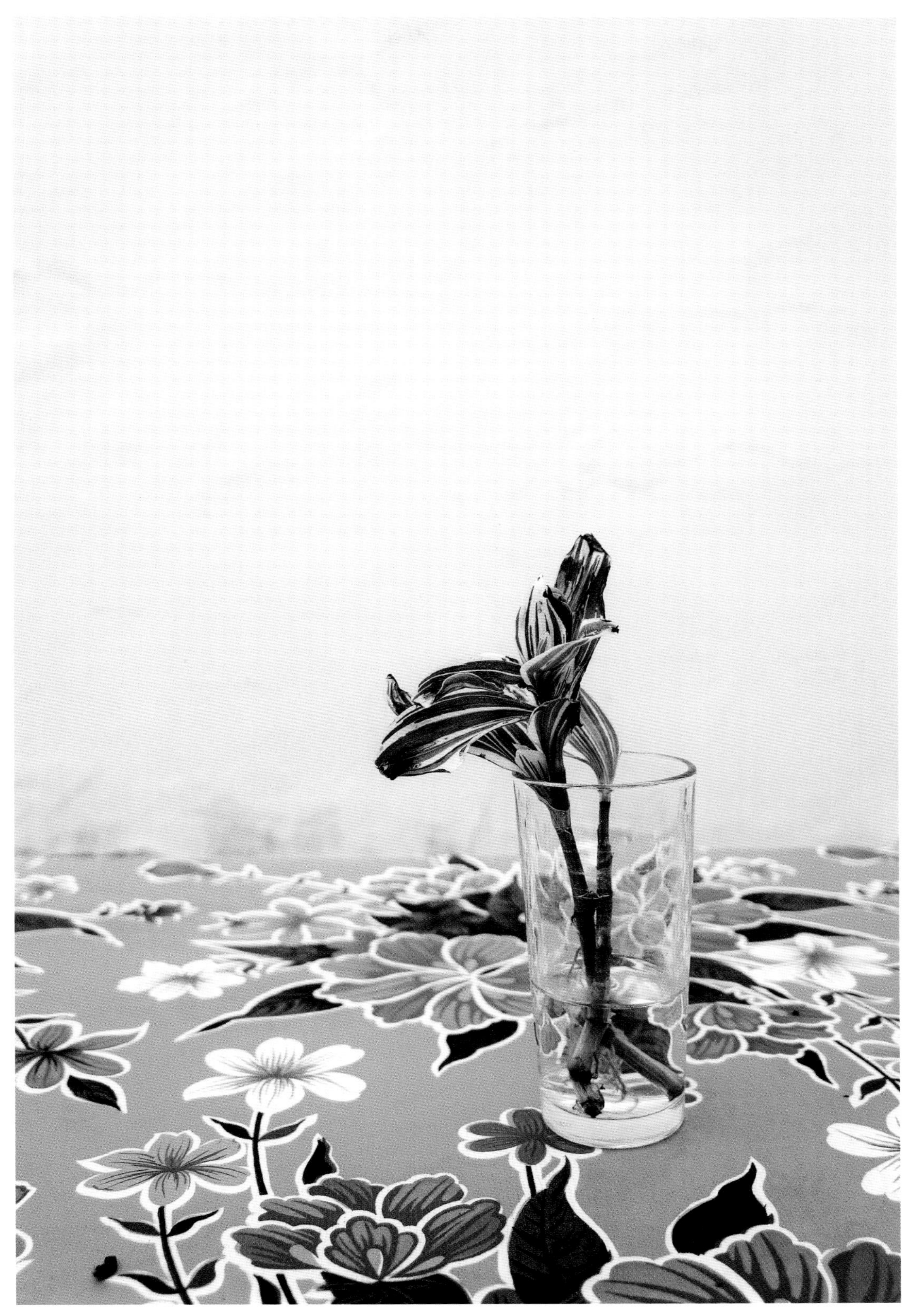

JESSICA BACKHAUS
Promise, 2019

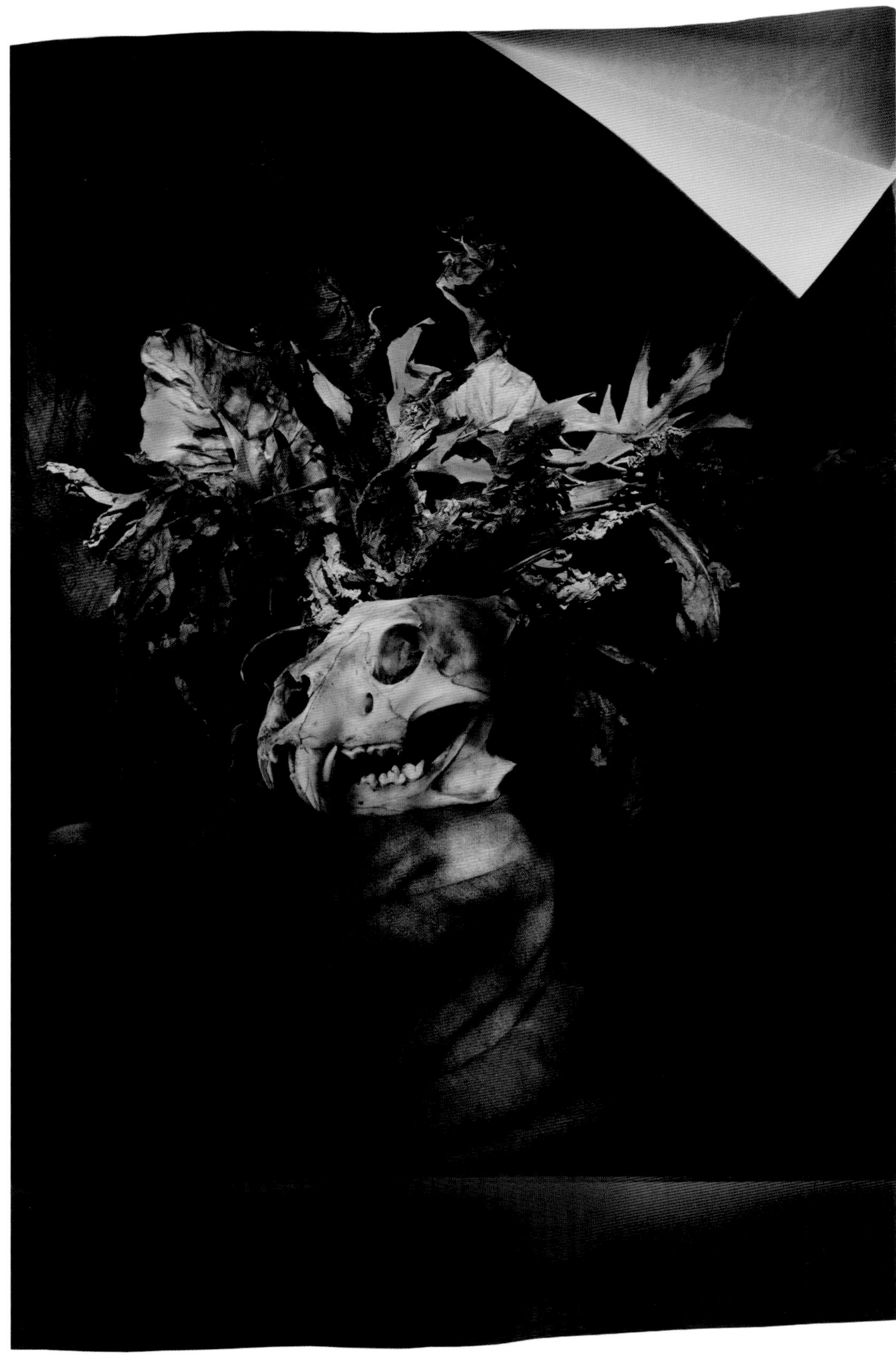

CHLOE SELLS
Obstacle to Conquest, 2013

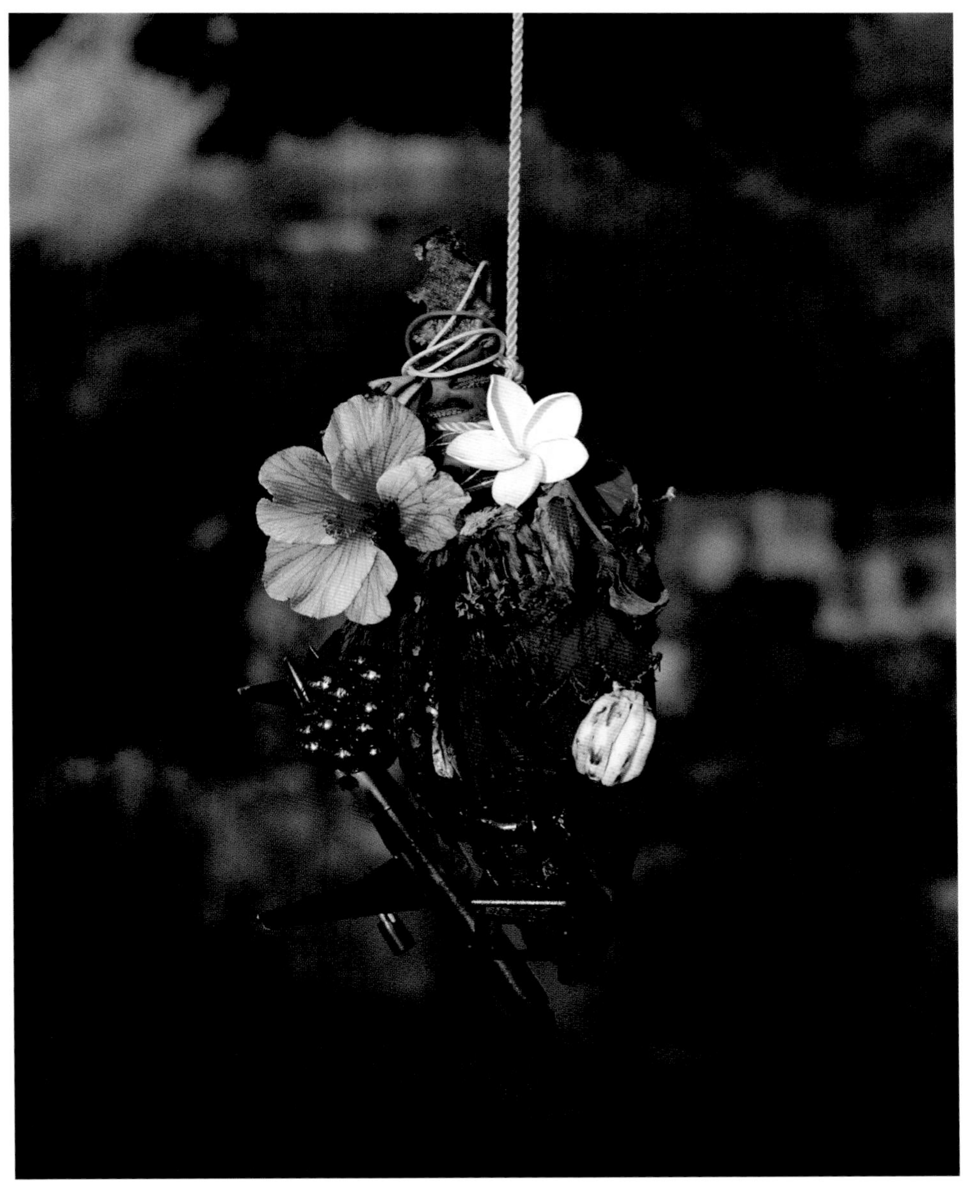

ELSPETH DIEDERIX
Banana still life, 2003

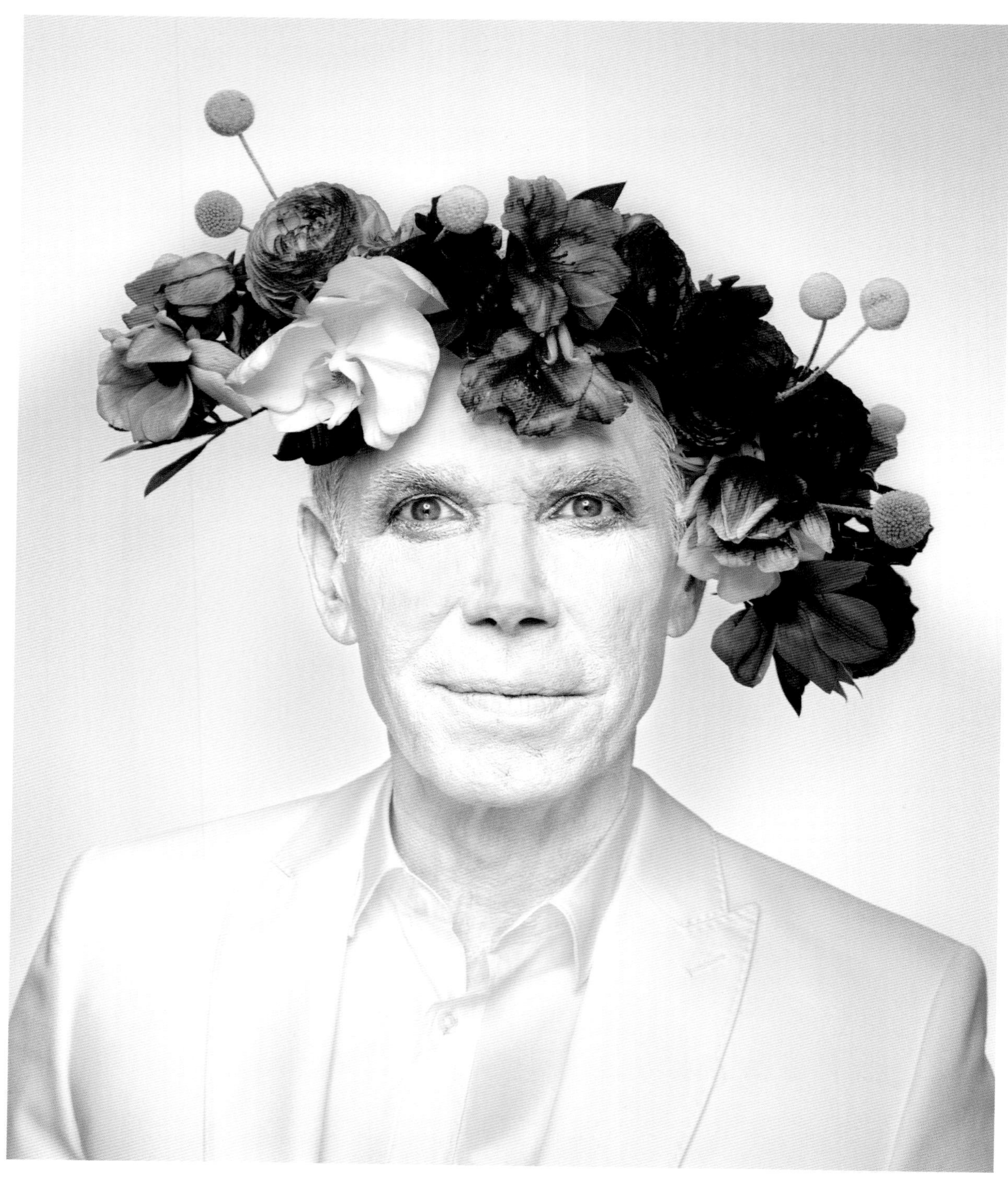

MARTIN SCHOELLER
Jeff Koons with Floral Headpiece, New York, NY, 2013

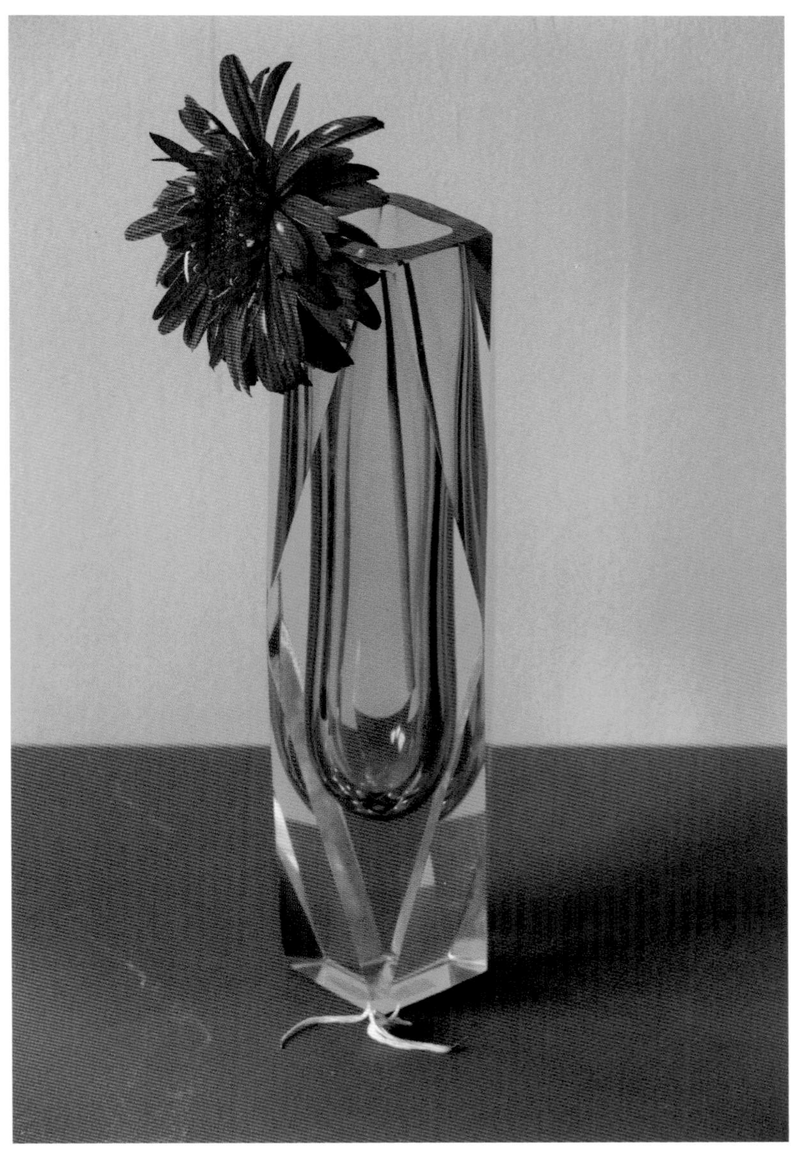

PEDRO ALMODÓVAR
Depending on the Red Gerbera, 2019

TWO STREAMS

Flowers...have come to the confluence of two streams, that of representation and that of memory. It is the ground of art itself, the good ground of reality, harrowed and ploughed by the artist.

Odilon Redon[4]

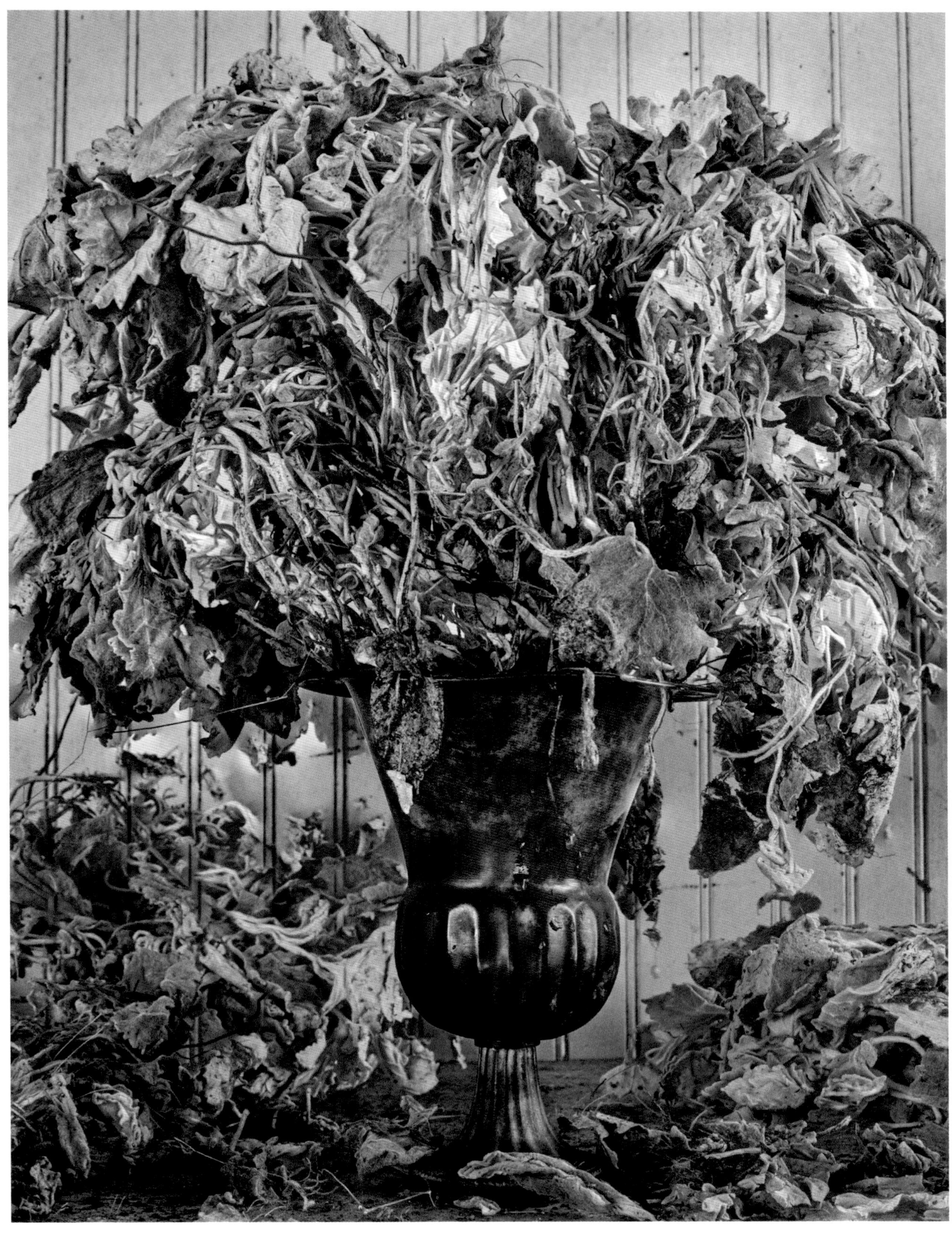

ABELARDO MORELL
2017 – Flowers for Lisa #47, 2017

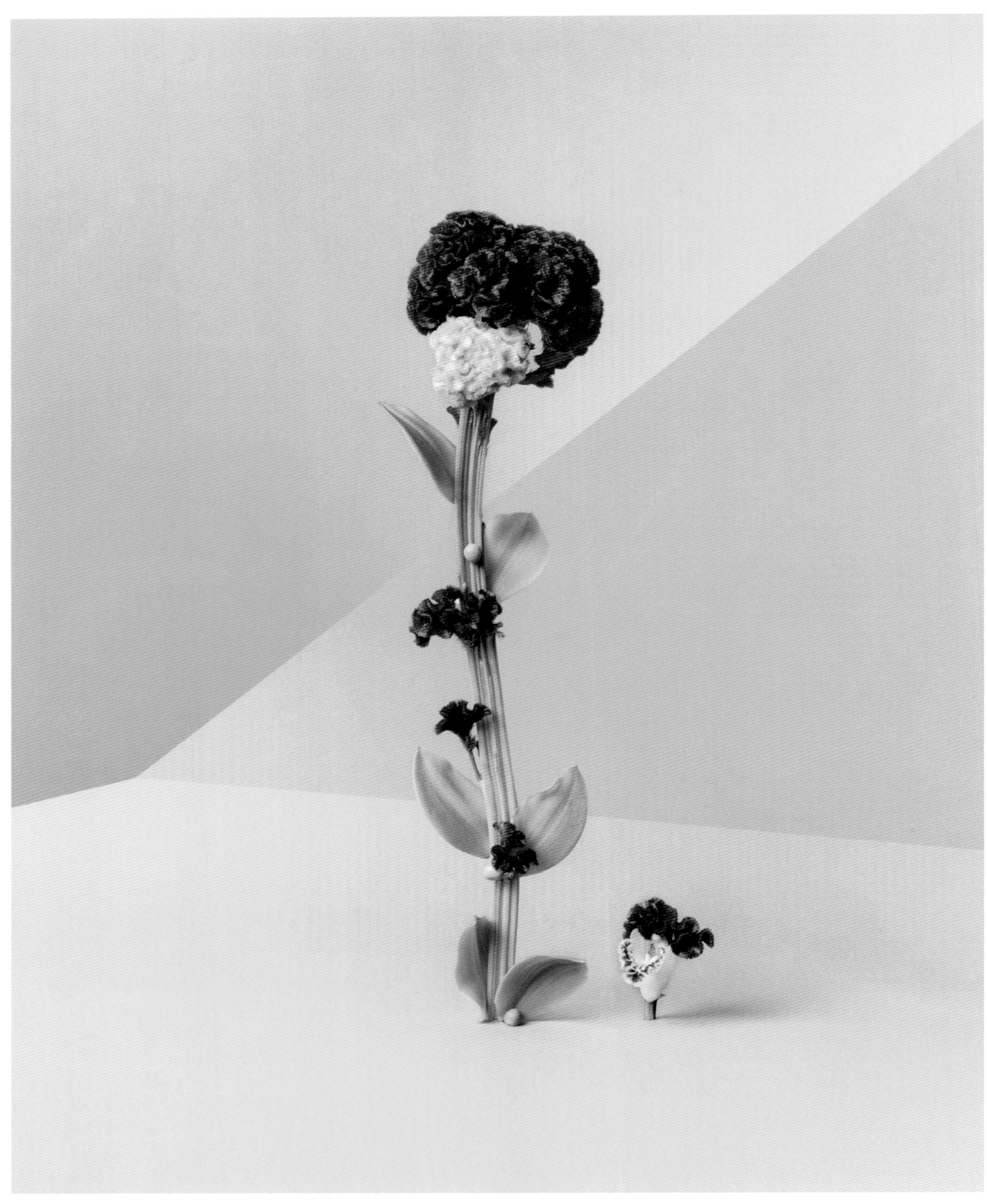

CARMEN MITROTTA
Tall Flower, 2016

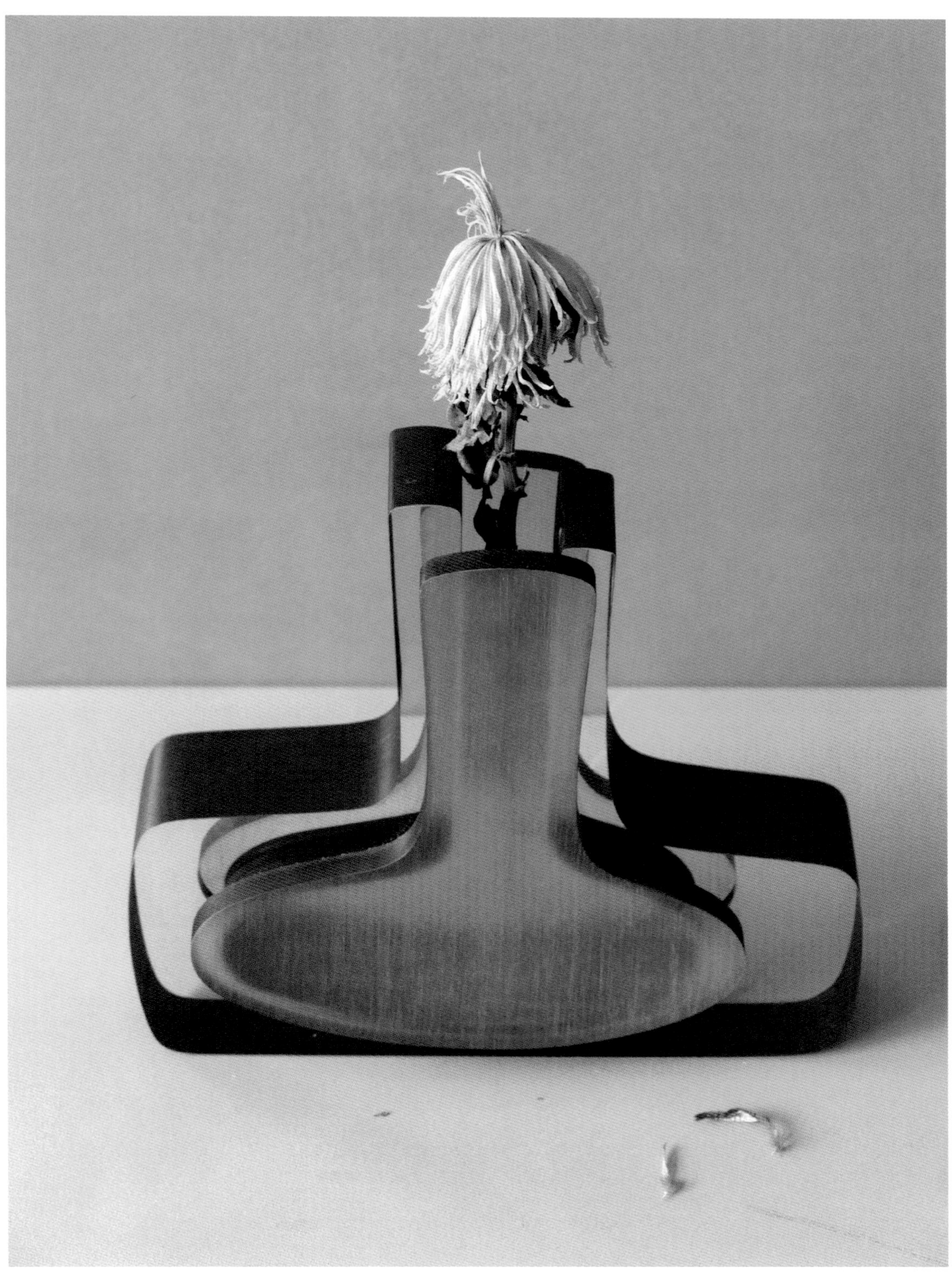

PEDRO ALMODÓVAR
Menina, 2019

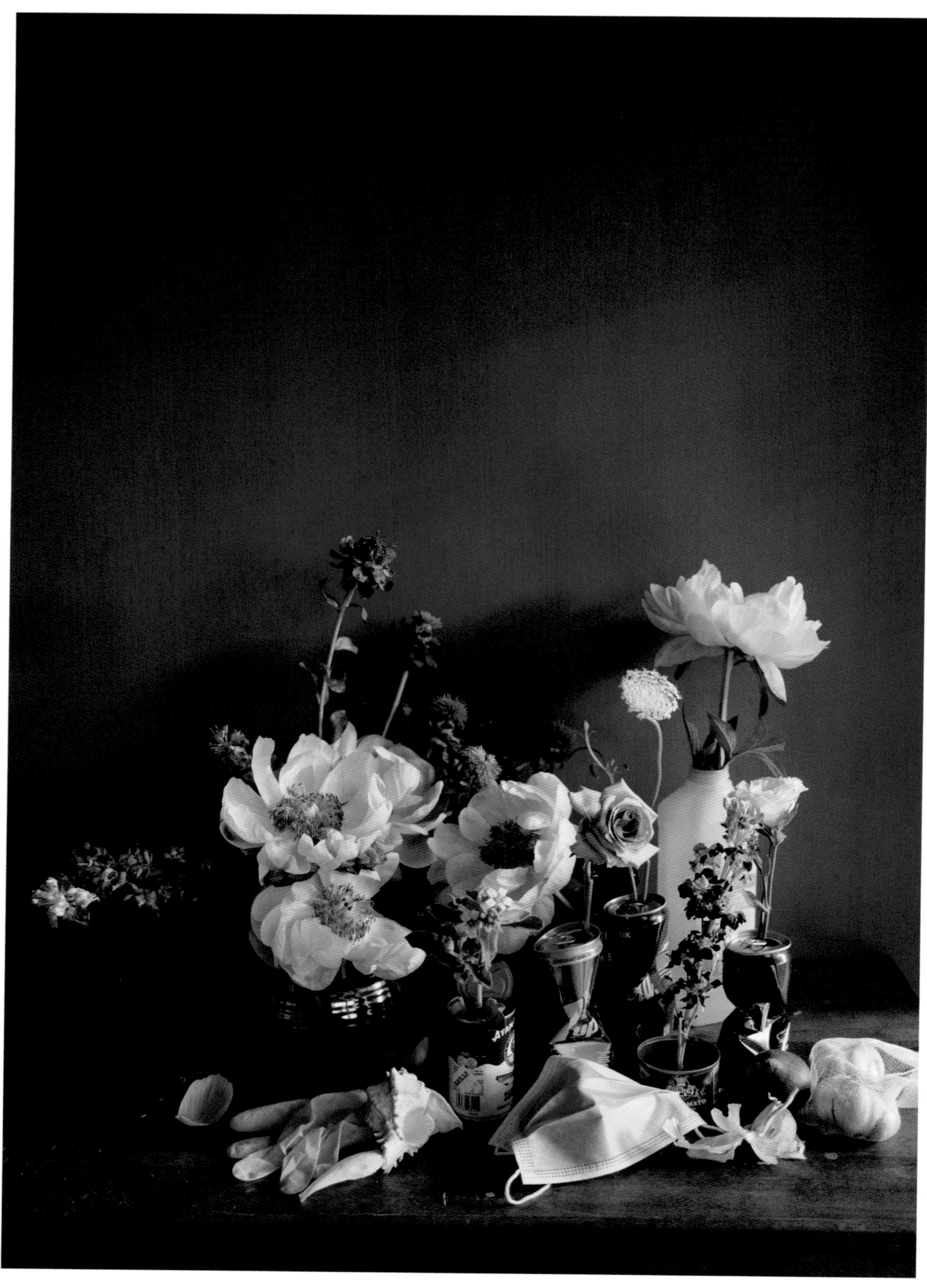

NADIRAH ZAKARIYA
All Purpose Flower: MCO Day 59, 2020

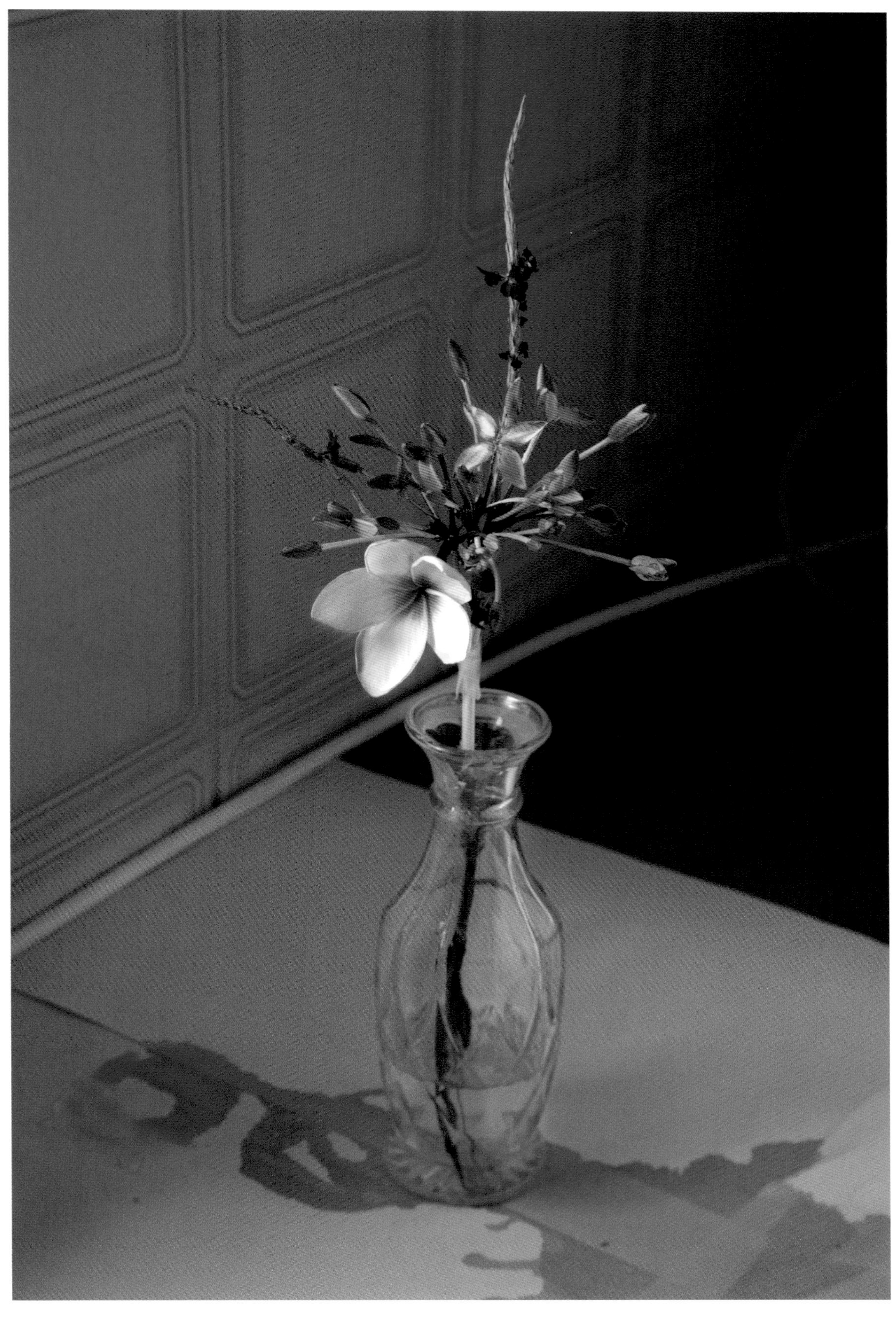

ELSPETH DIEDERIX
Frangipani firework, 2014

RAISING FLOWERS

I have learned more about people and human nature from raising flowers than you would believe…. Some varieties are just like a lot of happy-go-lucky humans; they'll go right on being themselves, neither showing any rare qualities in color or size or form, nor falling down on you and failing to bloom faithfully no matter how you treat them – just like people…. Flowers have verified all my concepts of human behavior.

Edward Steichen[5]

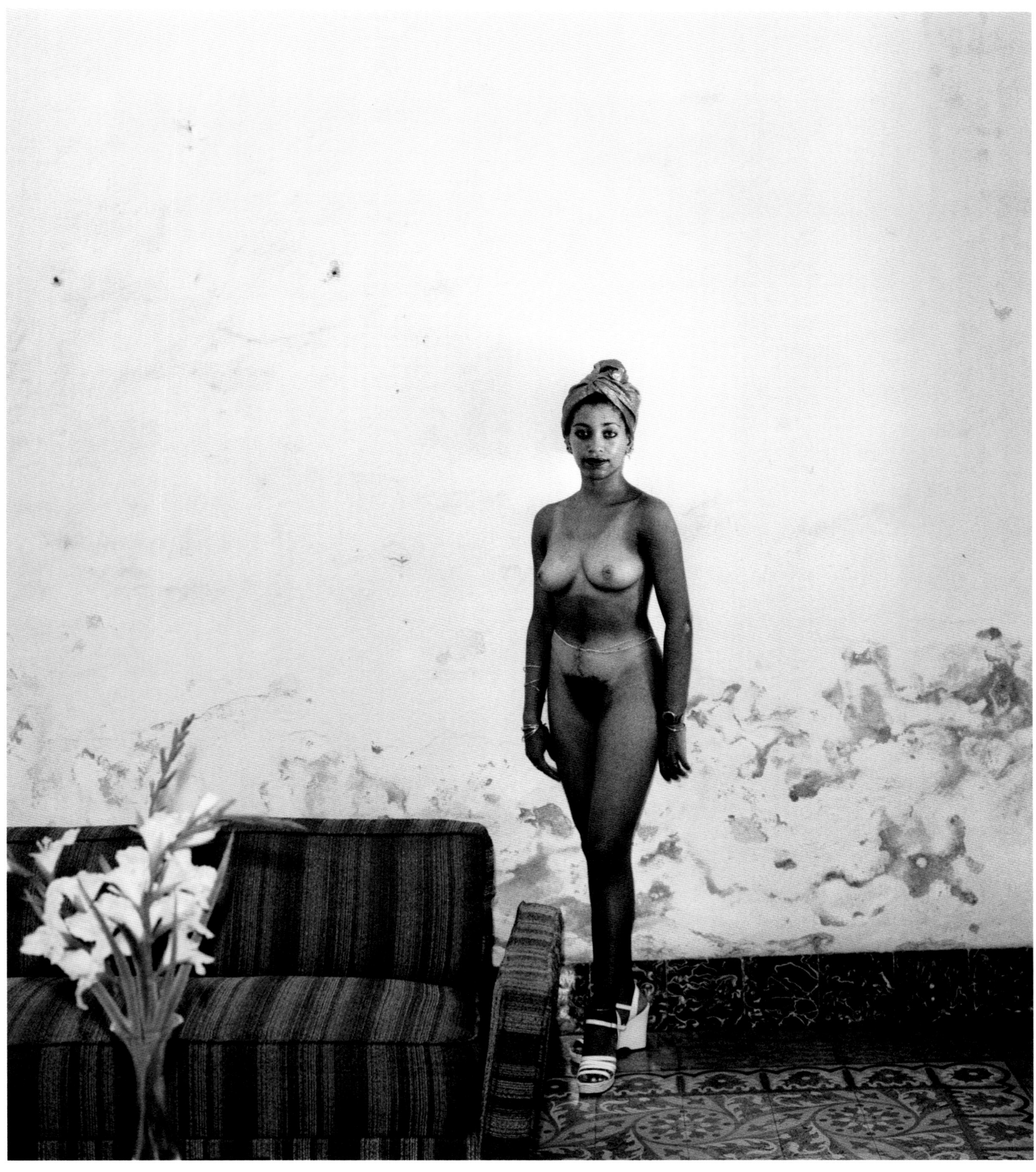

NADAV KANDER
Dunia, Havana, Cuba, from the series *Dream Girls*, 1998

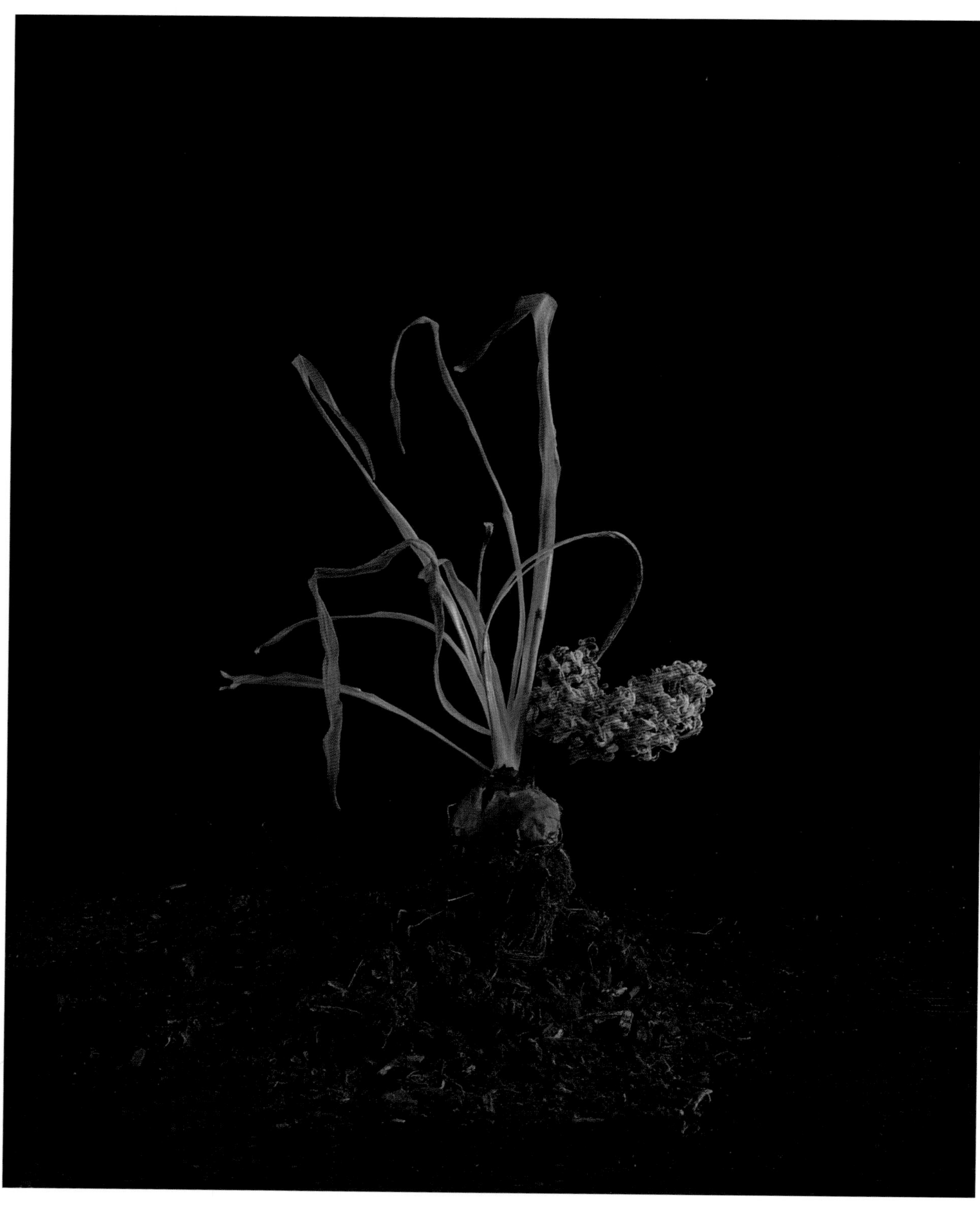

BRIGITTE LUSTENBERGER
Flowers IX, from the series *Still Untitled*, 2014

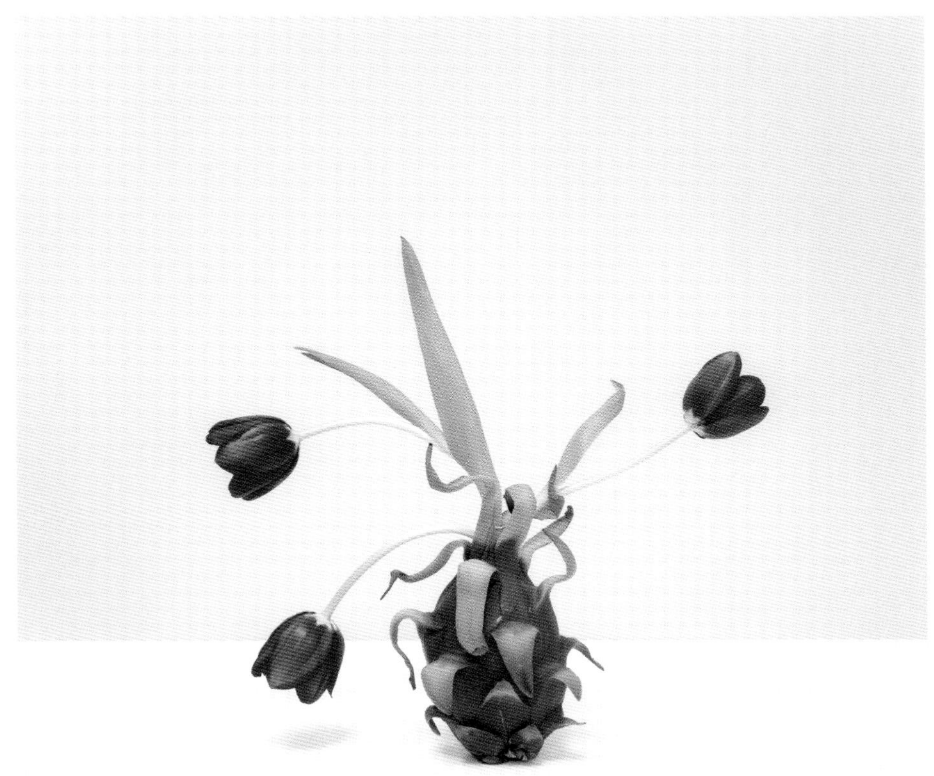

ADELE SPENCER
Tulips with Dragon Fruit, 2019

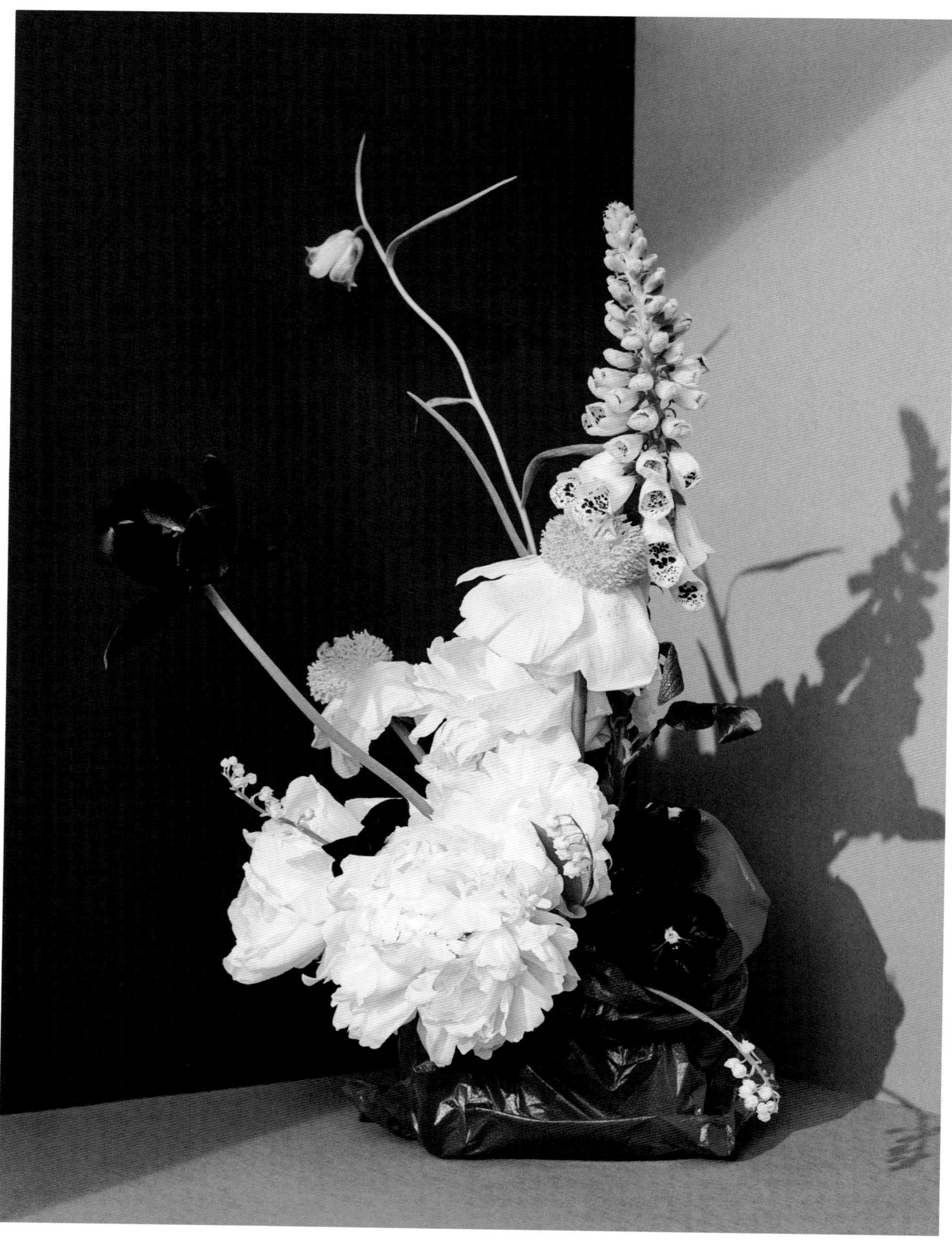

VICTORIA ZSCHOMMLER
At Bloom, 2016 (flower arrangements by Simone Gooch of Fjura)

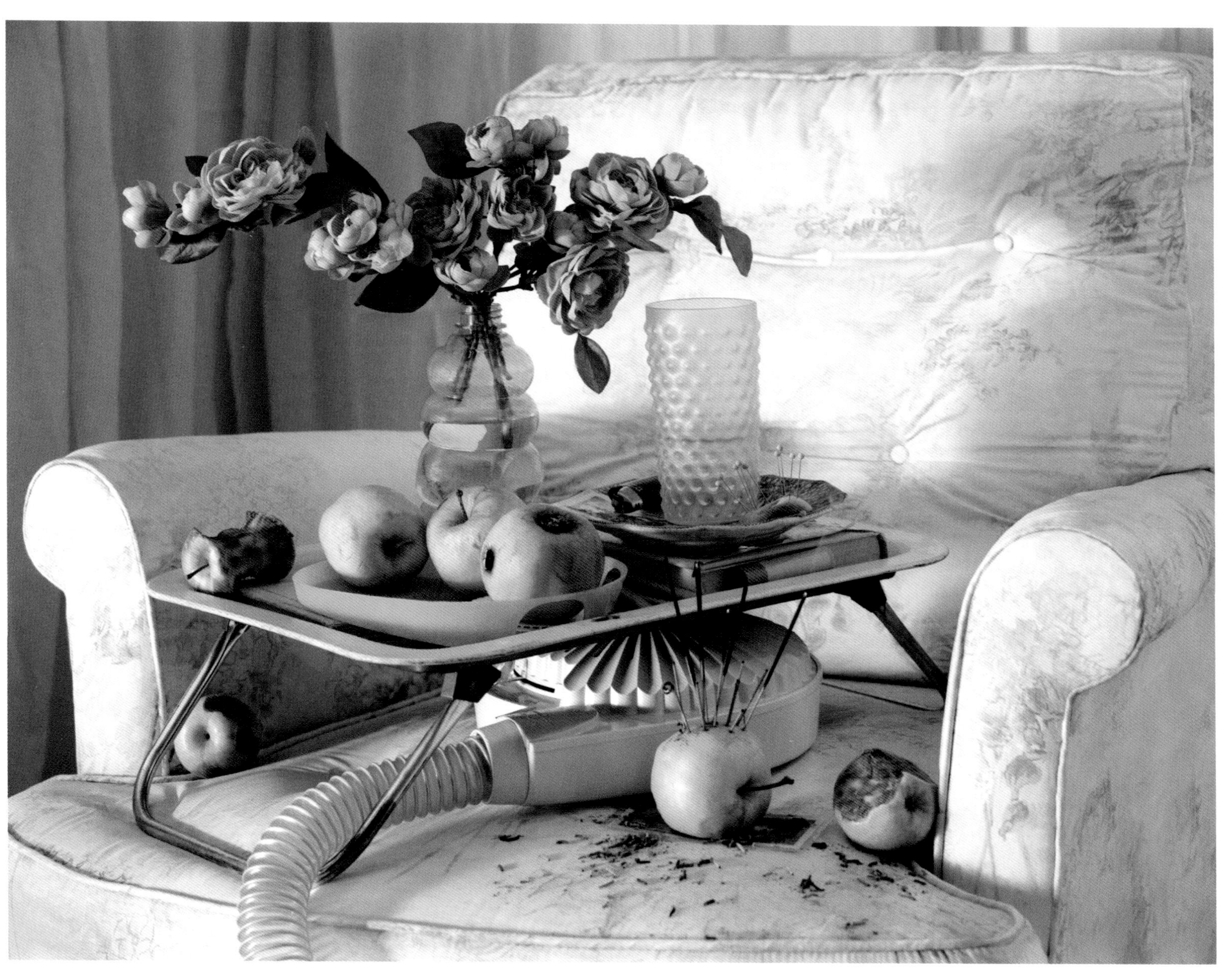

JEFF BARK
Slow Burn, from the series *Paradise Garage* shown at the Piazza della Esposizioni in Rome, 2019

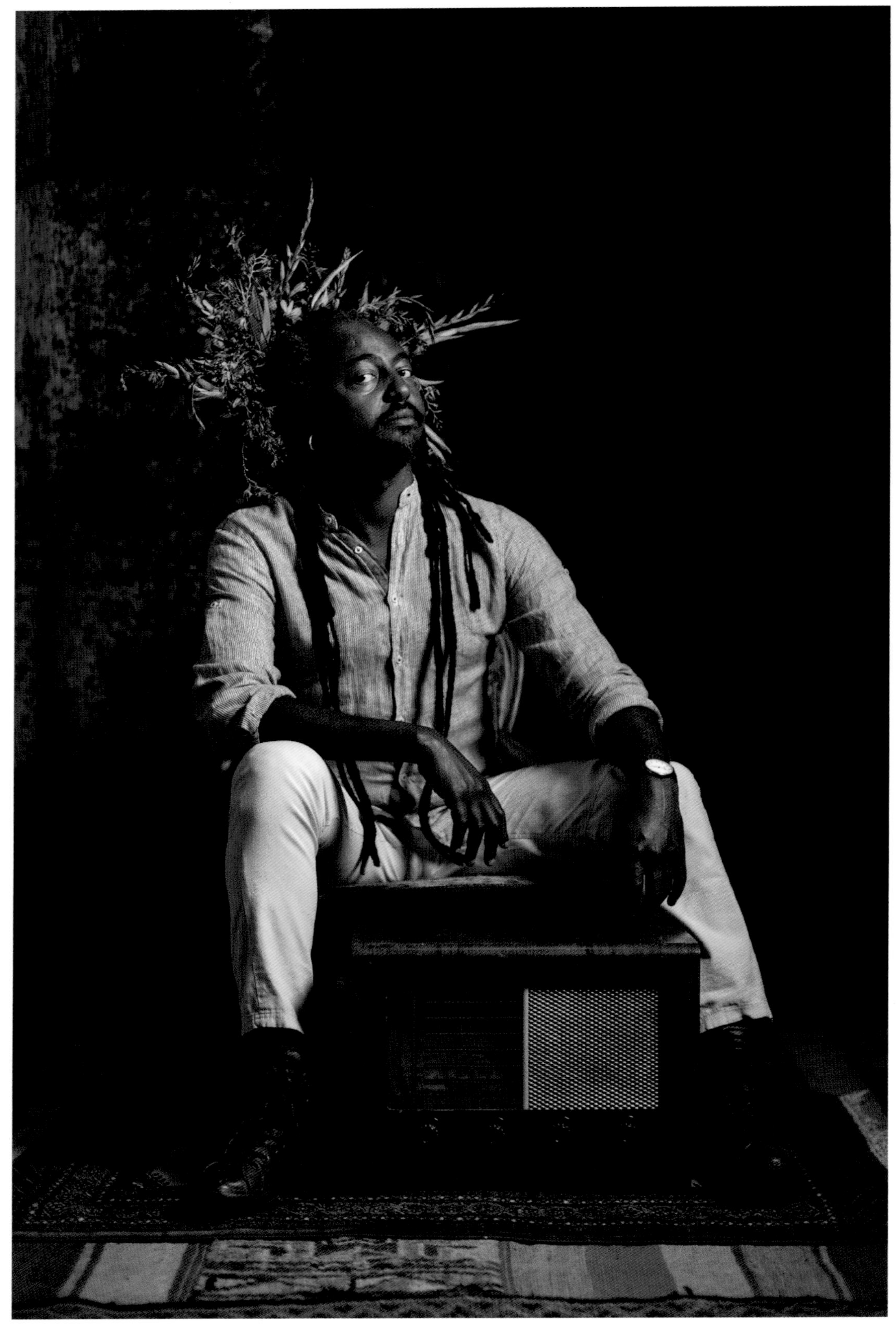

NICHOLE SOBECKI
Zelalem Mulat Teklewold, Ethiopia, from the series *afriMAN*, 2018

afriMAN is an exploration of evolving understandings of manhood on the African continent, and how traditional expectations are being subverted by individuals.

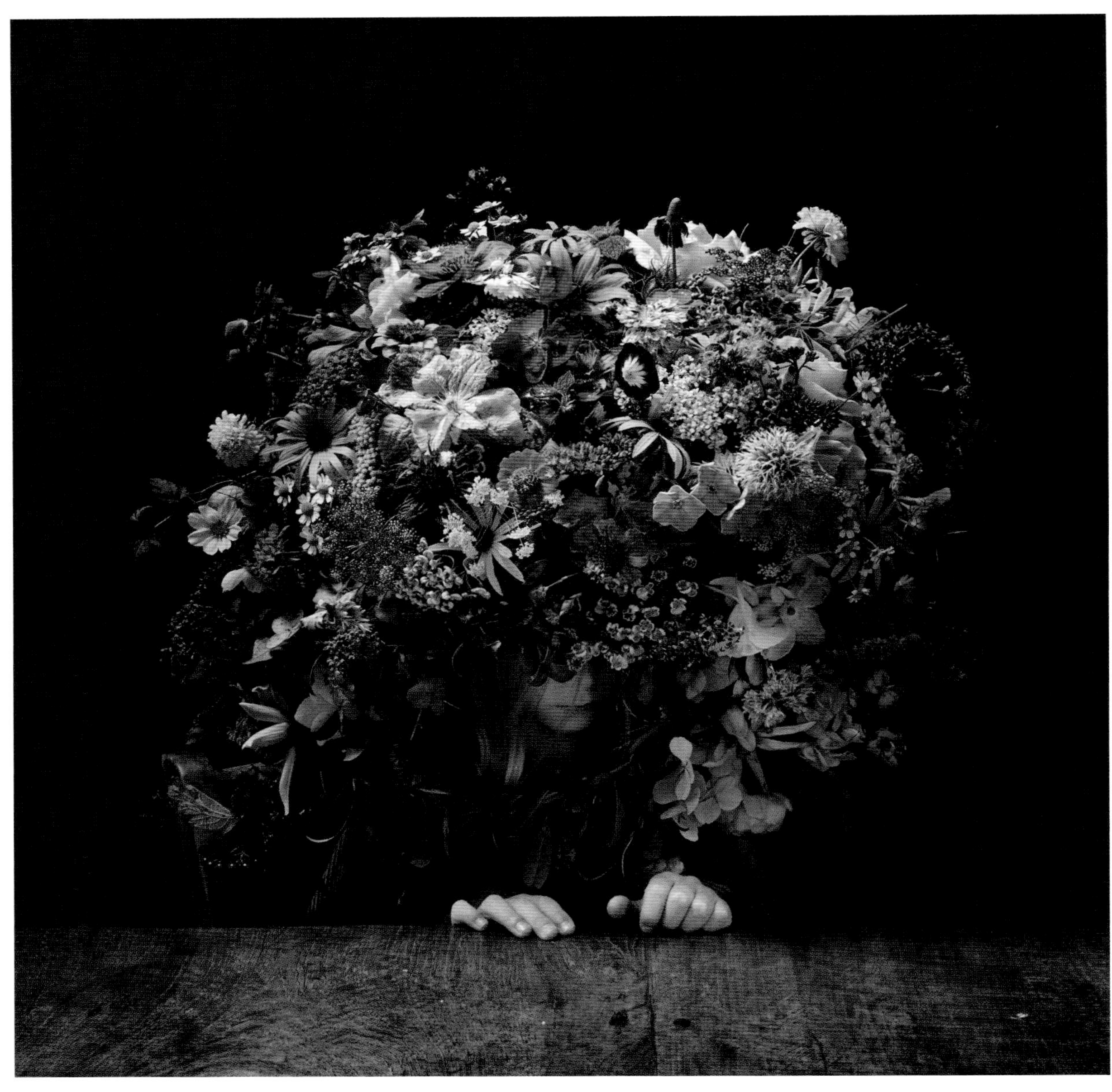

AIMÉE HOVING
Het Boeket, from the series *Pictures of Her*, 2017
(flowers by Brigitte Grentis Van dam Merret)

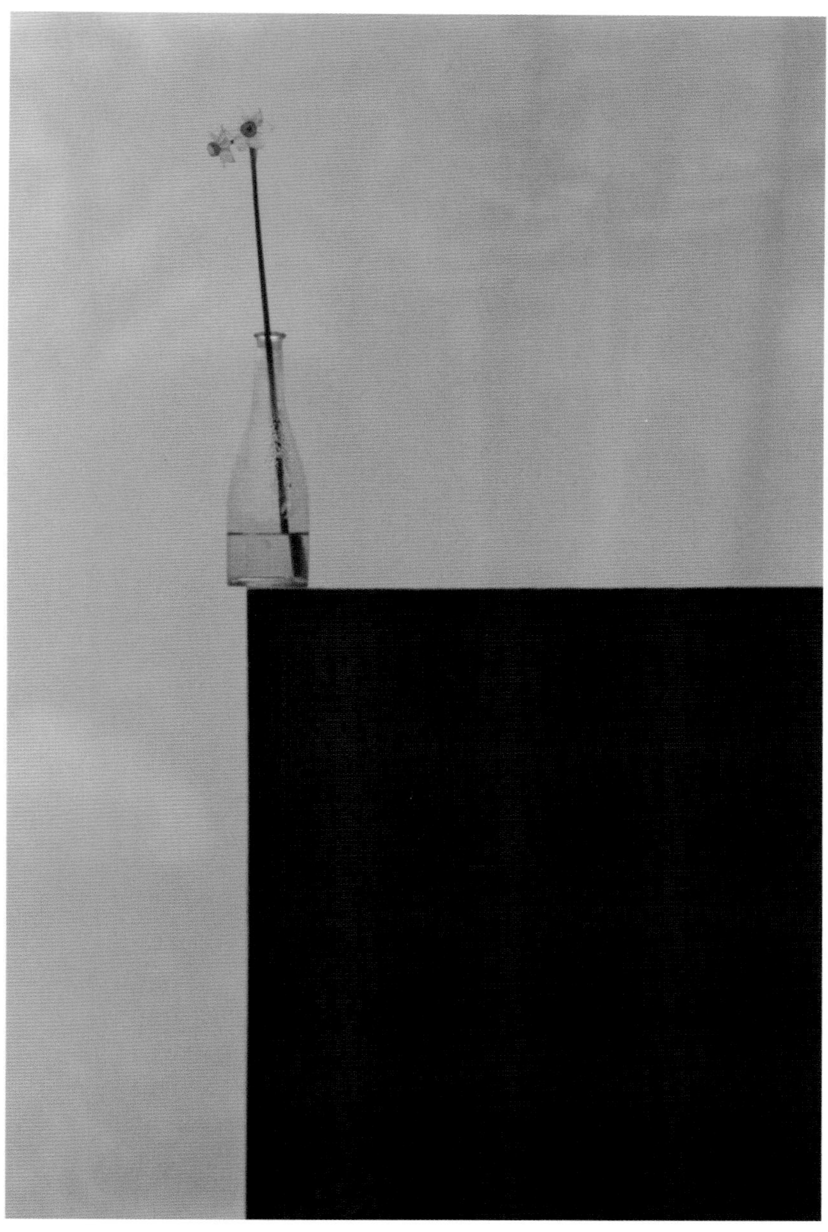

YAMAMOTO MASAO
A Box of Ku #156, 1995

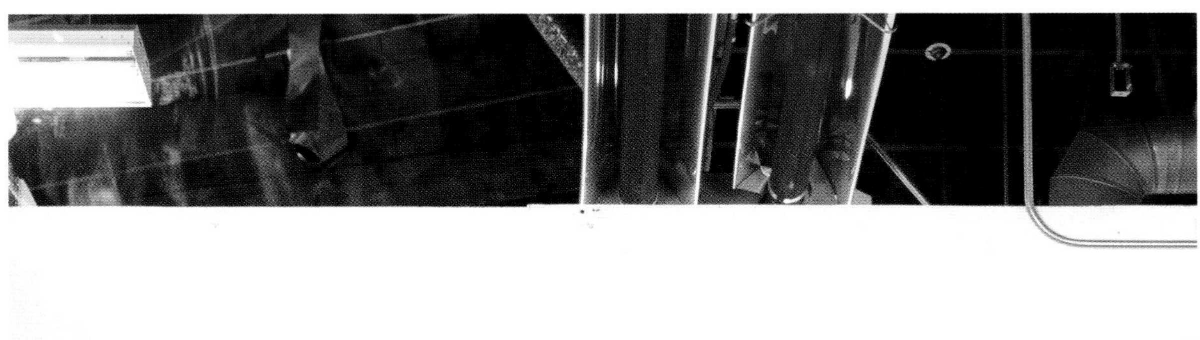

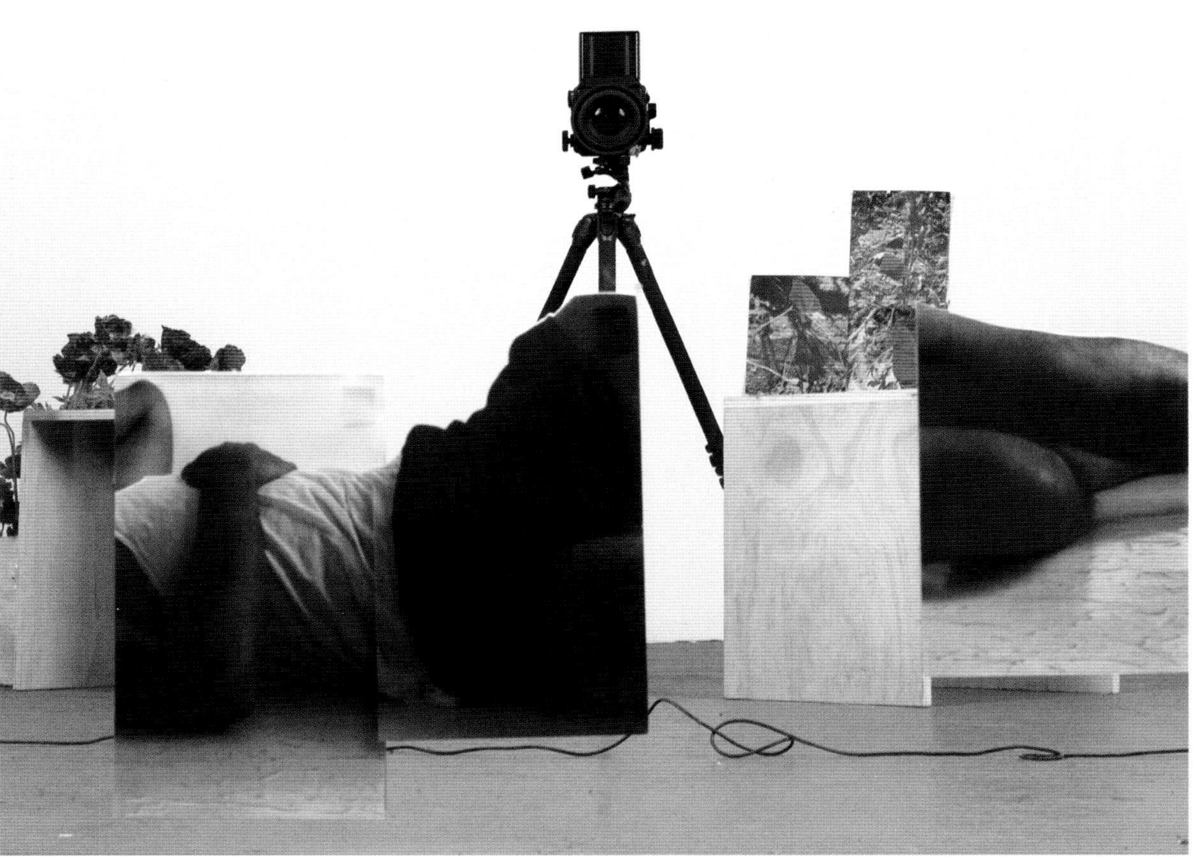

PAUL MPAGI SEPUYA
Figure with Poppies, after R.B.N. (2604), 2015

ESSENCE

When we speak of the essence of something, we mean that quality, that ingredient which is fundamental to it, and without which that thing would cease to be. It implies a zeroing in, a pushing aside of extraneous information. Where flowers are concerned, 'essence' has several meanings: 'essence therapy', for example, is a widespread form of alternative medicine, based on the ancient idea that flowers have a healing energy. The era of the modern essence begins in the 1930s, when Edward Bach, a British physician, argued that human emotions could be balanced by extracting the energy of plants.

To the botanically minded photographer, essence has to do with showing clearly what is absolutely typical of the species, leaving any aesthetic quality in a supporting role, an agreeable by-product in that it may attract the attention of a lay public. However, to the art photographer following his or her own path, 'essence' is a more nebulous concept: it means capturing, and conveying, a feeling or a sentiment – even *soul*. But both kinds of image-maker tend to gravitate to the single flower, as opposed to fields of them. The assumption is that the individual flower is all that is required to understand the 'family' – perhaps an anthropomorphic assumption based on our human culture of privileging the individual over the collective, as we do with the human face in portraiture wherein people have a horror of not standing out from the herd. But *this* rose stands for every *other* rose. Might we not question that?

More pragmatically, a field of flowers is usually taken in at a glance – seldom do we give any individual bloom or blossom close scrutiny. For the most part in photographic practice, a flower is removed from its natural habitat, brought to the studio, lit carefully and photographed in suitably high definition in order to give the viewer maximum information. Flowers are almost always photographed against a smooth monochrome surface, often of a complementary colour, which in turn is sometimes modulated to enliven the image.

In his passionate argument for a revolution in our thinking about the nature of the world (and/or the world of nature), and the central role in it of plants, the philosopher Emanuele Coccia posits that 'the world has the consistency of an atmosphere and that the leaves are witnesses to this fact.' He goes on to 'ask the roots to explain the true nature of the earth. Finally, it is the flower that will teach us what rationality is, when measured not as a universal capacity or power, but as a cosmic force.'[1] Perhaps, then, true essence is in the aggregate, not the individual; perhaps the search of photographers for truth (each with their own idea of it) is best seen as a collective endeavour.

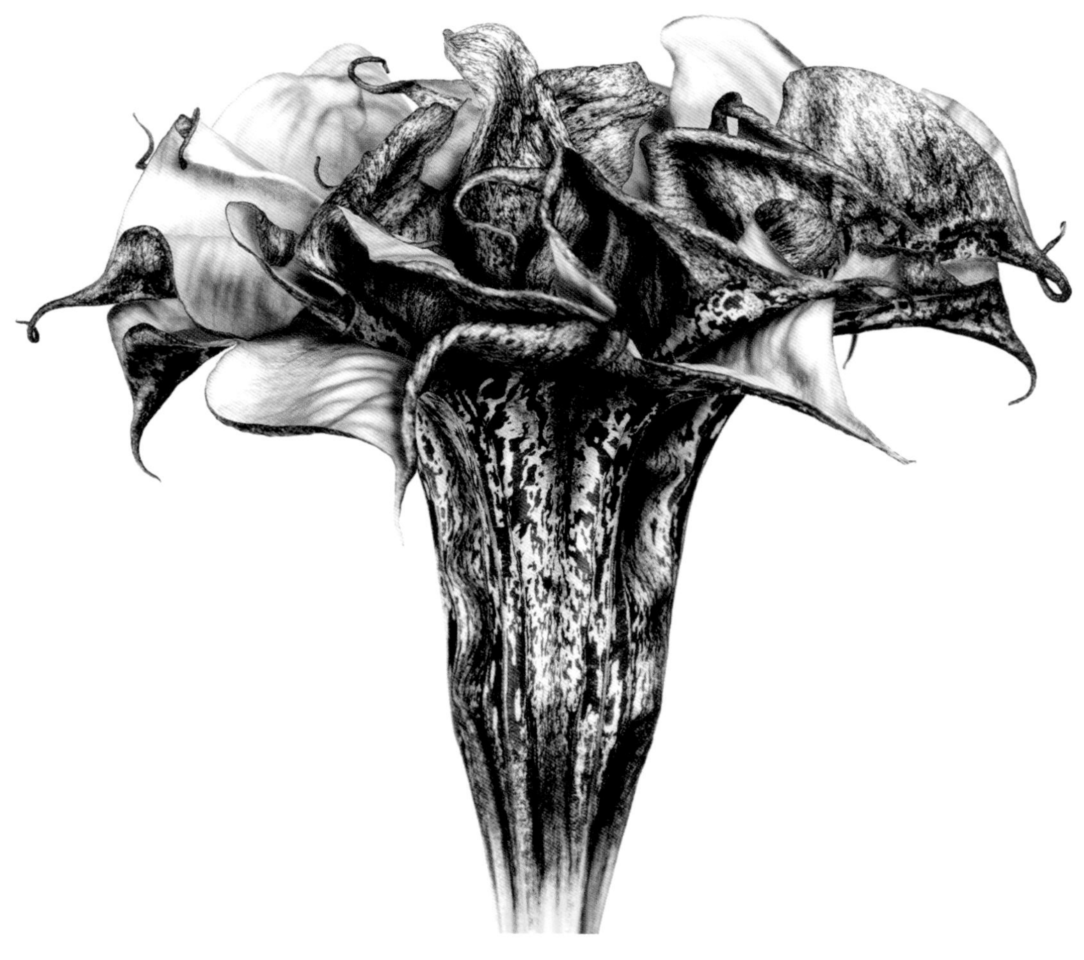

ANDREW ZUCKERMAN
Datura fatuosa Double Purple 6, 2012

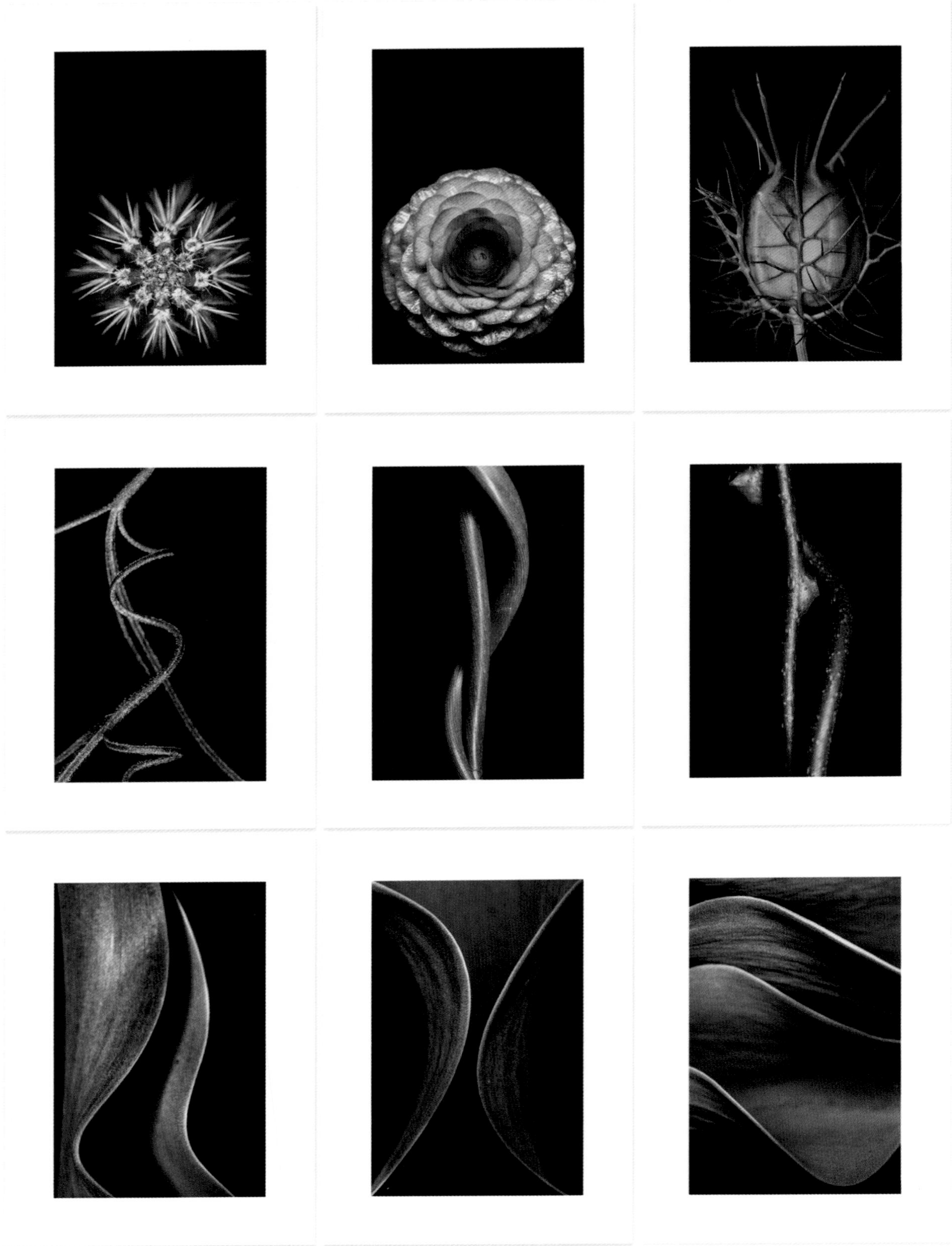

ANNA AGOSTON
The Garden of Epicurus, 2016

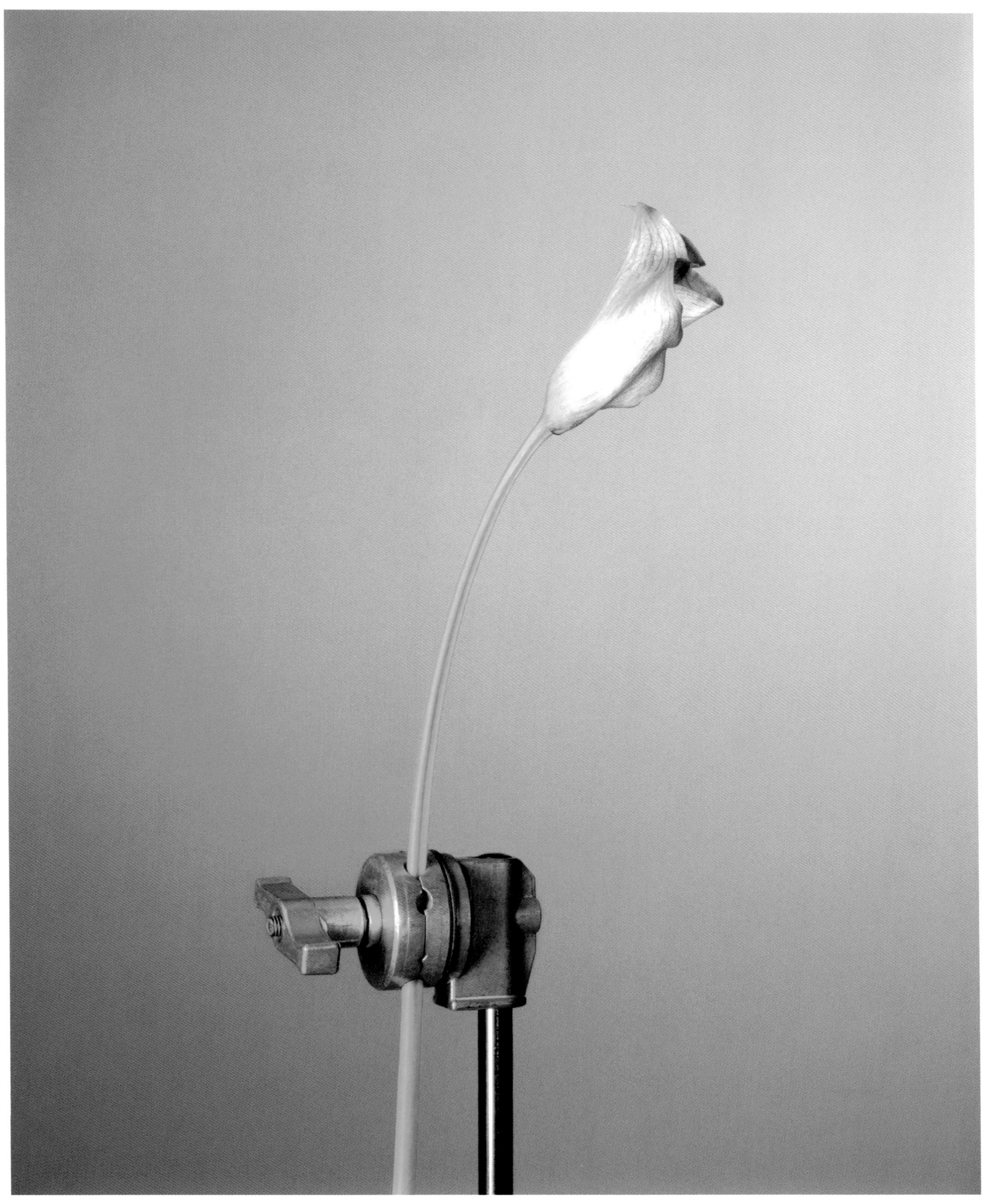

FELICITY MCCABE
White Lily in Clamp, 2013

GARRY FABIAN MILLER
Delphinium 1–8, Homeland, Summer 1990, flower, light, dye destruction print, 1990

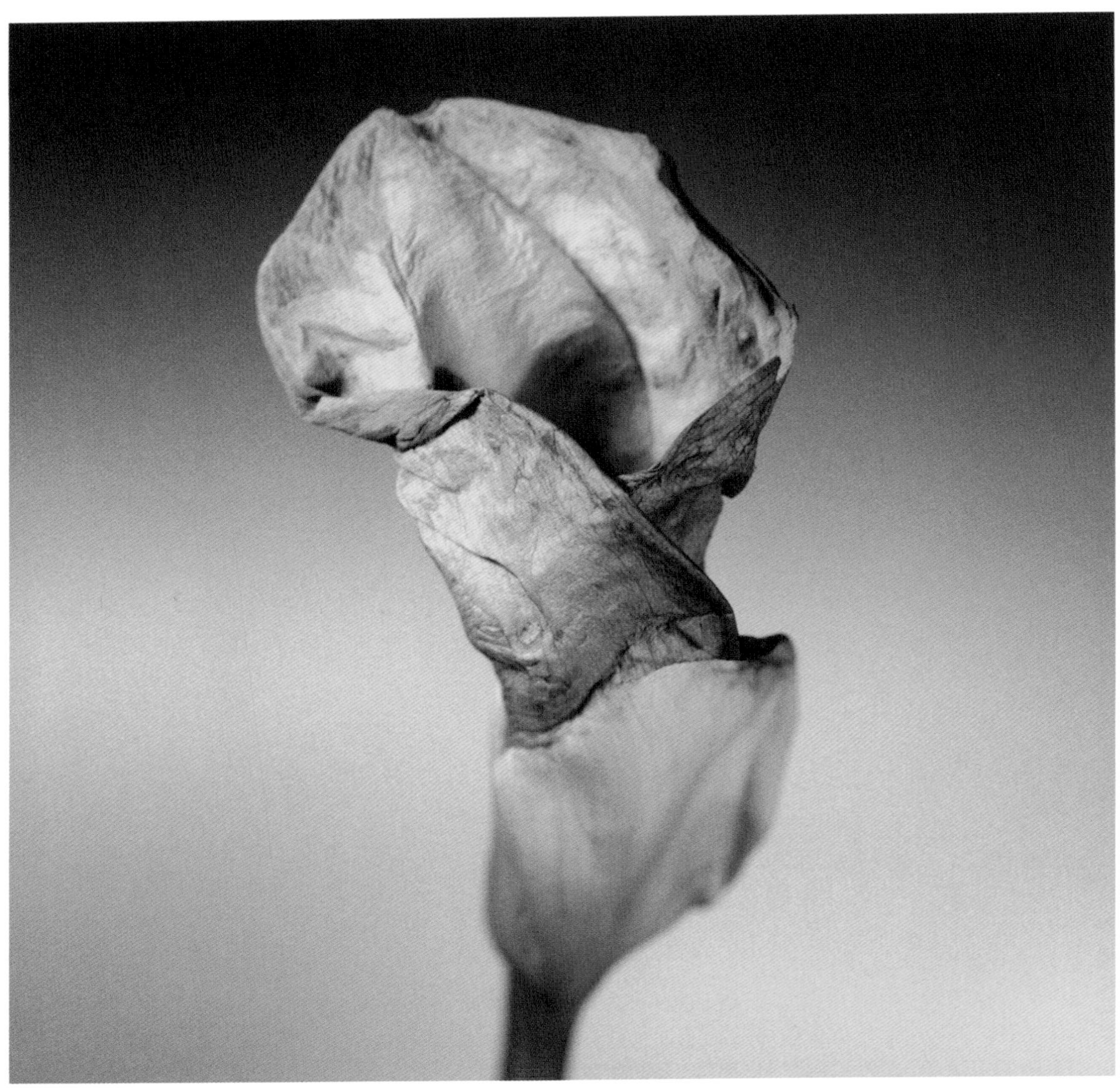

AMIN EL DIB
R 901-03, from the series *CutFlowerImages*, 1999

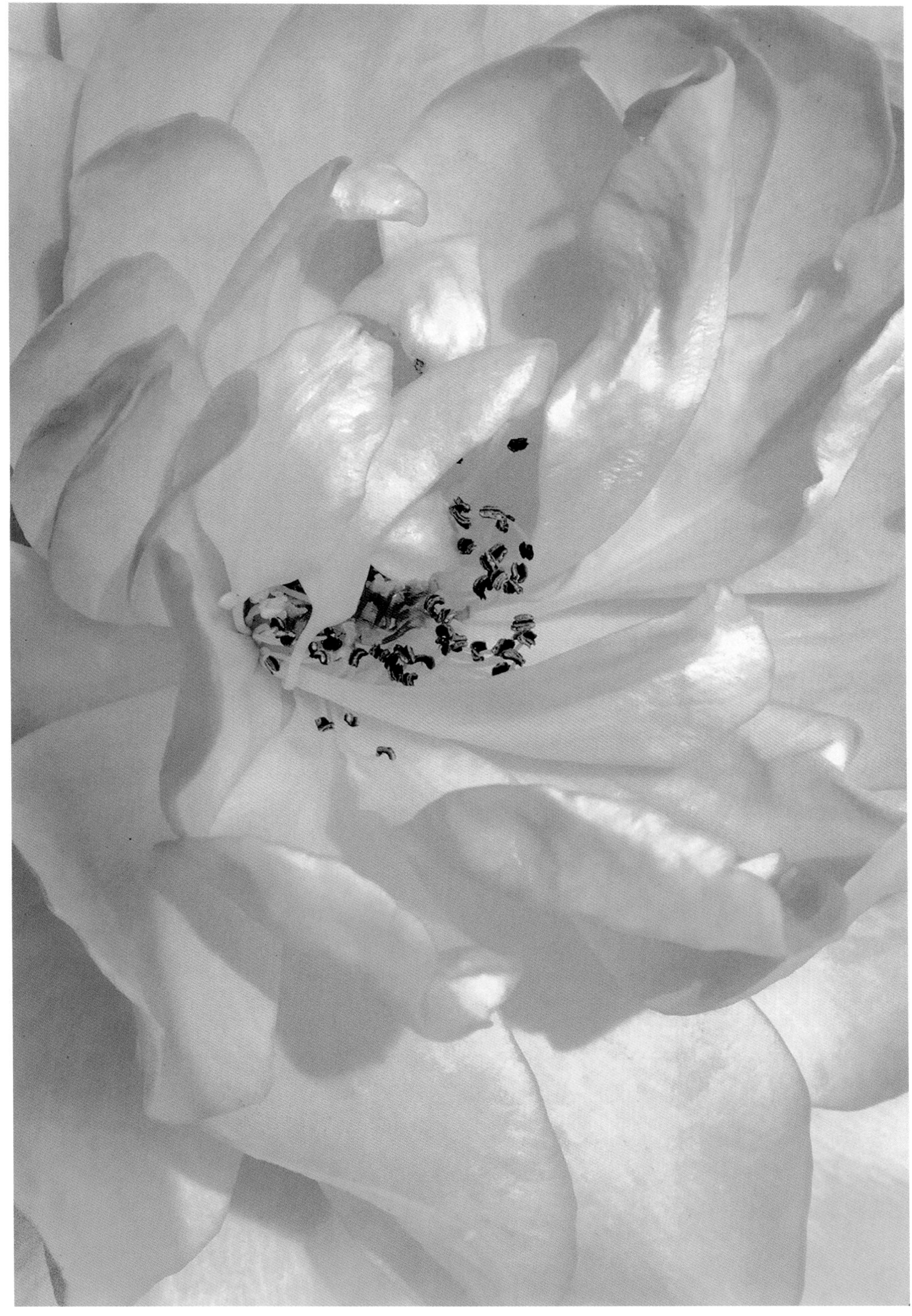

XUEBING DU
Mother of Pearl, from the series *Mother of Pearl*, 2018

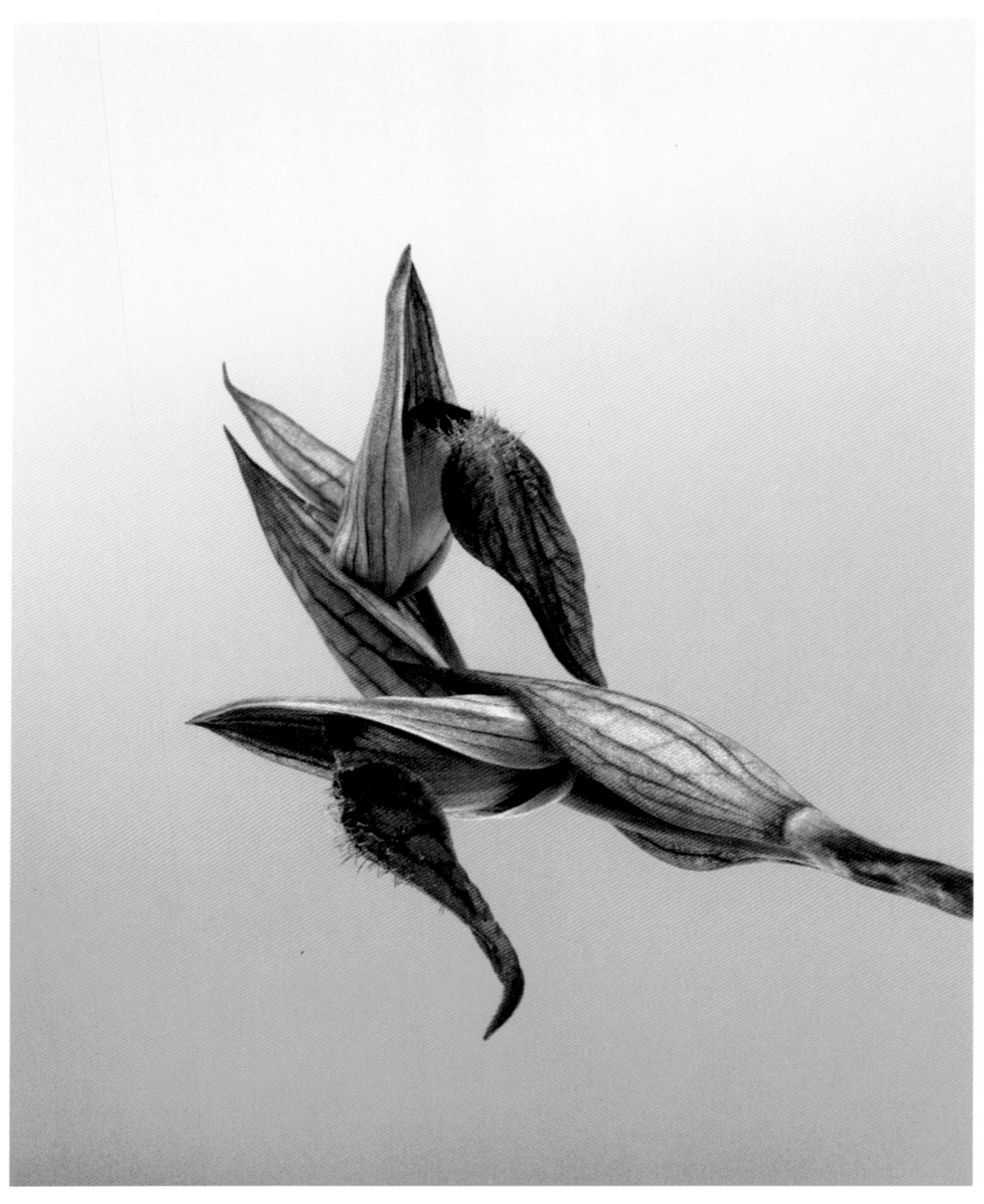

ERWAN FROTIN
Serapias neglecta, from the series *Flora olbiensis*, 2007

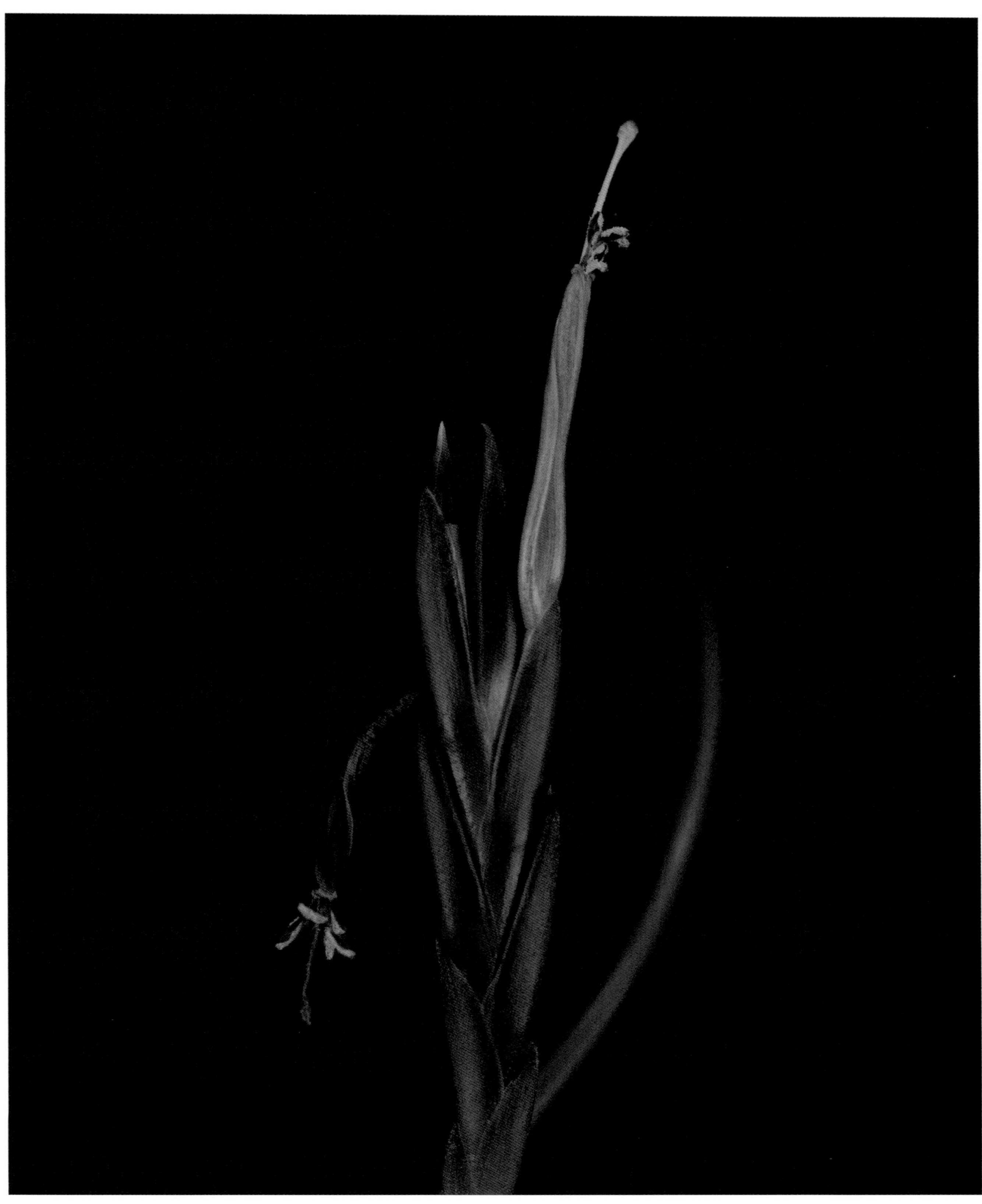

RON VAN DONGEN
Tillandsia caput-medusa, 2013

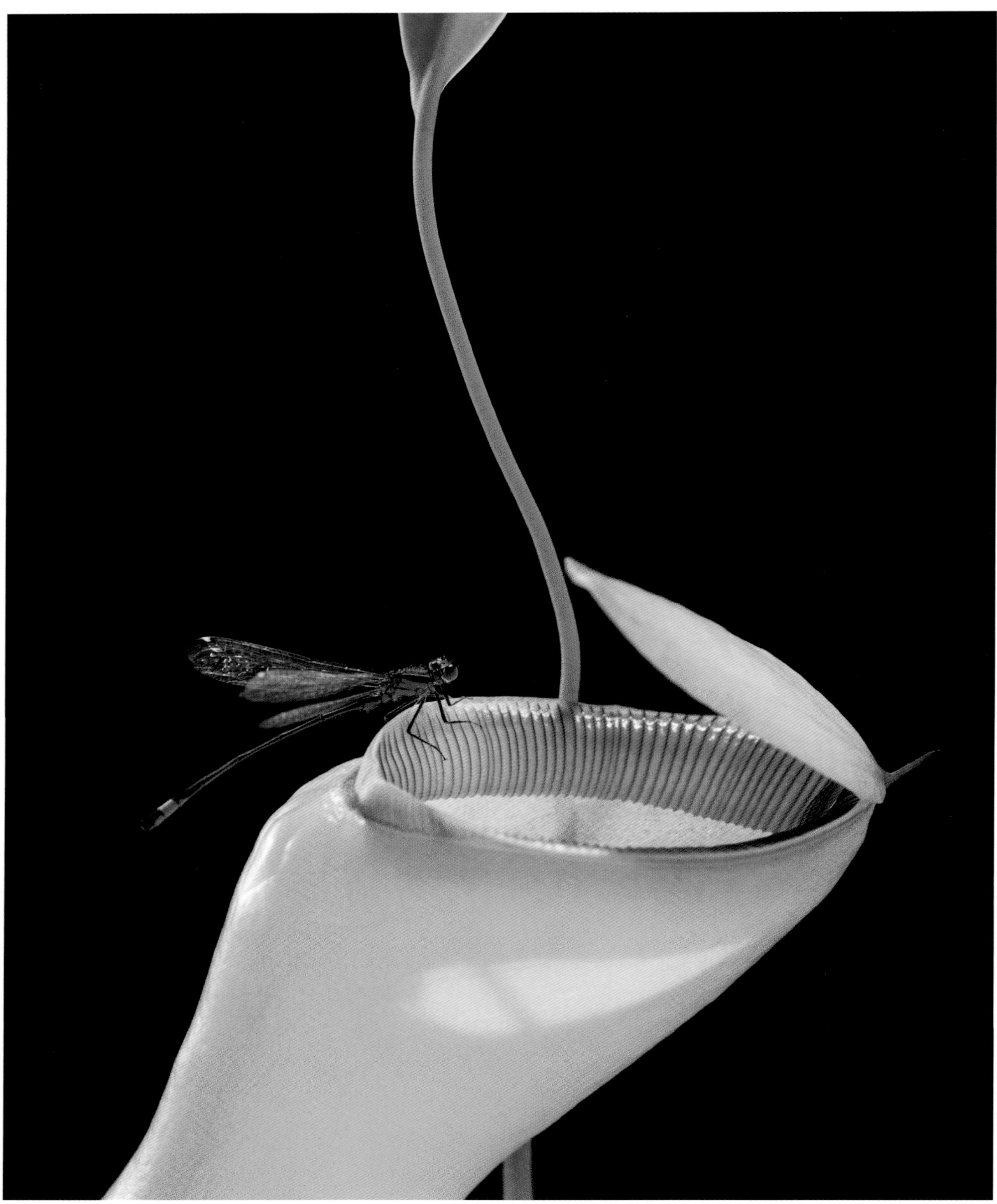

HELENE SCHMITZ
The Nepenthes and the Dragonfly, from the series *Carnivores*, 2010

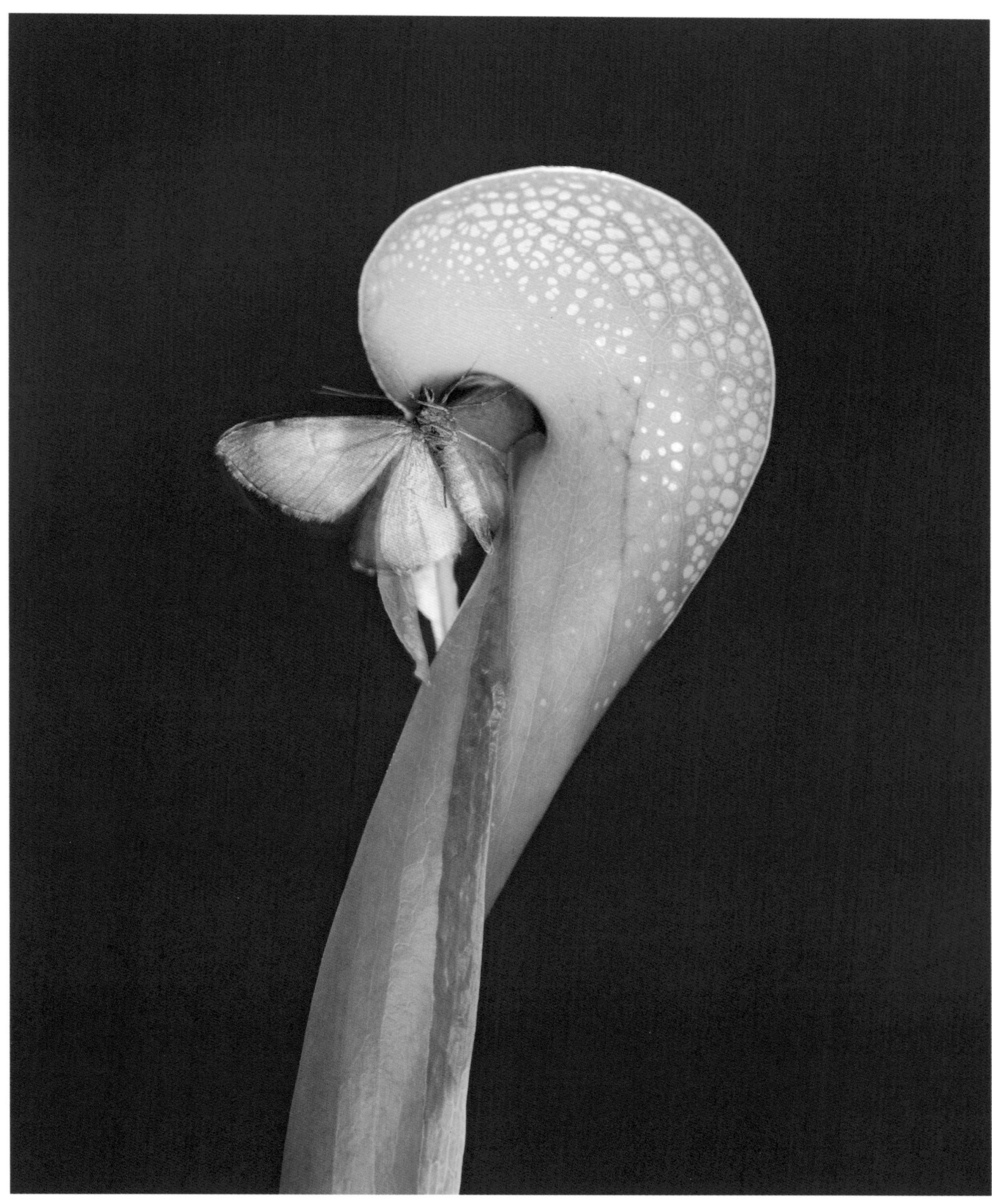

HELENE SCHMITZ
The Darlingtonia and the Moth, from the series *Carnivores*, 2010

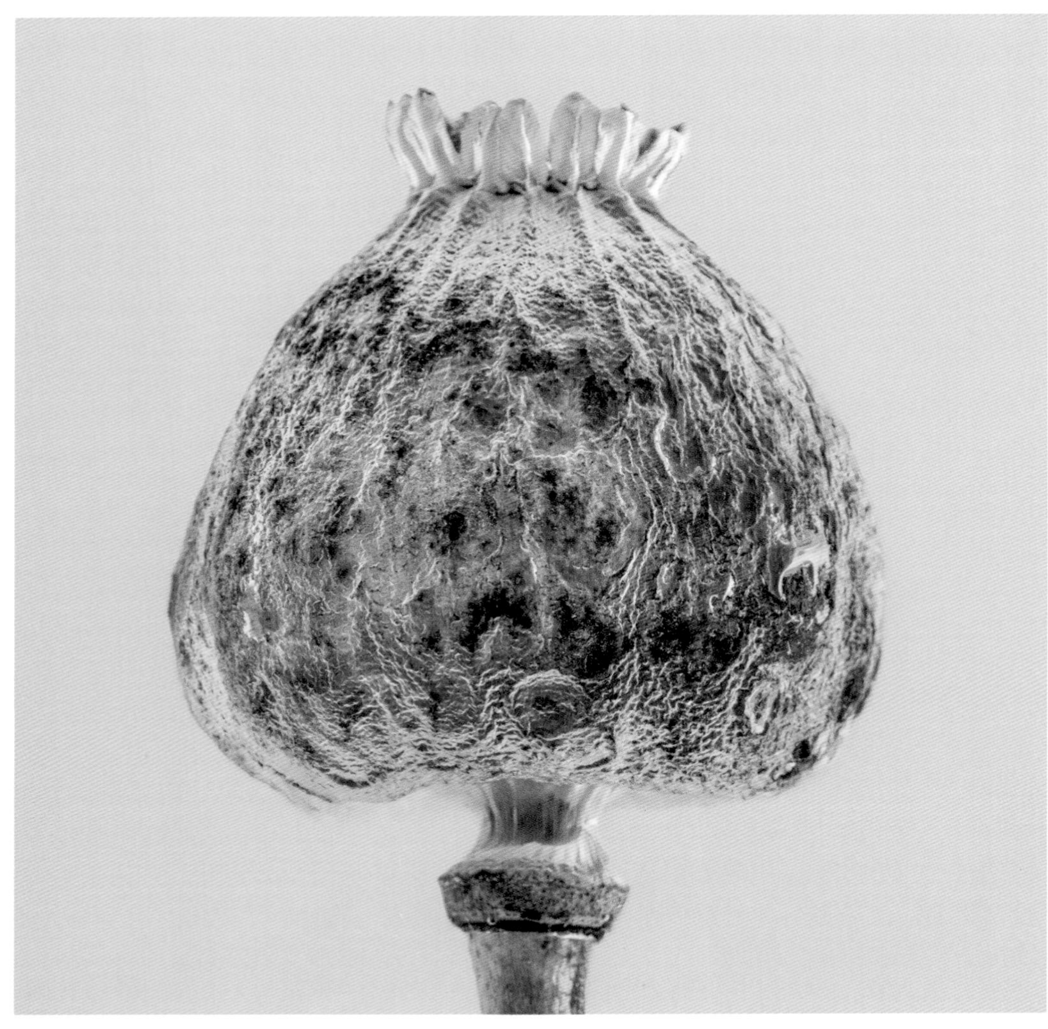

KATHRIN LINKERSDORFF
R-N 03, from the series *Re-Naissance*, 2014

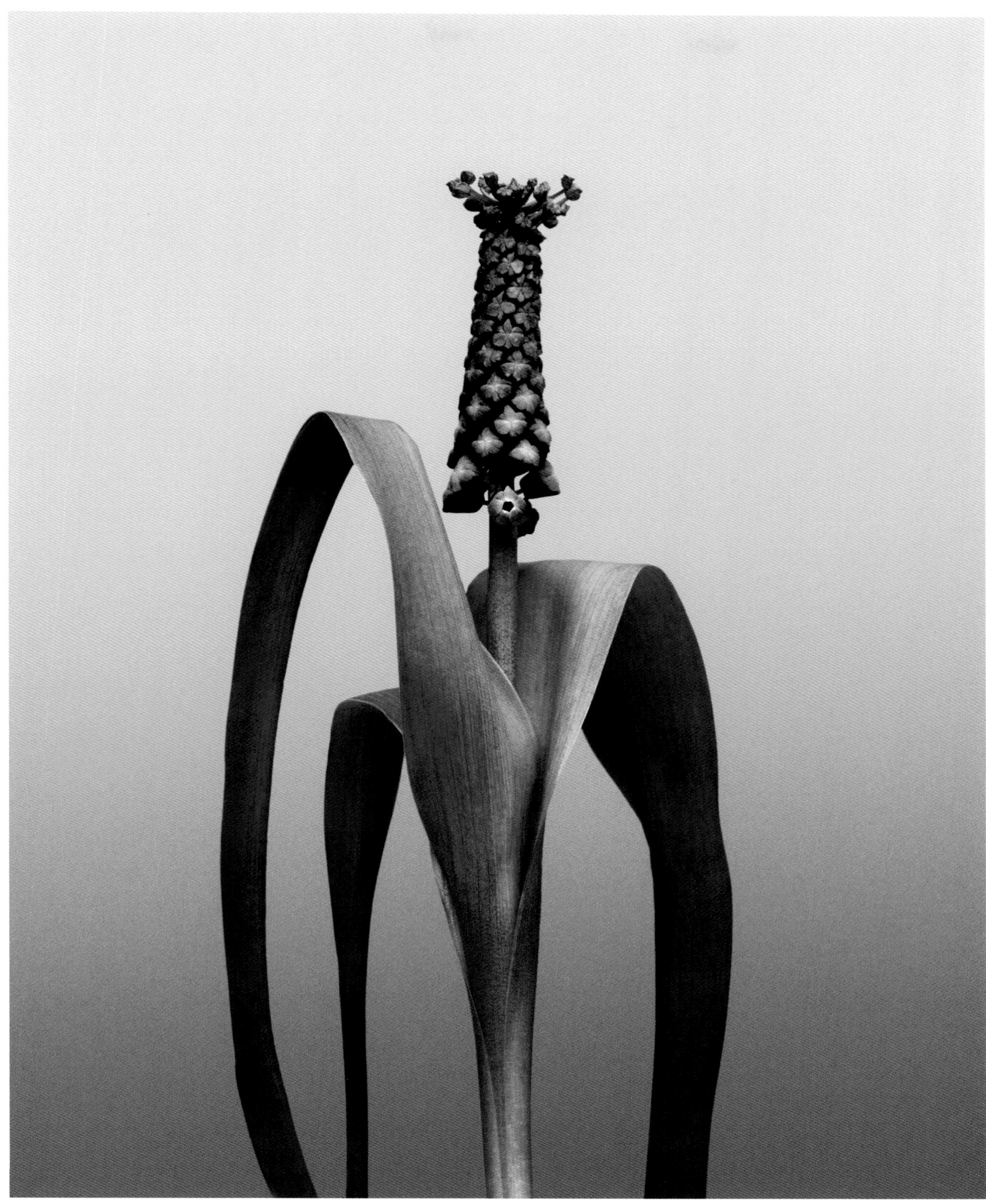

ERWAN FROTIN
Muscari comosum 2, from the series *Flora olbiensis*, 2007

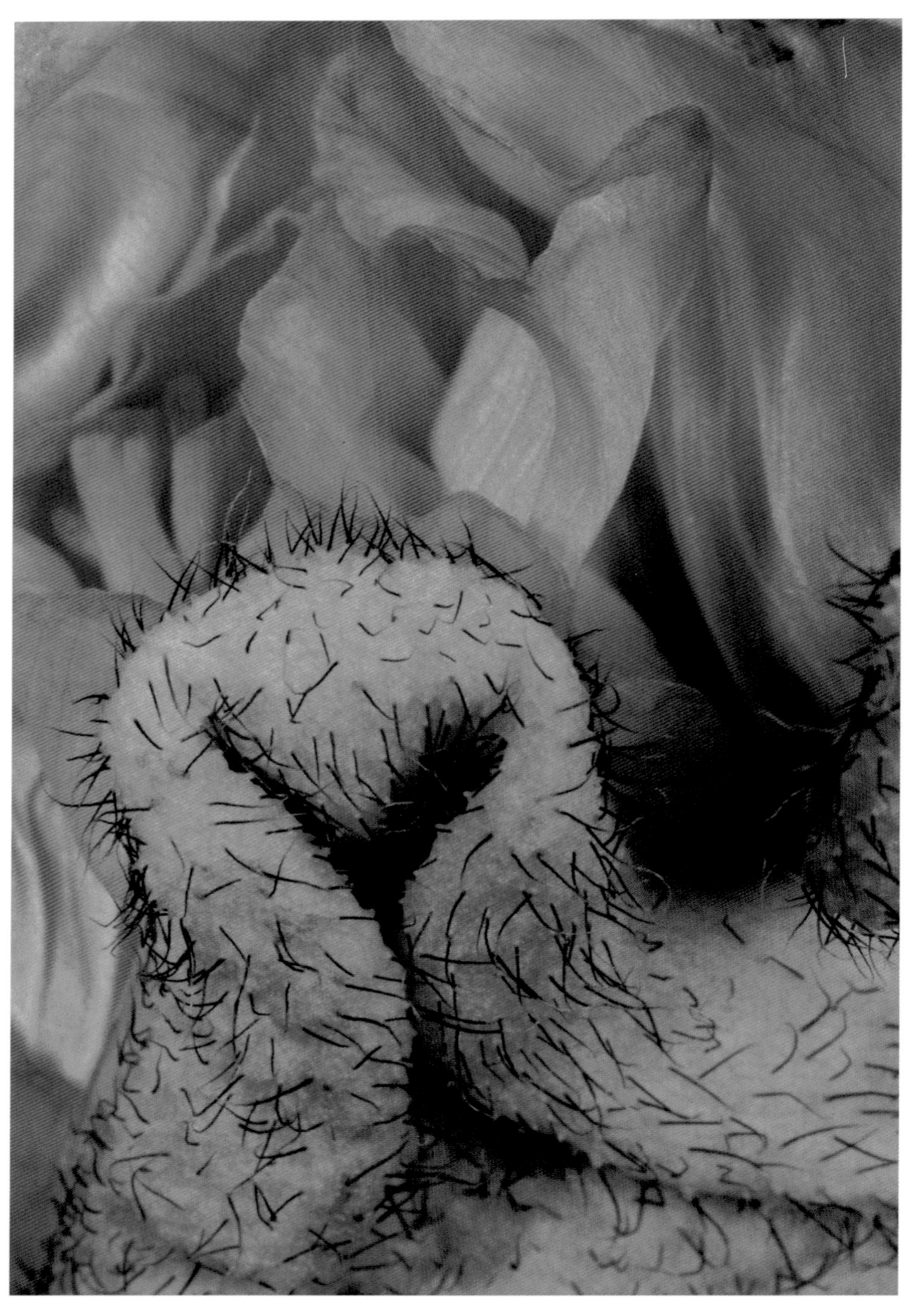

ANNA HALM SCHUDEL
Mohn, from the series *Blumenporträts*, 2004

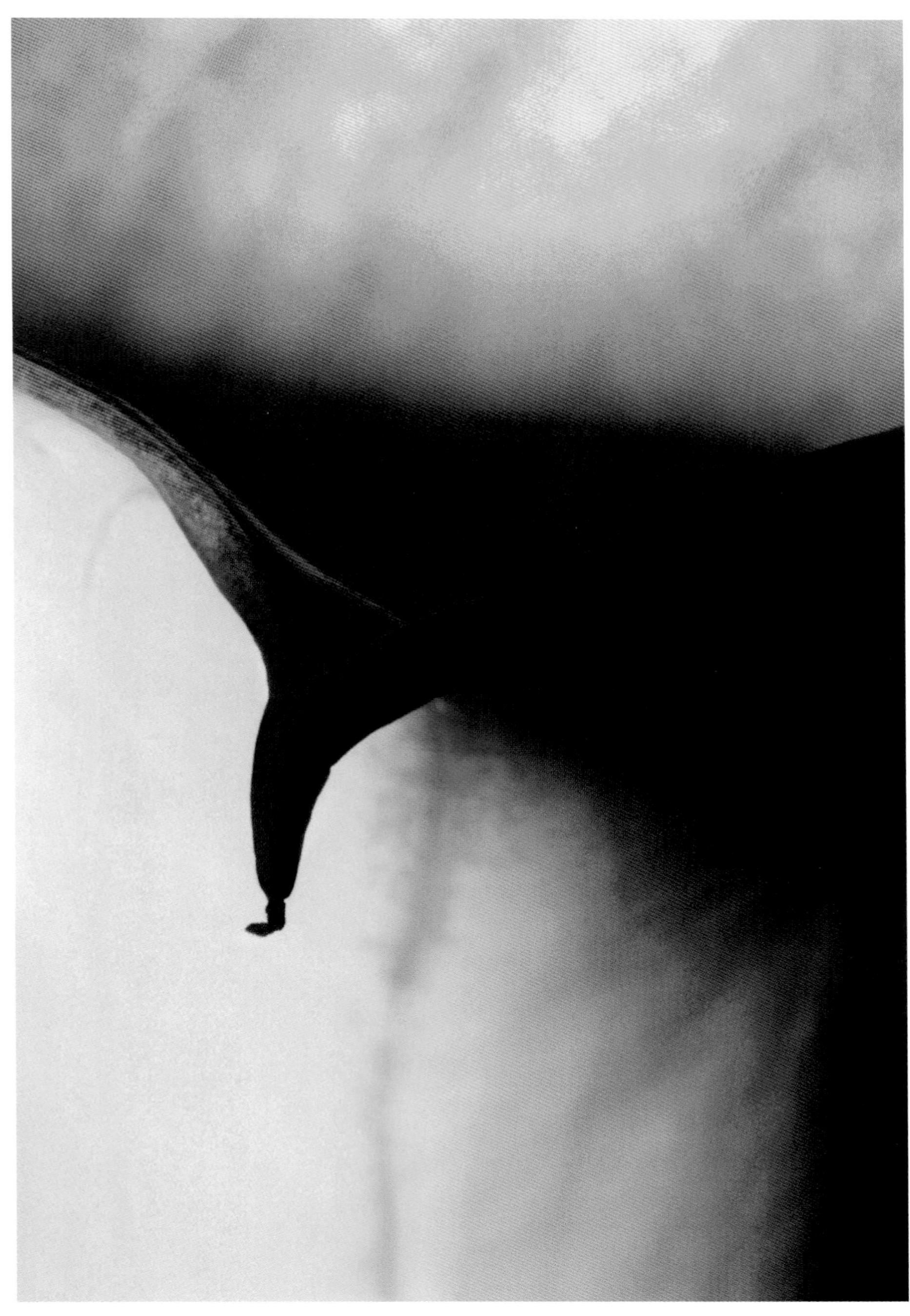

ANNA HALM SCHUDEL
Calla, from the series *Blumenporträts*, 2002

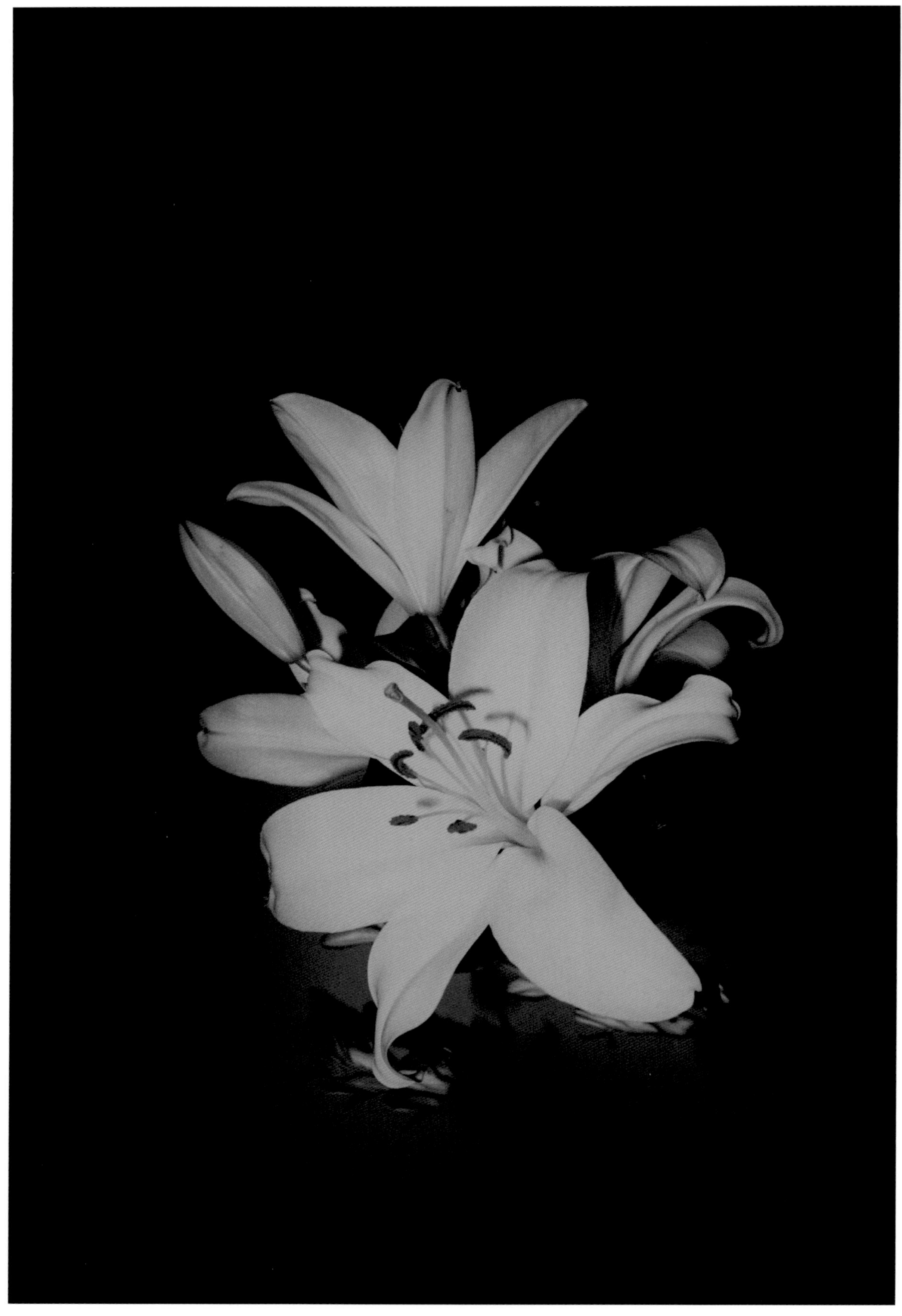

PAUL CUPIDO
Indigo II, 2021

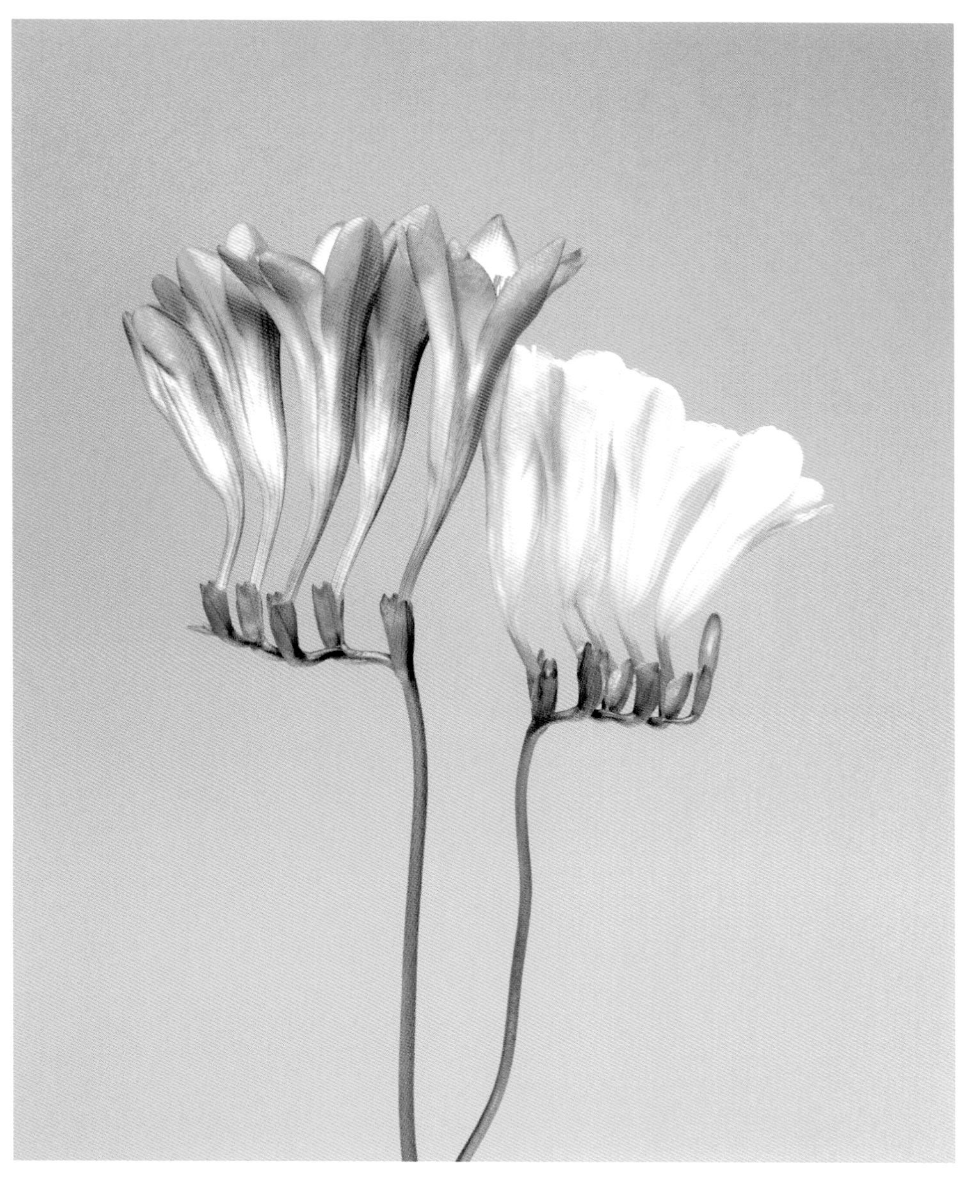

ERWAN FROTIN
Freesia sp., from the series *Flora olbiensis*, 2007

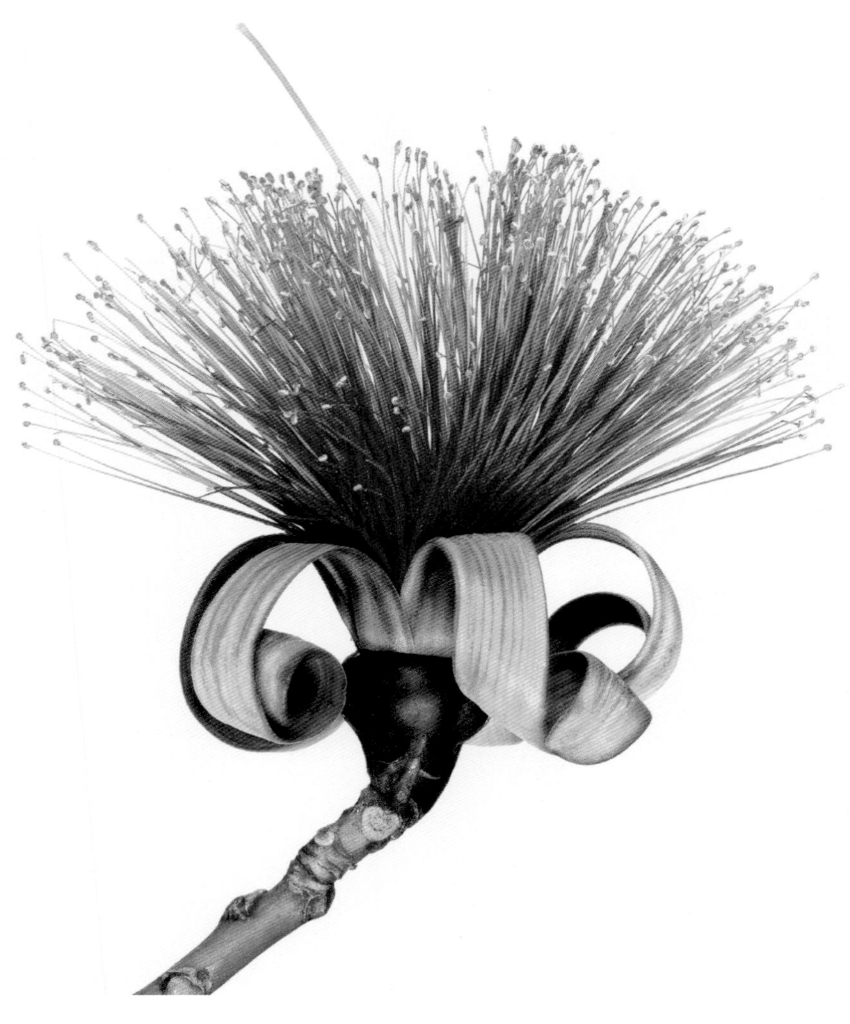

ANDREW ZUCKERMAN
Pseudobombax ellipticum 12, 2012

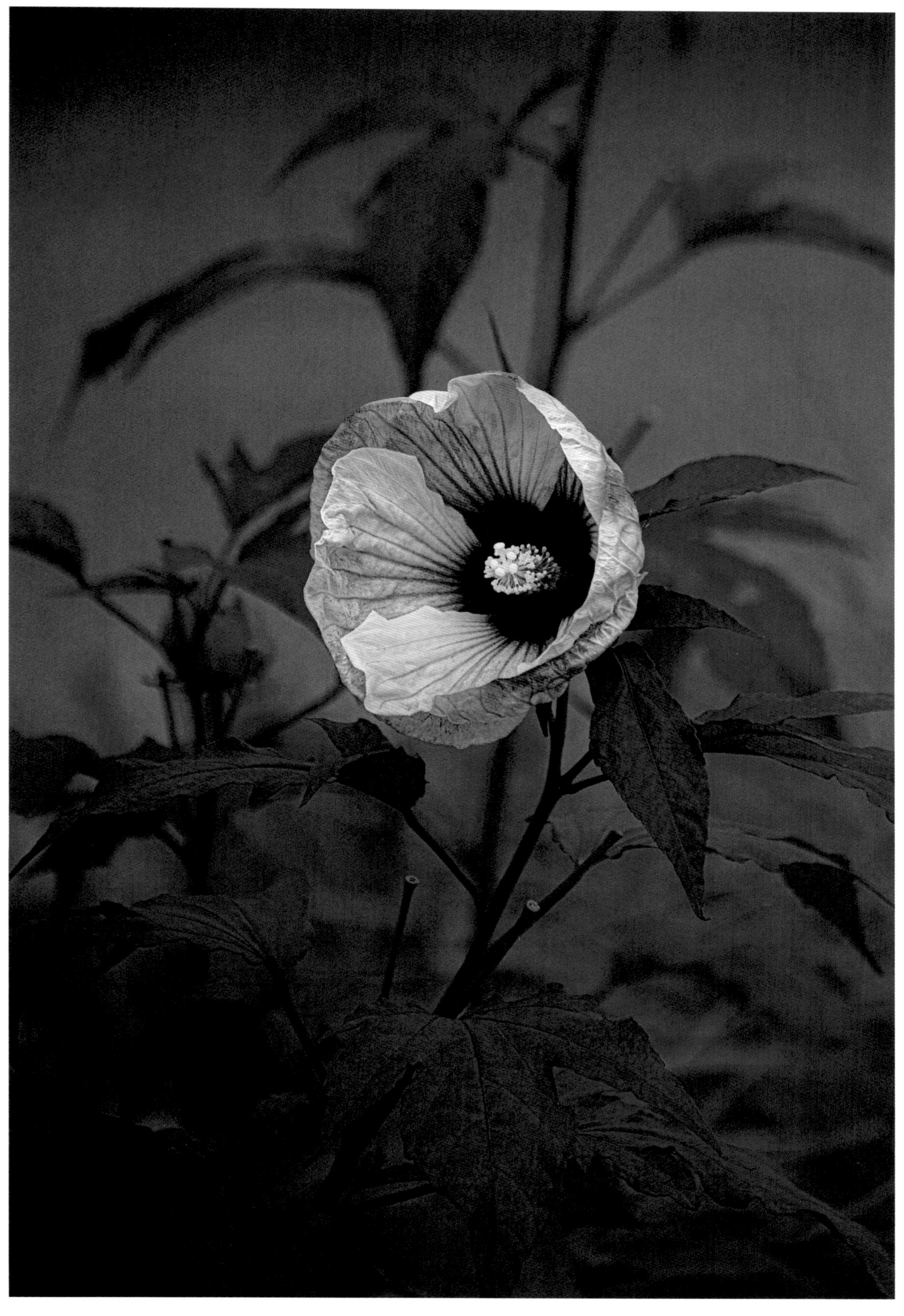

HUA JIN
2020-09-28 Blooming Hibiscus, from the series *2020 Visual Diary*, 2020

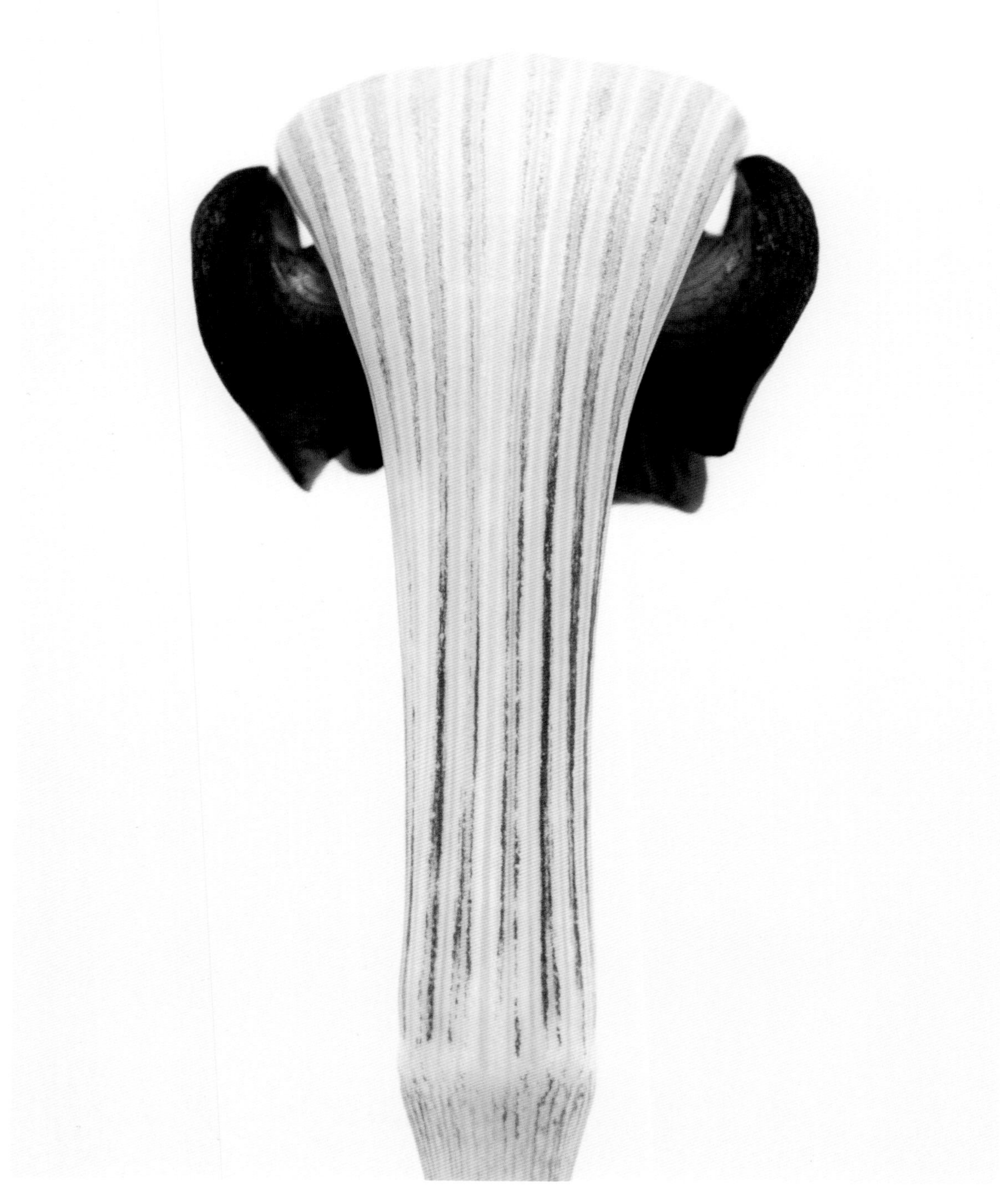

RON VAN DONGEN
Arisaema ringens, 1999

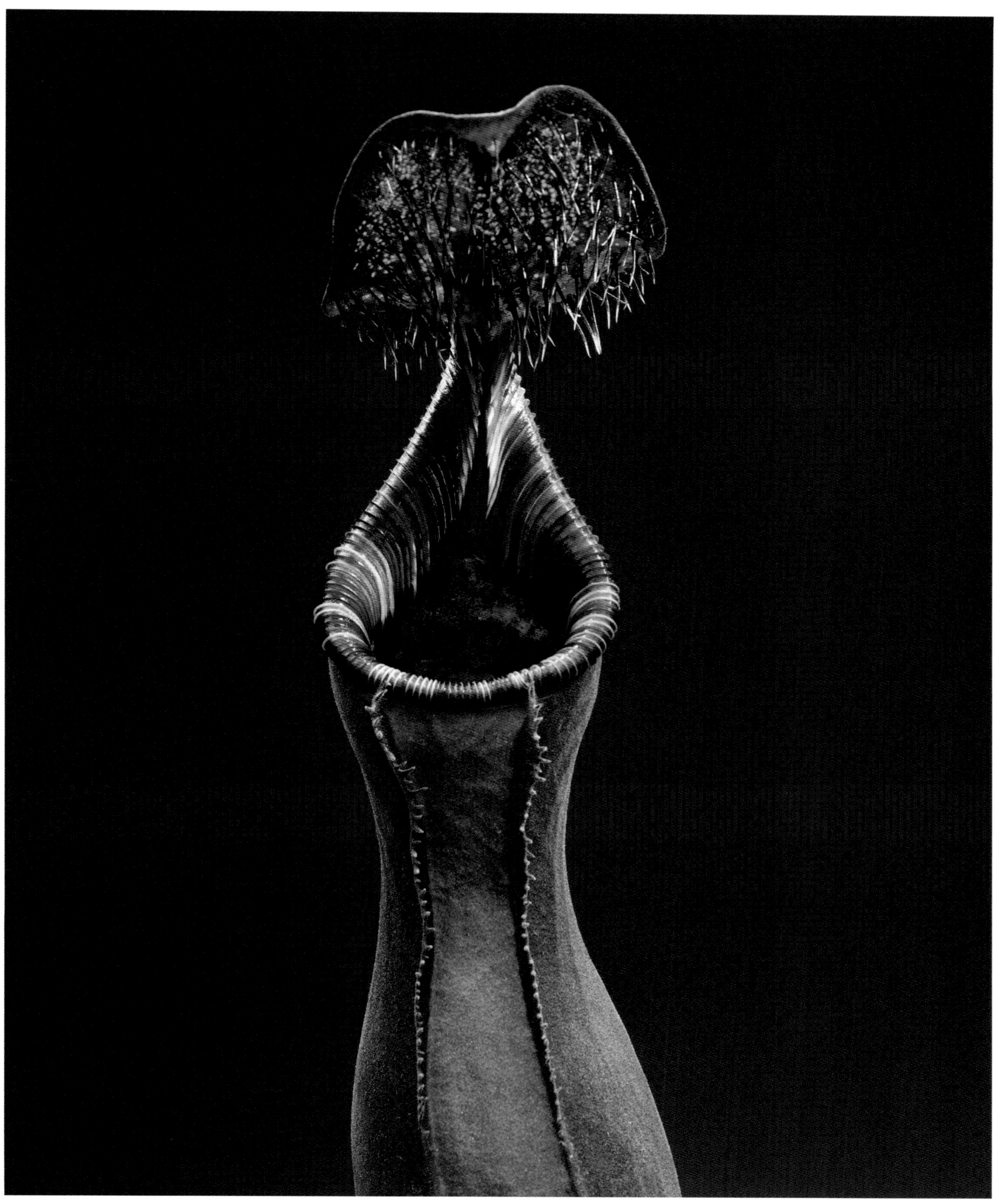

HELENE SCHMITZ
Nepenthes lowii, from the series *Carnivores*, 2010

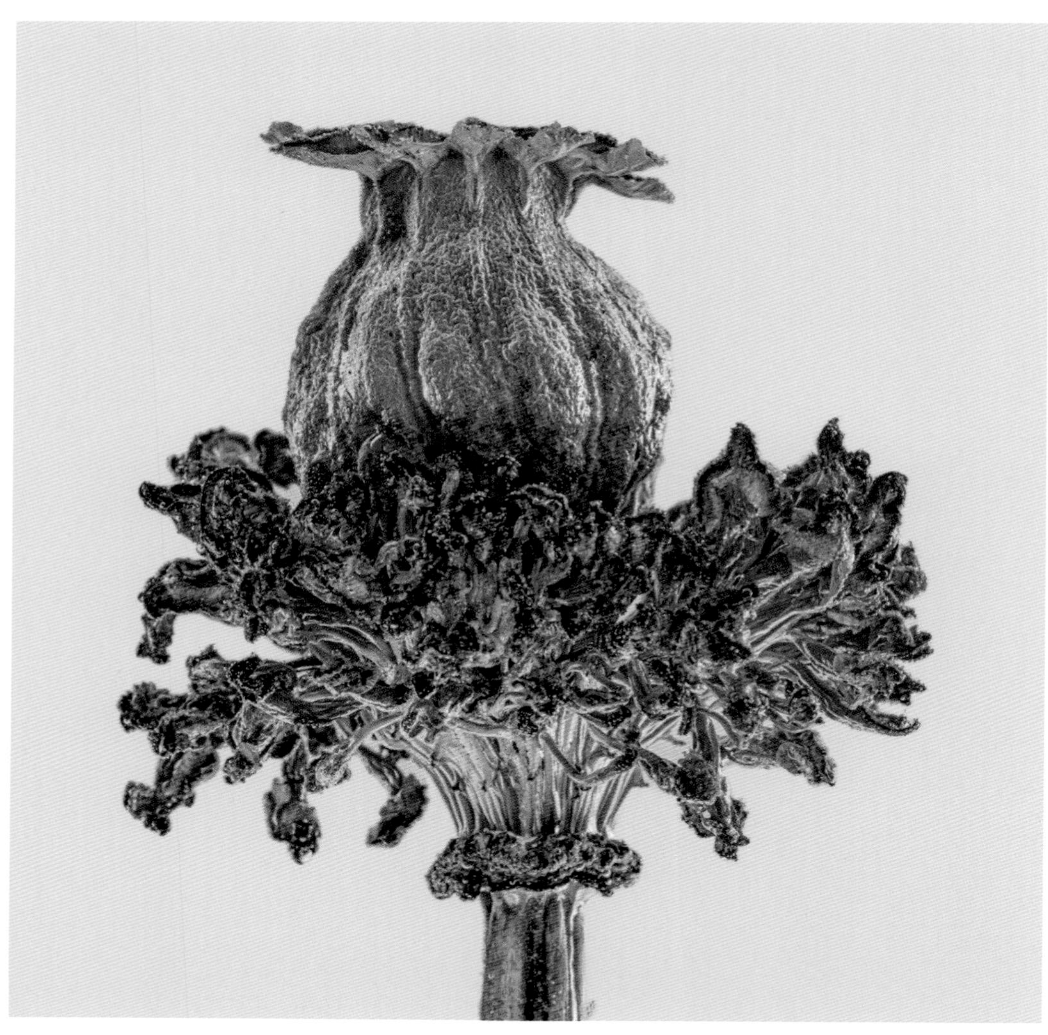

KATHRIN LINKERSDORFF
R-N 01, from the series *Re-Naissance*, 2014

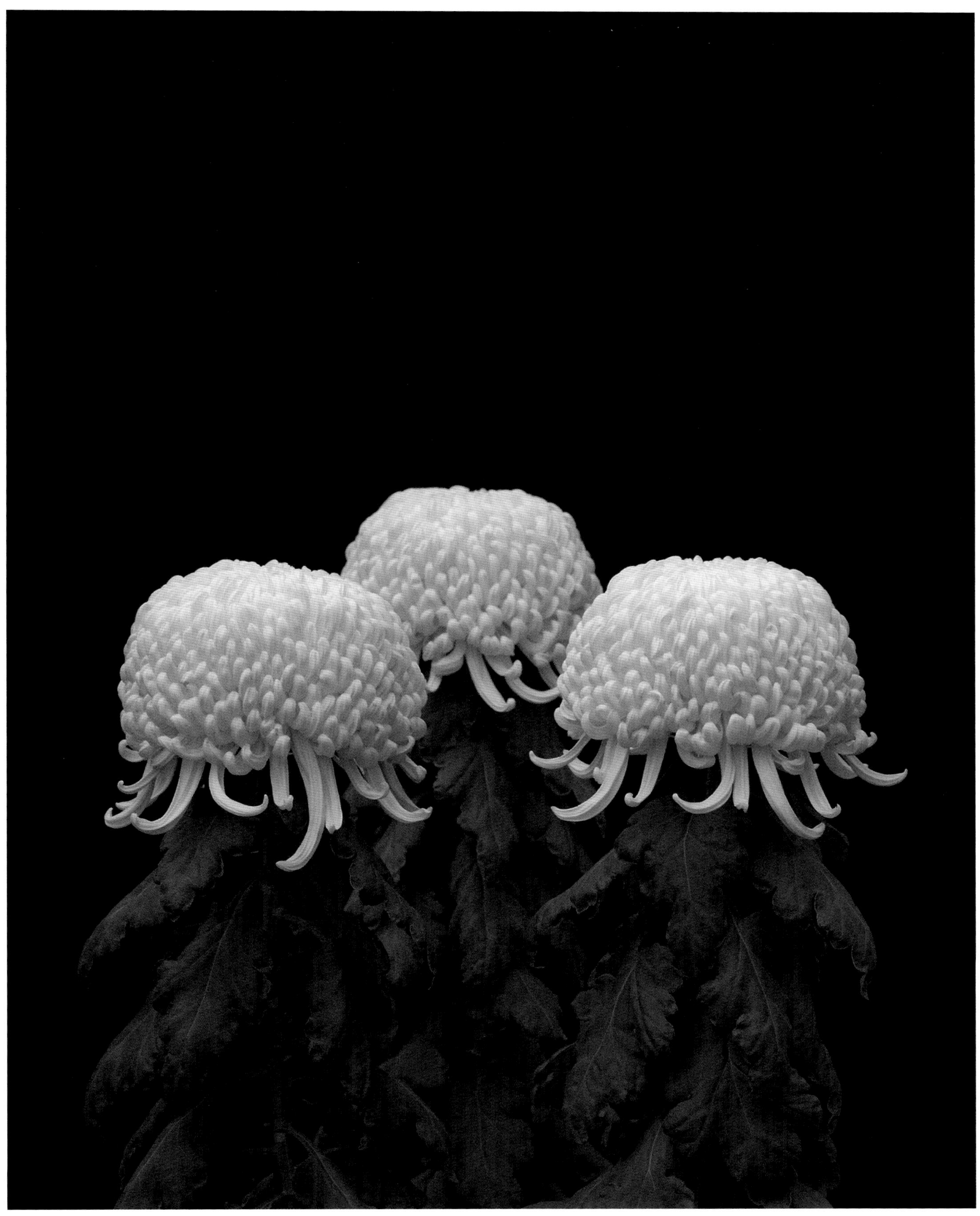

TOMOKO YONEDA
Chrysanthemums, from the series *Cumulus*, 2011

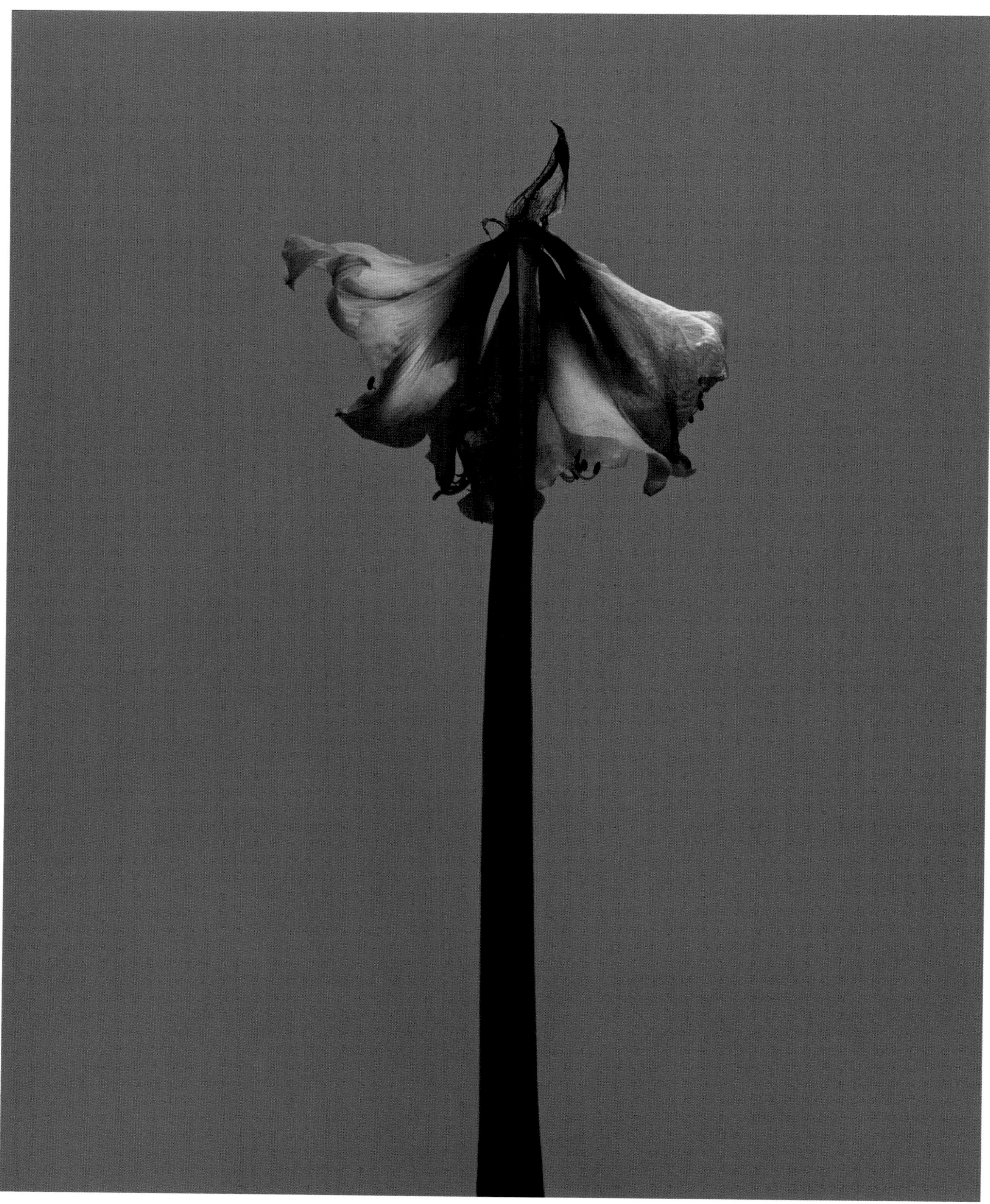

ROBERTO GRECO
Fig. XI, from the series *Œillères*, 2017

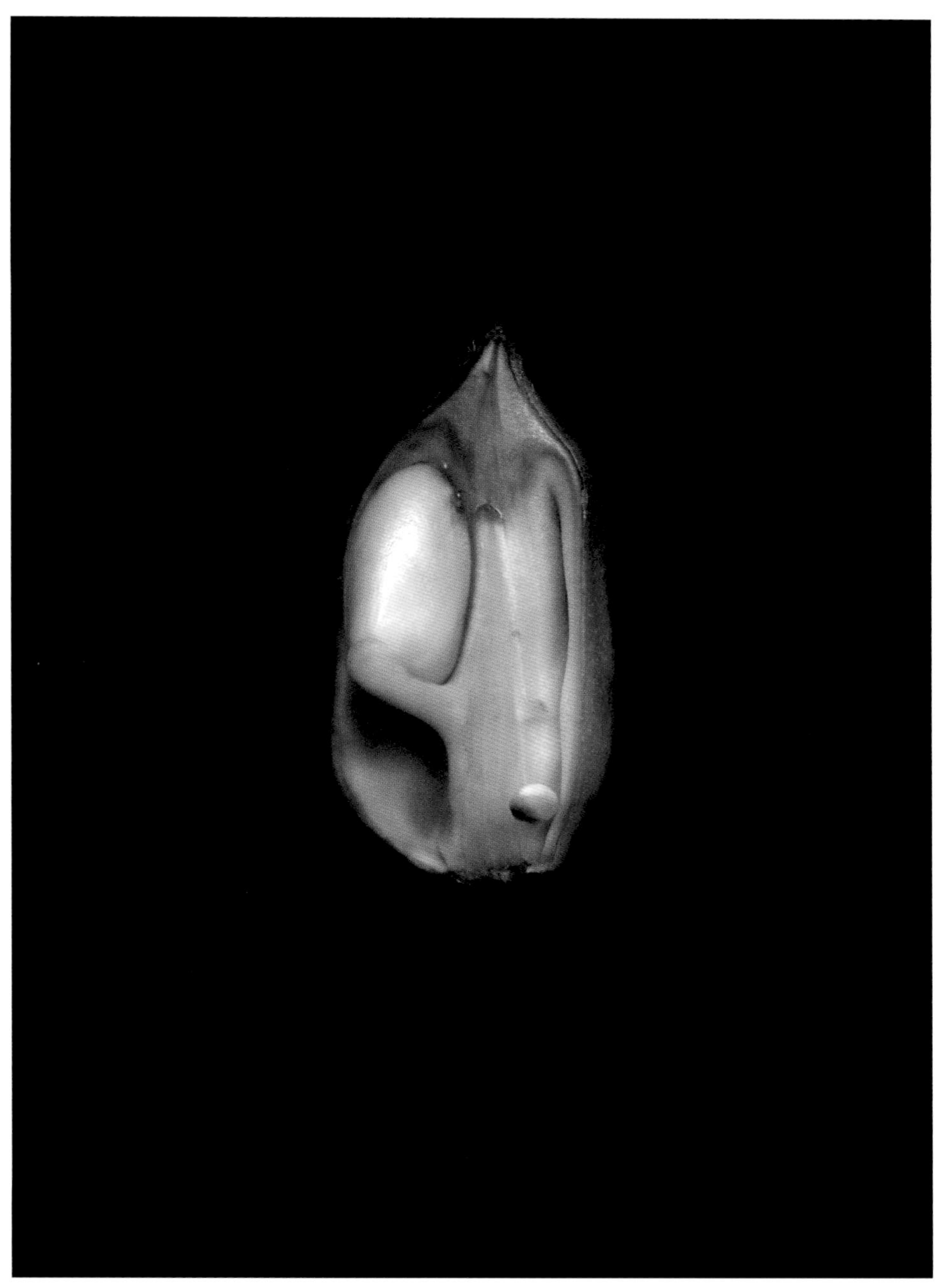

ELAINE DUIGENAN
House, from the series *Sex Pistils*, 2020

IMPOSTERS

An imposter is a person who pretends to be someone else in order to deceive others, especially for fraudulent gain. We might also have used the word 'counterfeit' – an exact imitation of something with the intention to mislead or defraud – for this chapter.

But these designations might be unfair where artificial flowers are concerned. While they are certainly intended to deceive the eye – silk roses are, after all, complete to the thorns – it is not usually for criminal purpose. The artificial-flower industry is above-board, legitimate and very, very lucrative. Whether silk, cotton or plastic, such flowers upstage nature's own creations with their low maintenance and longevity. The industry prefers the terms 'faux flowers', the more scientific-sounding 'permanent botanicals' or even the sweet-phrase 'everlasting flowers', and it is true that some of these marvels of deceit have to be touched to be distinguished from the real thing; some are even given distinctive fragrances by their makers.

'The employment of artificial flowers outside the season, and for purposes to which fresh flowers are inappropriate, has as long a history as the use of cultivated ones, both in the West and the East,' the anthropologist Jack Goody reminds us.[1] The practice goes back millennia, and probably originated in China through the cultivation of silkworms, although European craftsmen mastered the art some time in the twelfth century. But well before that, more than a thousand years earlier, Pliny the Elder could tell us that Romans turned to artifice during the winter, and that they could choose from 'multi-coloured forms steeped in perfumes'.[2] By the Victorian era, the fruits of the Industrial Revolution meant one could choose from satin, velvet, muslin, calico, crepe, wood, porcelain, paper, latex, rubber, polyester, rayon, wax or metal, including silver and gold. 'The luxury of nature', wrote the historian Georges Bernard Depping in 1837, 'was set aside in favour of the luxury of art.'[3]

Not all this artifice worked. A brief period of highly flammable celluloid flowers risked disaster – newly-weds might find their beautiful bouquets bursting into flame. Plastic, however, had become the mainstay of the industry by the middle of the twentieth century, and species multiplied. Manufacturers have since become acutely attuned to trends in fashion and interior design.

And what of 'faux flowers' in photography? In a sense all flowers are fake in photography, leaving traces on paper with the help of silver salts, dyes and pigments, or printed in books in ink, or rendered in pixels on a screen. Once captured in a photograph, the mystery of the false or real original is moot; it can never be resolved.

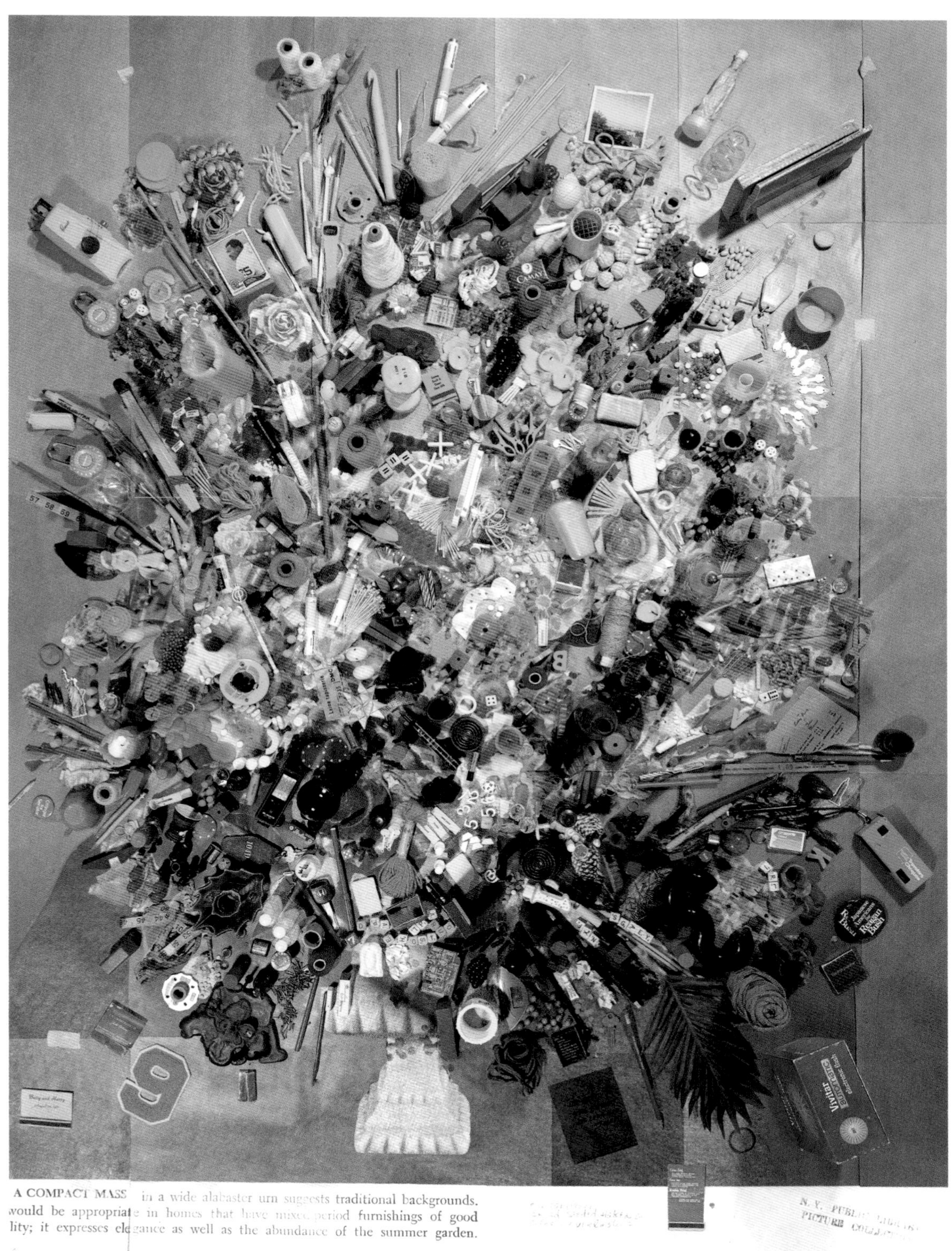

SARA CWYNAR
Contemporary Floral Arrangement 5 (A Compact Mass), 2014

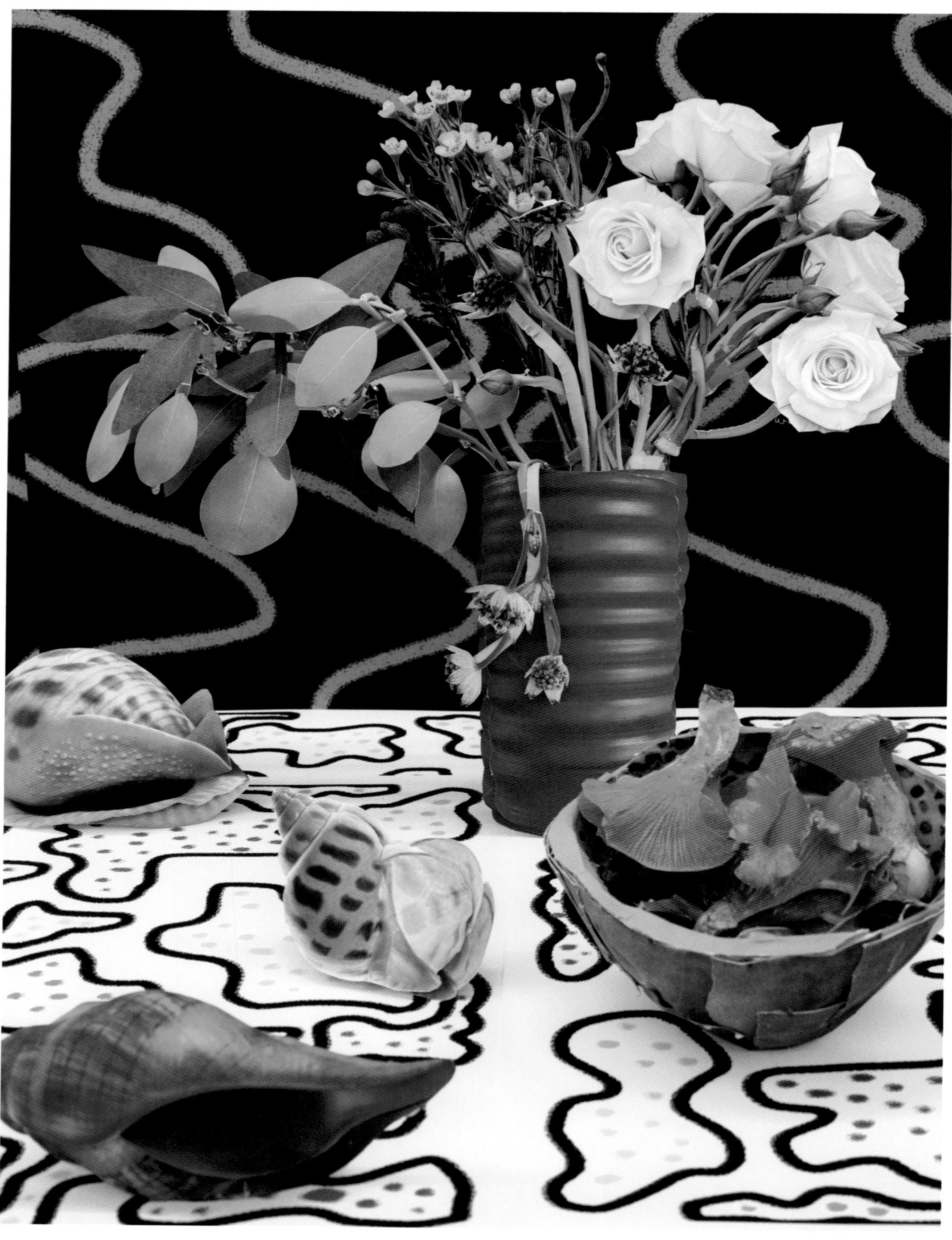

DANIEL GORDON
Seashells and Chanterelles, 2021

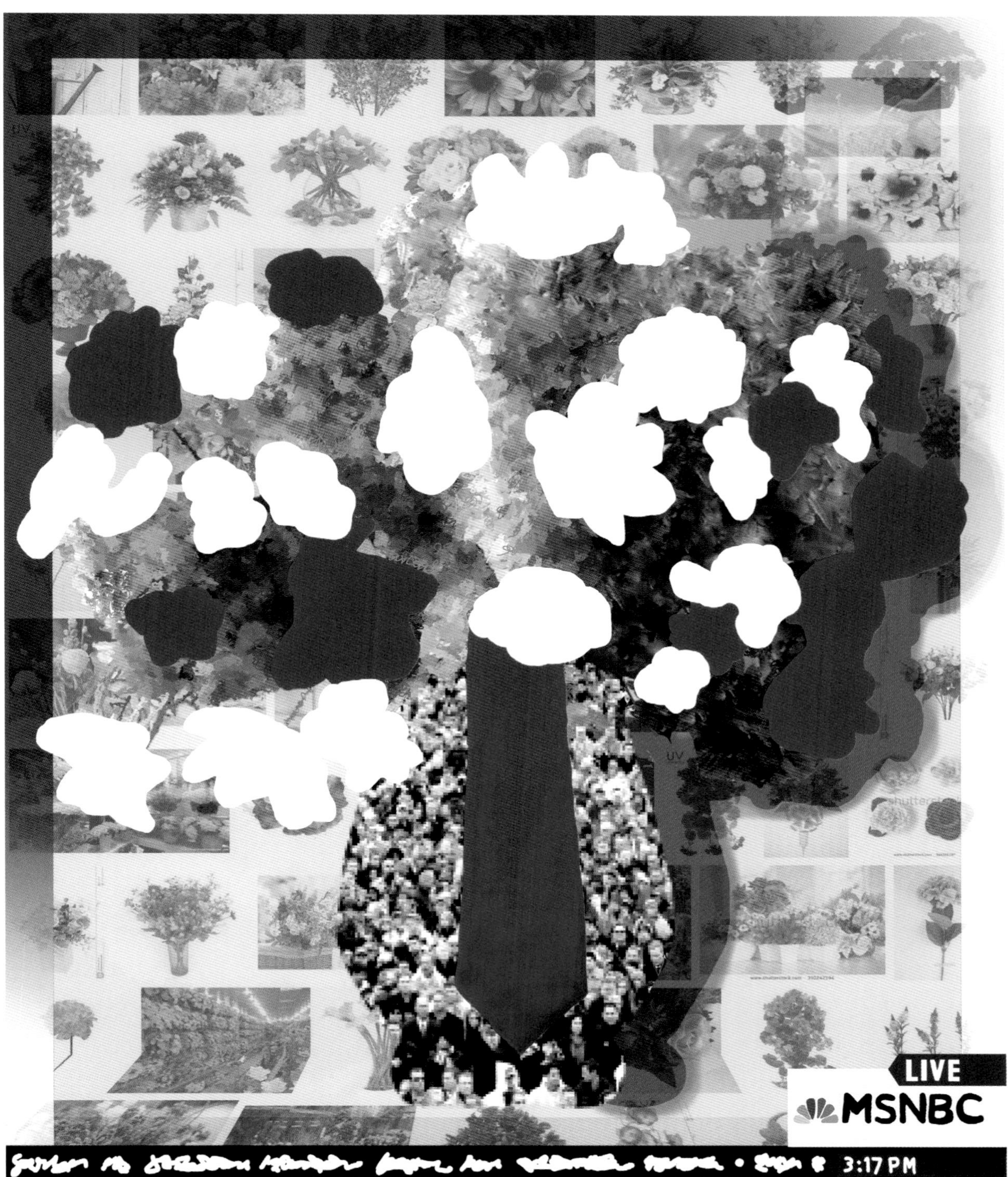

GREGORY EDDI JONES
Flowers for donald #13 (artificial flowers [with power tie]), 2017

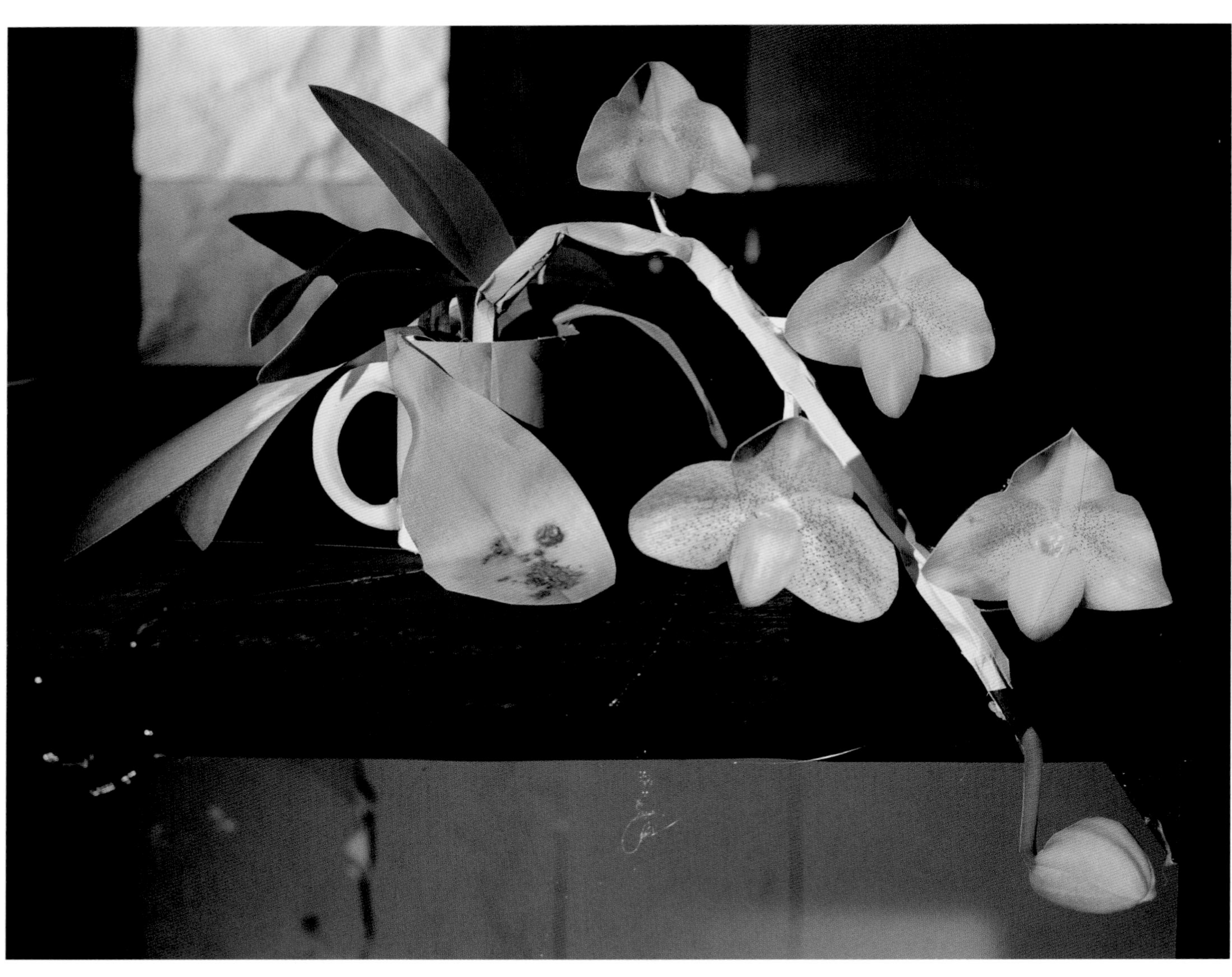

DANIEL GORDON
July 21, 2009, 2009

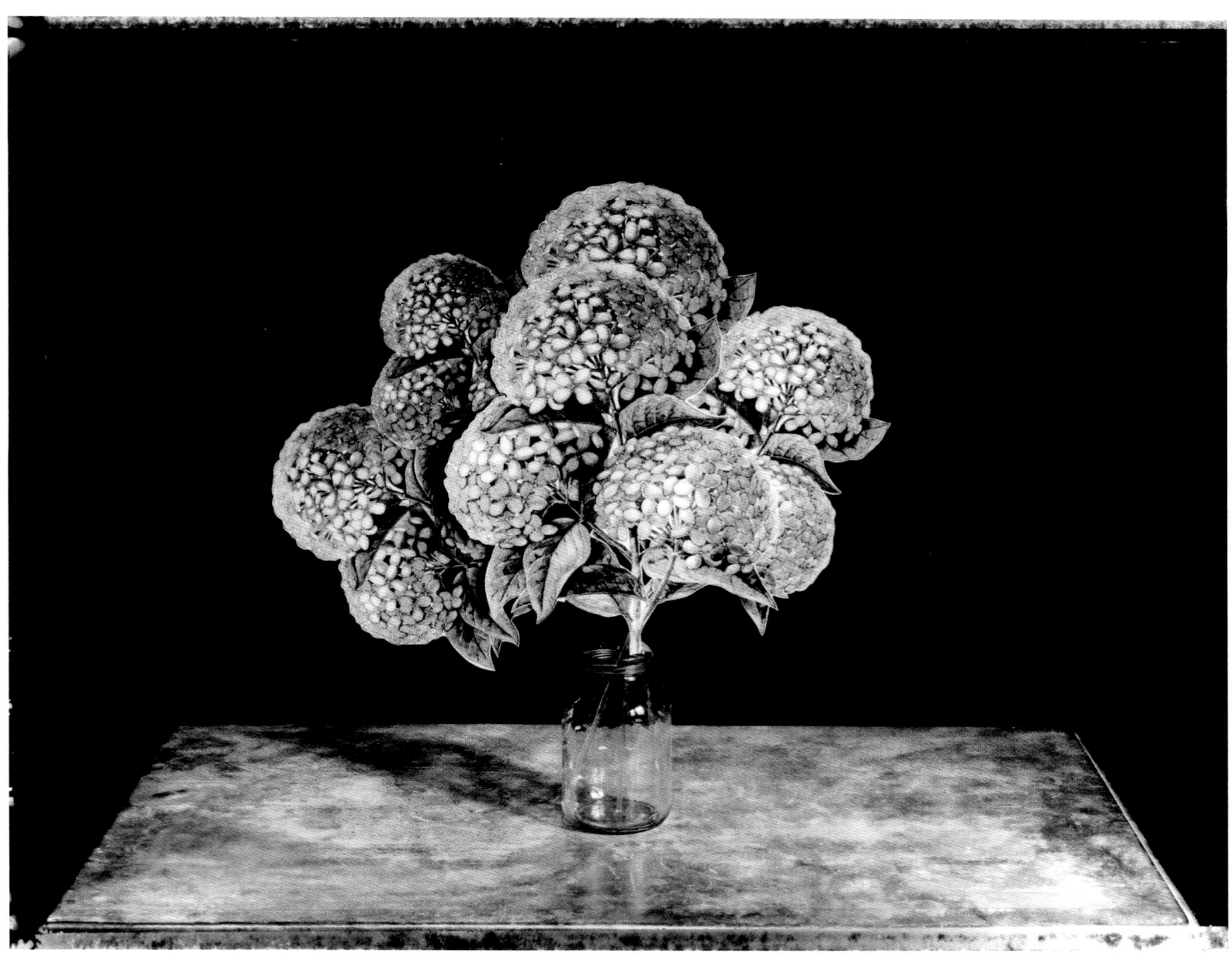

PAMELA ELLIS HAWKES
Paper Hydrangea, 2000

PHOTO-HYBRIDS

Artificial flowers go back to the Romans and the Egyptians: convenience and durability trumped vitality and ephemerality. In the first century AD, *Pliny the Elder could write of silk flowers 'steeped in perfumes', and the elite could parade their status wearing flowers of silver and gold.*[4] *Today the artificial-flower industry is worth billions, and new materials such as 'permastem' and 'permasilk' are making the illusion of reality ever sharper. Of course, a* trompe l'œil *painting of a flower is a form of artificial flower, and in that sense all photographs of flowers are artificial flowers, too. Photographers today happily photo-hybridize, breezily dismissive of genetic constraints.*

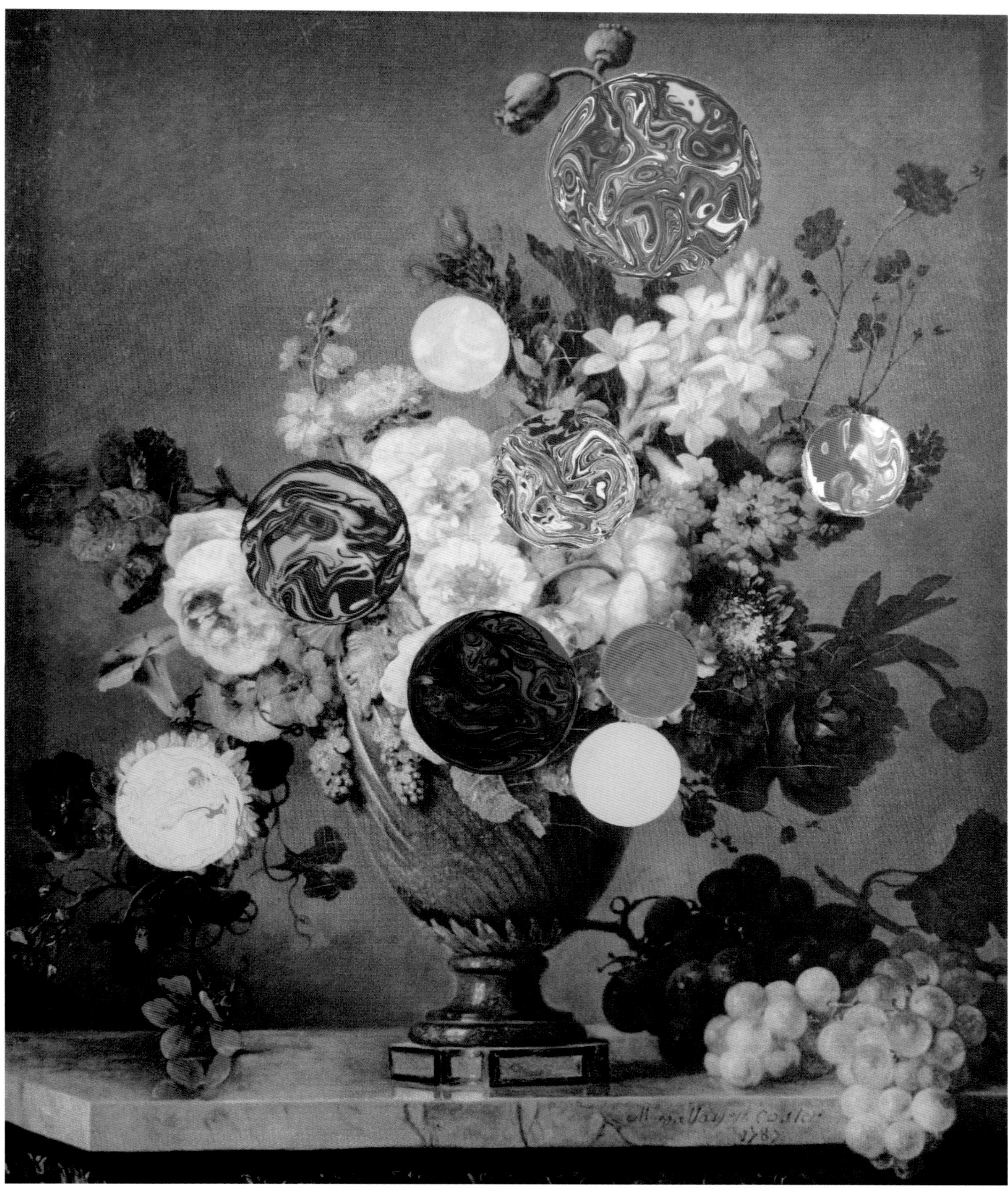

JULIE COCKBURN
Plasticine Flowers, plasticine and poster on wood, 2010

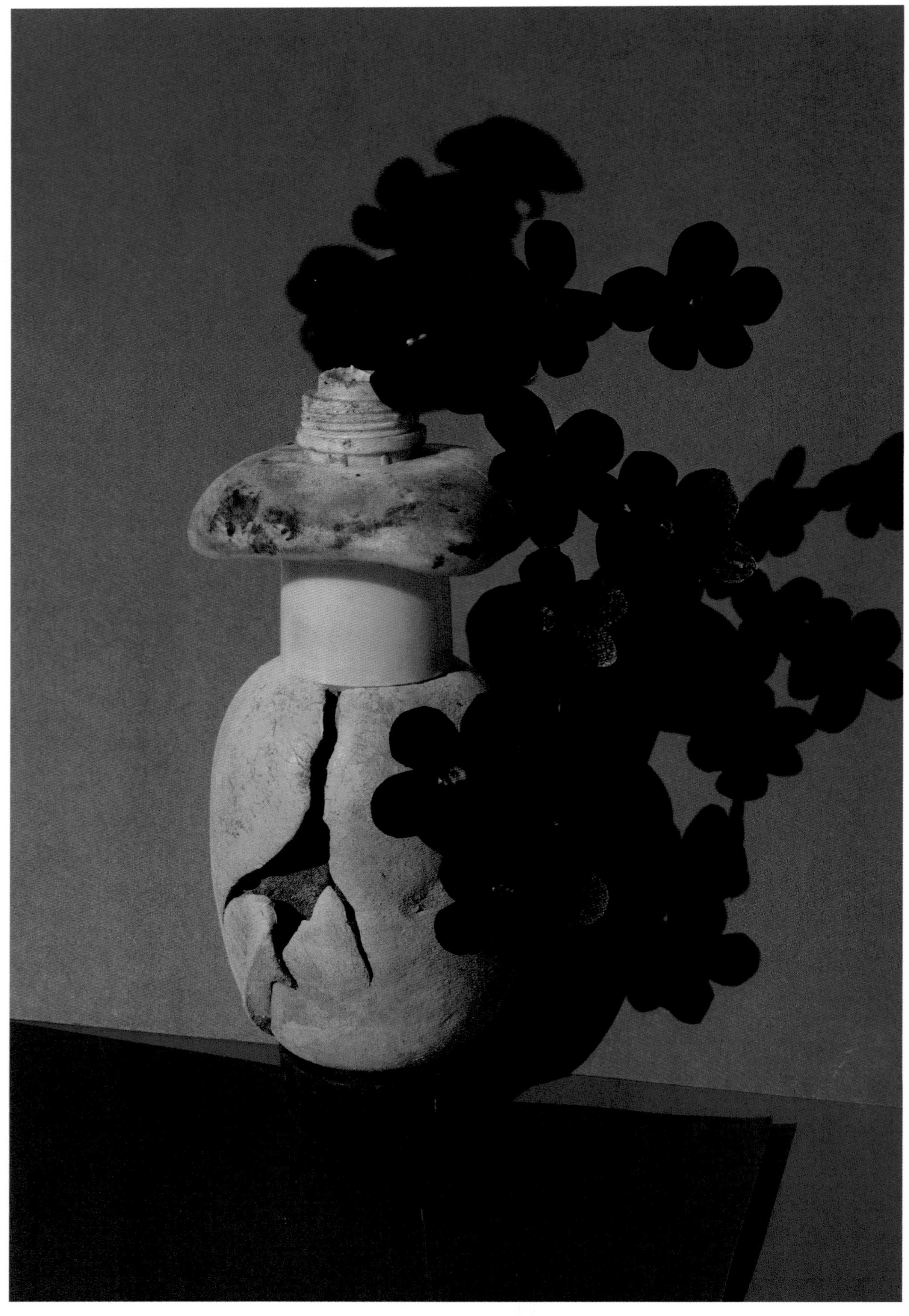

THIRZA SCHAAP
Vanda, from the series *Plastic Ocean*, 2020

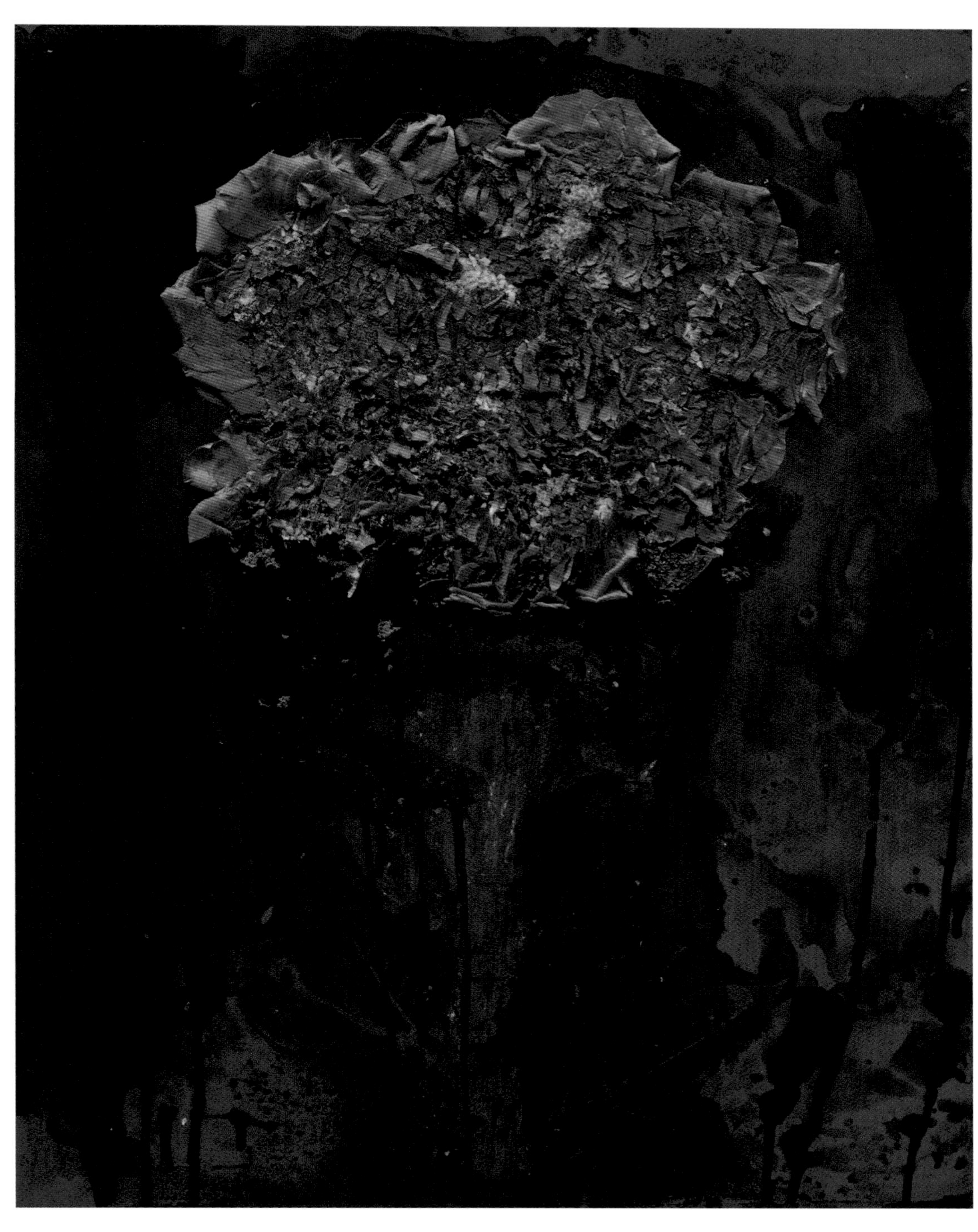

ADAM FUSS
Theia, 2019

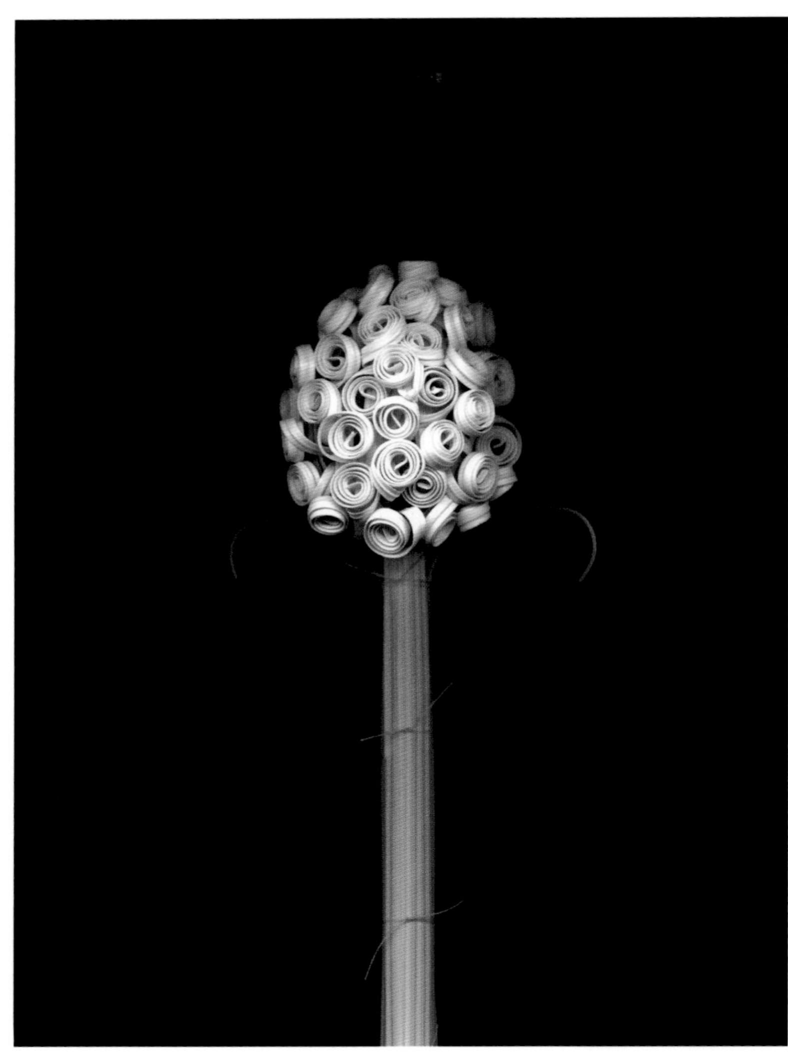

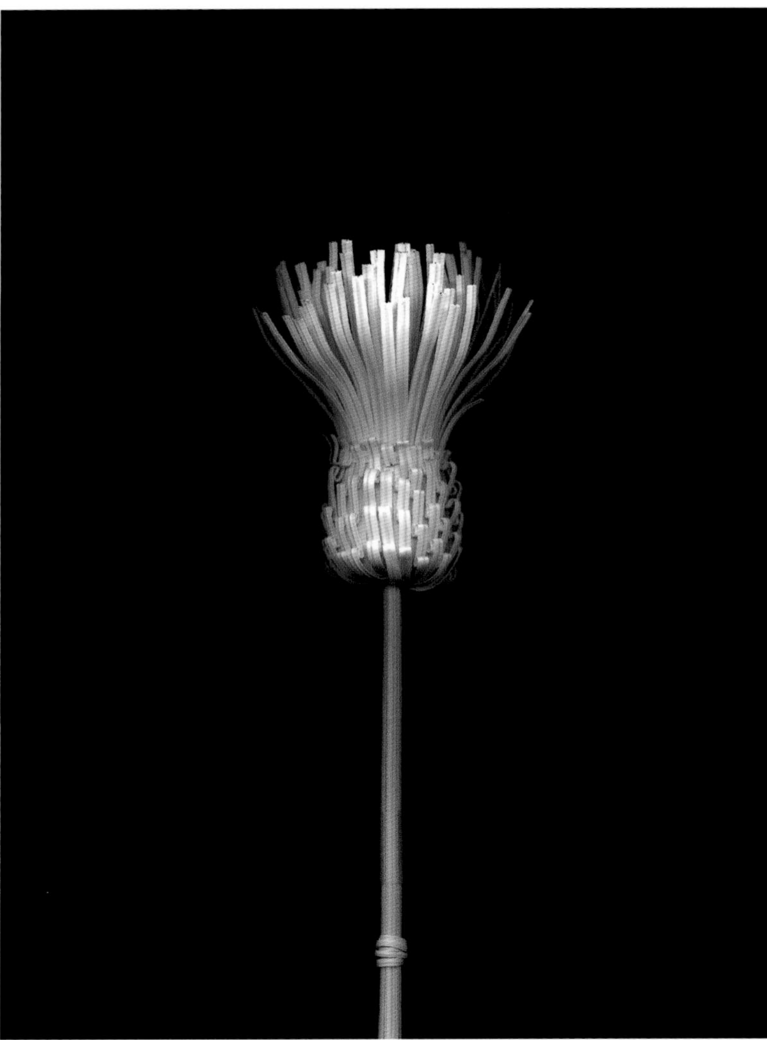

ELAINE DUIGENAN
Butterbur (left) and *Grey Thistle*, from the series *Blossfeldt's Apprentice*, 2016

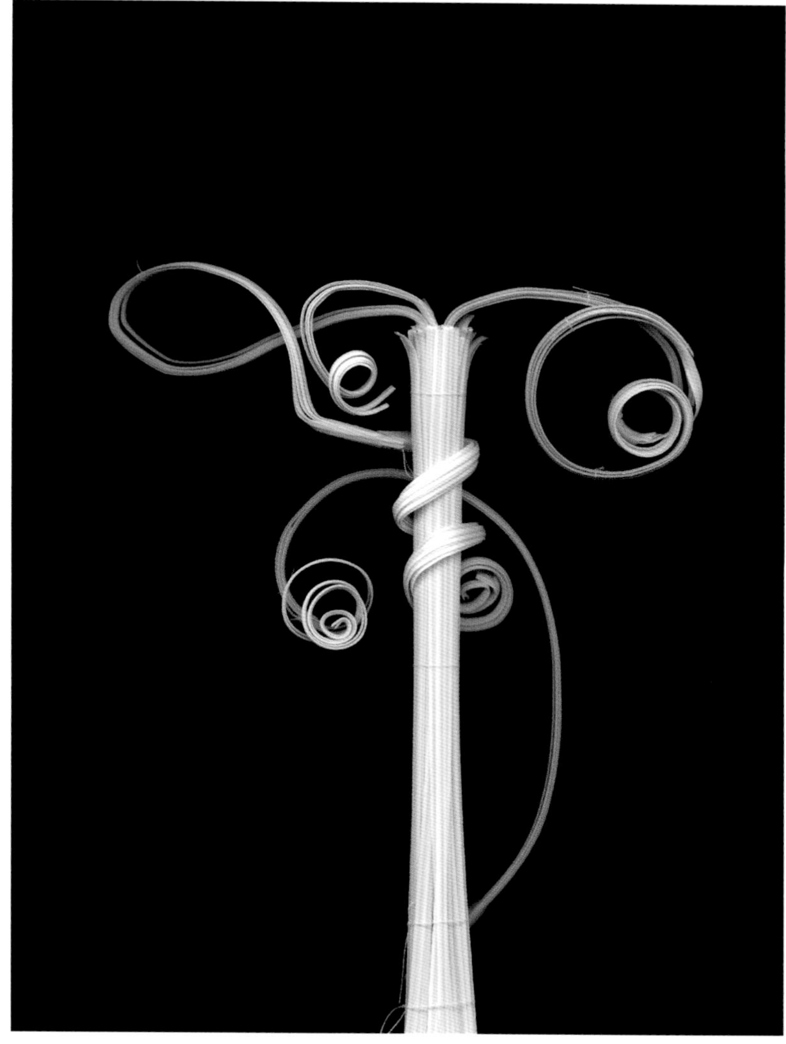

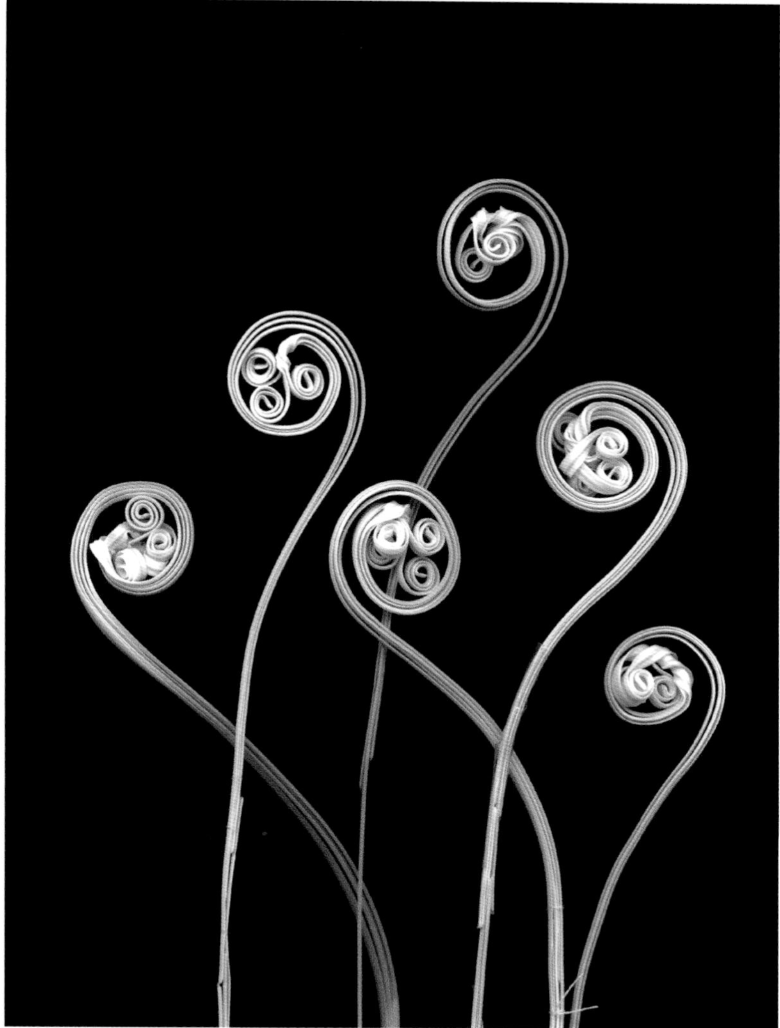

ELAINE DUIGENAN
Pumpkin Tendrils (left) and *Maidenhair Fern*, from the series *Blossfeldt's Apprentice*, 2016

FORMS UNAGEING

We read earlier the argument against *artificial flowers, which finds its echo from many directions, among them the early twentieth-century poet Wallace Stevens. 'Death is the mother of beauty,' he wrote, a sentiment that encouraged an anonymous writer to add, 'Only the perishable can be beautiful, which is why we are unmoved by artificial flowers.'* [5] *The computer scientist David Parnas used faux flowers in an analogy to disparage the concept of artificial intelligence, which, he believed, 'has the same relation to intelligence as artificial flowers to flowers'.* [6] *In other words, the gap between nature and artifice is simply too wide ever to be bridged. But others could mount vigorous defences of artifice, and for one of them we turn to the hymn-like words of the distinguished Greek poet Constantine P. Cavafy: 'Give me artificial flowers – porcelain and metal glories – neither fading nor decaying, forms unageing.'* [7] *Living forever: isn't that the eternal human dream?*

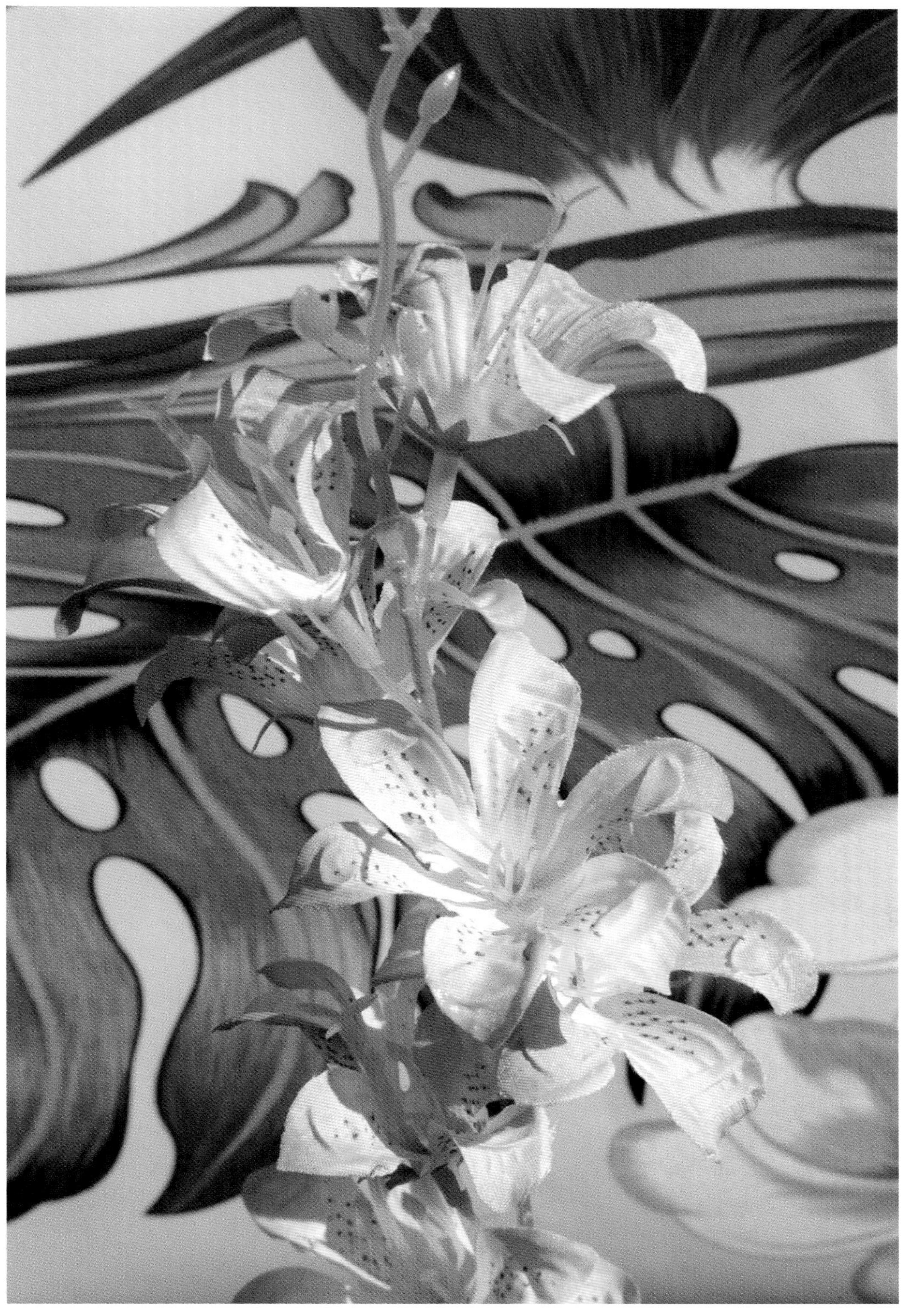

ROBERT WALKER
Flora plastica #01, 2020

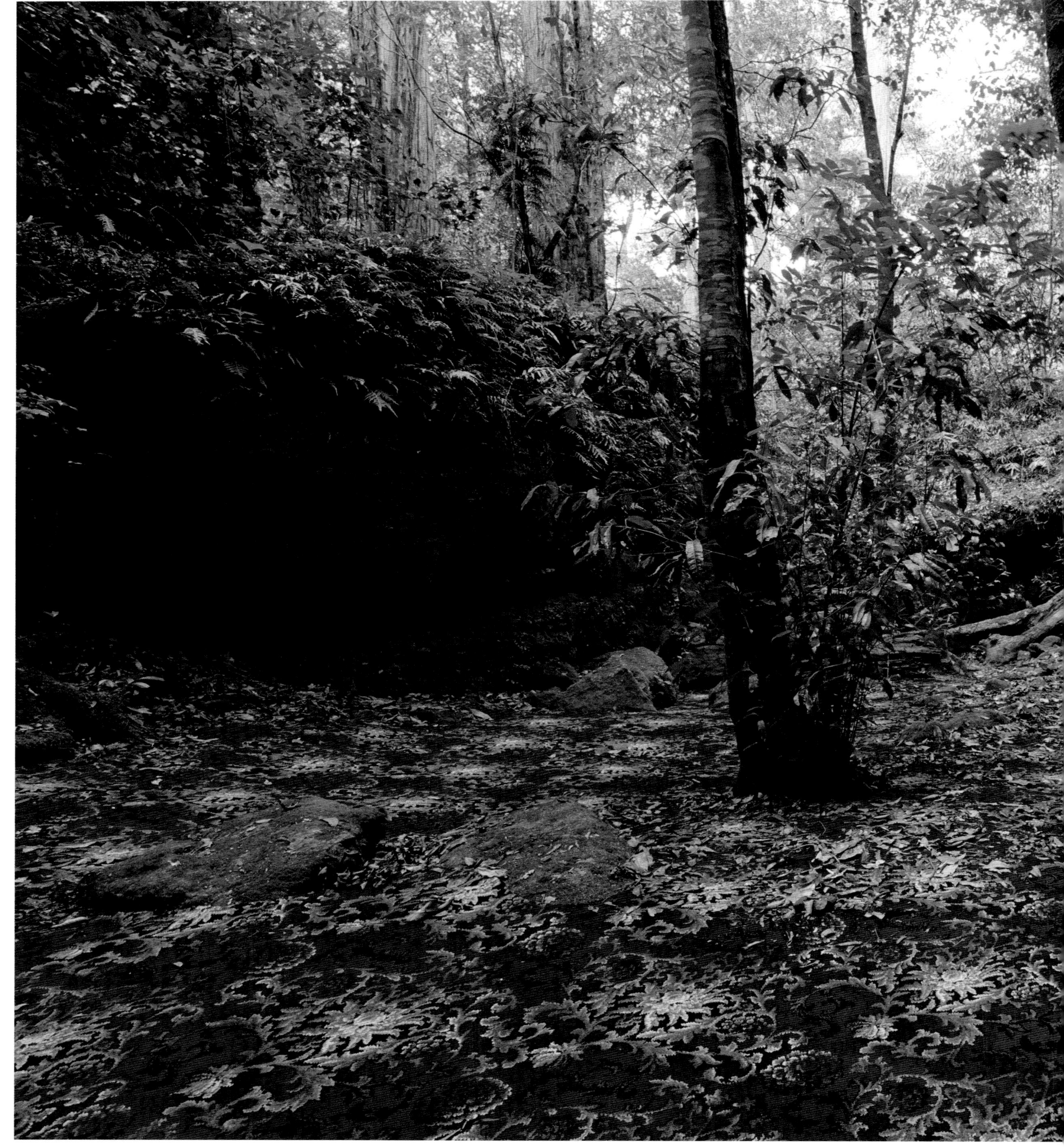

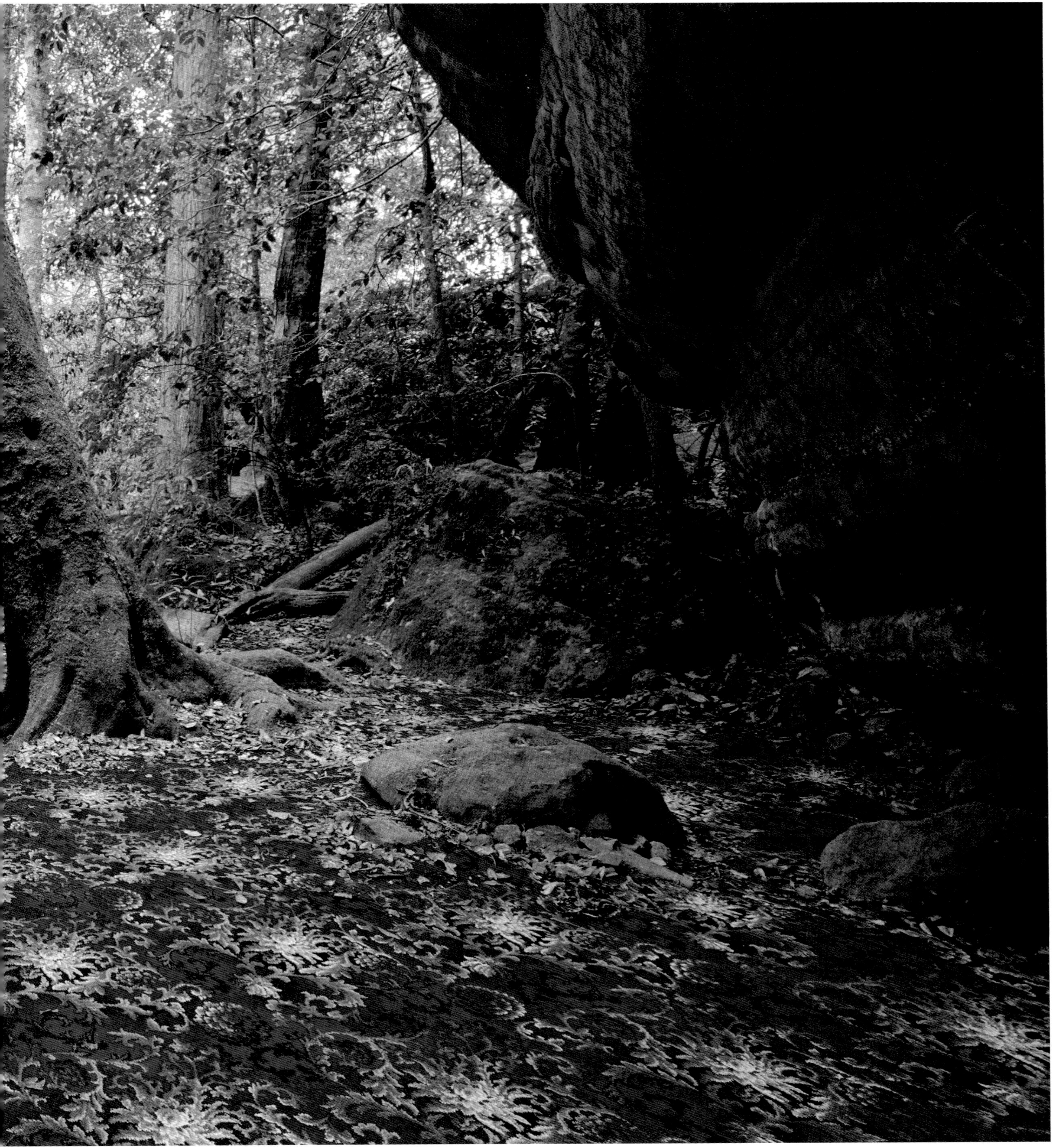

ROSEMARY LAING
groundspeed (Red Piazza) #2, from the series *groundspeed*, 2001

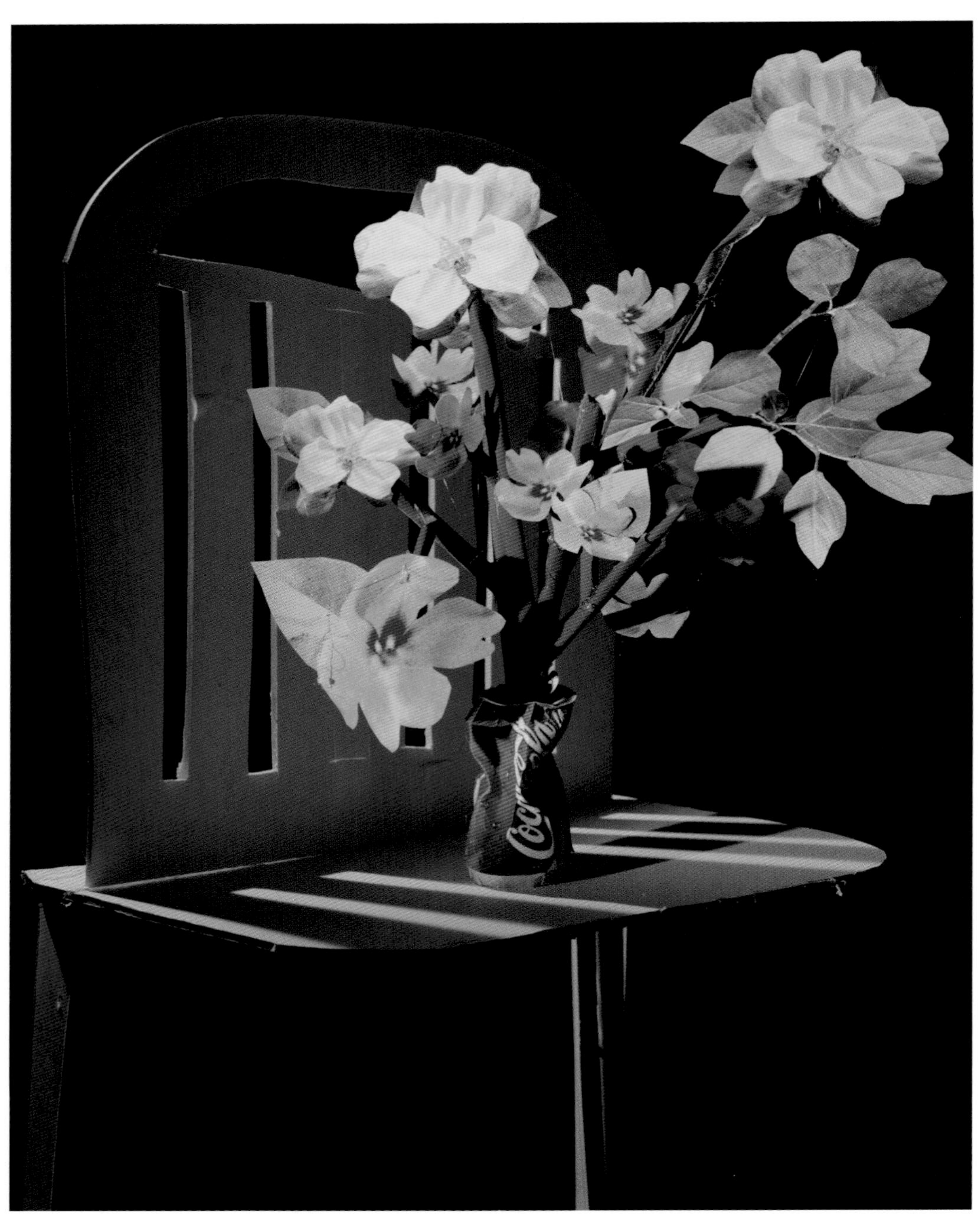

DANIEL GORDON
Apple Blossom, 2008

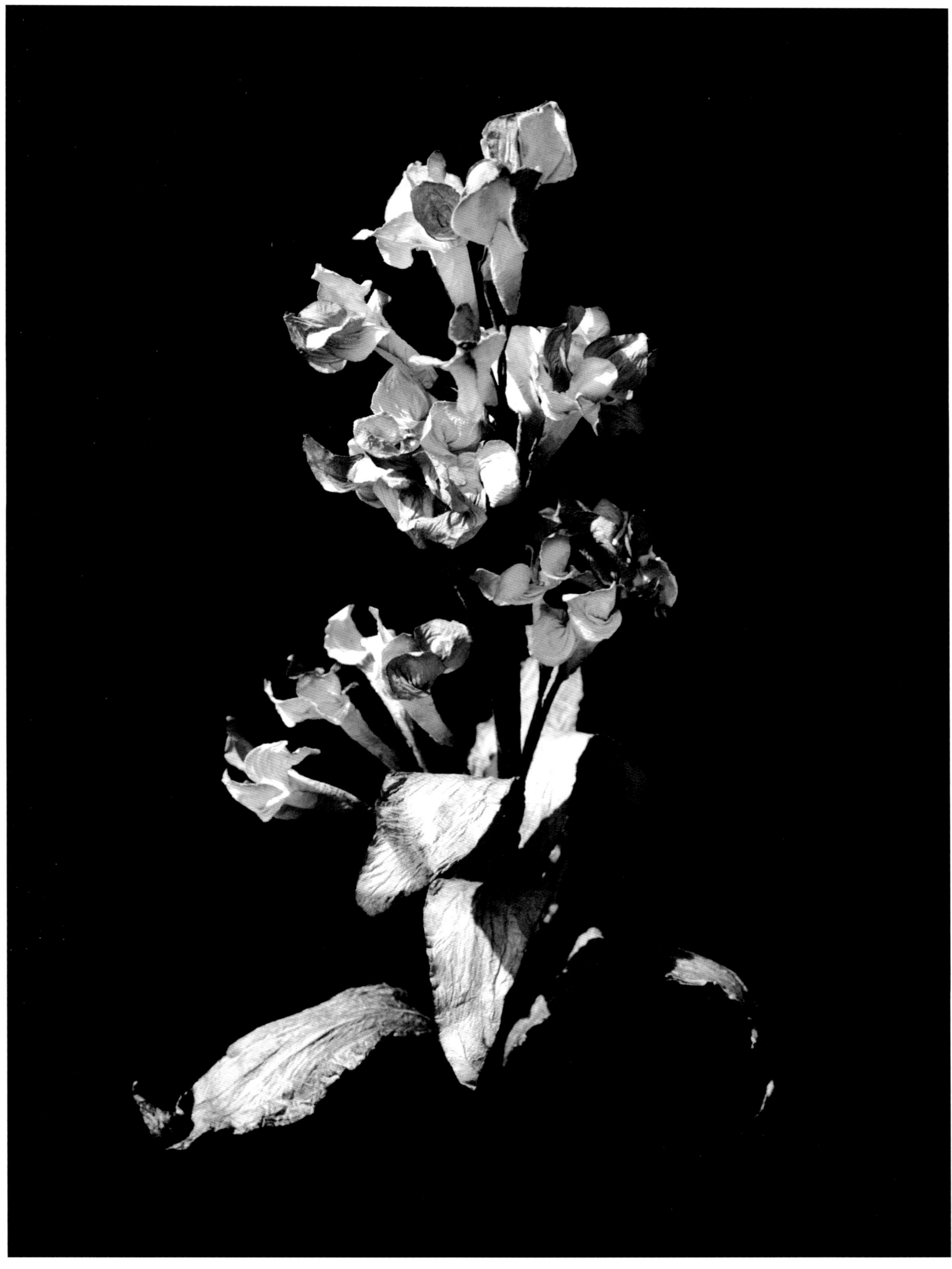

VIK MUNIZ
Cheiranthus cheiri (Wallflower), from the series *Flora Industrialis*, 1998

FLEURS DE FANTAISIE

Fake, faux, artificial… These are words that discomfit those many people who prefer the messy, ephemeral reality of living flowers to the more secure (if illusory) stability of the human, or machine-fabricated, variety. Some 250 years ago the master of decorative art Jean-Baptiste Pillement of Lyon felt free to invent flowers, which were then sewn into silk fabrics. He called them fleurs de fantaisie. *A century or so later Odilon Redon would feel that same urge, inventing vibrant flowers in watercolour, about which Alain-Fournier could write, 'they are all there, like a hundred suns.'*

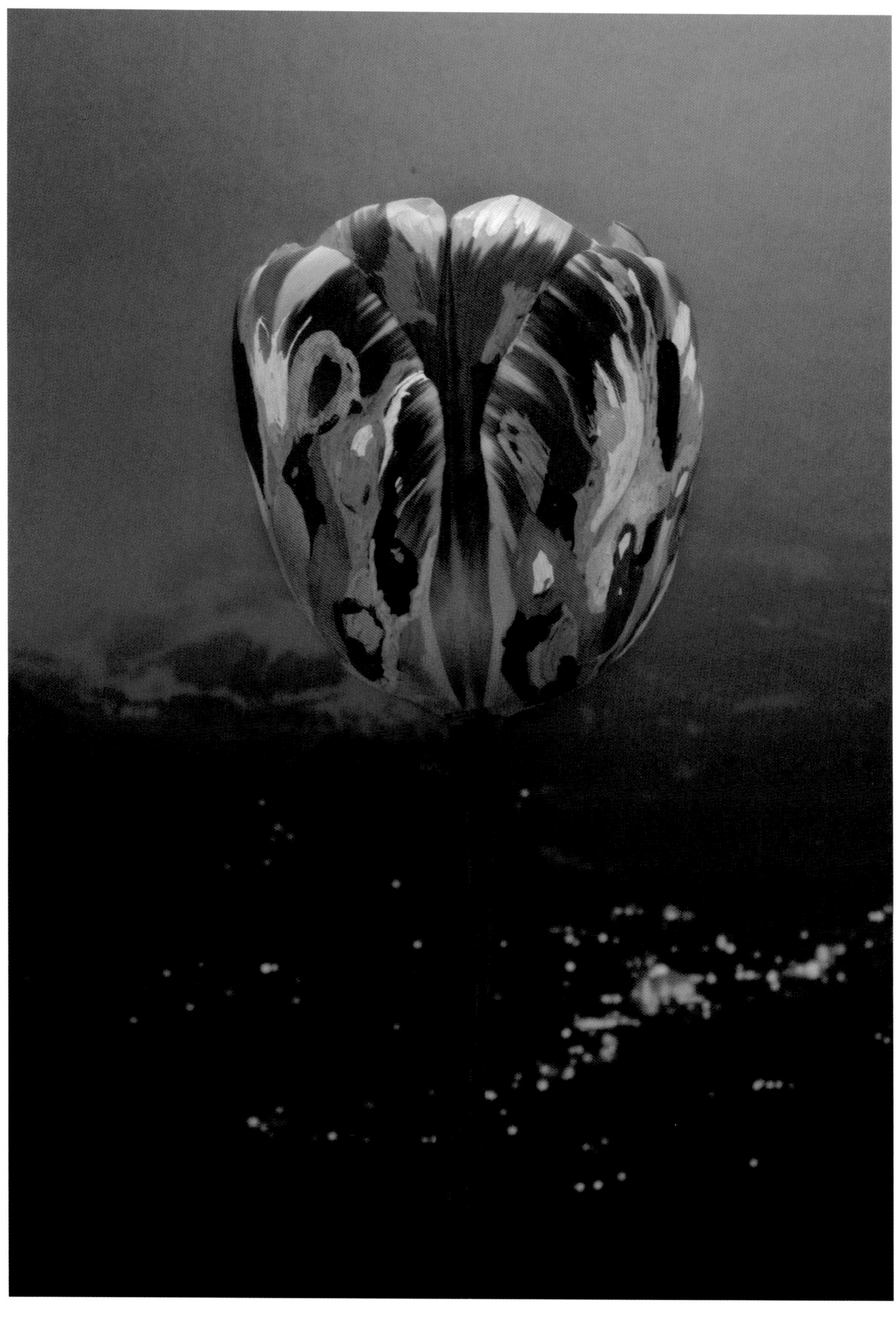

ELSPETH DIEDERIX
Tulipa, 2015

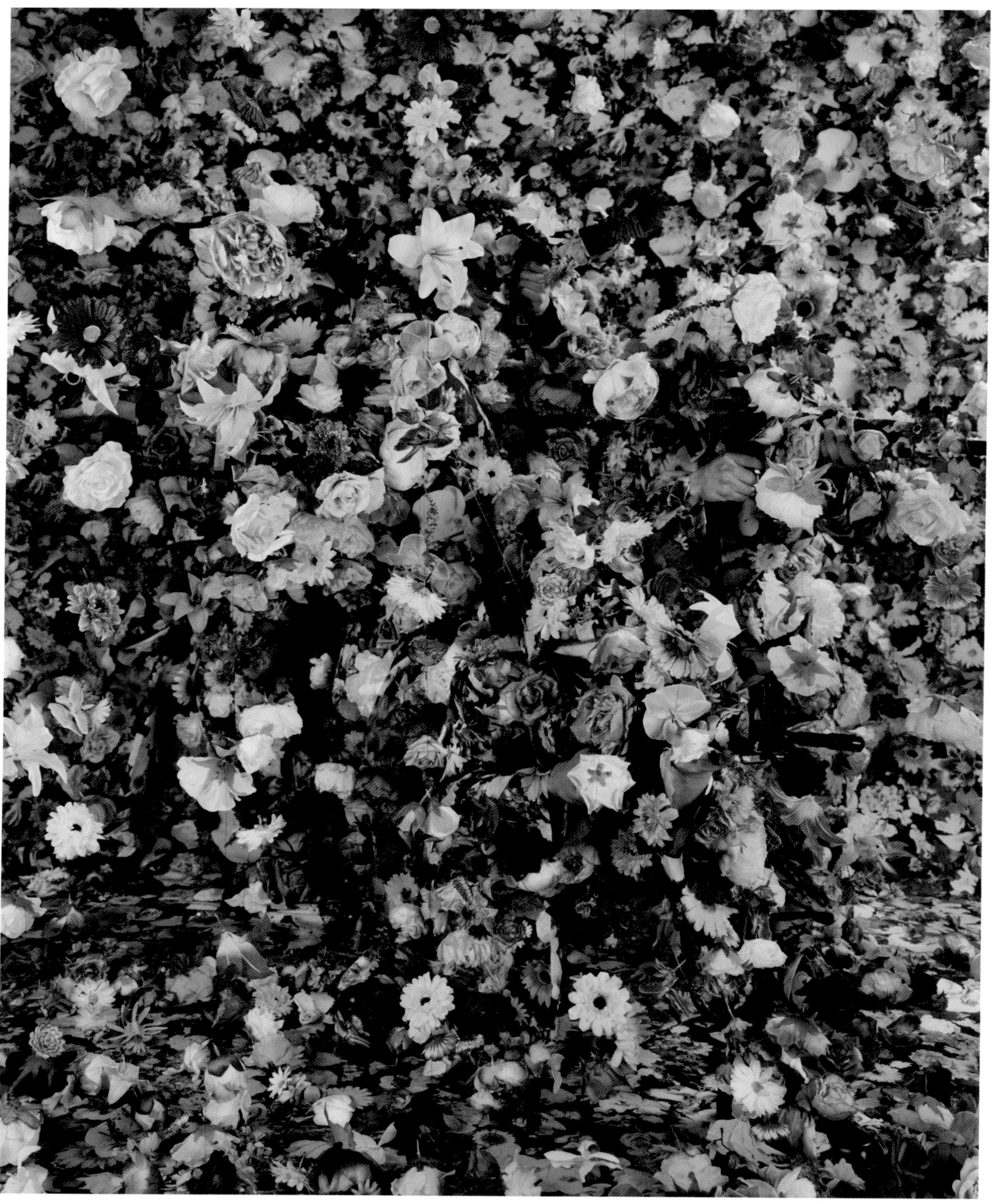

YONGBAEK LEE
Angel-Soldier No. 5, 2011

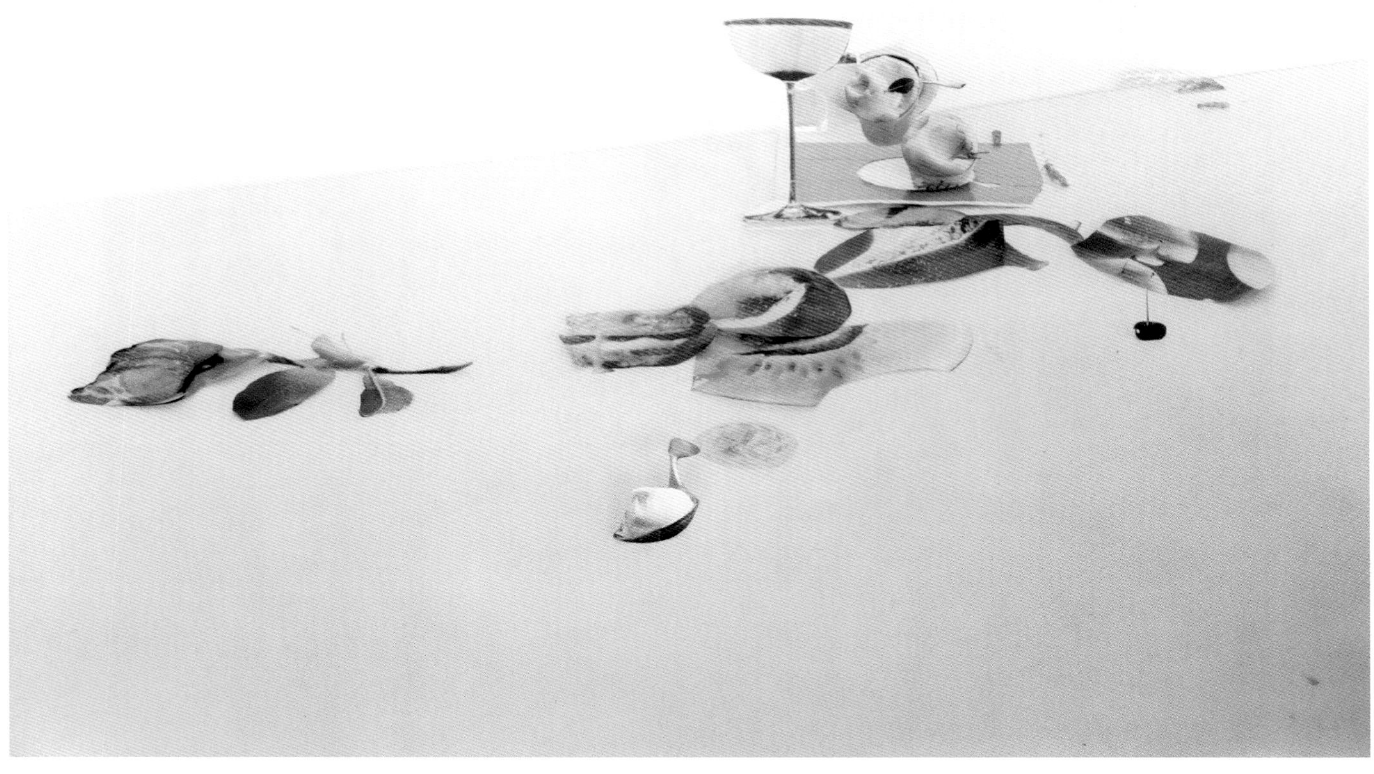

LAURA LETINSKY
Untitled 8, from the series *III Form and Void Full*, 2010

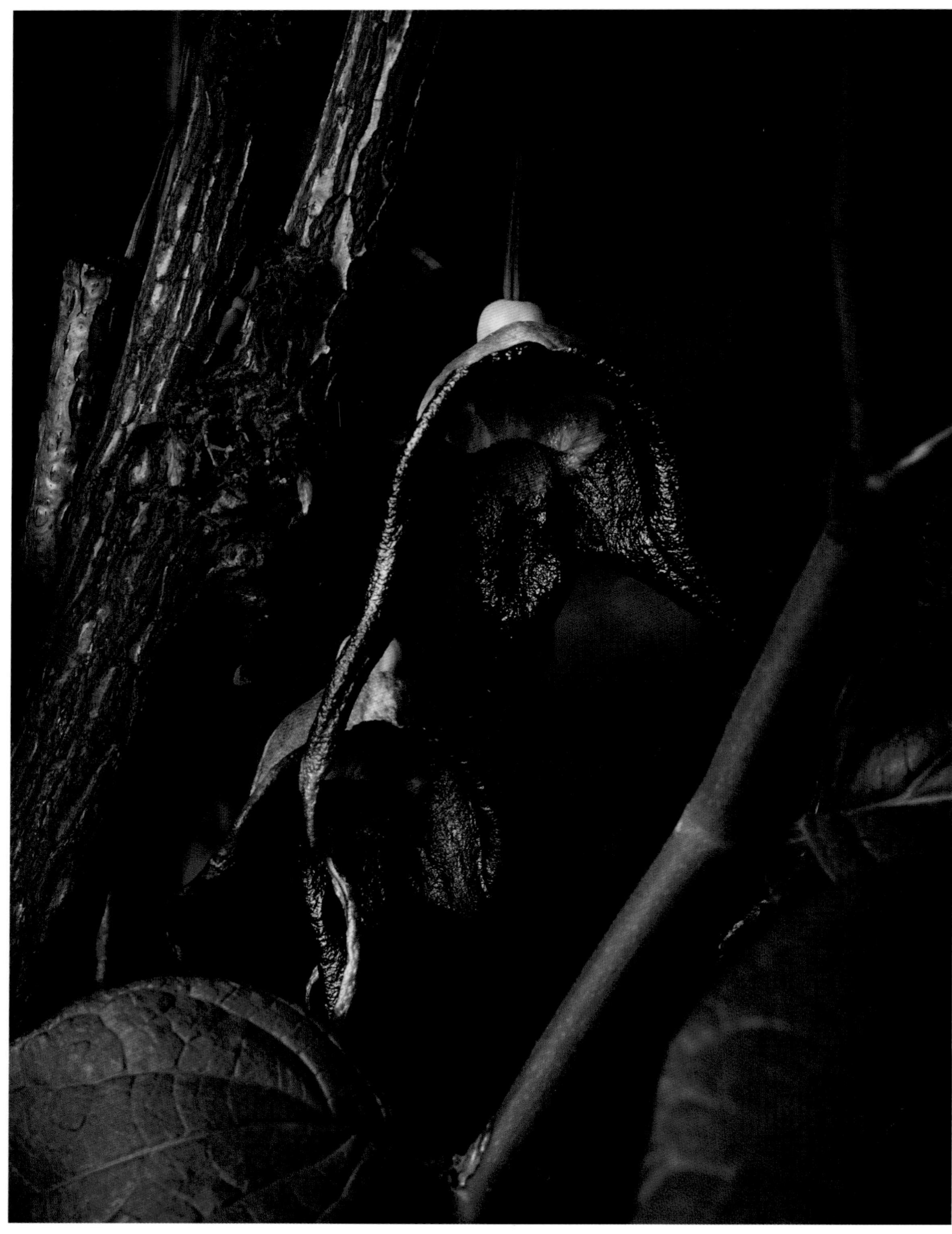

MARCEL RICKLI
Atomic Flower II, from the series *AEON*, 2019
Influenced by the first successful genetic modification of crops in the early 1980s, the Polish philosopher and science-fiction author Stanisław Lem proposed breeding an 'atomic flower' that would bloom only if radioactivity were to escape from a repository.

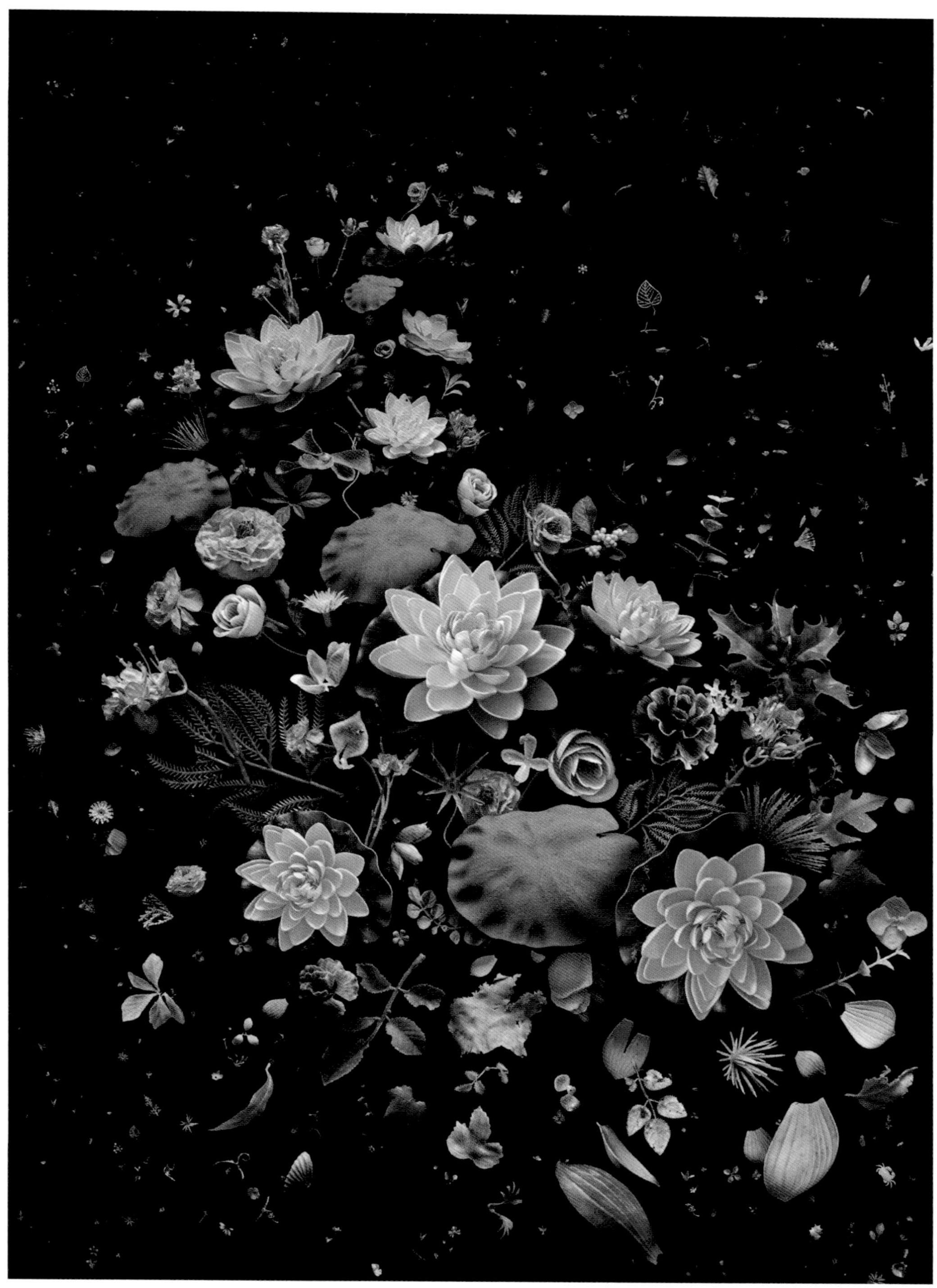

MANDY BARKER
Hong Kong Soup: 1826 – Lotus Garden, 2014
A collection of different species of discarded artificial flowers that would not exist at the same flowering time in nature, and should not be found in the ocean. The flowers were recovered from various beaches in Hong Kong over three years. (Image includes lotus flowers, leaves and petals, peony, carnation, rose, blossom, holly, ferns, castor-oil plant and ivy leaves.)

IN FULL BLOOM

THE FLOWER IN CONTEMPORARY PHOTOGRAPHY

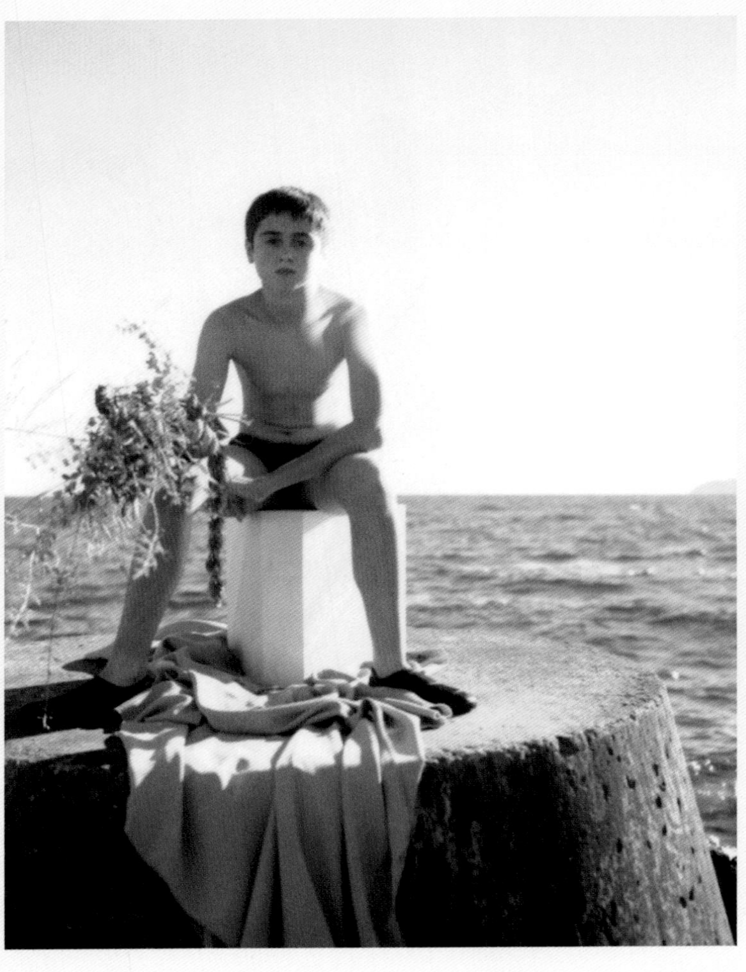

CAMILLE VIVIER
Toulon, été 2015, 2015

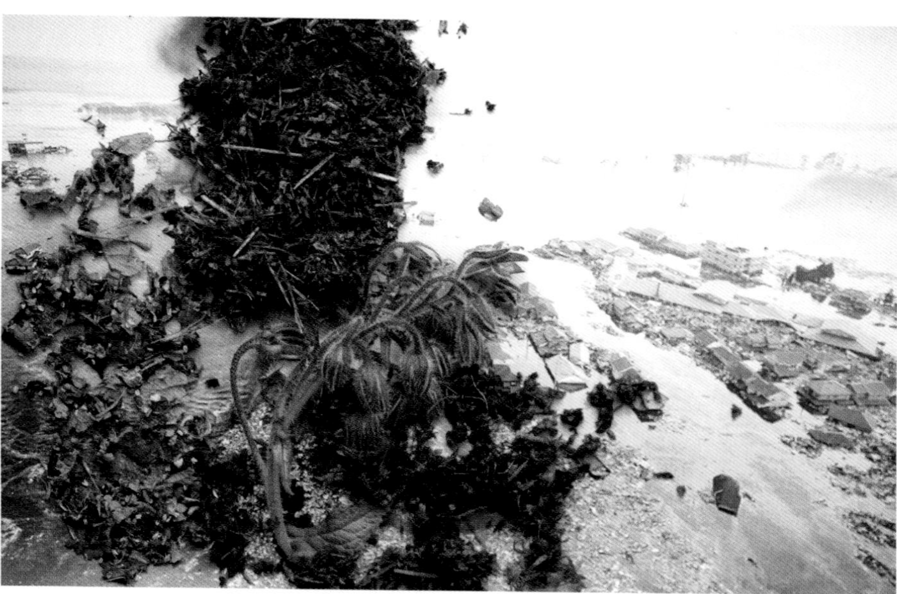

LAURENCE AËGERTER
Cannabis sativa *i.a.* – *Coastal Japan*, from the series *Healing Plants for Hurt Landscapes*, 2015

Shaped by nature over millions of years to lure insects into their folds, flowers exercise a similar fascination over humans, who have appropriated them as symbolic goods for millennia, employing them for embellishment and as spiritual offerings to the gods, as well as medicine or dyes, for example. Then and now, as common gifts and home decorations, they embody the attention paid to a host, a love interest or an ailing relative, and instantiate one's good taste, culture or wealth–or all three, as exemplified by the fashion designer Halston's alleged six-figure annual orchid budget, to name just one legendary floral aficionado.[1] It is thus unsurprising that they abound in art history, in particular across the periods and genres where artworks fulfilled similar–if on average much more expensive–decorative and social functions.

In his essay, my co-author, William A. Ewing, has sketched a history of what Jack Goody has called 'the culture of flowers', setting the stage for the recent arrival, relatively speaking, of photography. On the canvas, painted flowers have conveyed a broad range of meanings, from the straightforward representations of nature to complex symbols, such as the Christian allegories of the red rose (standing for the shedding of Christ's blood).[3] From the seventeenth century onwards, despite its innocuous appearance, the flora depicted in European still lifes could also hint subtly at world domination, with artworks bringing together rare and exotic goods from various parts of the world in the midst of conquest at the hands of Western nations.[4] For the artists themselves, not always personally concerned with such endeavours, arranging stems for a 'flower piece' or a still life, before painting them in exquisite detail, amounted to a showcase of their skill that could bring spectacular success, in terms equally of fame and of wealth. No one exemplifies this better than the Dutch painter Rachel Ruysch (1664–1750), whose distinctive and exceptionally realistic still lifes commanded prices 'high enough that she only had to paint a few pictures per year', and made her internationally and durably famous.[5]

When photography was invented in the middle of the nineteenth century, the flower had been a complex and ubiquitous artistic motif for more than two millennia. In the early days of the medium, when it came to flowers, the photographic image was impeded by both an inability to satisfactorily represent the colours and individual details of a specimen, and the absence of an existing visual language to propose new representations not indebted to the conventions of painting or engraving. Nonetheless, photographers rose to the challenge and set out to master this subject, developing new styles and approaches to do so. Some beginnings were indeed humble and are today intriguing footnotes in the medium's history (pp. 8 and 9). Other early attempts, however, such as the first photography book, *Photographs of British Algae: Cyanotype Impressions* (1843) by the English botanist and photographer Anna Atkins, retain a major influence today. While she intended primarily to produce botanical illustrations, and understood early the potential of photography in this matter, her impact went well beyond that field. To cite only one contemporary example of a successful interpretation of this seminal work, her blue cyanotype photograms directly inspired the ongoing body of work *Virtual Botany Cyanotypes (2016 - present)* by Alan Butler, a series of cyanotypes of the plants populating video games.

While Atkins's work was rooted in scientific research, much in the depiction of flowers at this time can be understood as an impossible–and thus irresistible–exercise in style. If photography, with all its presupposed shortcomings, could successfully propose original and breathtaking takes on the topic, wouldn't it be the decisive confirmation of its relevance and singularity as one of the visual arts? Although it was never, as far as we know, stated in these terms, it could be argued that we can approach it as a marker of photography coming of age. In some of its most successful early iterations, the flower was approached not as a symbol or botanical study, but as a challenge to prove the virtuosity of the photographer

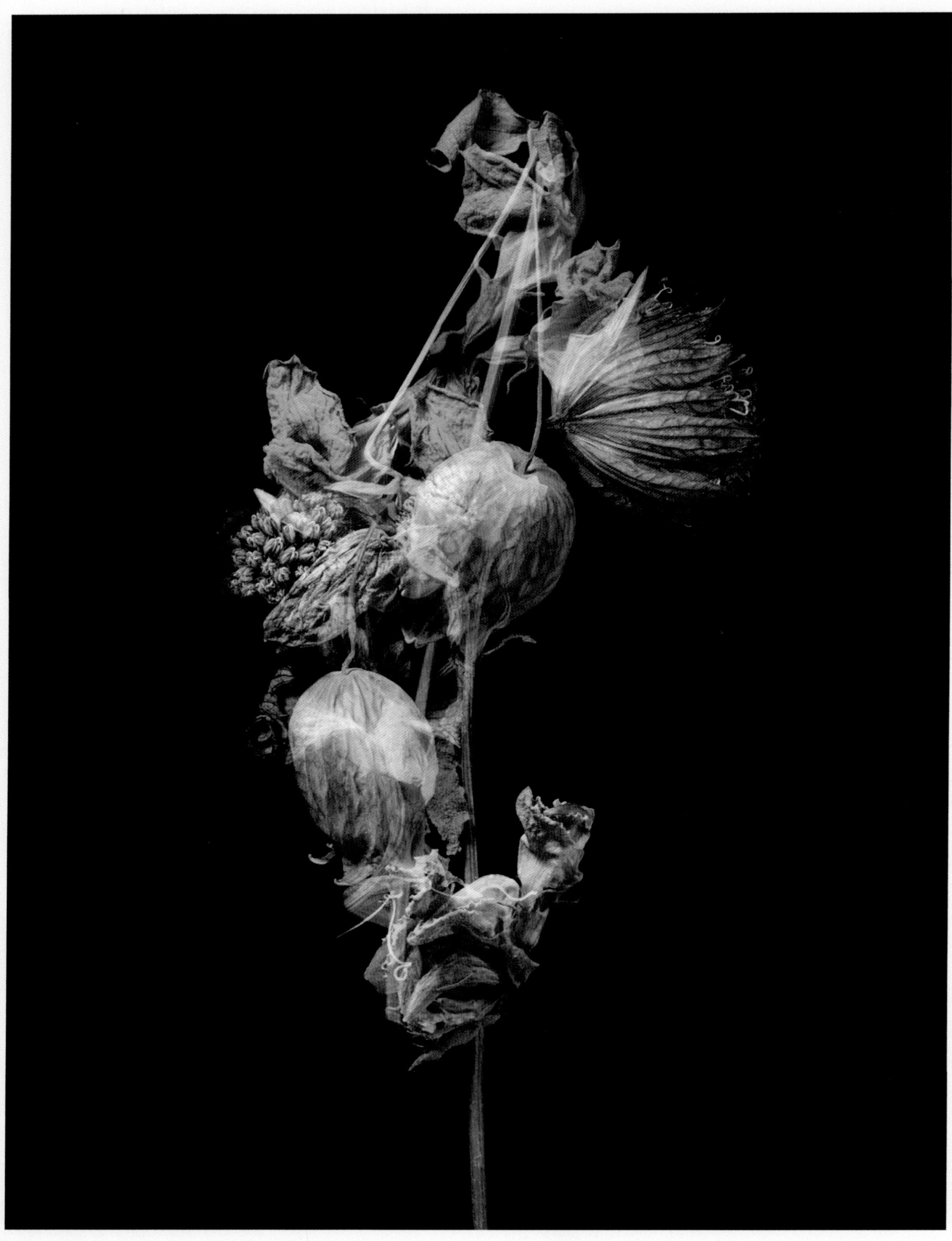

OLGA CAFIERO
Promenade 2, from the series *Flora Neocomensis*, 2019

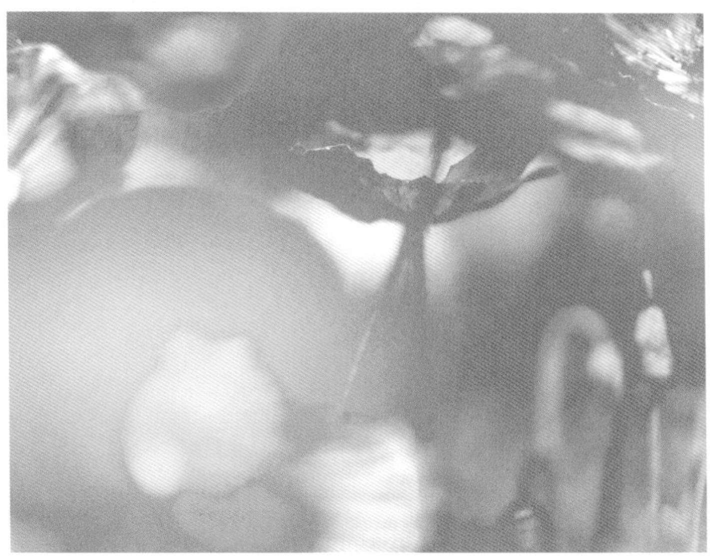

MATTHIEU GAFSOU
Sans titre, from the series *Vivants*, 2019

and the potential of the medium, their capability of creating masterpieces – not unlike the still-life masters of the seventeenth and eighteenth centuries. With pioneers such as the German photographer Karl Blossfeldt (1865-1932), equally renowned at the end of his life as he is now for his stunning, rigorous close-ups of plants emphasizing their sculptural structures, photography gradually established itself as a force to be reckoned with in the artistic and scientific representation of flora. The young medium did struggle to be admitted as one of the major arts for well over a century, and botany remains to this day reluctant to accept it. Nonetheless, from the nineteenth century onwards, photography produced landmark images that have durably shaped Western visual culture.

To this day, photographers continue to expand the rich history of the motif and its allegories. Transitoriness and the ineluctability of decay – which we can observe in the paintings of Ruysch, with their gently withering blooms about to succumb to the pull of gravity – still fascinate countless contemporary artists, such as Gary Schneider (p. 186), Amin El Dib (p. 132, 242), Roberto Greco (p. 150) and Brigitte Lustenberger (p. 35), who skilfully reinvent them to propose compelling new images.

In the visual arts, flowers are expected to be symbols, though often of fluid and ambiguous signification. We understand a white bloom as a symbol of innocence or purity, or, at the other end of the spectrum, an orchid or anthurium as a metaphor for sex. Floriography, as the 'language of flowers' is known, describes the use of flowers and arrangements as coded messages. It has existed since biblical times. However, with hardly any fixed meaning and with common plants being associated with several, sometimes conflicting significations, it has never stabilized into more than a handful of conventional interpretations.

Nonetheless, the very notion that flowers have symbolic meanings and are able to express precise sentiments endures, and remains central to the work of many contemporary artists. For instance, Paul Harfleet collects pictures of the pansies he plants at the sites of homophobic aggression (pp. 86–87). The flower, chosen for its homonymy with a homophobic slur, acts here as a temporary memorial. Similarly, many symbolic depictions of flowers in art are based on anthropomorphism: the plant is invested with concepts and sentiments relevant only to the human condition. The flower is also frequently associated with the human body. The phallic forms of anthuriums, the alluring cavities of orchids, the delicate, easily bruised, skin-like texture of petals, the evocative dewy secretions: these parallels have been explored in images of intoxicating erotic tension.

An overabundance of symbolic expectations with few fixed conventions contributes to making the flower a relevant and constantly renewed motif in contemporary photography. Most remarkably, artists often elude the expected conventions of the genre: the mastery of the photographic technique accompanied by an allegorical meaning indebted to the historical tropes of the flower. For instance, Elaine Duigenan's floral series explore, with a feminist perspective, themes such as fecundity, reproduction, gender and sexuality, ageing and decay in a singular and original visual language (p. 151). She, among many others, demonstrates the ability of photographers to assimilate centuries of floral depiction while still proposing new interpretations, in no small part because they relate to the contemporary world, its condition and values.

In contrast, Laura Letinsky's still lifes, for instance, attest to the infinite possibilities of successfully reinterpreting a particular genre with a contemporary twist (pp. 19 and 173). Her work is even more outstanding when we consider that her images are made with a scarcity of material, and myriad shades of white. Similarly, Victoria Zschommler creates stunning images with minimal elements: a few flowers, a plastic bag and sunlight. Others consider the flower arrangement an opportunity to push the boundaries of the medium itself, often appropriating what had been considered unsightly mistakes. Countering the extreme control offered by the environment of the studio with its professional cameras and lighting, Olga Cafiero (left) does blind multiple exposures of single stems. She names the morphing shapes that emerge *Promenades*, since

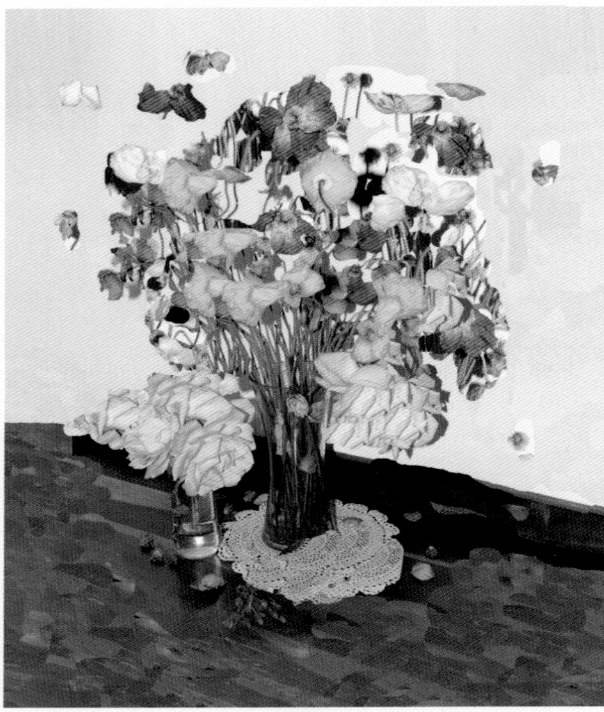

NICO KRIJNO
Flowers From My Brother, 2016

they offer the eye new wanderings in the shapes and compositions obtained with this process. Nico Krijno (p.180) uses tools designed to erase details and flaws in a photograph 'wrongly' in order to create pictures with singular texture and pattern. These 'mistakes' generate a new and intriguing visual language. Paul Rousteau uses exaggerated visual aberrations and distortions–the likes of which engineers have taken great pains to correct and reduce over the centuries in the lenses of cameras and the chemical layers of film–to create dreamlike enchanted worlds (p. 240). All these strategies allow new and engaging representations, entirely refuting the tired notion that 'everything has been done before.'

We can thus liken the flower to a relatively blank page, poised to be imprinted with allegories and metaphors related to human emotions and bodies. Many contemporary photographers harness this potential to explore political issues where the flower can act as a symbol or has direct political implications. This might reflect a political turn that we observe in contemporary photography over the last decades, as the old art/documentary binary roughly separating the lens-based practices into two groups gave way to more intricate approaches to the photographic image, blurring these artificial divides.

Examples of political flowers abound in this book, even if the blooms in their images do not, immediately, reveal their nature. The image that opens this publication, by the Polish photojournalist Jędrzej Nowicki, appears at first glance to be an innocent picture. In reality, it was taken during the protests in Belarus in 2020, which were violently repressed by the government. The flower is not serendipitous: white and red flower bouquets and ribbons are symbols worn in protest against the regime of Alexander Lukashenko, in particular by women. These are the colours of the opposition, and the regime perceives them as enough of a threat that carrying any item in these colours at some point became a cause for arrest, detention and potentially extreme violence at the hand of the authorities. The white flower bouquet and ribbon are here a defiant sign of political resistance, making this image fraught with tension and danger as we understand its full meaning.

The history of botany is tied to that of world exploration, and thus with conquest and colonization. The ways knowledge was extracted and constructed through expeditions by Western scientists, adventurers or military forces, and how their particular interests, world views and values framed and informed their research, is currently being re-examined and re-evaluated in different fields. Artists too are undertaking critical research in that area, for instance into the medicinal and social uses of plants that have been sidelined and sometimes almost forgotten since the Westernization of medicine across the globe. One such example is Ann Shelton, who since 2015 has been investigating the traditional medicinal use of plants against the background of colonialism and of the marginalization of certain knowledge and practices (pp. 68–69). Her flowers represent the way women (in particular) prepared herbal tonics and tinctures to bring on menstruation, induce abortion, act as contraceptives or increase fertility, among other functions. Beyond documenting and preserving this knowledge–which sometimes involves growing the plants herself–this work engages with the political aspects of women's health and the millennia-long struggle to retain agency over one's own body and reproductivity, notably in colonial and patriarchal contexts.

Roberto Greco's work *Porter sa peau* (Wearing One's Skin) echoes similar concerns in the use of plants as a symbolic act of affirmation of one's identity and culture. In this series, he explores

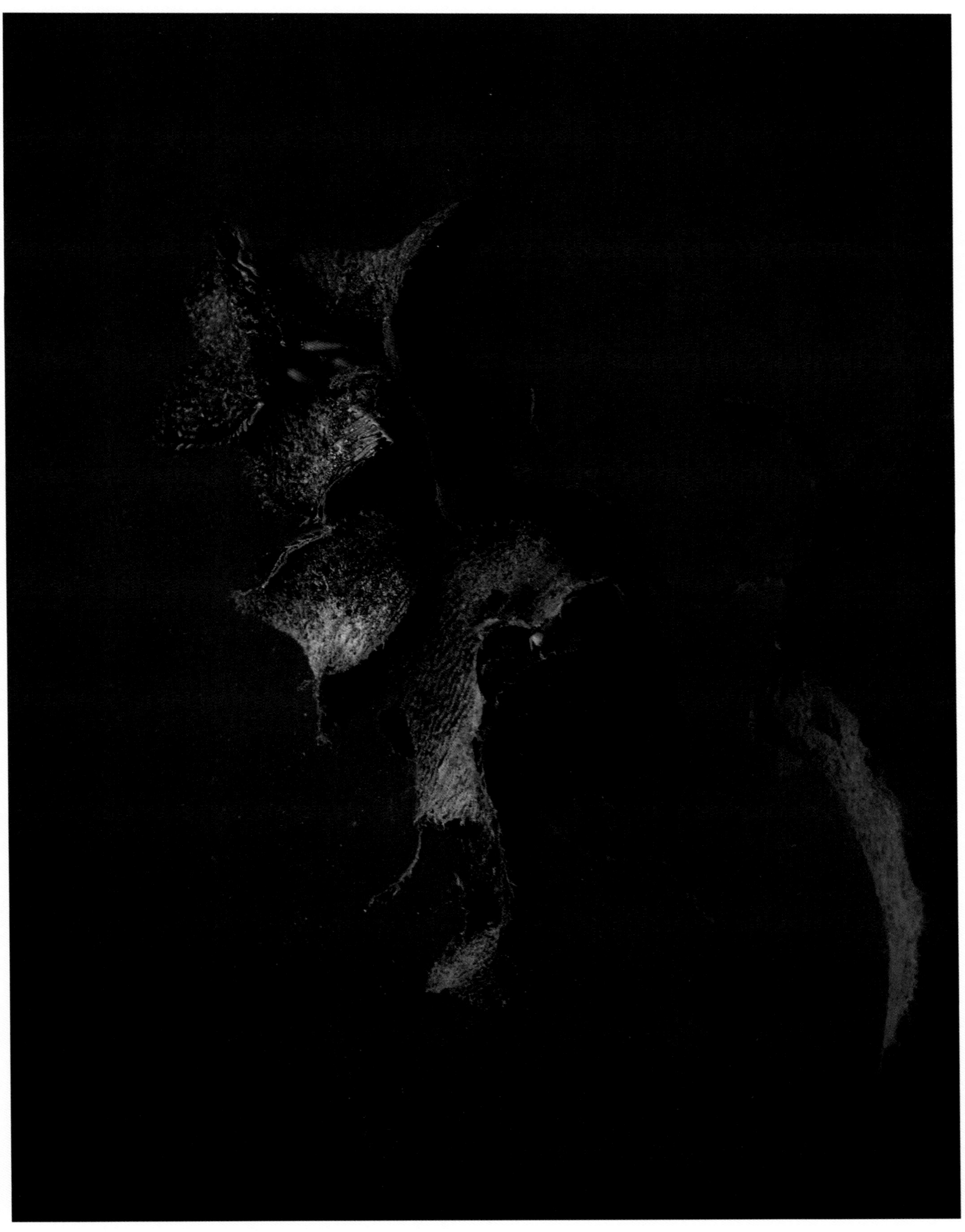

AKOSUA VIKTORIA ADU-SANYAH
Macrocystis pyrifera [Patagonia], from the series *Behold the Ocean*, 2020

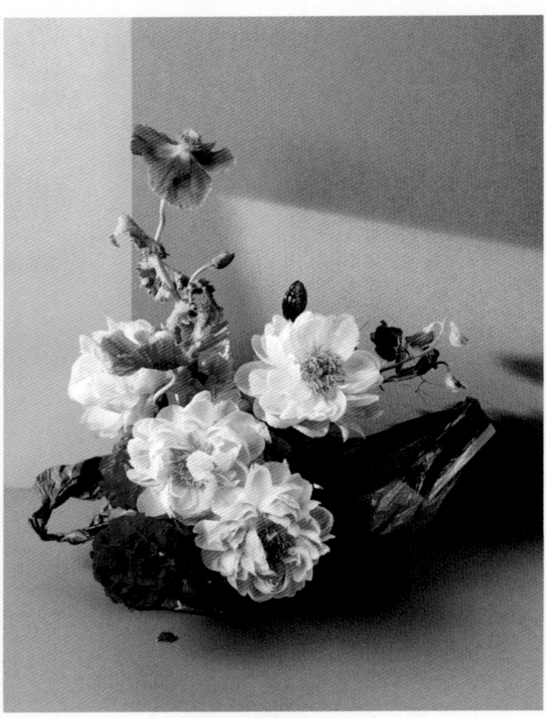

VICTORIA ZSCHOMMLER
At Bloom, 2016 (flower arrangements by Simone Gooch of Fjura)

his origins as an Italian born in Switzerland, and the prejudice surrounding this community. In *Les chiens et les Italiens dehors!* (Dogs and Italians Out!), in a chiaroscuro inspired by seventeenth-century paintings, an edelweiss (the national flower of Switzerland) and a bulb of garlic (associated with Italians and Italian cuisine in Switzerland) become eerily similar (p. 230).

Delving into a purely ornamental use of flowers, Taryn Simon's body of work *Paperwork and the Will of Capital* is nonetheless one of the most political works presented in this book (pp. 82–83). Each arrangement is meticulously composed of flowers identified by a botanist in the photographs documenting the signing of important accords, treaties or international contracts. These events are rigorously staged. They follow protocols designed to normalize these decisions as the rational outcome of deliberate negotiations balancing the interests of all parties. Flowers are a small but significant part of such precise choreography. They participate in the ceremony of power and add to a sense that the signing of these agreements is a cause for celebration.

Other works engage in documentary representations of flowers as an important industry. When we think of flowers as a commodity, what springs to mind is the tulip mania of seventeenth-century Holland. Its fame relies on exaggerated facts and stretched analogies with present-day speculative markets. It did not, indeed, crash the economy or ruin a vast number of people, although it does illustrate the enduring power of sensational reporting.[5] This historical episode is better known than the massive scale – mid-double-digit billions USD – of the global cut-flower industry.[6] It remains relatively uncontroversial considering its significant environmental impact (caused by high water use, intercontinental airfreighting and refrigeration, among other things). Three photographers featured in this book capture important aspects of this industry. Noor Damen's portraits of flower-pickers highlight the manual labour involved (p. 38). Gerco de Ruijter's almost abstract photographs of flower fields hint at the scale of industrial flower production and its impact on the landscape (p. 39). Finally, Henrik Spohler's images of a plant auction in the Netherlands unveil the monetary transactions involved in their trade (p. 12).

The work of Ruben Natal-San Miguel (p.183) is an example of another genre awash with flowers unexpectedly taking centre stage: street photography. One of his most renowned street portraits is *Lady Money Sings the Blues*, an image of a jazz songstress supplementing her income during the day by selling water bottles, photographed on the streets of Harlem, New York. It is part of a vibrant ongoing series capturing with undeniable tenderness the street cultures of that city, paying particular attention to areas and groups that are, for the moment, eluding gentrification. The flower here becomes a symbol of joy and resilience, countering the expression of the model, which hints at a rougher reality.

Other artists successfully combine the political and poetic potential of photography. Laurence Aëgerter's project *Herbarium Cataplasma* (p. 177) involved growing a garden of medicinal plants in Leeuwarden, the Netherlands. Local residents were then invited to partake in a symbolic healing ritual, laying selected plants from the garden over photographs of landscapes that have suffered natural or man-made disasters. Matthieu Gafsou's series *Vivants* (Living, p. 179) also harnesses the poesy and beauty of flower photography. He photographed a dwindling number of prairies with high biodiversity. Almost abstract, full of sensual, saturated colours, plants filling the frame without a horizon, the images invite us to confront ourselves with a gorgeous flora, against the background of their immediate

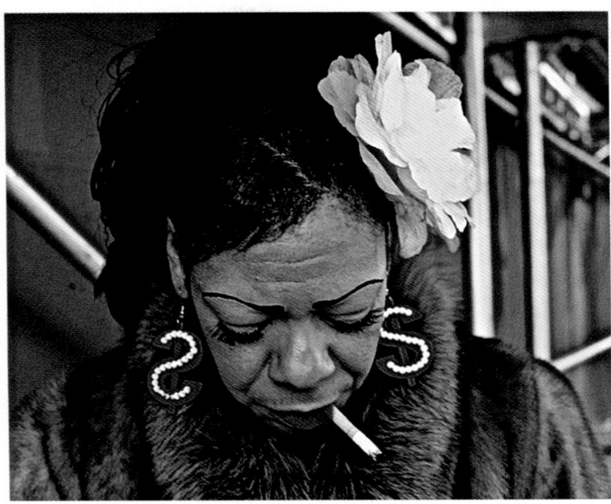

RUBEN NATAL-SAN MIGUEL
Lady Money Sings the Blues, Harlem, NYC, 2011

threat by human activities. These two works are part of a growing body in landscape photography that has shifted its focus from aiming to bring attention to threatened territories to exploring our emotional relationships with the landscapes we have failed to protect and our feelings of guilt, powerlessness, regret and longing.

Mandy Barker, Thirza Schaap, Marcel Rickli and Akosua Viktoria Adu-Sanyah (p. 181) explore similar themes of environmental threat. Barker's work from the last decade focuses on ecological topics, in particular the plastic pollution of the oceans. While her work is not directly documentary, it still aims at prompting action over the danger of marine plastic debris, and often involves collaborations with scientists. In the series *Hong Kong Soup: 1826*, made with objects collected on beaches in Hong Kong, she carefully lays out aesthetically pleasing arrangements of waste objects, encouraging the viewer to question their own use of plastic objects in daily life, and how it contributes to global pollution (p. 175). Similarly, Schaap uses plastic debris to craft beautiful flower arrangements, playing on the initial appeal of the sculpture and the disgust that follows as the viewer understands what they are looking at (p. 160). In a different vein, but equally thought-provoking, is Rickli's series *AEON*, which addresses nuclear energy and the long timeline associated with its waste (p. 174). His work explores how different disciplines – from engineering to semiotics – are facing the crucial but nearly impossible task of communicating the danger of nuclear-waste deposits to generations far removed from us in time. Part of his work documents the practical steps taken today to prevent spillage and danger to current and future human societies as well as flora and fauna, while other segments reflect the more prospective approaches taken by linguists or philosophers. Could the blooming of an 'atomic flower' warn future generations of radioactive danger? Using the very real (and intimidating-looking) Mexican flower *Aristolochia tricaudata* as a placeholder, Rickli invites us to ponder a world where seeing a single bloom would equal catastrophe. For *Behold the Ocean*, a project about vulnerability and contrast in climate research, Adu-Sanyah photographed a giant kelp forest in Patagonia. This seaweed provides habitat for marine species and plays an important part in sequestrating carbon in the ocean. Her image conveys the fragility and unfamiliarity of these ecosystems, despite their importance for life in and above water.

These contemporary works, and many more, engage in multifaceted ways with the pressing issues of our times. Each attests to the capacity of the flower to convey more than a handful of conventional meanings, and to overcome preconceived ideas about its limitations as a motif. Its innocuousness is refuted by the many political works articulated around it. Its undeserved reputation as an 'easy' way of getting a pleasant image is contradicted by the complexity of many works. The weight of art history is shrugged off by its capacity to embody new meanings relating to the contemporary world. The idea of the flower as a 'feminine' topic is undermined by the number of male artists professing their enduring passion for the subject, from Abelardo Morell to Pedro Almodóvar. Meanwhile, female artists are no longer pigeonholed or not taken seriously if they seize on the topic. The alleged fixed symbolic meanings of flowers, peddled by keen Victorian marketers and based on a very narrow range of examples, are consistently being disproved by new, and often unexpected, allegories and symbols. A simple stem opens up an infinite world of possibilities that contemporary photographers eagerly and strikingly take on. The only constant today? Harnessing the flower as a demonstration of skill, of conceptual and visual prowess.

HYBRIDS

Biologically (and botanically) speaking, a hybrid is the offspring of two plants of different species or varieties. More generally, it is something that combines two different elements. 'Is it art? Is it science?', asked the *Smithsonian Magazine* in 2013, addressing the work of Eduardo Kac, who at that moment was identified as 'the most radical figure in the biodesign movement', a champion of 'transgenic art'.[1] Kac had presented his *Edunia*, a petunia that harbours one of Kac's own genes. 'It lives. It is real, as real as you and I. Except nature didn't make it, I did.'[2]

Such an act would not seem overly radical for the photographers who refuse to take flowers at face value but feel the urge to fabricate their own hybrid imagery with whatever means they choose – from classic collage or montage to the subversive use of scanners and printers. While many photographers have as their goal a realistic depiction of a flower, in essence their final print being the closest thing to having the *real* thing in hand, many others have found in floral imagery a springboard for philosophical reflection.

No claims are made for scientific accuracy; it's not the proverbial window on the world they ask us to peer through, but the mirror they hold up, wherein we are faced with uncomfortable facts about the world, or about ourselves. This may mean the aforementioned subversive approach to the traditional still life, either by means of some established form of photomontage or collage, or, more recently, via pyrotechnic effects obtained by imaging edition software. The modern mind harbours suspicions about any claim to what is 'natural' and 'right'. At the dawn of photography, flowers could be described, on the one hand, by the journalist Frederic Shoberl as 'the sweetest of nature's smiles', and on the other, in darker terms by the poet Thomas Haynes Bayly: 'The canker worm is at work within The Fairest of her flowers.'[3]

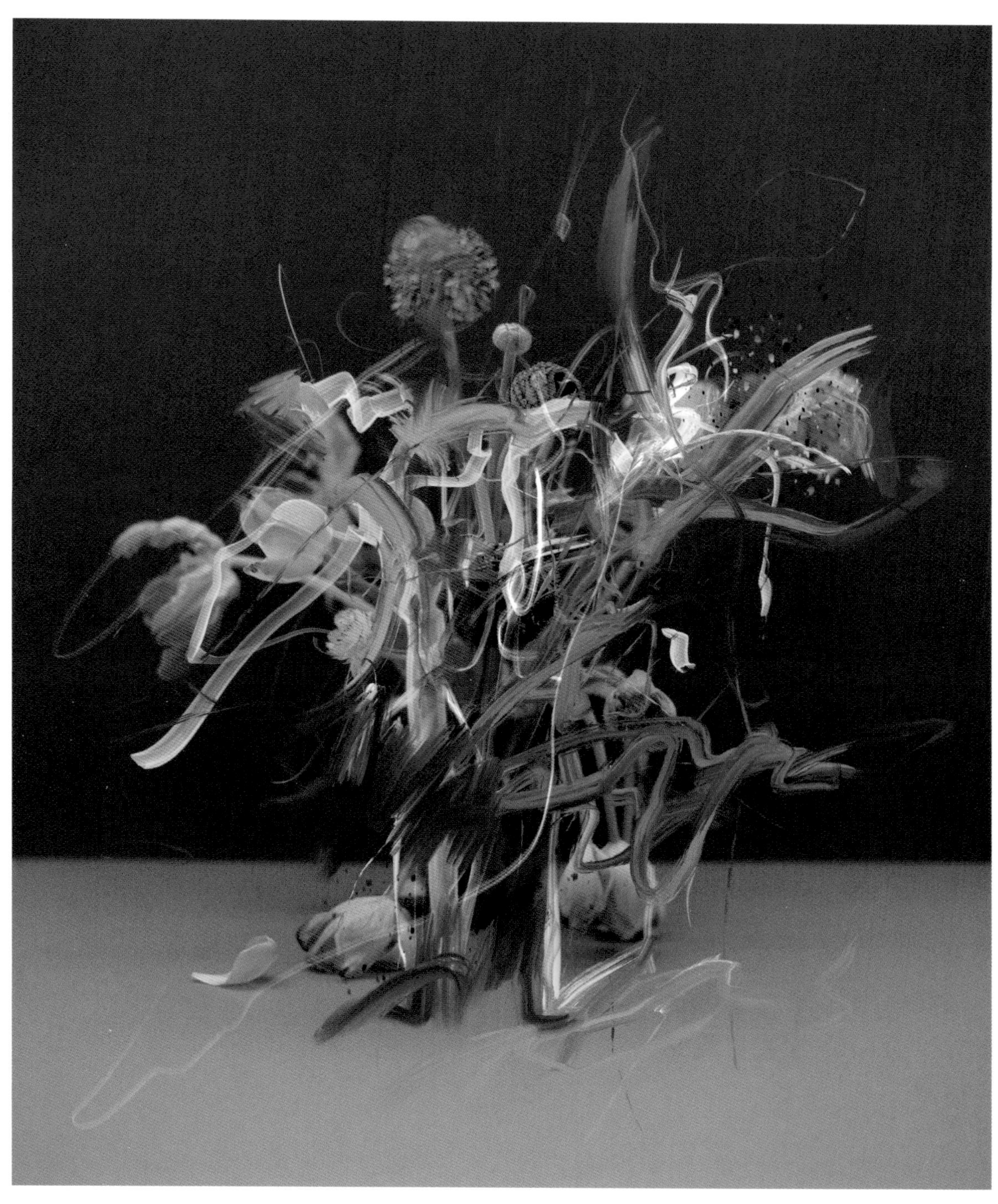

SANDRA KANTANEN
Still Life (Flowers I), 2020

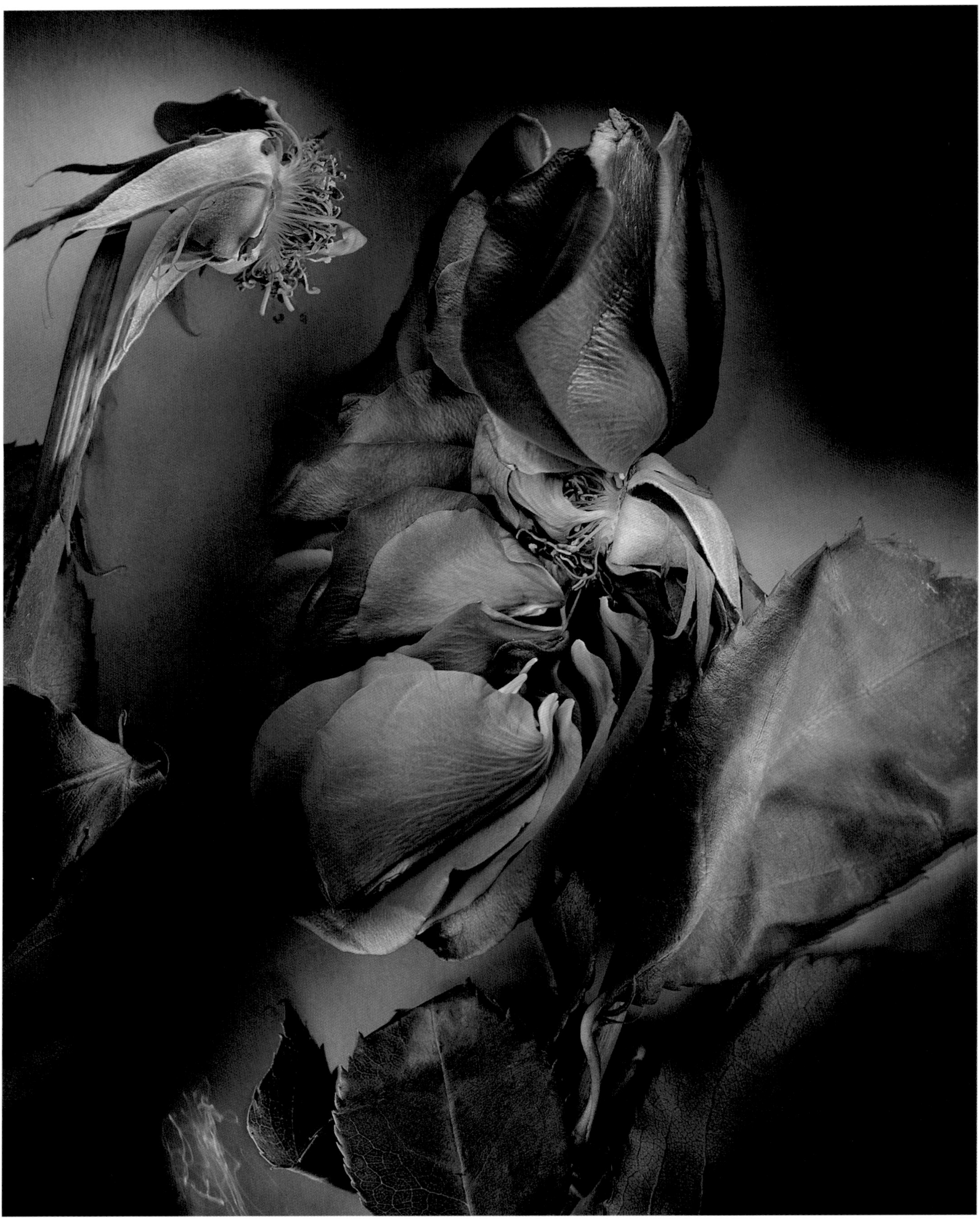

GARY SCHNEIDER
Rose, 1989

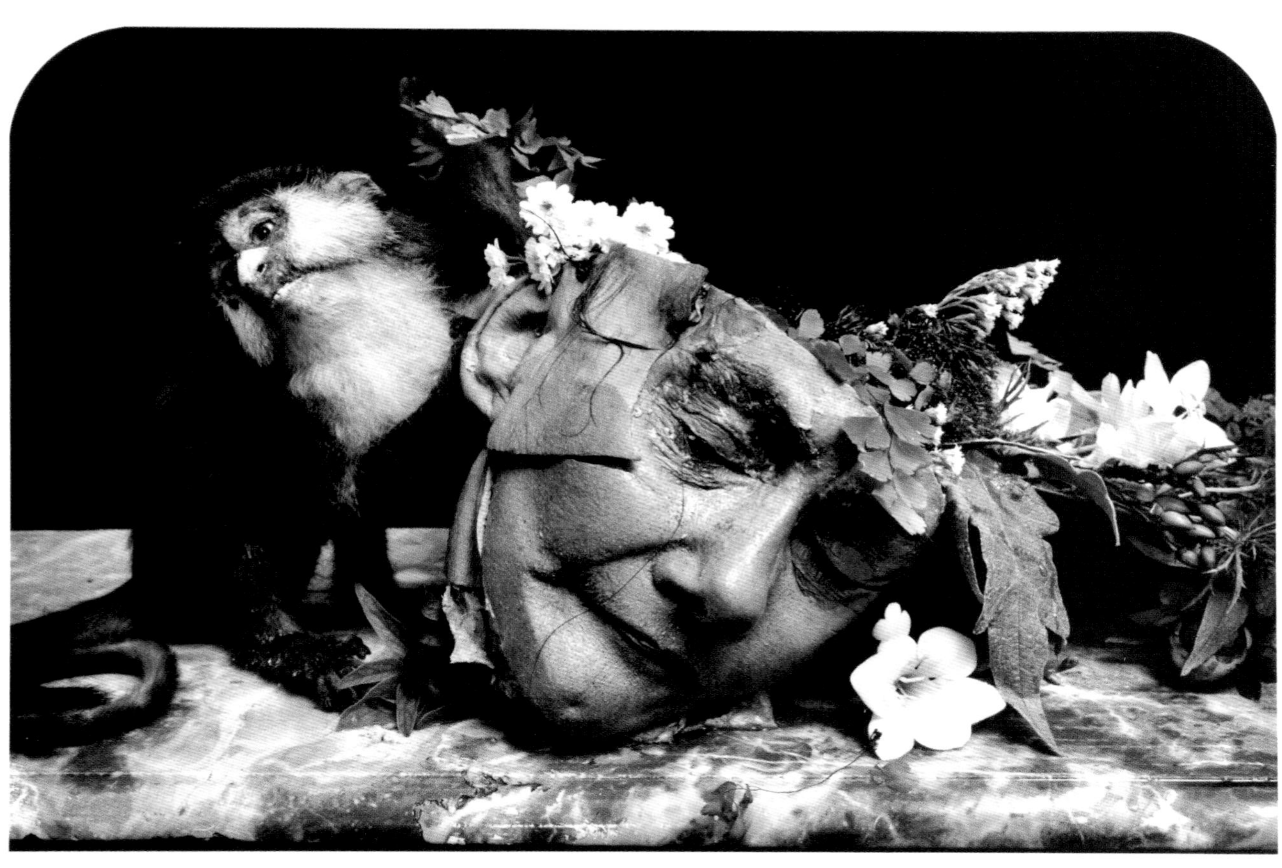

JOEL-PETER WITKIN
Face of a Woman, Paris, 2004

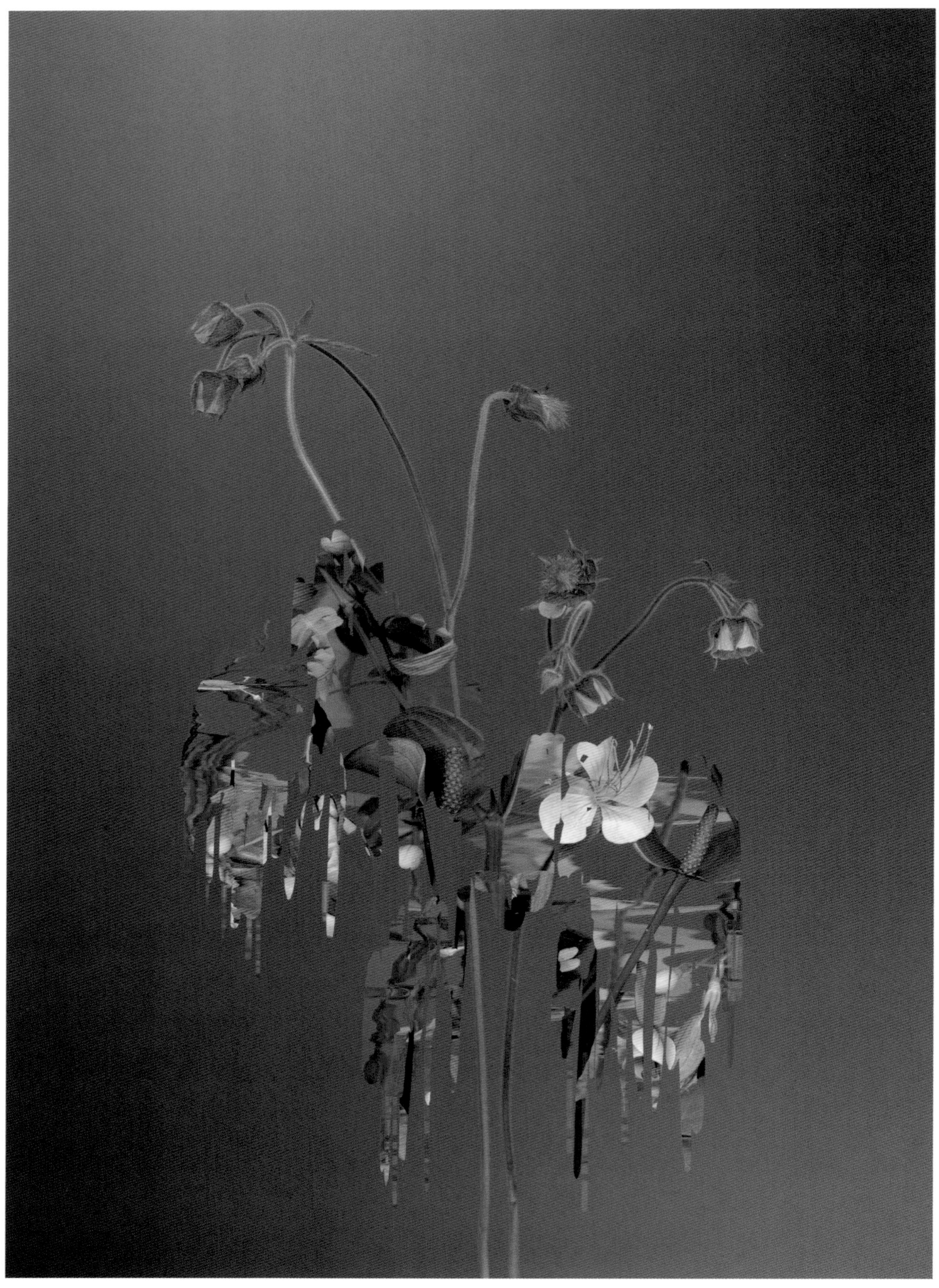

SANDRA KANTANEN
Untitled (New Distortion 3), 2018

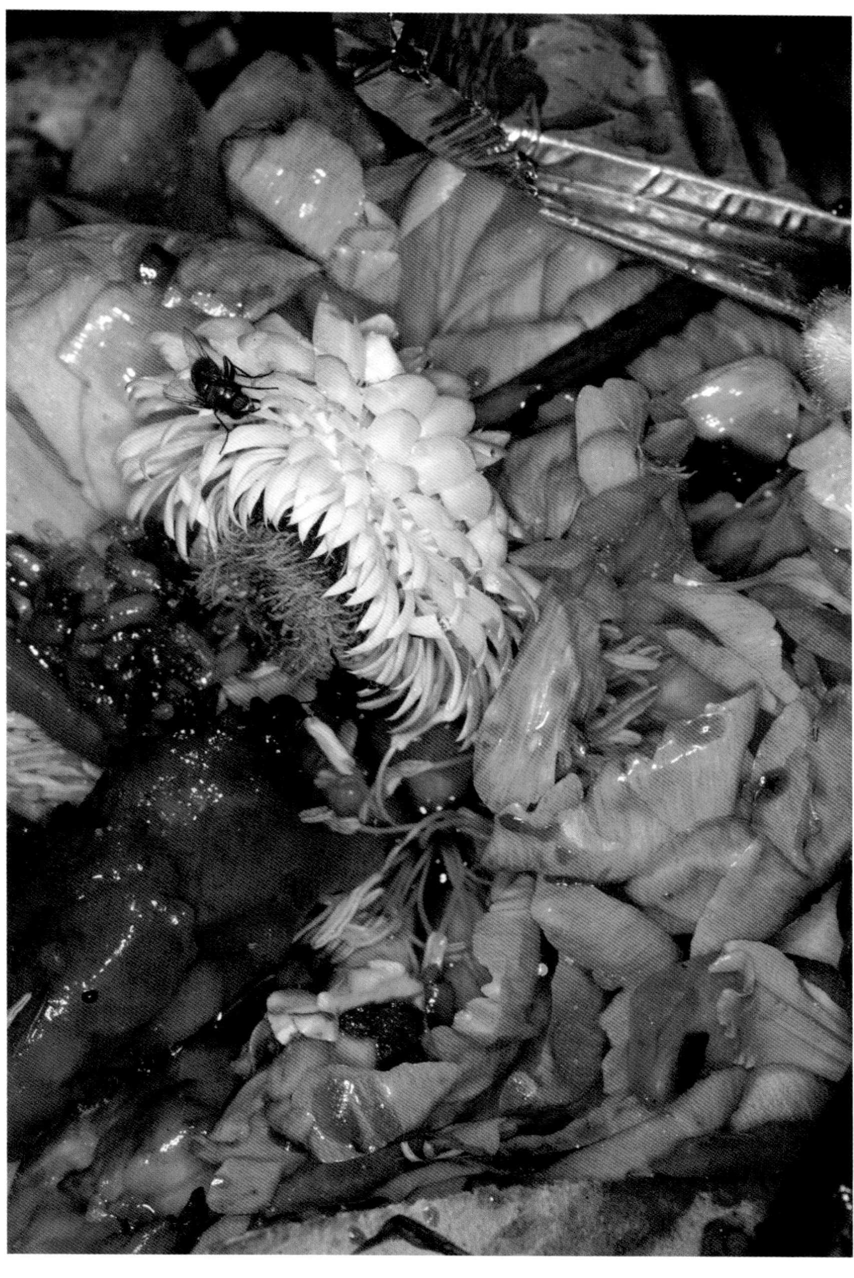

MAISIE COUSINS
Sweet & Sour 2, 2018

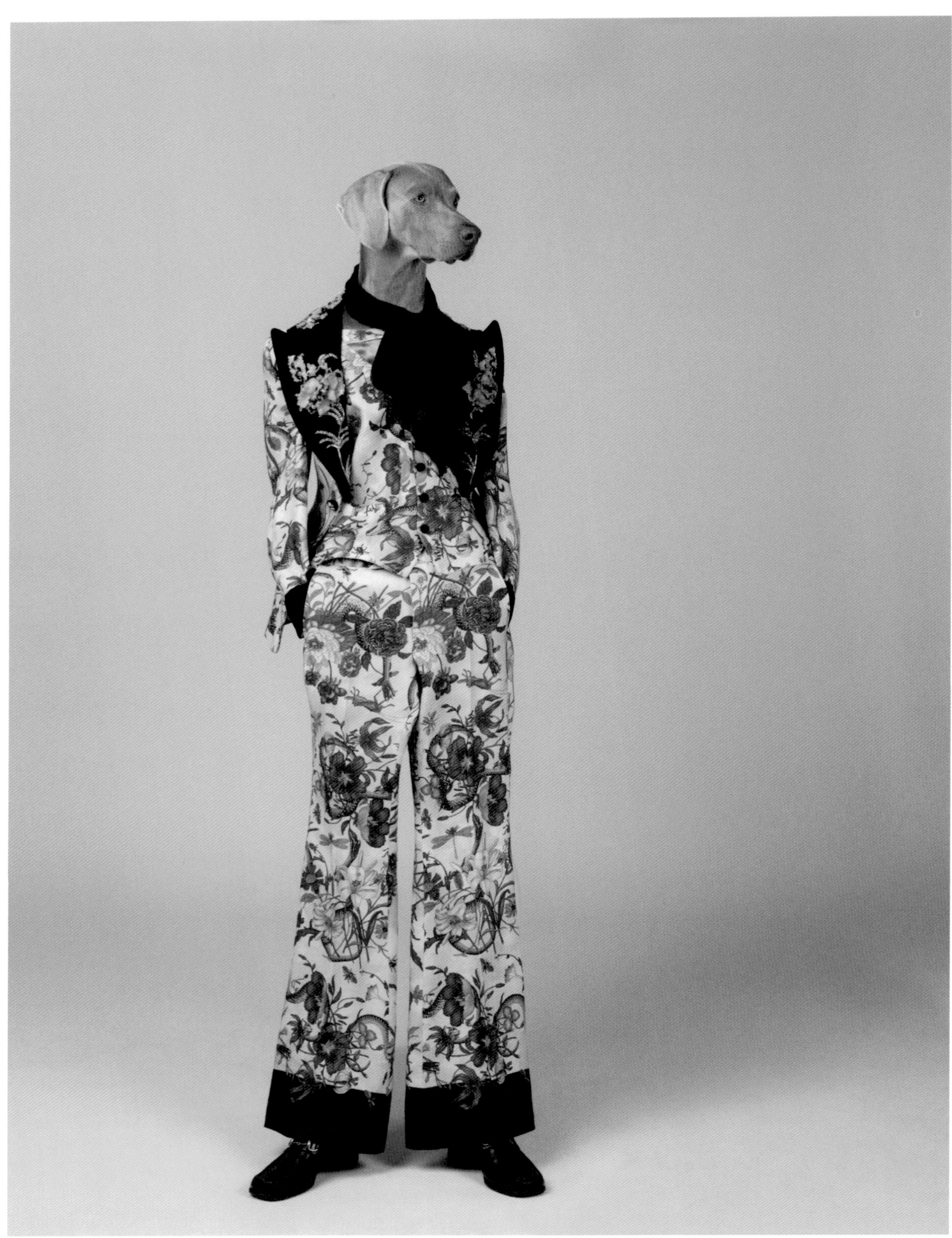

WILLIAM WEGMAN
Tall, 2017

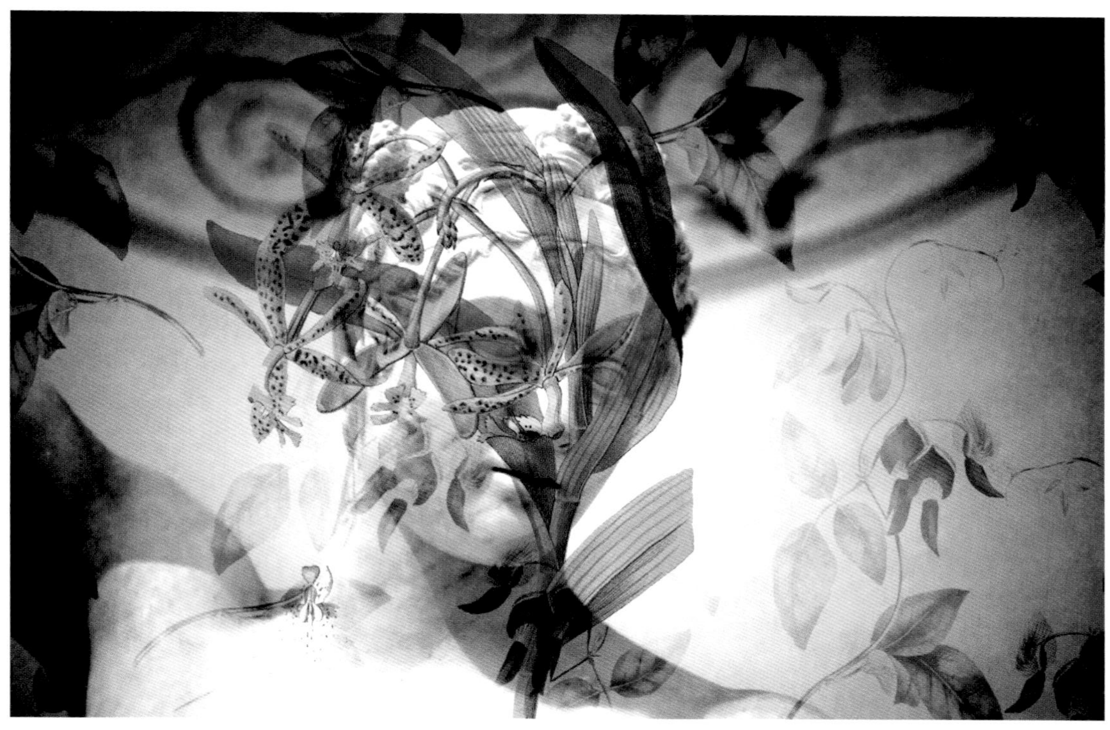

SOFIA BIANCHINI
Marmo #58, 2018–19

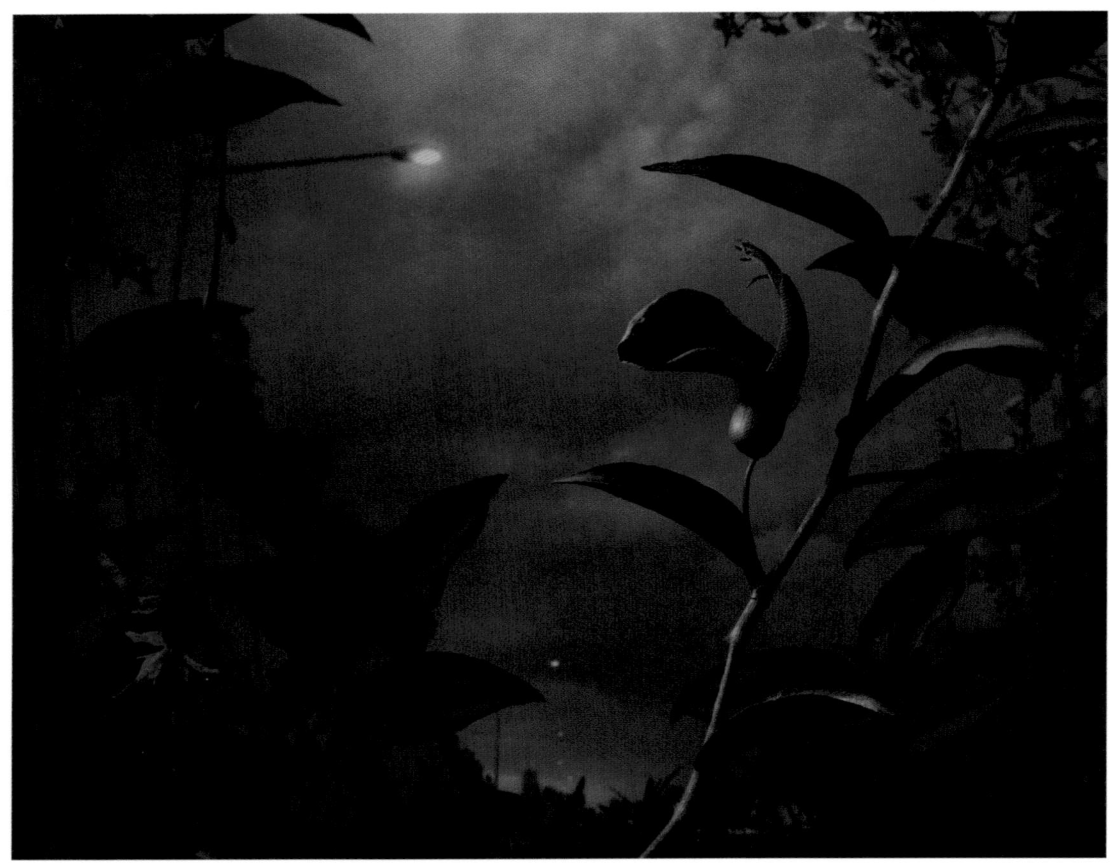

DANIEL SHIPP
Regeneration at Perimeter, from the series *Botanical Inquiry*, 2015

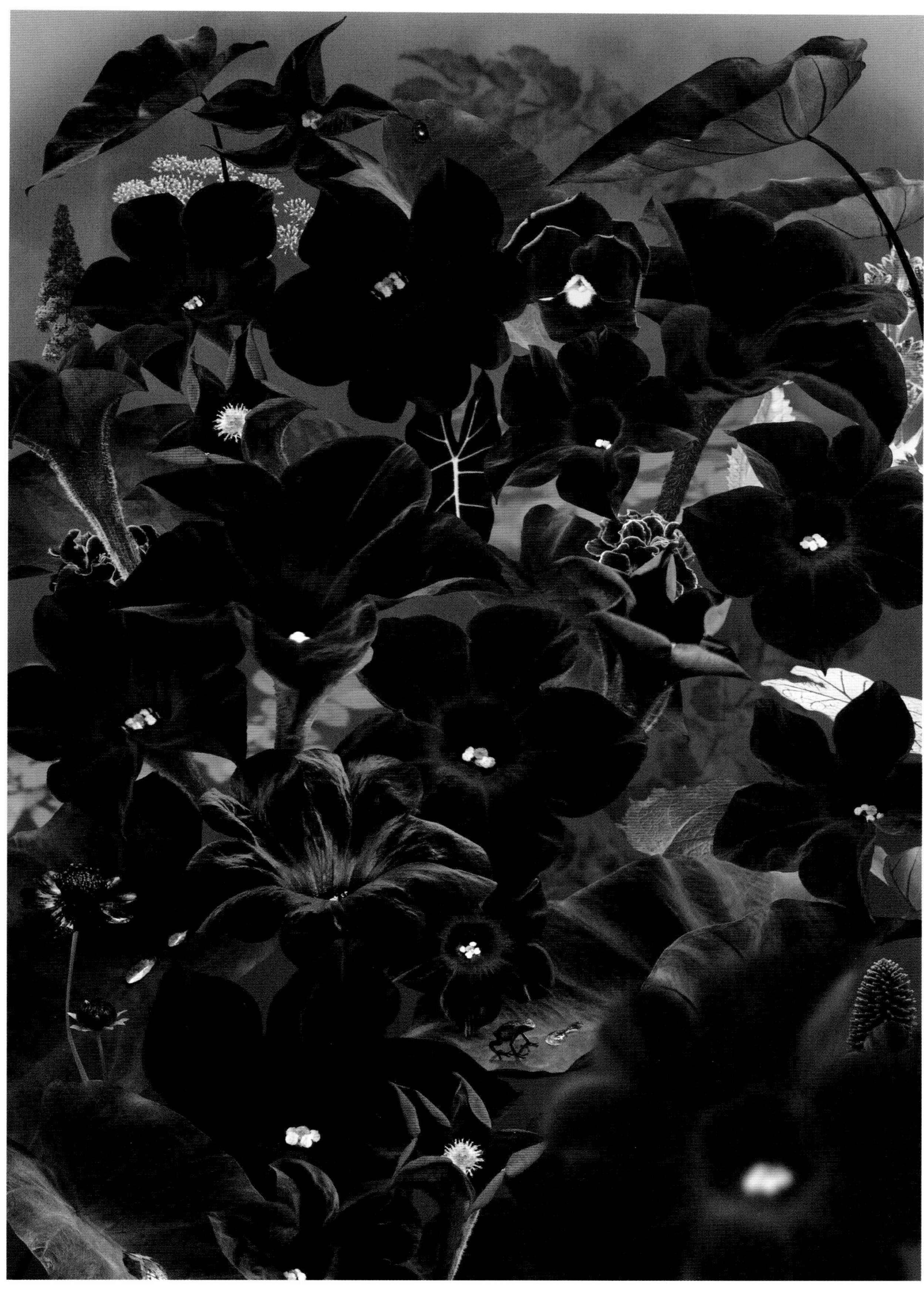

RUUD VAN EMPEL
Floresta Negra #1, 2018

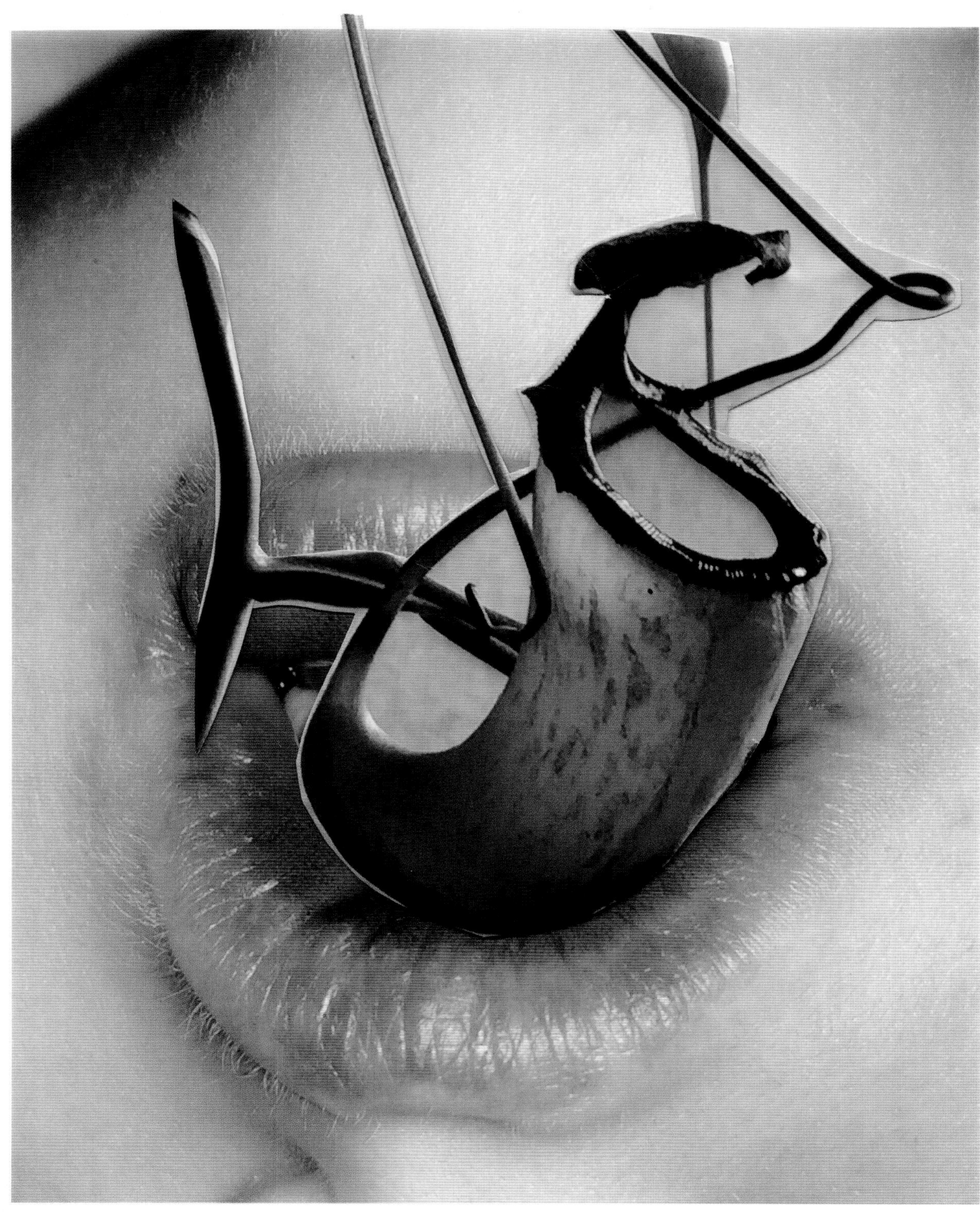

VIVIANE SASSEN
Nepenthes alata, from the series *Of Mud and Lotus*, 2017

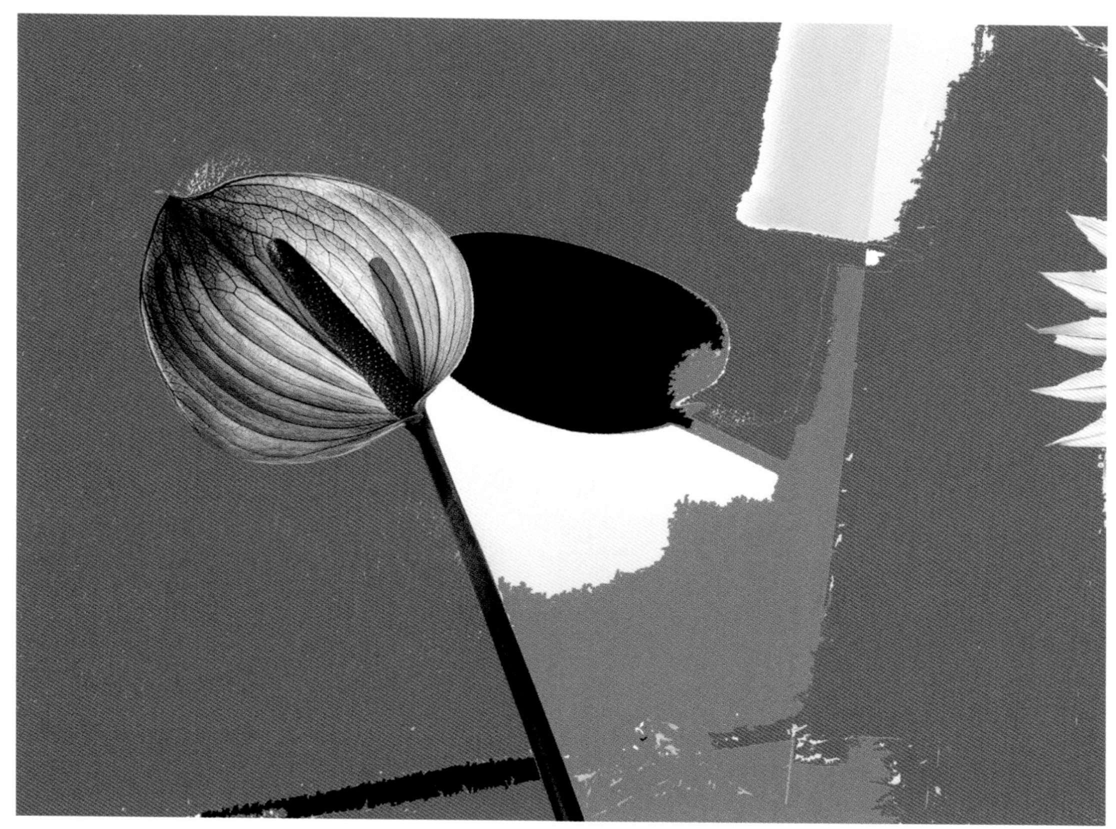

ANN MANDELBAUM
Anthurium Rose, 2000

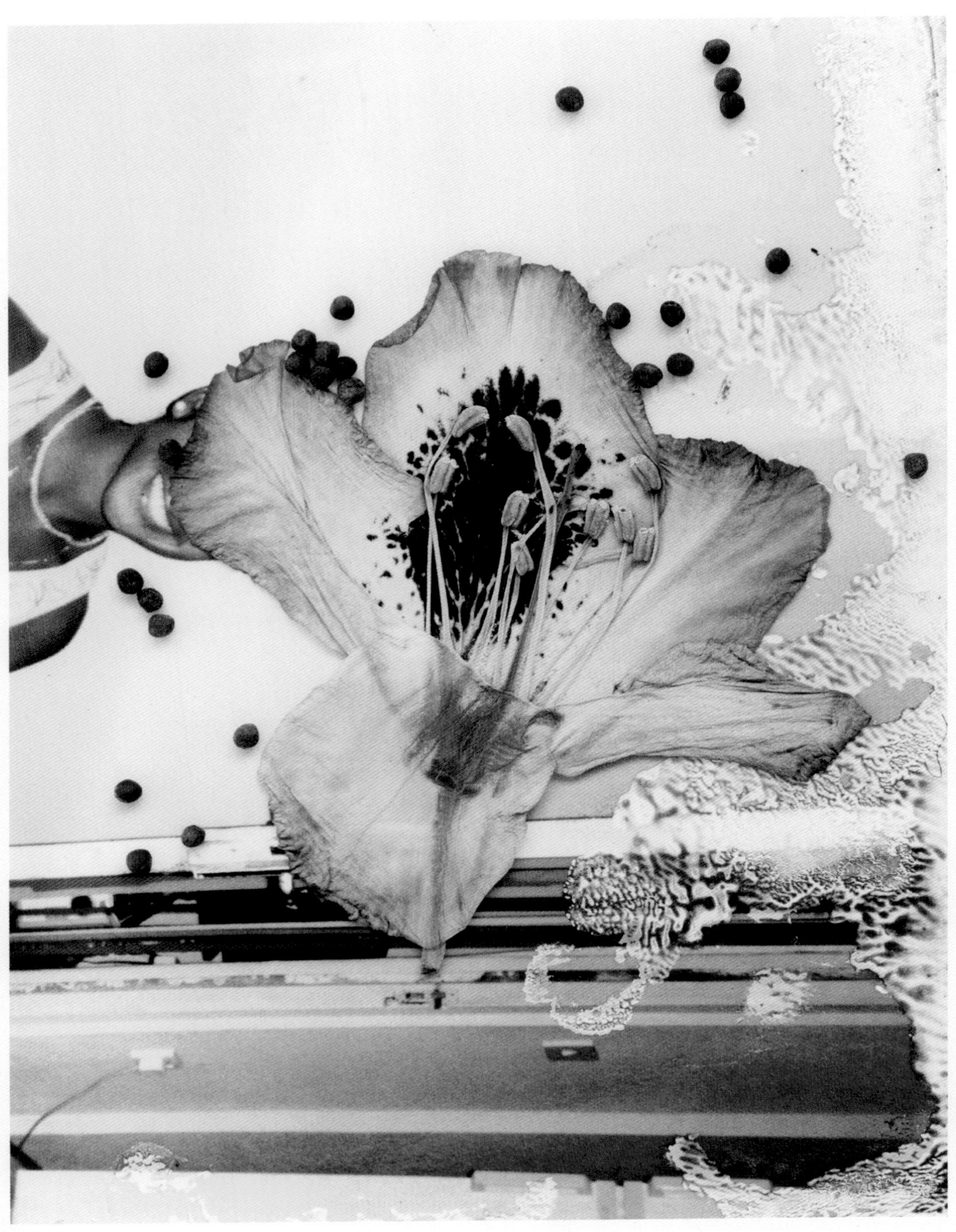

STEPHEN GILL
Untitled, from the series *Hackney Flowers 2004–2007*, 2007

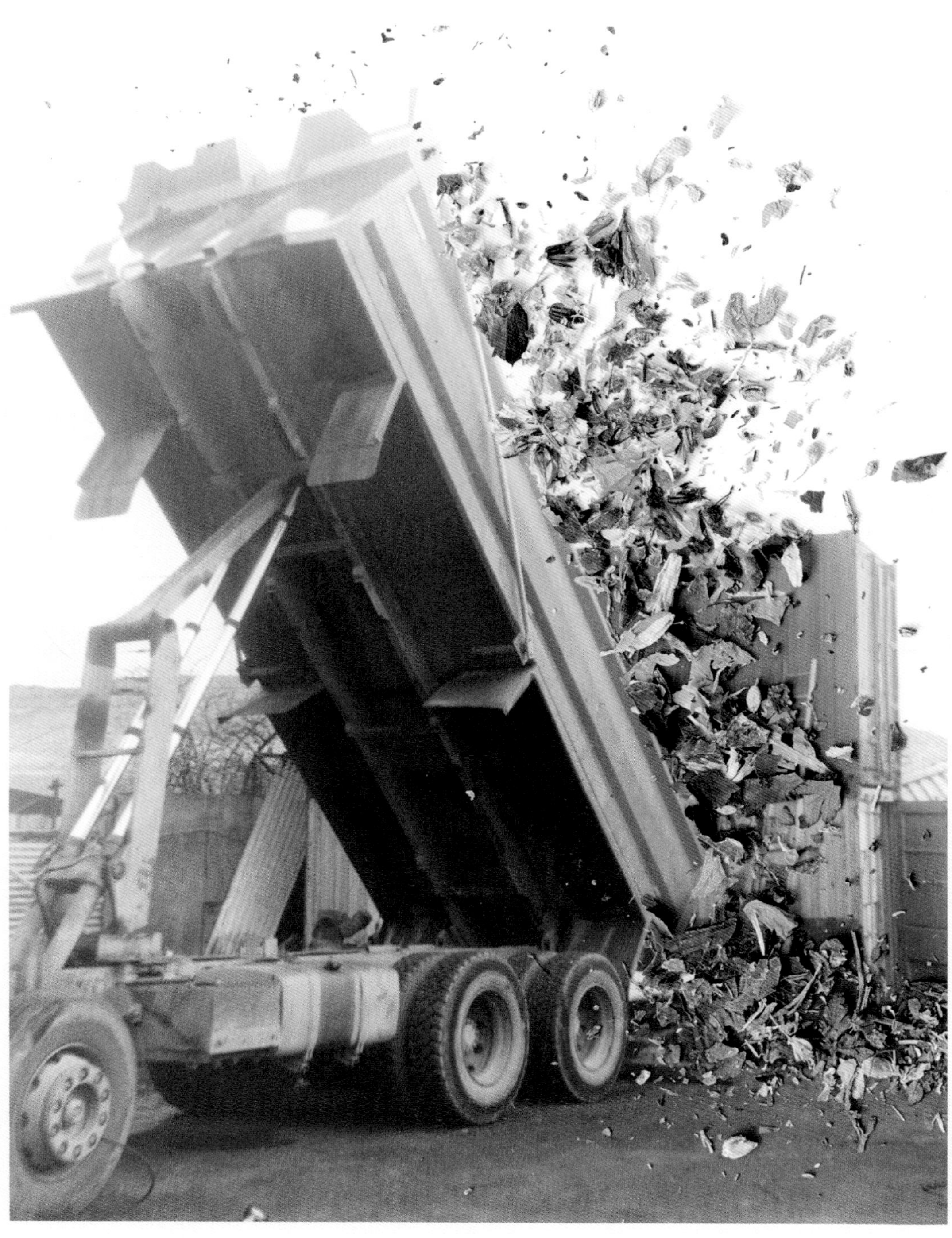

STEPHEN GILL
Untitled, from the series *Hackney Flowers 2004–2007*, 2007

THE GOODNESS OF PROVIDENCE

Our highest assurance of the goodness of Providence seems to me to rest in the flowers. All other things, our powers, our desires, our food, are all really necessary for our existence in the first instance. But this rose is an extra. Its smell and its colour are an embellishment of life, not a condition of it. It is only goodness which gives extras, and so I say again that we have much to hope from the flowers.

Arthur Conan Doyle[4]

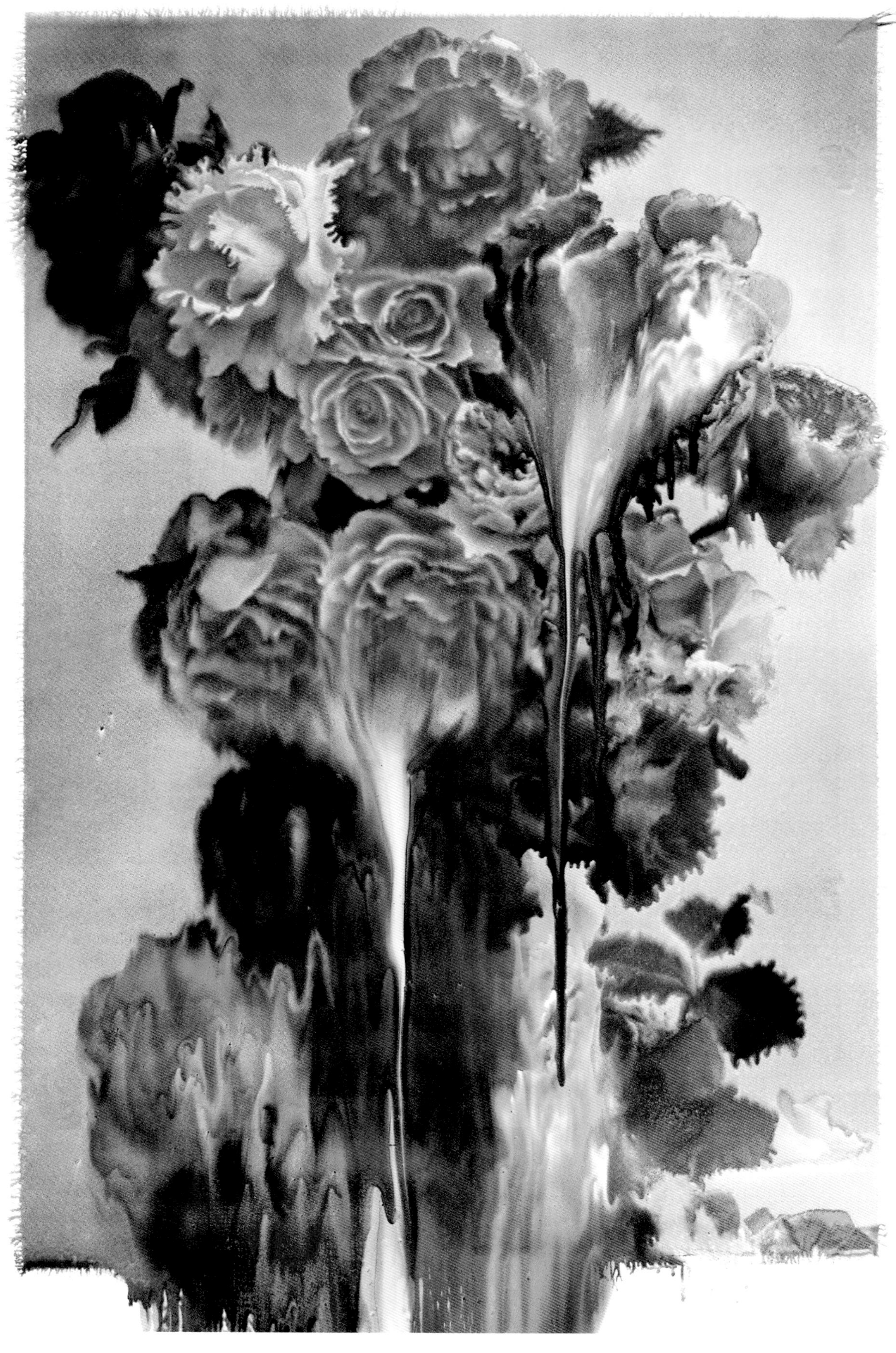

NICK KNIGHT
Rose II, from the series *Rose Photo Paintings*, 2012

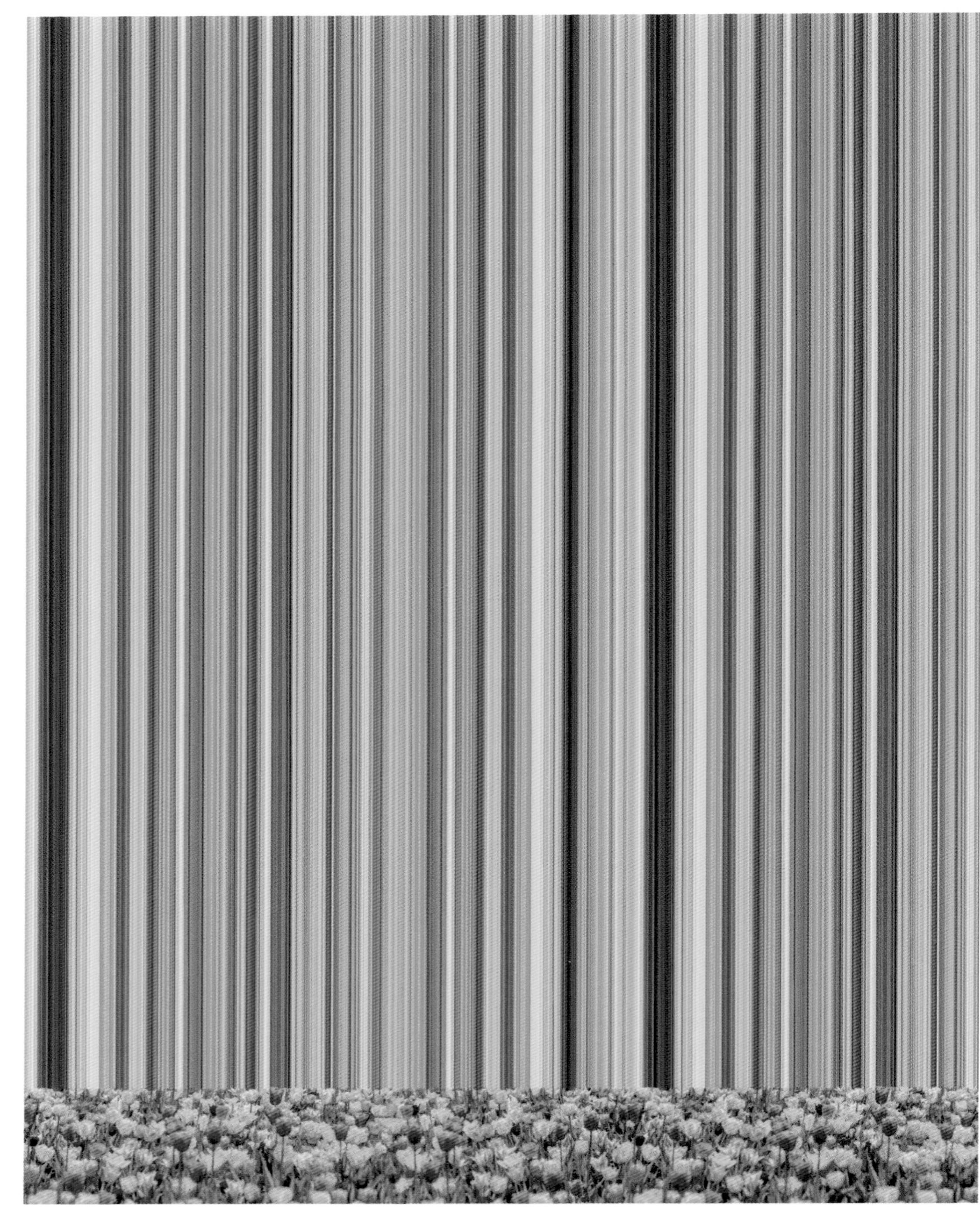

ERIK BERGLIN
Tulip Variation #101, 2021

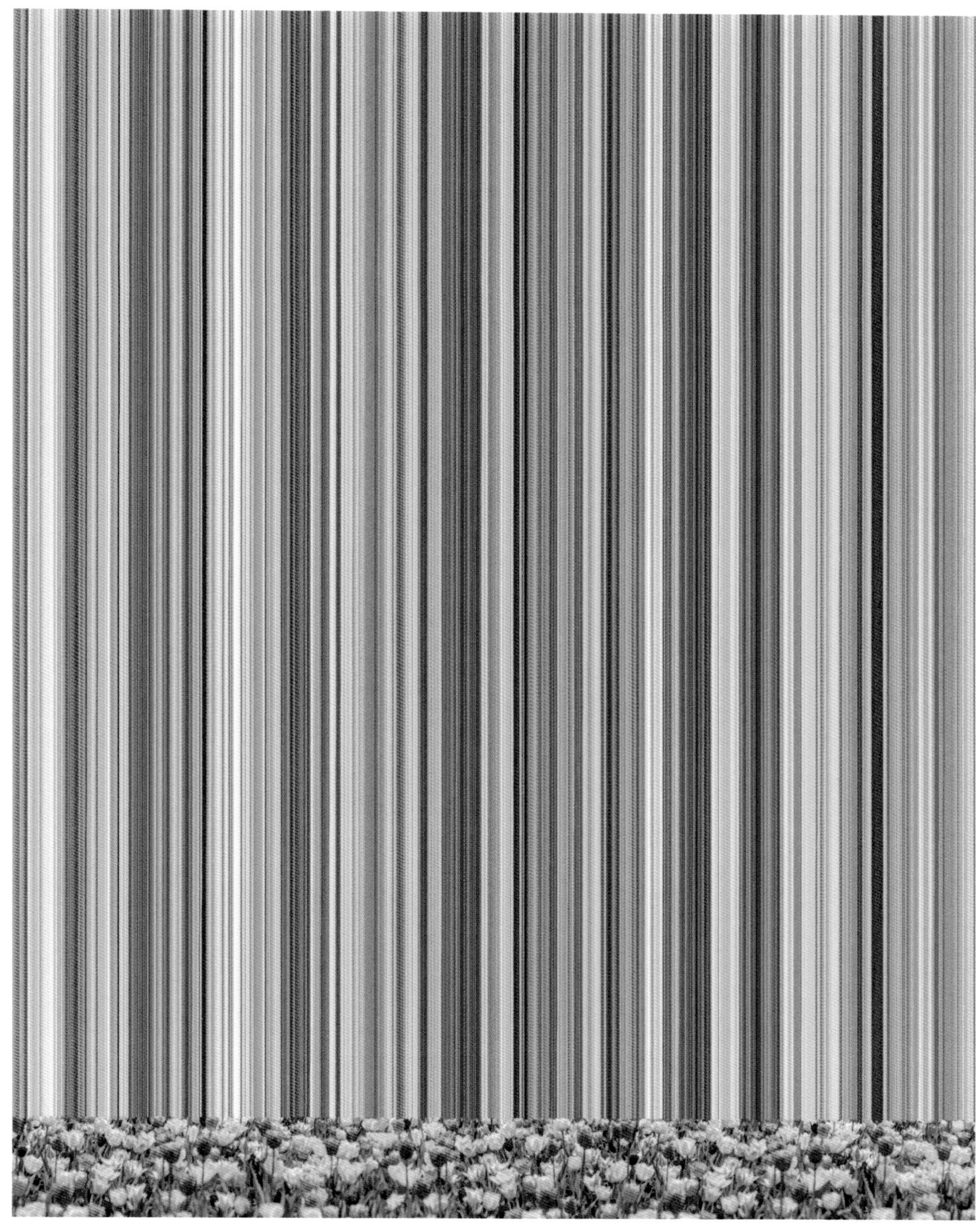

ERIK BERGLIN
Tulip Variation #105, 2021

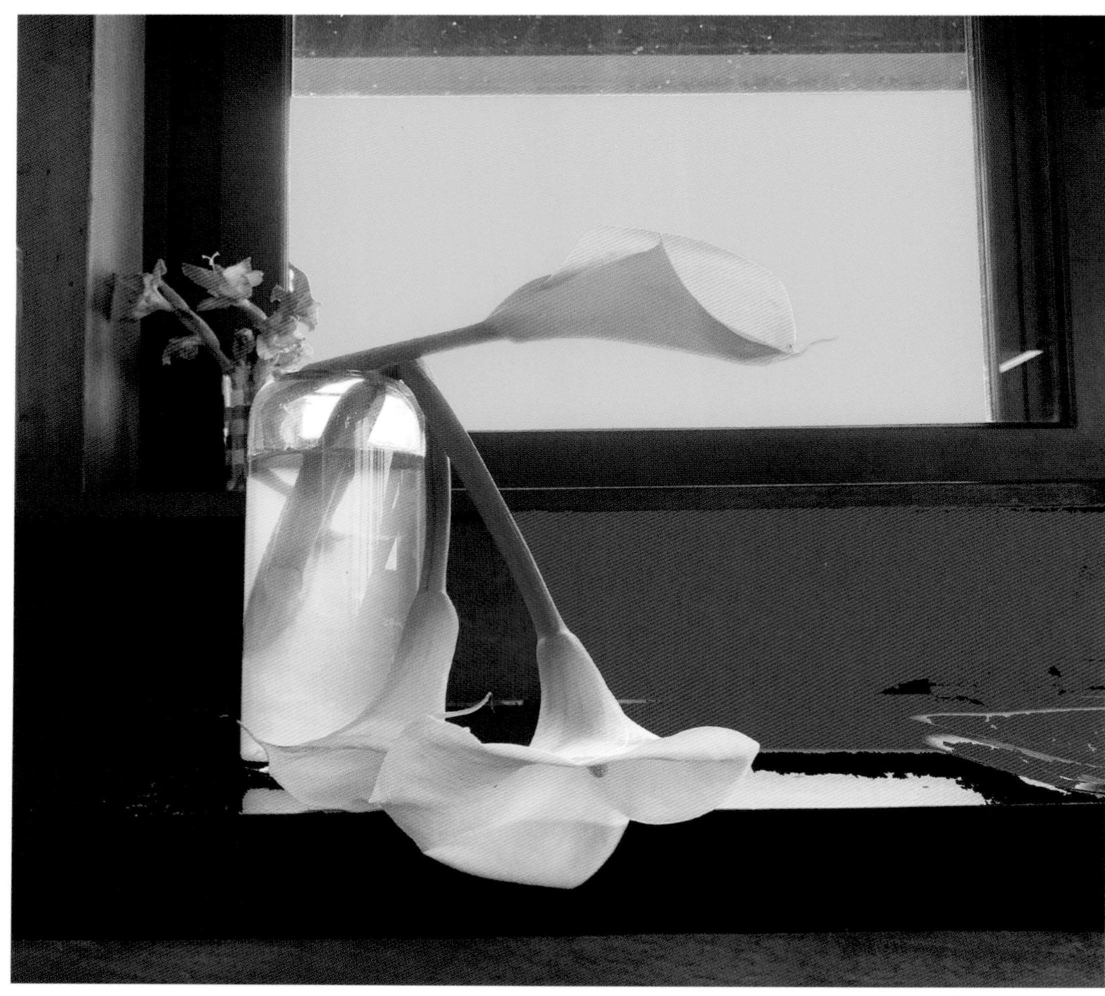

ANN MANDELBAUM
Red Lily, 2000

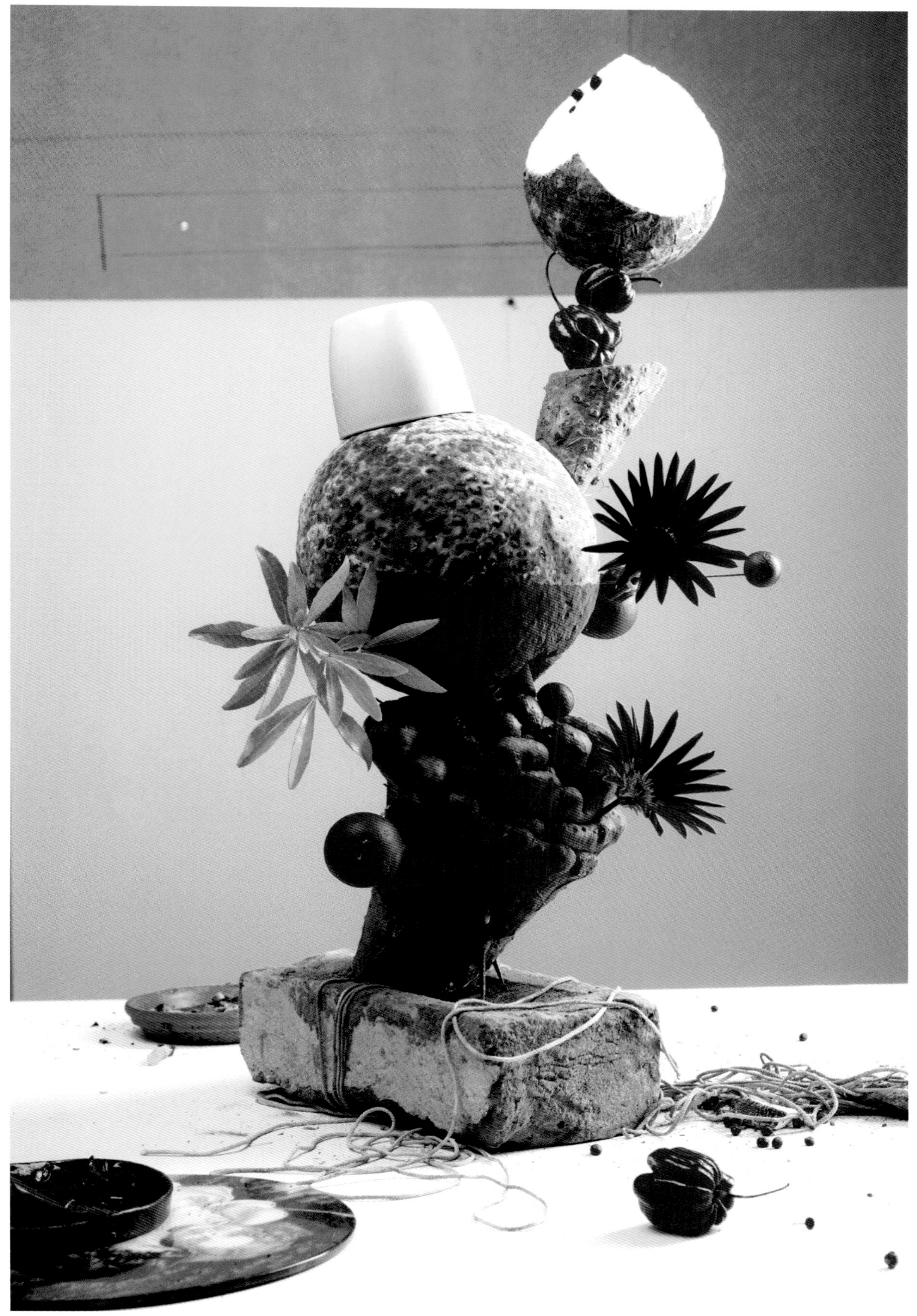

LORENZO VITTURI
Red #1, 2013

FUGUE

'Still life' was never a good fit where the traditional painted flower piece was concerned. True, in the early years, a convincing depiction of the flowers was enough of a challenge without trying to convey movement, but soon floral painting began to appear to move, much as if a light breeze were wafting through a room, and by the eighteenth century European painting shows absolute mastery of this effect.

In music, a fugue is defined as a play on a short phrase, which is overlapped, imitated or embellished in different voices. 'Flowers are the music of the ground,' wrote the poet Edwin Curran.[1] As for photography, we might use the term whimsically to indicate imagery that imparts a sense of movement, subtle or animated. After all, flowers in nature do move, and when they do, they tend to sway gracefully. Not surprisingly, they've inspired ballet, opera and popular music, from Tchaikovsky's 'Waltz of the Flowers' (1892) to Ed Sheeran's 'Supermarket Flowers' (2017). Studio-based photographers often compose their flower arrangements while listening to music. Perhaps the flowers are listening too; the idea that music can affect plant growth was popularized fifty or more years ago, most notably in *The Secret Life of Plants* (1973) by Peter Tompkins and Christopher Bird. Those who are sceptical of New Age thinking might do well to keep in mind sober scientific studies that showed the growth rates of plants increased decidedly when they were exposed to music.

When it comes to working with a flower arrangement, photographers learn quickly that their subjects like to shift about, despite efforts to keep them in their place. Photographers have often remarked how even supposedly dead flowers move about mysteriously if left alone for a while, overnight for example, or even during a break taken at lunchtime. Perhaps the will to make flowers appear to move has to do with that existential conundrum of photography: freezing movement in order to convey it.

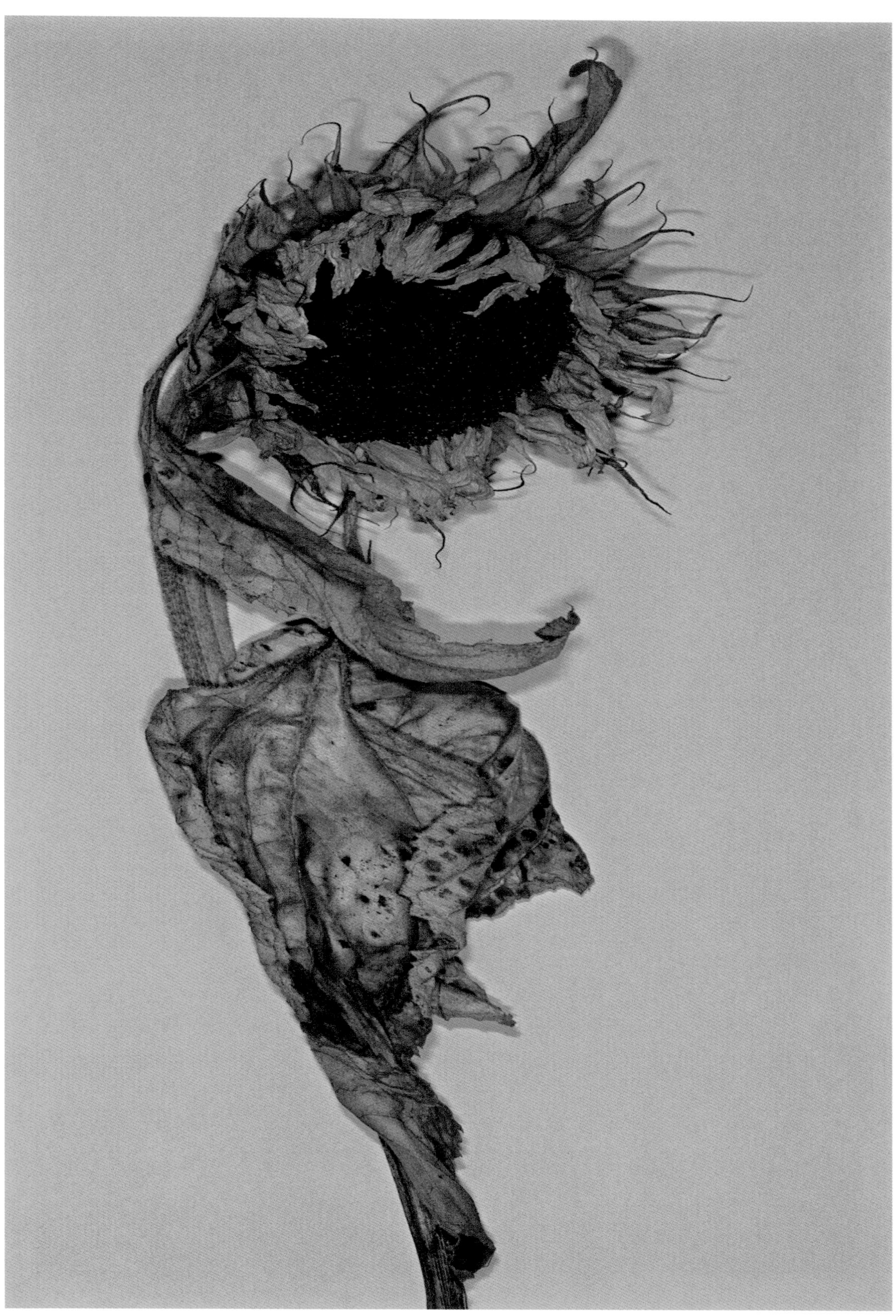

ANNA HALM SCHUDEL
Sonnenblume, 2007

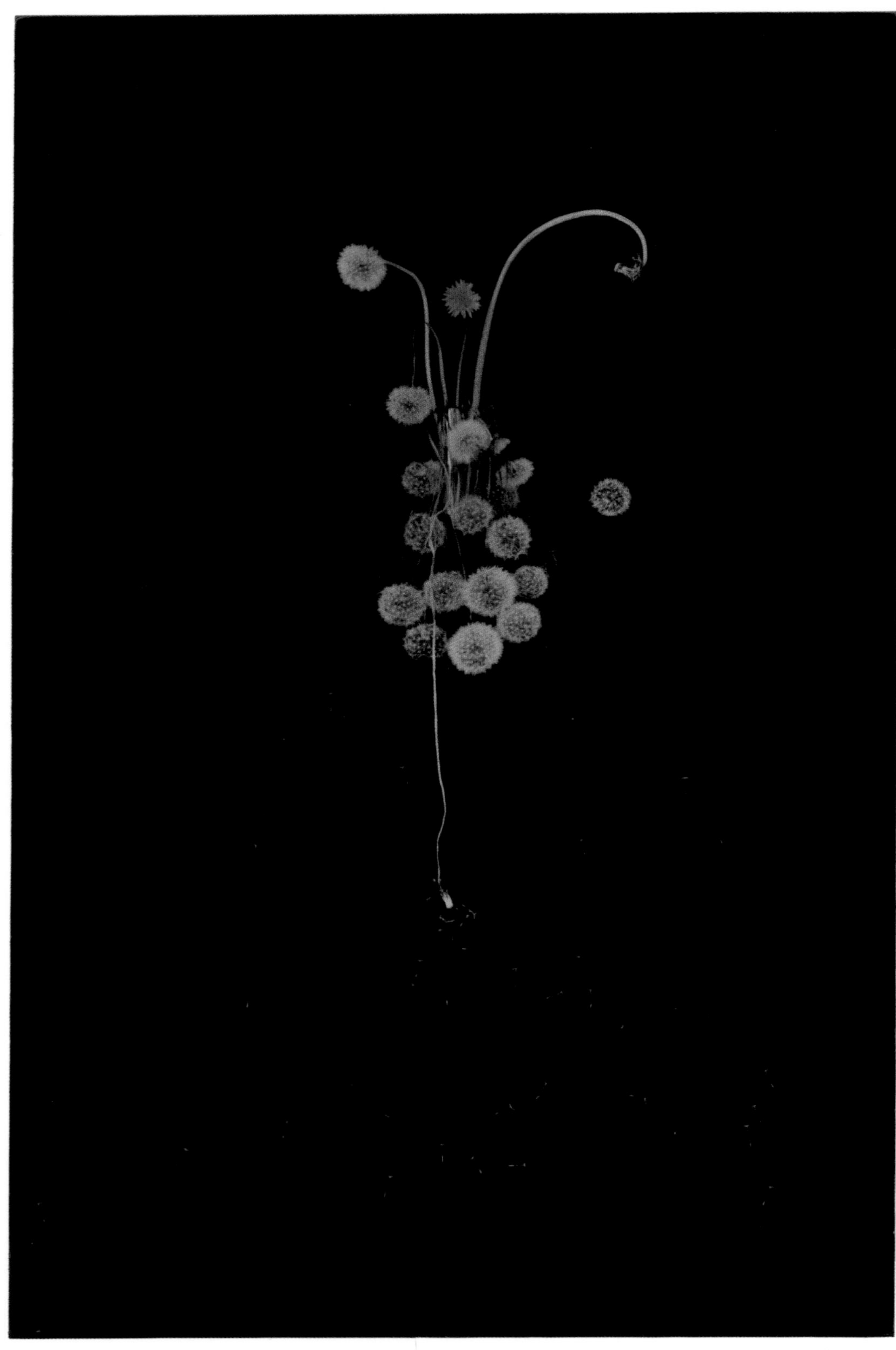

YAMAMOTO MASAO
A Box of Ku #36, 1992

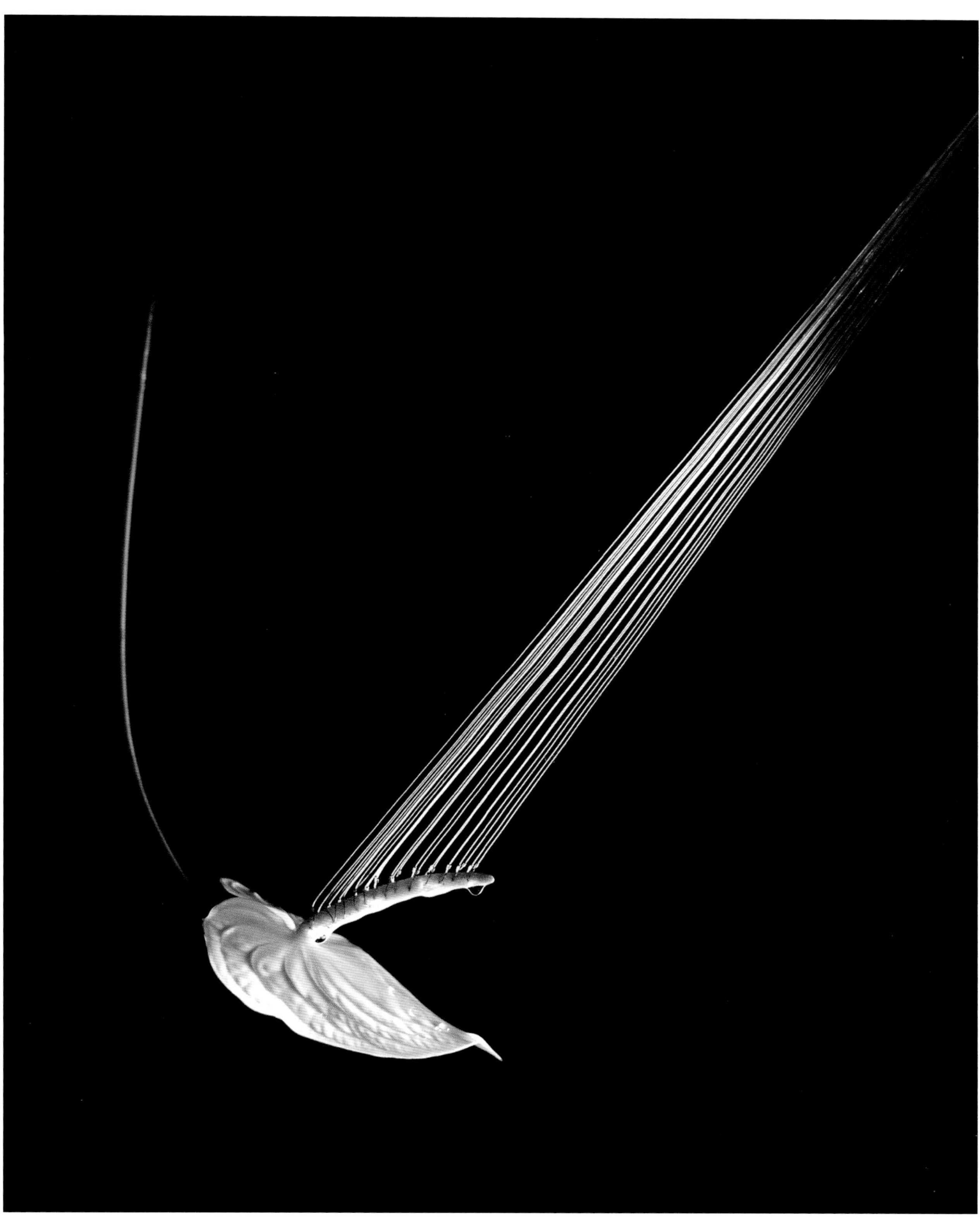

JIANG ZHI
Flowers No. 01, 2010

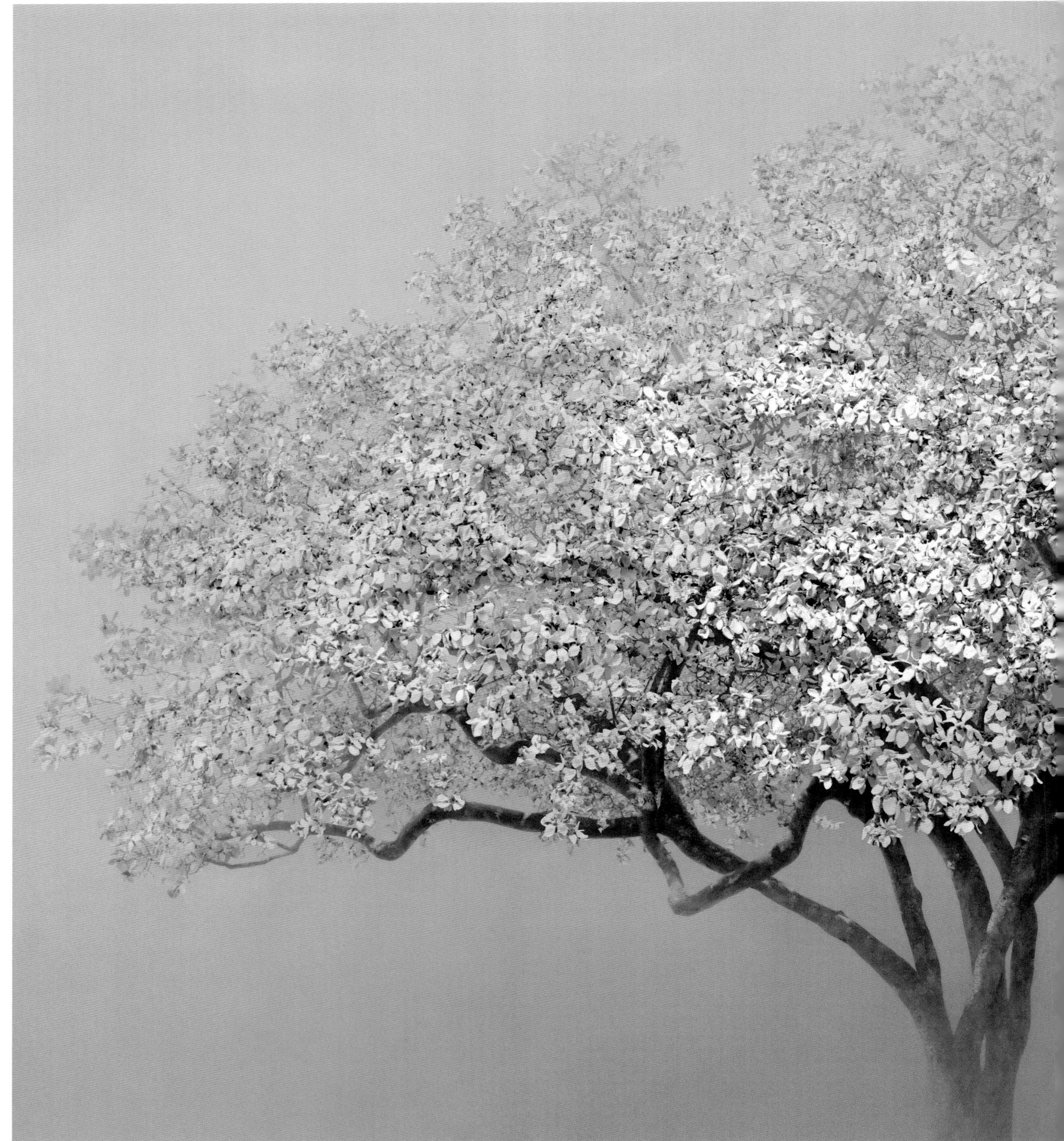

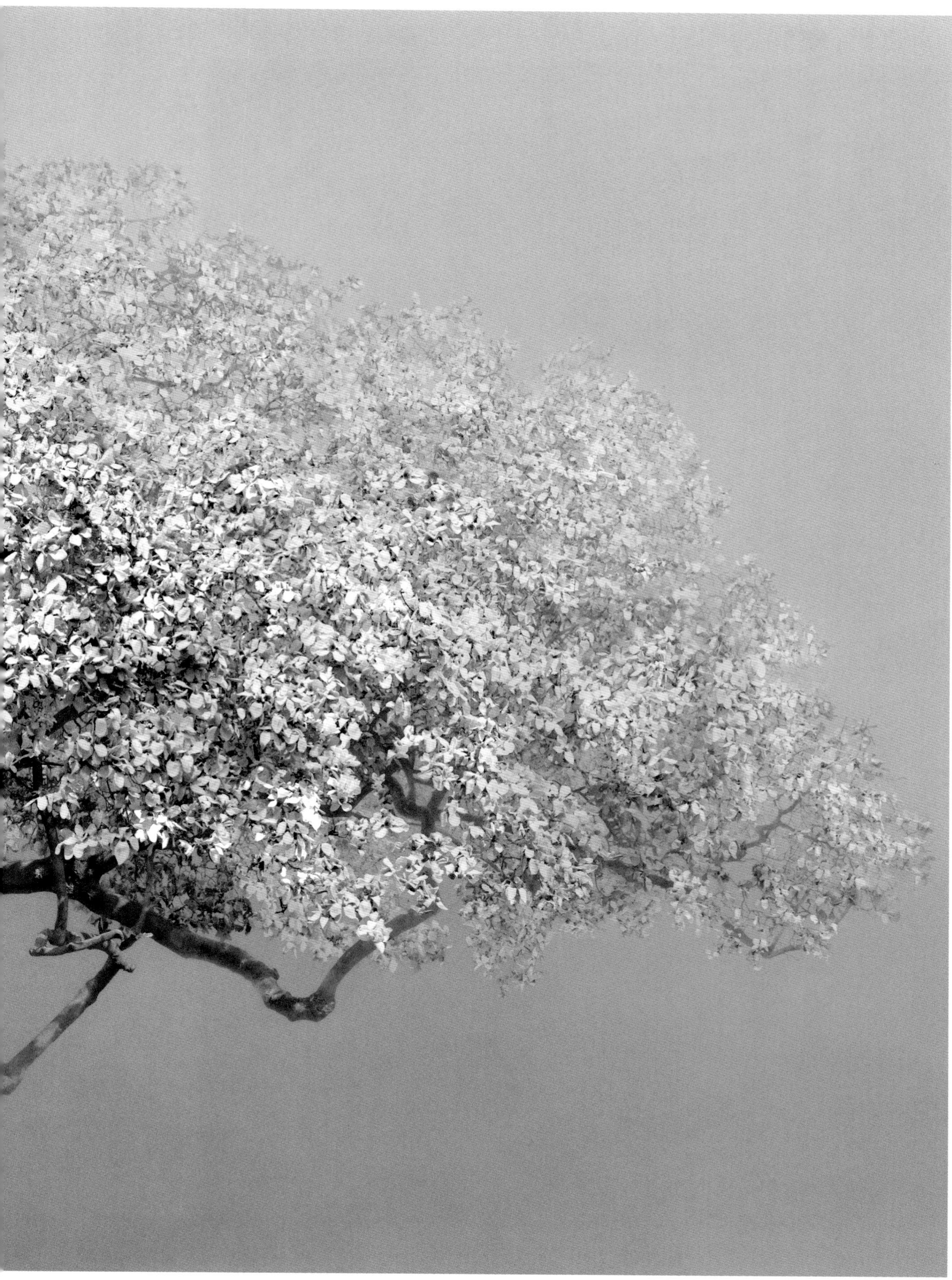

IRENE KUNG
Magnolia, 2013

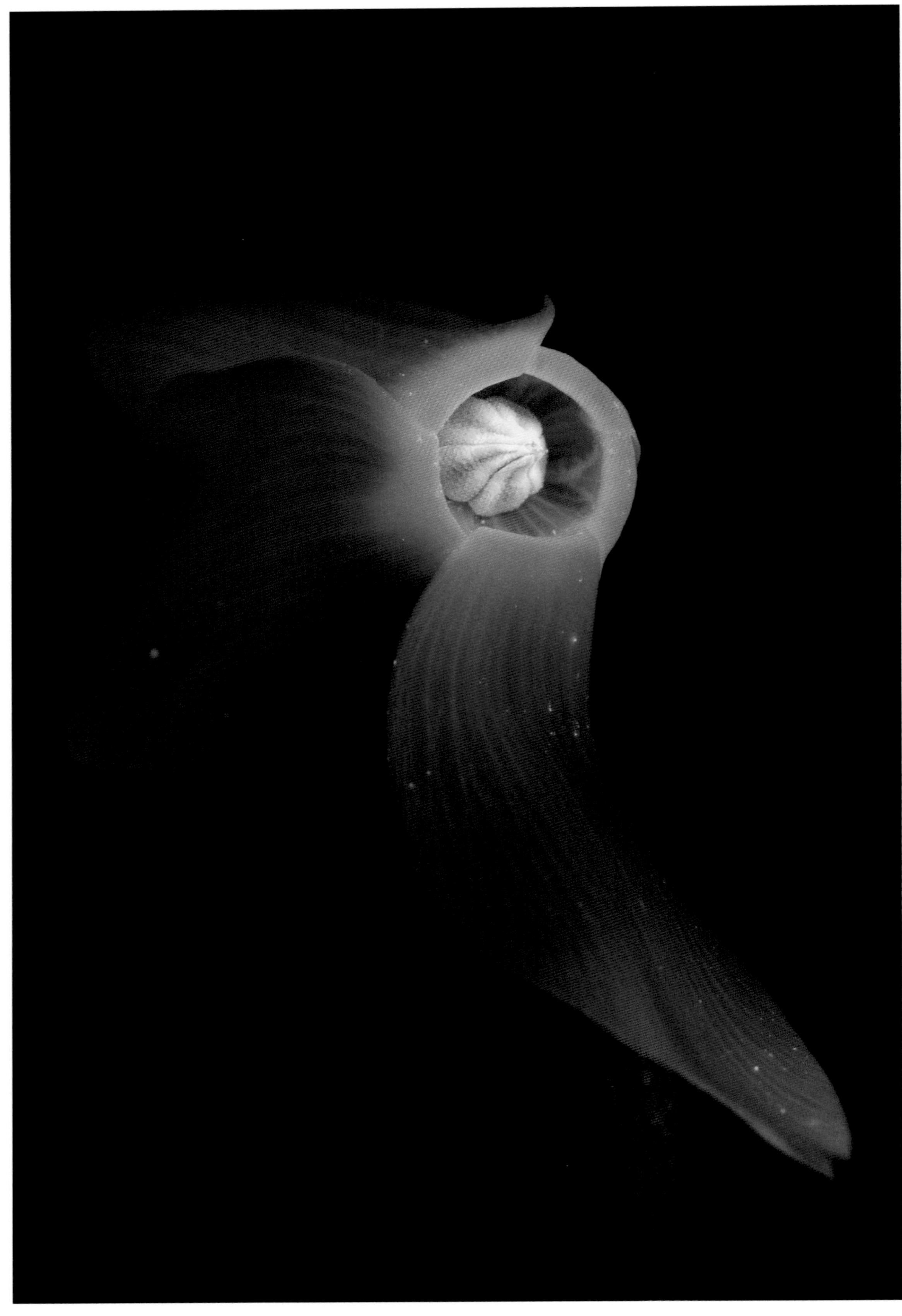

CRAIG P. BURROWS
Cyclamen, digital ultraviolet-induced visible fluorescence (UVIVF) photograph, 2017

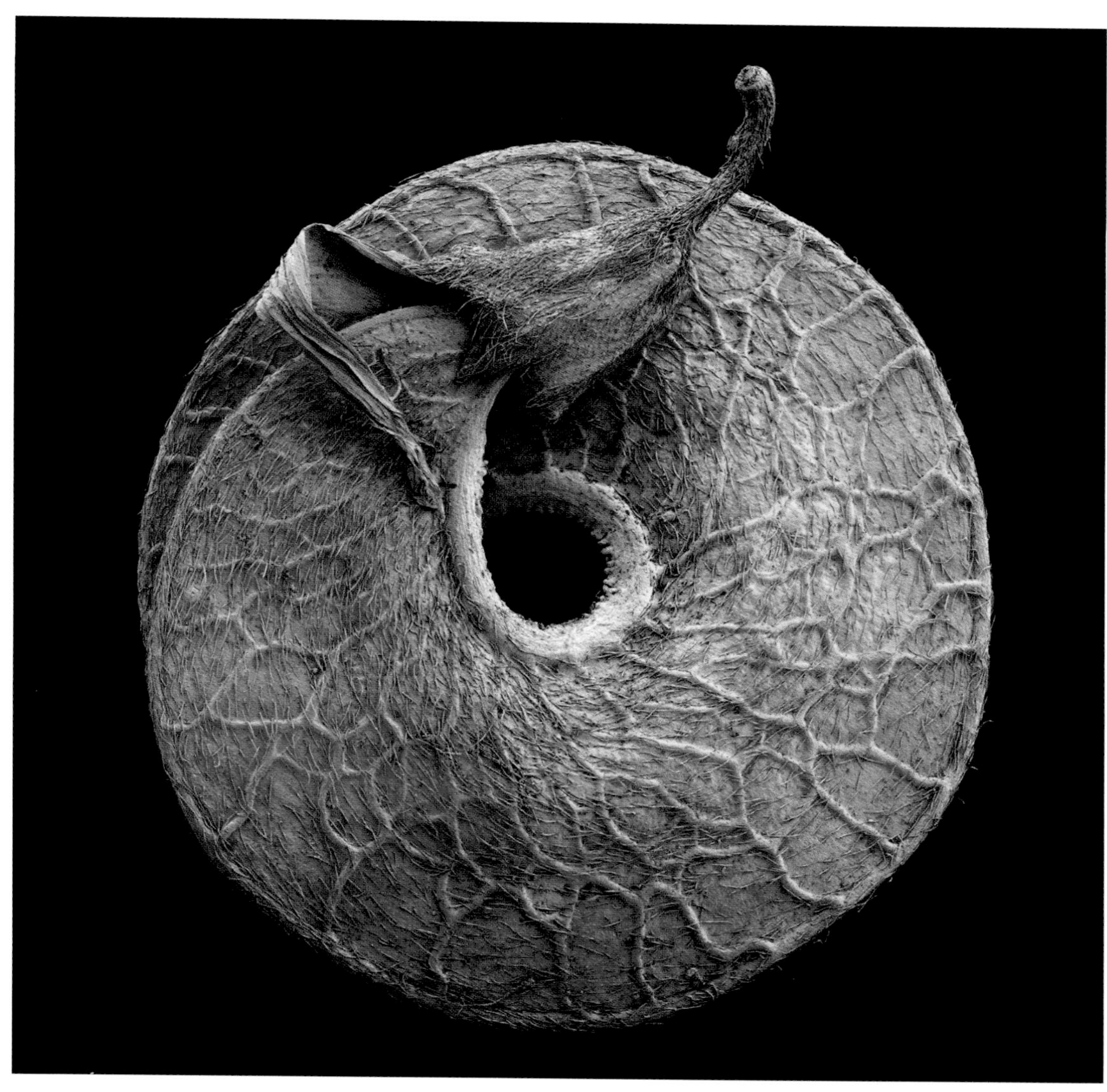

ROB KESSELER
Medicago arborea, hand-coloured electron micrograph, 2013

THE BORROWER

The Old Masters have proved that the artist, once he has established his own idiom, once he has taken from nature the necessary means of expression, is free, legitimately free, to borrow his subject from history, from the poets, from his own imagination.

Odilon Redon[2]

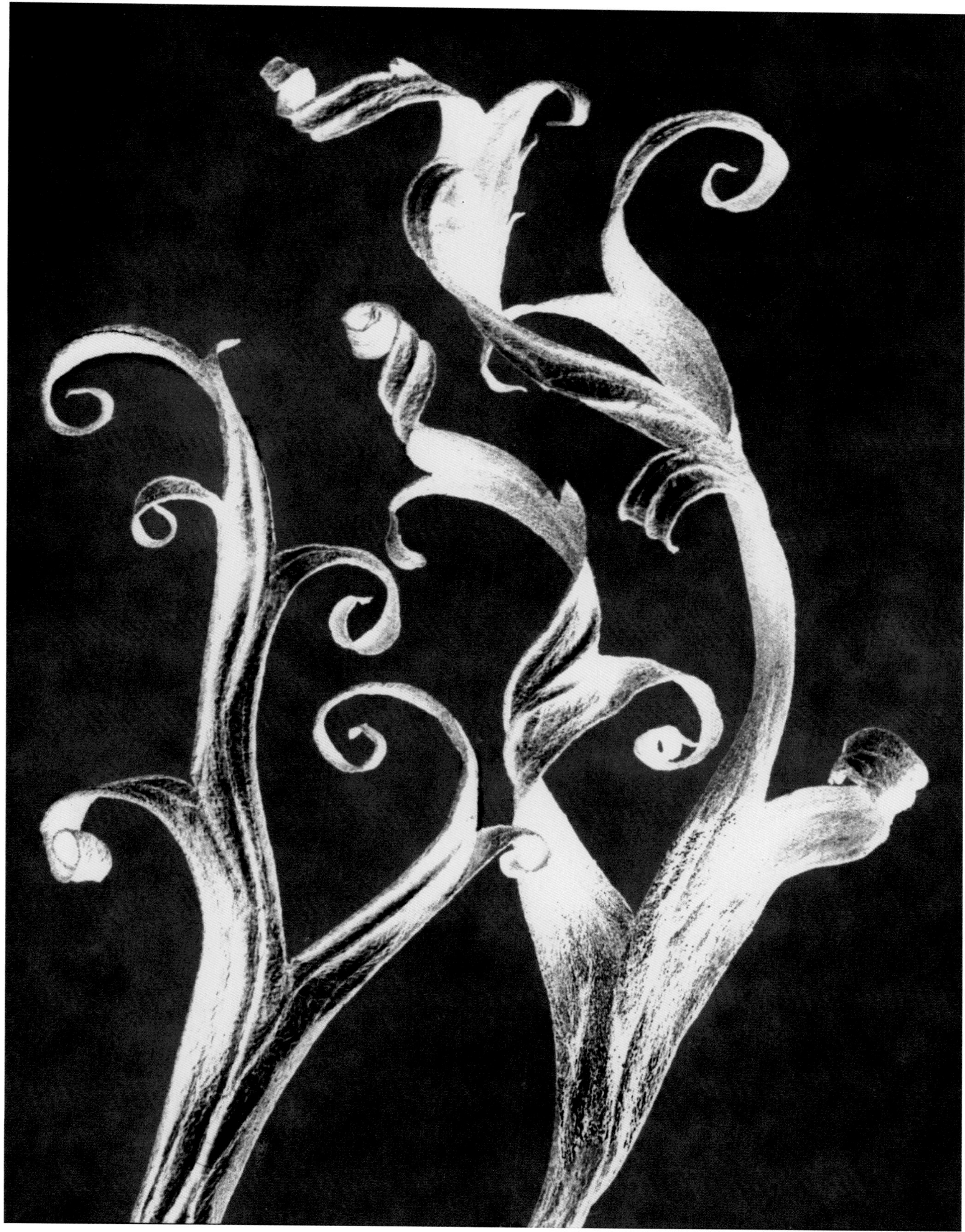

THOMAS RUFF
neg◊stil_06, 2015

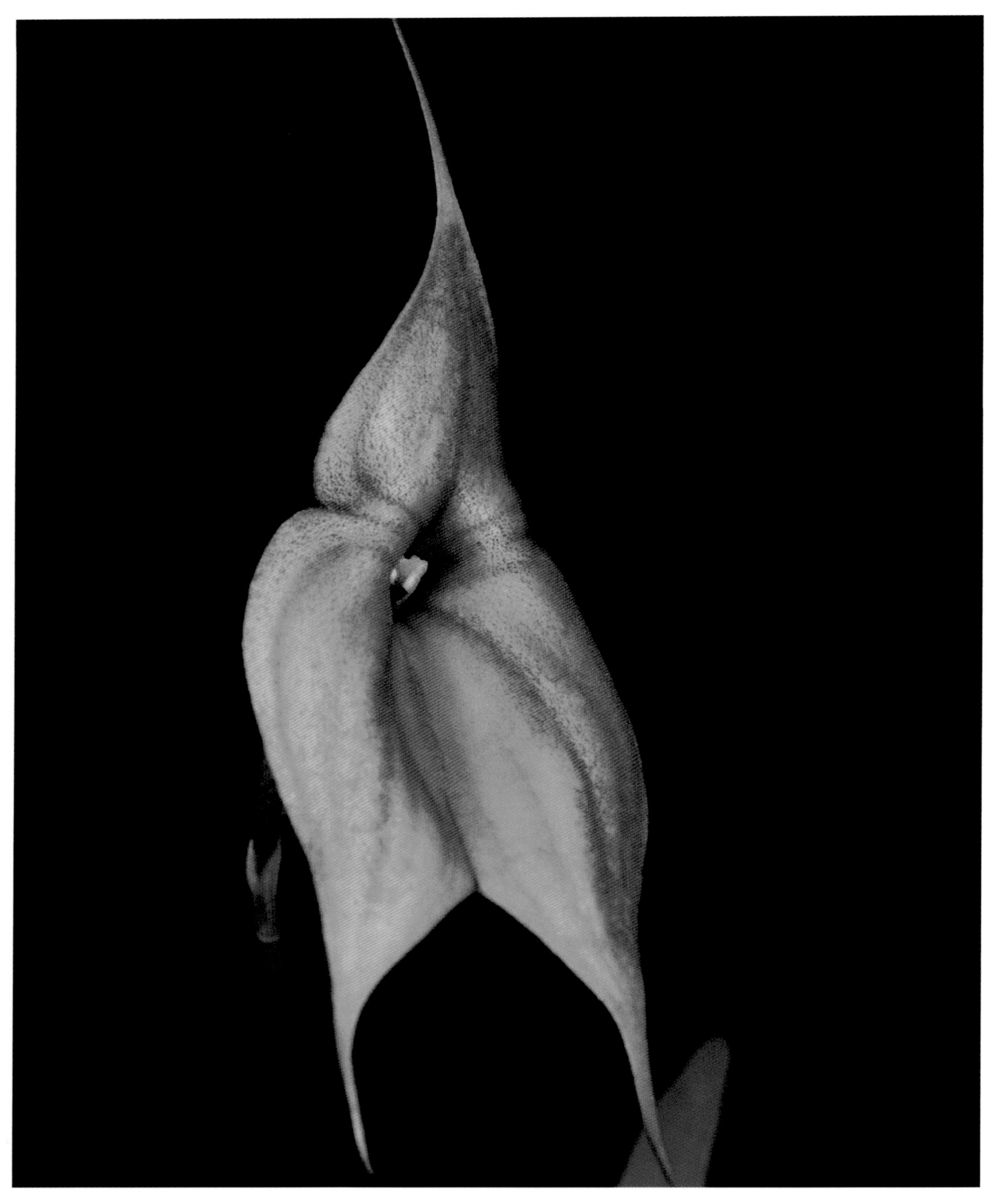

HELENE SCHMITZ
Masdevallia véitchiana, from the series *The Linnaeus Project*, 2007

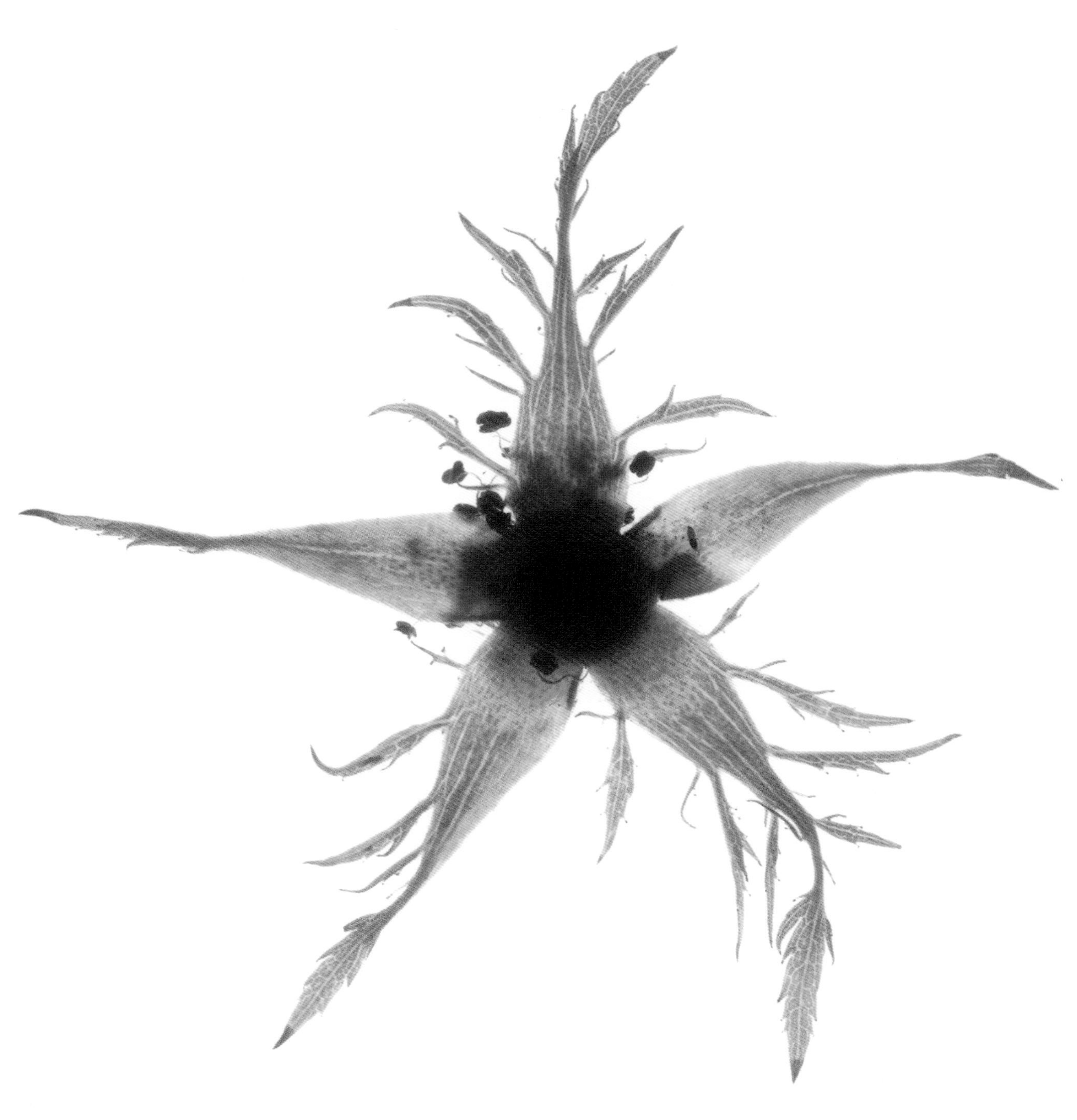

GARRY FABIAN MILLER
Dancing Sun 1, 2020

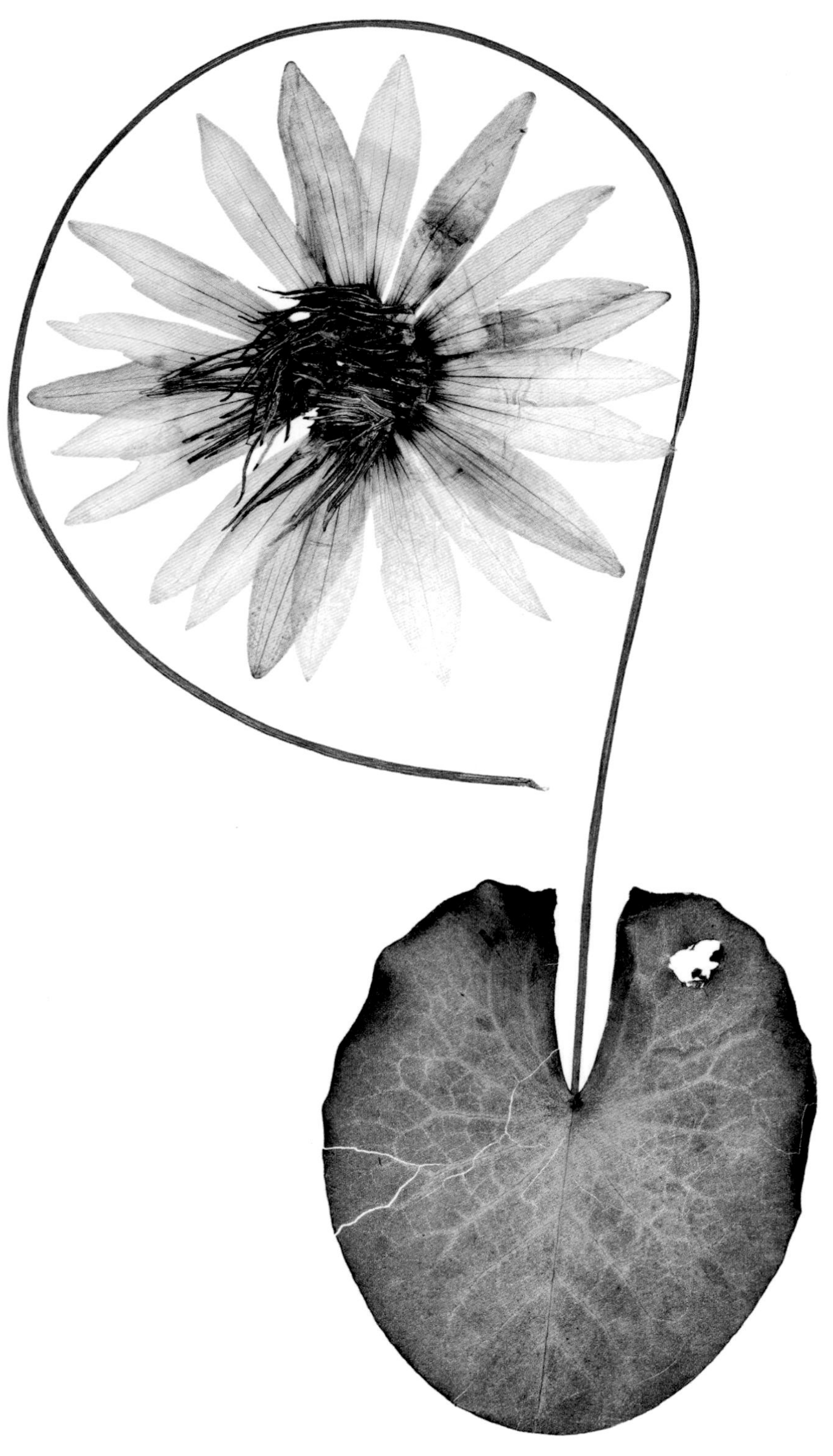

NICK KNIGHT
Nymphaeaceae, from the series *Flora*, 1994–97

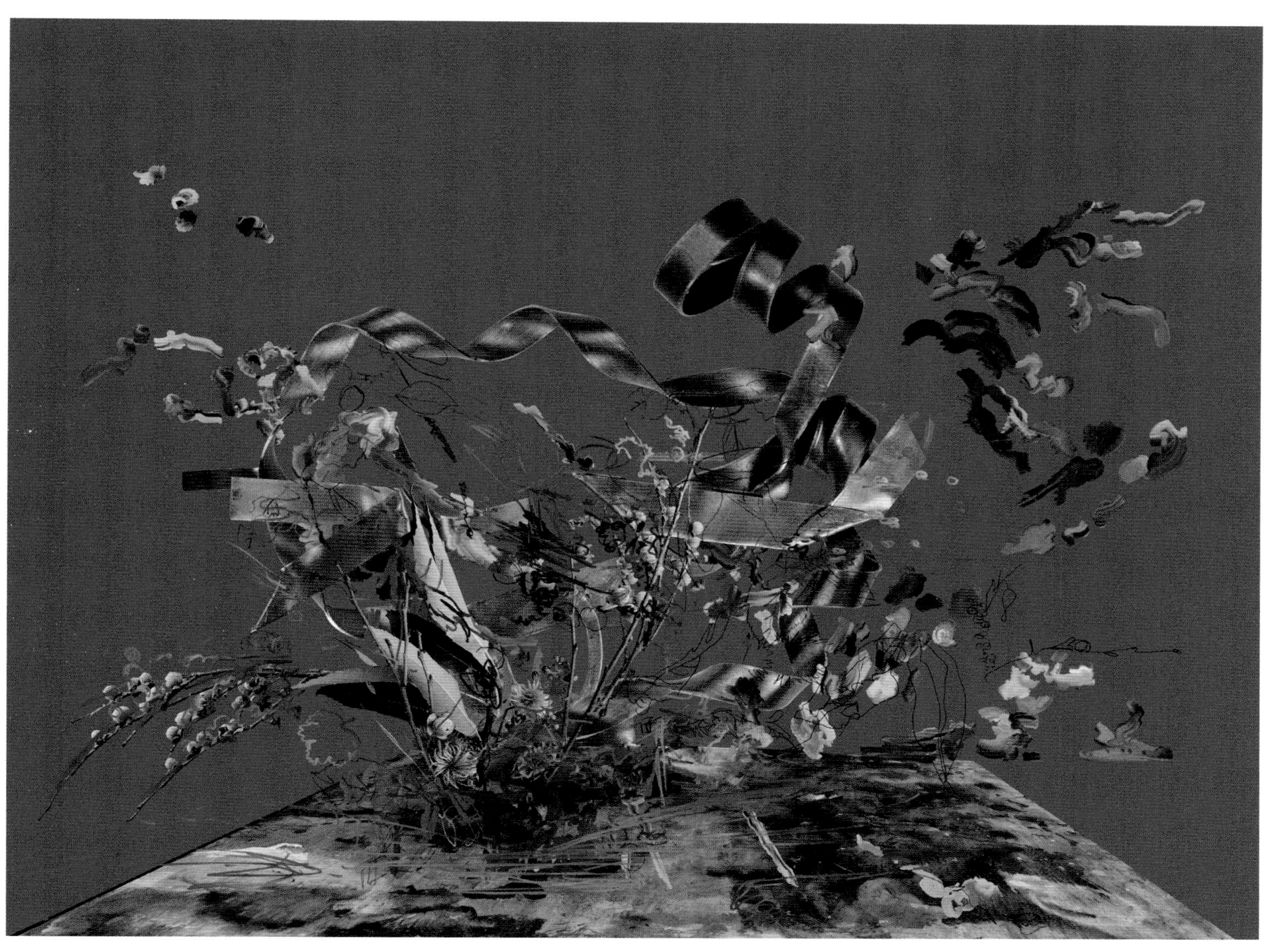

PETRA CORTRIGHT
Untitled, 2020

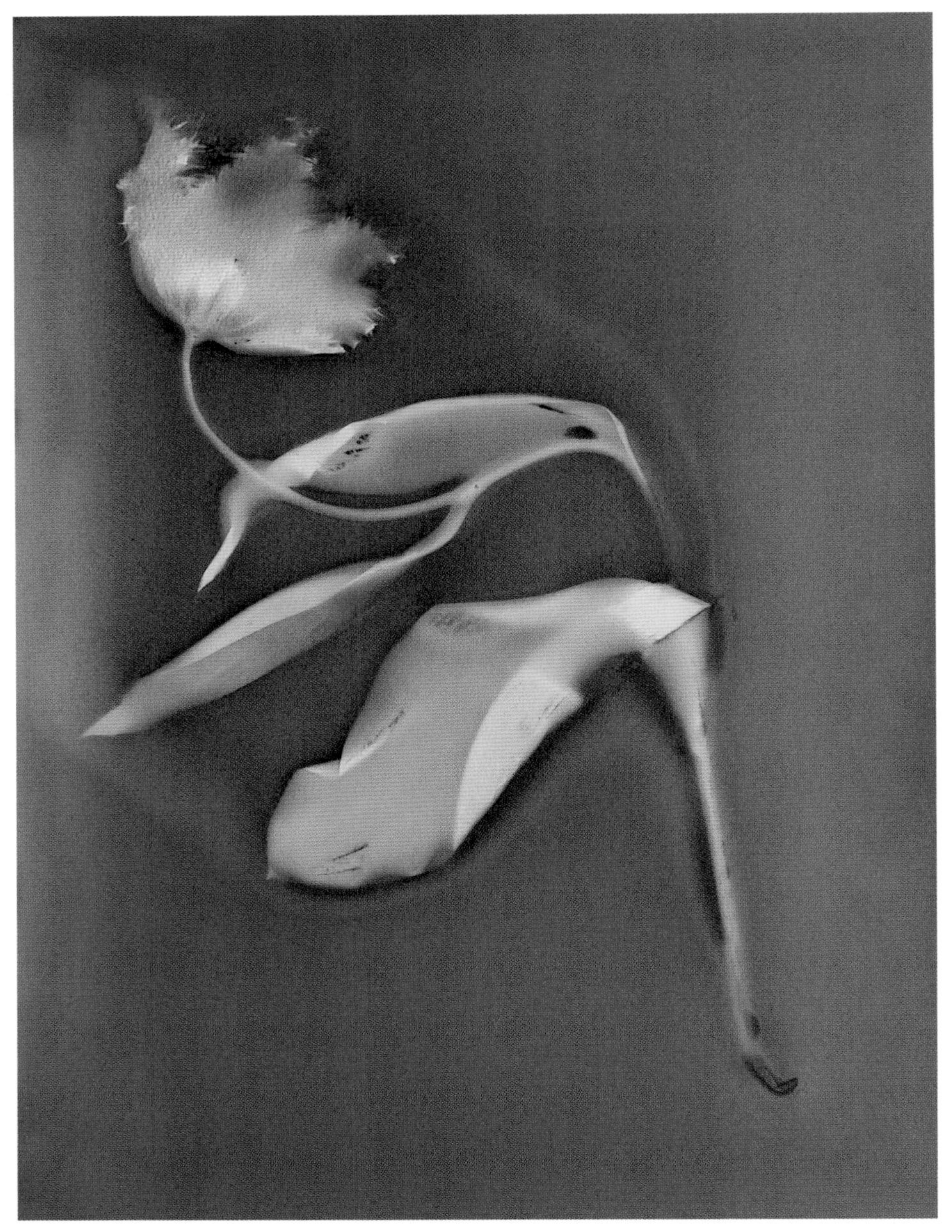

ANNA HALM SCHUDEL
Tulpe Fotogramm, 2003

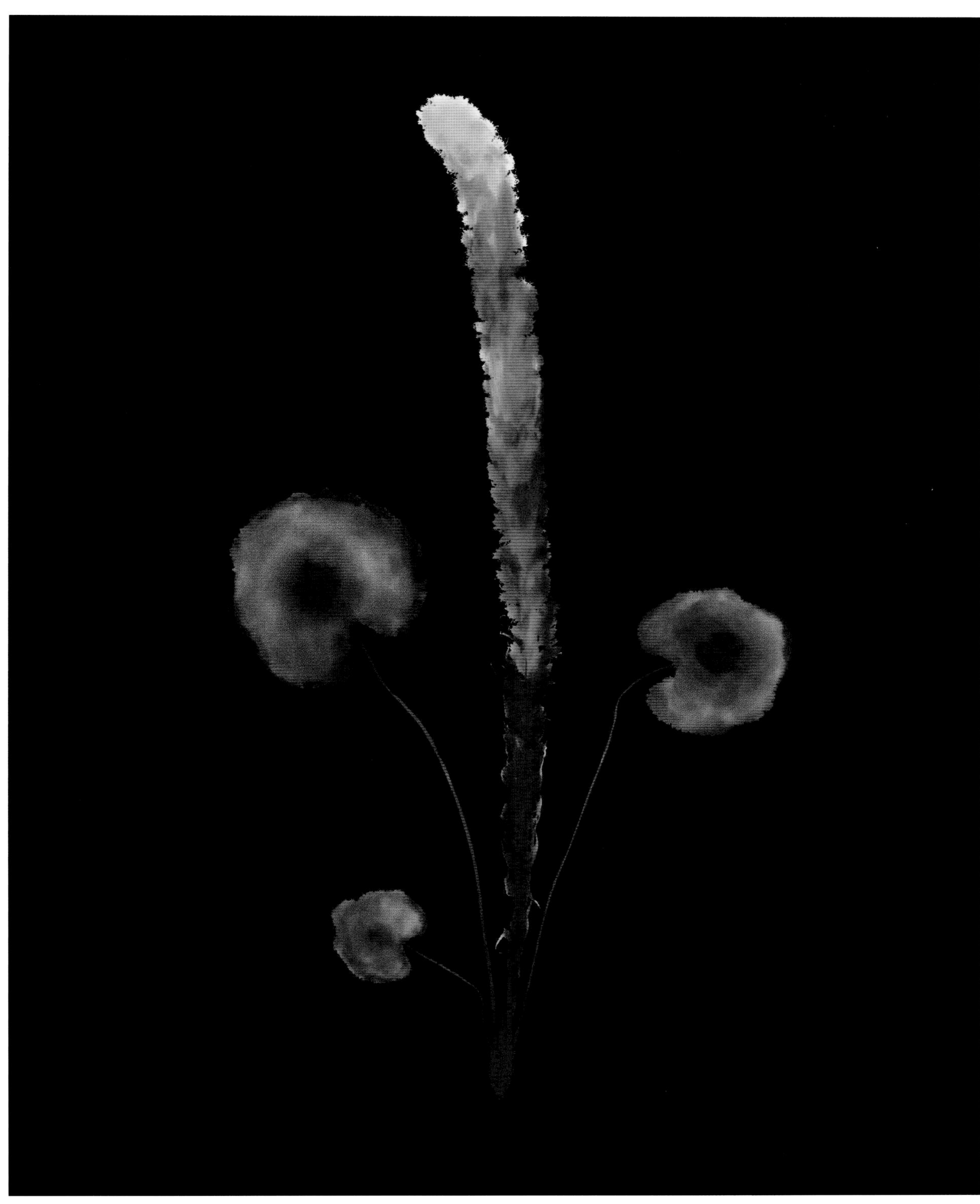

DAVID LEBE
Plant Specimen #20_vE, photogram, 1980/2013

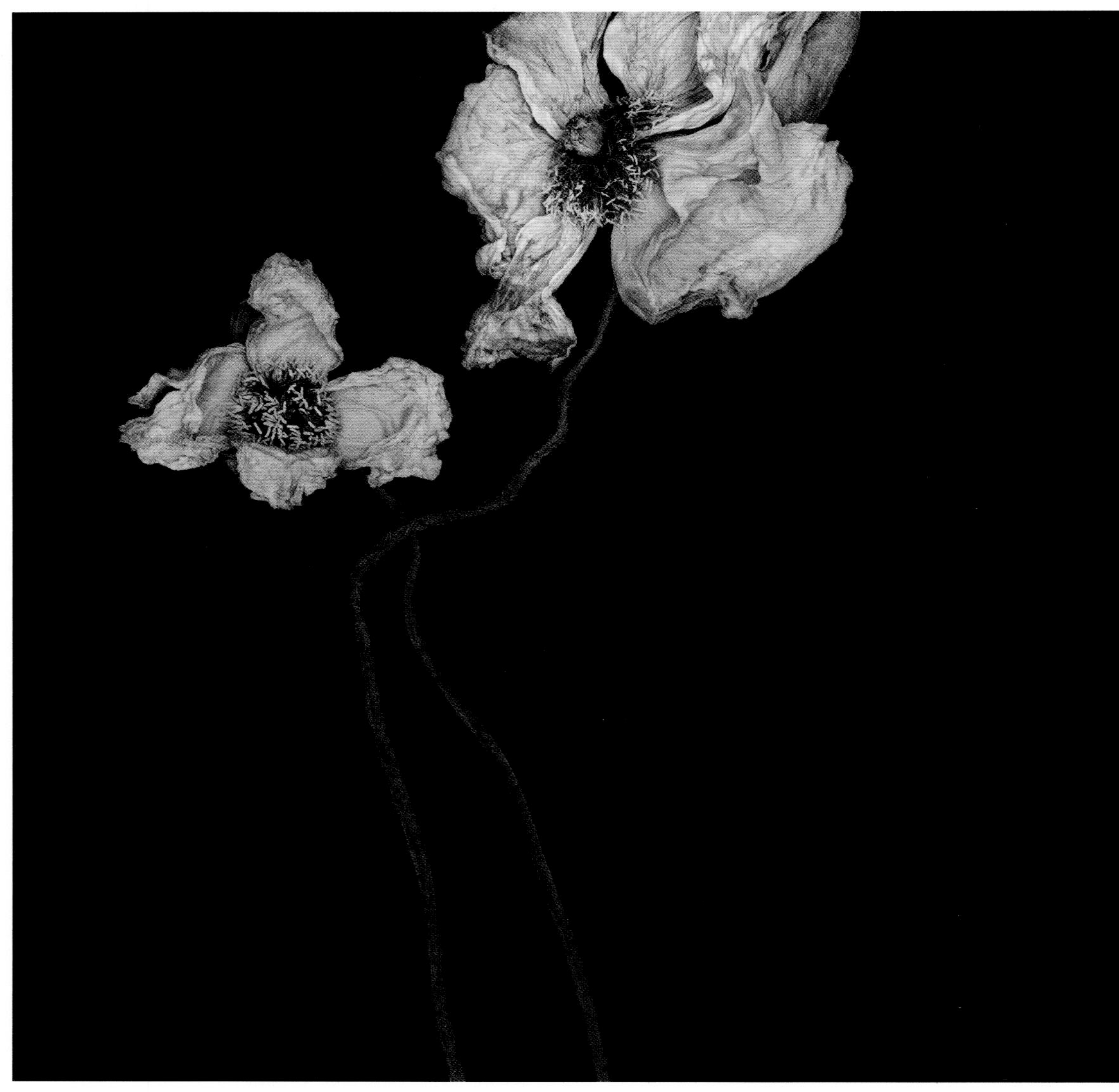

KATHRIN LINKERSDORFF
WS III/1, from the series *Wabi Sabi*, 2018

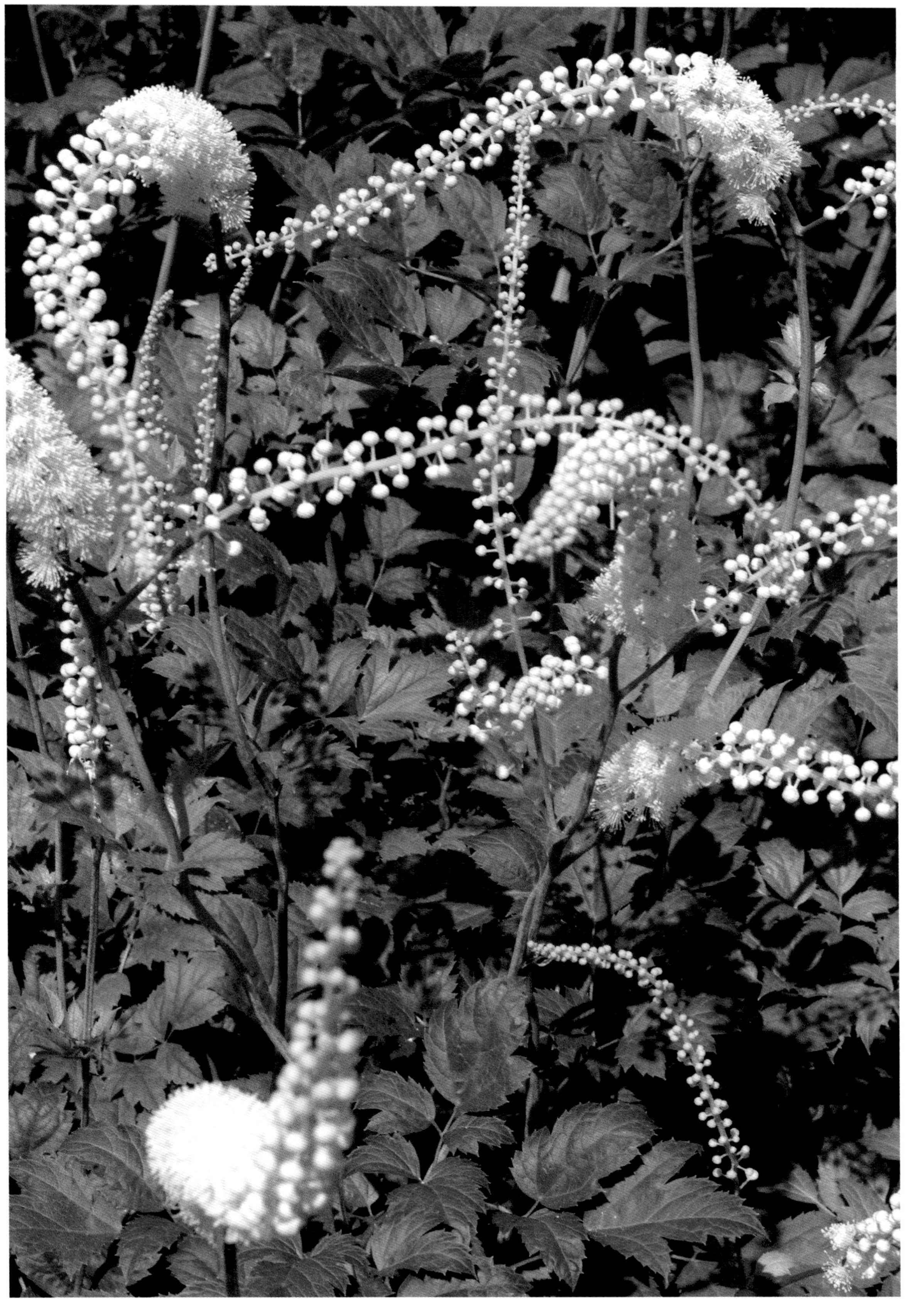

ROBERT WALKER
Montréal botanique #41, 2005

IMPORTANT PARTNERS

Many photographers, inspired by the swirling, pulsating forms of plant life, would share the writer and activist Edward Abbey's sentiments: 'I hold no preference among flowers, so long as they are wild, free, spontaneous.'[3] The primatologist Jane Goodall, famously associated with the animal kingdom, surprised many readers with her admission that plants and flowers had fascinated her since early childhood: 'The plants seemed to want me to share with the world my own understanding of their beingness, so that people might better honour them as important partners in so many of our endeavours.'[4]

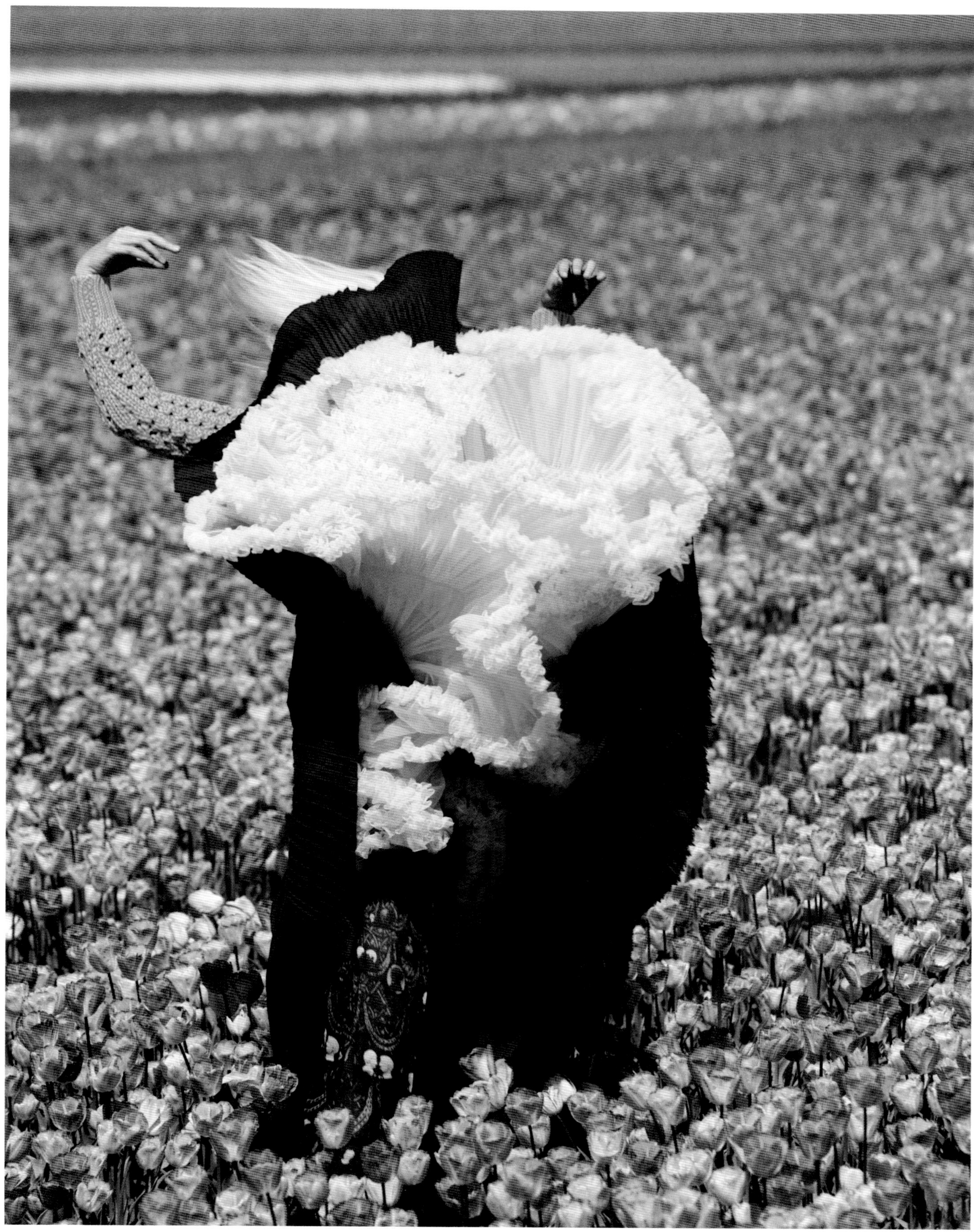

VIVIANE SASSEN
In Bloom, shot for *Dazed & Confused* magazine, 2011

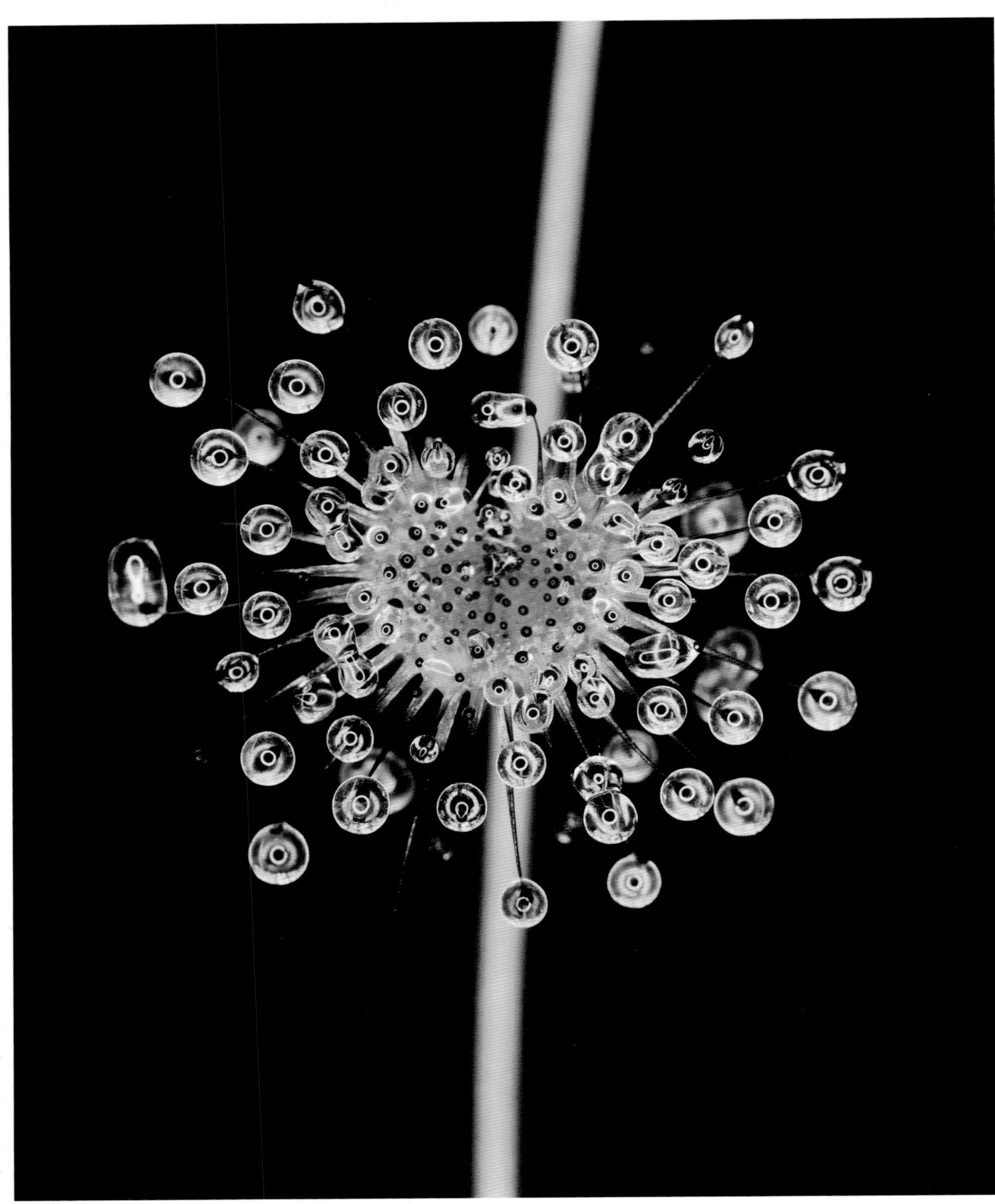

HELENE SCHMITZ
Drosera stolonifera, from the series *Carnivores*, 2010

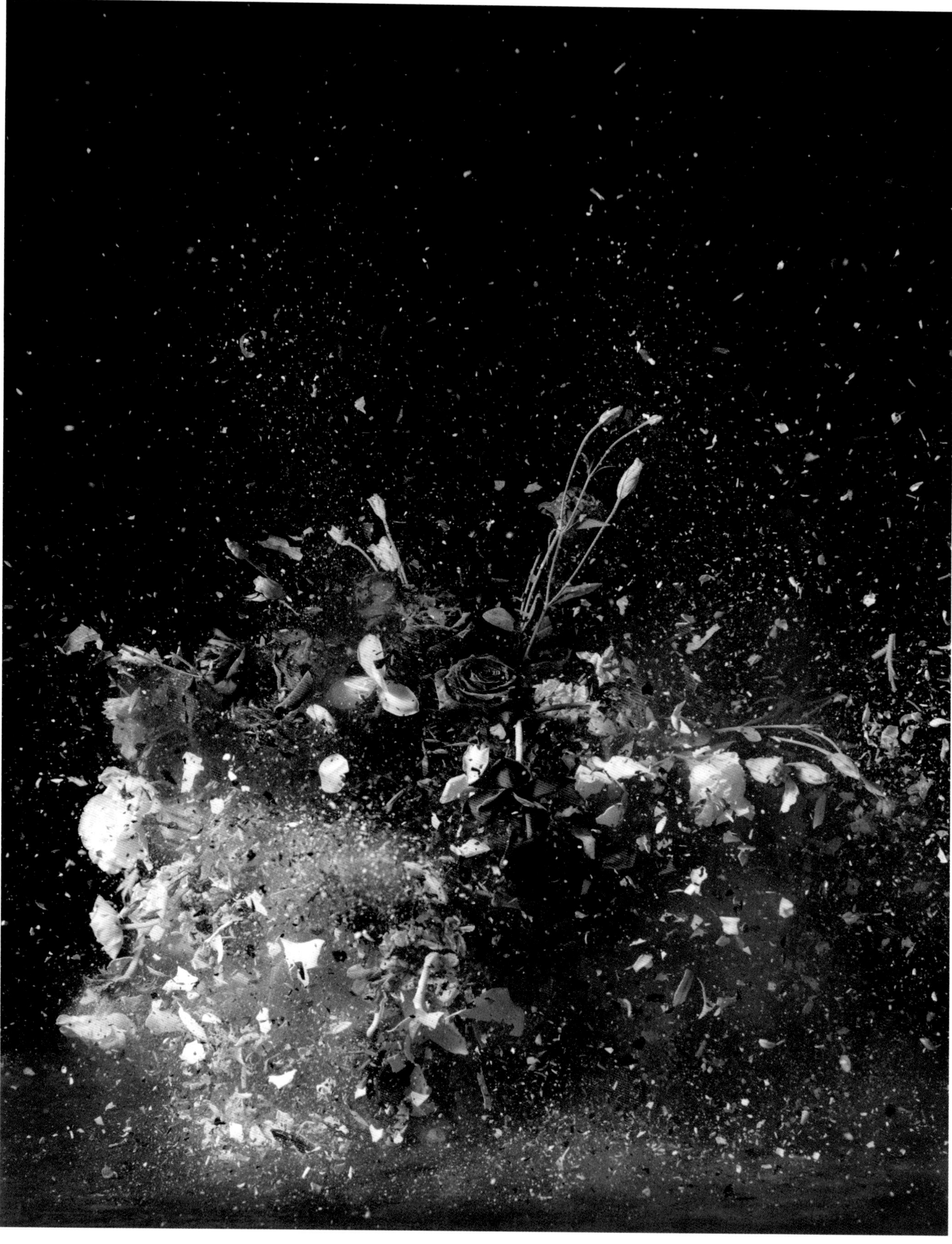

ORI GERSHT
Blow Up 03, 2007

REVERIE

Can one appreciate, even love flowers purely on an aesthetic level, for their glorious diversity of shape, colour and texture? Devoid of their symbolic attributes, which are so deeply embedded in culture? Perhaps, but with difficulty. Almost always symbolism suggests itself. Sometimes the symbols in a photograph are explicit, intended to be read as such; at other times the photographer is content merely to hint at a reading, preferring to leave it to the viewer's own associations.

Either way, it seems we cannot help but read meaning into *any* depiction of a flower, unless presented in a purely scientific manner as a botanical illustration. And even here we see one 'specimen' in terms of human and emotional attributes: this one is stronger and more vigorous; that one more joyous and youthful.

Even when an emphasis is placed on sheer beauty, photographers often weave their floral subjects into dreamlike frameworks, *reveries*. The rich tradition of the still life provides many time-honoured devices for conveying messages – the *vanitas*, for example. The collage, the montage, the photogram, the manipulated print...photographers refuse to be limited by conventional techniques.

The sentiments expressed in these reveries vary, however. There are the bright, positive fantasies, where the flower appears as a beacon of hope or spiritual uplift. Then there are dreamlike images where flowers are depicted *super*naturally, otherworldly, as a kind of Platonic ideal not to be found in the material world, or not quite so perfectly. But there are also dark and unsettling images, nightmarish even, where flowers – Charles Baudelaire's *Fleurs du mal*, perhaps – conjure up a world in disorder, or perhaps a disturbed psyche unable to cope with it.

In the very important and persuasive commercial domain, flowers are universally symbols of perfection (many firms have made a specific flower an emblem of their enterprise). Eternal youth, perfect health and flawless perfection are the beguiling messages here. But the serious artist sees the other side of the coin: death, disease, decay. A reverie can be bittersweet, too. 'Yes, flowers have their language,' wrote the journalist Frederic Shoberl in 1834, while William Henry Fox Talbot was experimenting with laying flowers on photosensitive paper. 'Theirs is an oratory that speaks in perfumed silence,' wrote another author anonymously at around the same time, 'and there is tenderness, and passion, and even the light-heartedness of mirth, in the variegated beauty of their vocabulary.'[1]

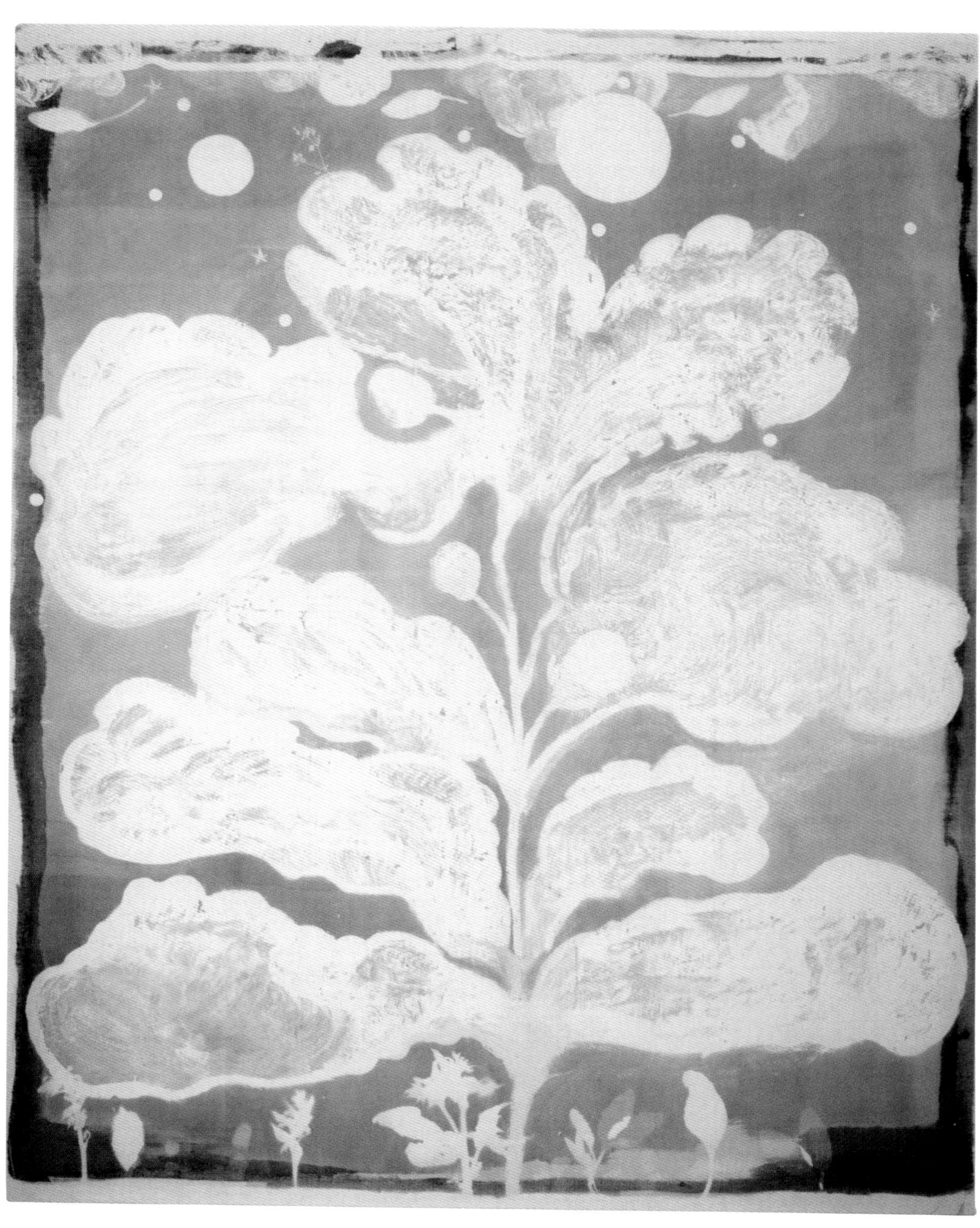

LISA LURATI
Nebulosa 2, 2020

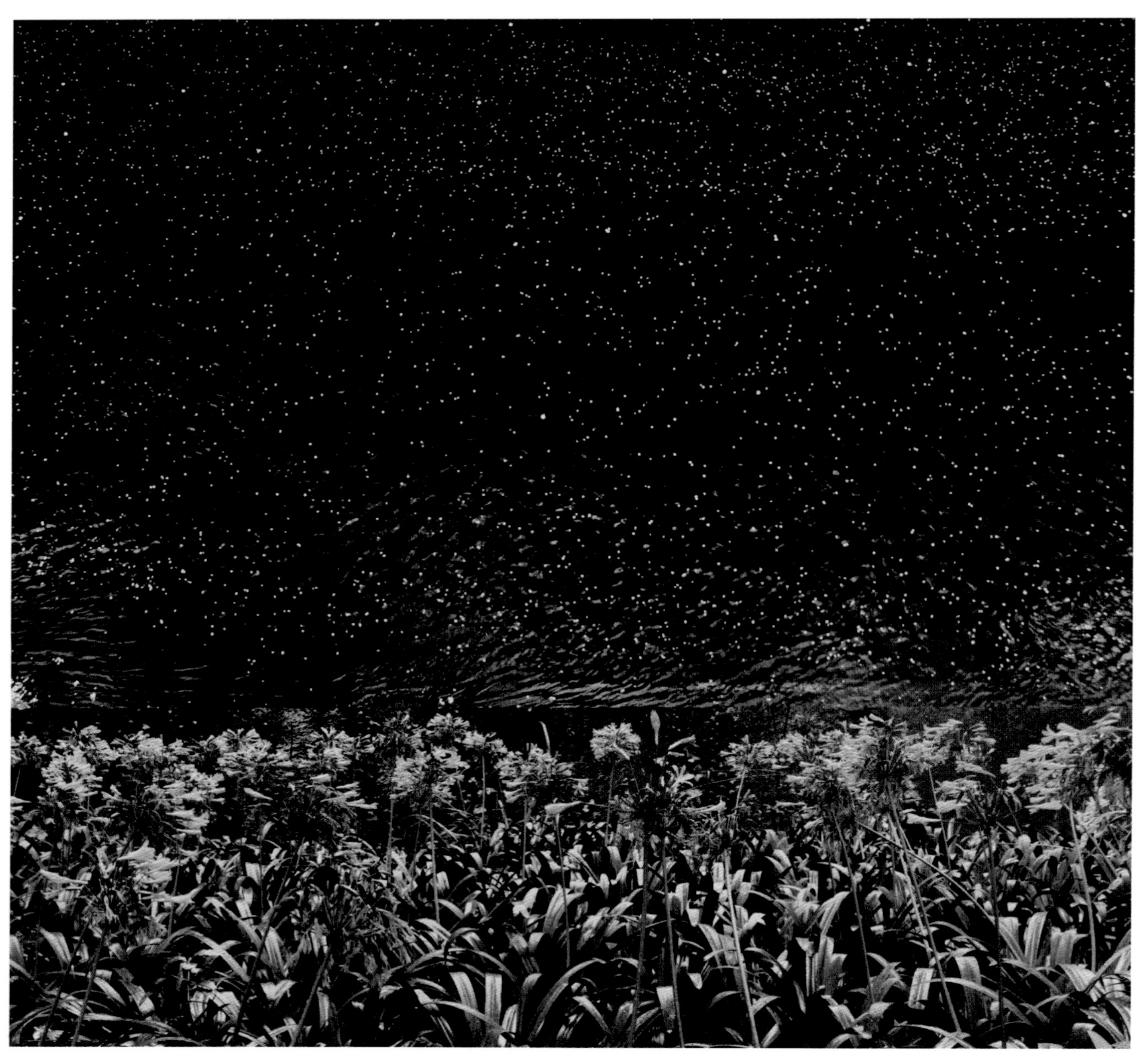

ALBARRÁN CABRERA
The Mouth of Krishna #172, 2013

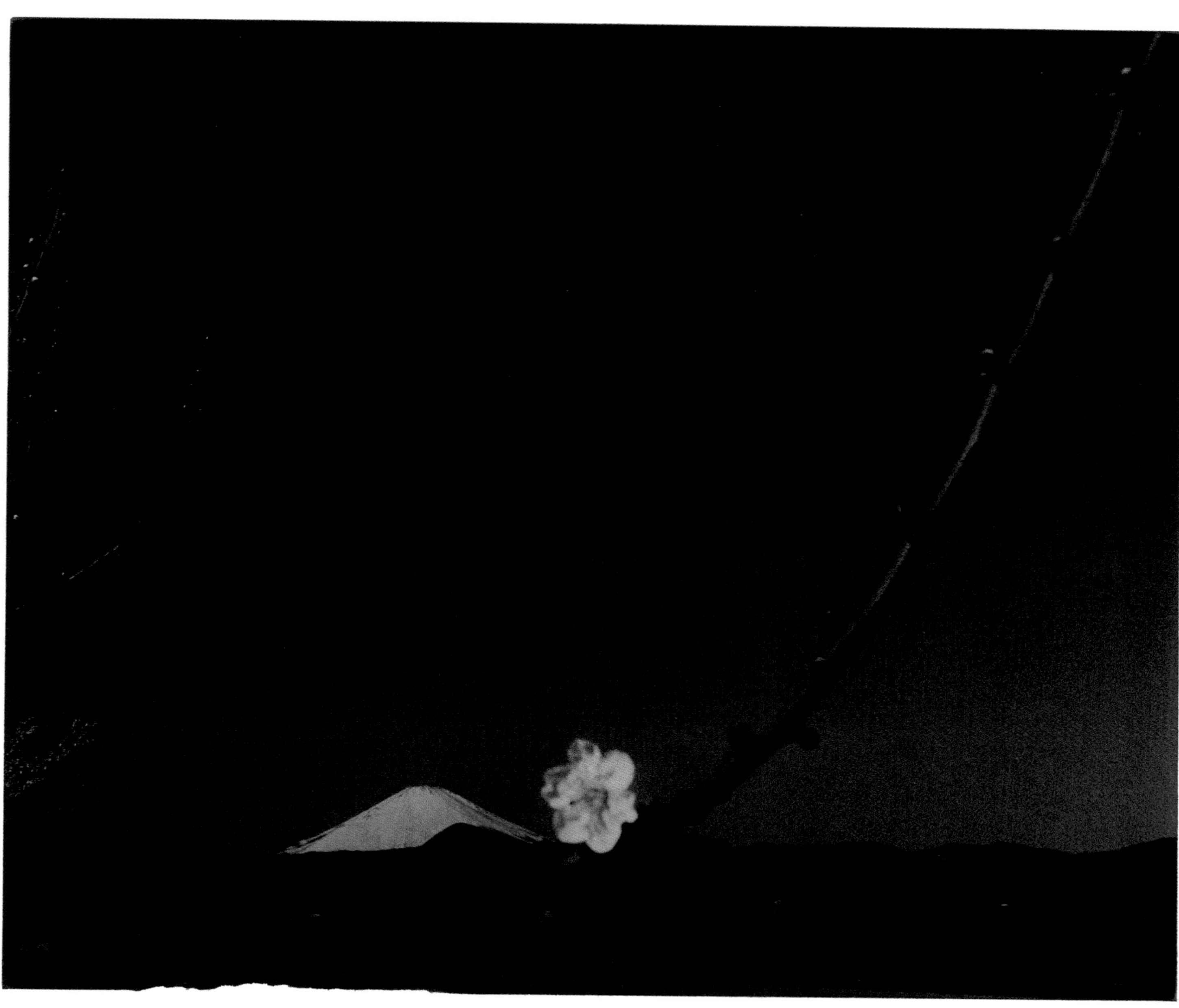

YAMAMOTO MASAO
A Box of Ku #764, 2000

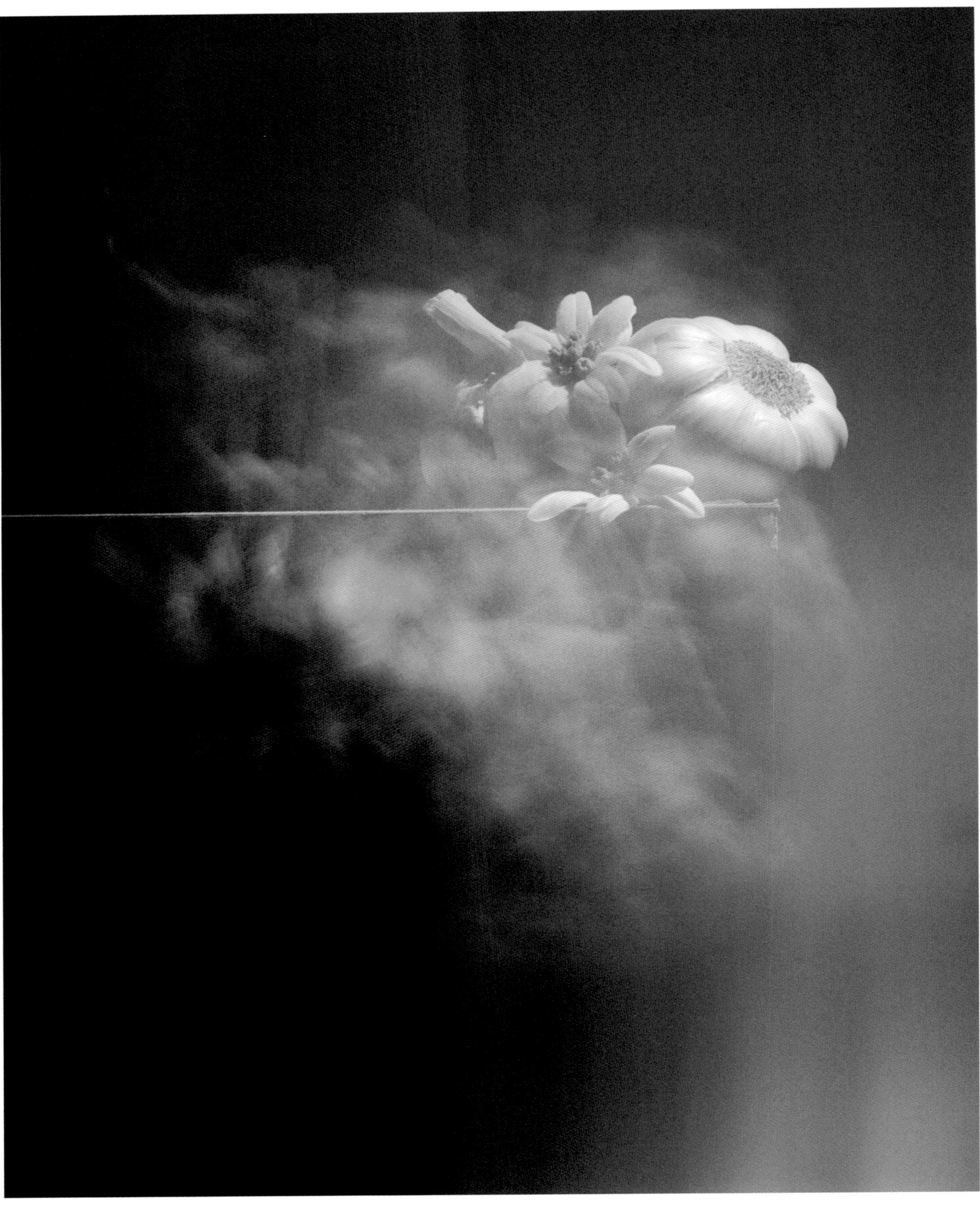

ROBERTO GRECO
Les chiens et les Italiens dehors!, from the series *Porter sa peau*, 2020

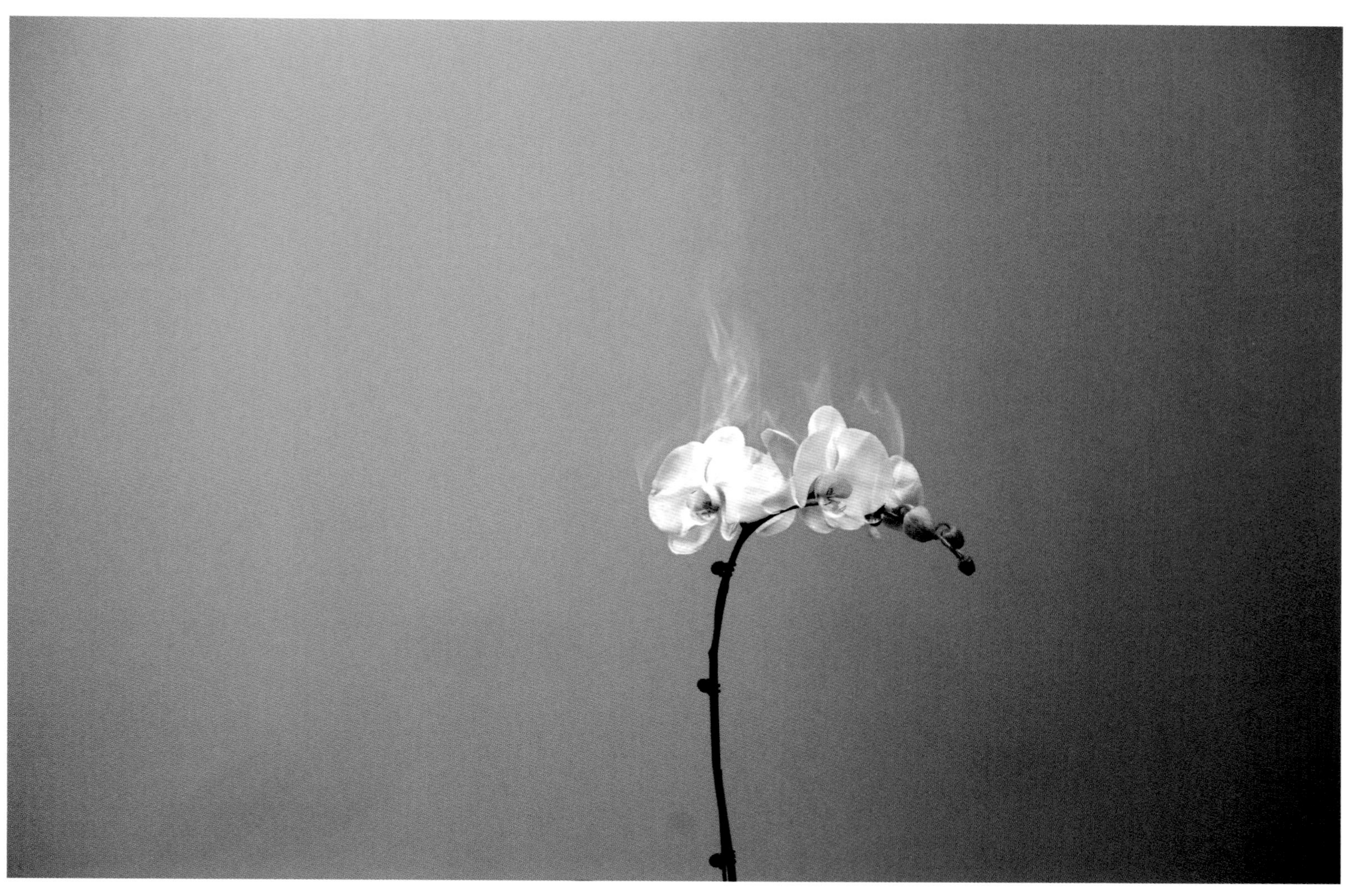

JIANG ZHI
Love Letter No. 05, 2011

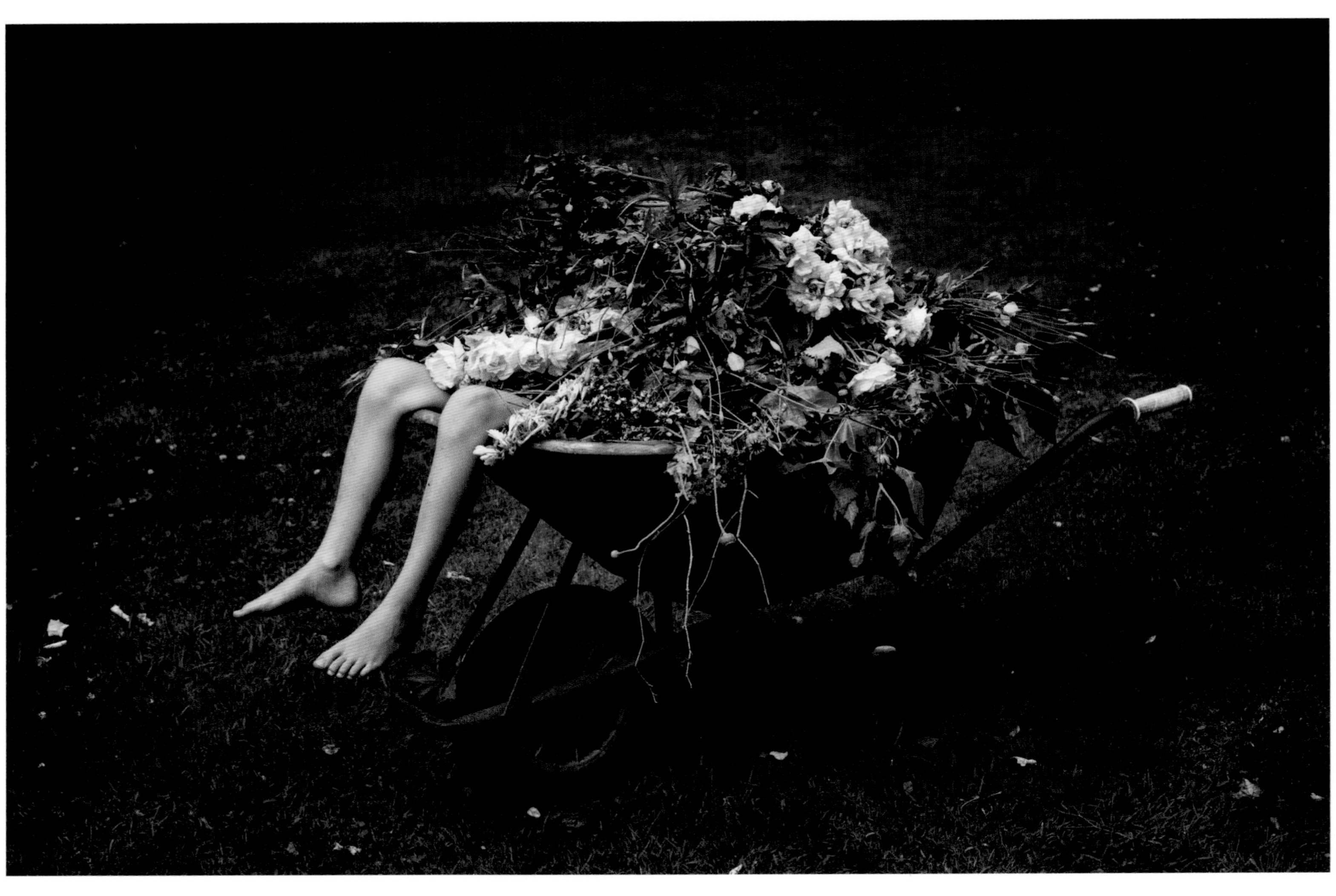

AIMÉE HOVING
Compost, from the series *L'Etre Aimée*, 2019
(flowers by Brigitte Grentis Van dam Merret)

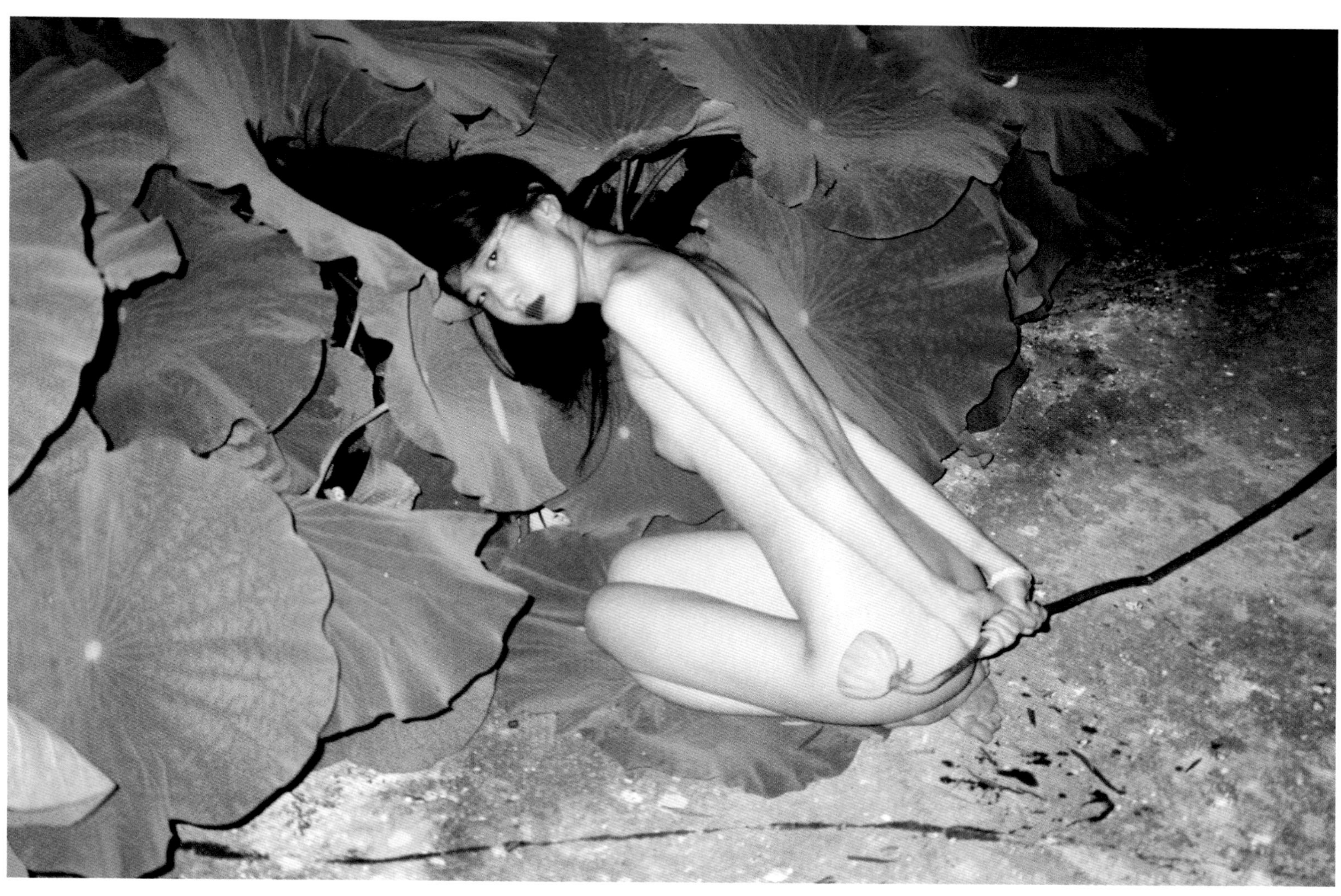

REN HANG
Untitled 03, 2010

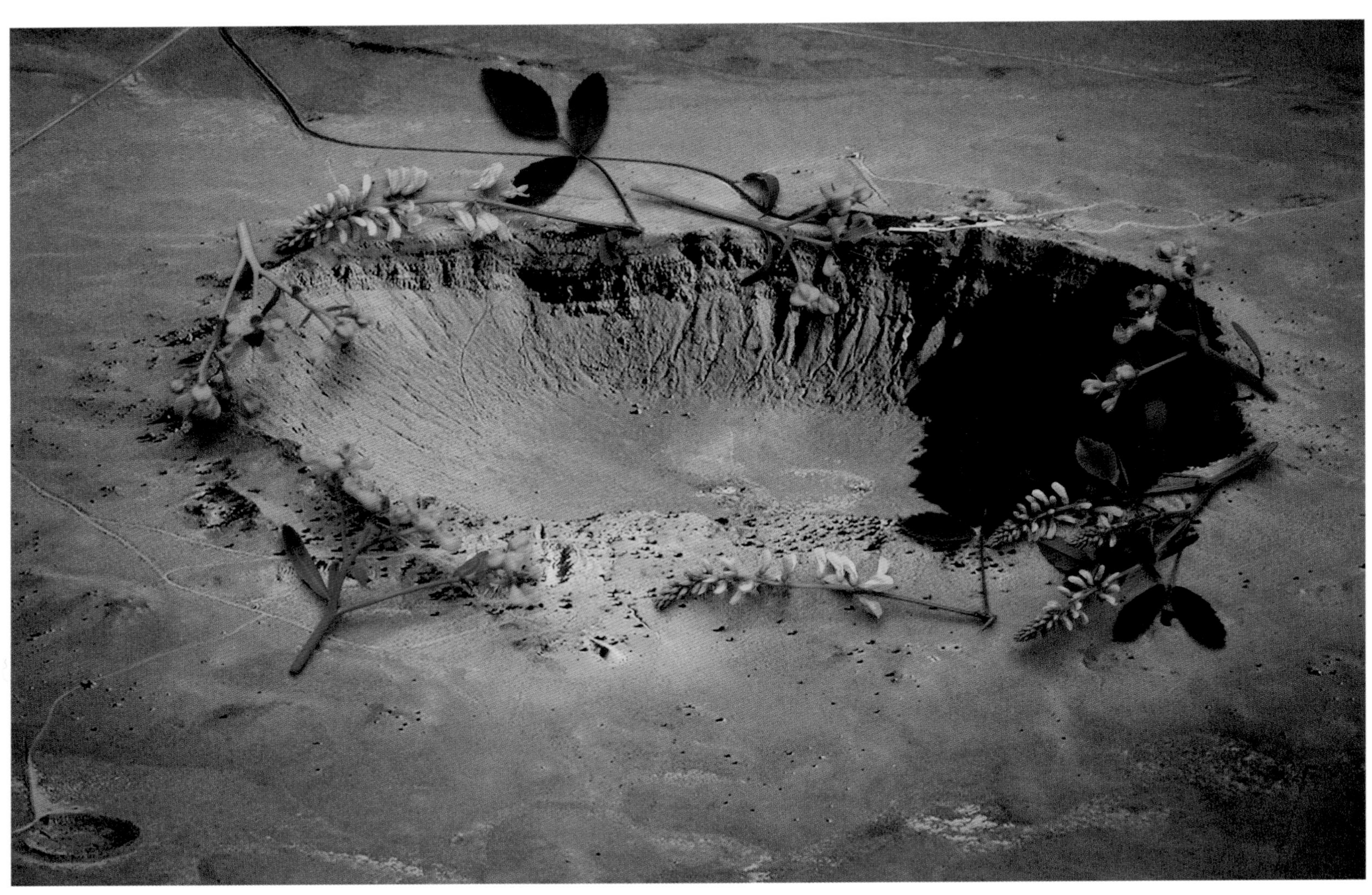

LAURENCE AËGERTER
Ruta graveolens i.a. – Barrington Crater, Arizona, USA, from the series *Healing Plants for Hurt Landscapes*, 2015

After a careful reconstruction of a medicinal garden in Leeuwarden, the Netherlands, Laurence Aëgerter invited the residents to a symbolical healing ritual. Participants were encouraged to 'treat' the photographs of destroyed landscapes with medicinal plants from the garden.

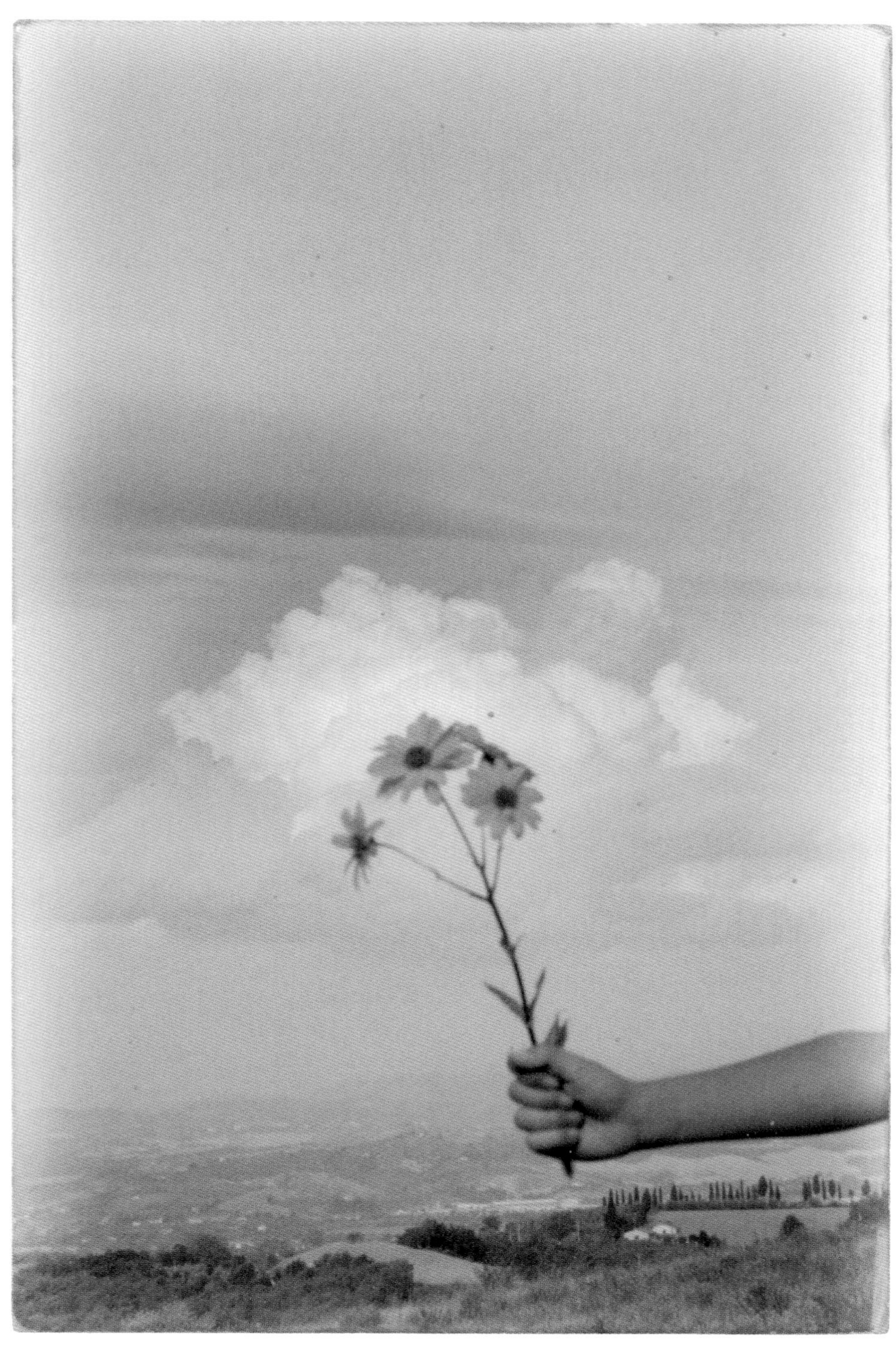

YAMAMOTO MASAO
Nakazora #1092, 2004

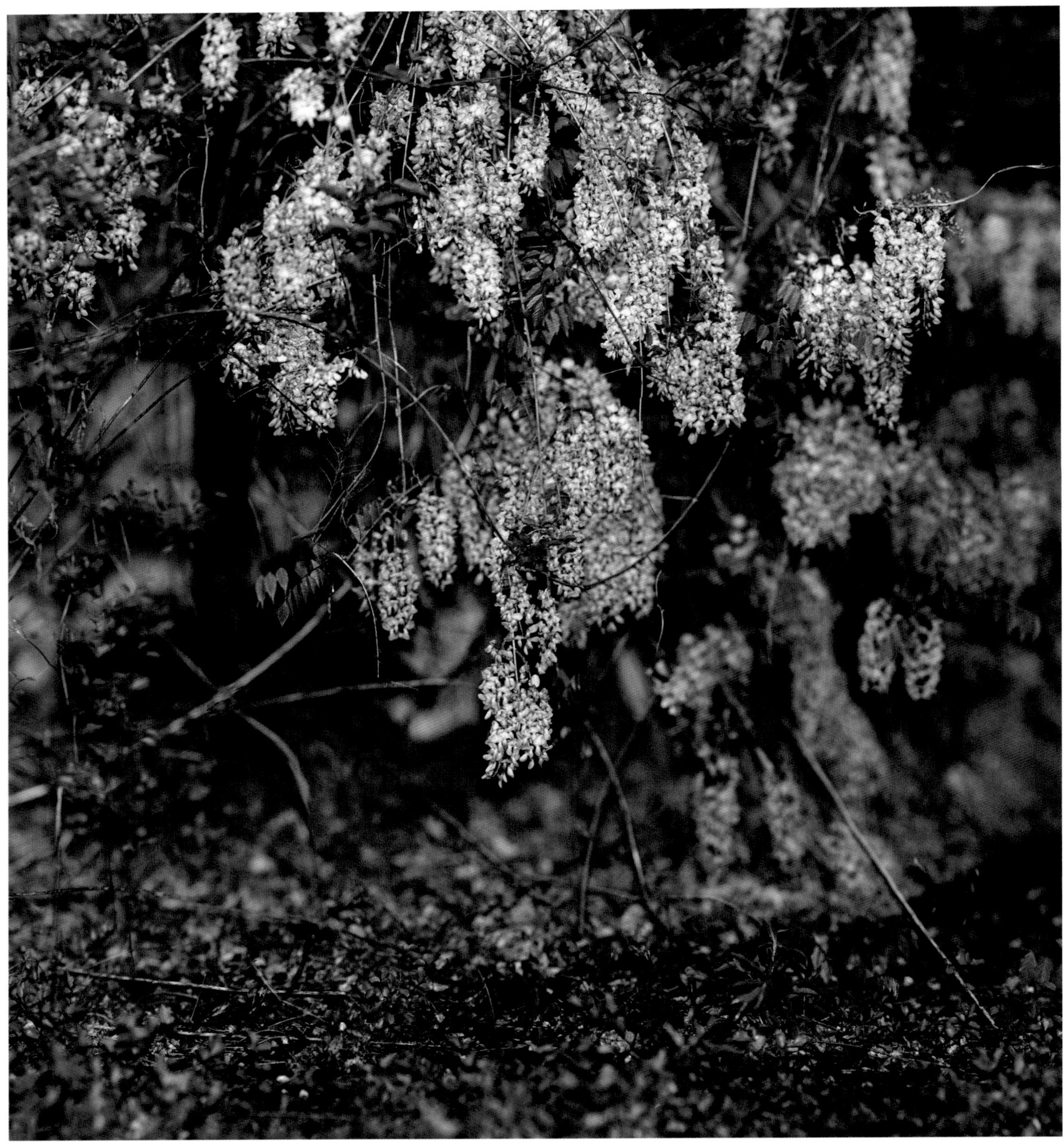

RUDOLF STEINER
Glycine 10, from the series *Ricochet*, 27 July 2019

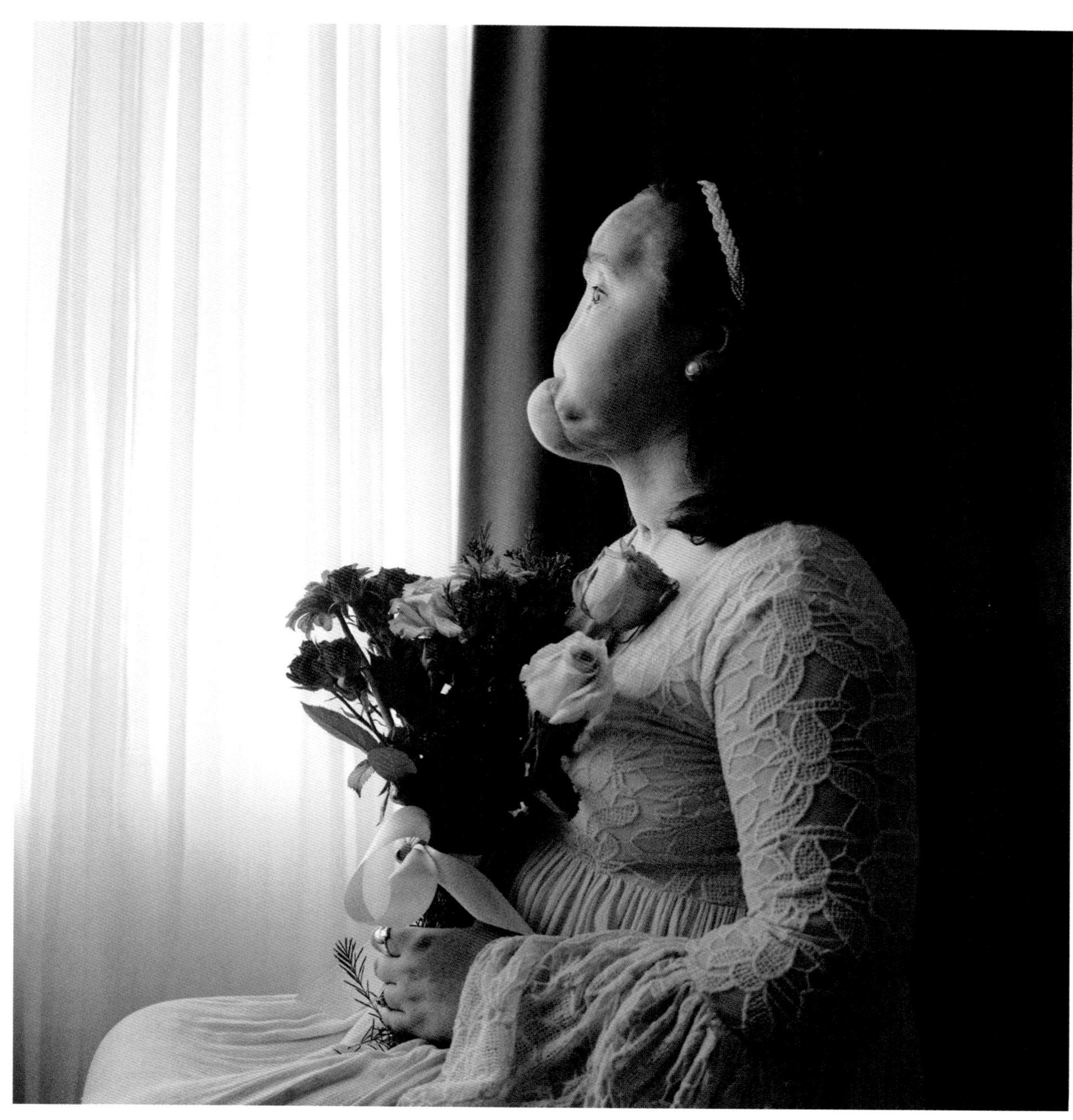

MAGGIE STEBER
The Girl Without a Face, November 2016

Maggie Steber followed the journey of Katie Stubblefield, a face-transplant recipient who lived for three years with a temporary face created by surgeons using flesh from her stomach and thigh after shooting her own face off with a rifle, until a face became available from a woman who overdosed on drugs. 'When I went to photograph the family, I would always do a portrait session with Katie and flowers to try to make something beautiful, even though Katie could not see it, having lost a lot of her eyesight. At least her parents could see it.'

If a man could pass thro' Paradise in a Dream, & have a flower presented to him as a pledge that his Soul had really been there, & found that flower in his hand when he awoke - Aye ! and what then?

Attributed to Samuel Taylor Coleridge[2]

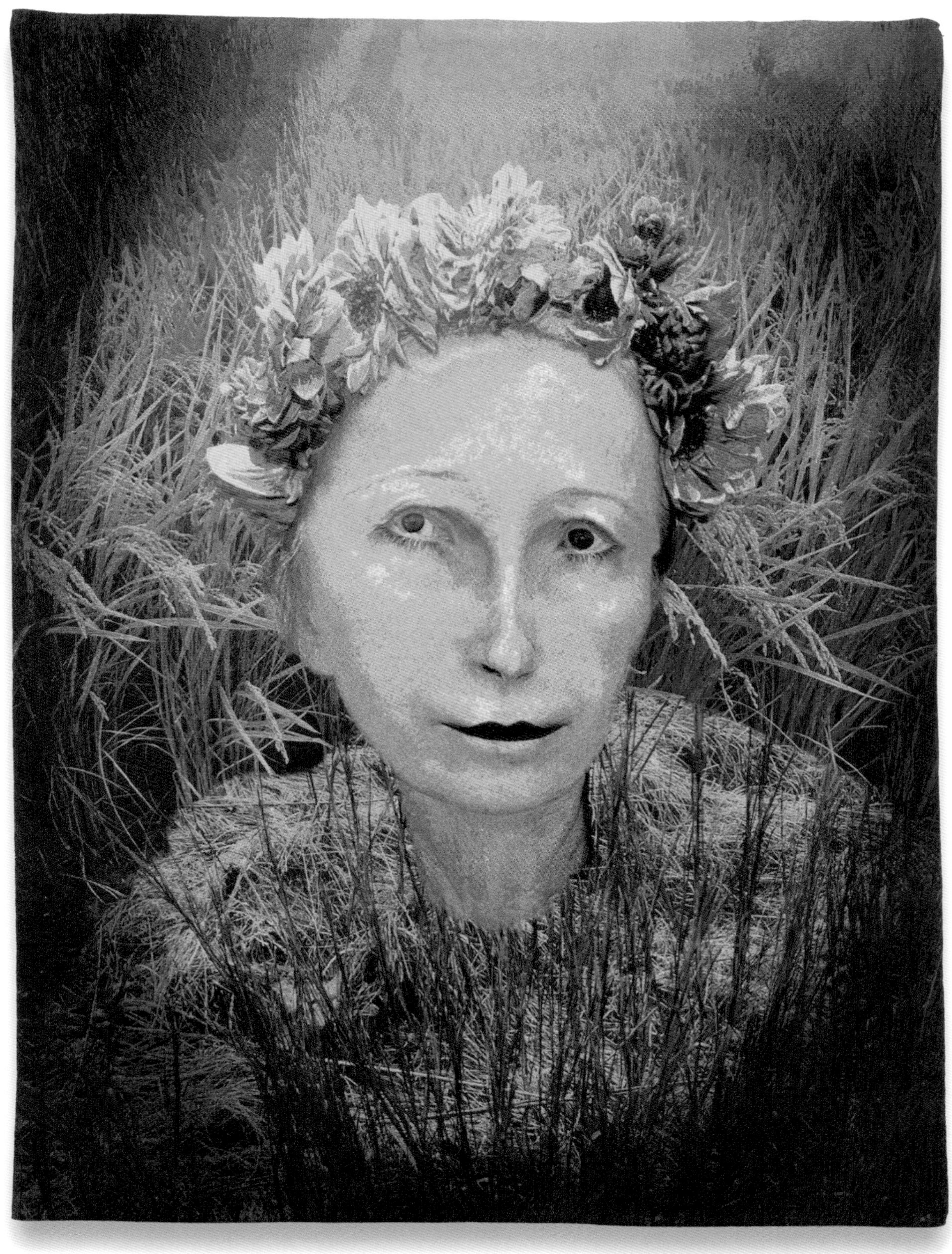

CINDY SHERMAN
Untitled, cotton, wool, acrylic, polyester and cotton mercurisé woven together,
285 × 214 cm (112¼ × 84¼ in.), 2021

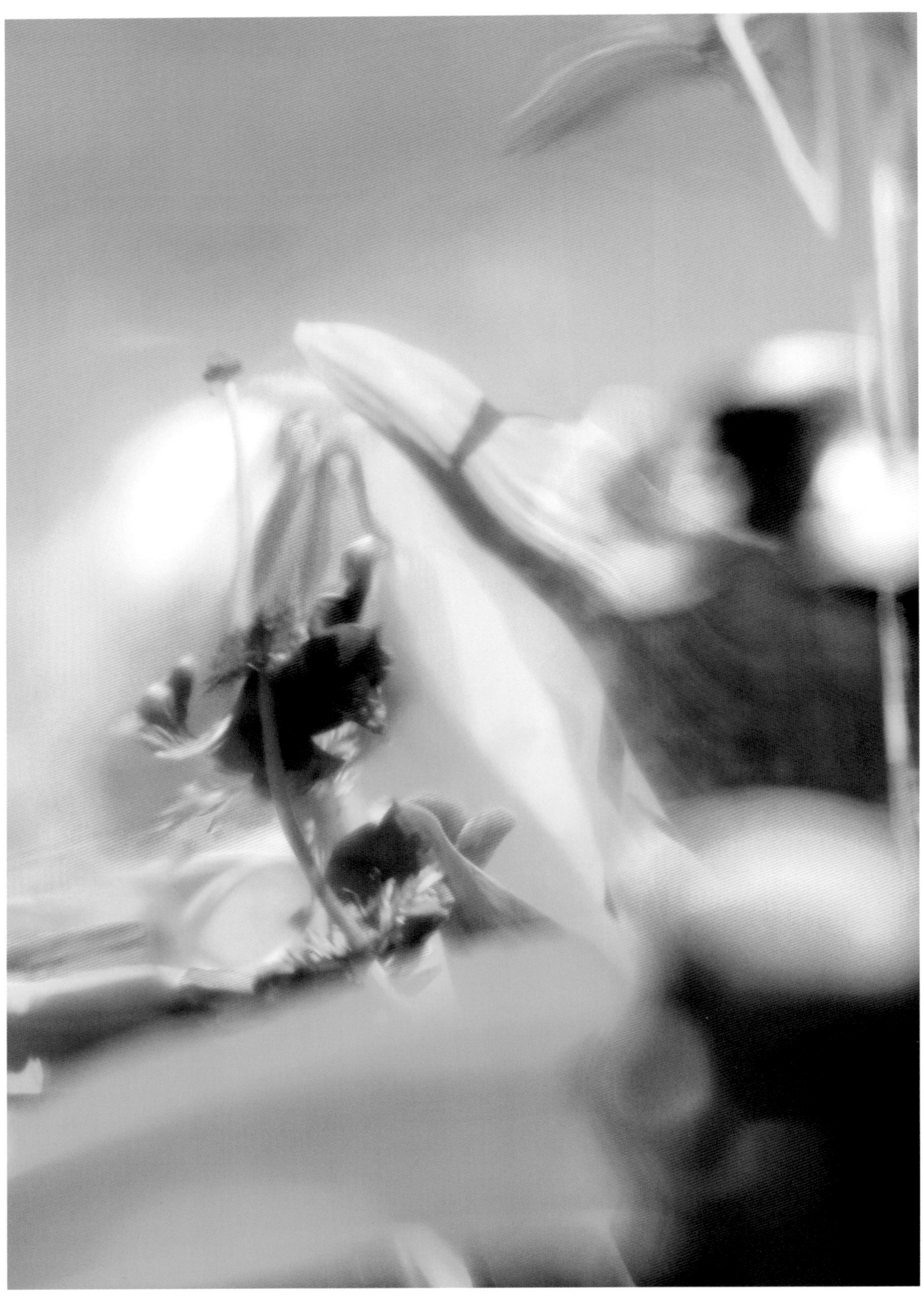

PAUL ROUSTEAU
Giverny, Beyond Photography, 2019

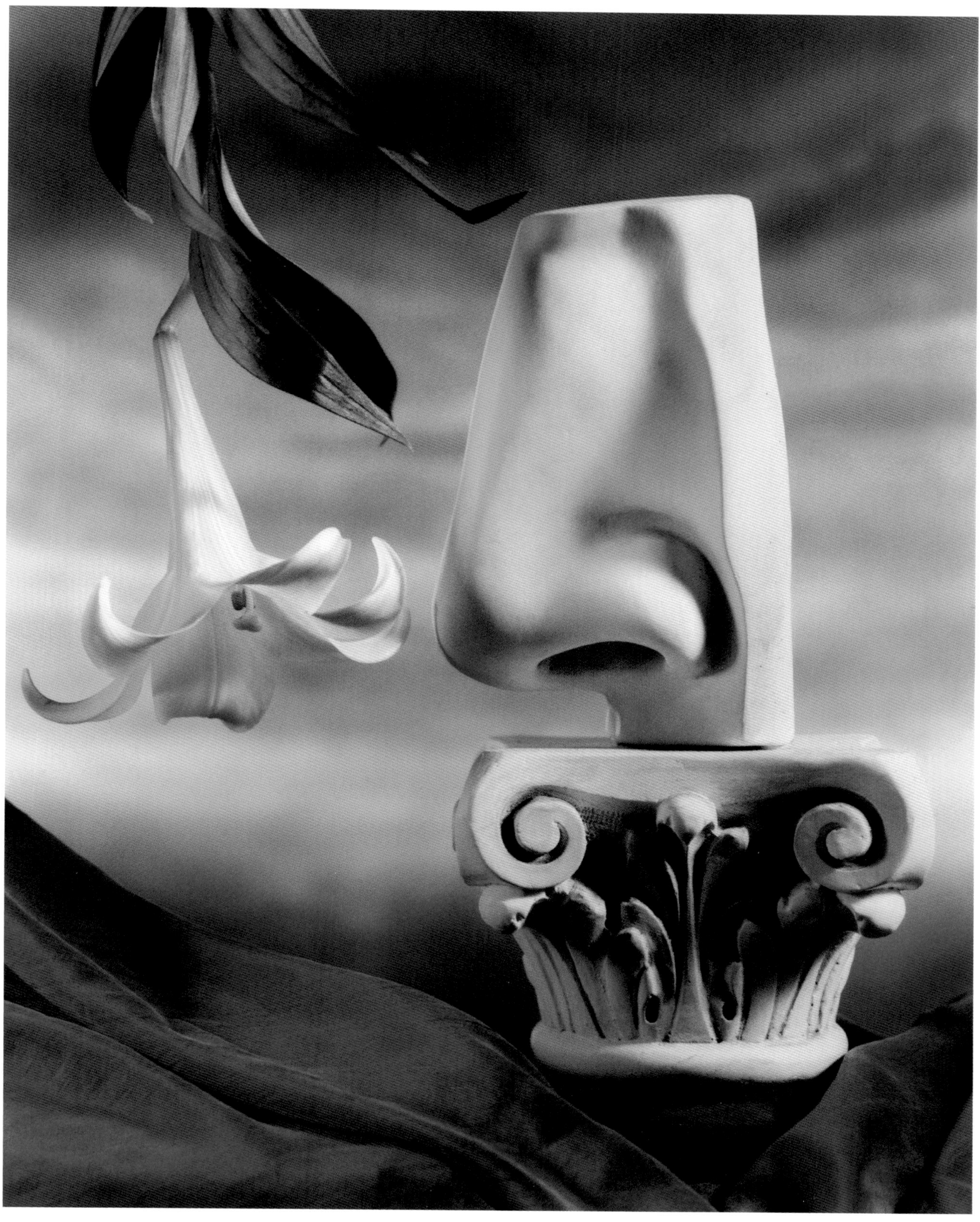

JO WHALEY
Knows No Scents, 1991

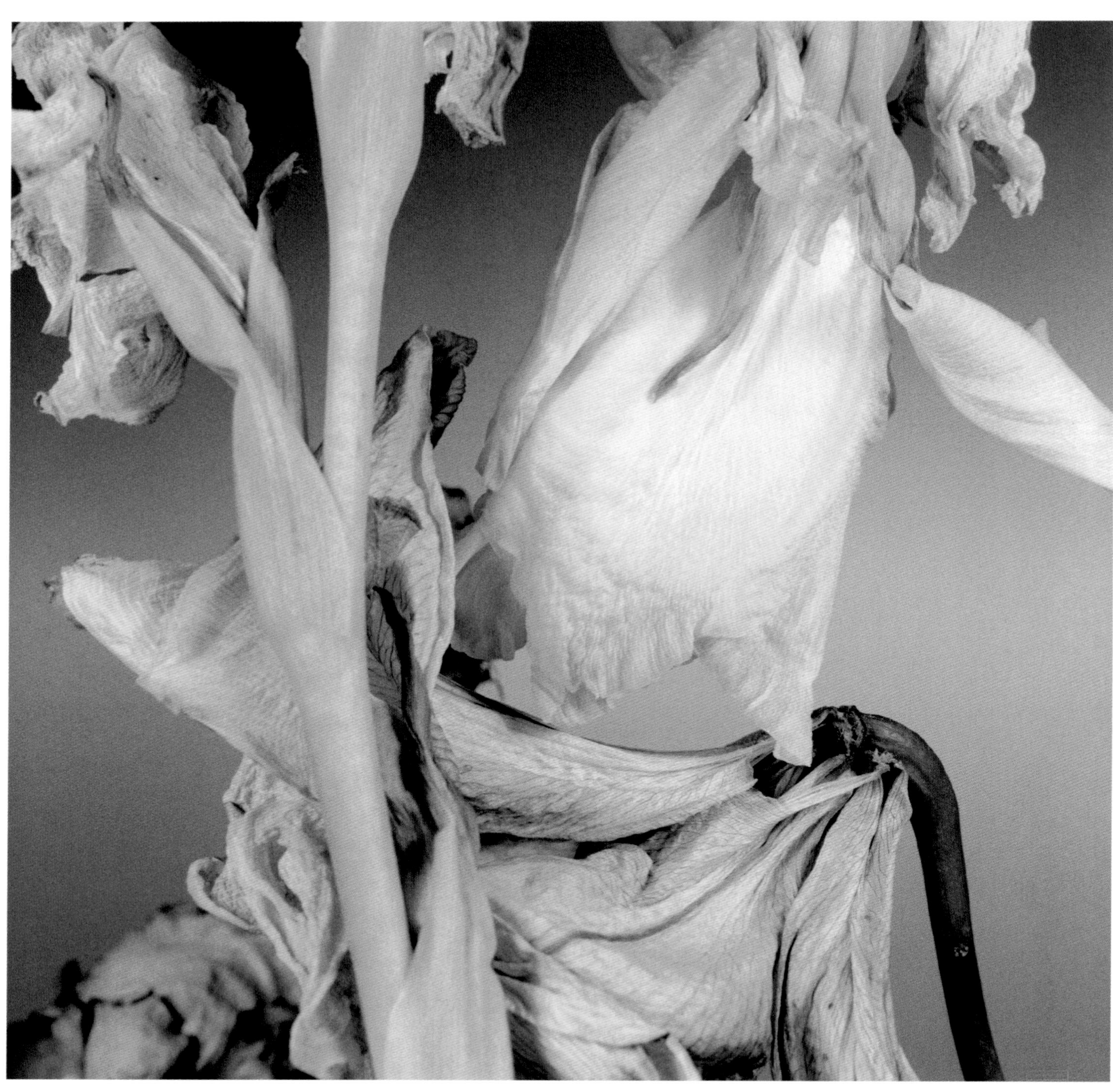

AMIN EL DIB
R 1029-08, from the series *CutFlowerImages*, 1999

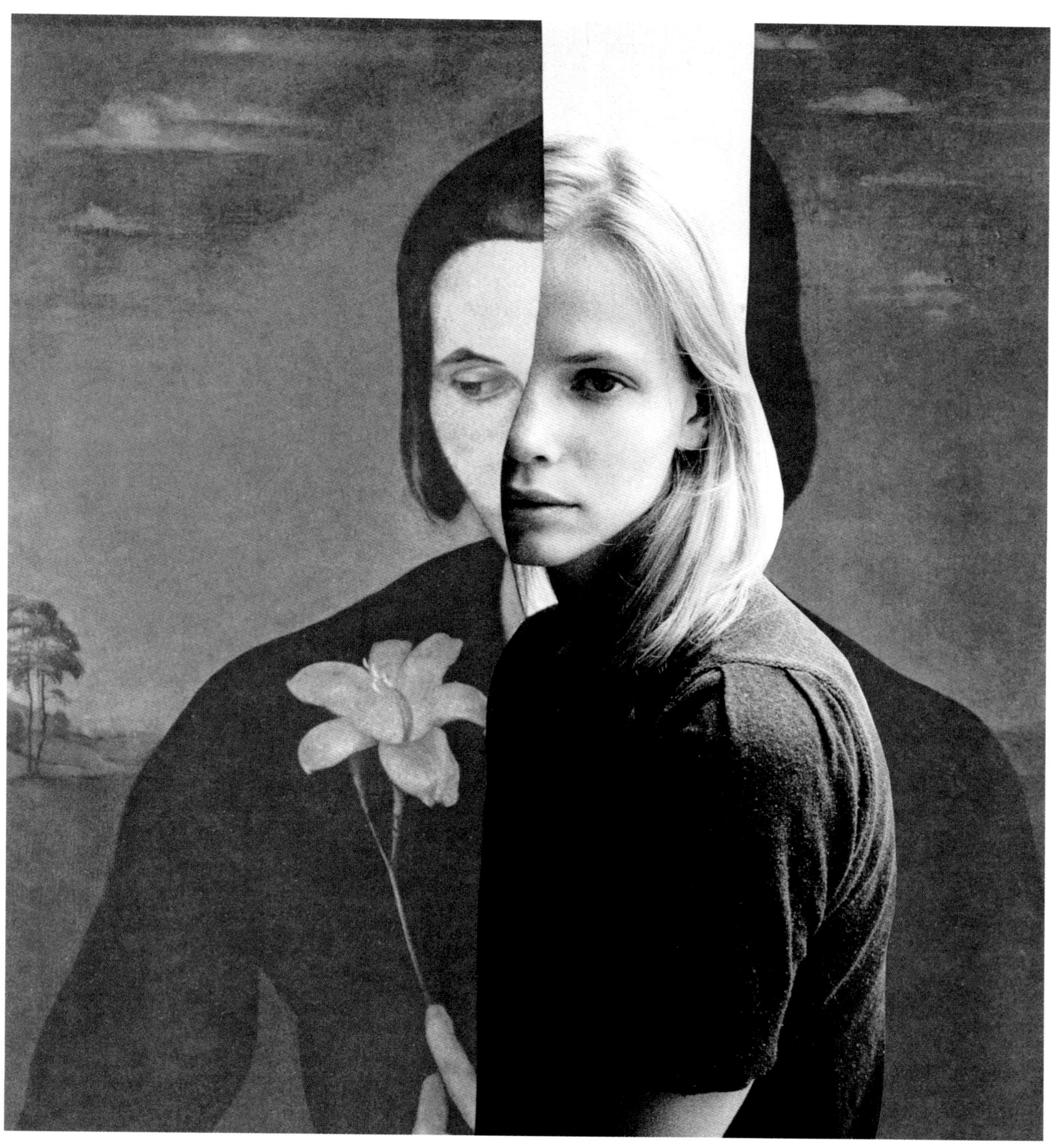

MIRIAM TÖLKE
Flower of Yesterday, 2019

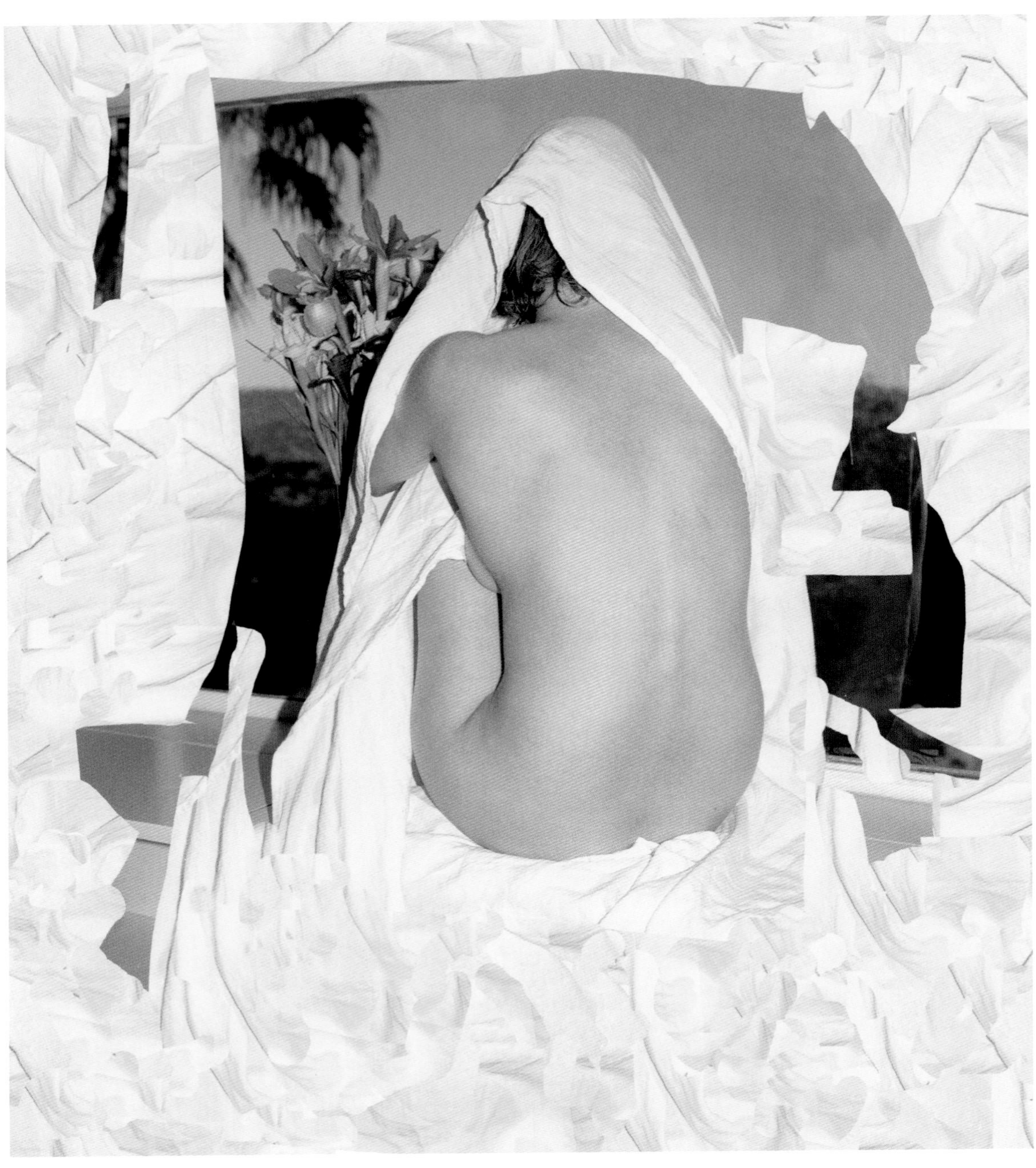

NICO KRIJNO
Mignonne with Iris, 2015

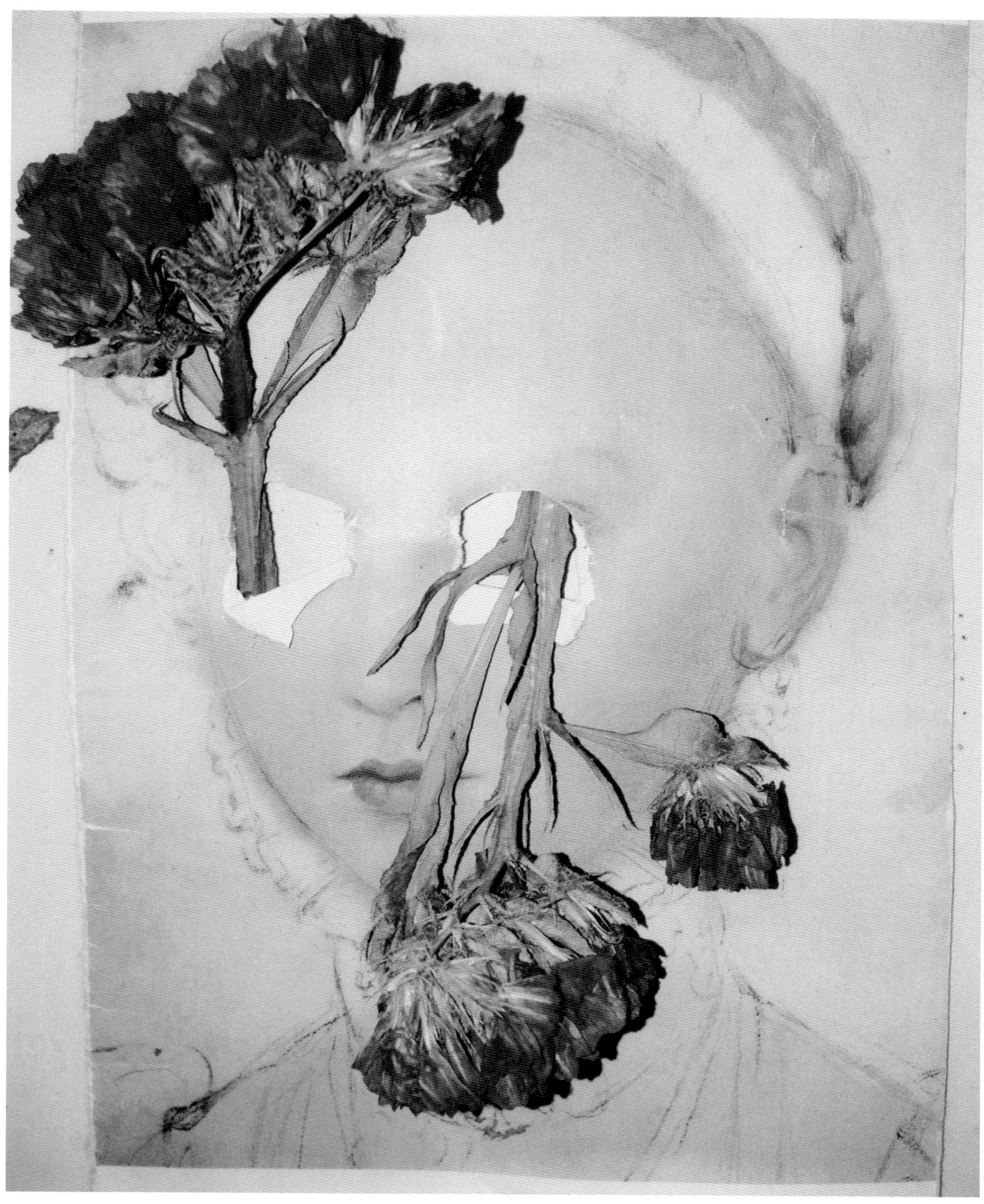

LISA LURATI
Morning Stretching Exercise for Flexibility, 2017

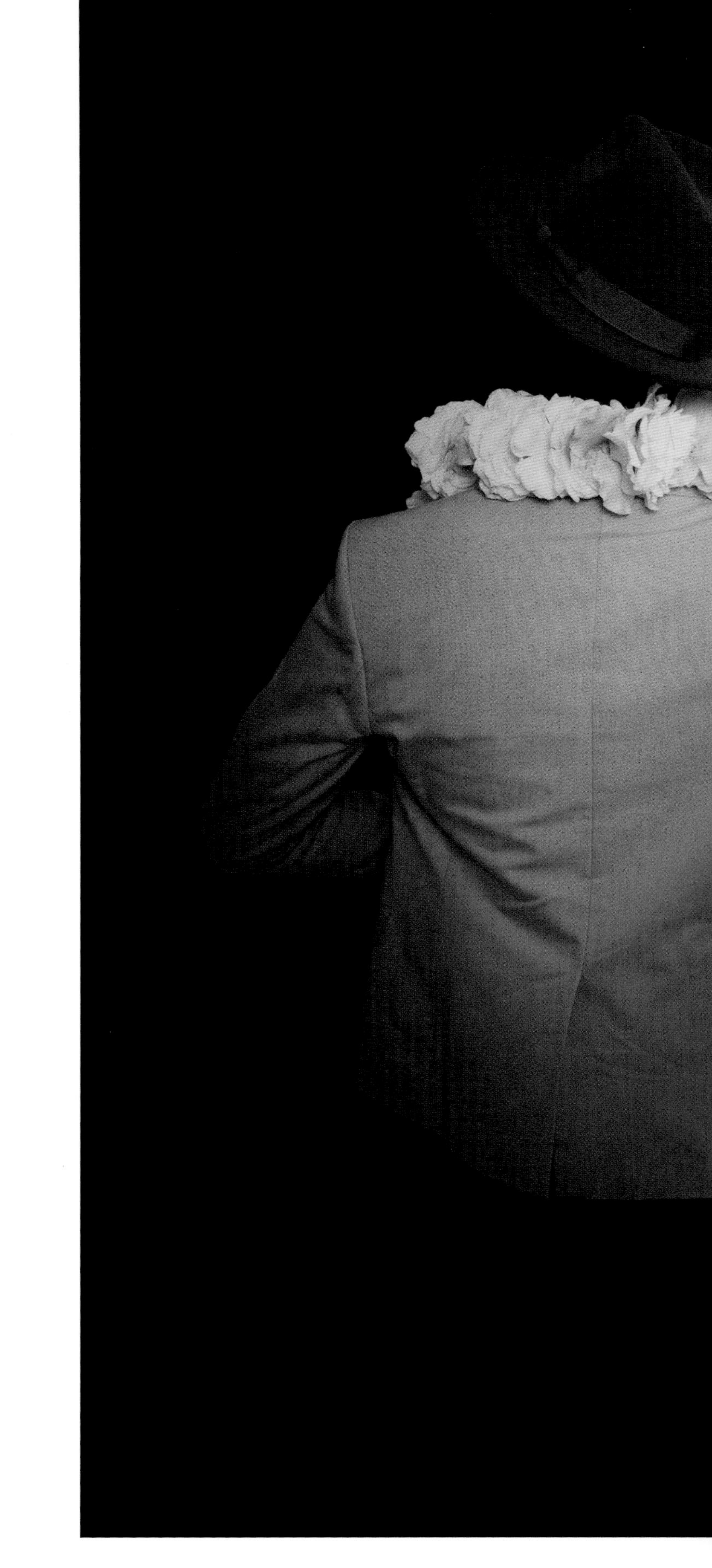

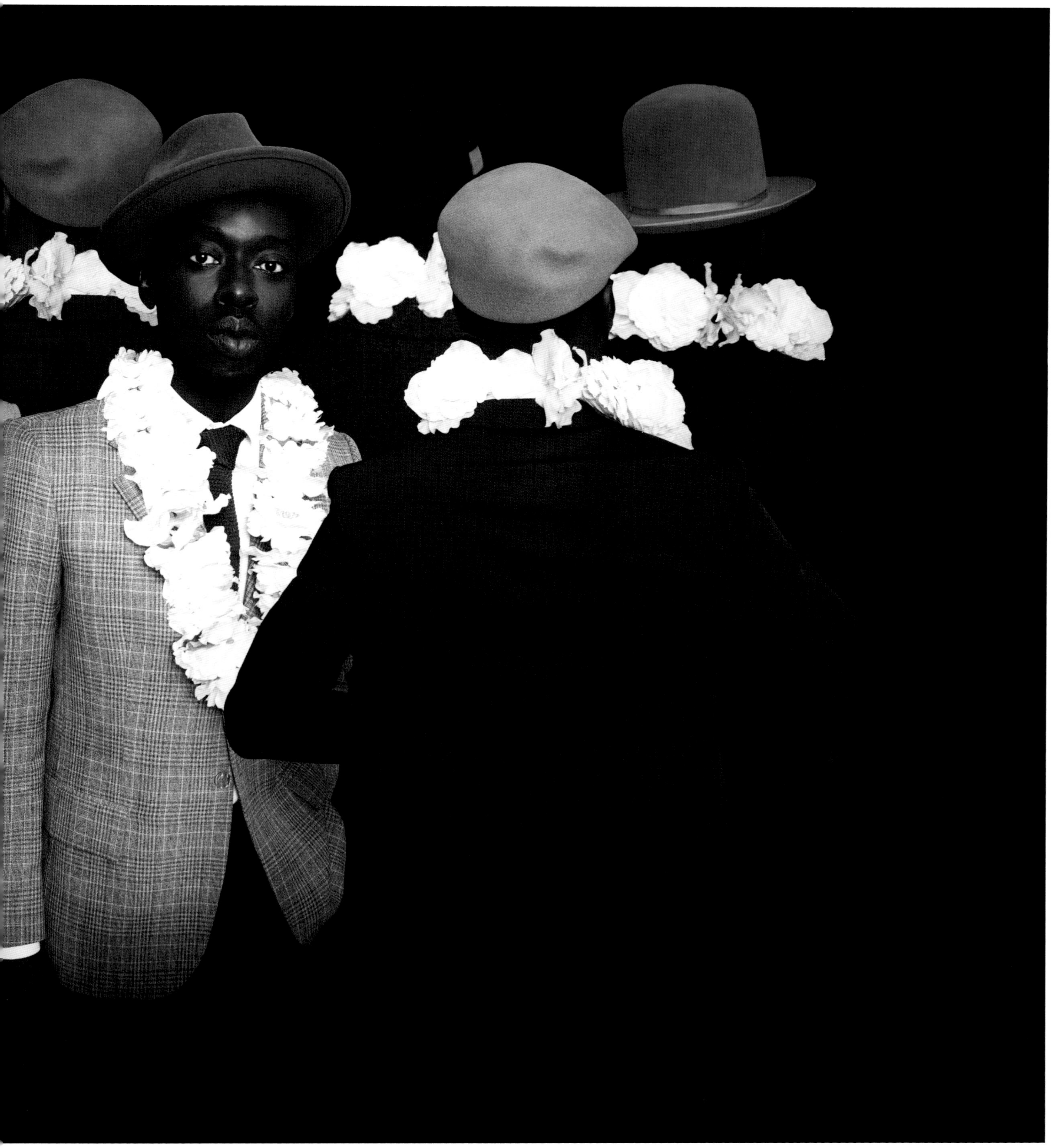

OMAR VICTOR DIOP
Selma, 1965, from the series *Liberty*, 2016

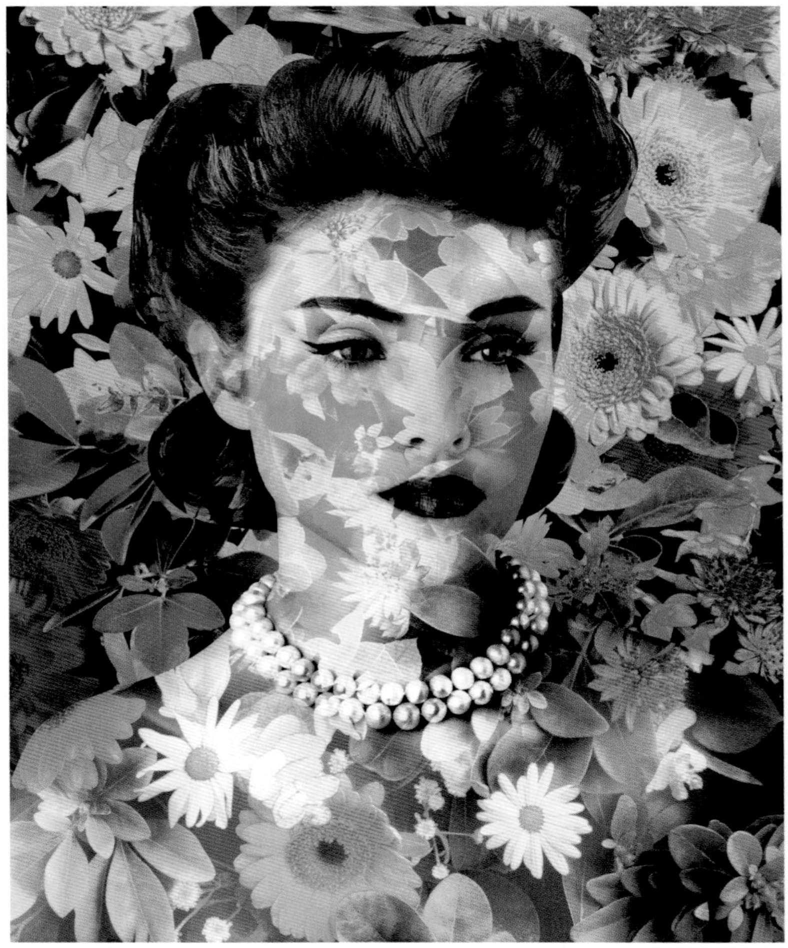

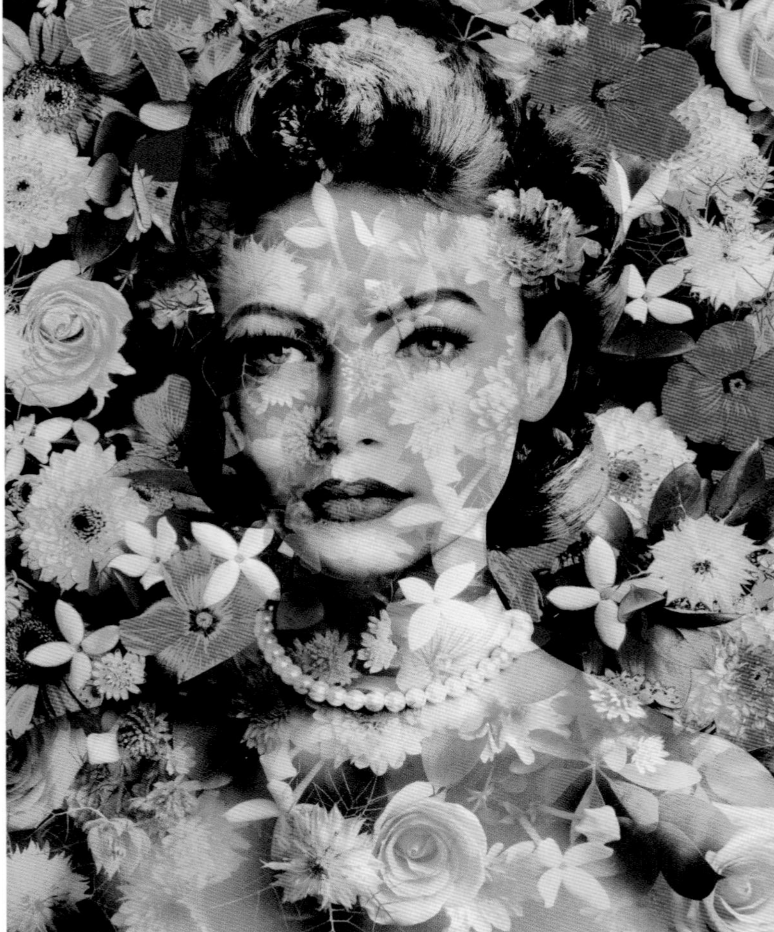

VALÉRIE BELIN
Arcotis fastuosa (Namaqua Marigold) (left) and *Astrantia major (Ruby Wedding)*, 2013

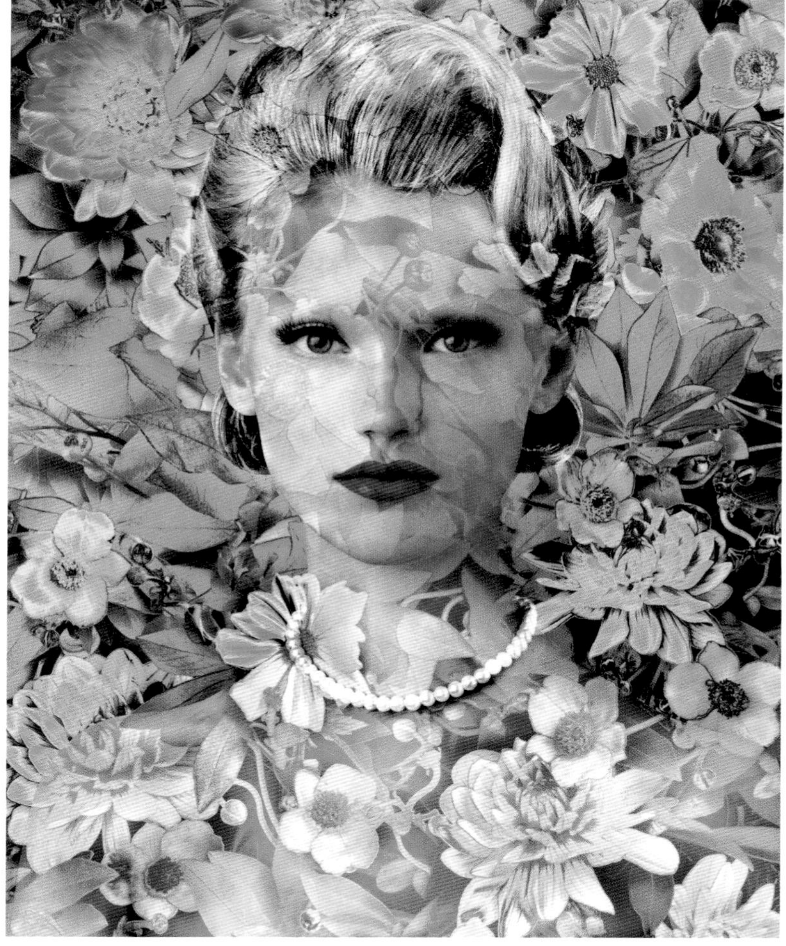

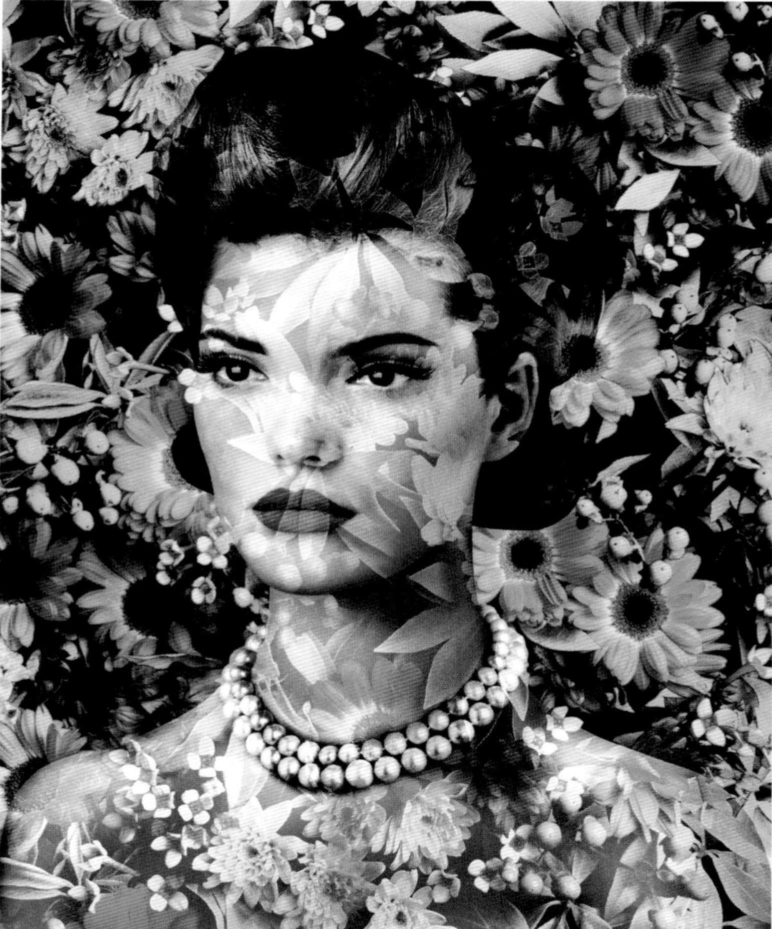

VALÉRIE BELIN
Giant Exhibition Aureole (left) and *Pieris japonica (Mountain Fire)*, 2013

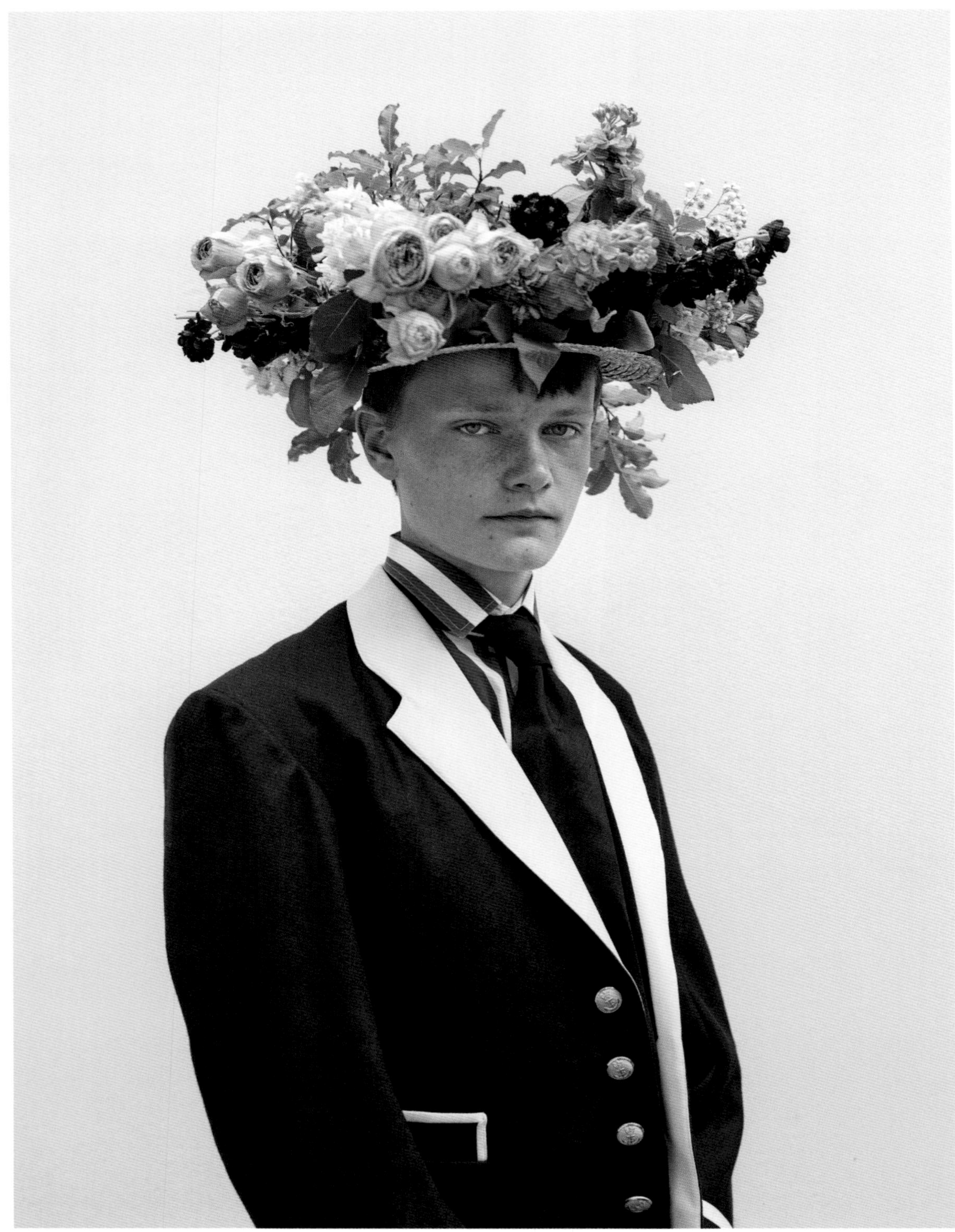

SIMON ROBERTS

Charlie Moody-Stuart, Procession of Boats, Eton, 2016

Eton College's famous annual celebration on 4 June includes the Procession of Boats on the River Thames at Windsor, where boys dress in historic naval uniforms and elaborate floral hats. The first procession took place in 1793 on the birthday of King George III, the school's greatest patron.

To Daffodils

Fair daffodils, we weep to see
You haste away so soon;
As yet the early-rising sun
Has not attain'd his noon.
Stay, stay,
Until the hasting day
Has run
But to the even-song;
And, having pray'd together, we
Will go with you along.

We have short time to stay, as you,
We have as short a spring;
As quick a growth to meet decay,
As you, or anything.
We die
As your hours do, and dry
Away,
Like to the summer's rain;
Or as the pearls of morning's dew,
Ne'er to be found again.

Robert Herrick

ARTISTS' STATEMENTS

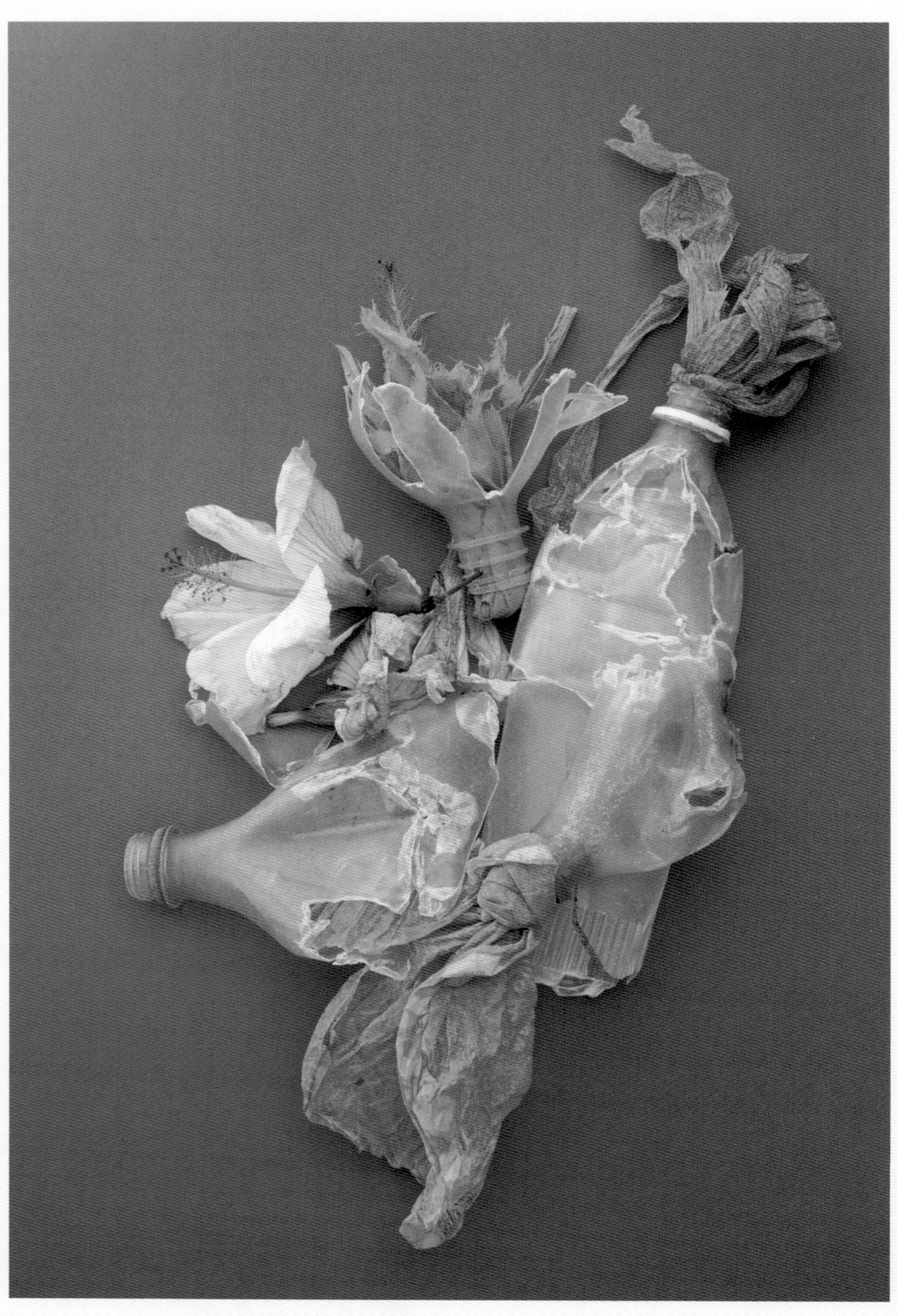

Thirza Schaap, *Splash of Pink*, from the series *Plastic Ocean*, 2017

The photographers were invited to contribute statements about their work, whether concerning the photograph(s) shown in this book, or their work in general. We believe that it is tremendously valuable to have the artists' own voices associated with their practice. On the other hand, a few photographers preferred to submit texts by others, and a few declined to contribute at all, believing that any further explanation is unnecessary.

AKOSUA VIKTORIA ADU-SANYAH

The giant kelp forest is an essential part of the blue carbon system that sequestrates half of all carbon circulating through the ocean. It is the largest of all seaweeds, reaching up to 65 m [213 ft] in length. Under the threats of climate change, the climate conditions of Patagonia's unique fjord channel system provide refuge for this vital marine algae. This photograph was taken on an oceanographic expedition from Punta Arenas to the glacier of Isla Santa Inés during the global pandemic in December 2020, when environmental scientific work was severely restricted in Chile. *Behold the Ocean* is a project about vulnerability and contrast in climate research.

LAURENCE AËGERTER

This series of photographs is the result of *Herbarium Cataplasma*, a community art project that I developed at the invitation of the city of Leeuwarden in Friesland, the Netherlands. I led a careful reconstruction of the plan of the medicinal garden of the medieval Abbey of Saint Gall [Switzerland] on an unused plot of land in Leeuwarden, which was once part of a convent. This project was realized in collaboration with the local residents. I invited the residents for a symbolic healing ritual of destroyed landscapes. I selected 100 images by searching the web for photographs of disasters created by nature and man throughout the world. Participants were invited to treat the photographs of destroyed landscapes with the medicinal plants from their newly built garden, using appropriate herbal therapies (e.g. cannabis for anxiety relief or ginger against pain from burns). Even if only a drop in an ocean of needs, the *Healing Plants for Hurt Landscapes* project connects the local realm to the global in an empathetic gesture.

LEONCE RAPHAEL AGBODJELOU

This new series looks at Porto-Novo's competitive bodybuilders who compete locally and nationally; the subjects aspire to one day achieve recognition beyond West Africa and work towards a better life in Europe. The bodybuilders have been a popular subject in African studio photography since the 1950s and 1960s, yet for this series I had them holding fake flowers, a somewhat incongruous touch. Plastic flowers have always been used in the traditional studios to show style and taste. I thought they added a nice contrast to the muscle men. I like what Coline Milliard wrote recently about them in *Modern Painters*: 'Although the images of these flower-adorned 21st-century bodybuilders function first as a social record, in this show they also seem to evoke issues about the objectification of the black male body.'

ANNA AGOSTON

The fine line between black-and-white photography and modern sculpture is blurred in my work. I produce print installations of forms to explore several existential themes, while highlighting the interdependence between humanity and the environment. I make my work by way of an innovative artistic process that depends on a device exclusive to digital cameras – the liquid-crystal display (LCD) screen. This device allows me to incrementally 'direct carve' my subjects (plant parts) in nature with light. Through this process, which involves not only carving, but also moulding and then detailing, I produce symbolic, metaphorical or anthropomorphic photographs of forms that I subsequently arrange into installations of between two and fifty-four photographs. *The Garden of Epicurus*, an installation of nine photographs, pays tribute to the garden where the philosopher advised his followers (women included) to lead modest, contemplative lives in friendly communities in order to achieve a good life.

ALBARRÁN CABRERA (ANNA CABRERA AND ANGEL ALBARRÁN)

For over twenty years we have been exploring the concept of reality from the point of view that humans are the eyes of the universe. Using photography, we can show that the very concept of universe exists because we all acknowledge its existence. Our conscience is like a wrinkle in the universe, a line of enquiry asking about itself. With every photograph, a new wrinkle is created. Thus, this 'wrinkle' is not only an image, but also a three-dimensional object that can function as a trigger for the mind of the viewer. In that sense, the series *The Mouth of Krishna* does not try to describe the element or object that appears in each print, but rather the experience of plurality generated by them.

PEDRO ALMODÓVAR

Since I began my brief life as a photographer I have always tried to imitate painting, not photography, without resorting to any special technique except waiting for the light that comes through the windows. My only task has been to wait for the exact moment, which varies depending on the season, and at times it's a matter of a very few minutes. Without intending to, I was photographing the passing of time, in the light and in the flowers. I don't know if I could have achieved all this digitally, but, for me, the physicality of it all was essential, the painted wood, the light from the window – almost always different – and the various vases of glass, resin or ceramic, as well as the decomposing flowers. It was a real adventure. I hope the photos bear witness to my pleasure and joy while I was taking them.

JESSICA BACKHAUS

I am a photographer. I mainly work on projects that develop over a period of several years. In my work I keep looking for new means of expression, which creates a fascinating interplay between the depiction of reality and enigmatic abstraction. I focus on everyday objects and situations. I try to see the world from unusual perspectives through my camera. My free combination with materials results in still lifes (sometimes staged), collages, and minimalist colour and light experiments. I am interested in what lies behind things, the world of thought behind what you can obviously see. The individual works are like visual poems for me. Emotional power always plays a formative role in my work. The immersion in new worlds, to move on uncertain paths and to take new approaches, stimulates me in my artistic work.

ALBERTO BARAYA

The Herbarium of Artificial Plants is a long-term collection of fake plants and data about the environments associated with them. The project is a modern attempt to compile a photo archive (*The InSitu Archive*, 1997–2020), including documentation of our social behaviour, and decorative categories involving different kinds of representation of the plant world. As an artist-traveller, my expeditions configure 'the Expedition' as a contemporary art practice (*Expedition Considered as a Fine Art*, AB, 2010). Pursuing an extension of the artist in the role of naturalist, I also took natural-history museums and new modified landscapes as a source for understanding the cultural and political identities of peoples, travelling, studying, contemplating and painting all those recomposed landscapes and dioramas where I find ecological disruption, including the automobile dystopia. *The Herbarium of Artificial Plants* is a way to see ecological complaints but also get further knowledge. *Tulip from Turkish Café* was collected on the Herbarium's expedition to Cologne, in June 2018, taking notes on actual scenarios of racism confrontation. In New York City *Another Amapola* was collected for an exhibition relating to narcotics.

JEFF BARK
When I start thinking about making a new picture, there is always something that triggers an idea, [and] often it's a colour. In this case it was when I bit into an apple from a nearby farm and I was surprised to see that the flesh of it was bright pink. This set the colour palette for finding the remaining objects I needed to tell a story. I always start from a blank studio and build these little vignettes with the idea that something is happening just outside the frame. In this case I imagined two best friends spending an afternoon together, doing their hair, listening to music and smoking pot.

MANDY BARKER
A collection of flowers and petals from several different species includes lotus, peony, carnation, rose, blossom and holly, with ferns, castor-oil plant and ivy leaves. Flora that would not normally exist at the same flowering time in nature but are presented in this arrangement brought together by the sea. Fake blooms that gave pleasure to many, perhaps displayed in a vase that once adorned a room. They now continue their journey as suspended plastic pollution recovered from the South China Sea and areas around Hong Kong. The grouping of seemingly 'natural flowers' represents a bigger picture of the disturbing statistics of man-made plastic items that have no boundaries.

BRENDAN BARRY
These images were created in a camera obscura, a room-sized camera that is operated from the inside, using two distinct analogue processes. One is a simple paper negative, the other is produced using a complex colour-reversal process that I have been developing over the last four years. These are wild flowers local to where I live, which I collect on morning walks and then carefully arrange in front of the camera to be photographed. Each one is unique, captured directly on photographic paper. The process is long and laborious and the photographs hard to achieve; it can take up to eight hours to create a successful exposure. As the ambient temperature in the room shifts, the colour balance fluctuates and the chemical concentration changes, [and] so too does the resultant image, meaning no two images will ever look the same. These are representations of flowers, of course, but they are also signs of a complex improvisation with chemicals, paper, light and time. I do not know what the image is going to be like at the start of the process; each one is a small revelation. Sometimes the strangeness of the result positions the everyday motif of the flowers in a new hybrid space between the chemical and natural, a fusion of the tradition of art that celebrates the transience of flowers, and a process that steals them away into an uncanny, chromatic image of an apparently permanent and artificial afterlife.

VALÉRIE BELIN
The *Black-Eyed Susan* series references the codification of female beauty in the 1950s. It is defined by its rigid, artificially 'mounted' forms (hair, jewelry, make-up) and recalls certain conventional icons of the day. But such is the fusion between the figure and the vegetal elements that the stereotype is dissolved in an organic, liquid flux: the icon reveals the mystery and charm of a creature coming into bloom.

ERIK BERGLIN
In recent years I have been exploring various randomized processes within a digital workflow, working with or against the pre-set algorithms found in image-processing software. I'm trying to find new approaches to working with photography in a digital age, making the computer the principal instrument of my practice. Each body of work follows a few strict conceptual rules, but I also like to add elements of change to impact the result. I want to be surprised by my own work, otherwise the creative process becomes boring to me. So I was happily surprised one day while making inkjet prints, when I accidentally removed the USB memory [stick] while the tiff file was being printed. The printer then repeated a single line of pixels. The result was minimalistic and abstract; it instantly intrigued me. But it was not at all clear in the beginning that this technique was going to be applied on images of tulips. It took a lot of trials with various images before the potential of the lines made sense to me. Another reason I choose flowers as subject matter is that they have always been a frequent motif in art, and it is said that the Dutch masters' apprentices had to paint tulips for years before they were allowed to make portraits. Such a well-known motif can easily become laboured and boring, so attempting to make something that could feel new in a long line of 'flower art' was one of my ambitions with this body of work. Another aspect of this method that I really like is that even though it might be possible in theory, it is highly unlikely [that I will] pull out the USB at exactly the same time twice. That means that this simple method transforms postcard pictures of flower fields into unique artworks.

SOFIA BIANCHINI
I had glimpses of this project flowering in my head and before my eyes long before I started putting all the layers together in 2017, and [it] finally saw the light in 2018. I knew that the cold white, stark marble would become my canvas for a while – my three-dimensional sculpture. I began a dreamlike journey, like a virtual tour, flying over marble faces and bodies and through fields, woods and forests; floral patterns and walls, botanic gardens and nurseries; wandering in and out of books, images and mystical flowering worlds. As if I was asking those still, emotionless and rigid figures to wake up and move. Filled with joy and excitement in 'drawing' these subjects, I discovered I could, with my eyes and fingers, manipulate their expressions and the connotation they were created for. And in return, it is as if they asked me to cover them with new meanings, reimagining the stories behind the marble. They are narrating for me the extraordinary beauty of a parallel, spiritual dimension, as I gently place my layers on their white skin...

CRAIG P. BURROWS
I began pursuing photography in 2010 without knowing at first what exactly I wanted to do with it. Despite that, from the beginning, there was a clear thread through the subjects of my images: I was compelled by the idea of a world absent of people. I found myself focusing on either the indirect manifestations of humanity or the absolute exclusion of it in nature. I began ultraviolet-induced visible fluorescence (UVIVF) in 2014, and through the technique I began to develop a stronger connection with life around me, particularly plants. I came to the conclusion that the botanical realm is the foundation of the modern world: not just the natural one, but the human as well. Despite the significant role plants play in our lives, they are usually only perceived as a pretty backdrop and easily overlooked. By utilizing the visual impact of my photography, especially the vivid colours resulting from the natural process of fluorescence, I seek to engage viewers in a relationship with plants and the life they support, especially as it concerns the future of life on Earth and the threats to its continuity.

OLGA CAFIERO
Within the frame of the *Enquête Neuchâteloise*, a photographic survey of the Swiss canton of Neuchâtel, I propose a census and an imagery of its flora, setting them within a strong historical context, going back and forth [between now and] the past. The status of these flowers – common, protected, invasive or even extinct – guided my visual approach and led me to develop seven photographic series in which I have brought together several disciplines and their different perspectives on nature. Botany, scientific imagery and history have informed my approach and nourished my explorations as much as the prospecting of my own walks. In the twenty-first century, Neuchâtel's municipalities are flourishing, as they did in the time of [Jean-Jacques] Rousseau, a key

figure in the field of botany in the canton of Neuchâtel, [and someone] to whom I often refer. Produced with a scanning electron microscope, these images present flowers in a poetic and unexpected way. The promenades also allude to Rousseau and his experience of the land. The pleasure of discovery is based on the creation of 'blind' images. 'Invasive' refers to undesirable plants, those whose spread threatens to choke other plants. This floral colonization is responded to by images saturated with information, to the point of blurring the reading of the image.

ROB AND NICK CARTER
Our work has always been focused on examining the boundaries between the real and the imagined, analogue and digital, the traditional and the contemporary. Our *Positive, Negative, Painting Photographs* take as their starting point watercolours and oil paintings by Jacob de Gheyn II (1565–1629). As the name suggests, *Positive, Negative, Painting Photographs* are positive prints produced from a black-and-white negative of the source material. We have taken the original oil painting and made a black-and-white negative from it, which we have then printed as a positive. The converse qualities of the Cibachrome prints underscore the intricate textures of De Gheyn's subjects and the subtle gradation in tone. They also reflect his early practice of working in reverse with engravings and etchings.

SHARON CORE
The photographs in the series *1606–1907* explore three centuries of the floral still-life tradition in Western art and its stylistic progression over time from its early beginnings in the Netherlands and Flanders up to the Modernist period, until 1907, when colour photography was born through the invention of the autochrome. The genre of still life is a family of images historically rooted in illusionism, *trompe l'œil* and themes of temporality. It is my intention to complicate and invert this relationship through the use of photography's descriptive abilities and [its] reliance on reality and time. I make copies, reproductions from reproductions of iconic floral works [by artists] from Brueghel to [Odilon] Redon. The process begins in research, growing and collection of specific flowers, props, insects, etc., for the camera's lens, followed by arranging, set construction, lighting and composing for the fraction of a second the film is exposed. The goal is a mimetic image, one that evokes the memorial and the multi-temporal layers of its creation.

PETRA CORTRIGHT
I work with pixelated brushstrokes and flower motifs to create unique digital paintings that resemble floral landscapes and still-life photography.

PAUL CUPIDO
The veil is thinnest in the very early morning, at around 4 am. Many cultures consider this time to be the zone in which the boundaries between the physical and spiritual realms are nearly non-existent. The earliest morning is a thin veil through which the dream world of the night appears at its most magical. My most cherished values inspiring my work are wonderment and the ability to see the world like a child. Flowers symbolize these values because of their ephemeral beauty. A photograph is able to play the thin veil of the early morning–transient like life, yet partaking in the continuum of change, disseminating its image wherever the winds of culture blow.

SARA CWYNAR
I am an artist working in photography and video. My photographs often take the form of sculptural constructions that are photographed, printed, tiled and re-photographed as new images. My videos similarly combine existing images from photographic history and from a personal archive to remix and re-present familiar imagery. My work parses the ways that commercial images work on our consciousness, how they infiltrate our psyches. I combine digital and analogue technologies in my work, and I use design and commercial image-making techniques that I learned working as a graphic designer and art director as a way to critique the strategies of these fields. I am trying to situate an individual approach within the shared visual codes and references of popular culture and images.

NOOR DAMEN
The Netherlands is number one in flower culture. I noticed that there are people at work, small landowners who have a close bond with their product. From their slightly curved posture, I saw that they chose with care and dedication those flowers that were ready for picking, and that they were bundled by hand on the spot. Flowers are delicate and must be handled with care.

LIA DARJES
The Russian exclave of Kaliningrad is squeezed between Poland and Lithuania. Until 1945 it belonged to Germany as East Prussia, and then it became a Russian military territory with severely restricted access until the end of the USSR. Every day, small unofficial roadside markets pop up, where old women offer the modest harvest from their gardens or the nearby forest for sale to supplement their pension. The goods range from three apples, a bunch of currants and two garlic bulbs to perhaps two jars of homemade strawberry jam and a beautiful flower bouquet from their windowsill. The radiance of the goods and the way they are presented reminded me of the classical subjects in the baroque market still life. Over the cycle of a year, I documented them in a still-life study. With *Tempora Morte*, I explore how the genre of still life can be positioned in contemporary documentary photography.

VICTOR DE CASTRO
Things are…Whatever things happen to be is a visual research [project] into objects, their composition and disposition in everyday life. In linguistics, it would be a question of working on the arbitrariness of the sign, its motivation and the place of words in a sentence. Here, it is a question of identifying, through photography, a poetic link between form and content and their arrangement. These conscious or unconscious, functional or purely random compositions are attractive. Every object, every shape or assembly can potentially be a constituent part of a visual poem. Is there possible harmony in daily chaos? Could we consider a less intelligible order, an even more arbitrary, less categorical semantics? Is absolute order really necessary for the perception of things? Since conventions are the basis of common sense, could we assign new functions, new causes, new names?

GERCO DE RUIJTER
The relation between humanity and nature, the way we (try to) control and industrialize nature, is a returning theme in my work. This picture was taken with a camera on top of a fishing rod, capturing roughly a 10 × 10 m [33 × 33 ft] piece of land right in front of my feet, in this case the premises of a perennial-flower nursery in Noord-Brabant, the Netherlands. Delivery to garden centres is prepared. The perennials are taken outside and tagged with information. These yellow tags show the image of the full-grown flowering plant, its name and its best place: on the sunny side, needs watering twice a day. All these tags indicate the industrial scale of the plant market. This particular nursery has an annual production of over 7 million plants. Hopefully, they will end up full-grown and flowering plants, repotted in the right place in private gardens.

RICHARD DE TSCHARNER
I was at a family party at the castle of Amsoldingen [in the canton of Bern, Switzerland]. I had taken my camera with me, to capture some images of my cousins. Imagine my surprise when I realized that, instead, I had

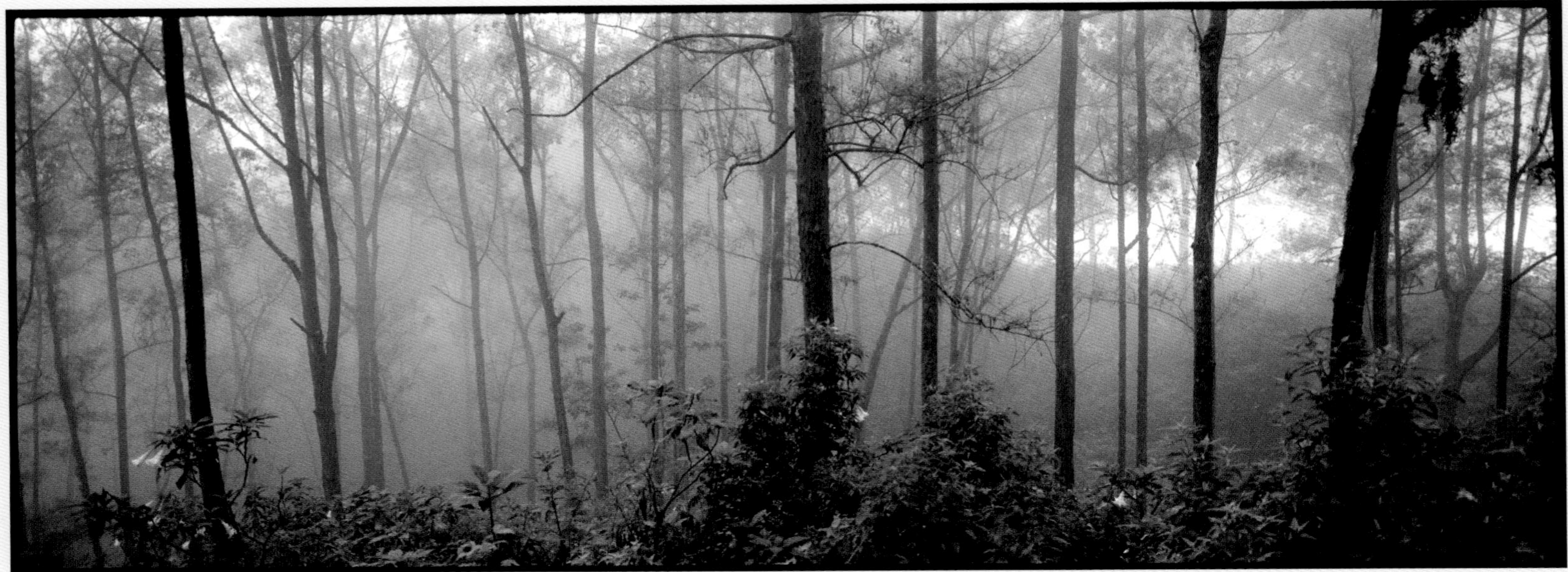

Richard de Tscharner, *Forêt enchantée, Indonesia*, 2011

only taken photographs of the sublime nature that was literally invading the veranda, where the aperitif was served. It was then that I saw an opening in the foliage that looked out into the park, like a window with the transparent greenery as a frame.

In Java, at the height of the rainy season, the weather is overcast and misty, with no sunlight. We had walked up the western slope of Bromo, not far from Gubukklakah and Ngadas, but our attempt to see the crater of the volcano from its caldera had to be abandoned due to the thick fog. As we made our way back down through the thick forest, we were suddenly enveloped in a mist that lent the forest an enchanted feel and the trees an air of mystery, with, in the foreground, wild lilies, the emblem of innocence and love.

ELSPETH DIEDERIX

There are moments when everyday objects suddenly lose their veil of familiarity and become abstract. The usual meaning that you give these objects is altered, and for a split second you are able to see them in a different light. This moment in time I use as a starting point for my images. [During] These past years I have also been captured by the magnificence of flowers and the world of growing and creating gardens. Flowers and plants are the new material I work with in order to create an image that will convey my fascination with the beauty of the ordinary.

OMAR VICTOR DIOP

From the beginning, the history of the relationship between African societies and Western powers was characterized by the denial of fundamental freedoms to the continent's population. The dominating powers admittedly imposed systems that allowed them to legitimize and organize various forms of exploitation of the continent and its wealth. The destiny of African societies, and subsequently that of the diaspora, was forever changed. Throughout the entire era starting with the slave trade, continuing with the colonial period and followed by independence on the African continent and emancipation in America, black people of the continent and the diaspora have tried to restore and preserve what had been taken away from them: their freedoms. The concept of Black protest is therefore necessary to evoke a chronology of movements of affirmation, of revolt and of vindication for the dignity and freedom of the black people throughout the world.

In a game of visual references combining self-portraits and staged scenes, the series *Liberty* revisits a history that spans centuries on a territory covering several continents, and brings together a collective memory of Black protest.

XUEBING DU

Flowers are a celebration of love and beauty. I want my flowers to be beautiful, feminine and otherworldly. I like to capture roses in full bloom, that are opening themselves to the sun. Petals lie in full light, with soft, silky and soothing colours. I concentrate on representing organic forms and smooth textures. Light is essential while creating this body of work: the balance in the light and shade; the transition between light and dark. I want to create a tone that is almost surreal, and illuminated by a strong yet delicate touch of light. Inspired by the use of light in Renaissance paintings, I hope to bring pleasure to my viewers.

ELAINE DUIGENAN

I work with objects – natural, found or made. My key tool is a flatbed scanner that makes the modern equivalent of a photogram. *Sex Pistils* offers a bold allegory of procreation. The fruit of *Acanthus* is a shapely house of seeds, ripe and bursting with sexual analogy, a dissected drama of fecundity, gestation, expulsion, fruition. The language of plants and flowers is curiously connected to human experience, and this language defines multiple aspects of our lives – from the innocent to the erotic. In *Blossfeldt's Apprentice* the images are of objects hand-made with twist ties. They attempt to re-create plant structures that are shown in iconic photographs by the German artist Karl Blossfeldt. Blossfeldt wanted to encourage his students to pay attention. He made a camera that allowed magnification of up to 30x, and took hundreds of photos of plant forms. He was demonstrating that the best design had already been anticipated in nature. I pored over his images and became a latter-day student – twisting, tying and bending the material to my will. My imperfect specimens taunted me with their limitations. But embracing the flaws became the point of the work, and showing the joins and loose threads reveals the tension between perfection and imperfection.

AMIN EL DIB

CutFlowerImages

I was seized by curiosity.
For these strange forms, meant as beauty
in our homes.
They seemed to me, even as a child,
like summoned death.
I allowed them time to develop their
every scent.
A little light helped me see them,
like the anatomists of yore who cut open
the body in search of the soul:
I didn't find it either.
I found images.

JOANNA EPSTEIN

This untitled photo is from the series *Isolation (Self)*, photographed while in quarantine alone during the COVID-19 pandemic. The series (consisting primarily of self-portraits and a number of still-life and landscape photos tracking the growth, bloom, wilt and decay of the garden behind my apartment) is an exploration of myself during this period of isolation; of anxiety and loneliness; of disconnection and a longing for intimacy; of depression, numbness, grief and nightmares. And ultimately of my own discomfort with myself.

GARRY FABIAN MILLER

Flowers have formed an important part of my life. As a gardener they bring moments of great joy, [and] the act of cultivation brings us close. As an artist I think my investigation of flowers helped me to see photographic exposure in a new way. Watching the sunlight igniting the corolla of an oriental poppy or a delphinium like a flame made me consider how much lamplight – what dosage – would transfer the essence of a plant to the Cibachrome print. There would always be a prescription for the perfectly exposed print, one that accurately described a botanical form and its pigmented colour, but I began to see in what might ordinarily be called overexposure – in prints that contained so much light that they appeared to be almost erased from the surface of the paper – a flicker of pure colour only, the true pulse of the flower.

LEE FRIEDLANDER

In 1994, in the throes of aching knees and painful concern about them, I decided I had better prepare myself for a sedentary life. Thus, I began to pursue still life as a possibility and maybe a way of life, photographic life.

I tried a variety of subjects with a few good results. Mostly they were dull attempts, until I began to look at the fresh flowers [my wife] Maria put in glass vases in our dining area, on the table and the windowsills. I began looking at the whole vase and very quickly found myself interested in the stems. The months of February, May, June and December 1994 were spent in stem games. Not only would the stems fall into wild disarray; the vases produced with them a kind of optical splendour. They added a perverse note to the optical qualities of the fine camera lenses. Helter-skelter light refractions and optical exaggerations, as well as compound reflections, happened naturally. A kind of inflammatory effect. I made rough work prints to keep track of what I was doing, but didn't really make good prints until around 1997. During 1996 and 1997 I spent a lot of time trying to deal with my own personal inflammatory stems – my knees – with no real results, although I tried all that was available in the way of therapy, short of undergoing surgical replacement. I bit the bullet in 1998. I had both knees replaced and began the slow process of recovery. Three months passed, during which time I took no pictures, the only period in almost fifty years of working with such a gap.

In 1999, with great success in my rehabilitation, able to walk again without pain, I thought to re-apply myself to the fun of the stems and finish them off as a subject. I returned to the square format but also used 35 mm, which allowed a larger choice of lenses for close-ups. I realized that stems, like all good subjects I've encountered, could invite me to spend a lifetime working on them. However, my knees were good and tugging at me to leave Still Life, and soon, happily, I was back on the the streets and the trails.

ERWAN FROTIN

The series *Flora olbiensis* was commissioned by the Centre d'art Villa Noailles in Hyères, in the south of France. I visited the area regularly between 2004 and 2007, and in the course of the seasons I photographed some 100 wild flowers. Through their expressive poses, the enlargement of sometimes tiny details, and the coloured backgrounds that decontextualize them, the flowers appear almost like people, while by their variations they evoke a range of diverse emotions. Starting off from a documentary position, the work leads the spectator towards a more dreamlike contemplation: each of these portraits of a flower is, like every encounter, a mirror. Each is an invitation to reflect on the relation between ourselves and the other.

MATTHIEU GAFSOU

Il y a un mal contre lequel l'opium est souverain et ce mal s'appelle l'Angoisse (Antonin Artaud) I set out to 'find poetry where it is not expected'. From 2012 to 2014 I worked in the drugs scene in Lausanne, the city where I live. I wish to reveal a 'tragic form of exoticism close to home', and have managed to create an original body of work on a subject that society tries, I think, to make as invisible as possible. Photographed against a black background and with sophisticated lighting, addicts are distinguished by a quasi-pictorial treatment, inspired by the portrait tradition, and which gives the models a humanity that the system sometimes denies them. The meeting places and consumption areas are photographed with a careful treatment, while the night landscapes evoke artificial paradises and help to shape the ambiguity of the project, which deliberately escapes any moralism.

ORI GERSHT

The mirrors in *On Reflection* reflect what appears to be still-life paintings by Jan Brueghel, but the images are illusions – not only because they are mediated by mirrors, but also because each reflection is not of a painting but of a replica, featuring artificial flowers meticulously crafted by hand. The three replicas I created, each based on a different Brueghel bouquet, are comments on the nature of the original paintings, in which Brueghel chose to depict not wild flowers but blossoms that were the result of sophisticated horticultural intervention by man. The depiction of the simultaneous perfection of so many species that bloom in different seasons and in far-flung geographic locations – a fantasy of a desirable but never attainable reality – is an assertion of the power of art and craft, alongside the power of science and technology, to remake the world of objects. In contrast to the laborious and meticulous processes that led to the creation of the replicas of the bouquets in Brueghel's paintings, the compositions that were captured by the film camera at the instant the mirrors shattered were rapid and unpredictable. The use of the two cameras allowed me to record simultaneously two contrasting views of the same event. One focused close up on the glass surface of the mirror, the other on the reflection in the mirror of the vase of flowers. Because of the different focusing points and the limited depth of field, each camera captured an alternative reality, questioning the relationship between photography and a single objective truth. In the film I combined the two points of view, integrating the virtual images of the reflections with the physical presence of the sharp, shattering glass.

STEPHEN GILL

Stephen Gill has used his surroundings, as he often does, as the inspiration for the evocative series from which these two works are drawn. *Hackney Flowers* evolved from his series *Hackney Wick*. For *Hackney Flowers*, Gill collected flowers, seeds, berries and objects

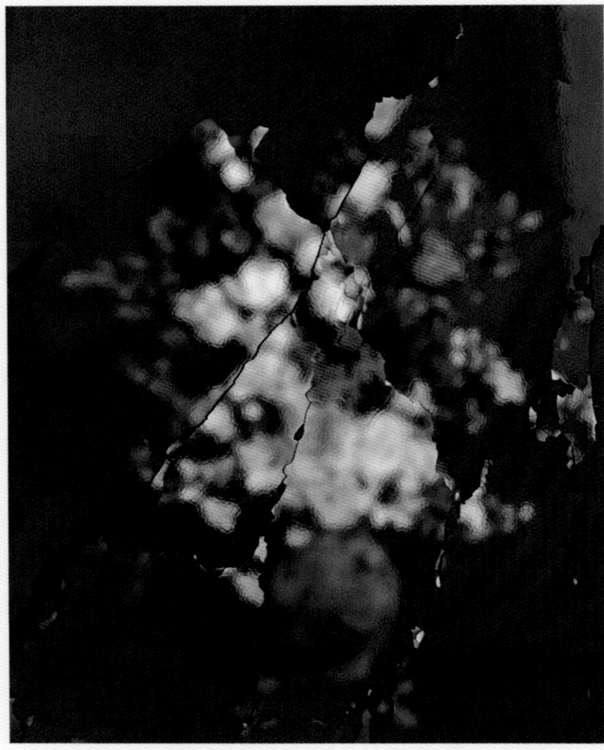

Ori Gersht, *On Reflection Material E07*, 2014

from Hackney, east London, which he then pressed in his studio and re-photographed alongside his own photographs and found ephemera, thus building up multilayered images. Some of the base photographs were buried in Hackney Wick, allowing the subsequent decay to leave an imprint upon the images, stressing the close association with place. A parallel series accompanied this elegant volume, showing members of the public in Hackney with floral elements on their dress. *Hackney Flowers* was conceived as a poetic and visually stimulating book, full of colours, emotions and rhythms extracted from a single, vibrant borough of London. A fuller context for Gill's floral imagery is provided by *Hackney Flowers* and his other publications: Stephen Gill Books (www.nobodybooks.com).

DANIEL GORDON

I came to representing flowers in my work through my interest in established art-historical tropes such as the still life. They are present in so many passages of our lives, from celebration to grief to our daily existence in between. They present an endless variation in form and colour, which allows me room to work.

ROBERTO GRECO

In the series *Porter sa peau* [Wearing One's Skin], I extract scenes from my memory in which my life is seen through distorting mirrors. The symbolism of the objects I stage is partly drawn from seventeenth-century art, or sometimes simply viewed through my own prism. Each scene explodes into several new compositions that bolster the main narrative. As murky and misty as memory, these images' asperities compel us to slow down in order to take them in more fully, at the risk of getting scratched by their hidden rough patches. Whether it is the way I envision my origins as an Italian born in Switzerland or [as] a father, or a tribute to my mother, this new photographic work is about me, leaning down to better see my own reflection.

ANNA HALM SCHUDEL

For more than twenty-five years, I have been photographing flowers. Their beauty saves me from my sadness. Tulips are my favourite flowers; they remind me of ballet dancers, they move gracefully as they grow older. The capturing of lively colours is essential in my work, but I also feel the desire to create fading shades. From earlier assignments lots of expired black-and-white photo paper accumulated in my drawers. After experimenting with different brands of paper, which always turned out in a faded pink, I placed a tulip on old Kentmere paper, weighed it down with a glass plate and placed it in the sun. The tulip began to sweat under the warm rays. This created, unexpectedly, a magical protective surrounding to the delicate tulip. Unfortunately, this type of paper is no longer manufactured, and the photograms become a sign of their time.

PAUL HARFLEET

I plant pansies at the site of homophobic abuse; I find the nearest source of soil to where the incident occurred and generally, without civic permission, plant one unmarked pansy. The flower is then documented in its location, [and] the image entitled after the abuse. Titles like 'Let's kill the Bati-man!' and 'Fucking Faggot!' reveal a frequent reality of LGBTQ+ experience, which often goes unreported to authorities. This simple action operates as a gesture of quiet resistance; some pansies flourish, others wilt in urban hedgerows.

PAMELA ELLIS HAWKES

Over the years I have been exploring and questioning the perceived reality inherent in a photograph and its relationship to the elusive and ethereal nature of imagination and memory. In a statement written twenty years ago I said, 'Because it is necessary to possess physical reality, photographers, as opposed to artists in other mediums, can't conjure up images from memory or imagination.' At that time I explored the use of 'surrogate objects' as an alternative to 'conjuring'. But, as the medium has quickly evolved since then, it has presented ever more possibilities for imagination as an alternative to physical reality. For instance, the degrading effects that can occur with subsequent generations of digital images are imposed on historic pieces that have been carefully restored and preserved for centuries. The results can be strange, fragmented and ephemeral. These concepts have fascinated and confounded me since making my first photographs, and my work is inspired by and explores the limits of these ideas.

AIMÉE HOVING
My work features my daughter Flavia. I am influenced by my Dutch heritage and together we create a specific atmosphere to express my feelings, childhood and imagination. My photography is like a mysterious curator of my life, of what I see in my head and would like to express of my past but through the eyes of an adult. My work has a painterly feel to it and is staged in locations I know well and that inspire me. The child is often alone and the centrepiece of the picture. All the details are very important in my pictures, and I try to capture the pursuit of a certain flawless perfection and beauty I was brought up with. I work alone, without a stylist or set designer, and most of the time in natural light.

HUA JIN
This photo is a piece from the *2020 Visual Diary* series, a project I started in March 2020, two days after the city of Montreal was locked down due to the pandemic. I photographed and recorded the changes in nature daily for 365 days. During this year of creation, I posted my photos with a short text on social media with the purpose of easing our nerves and bringing natural images to isolated people. This one was posted on 28 September 2020, with a short line: Visual Diary – 09-28 Discovered a book, *On Earth We're Briefly Gorgeous*, the author's name is 'Ocean'.

GREGORY EDDI JONES
Flowers for donald is a series of digital collage works begun in the days following the 2016 US election. The work borrows the symbolic potency of flowers to act as anchor points of protest, memorial and reflexive connotations of enduring beauty within the traditions of art history. Each *Flowers* image originates from a stock photograph of a vase of flowers and undergoes a process of stream-of-conscious re-authorship, engaging in digital mark-making, manipulation and web appropriation. Drawing from the legacy and strategies of Dada artists such as Hannah Höch and John Heartfield, *Flowers for donald* challenges the role and function of art itself in politically turbulent times, and embraces absurdism as a tool of critical reflection.

NADAV KANDER
For years I have disregarded any photograph of flowers as cheesy and simply out of bounds. I would have thrown flowers into the same bag as sunsets, kittens or nudes as difficult subjects to approach photographically. Difficult, I suppose, because of their popularity and overexposure. Pictures like these become mainstream, seen everywhere, easy prey, nostalgic, sweet, sentimental, and as a result it's hard to see the work as original. However, looking through my work, as I did with this publication in mind, I find flowers popping up all over the place. They are usually supporting or in contrast to what is central in my frame, like best supporting actors. A viewer can have a sense of the woman's personality more accurately in this constructivist photograph from *The Parade* because of the type and arrangement of her flowers. They support her, gently letting us know something about her, even as she turns away. Only long after photographing this did I notice the part the flowers play. In a closed-down, boarded-up film studio in Romania, I found this lonely bunch of dried flowers among what felt like an isolated dry desert of dust and blackness. I titled the series of photographs *Isolation*. *Dunia* from a series titled *Dream Girls* is seen more acutely because of the arrangement of flowers that accompanies her. A faded room in every way in contrast to the freshness and fleshiness of the flowers and her skin.

SANNA KANNISTO
I photographed this image in my field studio in the Costa Rican rainforest. The parrot snake was carefully placed on a *Heliconia* plant held by a lab stand. The studio is for me a kind of research laboratory or a theatre. It shows different scenes from nature, which I direct. It's one way to reduce and frame the abundance of the rainforest. When the object has been isolated, taken out of its original setting – out of nature – and put on to the stage, it becomes special. I'm interested in the strong impulse in photography to preserve something temporary forever. Through photography, I may preserve things as they were, forever in their 'glory'; it's an irony, a paradox. The still-life compositions have an allegorical nature. For me photography is a medium that in itself documents the transience of life.

SANDRA KANTANEN
Most of my work deals with the relationship between photography and painting. Flowers remind me, in a good way, of the impermanence of life, and in *Still life (Flower 1)* I have found a way to capture them in my work. In this image I made a traditional flower still life in ambient light. Then I used digital painting tools to obscure and distort the image. To me the question is what do we see first, the object or the surface? *Untitled (new distortion 3)* is made without a camera, using a scanner. The device once made to copy documents as accurately as possible is here used as a small-scale studio to portray flowers. The moving light makes the details almost hyper-realistic. I made several exposures, still and moving, piled on top of each other. The stripes reminiscent of paint are holes in the layers, revealing an optional image.

ROB KESSELER
For the past twenty years I have explored the creative potential of microscopy to reveal the spectacular array of diverse forms and structures of highly magnified plant specimens. Using scanning electron microscopy, black-and-white images of pollen, seeds and fruits are chromatically re-mastered, using multiple layers of colours to enhance their structures and reveal elaborate and fragile morphological traits with astounding clarity. Colour choices begin with referencing the original plant or specimen, and are additionally informed by artistic sensibility. In essence the results are complex plant portraits underpinned with scientific knowledge, and consequently have an aesthetic value bridging both scientific and artistic cultures. *Scabiosa crenata* is the dried floret from the flower head which contains the seed; the whole thing acts a parachute when it detaches from the flower head. Its graceful form suggests an exquisite balletic costume. *Medicago arborea* is a small seed pod from the tree medick, a member of the pea family, with its characteristic helical form.

IRENE KUNG
I found this tree in a park surrounded by many others. I was immediately struck by the sense of peace and balance that it conveyed. It evoked the feelings I had in China during my numerous wonderful trips there. It is a country I am learning to appreciate and admire for the ability of its art and Eastern sense of aesthetics to convey emotion and states of mind. For me, this has become a constant source of inspiration in combination with the magic and mystery that trees transmit. In my studio, I had to work on the image for long hours and days until I was fully satisfied that the still image could faithfully represent the emotion I felt when I first saw this tree. In the process I had to silence all rational actions and let my eyes and hands be guided solely by my emotions. The final photograph would have to convey the

sense of peace, calm and dream that the tree evoked in me. My purpose will thus be fulfilled.

ROSEMARY LAING
For the 2001 series *groundspeed*, Rosemary Laing undertook the careful and arduous process of physically laying Axminster carpet in the coastal forests of Morton National Park, New South Wales [Australia]. After months of preparation and installation, she then photographed the setting she had made, before removing all traces of her work from the location. Like much of her work, *groundspeed* is informed by issues of belonging to land and landscape, as Australia continues to reconcile its complex histories. On the one hand, the carpets and picturesque setting in the *groundspeed* series play on the comforts of domesticity used to create a meaningful sense of belonging and identity. On the other hand, the use of nostalgic European floral carpet motifs within the traditional country of the Yuin people also suggests a colonizing of the ground on which it is laid.

DAVID LEBE
I made photograms from the mid-1970s to the mid-1980s – constructing imagined plant specimens, gardens and landscapes. At the same time, I was working with other low-tech photographic processes and with techniques that allowed my hand to show: light drawing, handmade pinhole cameras and hand-colouring. During that time before sophisticated computer imagery, I was striving to connect the mechanical rendering of photography with painting and drawing. I was working to expand the way photographs were thought about then, while also mining for deeper expression. Photograms are a simple photographic process, but my workflow was mostly complex and layered, often culminating in the hand-application of colour. I had many successes but also frustrations; there were times when the medium was not flexible enough to allow me to go where I wanted, evolve the image or create the variations I wanted. Twenty-five years later, learning digital photography, I realized those limitations were gone, and I couldn't resist going back, reworking and reimagining some photograms – resulting in pictures with two dates. I also did this with pinhole pictures and a few light drawings. Even now I'm occasionally drawn back to evolve an old analogue image as I move forward digitally with new work. This work comes from a 2014–16 project called *Studies* (originally titled *Figures, Grounds and Studies*), a body of work made through photographing my camera's reflection in the mirror it faces in my studio, along with fragments of other images arranged on the surface of the reflecting mirror. They are not digital constructions or manipulations. They collapse the apparatus, the space of the studio, and elements and fragments of the external world into a single photographic picture.

VANESSA LEISSRING
We suffocate in plastic waste. About 400 million tons of plastic are produced every year. And too much of it ends up in the sea: two-thirds of all marine waste today consists of plastics. Today we even have plastics on beaches, in marine sediments, in sea strudels. Microplastics are a deadly danger for fish, marine mammals and seabirds, because conventional plastics such as PET are not biodegradable; they are only slowly decomposed by salt water and sun, and float forever in the sea as ever finer particles. In contrast, flowering plants are part of the natural material cycle. They grow, blossom, wither, are at some point biologically decomposed by micro-organisms and serve as the basic material for the creation of new life. And through photosynthesis they produce the oxygen on our Earth that is essential for life. *Polyflowers* is a photographic project that deals with these contrasts. Above all it is about the contrast between the natural and the synthetic colour spectrum: flowers in plastic bottles, nature in polymers. Through colour-blocking, plastic and nature are juxtaposed in their colours.

LAURA LETINSKY
Silver sparks dull on the wrinkly belly of an overripe apricot's skin moulting into the mottled edge of the tablecloth: my still-life photographs are reminiscent of seventeenth-century Dutch/Flemish painting. My photographs wrestle with the behemoth that is photography, that is, its proliferation as well as what and how it 'means'. If pictures 'mean' something, as do words, thinking of Gertrude Stein's 'a rose is a rose is a rose,' [can we also say] a photograph is a photograph is a photograph? A two-dimensional surface adorned with colour, line and texture, or is it what it pictures? Is the rose in my photograph a rose, or a photograph of a rose, or, to be more precise, a photograph of a photograph of a rose? All photographs of flowers are photographs first; 'of' flowers, not necessarily second, but [in] what order and to what effect is a quandary. Indeed, every photograph is both more and less than what it is 'of'. Pictures attest to a blush of pink just as they arrest this blush from fading. Theirs is an invitation to stop and smell flowers that cannot relinquish their scent. Using bits and pieces of others' pictures – Christie's catalogue, *Martha Stewart Living*, *New York Times* sports pages – as the building material in my compositions of table scenes, I thwart the monocular authority of the single lens through ambivalent spatial cues and conflicting perspectives and temporalities. My photographs afford another kind of pleasure, one that embraces the astonishment of the proposition itself.

KATHRIN LINKERSDORFF
Since the time I worked in Japan in the early 1990s, I have been fascinated by the clarity, simplicity, reduction and omnipresent influence of nature in traditional Japanese culture, in which a distinct sense of beauty is revealed. I learned the technique of *sumi-e*, Japanese inkwash painting, which sharpened my perception of the composition of colour and form. And in the aesthetic concept of *wabi-sabi* I discovered beauty as the acceptance of transience, imperfection and incompleteness. I am interested in the fleeting nature of flowers as a metaphor for the cycle of life. My photographic portraits fathom the essence and concealed structures of any living organism. Whereas I initially worked with a Hasselblad, I have used a digital camera since 2013. My otherwise essentially analogue practice consists of an extremely lengthy and meticulous process of preparing each flower for the moment of the photograph. The studio is rather an experimental laboratory dedicated to this process than a photographic studio. Following further specific interventions on my fragile subjects, I set up the camera in natural light, meticulously reflect all the shadows out, and shoot a staged instant of evanescent beauty. My ongoing series of dye-transfer or archival pigment prints are mostly square in format. In the photographs, I seek to achieve painterly quality and extreme sharpness. Only the experience of the original print can communicate the direct beauty of imperfection.

LISA LURATI
Through the use of a broad palette of techniques ranging from photography to sculpture and installation, my practice has lately developed around topics such as the relationship between nature, humans and non-humans, the idea of an interconnected cosmos of interspecies merging, [and] the concept of ruins in the contemporary world.

BRIGITTE LUSTENBERGER
Transience, the passing of time, and decay are central issues of my work. I do not feel fear or disgust but witness a lost, enraptured universe of withered and faded things: a beautifully wilted flower, the tenderness of a wrinkled petal, a hint of daylight on an almost forgotten world. Illuminated by natural daylight only, the flowers emerge from the shadows, unique and self-sufficient. The chiaroscuro still lifes reference

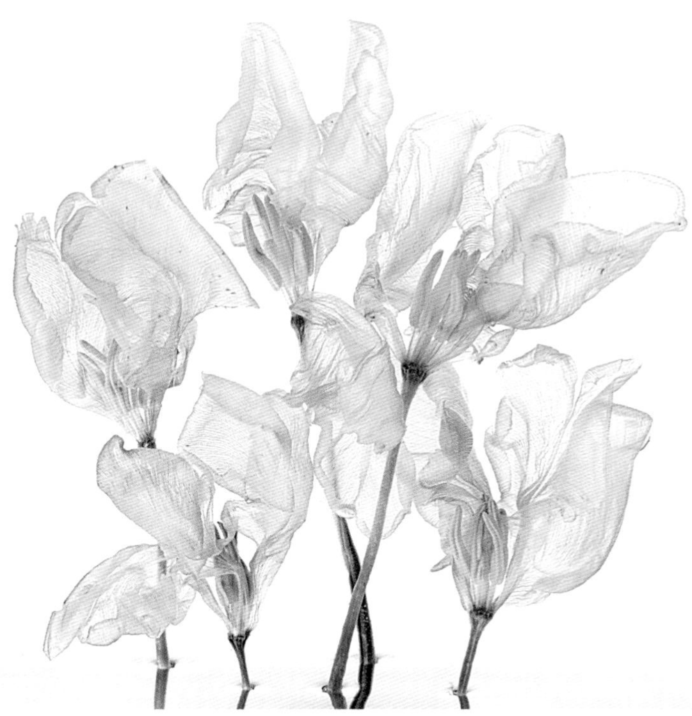

Kathrin Linkersdorff, *Fairies IV/12*, from the series *Fairies*, 2021

the original meaning of the word 'portrait', which descends from the Latin word *portrahere*, translating as 'to bring something to light'. The images hint at the paradox of photography by making us aware of the inescapable passage of time while photography as a technical medium was intended to preserve life.

FELICITY MCCABE
This image was one of my first forays into using flora in my pictures. There was a decadent bouquet that was about to be abandoned, and, as with most things, I felt panic at the thought of it being cast out into the rubbish bin, so I took the mix of stems into the studio to hopefully immortalize them before the inevitable happened. Around the same time, I'd been excited by a concept I'd heard about which was originally developed in 1927 by a British astronomer called Arthur Eddington. He had described the single, unswerving direction of the arrow of time. I found both an excitement and a horror in the knowledge that as time irreversibly marches on the flowers will certainly wilt and our mistakes will not be undone.

ANN MANDELBAUM
2D Flattens 3

what's more than perfection? what's left to remove?
what tool to tame beauty or coax a new rule?
the seed, a beginning, its pause a dull moan,
such glory itself is the story sewn full.

the miracle, bigger than brain can allow,
leaves little to add to the gift of its loan.
petals arranged...so familiar, so slow
any capture a loss, with less to be told.

the game of the lens lands a digital hand.
the couple then dances, the tune driven through,
repeating the facts is a waste of the act.
what's left is a start that begins a fresh bed.

searing all senses; jumping red outside line;
squeezing space into flat; twisting gesture to still...
the history of glory puts language on hold
as order reverses, surreal leads it all.

2D flattens 3

ZOÉ MENTHONNEX
I was born in 1996 in Switzerland, into a family rooted in the Vaud area. From my childhood between lake and forest, vineyards and mountains, I developed a deep love for the sensuality of nature. And whether in the woods or lost among the reeds, I was soon able to capture the mystery that surrounded me: from these half-dreamed moments, I would later create a universe that was renewed each time and fantasized each time; a soft, humid and impermanent cocoon. A world of my own, on the edge of reality. In my images, we find this ethereal nature, which like an unreal guide seems to capture the gaze and guide it towards a place that would be elsewhere and yet so present, so there; like an imperfect shadow that the eye perceives but does not quite see.

CARMEN MITROTTA
All my work is characterized by a careful study of colour and forms that paint my compositions. I don't stick to the expected, and it's that element of unpredictability that excites me to create my visions. This project, *Flowers*, was born from a dream. I imagined walking through an empty city in which new natural forms spontaneously arise. Nature invades the rational forms of architecture trying to imitate it. The flowers change and create parallel worlds because they are able to survive everything that hinders them.

ABELARDO MORELL
I chose to make pictures of flowers in dedication to my wife, Lisa, because they are lovely things, often exchanged between lovers. They are also part of the long tradition of still life in

art. Precisely because flowers are such well-known and conventional subjects, I felt a strong desire to describe them in new, inventive ways – I wanted to make them my own, so to speak. I love the way Jan Brueghel [the Elder], [Édouard] Manet, [Georgia] O'Keeffe, Irving Penn and Joan Mitchell reworked common flowers to show unexpected versions of them. The nominal subject of my photographs may be flowers, but to me they are more deeply about perspective, love, jealousy, hate, geometry, sex, agility, time and death.

VIK MUNIZ

I began collecting artificial flowers. Whenever I travelled, I would bring back the most beautiful ones I found – always asking where they had been made. I planned to analyse the materials used in them, to create a taxonomy of artificiality. I intended – although this ambition was never realized – to create a scholarly book about synthetic botany, with all the traditional methods used to classify the natural world transposed into a classification of the artificial. Where did they come from? Who were the craftspeople who made them? And, a question that perhaps was at the heart of my proposal: Did artificial flowers also have natural counterparts in the place where they were made? The complexity of the artificial flower is extremely interesting. In China and Thailand, for example, craftspeople reproduce flowers that they have never seen – and they commonly consider these flowers to be their own inventions. A tulip, say, grows in the fields of Holland, yes. But so what? How can its creator be denied a level of authorship – of invention? It is a perfect abstraction, valorized by the powerful abstract charge of the flower as an idea. My aim in *Flora Industrialis* was to re-create, with artificial flowers, a typical nineteenth-century botanic garden.

HABIBA NOWROSE

I am a photographer based in Dhaka, Bangladesh. I am particularly interested in exploring the construction of gender identities, mythology and perception through my work. I am more inclined to take portraits. Often my portraits are made after elaborate preparation. In my artistic process, I carefully take note of the objects, colours, patterns and locations that attract me repeatedly. These elements play a fundamental role in my image-making process. This process is psychological and interactive at the same time. I thoroughly enjoy this process as I enjoy image-making.

SARKER PROTICK

This photograph was made in one distant September of 2012, during an art residency in France. Around that time, I had been thinking of the word *lumière* [light]. I was on a road trip, and on my first stop I visited the town of Vendôme by the River Loir. There, inside an old church, I found a flower vase in one corner bathed in sunlight.

LAURENCE RASTI

On 24 September 2007 at Columbia University, former Iranian president Mahmoud Ahmadinejad said, 'In Iran, we do not have homosexuals like in your country.' While today some Occidental countries accept gay and lesbian marriage, in Iran homosexuality is still punishable by death. This sanction prohibits homosexuals from living their sexuality. Their only options are to choose transsexuality, a practice tolerated by law but considered pathological, or to flee. In Denizli, a city in Turkey, hundreds of gay refugees from Iran [wait in] transit: they put their lives on pause waiting to join one day a host country where they can freely live their sexualities. In this context of uncertainty, where anonymity is the best protection, this work questions fragile identity and gender concepts. It tries to give back to those people a face that their country has temporarily stolen.

MARCEL RICKLI

The *Atomic Flower* is part of my ongoing series *AEON*, which investigates the current issues of storing radioactive waste over a long period of time. Beside technical measures to ensure secure geological repositories, the project also questions how future generations in hundreds of thousands of years to come can be warned of the lethal threat of nuclear waste. On several occasions, semioticians and energy authorities have dealt with the central question of preserving data, knowledge and memories over generations – with partly pragmatic, partly fanciful solutions. In the early 1980s, influenced by the first successful genetic modification of crops, the Polish philosopher and science-fiction author Stanisław Lem proposed breeding an 'atomic flower' that would bloom only if radioactivity were to escape from a repository.

SIMON ROBERTS

T. S. Eliot once wrote that the point of any journey is to find out where you came from. This urge to document one's homeland and enquire into a collective identity is a powerful one, and has occupied writers and artists for centuries. In this vein, much of my practice over the past decade has been based on journeys around the British landscape photographing events, rituals and rites where people are drawn together in public, reflecting on the nature of our shared histories and communal experiences. Together, the work explores issues of identity, belonging and the complex relationship between history, place and culture. It reflects on our post-imperial predicament, the complications of New Commonwealth immigration, the Brexit schism and UK devolution, particularly the resurgence of a confident, forward-looking, flag-waving Scottish and Welsh nationalism.

ALESSIO ROMENZI

After days of hot weather that prevented any war activity, the day had arrived. All the soldiers carefully prepared their weapons and I was tremendously struck by the contrast between the feeling of death in the air and the joyful colour that surrounded us during the preparations for the attack.

PAUL ROUSTEAU

I use bright, radiant colours because they visually capture the emotion I sometimes feel when I see the world and its beauty. These moments are epiphanies. By epiphany I mean evidence of a manifestation from beyond, evidence of the miracle of creation. Abstraction is one of the ways of showing the border between the visible and the invisible, the complexity of things and of the living. This is where the doors of perception are, the border between reality and illusion. All this feeds my work. I have listed all the mistakes that a good photographer should not make, and I have tried to include them in my practice. These taboos have contributed to the development of my photographic writing.

THOMAS RUFF

Due to digital photography, the negative, which I have used nearly every day for more than twenty-five years, has almost disappeared. If I ask my daughters what a negative is, they look at me wide-eyed, for they've never seen or used one. The negative was actually never considered for itself; it was always only a means to an end. It was the 'master' from which the photographic print was made, and I think it is worth looking at these 'masters'.

VIVIANE SASSEN

Some of my earliest childhood memories are of flowers. I spent my years as a toddler in Kenya, where my father worked as a doctor in a local hospital. I vividly remember the gorgeous smell of the frangipani tree, which releases its scent in the evening when the sun has gone down. I remember the bright orange-red of the flamboyant tree in our garden, where the 'banana birds' used to nest. And the lovely lilac flowers paving the road when it was jacaranda season. Back in Holland, aged six, I found most of the Dutch flowers rather underwhelming in their scents, compared with the African flowers. But then again, the sight of multicoloured striped tulip fields till the horizon meets the sky isn't bad either.

THIRZA SCHAAP

The *Plastic Ocean* series combines sculpture and photography to examine our changing relationship with plastics and their overwhelming presence within society today. The images provide a clash between worlds, offering minimal and aesthetically pleasing compositions that, on closer inspection, instil a sense of ecological grief, asking questions about consumption, idolatry and what we value in our lives today. The effect is quirky, playful and pop: paradoxically, this debris does not disgust us. Their dainty look seems to gloss over the urgency of plastic pollution on our beaches, but this first impression soon fades. The use of flowers in *Vanda* contributes in providing a kind of *vanitas* for the twenty-first century. Traditional markers of mortality, ephemerality and wealth have been traded out for bottles, baskets and bowls: single-use items that are used and discarded, existing now as empty, destructive vessels. Flowers have [long] been symbols of the shortness of our existence and the fleeting nature of life's futility [and] of earthly possessions.

HELENE SCHMITZ

In my artistic practice as a photographer, I have focused on the Occidental world's way of studying, exploring and exploiting the natural world and its resources. A part of my practice has been the study of human attempts at categorizing and classifying nature. I was captivated by the famous Swedish botanist [Carolus] Linnaeus's obsession to create a [naming] system for all living organisms in the world. My photographs of flowers were published in the book *A Passion for Systems: Linnaeus and the Dream of Order in Nature* (2007), where I photographed flowers and their reproductive parts according to Linnaeus's 'sexual system', published in *Systema Natura* in 1735. I have also tried to capture the fascinating beauty and function of the carnivorous plants in the series *Carnivores* (2010). This project was published in *National Geographic* magazine.

GARY SCHNEIDER

For my *Botanicals* (1989–96), I studied late eighteenth- and early nineteenth-century pre-photography botanical engravings. Unlike those scientific studies, mine are a personal interpretation of the subject. I created a narrative by carefully composing the image, then lighting the specimen with a small flashlight (torch) in total darkness to pick out discrete details. Using the same sheet of 8 × 10-in [20 × 25-cm] film, I would accumulate one detail after another over a long period of time, sometimes months. This process was an adaptation of what I had learned in the darkroom while making prints by dodging the light and then burning-in with light. After making the first exposure of *Rose*, I turned it over to examine the other side. The flower had dried out while I was doing the lengthy composing. The petals fell away from the stem, denuding the inner flower, further revealing the reproductive parts.

MARTIN SCHOELLER

My idea was to turn Jeff Koons into an art piece by painting his face white to give him the appearance of a sculpture. The suit jacket hints at his financial success, and the flowers reference elements from his work.

CHLOE SELLS

Informed by extensive travel, residence and immersion in countries foreign to me, I explore the question of how places define us. Is a place fixed, or continually shifting? Do people shape the particularities of space as they encounter it, or does space transform people? When depicting a landscape through the fallible mechanism of memory, what becomes essential? I interpret my encounters with places through the utility of beauty, questioning what is familiar and exotic, known and unknown. For me, beauty creates an opportunity for consonance within, eclipsing our contemporary songs of despair, thus allowing the sacred and uncanny to converse. While experience is happening on many different levels simultaneously, there is a play between the immutable and the supple, which I embroider through my process. Image and imagination become entangled. To create my pictures I use a large-format camera and [make] prints in a darkroom. The printing process is both considered and spontaneous, and manipulates the alchemical foundations of darkroom practice to create kaleidoscopic images. Imposed textures retrace geographic contours. Image fragments and oddly cut prints have been sketched and painted on. This layering brings an intensity or clarity to the place, constituting a further mapping of the journey. Each outcome is unique.

ANN SHELTON

jane says is a photographic garden of flowers and herbs arranged and offset against a brightly coloured background. The featured plants – rue, peony, pennyroyal, poroporo among them – are drawn from millennia of human history in which they have been used medicinally in association with women's reproductive health as emmenagogues (substances that bring on menstruation), abortifacients (substances that induce abortion) or contraceptives, of varying strengths. Along with my research into the histories of botanical medicine, colonial practices of abortion and human relationships with these plants, this series of large-scale hyper-detailed images references the Japanese tradition of *ikebana*, which I learned, and its visual and conceptual qualities of structure and regulation. The series is accompanied by printed matter and performance-based components. By making these works, including constructing the arrangements myself and growing some of the more difficult-to-source plants, I intended to focus a viewer in on the profound knowledge nature holds. Set against the backdrop of the ongoing politicization of women's health, the #metoo movement, the ever-growing impact of the climate emergency and COVID-19, these artworks argue that our mismanagement of nature has engendered an incremental loss of knowledge and understanding that we cannot easily build back, and that continues to pose a danger to human existence.

DANIEL SHIPP

I'm interested in what we consider worthy or beautiful in the plant world and how urban nature is subjected to the dominance of human activity. When viewed with the naked eye, many of the plants featured in my images are considered unremarkable or even undesirable 'weedy' elements of urban living. I scour residential streets, industrial parks and forgotten parcels of urban land, taking clippings of found plants, which I then bring to my studio. Using a set and artificial lighting, I develop photographic compositions that evolve very gradually and quietly. There's a tension between the slow and exacting nature of how I work and the spontaneity of responding to the plants I find on a given day. Although captured digitally, the images aren't created in a computer, they are one shot created in camera using numerous visual-effect techniques derived from classic cinema.

TARYN SIMON

In signings of political accords, contracts, treaties and decrees, powerful men flank floral centrepieces curated to convey the importance of the signatories and the institutions they represent.

I saw an early image of Mussolini, Hitler and Chamberlain at the Munich conference in 1938 sitting in a room around this large bouquet of flowers, and it got me thinking about the performance of power, and nature as this sort of castrated accessory – this silent witness listening to those men and their belief in their abilities to control economies and geographies and the evolution of the world.

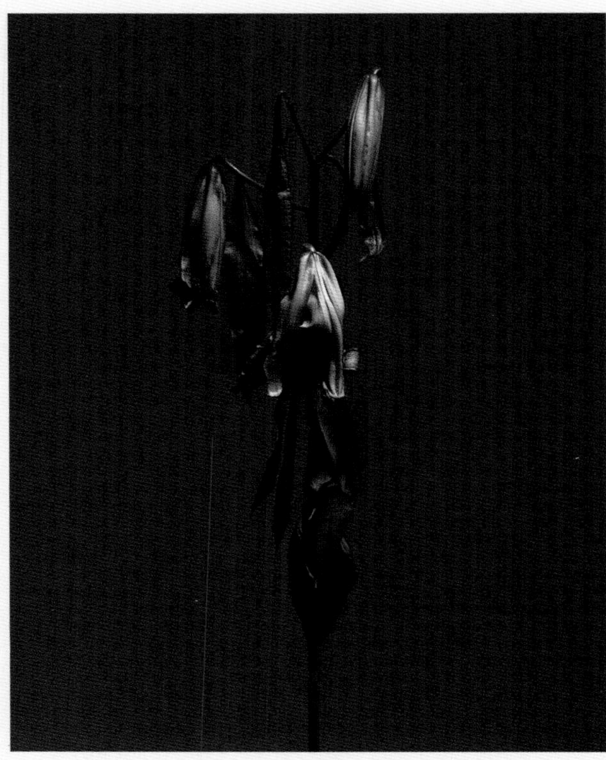

Roberto Greco, *fig. IV*, from the series *Œillères*, 2017

These ceremonial bouquets and the colour fields of curtains surrounding them are the component parts of the mathematics in the stagecraft of power.

I started researching archival images of signings and worked with a botanist to identify the flowers in them. I then sourced these flowers from the world's largest flower auction, in the Netherlands, and re-created the bouquets from those archival images with a focus on signings from 1968 onwards that involved countries present at the 1944 Bretton Woods Conference in New Hampshire, which addressed the globalization of economies after World War II and led to the establishment of the International Monetary Fund and the World Bank. They are all 'impossible bouquets' – a term that started to be used in early Dutch still-life painting alongside early murmurings of capitalism. The 'impossible bouquet' referred to an arrangement of flowers that could never be present in the same time and place [because of] geographical and seasonal limitations. It was a surreal flower arrangement. Now, these arrangements that were once possible only in a painting can exist in real life, thanks to this new chapter of global capitalism in which some [people] can have whatever they want, whenever they want.

Many of the agreements in this project represent broken promises – declarations that have been violated and withered.

NIKI SIMPSON

I began my experiment with digital techniques of botanical illustration in 2004. In time-honoured fashion I aim to convey a scientific visual description of the plant concerned, but photography now allows me to do this with a degree of realism that is difficult to achieve by painting. To others a white background is clinical, but to me it feels enabling. It allows me to give even the lowliest of plants their moment in the limelight. I want to portray them alive and kicking, neither laid out like corpses nor flattened like pressed herbarium specimens. The only hidden depths are those further features or micro-characters that can be revealed on magnification, especially by on-screen viewing, and which the photographic medium makes possible. If respect for the environment is to be felt, an understanding of plants is necessary. It is my hope that visually accessible information in attractive images can draw in those who have been blind to plants, to encourage them to go into and beyond the image. I want to share my love [of] and interest in plants and encourage everyone, especially the young, to take a closer look.

NICHOLE SOBECKI

afriMAN is an exploration of evolving understandings of manhood on the African continent, and how traditional expectations are being subverted by individuals. Conceived in collaboration with artists Zelalem Mulat Teklewold and Fitsum Berhe Woldelibanos, these portraits are our interpretation of Africa's modern-day chiefs – men defining their own sense of identity beyond gender essentialism. The interviews that accompany the portraits are an essential part of this project, preceding the making of images that were then conceptualized together with our subjects. The men here reflect the emergence of a fresh, unhindered image of gender that rejects the dominant masculine ideals of aggression, dominance and a closed emotional state. Their masculinity is not imposed on them by the outside world. It's not the masculinity of their fathers. It's not even a fixed state. 'Being a man', explains the writer Kevin Mwachiro, 'is just simply being comfortable in your own skin.' This is the *afriMAN*.

ALEC SOTH

This photograph was made while I was in Bogotá with my wife in 2002, adopting our daughter Carmen. We ended up staying there for two months while the courts processed the paperwork. While we waited, I wandered the city looking for pictures. I didn't have any big concepts or agenda. But looking back, it's easy to see that many of the pictures speak to themes of newness and fragility.

ADELE SPENCER

I am an avid amateur photographer from Dublin, Ireland. I like to create compositions that are minimal in nature, yet visually appealing. This image of a dragon fruit with tulips is part of a set of six still-life images that I created when I was experimenting with shape and form through the use of edible items and flowers/foliage.

HENRIK SPOHLER

In the photo series with the biblical title *The Third Day*, I examined the relationship between man and flora. Photos of monocultures or greenhouses that reach to the horizon show how the industrial cultivation of crops shapes and changes landscapes worldwide. Glimpses of research laboratories give an idea of what the future holds when humans themselves become creators, designing new plant species with increasingly profitable traits. The plant auction in the Netherlands shown in this book is indicative of the monetary relationship between humans and flora.

MAGGIE STEBER

When Katie Stubblefield was seventeen, a boy broke her heart. She tried to get past it with the help of her family, but one day she went to her brother's house, found a rifle that someone had given him, went into the bathroom and attempted to kill herself. She failed, but in so doing, she shot her face off. Her brother heard the rifle go off and found her in the bathroom. It was a miracle she lived. After multiple surgeries doctors created a temporary face for Katie using flesh and skin from her stomach and thighs. She had no nose, so she breathed through a hole in her neck and took medication and pills through a hole in her stomach. Her parents, Robb and Alesia, had to quit their jobs as teachers to take care of their daughter full time, taking her to doctor's appointments, speech lessons, physical therapy and mental-health therapists. For three years this went on, and so did more surgeries. Her surgical team at Cleveland Clinic Hospital in Ohio was comprised of twenty-five surgeons, and when the face became available, it took a twenty-five-hour surgery to place and sew the face to Katie's scalp. After much suffering and constant pain for several years, Katie's dream came true. A grandmother had donated the face of her granddaughter who was brain-dead from a drug overdose. Katie got a new face and a new chance at life, which is not wasted on her or her parents. When I went to photograph the family, I would always do a portrait session with Katie and flowers to try to make something beautiful, even though Katie could not see it, having lost a lot of her eyesight. At least her parents could see it. It was always a special day that we would end with a nice supper at their favourite restaurant. The gift of a face is a rare thing. People will donate organs of every sort, but the face is what describes us, is who we are, is the first thing people notice and [use to] judge whether they want to talk to us.

RUDOLF STEINER

This image was taken as part of a long-term photographic research [project] entitled *Ricochet*. A device called Gigapan, developed by NASA for high-resolution panoramic images of the Martian surface, was used to take several hundred individual images, which were then combined into a single image by computer. This recording technique is very precise under studio conditions and leads to extremely high-resolution results. In the wild, however, all meteorological conditions such as light changes, rain or wind write themselves into the recording and lead to unpredictable 'errors' in the final image. Additionally, using a telephoto lens with an open aperture creates a paradoxical effect in that the extreme reduction in depth of field manifests itself in an inherently wide-angle image. All these effects are more palpable than clearly visible in the shot of a fading glycine [wisteria] overgrowing an abandoned house in the immediate neighbourhood of my studio.

THOMAS STRUTH

In 1990 I was invited to create works for the patients' rooms of a Swiss hospital. What condition do all patients share, I asked myself, no matter what reason they found themselves at a hospital? Having parts of their body under alarming focus and being separated from their homes and loved ones, I thought. This led me to photograph flowers in a commensurate manner – with special focus and magnification – as well as generic landscapes of the surrounding hills and forests. Thirty years later the pandemic, the uncertainty of the world's political and natural future, and my own ageing drew my mind to mortality. The oriental poppies we had planted in our garden offered a symbol of startling beauty, decay and death, with the certainty of a return to beauty.

MARIA STURM AND CEMRE YEŞIL GÖNENLI

A symbol of schism and confluence, a transcontinental city, Istanbul has always been the inspiration for great stories. But this is not a story about Istanbul; it is a story from the female vantage point about how a group of men devote their lives to raising goldfinches and greenfinches: a mysterious bond full of contradictions, love, possession and pleasure; the contradictions between masculine and feminine; the female caress alongside the power of men; caregivers who compete for the bird that sings the best... And two women who learn how to listen and speak.

LARRY SULTAN

The cast and crew have gathered in the front yard of a ranch-style house, a few blocks from where I went to high school in the San Fernando Valley [California]. Women in six-inch heels sink into the lawn; men push around camera equipment, anxious about losing the light. They are preparing to film a scene in which four blonde housewives in a convertible are pursued and overtaken by two men in an appliance-repair van. In the golden afternoon light, the neighbours have come out to water their lawns and witness the scene. It is common for adult-film companies to shoot in tract houses – the homes of dentists and attorneys and day traders whose family photographs can be seen in the background, and whose decorating tastes give the films their particular look. It's as if one family has gone on vacation for a few days, leaving everything in the house intact, and another family, an odd assembly of unrelated adults, has temporarily taken up residence. While the film crew and talent are hard at work in the living room, I wander through the house peering into the lives of the people who live there. I feel like a forensic photographer searching out evidence. In these films, lazy afternoons are interrupted not by noisy children but by the uncontrollable desires of delivery boys, babysitters, coeds and cops. They crowd into the master bedrooms and spill out on to the patios and into the pools that look just like our neighbours' pools, like our pool. And by photographing this I'm planted squarely in the terrain of my own ambivalence – that rich and fertile field that stretches out between fascination and repulsion, desire and loss. I'm home again.

MIRIAM TÖLKE

The city and nature are my masters, they energize me. While I live as well in Berlin, I also find myself at home in the countryside. Nature follows an aesthetic perfectionism but the city is dense, full of snapshots and volatility. I see myself as a collector, a *flâneur*. Everything seems connected to me. My works are impressions that fall into a collage, showing a web of incidents.

RON VAN DONGEN
My interest in nature, and specifically gardening, started at a very young age, before I ever touched a camera. Years later, while attending art school, photographing flora began as a mere exercise. It allowed me to learn the ins and outs of working with a large-format camera, while my subject matter waited patiently in the studio. Little did I know that I was going to be able to make a living from gardening in the most unconventional way: first growing the plants and subsequently documenting the different and unique specimens. But I suspect that when all photographic activities have passed, I will still be tending my plants with love and care, whether it is in a lush garden somewhere in the countryside or in a few pots on a city balcony.

RUUD VAN EMPEL
The colours in nature are overwhelming. Whenever I make images of nature, I love to portray those intense colours. But there are also very dark colours; a very dark-black nature also exists – what would it mean? I made a small series of works in 2018–19 about the colour black in nature, and I photographed black plants and flowers everywhere I came across them until I had a good stock to work with. I then worked in my usual technique, cutting out elements from photos and combining them with other elements to create a whole new image. I use photography to create a fictional image; I link realism and dream: the inconvenience of the almost tangible reality versus the illusion.

LORENZO VITTURI
Dalston Anatomy is a visual celebration of the Ridley Road market in east London. The project was presented for the first time in 2013 as a photo-book, a month-long performance, and installations. I recognized the market as a unique place where different communities and cultures coexist, and decided to capture the energy and traces of this place before it transformed beyond recognition. In *Red #1*, organic materials are left to rot, manipulated with pigment, deconstructed and then rearranged into a composition and photographed against discarded market materials before and after its collapse. The ephemerality of this floral-like sculpture mirrors the impermanent nature of a rapidly changing neighbourhood, while its reintroduction in the exhibition space as photographic image allows reflections on constant cycles of production, destruction and re-creation.

ROBERT WALKER
For the past forty years I have photographed cities; nature has never interested me as a subject for photography. I suffered under the delusion that a rectangular image wrenched out of the landscape could only be arbitrary with no logical structure, or just a pictorial cliché, reminiscent of those on calendars and postcards. At a certain point, I felt obliged to take up the challenge, to face the beast of nature. I decided to limit myself to working with flowers. I adopted the same compositional strategy I use when photographing in places such as Times Square [Manhattan]. When looking through the viewfinder, I ignore the literal subject matter and compose the picture on the basis of purely abstract elements of form and colour. Forgetting the countless metaphorical significances usually associated with flowers, I compose my images as if on a blank canvas or flat surface. This often enables me to conjure up relationships between styles and techniques evocative of abstract painting.

WILLIAM WEGMAN
This is my tall dog Topper wearing a stunning flowery pant suit by Gucci. I love the wide lapels from which his arms appear to grow. How is it possible that he is so tall?!, you may ask. If I knew, I probably wouldn't tell you. Magicians never give away their tricks...or at least they shouldn't. He's sitting on a tall stool made especially for him.

MARCUS WESTBERG
Although it has never been a particular focus of my work as a photographer, in which I cover mostly conservation issues and various aspects of travel, I have always loved flowers. I spent my early childhood in Sweden, and during spring and summer would often come home with bouquets of freshly picked wild flowers for my mother. To this day, seeing wild flowers can't not make me happy. They add such colour and joy, in photography as well as in life, as was certainly the case on this Harar [Ethiopia] street.

JO WHALEY
In *Analytical Behavior*, an anthropomorphic magnifying device examines a Japanese anemone flower, while restraining a pinned Luna moth, engaged in a post-mortem flight. Meanwhile live snails investigate the drama. As actors on a stage, they are engaged in a mute dialogue. The painted backdrop and studio lighting are key to animating and unifying the disparate elements. Surprisingly, when the strobe lighting flashed, the snails retreated into their shells, and only with time would they retake their positions on the stage. The performance was concluded with one click of the view camera's shutter, exposing film, without digital manipulation. In *Knows No Scents*, against an acid-rain sky, an insentient nose attempts to inhale the intense fragrance of an Asiatic lily, from the glorified position on a plinth of *Acanthus* leaves. The apocalyptic sky is painted and the theatrical lighting bathes the scene in an ominous glow. Artifice and illusion are part of the theatrical tradition. The photograph is an updated version of the symbol-laden seventeenth-century Dutch floral paintings, both referring to the transitory nature of life and offering a cautionary tale, which considers the consequences of an engineered society at the expense of nature. My studio process is in essence the theatre of photography. Artifice and illusion are part of the theatrical tradition where the intent is to fuse the imaginary with the real in order to create a narrative fiction.

YAMAMOTO MASAO
I was impressed with the many forms of nature when I was shooting my early series *A Box of Ku* and *Nakazora*. The beautiful designs of the flowers and the wings of butterflies as well as the intricate rock patterns created by rivers and ocean water remind me how ordinary things keep changing. While some changes are internal, others are external. I reconstructed the wonder of nature in my own way and put them on photographic paper. Through my photographs, I have tried to be nature's messenger.

TOMOKO YONEDA
Chrysanthemums is one of the images from my series *Cumulus* (2011–12). I undertook these photographs right after the Great East Japan Earthquake in 2011. This natural catastrophe brought the tremendous tsunami and aftershocks that caused the meltdown of the Fukushima Daiichi nuclear power plant. This event once again reminds us all of that other nuclear catastrophe, the atomic bombs dropped on Hiroshima and Nagasaki [in 1945]. The chrysanthemum is a symbol of grace and the Japanese imperial and national crest, [and] I took this as a metaphor for [the] Japanese family: child, father and mother who stand firm but are also as lost as stray sheep to the unknown fate of Japan at the time of the disaster in 2011.

NADIRAH ZAKARIYA
All Purpose Flower was conceived and created during the Malaysian Movement Control Order (MCO) due to COVID-19 in May 2020. It began as a coping mechanism while in quarantine, creating flowers using items found in my home, from cut-out flowers from vintage kimono fabric to coconut-milk cartons to flowers made from raffia. Once the florists were back in business in Malaysia, I had some fresh blooms delivered for my birthday, and created arrangements as a form of self-portrait during quarantine, displaying household items that

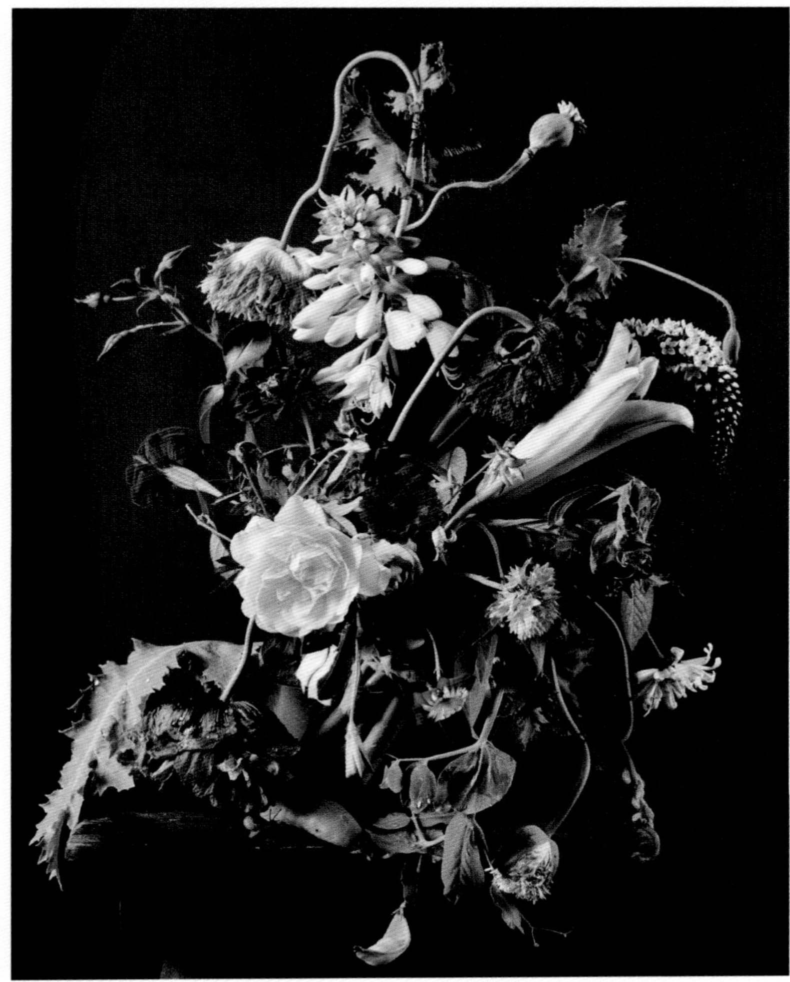

Sharon Core, *1720*, 2012

became part of the new norm such as gloves and masks, and items found in the pantry. On MCO Day 59, I wrote: 'As the peonies' colour transformed from vibrant pink to this dusty pastel shade, they also grew bolder and more beautiful each day. Though time seems to be standing still these days, I can feel something is changing within, just like the peonies, [and] I hope that I too am blooming.'

ANDREW ZUCKERMAN
With a lot of my projects, there's a preservationist impulse at work. In many ways, I think of the photographs as a kind of record-keeping in a world that's rapidly being depleted of its most exquisite subjects. By using photography as a recording device to create two-dimensional representations of three-dimensional living things, the images become physical documents of moments that have passed. I want to understand how things work, to lay them out in some kind of order, to consider them in a way I can understand. I have a desire to create clarity out of confusion, and investigating the botanical world appeals to this impulse. It's fascinating that the most astonishingly beautiful qualities of flowers are purely survival mechanisms. I love that every flower is a dependent half of an ecosystem, and structurally, they evoke their insect counterparts. Very early on in the making of this project, I had the opportunity to photograph the extremely rare Darwin's star orchid [*Angraecum sesquipedale*], which was instrumental in [Charles] Darwin's formulation of the theory of evolution. He postulated that because of the 11-in [28-cm] spur extending from its blossom there had to be an insect with some kind of appendage long enough to pollinate it. No one believed him, but forty years later entomologists discovered a moth with a furled tongue that was four times longer than its body.

Introduction
1. Colette, *Prisons et Paradis*, Paris, 1932. Colette admitted to what she wryly called a 'disinterested botanical passion'.
2. See Karl Blossfeldt, *Urformem der Kunst: Photographische Pflanzenbilder* (Archetypes in Nature/Art Forms in Nature), Berlin, 1928. The book became an international bestseller and established the photographer's reputation virtually overnight.
3. Edwin Hale Lincoln self-published his platinum prints in elegant volumes under the title *Wildflowers of New England* between 1910 and 1914.
4. The X-ray was invented in 1895, but we hear of a flower as a subject only in 1912, when Pierre Goby exhibited one at the Royal Photographic Society in London; it took Tasker's efforts in the 1930s to bring the practice to public attention. Hans Busch invented the electromagnetic lens in 1926, but did not construct a microscope. That honour goes to the physicist Ernst Ruska and the electrical engineer Max Knoll, at the University of Berlin in 1931.
5. Noel Chanan, *The Photographer of Penllergare: A Life of John Dillwyn Llewelyn 1810–1882*, London, 2013, p. 52.
6. *Photographic News*, May 1887, p. 371.
7. *Photographic News*, 10 September 1858, p. 1.
8. Jack Goody, *The Culture of Flowers*, Cambridge, 1993, p. 49.
9. Sean Sexton and Robert Flynn Johnson, *Plant Kingdoms: The Photographs of Charles Jones*, New York, 1998, p. 21.

Roots
1. Quoted in Theodore Stebbins, Jr, and Norman Keyes, Jr, *Charles Sheeler: The Photographs*, New York, 1987, p. 4.

In Situ
1. Edwin Smith, *All the Photo-tricks: Ways and Ideas Off the Beaten Track*, Waltham, MA, 1947, p. 272.
2. Maurice Maeterlinck, *The Intelligence of Flowers*, 1907, p. 11.
3. Margaret Ann Donnell, 'Floral Imagery within Wartime Era Poetry: How its Usage Transforms Memory and Remembrance', History Class Publications, Ouachita Baptist University, December 2018, p. 3.
4. Ernst Jünger, *The Storm of Steel: From the Diary of a German Storm-Troop Officer on the Western Front* [1920], trans. Basil Creighton, London, 1920, p. 1.
5. Ralph Waldo Emerson, 'Gifts', *Essays: Second Series*, 1844, available at www.archive.vcu.edu/english/engweb/transcendentalism/authors/emerson/essays/gifts.html.

Enquiry
1. David Deutsch, 'Why Are Flowers Beautiful?', Chapter 14 in *The Beginning of Infinity: Explanations that Transform the World*, New York, 2012. Also available on YouTube as a lecture given at the Irish Museum of Modern Art, Dublin, 27 January 2007.
2. James Mew, 'Photographic Botany', *Photographic News*, April 1892, p. 259.
3. See Artists' Statements for Olga Cafiero, p. 254, and Craig Burrows, p. 254
4. In conversation with photographer Niki Simpson.
5. John Riddle, *Eve's Herbs*, Cambridge, MA, 1997, p. 254.
6. R. H. Noailles, *The Hidden Life of Flowers*, New York, 1954.
7. Antonin Artaud, 'Lettre à Monsieur le législateur de la loi sur les stupéfiants' (Letter to the legislator of narcotics), available at www.guillaumehoogveld.net/2012/08/artaud (accessed 14 September 2021).
8. Victor Hugo, letter to Baudelaire, 30 August 1857.

A Photo-synthesis
1. Raymond Williams, *The Country and the City*, New York, 1975, p. 120.
2. Matthew K. Chew, 'The Monstering of Tamarisk: How Scientists Made a Plant into a Problem', *Journal of the History of Biology*, 42:2 (Summer 2009), p. 235.
3. Jack Goody, *The Culture of Flowers*, Cambridge, 1993, p. 425.
4. Maurice Maeterlinck, *The Intelligence of Flowers* [1907], trans. Philip Mosley, New York, 2008, pp. 41–2.
5. David Deutsch, 'Why Are Flowers Beautiful?', Chapter 14 in *The Beginning of Infinity: Explanations that Transform the World*, New York, 2012. Also available on YouTube as a lecture given at the Irish Museum of Modern Art, Dublin, 27 January 2007.
6. Jeannette Haviland-Jones, Holly Hale Rosario, Patricia Wilson and Terry R. McGuire, 'An Environmental Approach to Positive Emotion: Flowers', *Evolutionary Psychology*, 3:1 (January 2005), pp. 104–32.
7. Goody, *Culture of Flowers*, p. 12.
8. Truman Capote, *The Essays of Truman Capote*, New York, 2007.
9. Goody, *Culture of Flowers*, p. 2.
10. Ibid., p. 291.
11. See www.bloomandwild.com/floriography-language-of-flowers-meaning (accessed 20 July 2021).
12. See, for example, Jane Carruthers et al., 'A Native at Home and Abroad: The History, Politics and Aesthetics of Acacias', *Diversity and Distributions: A Journal of Conservation Biogeography*, 17:5 (8 August 2011), p. 811. The authors explain how botanical symbols of all the British colonies were embroidered on the Coronation stole of King George V in 1911. The recently established Union of South Africa had not yet decided on its national flower, so a thornless acacia-like flower was used to represent it. The lack of thorns meant it was clearly an Australian import, rather than a native African species, a fact that caused much consternation; the compromise was to add thorns. Another international incident occurred in 2005, when the Nomenclature section of the International Botanical Congress altered the type specimen of the genus *Acacia* from an African to an Australian species, causing heated debate.
13. Goody points out that 'Mao was constantly referring to flowers (as well as to the notion of the "soul") in his many speeches.' *Culture of Flowers*, p. 405.
14. Lucia Tongiorgi Tomasi and Gretchen A. Hirschauer, *The Flowering of Florence: Botanical Art for the Medici*, National Gallery of Art, Washington, DC, 2002.
15. Peter Mitchell, *European Flower Painters*, New York, 1973, p. 25.
16. William A. Ewing, *Flora Photographica*, 2nd edn, London, 2002, p. 31.

Arrangement
1. Odilon Redon, 'Le Salon de 1868', *La Gironde*, 19 May 1868.
2. Yasuhiro Ishimoto, *Hana*, San Francisco, 1989, n.p.
3. Ronald J. Gedrim, 'Edward Steichen's 1936 Exhibition of Delphinium Blooms: An Art of Flower Breeding', *History of Photography*, 17 (1993), p. 361.
4. Odilon Redon, *A soi-même: Journal, 1867–1915*, Paris, 1961, p. 120.
5. 'Steichen Roars Denunciation', *New York World Telegram*, 24 June 1936. Peter Mitchell, European Flower Pianters. A. & C. Black, London, 1973, p.209

Essence
1. Emanuele Coccia, *The Life of Plants: A Metaphysics of Mixture*, Cambridge, 2019, n.p.

Imposters
1. Jack Goody, *The Culture of Flowers*, Cambridge, 1993, p. 62.
2. Quoted in ibid., p. 52.
3. G. B. Depping, *Réglemens sur les Arts et Métiers de Paris...*, Paris, 1837, p. xxviii.
4. Quoted in Goody, *Culture of Flowers*, p. 52.
5. Wallace Stevens, 'Sunday Morning', in Harmonium, New York, 1923. The second phrase has often been wrongly attributed to Stevens, perhaps because his sentiment is illustrated so aptly by the case of artificial flowers.
6. D. L. Parnas, 'Software Aspects of Strategic Defense Systems', *American Scientist*, 73 (September–October 1985), p. 438.
7. C. P. Cavafy, 'Artificial Flowers', February 1903. Original poem in G. P. Savvidis, ed., *Anekdota Poimata*, Athens, 1968.

In Full Bloom
1. Christian Josi, 'Halston's Personal Orchid Man on the Netflix Series, Studio 54 and Tending Flowers for the New York Élite', *InsideHook*, 11 June 2021, www.insidehook.com/article/style/halstons-personal-orchid-man.
2. Tristan Bravinder, '7 Favorite Flowers from Renaissance Manuscripts and their Christian Symbolism', *Iris* blog, Getty, 20 December 2017, https://blogs.getty.edu/iris/7-favorite-flowers-from-renaissance-manuscripts-and-their-christian-symbolism.
3. Julia Fiore, 'In Dutch Still Lifes, Dark Secrets Hide behind Exotic Delicacies', *Artsy*, 4 September 2018, www.artsy.net/article/artsy-editorial-dutch-lifes-dark-secrets-hide-exotic-delicacies.
4. Alexxa Gotthardt, 'Rachel Ruysch's Exquisite Still Lifes Revolutionized the Form', *Artsy*, 21 May 2020, www.artsy.net/article/artsy-editorial-rachel-ruyschs-exquisite-lifes-revolutionized-form.
5. For a more accurate account and detailed sociological analysis of tulip mania, see Anne Goldgar, *Tulipmania: Money, Honor, and Knowledge in the Dutch Golden Age*, London, 2008.
6. 'World Floriculture Map 2016: Equator Countries Gathering Speed', Rabobank, November 2016, https://research.rabobank.com/far/en/sectors/regional-food-agri/world_floriculture_map_2016.html.

Hybrids
1. Megan Gambino, 'Cracking the Code of the Human Genome: The Story of How an Artist Created a Genetic Hybrid of Himself and a Petunia', *Smithsonian Magazine*, 22 February 2013.
2. Quoted in ibid.
3. Frederic Schoberl, *The Language of Flowers; With Illustrative Poetry*, 1834; Thomas Haynes Bayly, *Oh, This World of Ours*, c. 1830.
4. Arthur Conan Doyle, *The Adventure of the Naval Treaty*, www.sherlock-holm.es/stories/pdf/a4/2-sided/nava.pdf, pp. 6–7.

Fugue
1. Edwin Curran, 'Flowers', *c.* 1920.
2. Odilon Redon, 'Le Salon de 1868', *La Gironde*, 19 May 1868.
3. Edward Abbey, *Desert Solitaire*, Chapter 4, 'Cliffrose and Bayonets'. Abbey (1927–1989) was an American naturalist and writer who worked in the southwestern United States. His best-known works, *Desert Solitaire* (1968) and *The Monkey Wrench Gang* (1975), did much to inspire radical environmental activism.
4. Jane Goodall, *Seeds of Hope: Wisdom and Wonder from the World of Plants*, 2013, n.p.

Reverie
1. Frederic Schoberl, *The Language of Flowers; With Illustrative Poetry*, 1834; Anon., *The Language of Flowers*, Philadelphia, 1835, p. v.
2. The Notebooks of Samuel Taylor Coleridge, Volume 3, Routledge 1973, entry 4287

Unless otherwise stated, all works are courtesy the artist.

p. 6 Courtesy Howard Greenberg Gallery, New York.

p. 8 Reproduced by permission of the Bodleian Libraries, Oxford, U.K. https://archives.bodleian.ox.ac.uk/repositories/2/resources/2837.

p. 9 Courtesy, Private Collection

p. 10 Courtesy, Sean Sexton and the Sexton Collection

p. 11 © Estate of Larry Sultan Courtesy of Casemore Kirkeby, San Francisco; Yancey Richardson, New York; Galerie Thomas Zander, Cologne; Estate of Larry Sultan.

p. 13 Courtesy, Private Collection

p. 15 © 2021, ProLitteris, Zurich, Courtesy Mai 36 Galerie, Zurich

p. 18 Courtesy of Rob and Nick Carter

p. 20 Courtesy by Robert Morat Galerie, Berlin

p. 23 Photograph by Abelardo Morell, Courtesy of Edwynn Houk Gallery

p. 24 Photo: Julia Hetta / Art + Commerce

p. 25 Photograph by Abelardo Morell, Courtesy of Edwynn Houk Gallery

p. 28 © Lee Friedlander, courtesy Fraenkel Gallery, San Francisco and Luhring Augustine, New York

p. 35 Courtesy Christophe Guye Galerie

p. 37 Courtesy of the artist

p. 38 Courtesy Gallery Zerp Rotterdam

p. 39 Courtesy Galerie Cokkie Snoei, Rotterdam

p. 41 © John MacLean, Courtesy of Flowers Gallery

p. 43 Courtesy of Gallery Stigter van Doesburg

pp. 44-45 Courtesy of Robert Morat Gallery

p. 48 © Michael Wolf, Courtesy of Flowers Gallery

p. 53 Courtesy: the artist

p. 54 Courtesy of Flowers Gallery and Howard Greenberg Gallery

p. 59 Courtesy of Flowers Gallery and Howard Greenberg Gallery

p. 60 © Thomas Struth

p. 61 © Michael Wolf, Courtesy of Flowers Gallery

pp. 66-67 © Niki Simpson www.visualbotany.co.uk

p. 73 © Jo Whaley, 1994

p. 74 Courtesy of Galeria Nara Roesler, SP, NY

p. 75 Courtesy of Galería Fernando Pradilla - Madrid

p. 79 Courtesy of Rob and Nick Carter

pp. 82-83 © Taryn Simon. Courtesy Gagosian

pp. 86-87 Paul Harfleet of The Pansy Project

p. 89 Courtesy Galerie C

p. 90 Collection Noel Chanan, Taunton, U.K.

p. 93 Courtesy James Abbe Collection, New York.

p. 94 Collections du Musée suisse de l'appareil photographique, Vevey, Switzerland.

p. 96 Courtesy of the photographer

p. 97 Courtesy Implenia Schweiz

p. 99 Courtesy Jack Bell Gallery, London

p. 102 Copyright Pedro Almodóvar

p. 105 Courtesy by Robert Morat Galerie, Berlin

p. 107 Courtesy of Gallery Stigter van Doesburg

p. 108 Courtesy Camera Work

p. 109 Copyright Pedro Almodóvar

p. 111 Photograph by Abelardo Morell, Courtesy of Edwynn Houk Gallery

p. 113 Copyright Pedro Almodóvar

p. 115 Courtesy of Gallery Stigter van Doesburg

p. 117 Courtesy of Flowers Gallery and Howard Greenberg Gallery

p. 118 Courtesy Christophe Guye Galerie

p. 124 © Yamamoto Masao

p. 125 Courtesy of the artist

pp. 130-131 © Garry Fabian Miller

p. 142 Courtesy of Bildhalle

p. 149 Copyright the artist. Courtesy ShugoArts

p. 153 Courtesy Sara Cwynar and The Approach, London, Cooper Cole, Toronto and Foxy Production, New York

p. 154 Courtesy of the artist and M+B, Los Angeles

p. 156 Courtesy of the artist and M+B, Los Angeles

p. 159 © Julie Cockburn, courtesy of Flowers Gallery

p. 160 Courtesy Bildhalle Zurich

pp. 166-167 © Rosemary Laing, Courtesy Tolarno Galleries, Melbourne

p. 168 Courtesy of the artist and M+B, Los Angeles

p. 171 Courtesy of Gallery Stigter van Doesburg

p. 179 Courtesy Galerie C

p. 180 Courtesy The Ravestijn Gallery

p. 185 Courtesy of the artist Sandra Kantanen and Purdy Hicks Gallery

p. 187 © Joel-Peter Witkin, courtesy baudoin lebon

p. 188 Courtesy of the artist Sandra Kantanen and Purdy Hicks Gallery

p. 189 Courtesy TJ Boulting

p. 192 Photograph Daniel Shipp

pp. 196-197 HACKNEY FLOWERS 2004-2007 © Stephen Gill, published by Nobody Books in 2007. A survey retrospective exhibition of Stephen Gill's work spanning 39 years will take place at the Arnolfini in Bristol from 16 October 2021 to 16 January 2022 https://arnolfini.org.uk/whatson/stephen-gill/.

p. 199 Image courtesy of Nick Knight

p. 203 Courtesy of the artist

p. 206 © Yamamoto Masao

p. 207 Copyright Jiang Zhi. Image courtesy of Jiang Zhi and Blindspot Gallery

p. 213 © 2021, ProLitteris, Zurich, Courtesy Mai 36 Galerie, Zurich

p. 215 © Garry Fabian Miller

p. 216 Image courtesy of Nick Knight

p. 219 Courtesy the artist

p. 228 Courtesy of Albarrán Cabrera

p. 229 © Yamamoto Masao

p. 231 Copyright Jiang Zhi. Image courtesy of Jiang Zhi and Blindspot Gallery

p. 233 Copyright Estate of Ren Hang. Image courtesy of Estate of Ren Hang and Blindspot Gallery

p. 235 © Yamamoto Masao

p. 239 © Cindy Sherman Courtesy the artist and Hauser & Wirth

p. 241 © Jo Whaley 1991

p. 244 Courtesy The Ravestijn Gallery

pp. 246-247 © Omar Victor Diop Courtesy Galerie MAGNIN-A, Paris

pp. 248-249 Copyright Valérie Belin 2013, Courtesy galerie Nathalie Obadia Paris/Bruxelles and Edwynn Houk Gallery New York

p. 250 Courtesy Flowers Gallery, London

p. 252 Courtesy Bildhalle Zurich

p. 256 Courtesy of the artist

We very warmly thank the artists for participating in the project, trusting our vision, and sharing their work with us.

We are deeply grateful for the assistance of gallerists and studios in obtaining the works of many artists:
Jack Bell, Oliver Durey, Georgia Currell and Rosie Ward at Jack Bell Gallery; Rosa Bacile and Sophie Nurse at Hauser & Wirth; Jason Burch; Christine Burgin; Desiree Cannon Wattis; Mirjam Cavegn at Bildhalle; Mimi Chun at Blindspot Gallery; Apollonia Colacicco and Howard Greenberg at Howard Greenberg Gallery; Giulia Derege-Thesauro; Dillon DeWaters, Erika Benincasa and Evan Jorgensen; Nico Dregni; Christian Egger at Galerie C; Jan Erting; Elena Frohlick and Charles Buchan at Wylie Agency; Susan Gin; Pauline Giroux and Hugo Brami at MAGNIN-A; Christophe Guye at Christophe Guye Galerie; Justine Hauer at Mai 36 Galerie; Belén Herrera at Galería Marlborough; Jana Hofmann; Ethan Jones; Marloes Krijin; Max Labelle; Jaybe Lee; Lindsay Macdonald Danckwerth at Galerie Lelong; James McKee and Kelso Wyeth at Gagosian; Robert Morat at Robert Morat Galerie; Reina Nakagawa at Art + Commerce and August Rehnberg; Nayuta Otani at ShugoArts; Douglas Parsons; Laurie Paton; Adrian Porikys; Emma Robertson and Jędrzej Nyka at The Approach; Rebecca Robertson and Amy Whiteside at Fraenkel Gallery; Marie-Josée Rousseau at La Castiglione; Pedro Sampaio and Irene Mc Allister at Nara Roesler; Valerie Schultz; Michel Soskine at Michel Soskine Inc.; Moto Takeda and Flavia Souza; Amy Thornett and Anna Selleri; Uyeda Seiko and Yamamoto Reiko; Hannah Watson at TJ Boulting; Natasha Woolliams at Flowers Gallery.

We would like to warmly thank for their invaluable help during our research, for bringing many artists to our attention, and facilitating the obtention of some artworks:
Anton Affentranger; Katia Bonjour; Noel Chanan; Luc Debraine; Joe Helman; Nathalie Herschdorfer; Richard Ovendon; Holly Roussel; Mario Santoro; Kelly Sultan; Sean Sexton; Cornelia Widmer at Implenia Schweiz; The Estate of Michael Wolf.

We are extremely grateful to the team at Thames & Hudson for their trust and support in every phase of the development of this book:
Sarah Boris; Rosanna Fairhead; Julia MacKenzie; Sophie Mead; Ramon Pez; Andrew Sanigar; Nella Soušková.

As well as to the team of the Foundation for the Exhibition of Photography for their support during the research:
Todd Brandow; Justine Chapalay; Laura Gomez Schaer; Juliette Hug; Audrey Zimmerli.

References to illustrations are in *italics*.